A RENAISSANCE EDUCATION: SCHOOLING IN BERGAMO
AND THE VENETIAN REPUBLIC, 1500–1650

A litteras. A.b.c.d.e.f.g.h.i.k.l.m.n.o.p.q.r.f.f.t.u.x.y.z.
Da falutationem beatæ Virginis. A ue Maria gratia plena:
dominus tecum: benedicta tu in mulieribus: & benedictus
fructus uentris tui Iesus: Sacta Maria mater dei ora pro no
bis peccatoribus. Amen. Da orationem dominicam. Pater
noster qui es in celis fanctificetur nomen tuum. Adueniat
regnum tuum. Fiat uoluntas tua: ficut in cælo & in terra. Pa

Niccolo Perotti, *Rudimenta grammatices* (Venice, 1493). This image, from a 1493 grammar textbook, depicts different levels of learning. The illiterate, naked monkey symbolizes the total absence of education. The young boy on a low stool points to the individual letters displayed on a *tavola* (a wooden primer) as he instructs the monkey. (The letters of the alphabet are repeated in the first line of the text below the image.) A slightly older boy, having discarded his primer, sits on a higher stool as he reads a simple book. The book probably contained the simple prayers and phrases written out at the bottom of the page (i.e., the *Ave Maria*, the Lord's Prayer). A whip lies discarded on the floor to his left. More advanced students sit on benches, dressed in traditional academic robes, studying a text. The senior students sit in direct view of the master; the younger students are arrayed behind them or perhaps across the classroom. It is significant, and in the case of Bergamo a bit unusual, for so many students to have a personal copy of the text. The master sits in his *cattedra* (chair), pointing to a specific line in the text, with his copy of the text open before him. Above the head of the *maestro* is inscribed the first rule in all schoolrooms: 'SILENTIUM.'

CHRISTOPHER CARLSMITH

A Renaissance Education

Schooling in Bergamo and the Venetian Republic, 1500–1650

UNIVERSITY OF TORONTO PRESS
Toronto Buffalo London

© University of Toronto Press Incorporated 2010
Toronto Buffalo London
www.utppublishing.com
Printed in Canada

ISBN 978-0-8020-9254-0

Printed on acid-free, 100% post-consumer recycled paper with
vegetable-based inks.

Library and Archives Canada Cataloguing in Publication

Carlsmith, Christopher
    A renaissance education : schooling in Bergamo, 1500–1650 /
    Christopher Carlsmith.

    Includes bibliographical references and index.
    ISBN 978-0-8020-9254-0

    1. Education, Secondary – Italy – Bergamo – History – 16th century.
    2. Education, Secondary – Italy – Bergamo – History – 17th century.
    3. Education – Italy – History – 16th century.
    4. Education – Italy – History – 17th century.
    5. Renaissance – Italy – Bergamo.   6. Bergamo (Italy) – History.
    I. Title.

    LA799.B47C37 2010   370.945'2409031   C2009-903767-X

University of Toronto Press acknowledges the financial assistance to its
publishing program of the Canada Council for the Arts and the Ontario
Arts Council.

University of Toronto Press acknowledges the financial support for its
publishing activities of the Government of Canada through the Book
Publishing Industry Development Program (BPIDP).

Contents

Maps and Illustrations

Maps

Illustrations

A Note about Money, Quotations, and Names

I have left all references to money as they appear in the original documents. In Bergamo the value of a scholarship or a teacher's salary was usually described in a 'money of account' known as imperial lire (*lira imperialis*). This currency was divided into three levels: *lire, soldi, denari* (e.g., a teacher might be paid L. 200 s. 12 and d. 4.) One lira equalled twenty *soldi*; one *soldo* equaled twelve *denari*.[1] Other denominations appear occasionally (e.g., *scudi, marchi, fiorini, lire grandi, lire piccoli*). For most of the sixteenth century, one *scudo* equalled between six and seven lire.

The value of currency in Bergamo can be roughly estimated by its buying power. Annual teacher salaries in the early sixteenth century ranged widely: a minimum of 40–80 lire for an assistant teacher; 200–300 lire for a master teacher; and as much as 800 lire for a prestigious professor. Outside of academia, a fifteenth century stonemason might earn 180 lire annually as a journeyman, 280 lire as a master stonemason, and 350–500 lire as a master builder. A lawyer or doctor with the benefit of a university degree could earn 30–50 lire in a day for assisting a client or patient. Student scholarships ranged from 18 to 100 lire per year and could be extended for up to six years. Confraternities sometimes awarded financial aid or scholarships in much smaller amounts, such as a few denari or even a pair of shoes or a bundle of firewood. A house might be rented for 30 to 80 lire per year, and could be purchased for anywhere from 100 to 1000 lire.

All quotations in the text have been translated into English. The original Latin or Italian text has been included in a footnote when that material is available only in an archive or is similarly inaccessible; if a transcription of the original quotation has been published elsewhere, it is cited in the footnote.

With regard to personal names, I have usually Italianized names in the text but have left the original version in the notes and appendices. The primary sources frequently oscillate between different versions of the name (e.g., Giovita Ravizza and Jovita Rapicius), and previous scholars have employed no consistent policy. Book titles and individuals that are well known in English (e.g., Cicero's *On Offices*) I have rendered in English. Unless indicated otherwise, all translations are my own.

Acknowledgments

I would like to thank Professors Duane Osheim and Anne Schutte of the History Department at the University of Virginia, who guided the research that served as the foundation of this book. Their thoughtful comments, good humour, and steadfast encouragement have immeasurably improved the quality of my scholarship. One of the pleasures of writing this book has been the opportunity to become acquainted with fellow scholars who share my intellectual interests. Paul Grendler's erudition and generosity have been invaluable, and his numerous publications have served as both a guide and an inspiration for my own research. The work of other scholars on late medieval and Renaissance education in Italy, such as Robert Black, Gian Paolo Brizzi, Kathleen Comerford, Paul Gehl, David Lines, and Maurizio Sangalli, has enhanced my understanding of the period even when we have come to diverse conclusions. Other scholars, including Naomi Andrews, Ann Blair, Konrad Eisenbichler, Paula Findlen, Brad Gregory, Michael Knapton, Lance Lazar, Tara Nummedal, John O'Malley, Nicholas Terpstra, and my colleagues at UMass Lowell, all shared their wisdom with me.

In Bergamo, I am grateful to Director Orazio Bravi and the *personale* of the Biblioteca Civica 'A. Mai,' especially Sandro Buzzetti, Marta Gamba, Francesca Giupponi, and Elisabetta Manca. The BCBg became my scholarly home for nearly two years, and the staff there were always supportive and *disponibile*. Vincenzo Marchetti, formerly archivist of the ACVBg, helped me to understand the intricacies of Church history and sixteenth-century palaeography. Alessandro Marchi generously volunteered his time so that I could study the records of the parish of Sant'Alessandro in Colonna, just as Giovanni Ghidini graciously permitted me to work in the parish archive of Sant'Alessandro della Croce.

Pier Maria Soglian and Lester Little listened patiently while I tried out new ideas, and Maria Mencaroni Zoppetti shared her enthusiasm, her knowledge, and her family with me throughout my stay in Bergamo. My fellow bibliophiles and archival cognoscenti in Bergamo kindly shared their discoveries with me, and include Rodolfo Vittori, Marino Paganini, the late Lelio Pagani, Gian Mario Petrò, Roberto Rossi, Andrea Zonca, and many more. My *padrona di casa* for two years, the late Maria Battaggion, made returning home from the archive something to look forward to. To my numerous other friends and colleagues in Bergamo, especially Sonia Ricelli and Francesca Villa, *grazie del cuore*.

Closer to home, Laura Fuller's love and support helped to make this book a reality. The support of numerous family and friends on both the East Coast and the West Coast has been critical to the success of this project. They have provided encouragement – and distraction – as needed, and I am grateful to all of them. During the long gestation of this book, two children of my own have come into the world, and I hope one day that they will read the book and understand why we went to Italy so often.

Preliminary versions of some of my findings have been published in other places. I wish to acknowledge the use of passages from these publications: Christopher Carlsmith, 'A Peripatetic Pedagogue: G.B. Pio in Bergamo, 1505–1507,' in *Ritratti: La dimensione individuale nella storia (secoli XV–XX)*, ed. Silvana Seidel Menchi and Robert A. Pierce (Rome: Edizioni di Storia e Letteratura, 2008), 45–55; idem, 'Troublesome Teens: Approaches to Educating and Disciplining Youth in Early Modern Italy,' in *The Premodern Teenager: Youth in Society, 1150–1650*, ed. Konrad Eisenbichler, Essays and Studies, 1 (Toronto: Centre for Reformation and Renaissance Studies, 2002), 151–71; idem, 'The Jesuits in Bergamo, 1570–1729' *Archivum Historicum Societatis Iesu* 70, no. 139 (Jan.–Jun. 2001): 71–93; idem, 'Il Collegio Patavino della Misericordia Maggiore di Bergamo, 1531–ca.1550' *Bergomum* 93 (1998): 75–98; idem, 'Una scuola dei putti: L'Accademia dei Caspi a Bergamo' *Atti del Ateneo di Scienze, Lettere, ed Arti di Bergamo* 61 (1997–8): 291–302; idem, 'Le *scholae* e la scuola: l'istruzione *amore dei* a Bergamo tra '500 e '600,' *Atti del Ateneo di Scienze, Lettere, ed Arti di Bergamo* 60 (1996–7): 235–56. All excerpts are published with permission.

I am beholden to several institutions for providing the resources that allowed me to complete this project. The Italian Fulbright Commission and the Monticello Foundation's Dumas Malone Fellowship made it possible for me to spend 1996–8 in Bergamo conducting dissertation research. The History Department and the Dean's Office at the University of Virginia granted tuition assistance, teaching opportunities, and an Alfred Dexter Whitehead writing fellowship. The University of Massachusetts Lowell awarded a teaching reduction in Fall 2005 and a sabbatical in 2008–9 that allowed me to complete the manuscript. Boston University's Mugar Library and Stanford University's Hoover Insitution each offered a quiet sanctuary in which to write.

The three anonymous readers for the University of Toronto Press shared their expertise and helped to improve the quality of the book. Such thoughtful and stimulating critiques are hard to find, and I am grateful to each. Jenna Venturini assisted with preparation of the maps; Paul Coppens helped with the illustrations in the book. Suzanne Rancourt, Barb Porter, and the staff at the UTP demonstrated patience and determination in bringing this book to completion, and I am grateful for that.

The book is dedicated to Lyn and Merrill: the finest parents, professors, and pedagogues that a son could ever ask for.

CHC
Lowell, Mass.

Abbreviations

Archives and Libraries

AAUPa	Antico Archivio dell'Università di Padova, Padua
ACVBg	Archivio della Curia Vescovile, Bergamo [now Archivio Storico Diocesano, Bergamo]
APSACol	Archivio della Parrocchia di S. Alessandro in Colonna, Bergamo
APSACro	Archivio della Parrocchia di S. Alessandro della Croce, Bergamo
Arch. MIA	Archivio della Misericordia Maggiore, in BCBg, Bergamo
ASemBg	Archivio Storico del Seminario Vescovile Giovanni XXIII di Bergamo
ARSI	Archivium Romanum Societatis Iesu, Rome
ASBg	Archivio di Stato, Bergamo
ASBs	Archivio di Stato, Brescia
ASCClusone	Archivio Storico del Comune di Clusone
ASCRomano	Archivio Storico del Comune di Romano di Lombardia
ASPd	Archivio di Stato, Padua
ASPSGe	Archivio Storico dei Padri Somaschi, Genoa (*aka* Archivio della Maddalena)
ASV	Archivio di Stato, Venice
ASVr	Archivio di Stato, Verona
BCBg	Biblioteca Civica 'Angelo Mai,' Bergamo
BMC	Museo Civico Correr, Venice
BMV	Biblioteca Marciana, Venice
BQ	Biblioteca Queriniana, Brescia

Printed Sources

AVASC   *Gli Atti della visita apostolica di San Carlo Borromeo a Bergamo, 1575.* 5 vols. in 2. Edited by Angelo G. Roncalli (John XXIII). Florence: Leo S. Olschki, 1936–57.

Belotti   Bortolo Belotti, *La Storia di Bergamo e dei Bergamaschi.* 9 vols. Bergamo: Bolis, 1989.

DBI   *Dizionario biografico degli italiani.* Vols. 1–71. Rome: Istituto della Enciclopedia Italiana, 1960–pres.

DIP   *Dizionario degli istituti di perfezione.* 10 vols. Edited by Guerino Pelliccia and Giancarlo Rocca. Rome: Edizione Paoline, 1974–2003.

Locatelli   Giuseppe Locatelli, 'L'istruzione a Bergamo e la Misericordia Maggiore.' *Bergomum*: *Bollettino della civica biblioteca di Bergamo* 4, no. 4 (1910): 57–169, and ibid., 5, no. 1 (1911): 21–99.

Chronological Terms

Trecento	1300–1399
Quattrocento	1400–1499
Cinquecento	1500–1599
Seicento	1600–1699
Renaissance	ca 1400–1530
Early Modern	ca 1500–1700

Archival References

a. = year [anno]
arch. = archive
b. = envelope [busta]
bis. = twice
cap., ch. = chapter
f. = folio
fald. = binder [faldone]
fasc. = booklet [fasciolo]
ff. = folios
ms. = manuscript
n. = note
no. = number

perg. = parchment
pt. = part
r. = obverse [recto]
scat. = box [scatola]
tom. = tome
v. = reverse [verso]
vol. = volume
vols. = volumes

A RENAISSANCE EDUCATION

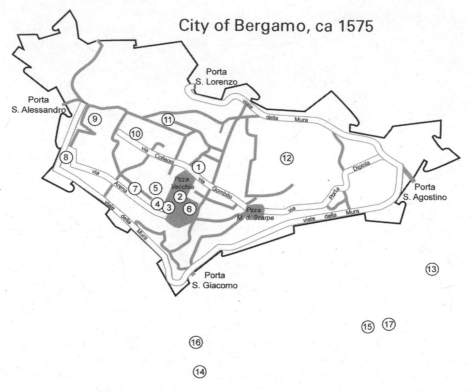

City of Bergamo, ca 1575

1. Biblioteca Civica/Palazzo Nuovo
2. Palazzo della Ragione
3. Basilica of Santa Maria Maggiore
4. Colleoni Chapel
5. Episcopal Palace
6. Cathedral of S. Alessandro
7. Palazzo della MIA
8. Current Seminary (John XXIII)
9. Citadel
10. Church of S. Agata (Theatines)
11. Original Seminary (Seminarino)
12. Fortress (Rocca)
13. Church of S. Alessandro della Croce
14. Church of S. Alessandro della Colonna
15. Convent of Matris Domini
16. Monastery of S. Stefano
17. Caspi Academy

Introduction

This book examines the educational network that existed in northeastern Italy between 1500 and 1650, with a particular emphasis on the city of Bergamo. The focus is primarily upon pre-university education – what today we would call high school – but cases of elementary schooling, pre-professional training, and university instruction provide important points of comparison and thus are included. A close analysis of civic, ecclesiastical, confraternal, and family records not only paints a vivid portrait of how schooling functioned in one city but also explores this small city's dynamic interconnections with other locales and with larger regional processes.

The importance of an accurate understanding of Bergamo's educational past became clear to me in a *gelateria* one summer afternoon in 1997. I had been reading in Bergamo's archives for about a year and was increasingly surprised by the frequent references to schooling and the intricate web of educational options that existed in the sixteenth century. The staff at the ice cream shop were naturally curious as to why an American would spend so much time with dusty books of five hundred years ago. When I explained that I wished to unearth the history of Renaissance education in Bergamo, they laughed uproariously and told me that earlier residents of the city had been largely illiterate. If any schools had existed, they informed me confidently, they were either under the thumb of the bishop or restricted to just a few aristocrats. This stereotype – of Bergamo and neighbouring areas as ignorant towns in which only priests or wealthy patricians could read and write – is based upon several factors. Bergamo's undeserved reputation for illiteracy and stupidity grew out of the region's grinding poverty, its famously guttural dialect, and, most importantly, the character of Arlecchino (Harlequin) in the Italian theatrical tradition known as *commedia dell'arte*.[1] These circumstances have distorted the truth about Bergamo's educational achievements for centuries, even for the city's own residents. In reality, an array of schooling options was available to the populace of Bergamo and its sister cities. These options appealed to a diverse audience that certainly included priests and patricians but also encompassed ambitious merchants, aspiring bureaucrats, and secular scholars. As we shall see, schooling in Bergamo was often representative of a larger reality, rendering this local study a microcosm of greater trends. The story of who studied what, with whom, and why forms the subject of this book.

For centuries, Italy has played an innovative and important role in the development of primary, secondary, and university education. The medieval universities of Bologna and Padua contributed to critical advancements in law and later in medicine, while the humanist academies of the Renaissance promoted the rebirth of Graeco-Roman literature and philosophy. The Jesuit colleges of the Catholic Reformation provided a model of classical secondary instruction that endured well into the modern era, just as the nineteenth-century theories of Maria Montessori shaped elementary schools across the globe.

I suggest that the period from the late fifteenth century through the mid-seventeenth century constitutes an especially key phase in this history. In the fifteenth century Italian humanists sought to introduce a new kind of pedagogy, one that they hoped would inculcate morality and virtue through the careful study of Ciceronian grammar, Roman literature, history, and philosophy. Humanist scholars like Vittorino da Feltre and Guarino da Verona established residential academies where elite students were trained in good letters and good behaviour (*buone lettere e buoni costumi*). In the sixteenth century the structure and purpose of instruction shifted in response to new economic demands, the printing 'revolution,' and the formation of regional states. Meanwhile the Protestant and Catholic Reformations also deeply influenced the composition of education from elementary school up through university. Pedagogues on both sides of the confessional divide, including Johan Sturm, Juan Luis Vives, Roger Ascham, and Erasmus of Rotterdam, wrote extensively about how children should be instructed. To put it simply, schooling of all kinds flourished after 1450: municipal schools, catechism schools, seminaries, academies, and private tutors, not to mention universities and colleges. Poor students learned their ABCs and elementary mathematics; aspiring priests studied Latin

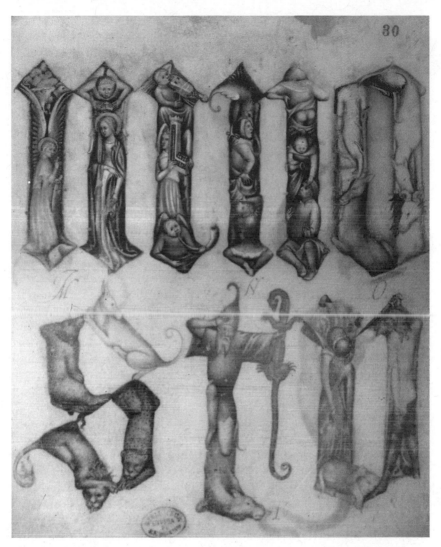

Giovannino de Grassi, *Alphabeto* (1390). These Gothic letters, representing the letters 'm-n-o' (top) and 's-t-u' (bottom), were illuminated on parchment, presumably to help new readers. Only the wealthiest of students would have been able to afford such an elaborate and costly work. The artist has used an inventive array of human and animal figures in diverse poses to constitute each letter. De Grassi was a court artist for the Visconti family in late four-teenth-century Milan.

grammar and theology; and elite children acquired the elegant manners and social graces idealized by Baldassare Castiglione in *The Courtier*.

Where does Bergamo fit in and why does its educational history matter? Located close to Milan, but under Venetian domination from 1428 to 1797, Bergamo occupied a strategic military and commercial position in the balance-of-power politics that characterized Renaissance Italy. A study of schooling in this liminal city reveals the extent to which the Republic of Venice sought to control its dominion cities, and illustrates the strategies by which a small city could survive, and even prosper, between two larger powers. Local historians have studied Bergamo's economic and political history but with one exception have inexplicably avoided the history of education.[2] Yet vast holdings provide a wealth of primary sources. Furthermore, although it is true that Bergamo possessed neither an internationally known schoolmaster nor a world-famous educational institution like Vittorino da Feltre's *Casa Giocosa* in Mantua, its very ordinariness allows the city to serve as a benchmark for the 'typical' types of schooling available in small and medium-sized provincial Italian cities. For example, Bergamo's inability to sustain its commitment to communal education was rather typical, as was the resurgence of post-Tridentine Catholic education. At the same time, Bergamo's schooling displayed certain idiosyncrasies and exceptions that serve to remind us of Renaissance Italy's myriad political systems and linguistic diversity. As Robert Black has demonstrated for education in Florentine Tuscany and its neighbouring cities, an awareness of local variations is crucial for accurate historical understanding.[3]

A rapid overview of Bergamo's history will help to situate the city within the broader developments of late medieval and early modern Italy. An independent commune in the twelfth century, Bergamo fell to the Sforza and Visconti families of Milan from 1264 to 1428. Under the generalship of its native son Bartolomeo Colleoni (ca 1395–1475), in 1428 Bergamo passed under Venetian hegemony. With the exception of a decade during the War of the League of Cambrai (1508–16), Bergamo remained loyal to the Venetian Republic until 1797. As noted in subsequent chapters, the *podestà* (governor) and *capitano* (captain) in Bergamo were always appointed by the Venetian Senate; similarly, Bergamo's bishop was always a Venetian patrician, Bergamo's students were required to attend university within the Republic, and Bergamo's cultural life gravitated toward Venice. Bergamo's natural resources in the sixteenth and seventeenth centuries – carefully monitored by Venice – included wool, iron, silk, and wine, as well as the many labour-

ers who emigrated to the Venetian lagoons. Aside from Bishop Vittore
Soranzo (1547–59), Bergamo's episcopal leadership remained staunch-
ly orthodox during and after the Council of Trent, including Federico
Cornaro (1561–77), Girolamo Ragazzoni (1577–92), and Gregorio Barbarigo (1657–64). The enormous walls that encircle Bergamo today
were constructed by the Venetians during the later sixteenth century
(1561–1620) to discourage Milan from expanding north as well as to
limit the flourishing contraband trade. If submission to Venice marks
one key turning point in Bergamo's history, and the fortification of Bergamo constitutes a second, a third would surely be the great plague of
1630–2. Memorialized by Bergamo's secretary Lorenzo Ghirardelli and
the inspiration for Manzoni's novel *I Promessi Sposi*, this catastrophe
decimated Bergamo's population and economic production. During the
later seventeenth century Bergamo would slowly rebuild itself, gaining
fame for its musical tradition and its annual *fiera* (fair) for merchants.

In terms of schooling, although scattered references to education
in Bergamo exist during the fourteenth and fifteenth centuries, only
around 1500 did the commune consistently begin to sponsor public instruction and only in 1506 did the confraternity of the Misericordia Maggiore open its first school. Schooling was never widespread or available
to all, but during the first half of the sixteenth century it became a more
visible and regular facet of urban life for a broader segment of Italian
society. By mid-century an array of possibilities was available at the
primary, secondary, and even university levels (although the latter was
carefully regulated by Venice). This strong interest in education continued during the later sixteenth century, even as the commune's involvement waned and other institutions, such as confraternities or religious
orders of men, intervened. The Catholic Church especially assumed a
stronger presence in delivering education to lay and religious children
in the late sixteenth and early seventeenth centuries. The devastating
plague of 1630–2 shuttered schools in Bergamo and elsewhere, but the
subsequent two decades witnessed much rebuilding and therefore I
continue the story to circa 1650.

As the sceptical staff in Bergamo's gelateria asked me during a later
visit, what kinds of documents reveal the history of schooling? The
commune of Bergamo and the various confraternities in the city each
produced copious arrays of reports, budgets, minutes, petitions, inventories, statutes, and letters. They also conserved schoolbooks, maps,
building plans, and even depositions. Pastoral visitations, episcopal
decrees, and other confraternal records are preserved in ecclesiasti-

cal and parish archives, while hundreds of notarial cartularies contain contracts, wills, and assorted legal documents. In addition, libraries in Venice, Rome, Brescia, Verona, and Vicenza hold printed materials on schools and schooling, such as treatises and handbooks. With the exception of occasional reports or petitions, most of this documentation was neither created nor preserved for the purpose of recording how schools functioned. Many documents are prescriptive, declaring what the teacher or institution wanted to happen; others are descriptive, illustrating what actually happened. Both types are important in order to delineate how schooling in Bergamo and its environs was conceived, organized, and delivered.

Institutional records are the foundation of this study. Sometimes the entries are maddeningly terse, and at other times numbingly formulaic. Yet the archives are also rich with details about communal, confraternal, and religious life. Bergamo's Civic Library 'Angelo Mai' contains the two most important archives upon which my work is based. The Archive of the Commune includes a nearly unbroken run of city council deliberations from the 1470s through the end of the eighteenth century, as well as municipal budgets, correspondence, legal documents, etc. In addition, the Civic Library contains twelve thousand books published in the sixteenth century (cinquecentini), twenty-four thousand incunabula and parchments, and the various statutes and decrees that governed the city and its surrounding region. The second critical source is the Archive of the Misericordia Maggiore confraternity. It too incorporates council minutes, letters, tax records, property holdings, privileges, and much more. Petitions from teachers, squabbles over inheritances, inventories of household goods, treatises on how children should be taught – these two archives contain numerous documents on civic and intellectual life in Bergamo.

Other archives in Bergamo have contributed to this study in important ways. The Episcopal Archive, located across the piazza from the Civic Library, offers hundreds of volumes of pastoral visitations as well as papal and episcopal decrees, synodal records, ordination registers, and personnel lists. The Episcopal Archive also holds the original documents concerning the Caspi Academy as well as those on the Schools of Christian Doctrine. The adjacent Seminary Archive contains important documents about the financial and administrative history of the diocesan seminary in its early years. Equally useful, although much smaller, are the parish archives scattered throughout the city. I focused in particular on the archives of Sant'Alessandro in Colonna and

Sant'Alessandro della Croce, each of which contained the minutes of the parish executive councils and their negotiations with teachers and parents. The State Archive of Bergamo boasts a substantial collection of testaments and notarial cartularies as well as the records of selected convents. These were useful for looking up specific contracts or wills that pertained to teachers, but the lack of a master index hampered a broader enquiry into notarial documents. In addition, much of the material that might normally be contained in a state archive has previously been deposited in Bergamo's Civic Library.

Outside of Bergamo, the archives of the Somaschan order (in Genoa) and of the Jesuit order (in Rome) furnished important information about how those orders contributed to schooling in Bergamo and in the Venetian Republic. Treatises, letters, memos, and notes from annual conventions all help to shed light upon the pedagogical mission of these two religious orders. The State Archive in Venice holds all of the reports submitted by the podestà and capitano as well as ducal pronouncements, acts of the Senate, and materials pertaining to the university in Padua. Additional information about Bergamasque students in Padua was obtained from the University of Padua archives. State archives in Brescia, Verona, and Vicenza each contain the city council minutes that were so valuable to me in Bergamo, and I used them to draw comparisons between these different cities of the Veneto. Lastly, a number of provincial archives (e.g., Clusone, Chiari) helped me to unearth how education was organized in the small towns and villages of the region.

Although archives in Bergamo and the Veneto are rich, there are some primary sources that do not form part of this study. Unlike the Florentines, the people of Bergamo did not keep ricordanze in which to record personal and commercial affairs.[4] Nor did the Bergamaschi typically record events in journals or diaries as, for example, Marin Sanudo of Venice famously did. The well-studied, and unique, Florentine catasto of 1427, with its detailed tax returns on each of Florence's inhabitants, has no counterpart in Bergamo. Lectures, commentaries, glosses, and student notebooks can provide tremendous insight into classroom practice, as David Lines has shown us for Bologna, but such sources are more abundant in university towns; I have found very few of these for sixteenth-century Bergamo.[5] Town chronicles often provide an insider view of town politics or a consistent perspective over many years, and I utilize chronicles by Giacomo Filippo Foresti (1492), Giovanni da Lezze (1596), and Thomas Coryat (1612) as needed. However, these journals or diaries do not often comment on education per se, and thus are less useful for my purposes. A significant collection of sixteenth-century books is held in Bergamo's archives, but these *cinquecentini* usually do not contain notes of possession, rendering it difficult to argue that a particular book was used by an instructor or a student. Book inventories do survive for a couple of teachers in Bergamo, and these certainly tell us something about the intellectual interests of these pedagogues, but they reveal little about actual classroom practice. The declarations of faith (*professioni di fede*) in late sixteenth-century Venice provide valuable data about teachers, as Paul Grendler and Vittorio Baldo have shown, but these documents have not been carefully conserved in Bergamo. One purpose of this book is to stimulate further research into education in Bergamo and other cities of its kind; I hope future scholars will unearth additional sources to those utilized in my study.

This book advances a number of arguments, both explicitly and implicitly, that pertain to important developments in education between the fifteenth and seventeenth centuries. In the paragraphs that follow, I briefly lay out some of the crucial themes and issues. For example, the transition from 'Renaissance education' to 'early modern schooling' represents one of the key elements in this book. The former represented a humanist-inspired form of instruction that sought to train a small number of elite boys in classical literature, history, and rhetoric in preparation for civic responsibilities, while the latter was a more broad-based approach that included the pedagogy of Protestant and Catholic reforms. This transition was neither a linear process nor one that can be charted year-by-year. Yet during the long sixteenth century pedagogues, parents, and politicians in Bergamo experimented with an astonishing array of options to teach children and adults. I argue that this pluralism of educational choices represents part of the movement from medieval to modern society. Bergamo is not alone in having a selection of schools and academies for students, but this wider choice of alternatives for classroom instruction signifies an expansion of opportunity for greater literacy and numeracy. If access to information constitutes one of the hallmarks of our contemporary society, surely the origins of that tradition can be found in the increased number of schooling opportunities available in the sixteenth century. This is not to suggest that education was 'universal,' nor even widely disseminated beyond select groups. And we must be aware that the sixteenth century introduced a barrage of propaganda and state control over information. Nonetheless there was for the first time a growing number of educational choices that allowed boys, and sometimes girls, to explore a wider intellectual and vocational world. It is precisely this paradox in the sixteenth century – between greater access to information via schools, printing, and rediscovery of classical sources, and greater control over information via censorship and confessionalization – that makes the study of education so compelling.

The proposed 'aristocratization' of instruction represents a second issue in charting the development of education. Early humanist schools, like those of Vittorino da Feltre, targeted elite children by offering a curriculum that emphasized skills necessary for public speaking, diplomacy, and civic or courtly life. Jesuit schools of the sixteenth and seventeenth centuries similarly catered to elite children by offering an advanced Latinate curriculum. Examples such as Bergamo's Caspi Academy and Brescia's Collegio Lambertino indicate that wealthy families did seek to isolate their children and restrict access to schooling. Nor was such exclusivity limited to schools: in 1557 Bergamo's College of Jurists declared *quod non admitatur bastardus* and in 1568 the same group refused to admit Marcello Viscardi to its ranks after he obtained a law degree, because his father had sold cloth, a 'vile and mechanical art' that precluded his sons from respectability.[6] An argument can be made that even if the number of schools in the sixteenth century grew, access to education became increasingly restricted, as middle- and upper-class citizens sought to protect their own socio-economic status. On the other hand, there is no denying that the number of schools did increase, and that literacy rates followed suit, suggesting a 'democratization' of schooling. The scholarship records of the MIA confraternity in Bergamo offer a telling example about the confraternity's' ambivalence regarding the social class of recipients: while the confraternity proudly claimed that it founded scholarships to assist poor boys, the majority of scholarships were awarded to scions of successful Bergamasque families. Perhaps the simple explanation of nepotism or corruption will suffice, but these cases also help to put the issue of social class into stark relief. Thus we must be cognizant not only of how many schools there were, but also of which students could attend and the extent to which such schooling conferred social and vocational mobility.

An additional issue in the transformation toward early modern schooling concerns the continuing struggle between secular and religious forces for the hearts and minds of the next generation. The later sixteenth century is renowned for the bitter religious battles waged among peasants, prelates, and princes, conflicts in which the schoolrooms of early modern Europe constituted a primary battlefield. Bergamo and the cities of the Venetian mainland had their share of territorial disputes and angry accusations over who should govern the classroom. Nor was this issue restricted to the early modern world, as recent debates over abstinence education or the prohibition of school prayer in the United States make clear. In both eras fervent concern has been expressed about the development of 'morality' and 'character' in the student body, with heated rhetoric from individual parents and from state bureaucrats. The documents in Bergamo speak again and again to the importance of developing a child's moral awareness, whether through the example of religious saints or classical heroes.

This book takes up other broad issues in the Renaissance and early modern world. I demonstrate that, for education at least, part of the 'Venetian myth' still holds true. Encouraged by Venice itself for centuries, this perspective idealized the *Serenissima's* religious tolerance, social stability, political inclusiveness, economic wealth, intellectual splendor, and diplomatic sophistication. Recent scholarship has systematically undermined each of these claims but the 'myth' of Venice can still encompass some broader truths.[7] In contrast to Florence and Milan, Venice did allow the cities in its dominion a fair degree of autonomy in setting educational policy. Individual city councils had considerable leeway in hiring and firing teachers, for example, and the Venetian governors typically ruled with a light hand. Although education represents only one facet of the relationship between the *Dominante* (Venice) and the *dominate* (subject cities), it confirms the independence and flexibility that existed between centre and periphery in the Venetian Republic.

This book reveals a surprising degree of cooperation between institutions and groups traditionally assumed to be at cross purposes: Church vs. State, urban vs. rural, public vs. private, parents vs. commune. I describe several examples of joint ventures between civic and ecclesiastical bureaucracies, between parents and clerics, between lay confraternities and religious orders of men. Such cooperation implies that schooling represented one area where common ground was often found. This is not to suggest that unanimity existed concerning who should teach, what should be learned, or how it should be taught; indeed, polemics abounded on these very issues. Nevertheless, schooling, at least in Bergamo, engendered more cooperation among institutions than is traditionally recognized. Here again we see the value of approaching education through an institutional lens, where relationships among associations and various corporate bodies can be viewed more clearly.

Literacy, both urban and rural, has captured the attention of early modern historians in the last few years.[8] Through an examination of how literacy and numeracy were achieved, and by whom, this work explains why Bergamo and the valleys to the north enjoyed an unexpectedly high literacy rate. In addition, I show that important elements of humanism, such as the revival of antiquity and the celebration of Cicero, were clearly present in Bergamo during the later Quattrocento (fifteenth century) and Cinquecento (sixteenth century). Bergamo never attained the critical mass of humanist scholars and teachers to be found in larger cities, but the humanist program was valued and promoted in Bergamo as it was in many other smaller towns. Comparing and contrasting Bergamo's well-documented educational experience with that of other cities and regions makes it possible to uncover the historical reality across a broader area.

The overlap between humanism and the Church constitutes an additional theme throughout the book. The crusade of fifteenth-century Italian humanists to shift the curriculum and pedagogy of schooling away from medieval Scholasticism and toward a new spirit of humanistic enquiry reflected a sea change in how man viewed his place in the world. One century later, through its establishment of seminaries and catechism schools, a revitalized Catholic Church fought to regain the primacy it had previously enjoyed in education of medieval European youth. The humanist revolution and the Catholic reformation are hardly new topics, but my analysis illuminates and contextualizes the practical impact of such movements on the ground.

Schooling in Bergamo was largely a male enterprise. With the exception of the Schools of Christian Doctrine in the early seventeenth century, male students and teachers dominated all aspects of instruction. The documents in Bergamo make only occasional reference to female pupils, and more often than not such girls were the daughters of teachers. To be sure, some female students, and perhaps female teachers, were hidden behind the use of collective (masculine) nouns when referring to a mixed group of boys and girls. Some girls doubtless received instruction in convents in and around Bergamo, and still others were certainly tutored at home. But such instruction has left few traces, particularly in comparison with the communal and confraternal schools that catered to boys. Students in early modern Europe received the education that was deemed useful and appropriate for their social class, gender, and future career. Upper-class boys thus studied the Latin curriculum and public rhetoric, while girls were more often limited to vernacular texts, catechism lessons, and instruction in needlework. If girls appear to be absent in much of the history recounted here, it is because they remain invisible in the documents.

A perennial question in the study of early modern education involves quantification: how many students actually went to school? What percentage of them could read or write? What was the ratio of students and teachers? How much did school cost? I have included statistics wherever the numbers seemed both reliable and useful toward a deeper understanding of instruction. Thus I analyse the number and gender of students in Bergamo's Schools of Christian Doctrine in the period 1609–10, one of the few cases for which we have good data. Teachers' salaries and scholarship payments offer two sources of information that can be compared both over time and among multiple cities. I have not been able to calculate with any degree of certainty the total number of students who attended school in Bergamo, nor can I estimate reliably the percentage of students (or adults) who were literate. Literacy varied widely by gender, class, location, and profession. Even in such a well-documented case as Renaissance Florence, scholars disagree on the literacy rate for adult males as well as the total number of students there.[9] Nearly all schools examined in this study were run by a single schoolmaster, and he would rarely have taught more than sixty students at one time. However, many assistant teachers (*ripetitori*) are recorded in the documents, and their presence would have allowed a larger number of students to be educated. Ultimately the book relies less on quantitative analysis than on a qualitative, narrative account of the educational network in and around the city of Bergamo.

Studies in the history of European education have tended to follow larger historiographical trends. As Robert Black has noted, the late nineteenth-century positivist movement initiated one trend by producing dozens of studies about Italian education.[10] Although the positivists were talented philologists and rigorous scholars, their work focused on prominent teachers and early printed editions, with little attempt to construct an overall synthesis or to identify broader intellectual movements. The best example of this approach in English is probably the work of William H. Woodward on Vittorino da Feltre and other Italian humanists. Woodward published translations of early Renaissance pedagogical treatises and offered short biographies of their authors, but his translations can be loose and he does not fully contextualize the authors. Giuseppe Locatelli's article on the educational activities of the Misericordia Maggiore of Bergamo also exemplifies this trend; driven largely by documents found in the archive, he makes no effort to integrate other sources or to do comparative history. Subsequent work on education in Bergamo, and in other cities such as Lucca, Pistoia, or Modena, suffers from a similar myopic focus. Giuseppe Manacorda combined many of these positivist studies to produce his monumental work *Storia della scuola in Italia* in 1914, but unfortunately his study covers only the medieval period.[11]

After the Second World War, Eugenio Garin led a new generation of Italian scholars who rejected their positivist predecessors, and sought instead to describe the impact and larger significance of humanism. Garin drew a sharp distinction between the medieval, scholastic curriculum that, according to him, emphasized theology and spirituality, and the new humanist lessons that promoted the revival of antiquity, self-knowledge, and *virtù*. For Garin, the humanists were champions of dialogue, discussion, and critical doubt; they interacted directly with classical sources and thought for themselves rather than relying upon past authorities. Furthermore, Garin argued that humanist pedagogy and commentaries were different (and better) than their Scholastic counterparts. Garin's optimistic view of the Italian Renaissance, although challenged in recent years, has strongly influenced the English-language interpretation of Renaissance schooling.[12]

Paul Grendler's *Schooling in Renaissance Italy*, and his subsequent work on universities, has generally followed Garin's interpretation of the Renaissance as a critical moment in the history of education, a period that could even be termed a 'revolution' for its impact upon curricula, texts, and teacher training.[13] Grendler's systematic research and mastery of the scholarship has made his book on secondary schooling a milestone in the field of Italian Renaissance education. He has emphasized the critical role of independent masters and devoted significant attention to the texts utilized for Latin and vernacular instruction. Focusing on the examples of Venice, Florence, and Rome in his opening chapters, Grendler lays out a vision of how schooling functioned across the Italian peninsula. He champions the innovations of the humanist pedagogues and demonstrates how they utilized new and traditional texts to teach grammar, rhetoric, and poetry.

An opposite interpretation is offered by Anthony Grafton and Lisa Jardine, who have challenged the entire notion of a humanist triumph. Their joint book *From Humanism to the Humanities* praises the rigour and clarity of the earlier Scholastic education and discredits the self-promoting claims of fifteenth-century humanists who promised virtue and morality through careful study of the Graeco-Roman classics.[14] Grafton and Jardine also criticize Garin's acceptance of the humanists' contention that good morals and character formation are affiliated with the study of classical eloquence. Through careful examination of the teaching program of Guarino da Verona, Grafton and Jardine argue that humanism succeeded only because it perfectly fit the needs of the new monarchs by training a class of docile, passive civil servants who were content to do their master's bidding. The governing elites, according to Grafton and Jardine, wished to emphasize rote learning rather than analysis and logical argument, and their success opened the door for the orthodoxy of the Catholic Reformation and later Protestant movements.

Grafton and Jardine's thesis spawned a flurry of debate and new research in the 1980s and 1990s as scholars sought to go beyond the humanists' idealized pedagogical treatises to discover what education was actually like on the ground. Robert Black's initial analysis of communal education in Arezzo provided one step in that direction, and his painstaking research on city council records has served as a model for my own research in Bergamo. Black properly calls for a more sensitive understanding of regional and local variations in Italian education, a point borne out by the example of Bergamo and its sister cities in the Veneto. Black's more recent works survey hundreds of manuscripts and grammar books in order to argue for the extended continuity of late-medieval pedagogy and texts in fourteenth and fifteenth-century Italy. In *Humanism and Education in Medieval and Renaissance Italy*, Black contends that the teaching of grammar remained largely unchanged between 1200 and 1500. He offers much detail on the history of *Ianua*, the medieval grammar that remained very popular in Italian classrooms, and he surveys the major and minor authors of the Latin canon. In the ceaseless debate among historians about whether change or continuity is more dominant, Black thus comes down firmly on the side of continuity and tradition. Black's second principal argument, drawn from close analysis of the glosses on school manuscripts, is that teachers and students were primarily concerned with philology rather than morality. Thus, Black argues, the humanists were not really doing anything new, and their claims to instil virtue through the study of classical texts is unfounded. In his more recent *Education and Society in Florentine Tuscany*, Black surveys in exhaustive detail the curriculum of Florence and its subject towns, as well as the identity and activities of teachers and pupils prior to 1500. He cites and transcribes hundreds of archival documents (e.g., *ricordanze* and *catasto* excerpts), thus providing a great service to other scholars. One of Black's surprising conclusions is the dominance of instruction in commercial mathematics in fourteenth-century Florence and the parallel lack of interest in Latin grammar instruction. Even more intriguing is that towns outside of Florence (e.g., Prato, Arezzo, Volterra) displayed exactly opposite tendencies. Such evidence underscores yet again the importance of looking closely at provincial towns; for Black, it provides additional evidence of humanism's weak hold in early Renaissance pedagogy. Black thus places himself squarely in opposition to Grendler and Garin, and indirectly allies himself with Grafton and Jardine.[15]

Although Grendler, Black, and other scholars cited above were principally describing Italian education at the primary and secondary levels, the debate resonates in university-level teaching as well. Some of the humanists taught in universities, of course, and distributed their ideas directly in Bologna or Padua. The university has traditionally been viewed as a bastion of conservative, Scholastic practice that was hostile to humanism. David Lines and Charles Schmitt have both suggested that this stereotype needs to be reevaluated.[16] In terms of education, Lines's thorough and erudite study of how Aristotle's *Ethics* was taught in Italian universities can tell us much about pedagogical theory and practice. He looks favourably upon Black's perspective, and argues that the humanists did not introduce any monumental change until the end of the fifteenth century. Yet in contrast to Grafton and Jardine, Lines does see – at least in the case of moral education – a clear distinction between humanist and scholastic methods of education. A second virtue of Lines's study, as noted previously, is the way in which glosses and annotations can reveal classroom practice. What emerges in his work is a dizzying array of pedagogical methods and motivations, even as the textbook remained the same. Lines's work concedes that the *Ethics* 'was among the more modest subjects in the universities'; it may be worth noting that Bergamo was only a 'modest' city but that it too saw a rising interest in education and a surprising variety of methods to achieve that goal.

Studies of education elsewhere in early modern Europe (e.g., Huppert and Carter on France, Strauss and Karant-Nunn on Germany, Moran and Orme on England) have a slightly different focus. Perhaps because they examine schooling outside of Italy, such scholars are often less concerned with the question of whether the humanists or the Scholastics 'triumphed' in the classroom. Instead, these scholars utilize a wide variety of primary sources, including episcopal visitations, tax returns, city council deliberations, wills, professions of faith, and marriage registers, to trace broader contours of schooling. In an attempt to move beyond mere intellectual history, historians of European education are posing broader questions about the interchange between schooling, religion, and society. They seek to include newer fields like the history of literacy or the history of childhood in order to construct a broader history of education. [17]

Similar to Grendler, Black, and others, my conclusions are based primarily upon the archival sources consulted in the course of my research. Although no historian can be a purely neutral observer, I have endeavoured to tell a story that accurately reflects the documents in Bergamo and elsewhere. In the historiographical debate outlined above, my methodology and conclusions are most akin to those of Paul Grendler. In my view, his interpretation of education in the Italian Renaissance is the most accurate. Nevertheless, there exist issues for which our sources and conclusions are markedly different. In a similar way, I agree with Robert Black's call to observe regional differences and an increased focus upon provincial cities even as I disagree with his conclusions about the humanist impact (or lack thereof) upon education.

Thus my book responds to and incorporates these recent movements, but it also breaks new ground in several areas. Previous studies of schooling have usually examined one institution or one type of education; mine is unusual in that it considers the whole *tableaux*. One result of this holistic approach is that I demonstrate the plethora of schooling options available in a city whose inhabitants were traditionally reputed to be ignorant and illiterate. These results force us to reconsider the intellectual and social contributions of Italian provincial cities. To put it bluntly, if a city with Bergamo's reputation for illiteracy turns out to have a complex and vibrant web of educational options, what does that suggest for neighbouring cities and towns? A second advantage of this holistic approach is the deep level of detail that can be obtained about the individuals and institutions involved in education. Case studies and microhistories provide a sense of intimacy and rich, telling examples that are necessarily absent from broader, more synthetic studies.

The humanist teachers of the Quattrocento disdained the 'corrupt' Latin of the medieval Church and sought instead to restore the classical Latin of Cicero and Virgil. Their attention to semantics and word choice serves as a reminder that we too must strive to be precise in how we define important terms. To that end, I offer a few observations about my own use of important words in this study. I prefer the term

'schooling' because instruction was often provided on a more individualized or ephemeral basis than is implied by the term 'schools,' with
its connotation of buildings, curricula, and multiple classrooms. Other
scholars have also argued for a looser definition of schooling that includes a variety of forms of instruction.[18] In those cases where a 'school'
clearly existed (e.g., the Caspi Academy, a Jesuit college, the Academy
of Clerics of the Misericordia Maggiore [known as the MIA]), I use that
term. Unlike Italian, in which 'istruzione' generally refers to academic
instruction, while 'educazione' usually means training in behaviour,
comportment, or proper manners, the English language does not really distinguish between 'instruction' and 'education,' and so I use the
terms interchangeably.

The word 'Renaissance' has become so fraught with connotation that
many historians prefer the more generic 'early modern.' The term 'Renaissance' implies a rebirth of classical traditions and revived interest
in Graeco-Roman philosophy and literature usually associated with
fifteenth-century Italy, while 'early modern' can be used to describe a
broad range of disciplines (e.g., literature, economics, anthropology)
and places more emphasis on how the period 1500–1789 anticipated
and shaped our contemporary society.[19] 'Renaissance' education is thus
viewed as the triumph of the humanist program, first in Italy and later
in Northern Europe; 'early modern' schooling includes the humanist
contributions but also encompasses developments from the Catholic
and Protestant Reformations to the pre-Enlightenment thinkers. It is
true that scholarship about the Renaissance often seems triumphalist or
Whiggish in its praise of the glorious past. Medievalists have objected
to the tendency to begin 'modern' history with the Renaissance, while
many putative historians of the Renaissance have debunked the mythic
achievements of that era. Recent decades have thus provided a necessary corrective and forced us to carefully consider just what the actual
achievements of the Renaissance were. Nonetheless, the documents in
sixteenth century Bergamo suggest that there was a fundamental shift
in how students, teachers, parents, and politicians viewed education.
They saw increased value in a 'classical' or 'humanist' education, and
to that extent the term 'Renaissance' is appropriate.

As noted earlier, the individual chapters of this book examine the
development of schooling in and around Bergamo chiefly through the
lens of the various groups that supported instruction: the commune,
lay confraternities, religious orders, the episcopate, and parents. When
residents of Bergamo envisioned their educational options, it was these

'sponsors' of instruction that occupied their vision. Avoiding a rigid chronological or teleological framework also allows for comparative treatment of relevant topics (e.g., curricula, teacher contracts) across institutions and time periods.

At the risk of engaging in historical anachronism, it may be useful to frame the issue in twenty-first century terms by imagining Bergamo's schooling as either a network or as a marketplace. Like the Internet (and unlike Microsoft), Bergamo did not possess one 'operating system' of education for all users. Rather, there were multiple independent sites that offered knowledge and skills appropriate to the desired outcome: for example, jurisprudence for lawyers, theology for priests, liberal arts for bureaucrats. If one part of the network crashed (i.e., a school closed), the other sponsors continued to offer schooling and scholarships. Just as the World Wide Web connects disparate users across time and space, Bergamo's educational network offered figurative and literal links beyond the city walls. Students could (like Niccolò Machiavelli in Tuscany) converse with the ancients in Ciceronian Latin through recovered texts, and they could also meet fellow scholars in a classroom. The most important aspect of this analogy, however, is the absence of centralized authority. There was no 'education czar,' no 'system administrator,' nor even a regional superintendent who oversaw all schools. Instead, independent masters offered their services to princes, cities, and parents. Examining this broad group of schoolmasters through the various civic and ecclesiastical institutions of the day, however, allows for a more systematic approach.

Schooling in Bergamo can also be conceived of as a village marketplace, where producers and consumers negotiated face-to-face for the exchange of goods and services. Here again the emphasis is on individual action and independent decisions, mediated through long-term institutions. Unlike lawyers and doctors, pre-university teachers were not usually members of a guild that regulated their services closely. Institutions in Bergamo may have exercised a monopoly over scarce resources, such as benefices or degrees, but consumers could also shop around for comparable wares. As in other local markets, consumers weighed price, quality, reputation, and durability in calculating their consumption of education. Some could purchase liberally for themselves and their families, while others could only stare longingly at the storefront. Bergamo's educational marketplace/network expanded substantially between 1500 and 1650, both in absolute size and in the diversity of its offerings.

What types of schools existed in Bergamo and across the Venetian Republic? There are several ways to answer this deceptively simple question. One is to categorize schooling by its institutional sponsor, the method that I adopt throughout the book. Such an approach is not only the most faithful to the runs of primary documents on which this study is based, but in my opinion most closely resembles how the people of Bergamo and elsewhere perceived their educational options. Those institutions included the commune, the confraternity, the episcopate, and religious orders of men, as well as parents acting in concert.

A second approach might be to divide students by age: elementary, secondary, university, and 'adult' education. While this method is appealing because it closely resembles our current practice, it paints a false picture of the Renaissance and early modern period. Elementary students might study advanced Latin grammar; university students might be as young as twelve or thirteen; adults could be functionally literate in Italian or dialect. Thus a purely age-based framework is impractical.

A third way to count schools would be to divide them by language of instruction: Latin on the one hand, Italian on the other. The Latinate schools taught Latin grammar and composition through works of history, literature, poetry, and rhetoric from classical antiquity, while the vernacular schools offered a broad range of adult texts including chivalric romances, morality stories, hagiographies, dramatic narratives, and so forth. Vernacular schools usually included commercial mathematics, bookkeeping, and rudimentary instruction in reading and writing skills.[20] Schools in Bergamo and neighbouring cities certainly offered instruction in Latin grammar and literature, for example in the Caspi Academy and in the Misericordia's Academy for Clerics, just as vernacular instruction was available in the Schools of Christian Doctrine. However, such a division is a blunt instrument that can obscure the important distinctions and sub-categories within schooling. Equally important, as both Paul Grendler and Robert Black have observed, students in the thirteenth through fifteenth centuries often learned to read for the first time in Latin rather than in the vernacular; thus we cannot automatically associate Latinate education with more advanced instruction.[21]

A fourth approach is to organize instruction by the subject matter being taught (e.g., grammar, abacus, notarial skills).[22] For Bergamo I have found little evidence of schools identified explicitly in this way; almost never is there a 'scuola di grammatica' or 'schola dei notai'. Nevertheless, such a categorization can be useful for summarizing what kinds of schools existed. Occasionally the founding charters will specify what kind of instruction is intended, but more often we must rely upon the job titles used in contracts, letters, and other official documents to describe teachers. These range from *rector scolarium* and *professore di grammatica* to *maestro d'umanità, precettore, ripetitore,* and *insegnante.* Some job titles appear to be primarily administrative (*rettore*), while others are highly specific about the subject being taught (*lector Institutiones, ad docere scribendam*).

The documents make clear that secondary schooling in grammar was available in several places in Bergamo, including the schools sponsored by the commune, as well as those run by the confraternities of Sant'Alessandro in Colonna and Sant'Alessandro della Croce. The college operated by the Somaschans in the seventeenth century appears to have had a similar grammar-oriented curriculum, as did the Caspi Academy for younger students. Schooling in grammar was also available to seminarians, along with catechism, singing, and 'sacred subjects' (which would not include theology, a topic reserved to the university). The grammar syllabus was intended to teach Latin composition (*lattinare*) and later to introduce Latin literature and rhetoric.[23] Sometimes pupils learned through an exclusively Latinate curriculum, including a textbook completely in Latin, but during the fourteenth to sixteenth centuries there was a slow transition to vernacular/Latin word lists, prose translation exercises, and so forth. Traditional (Latin) grammar schools taught the *auctores maiores,* such as the Roman classics in poetry (Ovid, Horace, Virgil) and prose (Cicero, Sallust).

Beyond the traditional (Latin) grammar schools, there were other options. Lessons in law were occasionally offered, although with such inconsistency that we cannot call it a 'school.' Instruction in reading and writing was certainly available through the Schools of Christian Doctrine, and from the smaller parish-based schools. Although more modest in their goals, such schools certainly taught a greater number of students than the more elite grammar schools. Aspiring notaries appear to have been trained in apprenticeships, for there are no records of any notarial school in Bergamo. Similarly, Bergamo has only scattered references to instruction in mathematics, commonly known as *abbaco.* Only two instructors, both hired by the confraternity of Sant'Alessandro in Colonna in 1575–6, were exclusively tasked with teaching mathematics. About a dozen references to the teaching of abbaco appear elsewhere, but it is nearly always cited in conjunction with other subjects to be taught. The absence of abbaco from the curriculum is surprising, for

Bergamo had a strong merchant class, even if it never compared to that of Verona or Florence, where abbaco instruction was much more common. In sum, the emphasis in Bergamo seems to have been primarily upon grammar (i.e., Latin) schools, even as other kinds of instruction were also available.

Chapter 1 analyses the efforts of the commune of Bergamo to instruct local youth at the pre-university level between 1482 and 1632. The city's efforts at 'public' instruction can be divided into four thematic sub-periods. Prior to 1482 education was dominated by noble families and the Church, and humanism had not yet taken firm hold. From 1482 to 1524 the commune took a more active role, beginning in the early Cinquecento with the appointment of such notable humanists as Giovanni Battista Pio and Giovita Ravizza to teach grammar and rhetoric. The period 1525–1632 witnessed the reascendancy of the Catholic Church and a corresponding decline in the commitment of the city council. This era also witnessed a spate of innovative attempts to move beyond conventional forms of instruction by experimenting with joint projects and new topics. The final portion of this chapter concentrates upon the teaching of law, such as that by the jurist Giacomo Carrara Benaglio in the seventeenth century. Each of these periods reflects changing support for education; as we will see, the commune's allegiance waxed and waned with external political forces and economic changes. Yet such efforts also reflected the desire of merchants and middle-class professionals to have a more secular education available to their children at public expense.

In chapter 2 I argue that lay confraternities' support for education, which reached back to the late thirteenth century and expanded significantly post-1550, was a crucial factor in Bergamo's educational network. These charitable organizations founded schools, hired teachers, and offered scholarships to educate (mostly male) children and future priests. The most important confraternity in Bergamo, the MIA, utilized its immense wealth and political influence to promote schooling at all levels. These efforts included several academies to train priests as well as a residential college in Padua for young men attending the university. The actions of the MIA were complemented by those of other, smaller lay confraternities in Bergamo's neighbourhoods such as Sant'Alessandro in Colonna and Sant'Alessandro della Croce.

Beginning with the Council of Trent (1545–63), the Catholic Church sought to re-establish its prior dominance in education. This phenomenon is explored over the course of two chapters. In chapter 3 we follow the Schools of Christian Doctrine in Bergamo as they cast a wide net in efforts to teach reading, writing, and the rudiments of Christian faith to boys and girls across Italy. The irony is that such efforts were largely staffed by *lay* men and women. In vivid contrast, the diocesan seminary offered an exclusive, rigorous, orthodox education to boys intending to pursue an ecclesiastical career. Although these two examples represent divergent approaches to schooling in terms of audience and pedagogy, after a rocky start each eventually would enjoy considerable success.

Chapter 4 considers the activities of the Jesuits and the Somaschans in Bergamo from the mid-sixteenth to the mid-eighteenth century. The sixteenth century witnessed the birth of many new religious orders, like these two, that gravitated toward education as their primary ministry. Despite a lucrative benefice, papal support, and an eager bishop, the Jesuits were repeatedly rejected in their efforts to enter the city as schoolmasters. This complex tale of ambition, deceit, and repeated failure reveals much about the educational goals of both individuals and institutions in Bergamo, particularly in comparison with the success of the Somaschans at supervising orphanages and public schools within the city. I carry this part of the story forward to the eighteenth century because only then did the Jesuits actually arrive in Bergamo and their later presence reveals much about these earlier events.

In chapter 5 I discuss parental efforts to educate their own children through private tutors, home schooling, and especially the creation of a private, cooperative boarding academy with a classical curriculum known as the Caspi Academy. A residential institution for young children was quite rare, particularly in a provincial city like Bergamo. Fortunately, one volume of papers for the Caspi Academy has survived largely intact, allowing us to reconstruct some of the financial arrangements, pedagogy, texts, and physical space inside its walls. Our knowledge of private tutors, by contrast, is much more limited, even with extant contracts, inventories, wills, and other legal sources about their activities. Nonetheless we can evaluate the role of tutors and private instructors, and seek to unravel the mystery of why Bergamo had fewer tutors than its sister cities.

Chapter 6 looks to the broader tapestry of northern Italy in order to understand the extent to which Bergamo's schooling did or did not match that of its neighbours. Comparisons with local towns of the *bergamasco*, with the larger cities of Brescia, Verona, and Vicenza, and with the capital city of Venice itself, permit preliminary conclusions about education on the Venetian mainland. Bergamo was simultaneously unique and yet entwined with a larger movement to transform education. For example, Bergamo's repeated rejection of the Jesuit fathers contrasts starkly with that order's success in Brescia and Verona. The wealthy and powerful 'maxi-confraternity' of the MIA resembled the *scuole grandi* of Venice, but its existence in a smaller, provincial city permitted Bergamo to have schools and offer scholarships that normally would have been beyond reach. Similarly, the city's negotiations with outside schoolteachers, and its institution of free public lessons in civil law, were unusual but not unheard of in sixteenth- and seventeenth-century Italy.

Through an analysis of the skills, ideas, and behaviours that parents wished to transfer to their children (or that rulers wished to impose upon their subjects), we can obtain a clearer sense of the dominant concepts and values in a society. Thus a study of schooling provides a window into the collective *mentalités* of a society in any age. The fundamental transformations in political, social, religious, intellectual, and economic practices and beliefs of Italy between 1500 and 1650 make the schooling of this period especially important. The consequences of this 'new schooling' have influenced every generation of schoolchildren from the early Renaissance to the early twenty-first century, and are likely to do so into the future too.

1 *Comune*: Schooling and the City[1]

For centuries parents, philosophers, and politicians have wrestled over the structure and function of public schooling. From Quintilian's observations in first-century Rome and Thomas Jefferson's plans for 'publick' education in colonial Virginia, to more recent debates over vouchers and charter schools, the struggle to shape public instruction has long been an impassioned one. Issues of curriculum reform, teacher qualifications, school prayer, student morality, corporal punishment, and tax-supported schools are not limited to modern U.S. history, but trace their roots to late medieval and early modern Europe. The international universities, humanist academies, and highly urbanized society of Renaissance and early modern Italy represent a critical turning point in this history of public education. A close examination of Bergamo's efforts to implement communal education between the late fifteenth and the mid-seventeenth centuries reveals both the challenges and the accomplishments of public schooling five hundred years ago.

The definition of a 'public' school obviously varies according to the location and time period. A 'public school' in contemporary Britain, for example, refers to a small circle of elite, highly competitive secondary schools whose equivalent in the United States would be termed 'private' or 'independent' schools. A 'public school' in modern-day North America usually refers to a publicly funded secular school open to all students residing within a defined geographical area. For the purposes of this book, I define 'public schools/schooling' as the scholastic instruction provided at the expense and direction of the commune of Bergamo for its citizens. Recipients of this public schooling were often asked to pay modest fees, just as modern students might for athletic programs or a school trip, but in both cases the education is clearly funded by government. Often this concept of a school might involve only one *maestro* [teacher], teaching in his house or in a public building owned by the commune – a far cry from the 'shopping mall high school' that frequently characterizes American education today. Nor was there any sense of a school 'system' in Bergamo; the various educational opportunities available are better described as a network in which the schools might be connected but without any no centralized direction. Finally, it is important to keep in mind that expectations for schools, students, and teachers five hundred years ago were vastly different than those of today.

The fifteenth century represented a golden age for Italian humanists and for the expansion of secular education. Spurred by a buoyant economy, the relative absence of war and plague after 1454, the invention of the printing press, and the re-emergence of works by Cicero and other Roman authors, humanists throughout Italy sought to promote a new type of education based on classical values and literature. This story is a familiar and traditional one, supported by centuries of scholarship, even as some of its specific components have been questioned in recent decades. Yet by any standard of measure, it remains certain that educational activity increased dramatically during the later fifteenth century. The impetus might be attributed to humanists, to Gutenberg's technology, to the rediscovery of classical sources, or to lack of opposition by the Church; what remains indisputable is the widespread interest in expanding public and private education. After the heyday of the Italian Renaissance, the humanists' position as arbiters of the new education was gradually supplanted by princes, city-states, and the Roman Catholic Church. Public education continued to prosper – or at least to survive – but the curriculum and the identity of teachers underwent a marked change. Religious orders of men and women assumed control of schools, catechism was promoted more rigorously, and censorship of texts was exercised more often.

Bergamo's case exemplifies many of these larger trends in public education, while at the same time providing a number of surprising exceptions that force us to rethink some of the most cherished stereotypes about 'humanist' and 'Catholic' education. From 1450 to 1650, the commune of Bergamo supported public instruction in grammar, rhetoric, humanities, and law. Through a variety of different means – salaries, tax exemptions, subsidized housing, joint ventures, and ultimately the foundation of its own school – the commune pursued its ambition to increase the number of literate bureaucrats, merchants, and clergy. As

Woodcut from *Donato al Senno* (Venice, 1564). This stylized image from a
woodcut shows a master lecturing to a small group of advanced students.
Only one of the students holds a book, emphasizing the importance of oral
communication and memorization. Both the students and the master are at-
tired in academic robes; the master's robe is trimmed with fur and he wears
the scholar's cap.

we shall see in successive chapters, other institutions in Bergamo (e.g., lay confraternities, religious orders of men) also promoted a multitude of activities to educate both lay students and those destined for a religious life. In many cases the chronology of these developments overlaps and the different institutions directly influenced each other. The public schooling of the commune thus represented only one avenue among many for a student who wished to obtain an education.

This chapter is divided into four related parts. The first is the period prior to 1482. Although the archival evidence can be thin for this period, it is important to grasp the historical background before the arrival of humanist pedagogy. From the earliest references through the fifteenth century, public education in Bergamo was characterized by indirect support of public education and only intermittent mention of teachers. Second is the period during the late fifteenth and early sixteenth centuries, when the commune made efforts to provide instruction in Latin grammar and humanities. From 1483 to 1524 the commune hired a series of famous masters from outside the city to share their learning in classical languages and literature. Communal support for education was strong in both word and deed. Third is the period after 1525, and continuing for just over a century. During this time, Bergamo experimented with a variety of different approaches: a joint venture with a local confraternity, a public college of its own, and the hiring of religious orders of men to supervise public instruction. This period witnessed a series of attempts to improve the kinds of schooling available to urban boys, while simultaneously trying to trim costs for the city. Nevertheless, there is no denying that the commune's support for education during much of the sixteenth century was inconsistent. Coupled with the increasing influence of the Catholic Church in education, this long period demonstrates a fundamental shift in who governed the early modern classroom.

The fourth and final part of this chapter examines the public teaching of law in Bergamo from the end of the fifteenth century through the middle of the seventeenth century. In examining the same chronological period but through a different lens, we will find some similar trends (e.g., little civic support prior to 1482, strong communal interest during selected decades). In accordance with city statutes of 1491, the commune hired a member of Bergamo's College of Jurists to lecture publicly on civil law, not only for the benefit of students seeking to study at the university in Padua but also for those Bergamo residents who simply wished to acquire more legal knowledge. The commune viewed the study of law as a distinct subject, one that had to be administered independently from the other subjects of public schooling, and thus it is examined separately here. Yet the commune was, if anything, even more inconsistent in supporting legal instruction than other subjects.

The central issue in this chapter is the extent to which municipal government was involved with public education. As the example of Bergamo demonstrates so clearly, civic support for communal education fluctuated dramatically. Such oscillation in public support for education was evident in other Italian cities of that era, and still remains a vibrant feature of public debate in the twenty-first century.

Despite the minimal amount of scholarship devoted to it, the history of public education in Bergamo is important for several reasons.[2] As noted above, the commune was willing to experiment with a wide variety of approaches. Although many of these efforts were inconsistent or under-funded, they remain important as an indication of the ways in which a provincial city responded to the larger movements of Renaissance humanism and Tridentine Catholicism. Bergamo's educational policy evolved from indirect support of public education to a more hands-on approach (e.g., from tax exemptions for teachers to hiring teachers and specifying the curriculum). The slow evolution of public schooling in early modern Bergamo also reveals the gradual resurgence of the Catholic Church. From 1482 to circa 1550 public schooling was staffed exclusively by lay teachers and financed entirely by the commune. From the mid-sixteenth to the mid-seventeenth century, on the other hand, the commune worked much more closely with confraternities, religious orders of men, and the Church hierarchy to achieve its educational goals. George Huppert describes a similar increase in religious influence over education in sixteenth-century France.[3]

Bergamo's experience also reveals the extent to which education remained a *local* prerogative in the Venetian Republic. In contrast to the centralizing tendencies of Milan and Florence, Venice usually permitted its subject cities a fair degree of latitude in determining local educational practice. There were exceptions, of course, particularly with regard to higher education or the admission of Jesuit and Somaschan teachers, but in general Bergamo exercised significant local autonomy in educational matters. Bergamo's location between the Duchy of Milan and the Venetian Republic also make it an unusual case. Politically beholden to Venice but with part of its territory subject to the archbishop of Milan, Bergamo's efforts to find a balance between these two powerful neighbours helped to shape its educational policy. Just as modern school boards or principals must seek accommodation with federal or state agencies that supervise public education, so Bergamo had to strike compromises while retaining its independence.

Public schooling in Bergamo served multiple purposes: to prepare students for more advanced study; to improve the quality of Bergamo's civil servants and ecclesiastics; to train students in virtue and morality; to keep school-age children out of trouble; and to demonstrate civic support for intellectual pursuits. Private tutors and Church-sponsored schools had similar goals, but the activities of Bergamo's public schools hold special interest because they reflect, at least in theory, the will of the city's residents. Public schooling may also help to explain Bergamo's surprisingly high literacy rate in successive centuries. Lastly, Bergamo's public education is important because of the extent to which its experience echoes that of other Italian cities. Although Bergamo's city council frequently extolled the benefits of education for both students and the city, it is hardly possible to call these efforts a 'triumph of humanism,' nor is it reasonable to accept that Bergamo set some kind of example for other cities to follow. Bergamo's sporadic attempts to support public education were, in fact, rather ordinary. Yet the very fact of its ordinariness may allow us to use Bergamo's experience as 'typical' of other small cities and towns in Renaissance and early modern Italy.

Schooling in Bergamo Prior to 1482

Aside from scattered lapidary references to a grammar teacher in Roman Bergamo, the first documented reference to schooling in Bergamo dates to 973, when Bishop Ambrogio donated a house and garden for the use of grammar and music teachers associated with the cathedral.[4] This was not a 'public school' but the long-standing name of the neighbourhood in which this school was located ('Antescholis') suggests that schools were often to be found on this site. A list of twenty-one teachers in residence during the brief period between 1160 and 1189 suggests the importance of education in Bergamo in the later twelfth century, as does an 1194 brief from pope Celestine III admonishing the canons of Nembro (a town near Bergamo) for refusing a benefice to Maestro Ambrogio.[5] Although the cathedral schools admitted lay students, and some of the twenty-one teachers might have been employed by the commune of Bergamo, most education at this time was directed by a bishop or by cathedral canons.[6]

In contrast, the commune's appointment of Bonifacio da Osio (or

Bonacio de Oxio) as *magister* (teacher) in 1291 clearly signalled a decisive gesture in favour of public schooling. The first of a series of renowned instructors invited by the commune of Bergamo to hold classes for the benefit of the city's youth, Bonifacio was born in Osio, near Bergamo, but educated at the University of Bologna. After taking his degree around 1252, he was offered a professorship at the university there, receiving praise for his outstanding erudition. In 1291 he returned to Bergamo and accepted a job offer from the commune to teach Latin grammar and rhetoric. Although he owned a significant amount of land in and around Bergamo, between 1291 and 1311 he rented at least half a dozen different houses for his lessons. In 1294 the podestà (governor) of Bergamo permitted several Milanese students to attend Bonifacio's grammar school. These references suggest that Bonifacio provided accommodations and private lessons to other students in addition to his public schooling responsibilities. It also implies that the commune was not yet willing to provide a space at civic expense where classes could be held. Bonifacio da Osio became a canon of the church of San Vincenzo in 1299 and later enjoyed a substantial benefice. Despite repeated pleas from his colleagues and his students that he return to Bologna, including an offer from the university to lighten his teaching load, he remained in Bergamo until his death in 1311.[7] Bonifacio da Osio's decision to remain in Bergamo, especially in light of a prestigious job offer at the university, is a first glimmer of the devotion to Bergamasque public education that would recur in centuries to follow.

Bonifacio da Osio was hardly alone in exercising the profession of *maestro di grammatica* (grammar teacher) in Bergamo. In 1298 Lorenzo Domenico de Apibus opened a public school in his own house on Via San Giacomo where he taught grammar and rhetoric for more than thirty years. Although little evidence remains of the activities of this initial school, we do know something of his life. Prior to becoming a public teacher, Lorenzo de Apibus had worked as a notary in Bergamo and from 1294 served as tutor to the nephews of Cardinal Guglielmo Longo in Rome.[8] Assisted by his sons Venturino and Jacopo, Lorenzo de Apibus became a wealthy and respected citizen. In 1317 he was nominated to settle a dispute between two political factions and simultaneously elected as *consigliere* (advisor) to the Misericordia Maggiore confraternity (known to all as the MIA). In 1319 the Crusaders of San Leonardo granted him the right to rebuild a house destroyed by fire and to keep all of the subsequent income. He raised four children and continued to acquire property until his death in 1337. In a will drawn up by the notary Gerardo Soiario, Lorenzo instructed his son Jacopo to support a poor student in his own house for a period of two years. Furthermore, he declared, if no male Apibus heir survived, his property was to revert to the MIA in order to fund a scholarship for poor boys.[9] Lorenzo de Apibus probably donated these funds and placed this burden upon his son as a demonstration of piety and to increase his chances for salvation. But his gesture also suggests that public education was not solely the province of the elite, at least in the eyes of this influential maestro.

Lorenzo's son Jacopo, nicknamed 'maestro Crotto,' studied under his father and eventually succeeded him as a grammar teacher. No record of his graduation from university survives, but it is significant that in notarial acts prior to 1347 he is referred to as a *magister*, while afterwards he was called either *professor artium liberalium* (professor of liberal arts) or *doctor grammatice* (doctor of grammar).[10] He began teaching around 1322 and continued to run a school in his house on Via San Giacomo for nearly forty years. In addition to teaching local students, Jacopo appears to have offered housing to boys from outside the city who wished to study with him. This father-son dyad thus taught in Bergamo's communal schools for six decades, a remarkable achievement in an era better known for instability and illiteracy.

Unfortunately, we know very little of the curriculum that Jacopo and Lorenzo de Apibus offered. A grammar book in Bergamo's Civic Library bears the name of the owner, Gerardo Soiario, and an inscription that 'he studied at the school of the teacher Jacopo.'[11] A second clue derives from a pair of letters written to Jacopo de Apibus by the famous Trecento poet Petrarch to request certain texts of Cicero, including the *Tusculanes*.[12] Petrarch opened his letter with an obvious bit of flattery: 'Rumour has it that of all Italians you are the most knowledgeable about and hospitable to Cicero.'[13] Not only does this request underline the extent of 'maestro Crotto''s fame among Italian scholars, but it suggests that in addition to grammar and vocabulary, his school taught literature and perhaps rhetoric. Of course it was standard practice for grammar teachers to utilize excerpts from Latin literature to illustrate points of grammar and syntax.

A 1342 petition of Jacopo de Apibus to the podestà of Bergamo requesting exemption from the tax rolls confirms that 'it was well known that he was working in a school where he taught grammar, dialectic, and rhetoric' for the good of the inhabitants and their children who otherwise ran the risk of remaining without an instructor.[14] Again we see the emphasis upon inclusion of all students within the school, not just of a few elites. In his will of 1361, Jacopo de Apibus left the bulk of his estate to the MIA confraternity, to be disbursed over time in the form of scholarships for poor students. Although the 'Apibus scholarships' certainly benefited the public, they were administered privately by the MIA and not by the commune, and are thus discussed in the next chapter.

Jacopo de Apibus's petition to the podestà for tax relief highlights an important means by which the commune supported public schools in Bergamo. Along with medical doctors, teachers were regarded as an asset to the public and therefore were often exempted from paying taxes. For example, in 1388, in response to a request by Nicolo Della Torre and other Bergamasque barber-surgeons (*magistri cirogiae in Pergamo*), the city council ruled that medical doctors be exempt from taxes on account of their utility and poverty.[15] Teachers were not exempt *de jure*, like ecclesiastics or fathers with more than ten children, but they were clearly exempt *de facto*, for they do not appear in the extended list of vocations compiled in fifteenth- and sixteenth-century tax returns. This tradition, begun when Bergamo was an independent commune, continued under both the Visconti dukes of Milan and the doges of Venice. The 1342 petition of Jacopo de Apibus, addressed to the podestà Cabrio Possobonelli, who ruled the city in the name of Giovanni and Luchino Visconti, points out that 'according to the law [Jacopo] has the right to enjoy the privilege of immunity from every real and personal tax, and he should not be included on the tax rolls, and this liberty has been and still is defended by a long-standing tradition of the governors and officials of the city of Bergamo, and therefore he asks that his name be stricken from the list of those who must pay taxes.'[16] A century later, just after the Venetians had assumed control over Bergamo, a tax return recognized the exemption of Spiciarus de Grandiniano because he was teaching school in the city.[17] In 1468 Bergamo's city council decreed that the grammar teacher Bartolomeo da Bonate Inferiore, by virtue of having opened a public school, had contributed sufficiently that he should be exempt from any further taxes. Two years later the council announced that all resident grammar teachers in the area should be exempt from personal taxes.[18] On 15 September 1475, in response to a request from Paolo Terzi, the rector of the city's public school, the council proclaimed that 'on account of their good and useful services to the city ... it is firmly declared that every public schoolteacher in the city and suburbs of Bergamo is exempt from every personal, property, or mixed tax, except for the customs tax.'[19] With the exception of a few academic 'superstars,' most schoolteachers were not particularly well paid. Similar to today, when school districts sometimes offer interest-free mortgages or forgiveness of student loans for teachers, the promise of tax immunity could have been a strong incentive to induce masters to stay in Bergamo rather than move to Milan or Venice. The commune of Bergamo was not always so generous to its teachers, however. For example, the city statutes prohibited grammar teachers, whether public or private, from accepting payment prior to Christmas for fear that teachers would cancel classes and the liberated students would engage in 'pernicious and abominable scandals and fights.'[20]

In addition to tax exemptions, the commune regularly allowed teachers to provide room and board to students and to receive additional payments for this service. The examples of Bonifacio da Osio and Lorenzo de Apibus demonstrate the roots of this tradition. The importance of this income is demonstrated by the fact that Giovanni Minoli, one of the grammar teachers hired by the MIA in the mid-sixteenth century, quit his job because he was not allowed to supplement his income by accepting student boarders.[21] Other public school teachers, such as Nicolò Cologno, also boarded students later in the century. Such boarding arrangements, important to the teachers' economic survival, could even be quite lucrative. These arrangements further serve to remind us that 'public' education was not necessarily limited to students who lived within the city, nor was it financed entirely by the commune. Students from Bergamo, including several members of the powerful Suardi family, regularly attended school in Brescia and vice versa.

The limited evidence presented thus far demonstrates that public schooling in late medieval Bergamo was viewed with some hesitation by the city fathers. Tax exemptions and permission for student boarders required no investment from the city council. Even this kind of indirect support, however, was inconsistent. In the absence of strong public support for education, independent masters probably filled the gap, as Paul Grendler has demonstrated elsewhere.[22] While the arrival of humanist scholars would usher in dramatic changes in some cities, the arrival of such men in Bergamo during most of the fifteenth century did not provoke much of a change.

One of the founders of the humanist movement, Gasparino Barzizza (1360–1430), taught briefly in Bergamo at the beginning of the fifteenth century.[23] In 1396 he and an assistant were paid by the chapter of canons of San Vincenzo for instructing individual students, but he may have also offered some public lessons in grammar.[24] He soon moved on to Venice, Padua, and Milan, where he taught students, published works on oratory and rhetoric, and emended editions of Seneca, Cicero, and

Saint Paul. In addition, he authored a Bergamasque-Latin lexicon that would prove invaluable to later generations. Bonaventura da Bergamo, author of a handbook on orthography praised by Alberico da Rosciate, appeared in Bergamo at about the same time to serve as a tutor.[25] Maffeo Vegio (1406/7–58), born in Bergamo but raised in Lodi, wrote a treatise entitled *De educatione liberorum* (On liberal education) along with numerous verses, elegies, and epigrams. Like his fellow humanists, Vegio bitterly criticized medieval schools and promoted new methods of study and learning, particularly in the field of law.[26] Although none of these men was directly hired by the commune of Bergamo, they illustrate that humanists did not confine themselves exclusively to the major urban centres or princely courts but travelled to smaller regional cities too.

One final example – that of Gian Mario Filelfo (1428–80) – perfectly summarizes the status of public schooling in Bergamo during the late fifteenth century. Gian Mario received a humanist education from his father, Francesco Filelfo, later a well-known courtier of the Sforza in Milan and the Medici in Florence. The elder Filelfo repeatedly found positions for his son as a teacher, including a post at Verona in the 1460s as instructor of *studia humanitatis* (humanistic studies). Around 1468–9 Gian Mario accepted the invitation of Bishop Luigi Donato to come to Bergamo; in 1470, with the assistance of Bergamo's most illustrious citizen, the Venetian captain-general Bartolomeo Colleoni, Filelfo obtained a position as a public school teacher. Although no direct evidence exists about Filelfo's pedagogy in Bergamo, his poor track record elsewhere, combined with his sudden request to move to Colleoni's court at Malpaga and his hasty departure to Ancona in 1471, suggests that his teaching was not well received.[27]

The examples of Filelfo and other humanists thus suggest that while the fifteenth century may have represented a golden age for humanism in Italy, public education in Bergamo did not flourish. Bergamo's hesitant embrace of public education is consistent with the experience of other provincial cities in northern Italy (see chapter 6). Nevertheless, at least in the short term, the tide would soon begin to turn in favour of communal support for education.

Grammar and Humanities, 1482–1524

This period of four decades represents the first significant shift in how Bergamo supported public education. Beginning in 1482 the commune hired a series of masters, several of whom were local but at least two of whom (Giovan Battista Pio and Giovita Ravizza) were well-known humanists with substantial records of scholarship. Many of the teachers in this period were more generously compensated by the city, sometimes with benefits beyond their salary and housing. For the first time the city council adopted humanist rhetoric to glorify the benefits of a liberal arts education. Also for the first time the council looked well beyond its own borders to recruit teachers. Occasionally this ambitious program ended badly, as when Pio departed unexpectedly to Bologna, but in general it was a successful time for commune-sponsored education. Certainly, the other institutions in Bergamo were largely dormant in this period with regard to education; neither the Church nor the various confraternities, with the exception of the MIA, displayed any initiative comparable to that of the city council. Following a brief review of those teachers hired in the late fifteenth century, we will turn to the more complicated cases of Pio and Ravizza, and the implications of these individuals for the story of public education in Bergamo.

Early in 1482 the commune decided to take a more active approach toward the issue of public schooling. By a vote of 36–16, the city council passed a motion to hire a doctor of humanities to lecture publicly in the morning and afternoon. The lessons were open to anyone who wished to attend, free of charge, presumably including adults. The teacher would be paid a monthly salary of eight imperial lire for a period of one year, with specified fines in case of repeated absences. For the first time, the commune was now actively engaged in the recruitment and supervision of its teachers, rather than relying upon financial incentives like tax breaks. Paolo Terzi was hired from 1483 to 1487 to teach grammar and logic at a salary of five florins per month, plus the contributions from his students. He was succeeded by Marco de Soltia, described as a *fisicus* (physician), who began giving instruction on 22 July 1487, presumably in the humanities, even though he had been trained in medicine.[28]

In 1491 the council declared that 'there is nothing that this city needs more for bringing up and wisely educating its youth than a good and modest orator and grammarian in the humanities who can teach publicly and privately.'[29] Although such humanists as Leonardo Bruni and Vittorino da Feltre had been trumpeting the benefits of a humanist education since the early fifteenth century, this was the first time that Bergamo's city council referred explicitly to the benefits that the city and its inhabitants would derive from a public, humanist education. The council nominated Francesco Romano da Crema, not only because of his outstanding abilities in grammar and rhetoric but also on account of his 'elegant public lectures on Dante and Virgil.' Although Romano's scholarship and erudition were already recognized by most of the learned men in Bergamo, the council nevertheless commissioned three deputies to investigate his character and previous teaching experience. Given the negative experience with Gian Mario Filelfo two decades earlier, such caution was warranted. After soliciting letters from several university professors, the deputies quickly submitted a report that lauded Romano as 'a very religious man, of excellent character, unquestioned honesty, superior knowledge, and quite above all others in the excellence of his conversation.' In order to demonstrate that Bergamo valued eloquent and virtuous men, the council offered him a gift of eighteen lire to help defray his living expenses prior to the official commencement of his job. In addition to the usual salary of five florins per month, Romano received permission to house boarders (*donzenarios contuberniales*) and other students in his house for a fee to be negotiated separately with parents. This offer represents the first time that the concept of a residence for students was explicitly approved by the commune of Bergamo. The city council's use of the word *contubernium* – the elegant Latin term preferred by Guarino Guarini to describe his boarding students – confirms that the commune had accepted some of the humanist message.[30] Romano taught for six years to the full satisfaction of both parents and the city council of Bergamo.

In 1497 the city council voted to hire Giovanni de Lolmo, *artium et medicinae doctor* (doctor in medicine and arts), to teach logic at a salary of eight imperial lire per month. Within two weeks he had begun teaching publicly in the city center; the curriculum and texts to be followed, however, were never specified.[31] In 1498 eight members of the executive council [Bina] proposed hiring someone else to teach logic and philosophy 'for the great and evident benefit of the commune of Bergamo and to more easily replenish the city with wise and virtuous men.'[32] This proposal made specific reference to the fact that such lessons were intended to help the less fortunate attain the path to virtue, thus reemphasizing the idea that the lessons were open to all. Surprisingly, the motion was defeated. The Bina immediately submitted another motion to hire someone to teach Latin grammar and rhetoric every day, with the salary to be determined by the entire council depending upon the diligence and competence of the instructor. After fierce debate, the second motion passed by a vote of 37–17. The city council minutes record neither the arguments for and against these motions, nor the identity of the instructor who was eventually hired.

Thus we can only speculate as to why one proposal failed and the other succeeded. Since the curriculum proposed in the first motion was more advanced, perhaps the majority of the council wished to keep these public lessons at an introductory level. Or perhaps, by varying a teacher's salary according to his qualifications, the council wished to emphasize control over its expenditures. A third possibility could be the 'aristocratization' of the city council; as the leading families of Bergamo solidified their hold on city council seats, they may have sought to limit public education to the fundamentals of reading and writing so that their own, privately tutored heirs would be assured of jobs in the civic bureaucracy. For instance, only two decades later in the midst of the chaos caused by the War of the League of Cambrai (1508–16), the Venetian Senate instituted a dramatic change in the election procedure for Bergamo's city council. The intention of Venice was clearly to break the stranglehold of the pro-Milanese Ghibelline aristocracy and to favour Guelf merchants, who supported Venetian policy. Regardless of the motivation behind the city council's actions, the trend toward greater involvement in education at the turn of the sixteenth century is clearly visible.

In contrast to the Byzantine manoeuvres of the late fifteenth century, the events surrounding the recruitment, hiring, and eventual resignation of Giovan Battista Pio and Giovita Ravizza at the beginning of the sixteenth century are well documented. These events mark an important shift in the city council's pursuit of public school teachers. Hiring Pio and Ravizza symbolized the city council's renewed desire to bring in a famous master and its willingness to pay the hefty salary necessary to recruit him. This experience also demonstrates that Bergamo's city council pursued multiple candidates simultaneously, a further indication of the seriousness with which it regarded this position.

A student of Filippo Beroaldo the Elder at Bologna in the late fifteenth century, Pio (1460–1540) was an accomplished philologist and ardent humanist who published numerous editions of, and commentaries on, various classical authors. As a peripatetic pedagogue and a participant in a plethora of polemics, Pio conforms to the archetypal image of the Italian humanist. Although he was educated in Bologna and taught rhetoric and poetry at the university there for twenty-six years, Pio held a number of other positions too: Latin tutor to Isabella d'Este in Mantua (1496–7), public school teacher in Bergamo (1505–7), tutor to Marc

Antonio Flaminio in Rome (1509–14?), professor of humanities in Lucca (1526–34), and finally professor of rhetoric at the university in Rome (exact dates unknown).[33] Widely recognized for his facility with Latin, Pio's love of philological detail made him an easy target for ridicule later in his career. In December 1506 Pio was attacked for his comments on Plautus by Giovan Francesco Boccardo, a Brescian humanist who used the pseudonym Pilade, to which Pio responded by publishing his vituperative *Apologia* in 1508. In 1512 Pio was drawn into the debate between Pico della Mirandola and Pietro Bembo over Ciceronianism and became a favourite target of the Ciceronians as the model of a boring and pedantic professor.[34]

Nevertheless, Pio was a prominent and important figure. Despite the relative brevity of his stay, his experiences and his network of acquaintances in Bergamo can be reconstructed in some detail. Furthermore, Carlo Dionisotti has argued that Pio's debate with Pilade represented the end of an era, when the humanists had to transform themselves from university professors into courtly scholars dependent upon the goodwill of the prince.[35] Subject city of the Venetian Republic, Bergamo could boast of neither a prince nor a royal court. Thus Pio's experience in Bergamo differs from his prior position with the Este family in Mantua or his subsequent appointment as a tutor in Rome. However, given that Pio was employed by Bergamo at the time of his famous debate with Pilade, his experiences within the city warrant examination. As we shall see, Pio's relations with the city council appear to have been cordial, but he was no sycophant trying to court favour with the city council of Bergamo.

Pio had been teaching rhetoric and poetry in Bologna in 1505 when Bergamo's city council authorized three deputies to find a 'superb teacher' willing to offer public lessons in letters, grammar, and rhetoric.[36] The lessons, announced the council, were intended to sustain the republic and ensure the well-being of the city by replenishing the number of wise men living there. A letter to Pio from one of the deputies, Paolo Zanchi, repeated the council's intention to find 'the most accomplished orator in the Italian world,' one who would 'nourish the habit of good studies and adorn [our] youth with the most splendid manners.' In late August the council offered the job to Pio, under conditions summarized by Paolo Zanchi:

> Contract between the Magnificent City of Bergamo and the excellent professor of both languages [Greek and Latin], Giovanni Battista Pio of Bologna.

- He will provide two public lessons every day in the lecture hall.
- He will set up a private school, and direct it in a suitable manner, receiving the appropriate fees and gifts from his students.
- [Salary of] one hundred gold [scudi] per year, with payment monthly or however he prefers; the payment by the public shall not be reduced on account of his private students.
- He will be given his own house free of charge.
- This contract may be renewed in either two years or three years as he prefers.[37]

Pio's salary was not only substantially higher than that earned by his predecessors but exceeded the salary paid to any other teacher in Bergamo during the next sixty years. The opportunity to teach private students must have been lucrative, particularly as no limit was specified for the number of students that he could tutor. In addition to his salary, the council offered Pio fifteen scudi toward the cost of finding a house and transferring his possessions. One month later, in an eloquent letter of thanks to the city council, Pio accepted the job and promised to arrive in October. City council minutes and the diary of Marco Beretta confirm that Pio arrived on 14 November 1505 for the purpose of teaching and lecturing publicly.[38]

In his first year Pio appears to have taught the required subjects without difficulty and without incident. In the spring of 1506 the city council signalled its appreciation by commissioning the carpenter Andrea Mangili to build several pieces of furniture, including a large wooden chair (*cattedra*) from which Pio could deliver his lessons on the principles of Latin grammar.[39] The chair, bench, and closet were apparently installed in the 'lecture hall' specified by the city council. Early in the summer Pio requested permission to be absent for two months in order to take care of personal business in Bologna. The council agreed, but in an ominous foreshadowing, Pio took his family with him to Bologna; the council therefore made arrangements to have one of the city council members receive the final instalment of twelve ducats if Pio were not present. Five months later Pio still had not reappeared in Bergamo. Upon expiration of Pio's contract in mid-November the council ordered the same three deputies to make arrangements with Pio's landlord, Nicolò Bonghi, in preparation for the arrival of a replacement master. Unexpectedly, Pio returned at Christmas, apparently swayed by a personal visit from the secretary of the city of Bergamo, Francesco Bellafino, and perhaps by the deposition of his Bolognese patron (Giovanni II Bentivoglio) earlier in the fall.

It seems probable that Pio taught students in Bergamo, including Bernardo Tasso, father of the poet Torquato, for the rest of the academic year 1506–7. In early May, however, two deputies were ordered to investigate how many lessons Pio had missed, and a week later Pio appeared before the city council to apologize for having skipped two weeks of classes at Easter. Pio offered to teach an additional class on Thursdays or else to forgo a percentage of his salary. The council must have accepted his explanation, for in late May 1507 they sent him the next installment of his salary. In August 1507 he was still in Bergamo, where he exchanged letters with Girolamo Suardi and loaned Suardi a copy of Angelo Poliziano's *Rime*. On 22 October 1507, however, Pio's appointment to teach rhetoric and poetry at the University of Bologna was renewed, and five days later he sent a resignation letter to Bergamo's city council.[40]

Why did Pio come to Bergamo in the first place? No doubt the high salary and corresponding benefits induced him to consider Bergamo. He also would have enjoyed considerable fame in a smaller city. Indeed, the extant evidence suggests that he was actively recruited and then coddled by the city council, attentions which doubtless would have appealed to Pio's vanity and pride. On a more practical level, Valerio Del Nero suggests that the arrival of Pope Julius II and the fall of the Bentivoglio family (Pio's patrons) in November 1506 may have induced him to look for work outside of Bologna.[41] With all of these reasons to stay, why might Pio have left early and often? Pio had a record of chronic absenteeism at Bologna too, so perhaps the truancy and indecision displayed in Bergamo represent part of a larger pattern of behaviour. His long absence from Bergamo in the summer and fall of 1506 might also be attributed to the publication of Pilade's vitriolic attack as well as the chaos in Bologna. Lastly, Pio's name appears infrequently in the acts of the university in Bologna, suggesting his isolation from his colleagues and his students.[42] Regardless of the specific motivation(s) behind his actions, Pio's presence was important to public education in Bergamo, not only because of his high salary and his notoriety but because he helped to solidify Bergamo's tradition of hiring a famous outside humanist.

Pio's successor, the humanist pedagogue Giovita Ravizza (1476–1553), boasts a similar career path: he taught publicly and privately in various Italian cities, engaged in frequent correspondence with other humanists, and published orations, poetry, and a pedagogical treatise during the first half of the sixteenth century.[43] Born midway between

Bergamo and Brescia, Ravizza began teaching in his hometown of
Chiari at the age of seventeen as a *ripetitore* (assistant teacher) for thirty
ducats a year before being promoted in 1499 to the position of master
in Caravaggio. The exact date of his arrival in Bergamo is not recorded,
but indirect evidence suggests that it was in the fall of 1508.[44] Ravizza
was ensconced as the master of Bergamo's public school by 1510 and
remained there for fourteen years, until he accepted a similar position
in Vicenza in the spring of 1524. He went on to hold the lower lecture-
ship at the School of Saint Mark in Venice in 1538, received Venetian
citizenship in 1543, and published important works in 1544 and 1551.
Ravizza is remembered primarily for his pedagogical treatise *De liberis
publice ad humanitatem informandis* (On public education of children toward the humanities), published in Venice in 1551 but first written under a different title in 1523 for the city council of Bergamo. *De liberis* was
utilized by scores of other teachers in the sixteenth and seventeenth
centuries owing to its practical advice about how to run a school.

With the exception of this important treatise, surprisingly little information exists about Ravizza's teaching career in Bergamo. Clearly,
he remained in Bergamo much longer than Pio, with the result that he
was more enmeshed in civic activities. Like Pio, Ravizza was hired by
a group of three deputies from the city council, of whom one was again
Paolo Zanchi. Upon the expiration of his initial three-year contract in
1511, he was reappointed for seven years with a raise in salary of twenty-five ducats, and in 1518 he was reappointed for an additional five
years. Ravizza, however, remained disgruntled. Dissatisfied with his
salary, he appeared repeatedly before the city council to ask for a raise
and was rewarded eventually with a supplement of 6.25 ducats per
month for an annual salary of 110 scudi. On 19 June 1523 he presented
the treatise *De modo in scholis servando* (On how to organize a school) to
Bergamo's city council. Ravizza received his final payment from Bergamo in May 1524, the same month that he began teaching in Vicenza's
public school. Ravizza was replaced by a monk who offered to teach
logic and philosophy in the Colleoni chapel free of charge, a proposal
accepted with alacrity by the city council.[45]

In addition to his salary, the council also provided Ravizza with ten
ducats to rent a room for teaching his lessons, probably in the Colleoni
chapel or the Palace of Justice (Palazzo della Ragione). The city council's investment in Pio's furniture and Ravizza's classroom suggests
that education was becoming more important to the commune. No
longer were indirect actions, such as tax exemptions, sufficient to sup-

port public schooling. The city council apparently desired to raise the profile of public schooling by removing it from the instructor's private home and placing it in a civic space near the centre of town.

The number and precise identity of Ravizza's students in Bergamo remain impossible to determine. A partial list of his students includes several boys who later became distinguished for their intellectual and professional accomplishments: Bartolomeo Pellegrino, Gian Gerolamo Albano, Guglielmo Gratarolo.[46] Several of his students wrote glowing encomiums about Ravizza's intellectual acumen, of which that by Panfilo Zanchi is typical.[47] Nor can we determine with any certainty the curriculum used by Ravizza, though it can be assumed that he taught the classic texts of Cicero, Virgil, Terence, Horace, and others. As we will see shortly, Ravizza was very familiar with Quintilian, so it seems likely that his students – like earlier generations – read the *Instituto oratoria*. In his pedagogical writings, Ravizza insisted that a large lecture be immediately followed by small classes of twenty-five students or less in which the teacher would explain and amplify the lesson that had just been heard. Furthermore, asserted Ravizza, the more able students should be assigned to help those who were weaker or younger. It seems likely that some of these pedagogical methods (discussed more fully below) would have been standard practice in his own classroom, even if Bergamo's city council never created the large, elaborate school envisioned by Ravizza.

In addition to his academic responsibilities, Ravizza participated in the civic life of Bergamo by delivering orations and congratulatory speeches. His 1510 funeral oration in honour of the temporary French governor of Bergamo, Gastone di Valenza, was followed by a funerary elegy for Giovanni Taberio in 1515 and another for Paolo Zanchi in 1520.[48] Ravizza was further asked by the commune to compose an appropriate discourse in celebration of the departure of the Venetian capitano, Nicolò Dolfin. On 6 November 1520 Ravizza even gave a speech at the wedding of Margherita Albani of Bergamo and Giacomo Fornario of Pavia.[49] He also corresponded with the Suardi family, and with Arrone Battaglia of Treviglio, who tutored Ravizza's son Eleuterio circa 1515.[50] Ravizza's letters to Battaglia reveal a tender and genuine concern about his son's progress.

Ravizza published very little during his tenure in Bergamo, either because he was busy with his classroom teaching or else because – as noted later in his will – he was devastated by the loss of his mother Elena, his brother Lorenzo, and his son, Eleuterio, in the year 1516–17.[51]

It must also be remembered that Bergamo suffered a series of military invasions and armed sieges during the battles of the War of the League of Cambrai, when the city oscillated between the Venetians, the French, and the Spanish. While such conflict may not have disturbed Ravizza's school, it doubtless hampered his ability to travel outside the city and to publish works in Venice or Milan (no books were printed in Bergamo until the middle of the sixteenth century).

In 1523 Ravizza presented a manuscript copy of his treatise *De modo in scholis servando* to Bergamo's city council.[52] The council promptly elected four deputies to consider the treatise; they in turn pronounced it to be excellent. The treatise is important in the context of this study for several reasons.

First, it reflected Ravizza's pedagogical experience in Bergamo; many of his written observations must have been founded directly upon his experiences within the city from 1508 to 1523. Giuseppe Gullino takes the opposite view, writing that the treatise owes much more to the model set by Vittorino da Feltre than to Ravizza's own pedagogical experience.[53] However, Gullino was analysing a later version, the 1551 *De liberis*, and he considered it in the context of Venetian education. Since we know from the preface of *De liberis* that it was explicitly *not* written for Venice, and indeed that Ravizza did not even edit this version himself, it makes sense that *De liberis* might not reflect Ravizza's own pedagogical experience in Venice. Regarding Bergamo, the situation is different: Ravizza wrote this treatise himself after teaching in Bergamo for fourteen years, and so the connection between his classroom experience and his written work was much more direct. Ravizza says explicitly in the preface that his work is based on three sources: Quintilian, Ravizza's own teachers, and, above all, his own didactic experience.

Second, Ravizza's treatise included practical elements often missing from humanist works on education. The treatise certainly contained lofty promises about how the study of ancient letters was the key to civic virtue and a well-founded government; as Gullino notes, Ravizza's treatise was 'completely soaked' in the rhetorical conventions and artifices that both the age and his profession demanded.[54] But it also contained practical details about installing a toilet or having sufficient sunlight, items not included by Vergerius, Vegio, and other humanist pedagogues. Third, as Paul Grendler has commented, Ravizza's text insisted that the state play an important role in support of public education.[55] In the 1551 edition considered by Grendler, 'the state' is represented by Venetian magistrates, but the 1523 version was obviously intended for

Bergamo's city council. This attitude represented a dramatic shift away from the previous and subsequent reliance upon confraternities, parents, or the Church to promote education, and instead assigned a fundamental responsibility to the government. While Ravizza was certainly not the only catalyst for this change of heart, his work stands as a clear example of how the perception of 'public' education was changing. In this context, his treatise supports the argument that Bergamo's city council became increasingly involved in public education after 1482.

Fourth, Ravizza does not suggest that the state should go it alone: a careful reading of his treatise reveals that parents were expected to play a key role in educating their children. Ravizza discourages the use of boarding schools, for example, believing that students learn more when they remain at home and receive positive feedback from their parents, particularly with regard to their behaviour and deportment. This example serves to remind us that the residential academies, seminaries, and colleges founded throughout Europe in the later sixteenth century educated only a minority of students; many more attended communal schools like the one envisioned by Ravizza. Fifth, the treatise demonstrates the renewed impact of Quintilian upon Renaissance pedagogy: the Roman schoolmaster is cited both directly and indirectly. Sixth, and lastly, Ravizza's treatise emphasizes the importance of instruction in morality and manners, a theme which assumed increasing importance during and after the Council of Trent (1545–63).

The treatise can be divided into several major subject headings: physical plant, academic schedule, teaching staff, pedagogy, curriculum, and external affairs.[56] According to Ravizza, the school building(s) must be spacious, sunny (*ne vel legentium vel audientium impedimento sit obscuritas*), free of drafts, and equipped with fresh water and a toilet (*locus, quo ad secreta naturae secedere liceat*). In addition to an auditorium large enough to hold all students simultaneously (*auditorium capax pro multitudine*), and a library well stocked with Greek and Latin texts, there should be eight classrooms and an office containing such school supplies as pens, ink, and paper, so that students need not waste time searching for these necessary items. Only one door should remain open during school hours, so that the *bidello* (i.e., porter) could keep track of students who arrive late or leave early.[57] The school day ought to begin early, according to Ravizza, with a general lecture for all students, followed by smaller classes in which the day's lesson would be analysed and explained in greater detail. After a recess for lunch, the students should return to the classroom to write a composition, which would be examined by the teacher later in the afternoon while the students listened to a second lecture in the auditorium.

Friday was to be devoted to a review session of the week's lesson: the students arrived an hour early and remained an hour and a half later so that there was sufficient opportunity for them to recite the poetry or prose or grammatical rules studied that week. Students who performed poorly were to be sent to the corner to review the lesson, with the threat of corporal punishment for those who were obstinate or lazy. In general Ravizza advocated prizes rather than punishment, urging teachers to use warnings and prevention rather than a heavy hand.[58] Top students regularly presented their work to other students or were chosen to engage in scholastic disputations on the weekends.

On Saturday students were again expected to arise early so that the time for bathing did not interfere with the literary competition (*in litterarium certamen descendant*) slated for the morning. Victors were rewarded with pens or paper, purchased with the income derived from fines levied against students who had not spoken Latin or who had committed other infractions during the week. Sundays were devoted to catechism and Christian piety, and perhaps to visits with family and friends. Holidays were specified: fifteen days at Christmas, eight days at Carnival, fifteen days at Easter, six days at Pentecost, and twenty days for the fall harvest.[59]

Ravizza recognized that the quality of teachers might vary substantially and thus designated different responsibilities to different teaching staff. The head teacher (*magister universalis*) should be the most accomplished and intelligent, and from his *cattedra* in the auditorium would offer daily lectures designed to stimulate and encourage not only students but also other teachers. In his interpretation of the key texts (not specified here), the head teacher ought to point out both the content and the style of these works in an effort to instil 'a love of truth and beauty' in his listeners. Similar to Quintilian, Ravizza recommended that students rewrite fairy tales (*fabulas puro sermone narrare*) and study history. The assistant teacher(s) (*magister specialis*) carried out diverse tasks: accompanying the students to and from the lecture, asking students to recite aloud, checking their pronunciation, and analysing the morphology and syntax of various orators and poets. Meeting with groups of twenty-five or thirty students, the assistant teacher(s) should walk students through a graduated series of lessons where one fact built upon another. The Jesuits would formalize and extend this approach in all of their colleges in the second half of the sixteenth century,

demanding knowledge and understanding of one level before promoting students to the next. Ravizza also adopted the venerable method of
using *decuriones*, whereby the students were divided into groups of ten
and the most able student led the group through exercises and recitations.[60] Clearly, he was promoting the idea that one learns best through
teaching others (*docendo discimus*).

The last chapter spells out the responsibilities of parents, above all
in the area of moral education and proper manners, which Ravizza
held to be supremely important. In a display of candid self-interest,
Ravizza urged parents to cultivate a relationship with their children's
teacher(s) by punctually sending payment on the first of the month and
by providing additional gifts in order to spur better teaching![61] Ravizza
even advocated a precursor of a parent-teacher association, proposing
a committee of elected citizens who would confer monthly with the city
magistrates about how the school ought to proceed. As noted above,
Ravizza firmly believed that the state must play a role in promoting
public schools, and his final chapter dispenses advice to city officials
about the benefits of studying the humanities.[62] Ironically, Ravizza
abandoned Bergamo's city officials within a year of submitting his treatise to them when he moved to Vicenza.

With its emphasis upon classical sources and a new style of pedagogy, Ravizza's treatise demonstrates the impact of humanist scholarship. It also speaks to issues of corporal punishment, parental support,
and the role of the state in public education – issues which continue
to be relevant in contemporary discussion about public schooling. The
presence in Bergamo of Ravizza, Pio, Filelfo, and others as humanist
educators testifies to the city fathers' desire to promote public schooling in the late fifteenth and early sixteenth centuries. This burgeoning
interest in education is reflected in other cities of the Veneto and in Renaissance Italy as a whole, but it was a movement soon challenged by
other forces.

Grammar and Humanities, 1526–1632

Despite the blueprint offered by Ravizza, the commune's interest in
supporting public education in Bergamo appears to have waned after 1525, particularly in the second half of the century. Scattered references to public school teachers indicate that the city continued to hire
masters, but less regularly than before. Although one master, Nicolò
Cologno, did achieve notable success as a lecturer at Padua toward the

end of the century, none of the subsequent teachers achieved the fame of Pio and Ravizza. No conclusive evidence exists to explain why the commune of Bergamo became less interested in bringing well-known *maestri* to instruct the city's youth. The city's economic position did not worsen significantly, nor did political or military issues pose a significant threat. Giuseppe Locatelli suggests that the Protestant Reformation might have damaged public schooling, but such a hypothesis is not supported by the evidence.[63] Noble Bergamasque families had traditionally sent their children to study in Brescia or other surrounding towns with prominent *maestri*, but it seems unlikely that this small percentage of wealthy students could have influenced the course of public schooling. There is always the chance that the relevant records concerning public education have been destroyed, but for the most part the *Azioni* and other serial records continue without interruption.

Perhaps the ebbing of the humanist tide led to a decreased belief in the virtues of civic humanism and a subsequent decline in the study of the humanities. Yet when the city moved to hire a teacher, the documents continued to proclaim the importance of public education for the well being of the city. A more likely scenario is that a reinvigorated Catholic Church may have swayed some students into attending clerical academies or the seminary rather than the public school. It is also possible that schooling sponsored by confraternities, which began in earnest after 1550, may have lessened the need for communal support of public schooling. However, the commune did not entirely abandon public education; indeed, it explored a joint venture with the bishop in the 1560s and with the Misericordia Maggiore in the 1570s. But the level of interest and support is perceptibly lower after 1525 than that for the preceding half century.

The mid- to late sixteenth century thus represented a period both of innovation and entropy for communal-supported education. For three decades (1525–56) the city was unable to sustain a long-serving maestro to supervise public instruction. Then in conjunction with the bishop, and later with a confraternity, the commune identified a superb teacher in the person of Nicolò Cologno between 1556 and 1579, although even he taught only intermittently for the city. From 1580 to 1610 there is no record of a teacher to manage public schooling, a gap which ultimately convinced the city to negotiate with the Theatines and later Somaschans to run a school on behalf of the commune. In short, this period witnessed a chronic instability in the commune's support of public instruction.

No record exists of an appointment to replace Ravizza in 1525. The next reference to public schooling appears on 10 December 1533, when the city council lamented the low number of grammar teachers and assigned five deputies to hire some more: 'Realizing that grammar teachers in this city are few and far between with respect to the goodly number of youth who need to be supervised and instructed in letters and proper behaviour, and that parents must send their children to board outside the city, with considerable inconvenience and expense, and [furthermore] that parents must ensure their children are not nourished on leisure, vice, and other bad qualities, but instead with wisdom and other praiseworthy activities, therefore a motion was passed that five distinguished, informed citizens be elected to identify some grammar teachers of good character, for this is the most important quality, and also of sound learning and knowledge.'[64] The five deputies were authorized to negotiate terms with these grammar masters and the motion passed with only two dissenting votes. Clearly, the city had not done a good job of retaining the teacher(s) previously employed in Bergamo. Although the reference to boarding schools outside the city suggests that this may have been a viable option for a small percentage of the well-to-do, it could not have been practical for most families. Six weeks later the council authorized a salary of 120 ducats to bring in a professor of grammar, but the school soon closed owing to an unspecified calamity.[65]

In 1539 the city appointed a blue-ribbon panel of noble citizens to bring in another teacher. After searching far and wide, the deputies hired a Bergamasque citizen named Nicolò Cologno, distinguished for his studies in both Latin and Greek.[66] Cologno promised to give a public lecture on Horace within a few days so that the townspeople could judge his erudition for themselves. The three-year contract specified that in exchange for teaching humanities and good letters five days a week, Cologno would receive a salary of four hundred lire. He was allowed to have private students as long as he taught them in a different building, and he also taught (catechism?) in the church on Sundays and holidays. Although his salary was significantly less than the 120 scudi authorized five years earlier, perhaps Cologno's other activities made up the difference. Cologno began teaching on 3 June 1539, but two years later he sent a letter of resignation to the city council.[67]

Between 1539 and 1543 the council was preoccupied with hiring someone to teach civil law publicly, which may explain why nobody replaced Nicolò Cologno. In 1545 a grammar teacher named Baptista

Benevolo approached the city council and offered to teach two lessons a week for fifty lire per year. This was clearly a temporary solution to the problem, and indeed in the spring of 1545 the council authorized a full-time teacher. A year later, however, Benevolo was still teaching grammar at the same salary, and in the absence of any other public school teacher we may assume that he continued to teach for a few more years.[68] In 1549 Benevolo was awarded twenty-five lire 'for the love of God,' suggesting that he had retired from teaching and needed charity from the city.

In the same year the commune apparently hired the *litterarum professor* Andrea Cato (Catto) of Romano to direct Bergamo's public school. Cato had been hired in 1547 by the bishop and a group of parents who wished to found a private elementary school for their own children, but he quit that job after only a year and was immediately hired by the commune.[69] While we know quite a bit about Cato and his activities in 1547, few records survive to document his employment by the commune. On 9 November 1550 Cato offered an encomium to the city council about Bartolomeo Pellegrino's work *De antiquitatibus divorum bergomensium*. As we will see, Inquisitorial records from 1550–1 accuse Cato of being a Lutheran and of skipping Mass. In 1551 he retired unexpectedly to Tirano, where he took a position teaching public school in the town. Despite the suspicions of heresy that lingered around him, Bergamo's city council approved his departure with regret and even sought to lure him back.[70]

By 1556–7 the lack of public education had become a serious problem. The absence of a visible maestro and the inconsistent efforts of the city council had encouraged alternative forms of education, particularly those associated with the Church. The Schools of Christian Doctrine were beginning to take root in various parish churches, and the MIA's school for clerics boasted an enrolment of sixty-three students who were busy learning grammar and the divine offices. The confraternity of Sant'Alessandro in Colonna decided to found a school for both clerics and lay boys in its own parish, an action quickly imitated by other confraternities. Publicly supported education seemed to be at risk of disappearing into irrelevance and oblivion.

The solution, unexpectedly, came in the form of a letter from Bergamo's bishop. Recognizing the benefit of a more literate laity, in 1556 Bishop Vittore Soranzo offered to pay half the salary of a teacher who would provide public instruction. Spurred by this generous offer, the city council asked Count Gian Gerolamo Albano and Giovanni Pietro

Pontano to find a learned scholar of the humanities for the universal benefit of the city's youth. The council recognized that it had not been assiduous in carrying out its responsibility, but claimed that there was simply a shortage of qualified men to be hired.[71]

The deputies immediately selected one of the canons of the cathedral of Sant'Alessandro, Nicolò Cologno, for a five-year contract with an annual salary of one hundred scudi.[72] Already familiar to the city council from his prior stint as a public school teacher from 1539 to 1541, Cologno had apparently used the intervening years to take holy orders and henceforth was always referred to as *Reverendissimo*. Cologno's academic career stretched over more than five decades in Bergamo and was capped by his appointment as professor of moral philosophy at the University of Padua in 1591. Cologno's contract of 1556 does not mention either housing or private lessons; combined with his position as a canon of the cathedral, this suggests that Cologno was already an established figure in the city. At the official signing of the contract in the bishop's palace, delegates of both the city council and the episcopal palace were present to ensure that their respective interests were represented. Cologno began teaching one week later; he continued to do so until at least 1561, and probably until 1564. Cologno thus represents the first full-time public school teacher in four decades to finish out his contract. It is telling that – even with assistance from the bishop – the city council was unable, or unwilling, to consistently hire and retain teachers.

In December 1564 the council renewed its search for a teacher of Greek and Latin but was unable to find a satisfactory candidate. The council minutes once again trumpet the importance of a public school teacher for Bergamo's boys: 'Whereas it is not only useful but absolutely necessary to have a master learned in the profession of humanities for the universal benefit and well-being of the youth of our city; [therefore] every effort must be made to identify and hire a man as was done previously ... in order that the youth of the city may flee from sloth (*fuggire l'otio*) and instead focus their minds on praiseworthy and virtuous studies.'[73] Despite such grand rhetoric, the council did not rehire Nicolò Cologno in 1564, nor did it hire anyone else. A decade slipped past with no mention of a public school maestro. The council again lamented that it was very difficult to find an appropriate master teacher, 'being that such men are extremely rare and in great demand.'[74] Interestingly, the council's lament also suggests that student input might have been considered, noting that any instructor selected by the council must be acceptable to a majority of the students. Once again we are faced with the question of why Bergamo could not, or would not, hire a teacher at public expense. Perhaps the city could not afford it without a partner; or perhaps there were sufficient other options available; or perhaps there was a genuine scarcity of qualified candidates.

In 1574 the city council decided to split the financial burden of a teacher with the Misericordia Maggiore. The previous successful experience with the bishop clearly encouraged the city council to explore alternative ways of financing the expense of a public school teacher. In addition, the MIA's Academy of Clerics had a good reputation in the city, and the confraternity was noted for its generosity toward education. The same five deputies who had attempted to find a teacher in 1564 were ordered to resume their search for an instructor of Greek and Latin who would teach virtue and wisdom to the boys. They chose the familiar figure of Reverend Nicolò Cologno, 'our fellow citizen, known, loved, and venerated by all for the kindness of his character, the excellence of his knowledge, and the outstanding method of his teaching.'[75] During the previous ten years, Cologno had continued to teach in several different contexts: he served as one of the directors of Bergamo's Tridentine seminary, taught in the MIA's Academy of Clerics, and tutored children in his own home. The city council deputies successfully appealed to Cologno's sense of patriotism to share his expertise 'with both the rich and the poor' so that his learning 'can be embraced by everyone in the years ahead.'[76] The MIA and the city council each agreed to contribute one hundred gold scudi, making Cologno the highest-paid teacher in Bergamo in either the sixteenth or seventeenth century.

According to Cologno's contract, classes were to be held Monday through Friday so that the assistant teachers could use Saturday to review the week's lesson with their own students. The MIA offered to hold the lectures in its recently renovated palace on Via Arena, where the Academy of Clerics was accustomed to meeting. In contrast to Ravizza's academic calendar, which suggested regular vacations throughout the year, the city council declared that the only vacation would be from the feast day of Saint Bartholomew to that of Saint Luke (24 August–18 October).

Cologno's high salary can be attributed to the fact that his job was more akin to a master teacher or supervisor than to a mere classroom instructor. He was expected to offer three lessons per day on the most important humanistic authors in prose, poetry, logic, rhetoric, and ethics. However, the lessons were not for a small group of his own students drawn from the MIA's Academy or chosen by the city council. Rather, the lessons were designed so that other teachers in the city might bring their students to Cologno for a morning or afternoon lesson before returning to their own classrooms. His contract states specifically that lessons were not restricted to students associated with the MIA's Academy or the commune, but were open to all who wished to be educated. Thus the lessons were 'public' in the broadest possible sense. This arrangement matches exactly that suggested by Giovita Ravizza a half-century earlier.

Cologno was further expected to visit the classrooms of the other teachers in the city, and to issue guidelines about how the students ought to recite what they had learned. He was even expected to participate in a sort of informal teacher training, so that the commune would not have to go begging for teachers from other cities.[77] Given the commune's difficulties in attracting teachers, this was a wise move. These expectations further imply that while the commune perceived a need for a master teacher within the city, it did not want to get involved in the logistics and details of regulating the necessary teachers. Instead, the commune preferred to hire one teacher who would serve as a supervisor of public instruction.

As noted, the council emphasized the *public* nature of these lectures, not only in terms of access but also for content and style: 'these lessons must not be read ostentatiously but for the benefit of the listeners, in such a way that every person will be able to understand them.'[78] Yet the curriculum of poetry, prose, logic, rhetoric, and ethics that comprised the *studia humanitatis* was clearly designed for advanced students. No mention of instruction in Latin grammar occurs anywhere in the document. Once again we see the unresolved tension in the commune's mixed feelings about the appropriate levels of public instruction.

A report generated by a subcommittee of the city council circa 1579 pointed to problems with the public school and suggested that the city might do better to invest its hundred scudi in another enterprise.[79] After gathering information from various sources, the deputies concluded that 'no objection has been raised against the lecturer [Nicolò Cologno], but for some time so few listeners have been attending that it seems that these public lessons serve the *chierici* of the Misericordia more than the others.' According to the deputies, the city should take steps to encourage the teachers and students of the academies and schools dispersed throughout the city to attend the lessons more regularly; otherwise, 'we think that the magnificent commune will be able to save this annual ex-

pense of one hundred scúdi, instead spending it on better and more necessary causes.' In the summer of 1579, exactly five years after Cologno's
first contract had expired, the city once again initiated a search for new
teaching staff. Although the council specified that the new teacher(s)
could not be paid more than the salary given to Cologno, there was
no mention of the MIA, suggesting that their joint venture had come
to an end. It is interesting to note the council's declaration that a task
as important as the education of young children must not be left to private means but must be supervised by the public. This sentiment again
echoes that of Ravizza and his insistence upon state support.

Nevertheless, from 1580 to 1610 there is a surprising and inexplicable
gap in the records regarding public education. Perhaps the commune
lacked the financial resources to support public instruction in both the
humanities and the law, or else it believed that public schooling was no
longer necessary. Certainly, there was no shortage of interest in expanding educational options in Bergamo: in addition to the seminary and
the MIA's Academy of Clerics, there were confraternal parish schools,
private academies, and even a Flemish professor of humane letters who
came to teach in Bergamo.[80] Private instruction was also available to
the sons (and to a lesser extent, daughters) of the wealthy elites who
could afford to bring in tutors or to send their children to Brescia to
be educated. It is true that many of the local, private academies suffered through hard times at the end of the sixteenth and beginning of
the seventeenth century. For example, both the seminary and the MIA's
Academy of Clerics received negative reports by Carlo Borromeo during his apostolic visitation in 1575. The Academy of Clerics underwent
a clamorous theft in 1594, and closed in 1610. In 1603 the son of the
ripetitore of the Academy in Borgo Pignolo grossly insulted seventy-
year-old Francesco di Gozzi, who lived next door to the academy, by
shouting obscene insults and then exposing himself in order to offend
the old man. Nevertheless, such anecdotal evidence still does not explain a thirty-year hiatus in public schooling. The most likely explanation is the resurgence of other options, particularly those sponsored
by the Church. The public schooling that did occur in the seventeenth
century was once again done in conjunction with the cooperation of
Catholic orders of men and with the implicit approval of the bishop.

In the spring of 1610 the city council opened negotiations with the
Theatine Fathers to teach logic, philosophy, theology, and catechism
publicly. Although logic, philosophy, and catechism were standard subjects for a school, the teaching of theology was traditionally reserved

to universities or the *studia* of religious orders such as the Dominicans, and remained a jealously guarded privilege for centuries. Bergamo's city council must have recognized that the Theatine lessons were more advanced than those previously offered, but there is no explanation in the documents for such a change. Founded by Gaetano Thiene and Gian Pietro Carafa (later Pope Paul IV) in 1524 and settled in Bergamo in 1590, the Theatines were one of many religious orders born at the dawn of the Catholic Reformation who chose education as part of their ministry.[81] Bergamo's city fathers, recognizing that the Theatines' school would benefit the city by providing more advanced instruction, therefore appointed three deputies to consider the circumstances. A week later, on 24 April 1610, the deputies declared that they had reached an agreement with the Theatines regarding location, curriculum, and other important details. The council immediately dispatched a letter to the Theatine vicar general in Rome, who responded favourably on 24 July.[82]

Despite such a promising start, negotiations soon stalled, and nearly two years passed with no result. In the spring of 1612, Bergamo's Executive Council intervened and admonished the deputies to conclude the agreement. The council noted specifically that the purpose of such lessons was to prepare students for more advanced public study, presumably at the university level.[83] Here we see again the shift away from a truly public, liberal arts education for all in favour of a curriculum targeted at elite students headed to university. The council seems oblivious to its earlier declaration of 1574 that public lessons must be accessible to all who are interested. Granted, forty years had elapsed, and the presence of a religious order may have substantially altered the city council's perspective. It is also true that providing students with a head start on their university courses had been one of the goals of courses offered in the study of law, as we will see shortly. There was no hint of opening an actual university, which would have involved significant additional expense and permissions, as well as a certain veto by the Venetian Senate.[84]

From 1612 to 1615 there is no mention of the Theatines' public school. In June of 1615, however, a detailed report was submitted to the Great Council summarizing the research conducted by three deputies about how to administer a public school.[85] The report implies that the Theatine school (here referred to as a *studio*) was never actually realized. Instead, following the council's directive of 24 March 1612, the deputies had spent three years studying the rules and regulations of colleges in Milan and Parma, 'which are reputed to be the finest in Italy.' The deputies also examined the organization and administration of the academies and boarding houses for students (*donzene*) in Bergamo. The deputies recommended the immediate establishment of a public college to ensure that the city's youth were adequately prepared for higher study. The first task was to rent a large and comfortable house in which lessons could be held and out-of-town students might be able to live. The college was to be run by three (later five) supervisors elected by the council.[86]

According to the deputies' report, the college should have two highly experienced principal teachers: one to teach history, poetry, philosophy, and letters (*humanità maggiore*), and the other to teach rhetoric and logic. They would be assisted by a third teacher, called the prefect, who would review lessons with the students and accompany them as directed by his colleagues. Students who wished to be admitted to the college had to be competent enough in the humanities to pass an examination administered by a committee of teachers, deputies, and supervisors. The number of *collegiati* (boarding students) was limited to thirty, but additional students might be admitted at the discretion of the supervisors and upon payment of one-half scudo per month. A later amendment stipulated that the college was intended primarily for *cittadini nobili bergamaschi* (noble Bergamasque citizens) rather than *giovani cittadini bergamaschi* (young Bergamasque citizens) as indicated in the original text. In a further sign of the drift toward education aimed at the elite, the deputies insisted that *every* student must pay the appropriate fees within three months or he would not be admitted to study. Perhaps in recognition of the 'aristocratization' process, the commune of Bergamo agreed to make an annual contribution of 150 scudi to defray the expenses of running the college.

In September of the same year, the Venetian governors wrote to Venice to confirm the Senate's approval of the new school.[87] The letter specified that a Theatine from Naples, Father Crescenzio, had been hired to teach logic and a Bergamasque Theatine named Lorenzo Biffi had been employed to teach rhetoric. A Milanese layman named Vernia was appointed to teach the humanities, along with a Bergamasque priest named Carrara as his assistant. Thus, although the school was staffed in part by Theatines, it appears to have been under the direct control of the city council. Despite such careful planning, this new college lasted less than a year. The reasons for its closure are not specified and it is difficult to speculate. Perhaps the council had lost its passion for public schooling, or perhaps some external political influence in Venice closed down the school. Whatever the cause, the commune's attempt to establish a more permanent public school was once again frustrated at its inception.

Fifteen years later, in the wake of a catastrophic plague, the commune would choose yet another route to provide public education. Once again it would import members of a religious order to staff the school, but there were important differences in curriculum, size, and goals. The 1630–2 contagion was the worst outbreak of bubonic plague in nearly three hundred years. Bergamo's population was decimated; harvests failed, trade declined, schools closed, and whole families were extinguished. The secretary of the city council, Lorenzo Ghirardelli, chronicled the events in a diary later published in 1681 as *Storia della peste del 1630, Il memorando contagio seguito in Bergamo l'anno 1630* (A History of the Unforgettable Plague Suffered by Bergamo in 1630). Ghirardelli's account would later be incorporated by Alessandro Manzoni into his novel *I promessi sposi* (The Betrothed). In his discussion of the effects of the plague, Ghirardelli pointed specifically to the effects upon education:

> Among the damages inflicted upon this city by the recent contagion, in addition to the deplorable ruin already described, was the fact that the teachers who were accustomed to educating the children were killed; with the schools being closed, the boys did not know what to do with themselves, and so they engaged in shameful leisure, wasting their talents in vain and indecent pastimes. Those who governed the city, knowing the education of children to be the foundation upon which every honest and praiseworthy action of our life is based, and that Republics would be badly governed without that training which is the basis of every good government, took various steps to bring in foreign teachers. Therefore the Somaschan Fathers were suggested, for part of their mission is the care and education of young children.[88]

Ghirardelli's observations are confirmed by the minutes of the city council of 5 December 1631. After noting that the Somaschans were a familiar presence in Bergamo, and well regarded for their zeal, frugality, and good reputation elsewhere in the Veneto and Lombardy, the council listed several more reasons why it was important to hire the Somaschans immediately. 'Recognizing the desire of the illustrious podestà to establish public schools where grammar and humanities can be taught by the Reverend Somaschan Fathers, and motivated furthermore by the desire to promote the public welfare, especially in these times when a majority of the schoolmasters have died of the plague ...'[89] Four months later the Somaschans signed an official contract to manage the public school of San Giuseppe in the parish of San Michele al Pozzo Bianco. The Somaschans continued to run this school, though with considerable difficulty, until they were transferred to the parish of San Leonardo in 1659. The story of the Collegio San Giuseppe is recounted in chapter 4, in the context of education sponsored by religious associations and institutions. The history of public education in Bergamo is not quite complete, however, for the commune had sponsored one additional – albeit sporadic – school in jurisprudence.

Law Schools, 1482–1650

In addition to supporting public education in grammar and the humanities, the commune of Bergamo also sponsored the study of law. Owing to the city's location on the border between Milan and Venice, and the varying traditions of law (civil, canon, Roman, Imperial, Venetian, Lombard) practised in the area, no single type of law predominated. Nevertheless, the municipal government made repeated, if erratic, efforts to provide a rudimentary legal education. Students who wished to train fully for a legal career went to study at the University of Padua; Bergamo never attempted to compete with the *Studio's* monopoly on higher education. Instead, the commune sought to offer courses in civil law that would both prepare Bergamasque students for university study, and provide training for residents who wished to improve their understanding of legal precepts. Despite the cooperation of the College of Jurists[90] (i.e., the lawyers' guild) and a statuary requirement of 1491 that the commune annually hire *uno bono jurisperito* (one accomplished jurist), efforts to hire and maintain a professor of law were inconsistent at best.

The commune got off to a good start, just as it had with schooling in grammar and humanities: in the last two decades of the fifteenth century it employed half a dozen legal scholars to offer public lessons. However, in the entire sixteenth century Bergamo offered public legal studies for only five years. Only in the 1620s did the city government finally establish a regular pattern of legal education, and even that success was marred by a bitter argument among the Venetian governors, the College of Jurists, and the inhabitants of the local valleys regarding who might teach and practise law.

Thus the commune's commitment to the teaching of law parallels its efforts in teaching grammar and humanities at the beginning and end of our period, but the situation is different for most of the sixteenth century. Why was this so? Such a paltry result might indicate that either the commune did not place much value on the study of law or else that there were alternative routes to receive legal training. Despite the strong reputation of Bergamo's jurists (see below), none of the city's own legal stars ever taught for the city. The teaching of law generally seems to have carried a lower profile. Perhaps law was perceived to be more about professional training and less about crafting good citizens; or perhaps there was less demand from city residents for this kind of education. Or perhaps the commune was unable to partner with another institution to share expenses. While it is possible to find some similar rhetoric about the importance of studying the law for the well-being of the republic, in this case Bergamo's actions speak louder than words.

Nevertheless, Bergamo boasted a proud legal tradition dating back to the late medieval period. For example, a letter of 1283 from the magistrates of Bologna to Jacopo Rivola in Bergamo attested to the magistrates' desire to have notaries and judges from Bergamo on account of their fine legal reputation. Marc Antonio Michiel's *Descriptio* (1523) makes a similar point concerning the profusion of legal scholars resident in Bergamo in the early Cinquecento. Bergamo's most famous legal scholar, Alberico da Rosciate, was a celebrated jurist of the fourteenth century who published important legal commentaries and a well-known *Dictionarium iuris*. Other jurists included Antonio Bonghi, described in 1474 as a *gravissimum iureconsultum* (very distinguished legal advisor); Gian Girolamo Albani, the author of numerous texts on canon law between 1535 and 1565; Pietro Alzano, elected rector of Padua's law teaching staff in 1591 and sadly assassinated one year later; and Ambrogio da Calepio, who wrote a three-volume handbook on criminal law.[91] In a less flattering light, one of the Venetian governors of Bergamo described the city's inhabitants as the most litigious he had ever encountered.

The Bergamasque tradition of studying law at university dates back to at least 1301, when the statutes of the College of Jurists of Bergamo declared that candidates for admission must have studied six years of law outside of the city. In 1361 Emperor Charles IV granted Bernabò and Galeazzo Visconti the right to open a public university in Pavia, and the Visconti informed Bergamo's podestà that all Bergamasque students must henceforth take their degrees at Pavia. When Bergamo submitted to Venice in 1428, the Most Serene Republic insisted that all Bergamasque students attend the university at Padua or risk a fine and exclusion from 'any rank, privilege, office, or honour conferred by the city of Bergamo.'[92] Although we know that Bergamasque students occasionally studied at Bologna, Pavia, or the *studio* in Venice, the vast majority did indeed pursue their degrees at Padua.[93]

The earliest reference to public instruction in law in Bergamo dates to 11 October 1476, when the commune authorized construction of a rostrum (*canzellum*) from which Giovanni Carlo Tiraboschi might read civil law to a public audience. In 1482, at the same meeting when it voted to hire a master of grammar and humanities, the city council declared that it wished to revive an 'ancient tradition' by hiring a judge to offer free public lectures on civil law. The lessons were not restricted to students but designed for the benefit of the general public (*per diversas personas ... pro utilitate publica*). Lessons were to be held daily at the Palace of Justice in the large meeting room near the offices of the podestà and the city council. The council specified an escalating series of financial penalties to be imposed if the teacher were absent without permission. At the end of the meeting, the council voted to hire [Iacopo] Agazzi for one year, and in the following year hired Giovanni Agostino Colleoni to replace him. These appointments were controversial: the city council minutes reflect debate about the qualifications of the various candidates and the reasons for their dismissal or election. In 1487 the council apparently proposed yet another motion to hire someone to teach 'the true spirit of the law' to Bergamo's youth.[94]

In 1491 the definitive version of Bergamo's city statutes was published; it stipulated the presence of a judicial expert to teach civil law. Although similar statutes existed for 1430 and 1453, the 1491 version remained unchanged for more than three centuries. All subsequent efforts to hire a professor of law make reference to this statute, which reads in part:

> For the great and evident benefit of the commune of Bergamo, such that the city itself might be filled with wise and prudent men, the commune of Bergamo is required to and must keep and maintain a good judge at a salary of 8 imperial lire per month. He shall be elected each year in December from the College of Jurists in Bergamo. He shall read, and is required to read, civil law at a public place in the city of Bergamo to all who wish to listen to it. If he fails to lecture for four days in a row, he loses a month's salary; and if he fails to lecture for ten days, he loses all of his salary; and

another person will be elected. He cannot and must not accept anything from his audience.[95]

The College of Jurists maintained a monopoly on this position for more than a century, selecting its own members and eventually raising the annual salary to 120 gold scudi. Such a monopoly was entirely appropriate for the lawyers guild, which wished to keep a close eye on who was teaching the subject in order to forestall any radical changes.

Both in 1482 and in 1491 the commune placed a strong emphasis upon the public nature of these legal lectures. Of course, the commune had used similar language in describing its ambition for public lectures in the humanities, and later failed to sustain that promise. Perhaps this desire for increased accessibility to education represented a specific faction that temporarily ruled the council in the waning years of the fifteenth century, or perhaps it genuinely reflected a broader sentiment among the populace. Late fifteenth-century Italy did witness an unusual period of freedom from foreign invasion and major military conflicts, which might have allowed Bergamo to focus on education and other issues eclipsed in times of war. At the same time, statutes are by their very nature prescriptive, and thus reveal more about what was desirable than about what actually happened.

In 1493 Guglielmo Suardi was elected to teach law *pro decorem civitatis* (for the honour of the city). The motion to elect Suardi specifically stated that his lectures were required for anyone from the city or province of Bergamo who wished to be considered for the position of procurator. Thus these public lectures were not just for students trying to get an early start on their university education, but also for those who wished to acquire a cursory knowledge of the law in order to improve their job prospects. In the following year, Bartolomeo Caleppio was appointed on the condition that he stop practising as a notary during his term as a teacher of law.[96]

In 1496 the city awarded twenty-five lire to Bernardo Colleoni in recompense for a booklet on civil law that he had written and offered to the city as a possible text.[97] In the same year Leonardo Comenduno resigned his position as the city attorney (*comunitatis defensorem*) in order to teach law publicly for one year. Comenduno would later play a key role in the struggle between the French king and the Venetian Republic for control of Bergamo. Like Suardi, Caleppio, and Colleoni, Comenduno came from one of the leading families of Bergamo. His appointment as professor of law reinforces the impression that this position was usually held by members of Bergamo's socio-economic elite, a marked contrast to the more inclusionary language stipulating a broad public audience. Each of these examples from the 1490s indicates the commune's good-faith effort to uphold the 1491 statute and to offer public education in the law.[98]

Owing to military invasions, repeated bouts of plague, and economic uncertainty, the teaching of law in Bergamo ceased during the first four decades of the sixteenth century. Given the political turmoil and economic hardship brought about by the War of the League of Cambrai, it is not surprising that the lessons would stop. However, the MIA confraternity continued to provide scholarships, Giovita Ravizza continued to teach in the city's public school, and the MIA's day school continued to operate. We also know that thirty-four Bergamaschi graduated with law degrees from the University of Padua between 1501 and 1537.[99] Not surprisingly, these students were drawn largely from the wealthy and powerful families of Bergamo, who perhaps were less influenced by the economic deprivation of these decades. Upon graduation, approximately one-third (13/34) joined the College of Jurists in Bergamo in order to practise law. A similar number (15/34) went on to become members of the Great Council at some point in their careers. These students may have received some preparatory lessons or private tutoring before enrolling at Padua, or they may simply have completed all of their studies in Padua. Regardless, it is clear that other forms of education continued apace in the early sixteenth century even as the teaching of law withered.

Why would the teaching of grammar and humanities have expanded just as the teaching of law declined? One obvious explanation is that the city council wished to promote only one of the schools at a time, and did not possess the financial resources to do more. Bergamo's valleys were famous for their penury. The Venetian governors' reports regularly attest to the region's poverty; in 1553, for example, Captain Francesco Bernardo noted that all but a handful of Bergamo's nobility were 'mediocre' in comparison with their counterparts elsewhere in Italy, because Bergamo's aristocrats averaged less than five hundred ducats income per year. The English traveller Thomas Coryat observed at the beginning of the seventeenth century that Bergamo's nobles dressed in accordance with the latest fashions but were forced to wear brass or pewter buttons instead of gold and silver.[100] Thus Bergamo may simply have not been able to afford public lessons in more than one area.

A second explanation might be a lack of qualified legal instructors in the early decades of the sixteenth century. Yet the membership of the College of Jurists does not appear to have declined substantially, and nearly three dozen new lawyers graduated from Padua in this period. In addition, the city council never hesitated to complain about the absence of qualified candidates for positions in grammar or humanities, yet there is no record of any such concerns for the teaching of law.

A third explanation might be found in the arrival of outside humanists like Pio and Ravizza. These men reinvigorated the teaching of the humanities by raising its public profile, and perhaps the corresponding lack of a notable legal scholar doomed that subject. It is always possible that the relevant records have been lost, but that seems unlikely as the city council records for this period are well-preserved and no other branch of city government would have hired a law teacher. Whatever the reason, nobody was hired to teach law between 1496 and 1538.

During this interval, a curious transformation occurs in the language regarding the appointments of the men hired to teach law. We have seen that those hired to teach grammar and the humanities went by a variety of different titles (e.g., master, rector, professor), even though they all performed a similar task. During the late fifteenth century, Bergamo's city council records invariably identify the teacher of law as a 'judicial expert' (*iuresperito*). As is clear from the examples cited above, this might include a sitting judge, a practicing lawyer, or even an intrepid notary. In most cases, the candidate already held another job in the legal profession, often a public office. Beginning in the 1540s, however, the professor is almost invariably referred to as the *lector institutiones*. This title indicates that he lectured about the *Institutes* of Justinian, which constituted the introductory phase of a legal education. Presumably once students had mastered this basic material, they could pursue more advanced lessons in Padua. The law curriculum in Padua is well documented: professors were expected to lecture on a set number of *puncti* (theses), a list of which was available from the university bidel. The texts to be studied were traditional: the *Institutes, Digest,* and *Codex* of Justinian, as well as Gratian's *Decretum* and papal *Decretals* of the late Middle Ages. Padua's professors were renowned both for the theoretical aspects of their lectures and for the practical help that they provided to students in preparing for exams and the practice of law.[101] Thus the focus of legal instruction in Bergamo appears to have shifted between the beginning and the middle of the sixteenth century, becoming more explicitly a preparatory step prior to university study.

At the end of 1538, in observance of the city statutes and in recognition of 'how useful and necessary the study and knowledge of law is to a well-organized republic,' the city council by a vote of 70–5 made a commitment to hire an outstanding professor of law. Baptista Botani, at the usual salary of eight lire per month, was elected as *lector institutiones* to teach those aspects of civil law that seemed most appropriate to him. Note that the council did not intervene to specify the curriculum, here or elsewhere, but rather left such decisions to the judgment of the teacher. Curiously, in contrast to all other classes in Bergamo that followed the conventional academic year (including subsequent classes in law), these legal lessons always began on the first day of March.[102]

The council next chose a series of distinguished jurists to fill this position. Francesco Suardi (appointed 1540) came from one of Bergamo's most illustrious families and served repeatedly on the city council.[103] Similarly, Girolamo Zanchi came from a prominent family that boasted three Lateran canons regular (Basilio, Dionigi, and Giovanni Cristostomo) and he served repeatedly on the city council before and after his appointment to teach law in 1541. A famous lawyer who joined Bergamo's College of Jurists in 1545, he authored a commentary in 1560 on the *Inforziato*.[104] Julio (Giulio) Agosti, appointed 1542, had been a student at the MIA's college for Bergamasque students in Padua from 1531 to 1541; despite taking ten years to do so, he obtained his degree in both civil and canon law and joined Bergamo's College of Jurists in 1545. He later became a canon of the cathedral of Camerino and in 1554 was nominated 'assistant, coadjutor, and vicar' of Bishop Vittore Soranzo. His loyalty to Soranzo – and his unwillingness to collaborate with the Inquisitor Fra Domenico Adelasio – soon resulted in an investigation for heresy in 1556, as a result of which on 1 June 1556 he was excommunicated and deposed by Paul IV. Nevertheless, the extant documents show that Agosti remained popular with the city council, which wrote to the Venetian Senate that 'until now messer Giulio has carried out his duties well and to the satisfaction of the city's inhabitants, earning a reputation as a reliable and sincere man … if this change is allowed to stand, our city will be very upset, and the honour of messer Giulio, who is innocent, will be very greatly damaged.' Nevertheless, Agosti was replaced by Giovan Battista Brugnatelli on 22 June 1556, after which Agosti was detained in the prisons of the Holy Office in Rome before his final sentence was issued on 6 March 1558.[105] Agosti's appointment to teach law, like those before him, was for only one year, and of course the encounters with the Inquisition were still more than a decade in the future.

In February 1543 the city council voted to *not* elect a law teacher for the following year.[106] No explanation was given, but for the period 1544–1608 there is no further mention of a *lector institutorum*, nor of the teaching of law in Bergamo. Given the steady stream of Bergamaschi who continued to graduate from Padua and to join the College of Jurists, such a lull is difficult to explain. The most likely explanation lies in the mid-century modifications to the statutes of the College of Jurists. In June 1557, the College introduced fifteen amendments, the first of which *required* that a candidate furnish proof of a university degree in order to be considered for membership. The second amendment confirmed that candidates still had to study outside of Bergamo for six years in a public university.[107] Since the College of Jurists now required students to come home with a degree in hand, the city (and students too) may have viewed lessons in Bergamo as superfluous. The requirement that the degree be completed entirely outside of Bergamo further rendered preparatory lessons in Bergamo unnecessary. In the seventeenth century the city council would petition Venice and Bergamo's College of Jurists to count the first year or two of study in Bergamo toward the degree, whereupon the frequency and popularity of lessons in Bergamo rose dramatically. It is also possible that private teachers replaced the public lessons, although no evidence of such tutoring has been found. An alternative explanation is that the College of Jurists lost interest in this exercise but refused to let the council select someone from outside their ranks, for fear that it might lose control of the process. Whatever the reason, it appears that from the mid-sixteenth to the early seventeenth century, the commune renounced its sponsorship of public lessons in civil law.

Reflecting the burst of enthusiasm for new schools and expanded educational opportunities that characterized the opening years of the seventeenth century in Bergamo, the city council announced on 14 December 1609 that it would appoint three deputies to identify a member of the College of Jurists who could begin the 'laborious task' (*fattuosa impresa*) of teaching civil law in January. With the usual rhetorical flourish, the preamble recounted that nothing was more pleasing to the city than to look after the education of its youth in order to create qualified men who would ensure the good government and tranquility of the city.[108] The deputies were also asked to develop the specific terms and conditions under which the new teacher would be hired. In a sign of its eagerness to move forward, and perhaps its frustration with the six-decade hiatus, the council authorized the deputies to hire someone from outside the College of Jurists if no member was willing to take on the job.

Nevertheless, nothing happened until 24 May 1625, when the council again appointed three deputies to report on a suitable candidate for the teaching of law within the city. Once again the council explained its motivation in lofty terms: 'the representatives of this city recognize that nothing is more important to the general public and the leaders of this city than the virtuous education of its children, and therefore ... a member of the College must be elected who will publicly teach civil law, the knowledge of which is the foremost foundation of any well-ordered government.'[109] The most important part of this motion, however, was a request to the College of Jurists that students might count up to two years of study in Bergamo as part of the requirement for six years' study outside the city. Such a change would have allowed students to live at home for the first phase of their legal education and save a substantial amount of money. It would also have heightened the value of the public lectures that the city was trying to promote. Since the College had for some time required an actual university degree rather than just attendance at classes, this change did not represent such an enormous shift as it might have a century earlier. Four months later the College of Jurists approved the request.[110]

In September of the same year, the three deputies submitted a revised version of the terms and conditions for hiring a law teacher. The council's strong desire to move forward on this issue is illustrated by the fact that this contract called for a four-year appointment at the substantial salary of 120 scudi per year. Lessons were to begin in early November, and continue until the middle of August. The teacher continued to be forbidden to hold any other public office, nor could he accept gifts of any kind from his students. In contrast to earlier contracts, the council was quite specific about its expectations:

> He is expected to offer a lesson about the *Institutes* on every day that is not a holiday, following the good and approved methods of other qualified lawyers. The lesson, to be conducted in Latin, should last about an hour, and will be held in the chambers of the executive council in the new palace. He will sit upon a teacher's chair [*cattedra magistrale*], to be constructed at public expense upon the order of the deputies. The lessons must begin on the calends of November and must be continued until the middle of August.[111]

Having approved the motion by a vote of 65–4, the council nominated a member of the College of Jurists, Giacomo Carrara Benaglio. Benaglio had earlier served as a member of the civic bureaucracy responsible for investigating corruption in other city offices.[112]

Benaglio continued to teach law in Bergamo for more than twenty years. His status as an 'insider' in city government surely helped him to obtain the position and to keep it as long as he did. Nevertheless, to judge from the reports of the deputies and the city council, he was an inventive, brilliant, successful teacher who attracted large numbers of students and prepared them well for further study at Padua. For example, Benaglio was praised for his 'diligent and careful attention' to teaching, which resulted in the 'notable advancement of many eager and industrious students.' Furthermore, his lectures 'not only bestowed honour upon the public, but were convenient and beneficial to more than a few of the citizens.'[113] The attendance of both citizens and students at Benaglio's lectures suggests once again that they were not intended solely for those aiming for a higher degree. The council records frequently noted the large number of students who crowded into his classroom, the pride with which parents sent their children to his lectures, and the benefit to the reputation of the city as a centre of learning. Furthermore, Benaglio was lauded for introducing new topics into his courses of study, thus keeping pace with the latest intellectual trends. At long last, it seemed, the city council had finally achieved its goal of hiring a brilliant lecturer on a long-term basis.

When his initial contract expired in 1629, Benaglio was quickly rehired. The salary, meeting place, curriculum, and punishments outlined in 1625 remained the same, but several changes were introduced. Vacations were specified, the academic year was shortened by eighty days, and the bidel was expected to record the lessons and bring them to the city offices so that the deputies could review them.[114] Students too had to write down the lessons, and a staff person was appointed to help clean the room and assist Benaglio. Benaglio was required to notify the deputies if any disciplinary problems occurred and to allow them to administer punishments as they saw fit. While the council removed the statement threatening a loss of salary for unexcused absences, it added a clause that Benaglio could still be fired after only a year if he violated any of the above conditions. These changes reflect the increasing scope of civic authority and the city council's desire to become more involved in managing civic activities. Although the council's closer supervision was unusual with regard to education, such developments were in keeping with the growing authority of the state in early modern Italy.

In 1635 Benaglio lodged a complaint with the council regarding either his salary or a fine that he had been forced to pay. In recognition of his excellent performance as a law teacher, the full council immediately replied that the deputies must reconsider their decision in light of Benaglio's appeals.[115] Unfortunately, neither the details nor the resolution of this particular argument survive, but judging from the continued praise that Benaglio received, it is probable that the issue was resolved in his favour. In 1636, perhaps buoyed by confidence in Benaglio's superior instruction, the city council submitted another request to the doge that students might study two years in Bergamo and four years in Padua to receive the doctorate. The College of Jurists had already assented to this change, and Bergamo wished to confirm Venice's agreement.[116]

Further testaments to Giacomo Carrara Benaglio's popularity can be found in the city council's actions of 1643 and 1645. The council declared that henceforth it would require students to sign up for Benaglio's courses by the end of July so that both the city and Benaglio himself would know how many students to expect. Requiring students to register in advance would allow Benaglio the time necessary to prepare his lessons, as well as reassuring parents that they need not make alternative arrangements for the instruction of their children. It also provided the city council with increased leverage over Benaglio's career and with greater authority over the residents who wished to enrol. Benaglio's contract would now commence in July, even if he would not actually teach until the middle of November when the harvest had been completed. Furthermore, he was to be appointed for a two-year term 'so that in this biennium the lecturer can cover the entire corpus of the *Institutes*, and the students can hear it without interruption.'[117] (This excerpt suggests Venetian assent to the proposal that the first two years of study in law be permitted in Bergamo.) In the spring of 1648, the council noted yet again how impressed it was with the large number of students who wished to enrol, but this time they elected Ludovico Cursino Petrobello to a two-year stint as *lector institutorum*.[118] The council continued to appoint members of the College of Jurists to teach civil law throughout the second half of the seventeenth century, though never again with the regularity or high praise that Benaglio had enjoyed. Still, it appears that Bergamo's government finally found a formula that worked for all parties in the teaching of law.

Legal education in Bergamo, however, was marred in this era by a bitter argument between the College of Jurists and the Venetian governors. In a meeting of 6 September 1638, the College of Jurists noted with dismay the increasing number of lawyers who were practising in Bergamo without a university degree or membership in the College.[119] There had always been a few men who utilized their legal skills to act as lawyers, solicitors, or procurators without obtaining a doctorate or joining the College. As one of the documents in the case noted, 'Quite a few of the procurators have spent time in Padua, although for reasons of poverty they could not continue their studies there.'[120] The College of Jurists became sufficiently concerned by the end of 1647 to file a formal complaint with the Riformatori dello Studio, the Venetian officials responsible for overseeing all aspects of higher education in the Veneto.[121] In the complaint, the College alleged that some of the solicitors employed by the podestà were writing, glossing, and interpreting the laws of the commune, the Venetian Republic, and the Holy Roman Empire. Not only was this illegal, they claimed, but it damaged both the reputation of the College and the quality of legal services offered to the public. Furthermore, according to the College, it was an affront to those members who had worked hard to earn their degree that others should enjoy similar fruits without similar effort and expense. The College asked the *Riformatori* to confirm that only College members be allowed to write legislation, interpret the laws, and act as judges in the city and province of Bergamo. The net effect of this request would have been to restrict most legal practice in Bergamo to members of the College.

Arrayed in opposition were the two Venetian governors of Bergamo and the representatives of the various Bergamasque valleys. In a letter of 25 July 1648, the podestà and the capitano wrote to protest the unjust petition of the College and to refute the points raised by the College.[122] The governors drew a distinction between a procurator and a solicitor: the former had to be 'sufficiently educated, with five years of residence in Bergamo, and be approved of by two notaries and three other procurators,' while the latter could possess only rudimentary legal skills. The governors attached numerous affidavits from judges, governors, and officials in other cities of the *terraferma* (the mainland domain of the Republic of Venice) to demonstrate that procurators in Brescia, Crema, and Verona routinely judged simple cases and argued on behalf of clients without owning all of the legal texts required by Bergamo's College of Jurists. Furthermore, claimed the governors, the procurators had often studied at Padua alongside the sons and members of the College, and many of them belonged to the College of Notaries which demanded similar (if less stringent) conditions for admission. In other words, the

social standing of these procurators should have been adequate for entry into the exclusive College of Jurists. Lastly, the governors noted that
many of the procurators travelled for weeks at a time through the various valleys to the north in order to serve as judges or advocates. Since
most of Bergamo's territory was isolated and poor in resources, valley
residents could neither afford nor reach the members of the College in
Bergamo. A supporting letter from Giovanni Andrea Locatello makes
the point very clearly: 'the wise Jurists [are motivated] not from a pure
zeal to do good, but from their own financial interest.'[123]

The Riformatori asked Alvise Valli of Bergamo to summarize the two
positions and to present a recommendation. Valli, identified as a doctor
of law, does not appear to have been a member of Bergamo's College
of Jurists. He wrote a lengthy, even-handed account of the dispute and
in conclusion decided in favour of the procurators and the governors.
In defence of his decision, he cited the public's right to choose its own
representatives, along with the lower cost and long-standing tradition
of allowing procurators to conduct certain kinds of legal work.[124] Shortly thereafter, the *Riformatori* accepted Valli's recommendation and the
case was closed.

Although the College of Jurists lost its stranglehold on some positions inside the city bureaucracy, this lawsuit confirmed that only a
member of the College could hold an appointment as *jurisperitum*. It
was probably small consolation to the members of the College who
won this battle but lost the war over the larger issue of who could practise and teach law. As noted above, the teaching of law in Bergamo was
intended both for students planning to continue at Padua and for those
seeking a new job as procurator. The city's commitment to the teaching
of law thus fluctuated from the late fifteenth to the mid-seventeenth
century: in times of peace and prosperity lessons were offered, but no
sustained effort to teach law was successful until the appointment of
Giacomo Carrara Benaglio from 1625 to 1647. Given Bergamo's poverty
and relative isolation, the city's production of so many lawyers and legal scholars is something of a surprise. Perhaps the law represented one
way for the residents of a poor frontier town to hold their own against
larger, wealthier, more powerful cities and individuals. These public
lectures on the law demonstrate that the city government of Bergamo
wished to promote the study of jurisprudence and the creation of an
educated youth to ensure the continued success of municipal government, even if the city could not always sustain such classes.

Conclusion

We have seen that the commune of Bergamo experimented with a variety of different approaches in order to provide public instruction in grammar, rhetoric, humanities, and the law. From tax exemptions and subsidized housing for teachers, to joint ventures with the bishop and the Misericordia Maggiore confraternity, the commune searched for solutions that would provide an educated youth at a minimal expense. Unlike other institutions in Bergamo that established long-lasting academies or seminaries, the commune of Bergamo was never able to maintain a stable school for more than a decade or two. Public schools in Bergamo tended to rise and fall with the ability of the individual masters hired by the city council. When a dedicated master such as Giovita Ravizza, Nicolò Cologno, or Giacomo Carrara Benaglio provided instruction, the lessons displayed some continuity. But after the retirement of these exceptional teachers, the commune found itself unable to sustain the pedagogical success of previous years.

As we have seen, public schooling in Bergamo can be subdivided into distinct thematic periods. The centuries prior to 1482 exemplify indirect support of public schooling, with individual teachers offering private lessons and boarding facilities to local boys. In recognition of teachers' civic value, the city council granted them tax exemptions, but was generally unwilling to invest in a more permanent public school. With the notable exception of Bonifacio da Osio, most teachers were independent masters, like Jacopo or Lorenzo de Apibus. However, during the last two decades of the fifteenth century and the first two decades of the sixteenth century, the commune became much more involved in the appointment and management of public school teachers. This civic commitment culminated in the hiring of Giovan Battista Pio from 1505 to 1507 and then Giovita Ravizza from circa 1508 to 1523. The city's willingness to bring in humanist scholars, and to pay the hefty fees that such scholars commanded, speaks to the increasing importance assumed by public education in these years. The subjects taught were generally (Latin) grammar, rhetoric, and humanities. Ravizza's important treatise of 1523, composed for Bergamo's city council, displays the educational philosophy that guided teaching and learning in this era of humanist revival.

The third phase of public schooling, a 'long century' from 1525 to 1632, witnessed three notable developments. First, the city's commitment to public education waxed and waned from one decade to the next. Sometimes the city was able to identify a strong maestro but the overall trend is clearly that of temporary appointments and broken promises. On a more positive note, a second development was the willingness of the commune (perhaps by necessity) to engage in joint ventures with other groups and institutions in order to offer schooling. Such arrangements – with the MIA, with the bishop, with the Theatines, and ultimately with the Somaschans – suggest that the city understood the importance of civic-sponsored schooling even as it was unwilling to assume the burden alone. A third development was the increasing role of the Catholic Church in offering education to lay and religious children alike. This expansion of ecclesiastical interest in education reflects the reforming impulse evident not only at Trent but in the creation of numerous new orders of men and women whose interest lay in teaching. Such a shift is clearly important to the commune's efforts to offer public schooling, and it may help to explain how and why the city council changed its focus in the later sixteenth century.

The teaching of law, which constitutes a fourth and final phase in communal-supported schooling, illustrates this inconsistent support for education too. During the late fifteenth and sixteenth centuries, references to instruction in law are few and far between. Not until the arrival of Giacomo Carrara Benaglio in the seventeenth century did the commune display a concerted effort to support such instruction. The *ad hoc* nature of lessons in jurisprudence in Bergamo may also reflect the changing requirements by Bergamo's College of Jurists and by the university at Padua concerning who could study and practise law.

This lack of continuity in 'public' schooling should not necessarily be construed as a failure. Other Italian cities struggled to provide education to their children too. Military incursions, harvest failures, rapacious princes, and other disasters contributed to the spotty record of cities and towns in supporting education. Indeed, this gap was one of the reasons that the Jesuits were so successful in their bid to open colleges all across sixteenth-century Europe. Although the Society of Jesus was unable to win permission to enter Bergamo until the eighteenth century, Bergamo's city council clearly looked to other representatives of the Church to assist with public instruction. Simply put, Bergamo's local government did not want the responsibility of administering a school. The commune preferred to hire one master to assume responsibility for all aspects of instruction, even when it must have been clear that a shortage of competent schoolteachers existed. Gradually the commune realized the necessity of *institutional* support for public education. In an effort to provide more consistent public instruction, the commune therefore attempted to share governance with the Misericordia Maggiore, the bishop, and religious orders of men. These and other institutions provided the necessary funds and teachers to ensure that children received an education (both spiritual and lay). It is to the study of these institutions that we turn next: confraternities in chapter 2, the Church in chapters 3 and 4, and parents in chapter 5.

2 *Misericordia*: Schooling and Confraternities

In 1549 the governor of Bergamo, Pietro Sanudo, lamented the poverty of the city's inhabitants: 'most of them are poor, and if there did not exist the many charitable institutions that are called *Misericordie*, many people would die of hunger and even as it is for the better part of the year they must survive on chestnuts and other wild foods.' Six years later another governor of Bergamo echoed this concern in his report to the doge of Venice: 'and truly, Most Serene Prince, so great is the number of the poor from the sterility of the land that it would be impossible for them to live if they were not assisted by charitable institutions [*luoghi pii*].'[1] Numerous other sources attest to the critical role of hospitals, schools, orphanages, and other charitable institutions in pre-modern Italy. Many of these institutions were managed by a confraternity: an association of lay people who joined together for socio-religious reasons and agreed to follow common rules. As Lester Little has demonstrated in the case of Bergamo, the twin purposes of a confraternity were to encourage religious devotion and to provide assistance to members of the confraternity and the poor.[2] Confraternities engaged in a wide array of philanthropic actions to benefit the community: they distributed bread and wine, cared for the sick, provided dowries, taught catechism, maintained chapels, ensured a respectable burial, and even furnished legal advice to prisoners. In Bergamo, as in other cities of northern Italy during the early modern period, confraternities also promoted education and literacy.

Confraternities are known by a variety of different names: brotherhoods, companies, consortiums, sodalities, fraternities, *ordines laicorum*, *luoghi pii*; in Venice they are called *scuole*, in Genoa *casacche*.[3] I define a confraternity as a voluntary association of laymen (and sometimes lay-

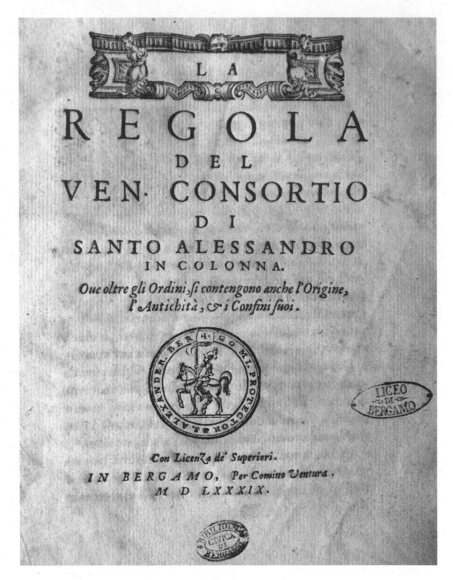

The Rule of the Confraternity of S. Alessandro in Colonna (Bergamo: Comin Ventura, 1589). This small pamphlet recounted the history, purpose, and guidelines for one of Bergamo's most important parish confraternities. In the Middle Ages it engaged in traditional charitable actions, such as the distribution of alms; after 1556 it began to offer scholarships and hire teachers to benefit the children of the parish.

women) who abided by certain rules in order to promote the honour of God, to perform philanthropic work for the needy, and to provide spiritual and material benefits for members. They should not be confused with monks and nuns: members of confraternities did not take formal vows, and they continued to live and work in the secular world. Nor should the term *scuola* be misinterpreted; confraternities in Bergamo and elsewhere were often referred to as *scholae* or *scuole*, but this term is independent of their interest in education.

The historiographical tradition of confraternity studies has only recently begun to move beyond the limited range of institutional and religious history. In comparison with other institutions of early modern Europe (e.g., convents, guilds, communes, seminaries), confraternities have been insufficiently studied or overlooked. Yet their contribution, in schooling as in other areas, was absolutely fundamental. In his study of late medieval confraternities in Bergamo, Lester Little notes that of all the orders within the medieval church, it is the *ordo laicorum* whose history is least known. He attributes this to the fact that 'the laity never had the clear identity, learning, need for record-keeping or even polemical interest with which to foster a tradition of historical writing.'[4] For the early modern period, Christopher Black, while agreeing that confraternities have been woefully understudied, points instead to a lack of readily available sources.[5] Adriano Prosperi confirms that confraternities have not received the attention they deserve; he cites the emphasis on hierarchical subordination after the Council of Trent, which placed the confraternities in an awkward position because they were an association that stressed equality and 'horizontal' relationships.[6] The last three decades have witnessed a substantial increase in the quantity and sophistication of historical writing on confraternities. In addition to the works just cited, Brian Pullan's magisterial work on the *scuole* in Venice has traced the history of elite confraternities in the Republic. For Florence, Ronald Weissman and Richard Trexler have emphasized the socio-religious importance of these associations, while Konrad Eisenbichler and Lorenzo Polizzotto have crafted in-depth studies of specific consortiums. Nicholas Terpstra's investigation of confraternities in Bologna has revealed their fundamental importance to civic affairs. More recently, Lance Lazar has considered the influence of Jesuit confraternities in Rome, while David D'Andrea's work on the confraternity of Santa Maria dei Battuti in Treviso has demonstrated the myriad important roles of a large confraternity in a small town.[7] Roisin Cossar's study of Bergamo's largest confraternity has carefully analysed lay religious culture through the twin lenses of gender and class.[8]

Despite the absence of a long, well-developed historiographical tradition, confraternity studies remain important for a number of reasons. First, many Italians were involved with confraternities, either as participants or recipients. When Archbishop Carlo Borromeo visited Bergamo in 1575, he found at least forty confraternities within the city, and more than a hundred in the province. Confraternities represented one of the most important manifestations of lay religious sentiment, reflecting the 'shock waves' of religious energy that pulsed through early modern Italy.[9] Confraternities may have helped to foster cooperation across lines drawn by class, trade, and urban geography, and thus moderated the fractious and competitive nature of Italian society. At the same time, they could also serve as elitist agents of social control on behalf of the city, the state, or the Church. Often lay confraternities served as an arena for political activity and influence by members of the middle class or elites who were denied access to politics in the state.[10] In addition to their quasi-political functions, these associations commissioned works of art, maintained churches, and helped to mitigate the ravages of famine, war, and plague.

In this chapter I analyse the efforts of confraternities in Bergamo to educate both lay boys and *chierici* (priests-in-training).[11] These confraternities provided scholarships, stipends, housing, books, lessons, clothing, and food to both students and teachers. As a direct result of such confraternal actions, Bergamasque children were instructed in grammar, rhetoric, law, medicine, arithmetic, and a host of other subjects at the primary, secondary, and university levels.

Confraternal history in Bergamo has been dominated by the Congregation and Fraternity of Saint Mary of Mercy, founded in 1265 and still in existence today. Known to all as the Misericordia Maggiore (commonly abbreviated as MIA), this confraternity served as a model to others and possessed the lion's share of bequests and philanthropic obligations. Its singular position within the city requires a very brief overview. Like the *scuole grandi* of Venice or the confraternity Santa Maria dei Battuti of Treviso, the MIA of Bergamo was a 'maxi-confraternity' that offered multiple types of assistance. It distributed weekly alms to the poor and to widows, offered dowries to members' daughters, and held masses for the deceased. It provided legal assistance to testators during plague epidemics as well as nursing care for dying individuals. The MIA supplied wet nurses for orphans and needy infants, compensated physicians who provided care to the indigent, and paid priests who comforted prisoners. Beginning in 1449, the confraternity assumed full responsibility for the maintenance and decoration of Santa Maria

Maggiore, the 'civic chapel' of the city and the second most important church in Bergamo after the cathedral. Furthermore, the MIA occasionally acted as a peacemaker between rival factions, and in the fourteenth century even stepped in to support the government. Lastly, the MIA supervised several smaller confraternities in Bergamo, sometimes absorbing their charitable responsibilities or governing their affairs.[12]

The MIA owned more than 1550 hectares scattered throughout the city, the valleys, and the farms to the south. Its coffers were further enriched by annual dues, testamentary bequests, and investment returns. As one of the largest landholders in the region, it was sometimes able to mediate between urban and rural interests. But the MIA was more than simply a wealthy corporation; it displayed a strong civic conscience and its officers consistently sought to ameliorate problems faced by the city. Such ventures included, but clearly were never limited to, education.

This chapter analyses confraternal actions in six distinct categories. Scholarships and subsidies provided by the MIA comprise the initial efforts to support education. The most famous of these scholarships, endowed by a public school teacher named Lorenzo de Apibus, distributed money to hundreds of students over the course of 250 years. The next three sections trace the MIA's different types of schools: a day school for chierici (founded 1506), a residential college in Padua (founded 1532), and a boarding academy of clerics (founded 1566). Each institution was closely supervised and financed by the MIA, but none survived more than fifty years. The impermanence of these three confraternal schools resembles those sponsored by the commune, as does the MIA's willingness to experiment. Even more than the commune, the MIA dared to try diverse approaches; when one school failed, the MIA's inclination was to open another one immediately. Although the MIA's educational ventures overshadowed those of smaller, less wealthy parish confraternities, by no means did the MIA hold a monopoly on instruction.[13] In the fifth part of this chapter, we consider other confraternities in Bergamo – Sant'Alessandro in Colonna, San Lorenzo, Santo Spirito, and Sant'Alessandro della Croce – that imitated the MIA's educational initiatives at the parish level after 1550. The chapter concludes with a brief look at the efforts of the MIA to provide instruction for chierici during the seventeenth century in its Collegio Mariano.

Scholarships and Subsidies, 1361–1611

From the mid-fourteenth to the early seventeenth century, the Misericordia Maggiore utilized two complementary strategies in dispensing scholarships and subsidies. First, in obedience to strict guidelines laid out in Lorenzo de Apibus's testament, the Misericordia Maggiore annually disbursed a fixed amount of money to a limited number of students who had met certain selection criteria. Second, the confraternity provided small amounts of food, clothing, money, or other items deemed necessary for study to poverty-stricken students upon their request. Although both methods were intended primarily to benefit the poor, scions of noble families often appear among the recipients. This suggests that paying for an education, especially at the university level, was a hardship even for those families near the top of the social pyramid. It further intimates that despite the MIA's claim to favour the poor, the confraternity was not immune to nepotism. Clerical and lay recipients were present in both categories in roughly equal numbers. Other Bergamasque confraternities sponsored schools but rarely granted scholarships or other direct subsidies to students and teachers. The MIA's virtual monopoly on scholarships is surely the result of its far more extensive resources; other confraternities in Bergamo simply could not afford to grant scholarships year in and year out. Until 1485, most recipients of the Apibus scholarship studied at university, but in the sixteenth century an increasing number of students used the funds to study Latin grammar in Bergamo. The essential point to remember is that the MIA supported education for hundreds of students over hundreds of years.

Scholarships

The story of the Apibus scholarships begins in late thirteenth-century Bergamo when Lorenzo de Apibus opened a grammar school in the neighbourhood of San Giacomo, where he was later assisted by his son Jacopo. As noted in the preceding chapter, Lorenzo's will of 1337 declared his intention to endow a single scholarship to be administered by the Misericordia Maggiore and asked Jacopo to house one poor student for two years. Guided by the example of his father, Jacopo in his will of 1361 directed the Misericordia Maggiore to use the income from his estate to create scholarships for poor students.[14] At the time of his death, Jacopo de Apibus owned more than a dozen pieces of land in and around Bergamo totalling approximately 11.5 hectares. With the exception of the house on Via San Giacomo that went to his daughter, nearly all of the land was inherited by the MIA, which administered this bequest for more than 250 years. In 1528 the MIA's notary reminded his confraternal brothers that all land from the Apibus inheritance was inalienable, and that the proceeds had to be used regularly for the support of poor scholars.[15]

Unlike the will of his father, Lorenzo, Jacopo's was very specific about the terms under which students were to be selected: they must be poor, eager to learn (*maxime habentes intentionem vivendi de lucro literarum*), competent in Latin, and at least eleven years of age. Students had to pass written and oral examinations in Latin, and could lose the scholarship if they behaved poorly or did not attend classes. The selection committee consisted of four members: a 'minister' (i.e., officer) of the MIA, a fellow of the College of Jurists, the prior of the Dominican church, and a grammar teacher to be selected by the first three members. The grammar teacher typically proposed three subjects to be discussed by the candidate, followed by one posed by the prior. The committee members were to be paid one florin annually for examining candidates twice a year, on the feast of Saint Michael (29 September) and around Easter. In contrast to the MIA's council of ministers, which always met in the confraternity's principal building on Via Arena, the Apibus selection committee met in many different locations. In order to ensure that the committee observed the stipulations of the will, the MIA's notary always copied out the full text of the covenant governing the election of each student, plus the names of the selection committee. Nevertheless, the MIA did exercise some discretion in its interpretation. For example, although the will specifically excluded relatives of the MIA's selection committee, in practice this prohibition was not strictly observed.

Recipients of the Apibus scholarship, who attended a solemn investiture ceremony at the convent of Santo Stefano, received eighteen lire per year for a maximum of five years. It is interesting to note that the amount of the scholarship remained fixed at eighteen lire per year, even as inflation steadily eroded its actual value. In comparison with scholarships awarded in other cities (e.g., the Salinguerro bequest in Treviso at 75 lire per year or the Lamberto bequest in Brescia at 100 lire per year), the Apibus scholarship may seem minimal.[16] However, smaller individual awards resulted in a larger number of students being able to study. Eighteen lire per year might have supported a frugal student lifestyle throughout the fifteenth century, but it would have been insufficient during the inflation-prone sixteenth century. As we will see shortly, beginning in 1532 the MIA awarded its top students in Padua the more generous sum of one hundred lire per year. A brief comparison may help to clarify the point. An Apibus scholarship worth 18 lire per year in 1350 would have been valued at 155,060 lire in 1956 and at 3,561,937 lire (=US$2,681.42) in 2004.[17]

The MIA faithfully carried out its responsibility for more than two centuries. From 1475 to 1540, for example, the MIA granted more than 140 scholarships, an average of three or four every year.[18] Half of those students received the maximum amount of ninety lire. The other half received varying amounts, depending upon the duration of the scholarship. Students could lose the Apibus scholarship for a variety of reasons: unsatisfactory performance, entry into a monastery, conscription as a soldier, failure to attend classes and take examinations, and of course death.[19] In this fifty-five-year period, more than a dozen students died while receiving an Apibus scholarship. The confraternity wished to be certain that the awards went to prepared, morally upright students who would honour their benefactor and themselves by satisfactory performance. An Apibus scholarship was sometimes passed down from one brother to another, as when the three Grignano brothers each received ninety lire; or multiple cousins could win a scholarship simultaneously, as happened to the fortunate Della Valle family.[20] Some students used the Apibus scholarship to study with private teachers in Bergamo, while others went to the university at Pavia (while Bergamo was under the Visconti) or at Padua (after it became subject to the Venetians).

Attending university in the fifteenth or sixteenth century was an expensive business. The average cost for a doctorate was 22 to 40 ducats (150–250 lire). Housing was substantially more expensive in a university town like Padua and could run 10–20 ducats annually. Students also had to pay for books, clothing, transportation, and food. Six years was the minimum amount of time to achieve a degree, and students often required ten years to get a degree in law or medicine. Thus the Apibus scholarships (and later the Collegio Patavino) certainly provided welcome assistance, but it never came close to covering the entire cost of an education, particularly if lost wages for the student are included. The cost, duration, and difficulty of university education meant that scholarships represented an important form of charity.[21]

Who were these students? Although children from Martinengo, Nembro, Olmo, Alzano, and other towns in the hinterland of Bergamo were occasionally selected, the MIA consistently favoured students from the city itself. The Apibus legacy was ostensibly designed to benefit poorer students, such as Vincenzo Pesenti, who in 1512 was 'burdened by a large family' but still sought to live *de lucro scientie*, or Giovanni Sebastiano di Pellegrino, a recipient in 1528, who listed his father as a lowly beret-maker (*beretario*).[22] Scholarships were often awarded to students whose fathers were identified as lawyers, notaries, and grammar teachers, which suggests that these professions were not particularly lucrative. Nevertheless, the list of recipients contains many of the leading families of Bergamo: Suardi, Colleoni, Agazzi, Zanchi, Bonghi, Benaglio, San Pellegrino, Tiraboschi, Roncalli, Rota. Prior to 1450, in fact, the list of recipients was dominated by nobles, but in a bid to limit the power of the old Ghibelline families and to increase political stability, the Venetian governors worked hard to promote new families and the more equitable distribution of scholarships.[23] Notarial acts recording the elections often specified the status of the student as either *clericus* or *scolaris* and suggest that the numbers were roughly equal. Jacopo de Apibus had specifically mentioned in his will that students who decided to take religious vows were not to lose their scholarships.

Very few explicit references to female education exist in these scholarship records. Indeed, the only one is dated 7 March 1493, when the MIA awarded twenty lire to the wife of Bartolomeo Stringari in order to pay the (female?) grammar teacher of her daughter.[24] The overwhelming majority of scholarships surely went to boys, who were viewed as the only ones needing an education in the 'public' disciplines of rhetoric and grammar. If girls were ever sent away to school, it was almost always to a convent; the first woman to earn a doctoral degree from the University of Padua was Elena Cornaro Piscopia in 1678.[25] Since the scholarship records of the MIA almost always listed the name of the student, we can be reasonably certain that Bartolomeo Stringari's daughter (whose name is not given) represented a remarkable exception.

The MIA regularly awarded Apibus scholarships until about 1540, when poor investments and new priorities dramatically reduced the amount of income from this bequest, with the result that virtually no scholarships were awarded during the second half of the sixteenth century.[26] In 1566 the MIA declared that funds from the Apibus legacy would be used to support the living expenses of twenty-five students in the MIA's new Academy of Clerics, 'in keeping with the will of the testator.'[27] In 1611, following the closure of the Academy of Clerics, the MIA announced that it had satisfied the conditions of the Apibus legacy and would no longer award scholarships in his name.[28] The confraternity donated part of the remaining funds to purchase two wooden sculptures by Andrea Fantoni for the church of Santa Maria Maggiore and gave the rest to the public schools of the city, thus encouraging the foundation of a commune-sponsored school in 1615. No explanation is provided for the final decision to shut down the Apibus scholarship, but presumably the endowment was close to depletion. In vivid contrast to nearly every other educational endeavour in Bergamo, the Apibus scholarship program had been successful over the long term and the MIA deserved to be proud of its record in administering this bequest.

While the Apibus legacy was certainly the most important scholarship fund administered by the Misericordia Maggiore, by no means was it the only one. The confraternity proved willing to manage other bequests designed exclusively to support members of a testator's family. In 1475 Cristoforo Biffi left half of the income from his property in Lower Oxio to the MIA for the specific purpose of sending his male descendants to study at Padua.[29] The exact amount was not specified, as it would have varied with the value of the property, but it was enough to permit a student to study law for seven years or medicine for six. Only one student at a time could hold the scholarship. If no member of the Biffi family presented himself for consideration, then a qualified legitimate male heir of the Ghislandi family (a distant relation by marriage) might be elected. As with the Apibus scholarships, the MIA was in charge of selecting the students and distributing payment. Another example comes from 1535, when the judge Giovanni Francesco di Mozzo left money to support his male descendants who wished to study at the University of Padua. Between 1535 and 1553 the MIA repeatedly awarded fifteen or twenty large gold scudi per year to sons of the Mozzo family.[30] Toward the end of the sixteenth century the Misericordia Maggiore received yet another legacy *pro studio filiorum Cannelli* (for the education of the Cannelli boys).[31] The MIA also accepted general donations on behalf of schooling; for example, in 1548 Giovanni Antonio Biffi left an unspecified amount of money to the MIA, which was immediately used to augment the salary of Bono de Lulmo, rector of the MIA's school.[32]

Subsidies and Assistance in Kind

In addition to scholarships, the Misericordia Maggiore distributed small subsidies in cash and in kind to students and their teachers on a regular basis.[33] One scholar has identified seventy-six examples of assistance by the MIA during the fifteenth century in favour of instruction or further study. For the period 1496–1500, there are entries almost every month recording the distribution of lire, wine, and bread. In contrast to the Apibus scholarships, the only requirement to receive a subsidy or goods in kind was demonstrated poverty. Most of these subsidies were intended to help students through a short-term crisis, not to finance an academic career. For example, the two orphaned sons of Vittoriano da Crema received 'two [bread] rolls per day for an indeterminate period of time,' and the cleric Baldassare di Giovanni da Trescore received just three lire in 1496.[34] In 1534 the MIA granted one gold scudo to Gelmino Marchese so that he might learn how to write, and in 1538 the teacher Alessandro di Brescia was paid four lire for teaching Nicolò di Mantua how to write.[35] In 1548 the pupil Filippo de Mozzo received a pair of shoes (*unum par caligarum*) so that he could attend school.[36] Repeated subsidies were possible, as when Alessandro Zonca received two bushels of grain, a *carro* (cart) of wine, and fifteen imperial lire; two years later he received another three gold ducats because he was assiduous in his studies.[37] The Misericordia Maggiore even awarded assistance *en masse*; in the winter of 1555 the confraternity provided one piece of coal per student per day to help heat a chilly classroom.[38] These awards appear to have been intended primarily for lower level study of reading, basic grammar, and the liturgy. Most students used these awards to study with private teachers or a local priest. Once in a while the MIA would hire someone directly to provide instruction on a very limited basis; for example, from 1546 to 1556 the confraternity hired Paolo Tiraboschi to teach writing and mathematics to a small group of four to six chierici. His students were usually assigned to him for a period of six months before being admitted to the MIA's regular school, implying that Tiraboschi was teaching at a remedial level.

   Although the MIA occasionally agreed to give money to individual students pursuing advanced degrees, it viewed such grants as one-time donations rather than annual scholarships.[39] For example, Jacopo Boselli received eight ducats to finish his law degree at Padua and become *virtuosus et doctissimus* (virtuous and learned); the two sons of Nicolo de Amanio each received two ducats to further their studies in Pavia; and Jacopo Antonio Benaglio was granted twenty-five lire *amore dei* (for charity) to earn his degree in medicine.[40] Bernardo Terzi of Gorlago requested charity from the MIA in 1588 to support his son Antonio in his efforts to become a surgeon. In 1597 Cesare Locatello submitted a similar request on behalf of his son Maffeo, the eldest of nine children; Maffeo had graduated from the MIA's academy and was now at the *studio* in Perugia. Nor were such requests limited to lay students. Giovan Battista Capodiferro obtained permission from the confraternity in 1586 to leave the academy and study canon law at Padua. Four years later, having finished his studies, he humbly begged the MIA to assist him with the expenses of his final exams.[41] It must be remembered, however, that nearly all such awards represented one-time grants-in-aid to individual students, not a multi-year scholarship or an effort to provide instruction for a group of boys. Such temporary, individualized assistance was doubtless necessary and valuable, but it is clearly different than a sustained commitment over multiple decades.

The Misericordia Maggiore also procured fundamental texts and loaned them to students for the purpose of study. In the winter of 1499, Giovan Pietro di Solza borrowed several volumes of Cicero's letters and a book of poetry by Virgil. In 1501 Alessandro Ceresoli, a cleric, was permitted to borrow a book of poetry by Terence and a grammar by Priscian.[42] Half a century later, the tradition continued: the MIA's notary, Hieronymo Pellegrino, purchased and delivered a Latin dictionary known as a *calepino*[43] to the cleric Antonio de Licinis in recognition of his virtue and superior performance.[44] Later in the same year, the MIA awarded Baptista de Mutio a book by the classical rhetorician Valerius Maximus and one-half of a scudo to purchase other books; when the MIA realized it did not have a work by Valerius Maximus, it substituted the epistles of Saint Jerome instead.[45] The MIA regularly drew up inventories of its possessions, and the same books often reappear on loan to different students. Works by Cicero, Terence, Virgil, and Boethius, in addition to grammar books, calligraphy books, and breviaries, circulated among the students sponsored by the confraternity.[46] The presence of such books reinforces the idea that the MIA was responding to the twin pressures of humanism and Catholicism by including a range of books in its lending library. The incomplete nature of these records, however, makes it impossible to determine which books were most popular. Nor can we generalize about classroom practice, given that we do not know precisely which books were used in the MIA's various schools. Some of these books were purchased, but more often the MIA received them from benefactors like Antonio Maffei, who donated sixty legal books at the end of the fifteenth century.[47]

The MIA did not limit itself to patronage of intellectual training alone. Particularly in the 1530s and 1540s, the confraternity began to pay for vocational education, placing students in apprenticeships where they might learn a craft. In addition, the MIA actively encouraged boys who wished to train for the priesthood by providing books, subsidies, and other necessities. Furthermore, the confraternity steadily increased its commitment to providing musical training to all clerics. In the seventeenth century this emphasis upon music would continue to grow until the MIA's school of music achieved an international reputation.

Throughout the distribution of scholarships, subsidies, and other kinds of assistance, the MIA's objective always remained the same: to train Bergamo's children to be literate, faithful, professionally qualified members of the commune. It is impossible to assign a precise monetary value to most of these scholarships, or even to know with any certainty how many students received assistance. But clearly the MIA granted scholarships and subsidies to hundreds and hundreds of students between the mid-fourteenth and mid-sixteenth centuries. The Misericordia Maggiore was not unique in this regard; the Trevisan confraternity of Santa Maria dei Battuti carried out similar actions.[48] Other small Italian cities provided scholarships to aspiring students, as in Treviso or Padua, but the history of financial aid in early modern Europe remains unwritten. The most important aspect of the MIA's educational philanthropy was its widespread scope. Despite testamentary guidelines, the MIA did not   with the exception of gender   encourage just one type of student or one field of study to the exclusion of others. Scholarship recipients were lay and religious, rich and poor, urban and rural; they studied grammar, mathematics, singing, the liturgy, law, and medicine; and the grants they received ranged from a few lire or a bundle of firewood to dozens of gold scudi for multiple years.

The MIA's Day School, 1506–66

By the dawn of the sixteenth century, in addition to providing books, shoes, clothing, and cash in support of education, the MIA had granted scholarships to at least a hundred students. The confraternity's charity permitted many students to obtain an education that otherwise would have remained beyond their reach. Not only did the MIA's actions dwarf the sporadic efforts of the commune to provide public schooling, but they would later serve as a model to other Bergamasque confraternities.

Nevertheless, the MIA remained dissatisfied with its efforts. Widespread ignorance and illiteracy, combined with a steady decline in the number and quality of boys serving in the church of Santa Maria Maggiore, prompted the confraternity to take decisive action. On 26 January 1506 the ministers of the MIA issued a ringing condemnation of clerical ignorance:

Considering that ignorance is the mother of all errors, if it is detestable
when found in the worshippers of the Church, it is even worse when encountered among the officials of the Church, the knowledge and doctrine
of whom ought to shine brilliantly, so that when they celebrate and explain
the sacred writings, they are not ignorant of what they say, as often hap-
pens. Nor should the maxims and holy lessons become mixed up and distorted with solemn erroneous declarations, which would certainly cause
great whisperings and scandals. It is necessary to ensure with every possible effort that this absolutely never occurs among the priests and chierici
celebrating [Mass] in the church of Santa Maria Maggiore of Bergamo. To
this church, almost the only one in the city which remains distinguished
and reflects the glory of the city, come not only commoners and labourers
to hear the divine offices, but men of wisdom and the patriciate of the city,
who attend frequently. The priests and chierici chosen by the council of
this consortium should possess such knowledge of letters that in carrying
out their duties they do not inflict tedium and nausea upon their listeners,
but rather bring happiness and joy, so that their audience remains more
attentive and more devoted in listening to the word of God.[49]

Preaching had been an important part of priestly offices for centuries, of
course, but the MIA's emphasis upon good rhetorical skills here may reflect the influence of the humanists during the previous century, and in
particular the arrival of Giovanni Battista Pio in Bergamo the previous
year. Recognizing that many chierici were too impoverished to obtain
instruction in grammar, the MIA's council of ministers unanimously declared itself 'eager to ensure that anyone who wishes to dedicate himself to virtue and to letters and to becoming wise should have the means
to become literate and educated.'[50] Therefore the council proposed to
hire a priest, for a maximum salary of 170 lire per year, who would provide daily lessons in grammar and good letters (*lectiones grammaticales
et auctores grammatici ... bonis et optimis litteris et non pedantariis*). He
was expected to act as a role model to his students, to instruct them in
proper behaviour, and to examine not only all the chierici who served
in Santa Maria Maggiore, but all others in the city who wished to learn.
Although on weekdays he might be excused from other canonical responsibilities, on Sundays and holidays he was required to celebrate
mass and to participate fully in all religious ceremonies. Curiously, the
MIA exhorted him to behave 'as if he were the master who held the first
chair of letters in the city' – perhaps a reference to the Bolognese humanist Giovanni Battista Pio? The Misericordia Maggiore specified fur-

ther that although this teacher was not to receive gifts or money of any kind from his students, the MIA would provide him with a house where he might live at the confraternity's expense. In theory, the number of students was to be capped at forty, although in fact this limit was rarely respected.

With this declaration of intent in 1506, the MIA founded a day school for chierici with the explicit goal of improving knowledge of letters and rhetorical ability. It was the first of several schools created by the confraternity, each with its own identity but all aimed at raising the bar for clerical training and performance. The MIA had mixed success with this day school. It kept the doors open every year and eventually trained hundreds of boys, yet it was unable to maintain a stable staff and was forced to expel boys on multiple occasions. As we will see, the MIA hired a series of teachers, including Fedrigino da Taliuno, Bono de Lulmo, and Michele Manili. Their respective contracts reveal details about salaries, housing, discipline, and other aspects of school administration. Several themes appear repeatedly, including the confraternity's penchant for rehiring familiar faces and its increasing concern about morality and discipline. While the MIA had garnered some experience with students through the administration of scholarships and subsidies, running a school (or even hiring a master and staff annually) presented knotty new problems. Ultimately, the MIA decided that it needed to exercise more control over its students and therefore transformed the day school into a boarding academy.

For the first half of the sixteenth century, however, the MIA relied upon two dozen *maestri* and *ripetitori*, as well as the confraternity's own deputies, to supervise schooling. The story of this school is told chronologically, primarily by reconstructing the expectations for various teachers and the degree to which those were met. Thus we often learn more about the administrative structure of this first school, and less about the content of its lessons. Such an approach may seem tedious at times, but given the extant documents, it is the best way to follow the school's history. Identifying the teachers and their concerns also allows us to focus on other issues (e.g., student life, textbooks) for subsequent schools when documents on those issues are more complete.

Just three weeks after its initial declaration in 1506, the confraternity reached an agreement with Bernardino Fogaccia of Alzano. In exchange for an annual salary of 160 lire and a respectable house, Fogaccia agreed to teach thirty-three students selected by the MIA and seven other students of his own choosing. The MIA permitted Fogaccia to have ten boarding students (*decem contuberniales sive donzenacios*), presumably drawn from the forty who were to attend his lessons. Fogaccia failed to show up, however, electing to remain in Alzano where he enjoyed a benefice and (ironically) tutored Giovanni di Giacomo Agazzi with the funds from an Apibus scholarship.[51]

The MIA immediately hired another priest, Marco da Brignano, as a replacement. His salary was fixed at 150 lire per year and an additional payment, not to exceed forty lire, for the rental of a house. Although his contract called for him to teach only forty students, the number of students who wished to enrol peaked at sixty, and the MIA therefore agreed to hire an assistant teacher (*ripetitor seu choadiutor*). The first twelve students chosen by the MIA were described as 'salaried' (i.e., on scholarship), while the remaining forty-eight assisted in the basilica during religious services and in return received instruction in grammar (i.e., work-study). This distinction between the two groups of clerics persisted for many years. After one year of teaching, Marco da Brignano asked to resign; the MIA granted his request, but demanded that he forfeit the year's salary.[52]

The MIA scrambled to find another teacher, and by 1 November 1507 had hired Antonio Lallio da Romano to teach thirty-three students, plus seven more to be chosen at his own discretion. Lallio's contract provided him with a salary of 150 lire per year for three years, a house rented from Jacopo de Muzo, and the option to house ten students privately. After he objected that his salary was insufficient, the MIA awarded him an annual raise of twenty lire on condition that he read a lesson from the Holy Scripture every Sunday. The MIA also awarded Lallio a one-time payment of twenty-five lire to assemble the necessary items for his trip, and on 9 December he received the first instalment of his salary. Barely five weeks later, however, he appeared again before the council to complain about the lack of heat in his house, which, he said, was endangering not only his own health but that of his students. The MIA's council grumbled that Lallio had approved of the house just a few weeks earlier, but wishing to please the maestro, they agreed to let him search for another house in the same price range. He found a house belonging to his assistant teacher, Bernardino Colombi. Although the MIA threatened to hold Lallio responsible for the balance of the rent on the first house, in fact they quickly relented and freed him from any financial obligation for either house.[53]

Two years later Lallio informed the council of the MIA that only one-third of the students were making satisfactory progress. The council immediately assigned its president, Marco Beretta, to investigate, and to expel or admonish students as necessary. When Beretta submitted his report (now lost) a few days later, the MIA drew up a new list of poor, eager chierici who would be more diligent in their studies. The council further instructed Lallio to report to them at once the names of any students who misbehaved and again assigned Bernardino Colombi to assist Lallio.[54] Pleased with Lallio's performance, in 1510 the MIA voted to renew his contract for three more years, and the following year the number of students in his school climbed to forty-one.[55] In the summer of 1514, however, Lallio became seriously ill and asked for a leave of absence in order to take a cure at the local mineral baths. Six months later he was still unwell, and the MIA accepted his resignation.[56]

Antonio Lallio's successor, the Reverend Fedrigino da Talluno (Val Calepio), served for thirteen years as *rector scolarium* (rector of students) of the MIA's school.[57] Praised repeatedly as the ideal schoolmaster for his young charges, Fedrigino taught forty boys every year in grammar and good behaviour, and brought much-needed stability to the MIA's young school. Like his predecessors, Fedrigino was permitted seven private students and ten boarders, who paid additional fees. When Fedrigino decided to move into a different house in 1518, the MIA agreed to pay the rent of twelve gold ducats to the owner, the jurist Ludovico Rota. Fedrigino held classes in this new, larger house, located in the neighbourhood of Antescolis, just behind the church of Santa Maria Maggiore.[58] The *terminazione* (register) of 4 January 1523 reappointed Fedrigino as preceptor for only thirty-three students 'because Quintilian's *Sentences* advises that a good teacher should not have to endure a larger crowd of students than he is capable of handling.'[59] The reference to the Roman pedagogue is telling here, especially as this reference coincides with Ravizza's presence in the public school. In order to forestall laziness and promote a good memory, the contract stipulated, daily recitations and frequent examinations were required. Fedrigino did not instruct the boys by himself: he was assisted in 1525 by the priest Giovanni Zanchi, who was excused from weekday religious services so that he could tutor half a dozen boys in Latin grammar. In 1526 the MIA sent six boys to a Father Martino in the neighbourhood of Borgo Canale for supplemental instruction after they had been to the lessons of Fedrigino.[60]

The performance of Fedrigino and the other *maestri* was regularly reviewed by three deputies assigned by the MIA to supervise the school. Elected every year between February and April, the deputies almost always included the president (*patrono*) of the MIA, a sign of the importance that the confraternity attached to its educational program. The deputies *ad scholam* (for schooling) had a number of responsibilities: to recruit and hire teachers, to visit the school monthly, to admit and expel students, and to update the school rules. The MIA's council of ministers had long included a number of standing subcommittees to supervise the confraternity's extensive landholdings and various charitable responsibilities, but no specific record of deputies for schooling appears prior to 1506. This suggests that the Apibus scholarships and other kinds of assistance provided to students and teachers were viewed as acts of general charity rather than specific support for education. The deputies responsible for schooling in the sixteenth century appear under a number of different titles in the MIA's records: *ad regimen scolarium, ad scholam et ecclesiam, ad gimnasium, ad praeceptorem et scolares, ad curam scolarium litterature et musice.* After the opening of the Academy of Clerics in 1566, they are often listed as *deputati ad accademiam*, and during the brief existence of the MIA's residential college in Padua (1531–42), there are references to the *deputati tam Padue quam Bergomi*. While it is possible that these different titles reflect only the vagaries of the notary recording them, it seems more likely that they reflect the changing educational emphases of the MIA over time. The deputies, who often served several consecutive terms, included members of Bergamo's most important families. The support of an influential deputy could be critical to the success or failure of a particular project (e.g., as we shall see, the repeated intervention of Francesco Bellafino to assist the Paduan College). In the 1550s and 1560s the number of deputies was increased to four, and later to five, reflecting the increasingly complicated and time-consuming responsibilities of this position.

In the spring of 1529 the MIA's deputies elected Nicolò Capitani of Val Scalve as *rector scolarium* (school rector). For a salary of 250 lire, plus two *brenta* (barrels) of wine and use of the house belonging to Ludovico Rota, he agreed to examine and teach the chierici and disciples assigned to him by the MIA, and to make sure that they became competent priests. All other conditions of his contract were similar to those of his predecessor, Fedrigino da Taliuno.[61] During the fall of 1529, however, the school was interrupted by military activity and a wave of plague, causing Capitani to withdraw to the town of Lovere near Lake Iseo. On 12 January 1530 Capitani wrote to the MIA to enquire about the status of the school and to proclaim that he was ready to resume his teaching duties. One month later he appeared before the council in person to ask for his salary. The MIA took a dim view of his absence, calling it an extended vacation and citing the maxim of Saint Paul that 'those who don't work, shouldn't eat.' In the end, however, the MIA agreed to give him ten gold ducats to settle all debts past and present. At the end of 1530, perhaps mollified by his teaching during the previous months, the MIA gave him two hundred lire but noted that he was not to receive any more payments even if he celebrated additional masses.[62] It seems unlikely that Nicolò de Capitani's tenure lasted much beyond 1530–1.

From 1531 to 1542 the MIA was preoccupied with the foundation and management of its residential college in Padua, the Collegio Patavino (described later in this chapter). Although the deputies possessed responsibility for both the Paduan college and the Bergamasque school, the lack of references to schooling in Bergamo during this period reflects the MIA's focus on the Collegio Patavino. In the spring of 1541, following a series of scandals at the Paduan college, the MIA issued a decree instructing the rector of the MIA's school, Giovanni Minoli, to include in his lessons at least one sacred book or treatise that praised and glorified the Holy Trinity. The selected readings, to be at a level appropriate for the students of the confraternity, were held to be especially important for the chierici, who read the divine offices every day. As the confraternity explained, experience had shown that everyone, from children to adults, needed (religious) instruction.[63] The MIA's concern with religious instruction may also have been a reaction to external events such as the Regensburg Colloquy of 1541 and the increasing success of Protestantism across Europe.

The MIA's concern over virtue and godliness was emphasized again in 1542 when it hired Bono de Lulmo (also Bono da Olmo) to teach seven students in grammar for thirty lire per year. Bono de Lulmo was chosen in part because of his exemplary moral behaviour, which the MIA held to be fundamental for anyone entrusted with the training of future priests. For the previous six years, de Lulmo had been employed by the bishop of Bergamo to teach grammar and offices of the Church to a dozen young scholars inside the episcopal palace.[64] Even for a part-time appointment, the Misericordia Maggiore was clearly preoccupied with the moral tone of its educational activities. As noted above, this preoccupation with morality may have been inspired by previous scandals at the Paduan College, or perhaps by preparations for the Council of Trent, not far to the north of Bergamo. In addition, a former student of the MIA's, Guglielmo Gratarolo, was investigated by the Inquisition at this time, and even Bergamo's bishop, Vittore Soranzo, would soon be under suspicion of heresy. The MIA, therefore, probably saw its school as a bulwark of orthodoxy and probity, and thus required its teachers to be exemplars of Christian morality.

Nevertheless, the choice of de Lulmo was a curious one given de Lulmo's history outside the episcopal palace. When Bishop Pietro Lippomano visited de Lulmo's parish of Sant'Antonio dell'Olmo in September of 1536, he found the parish *male tractatur* (poorly managed) because de Lulmo was not often in residence. Perhaps de Lulmo was simply following the example of his father, Antonio, who was mayor of the community and head of the local chapter of the Misericordia, against whom complaints were also lodged because of 'unequal' distribution of alms. Bono de Lulmo's probity might have been further questioned by the MIA had they been aware that in 1541 he owned a copy of Cardinal Iohannes Gropper's 1538 *Enchiridion*, or that the bookseller Pasino Canelli of Brescia indicated in 1539 to the Inquisition that he had sold a copy of a suspect work recorded only as *Consolationis Bibliae* to a certain 'presbiter Bonus.'[65]

In addition to the principal masters mentioned thus far, from time to time the MIA hired additional personnel to tutor students in writing, mathematics, Latin grammar, catechism, and theology. These supplementary teachers either provided instruction in subjects that the regular teachers could not or did not wish to teach, or else they handled extra students. The supplementary teachers were always identified as assistants, whereas the head teacher of the school received a formal contract and the title of *rector scolarium*. During this period the school added music to the curriculum so that the chierici would be able to sing counterpoint and harmony.[66] Three brief examples of assistant teachers must suffice.

Paolo Tiraboschi was hired on 29 November 1546 for three years, to say Mass, live in residence, and 'teach two boys assigned to him by the deputies of this confraternity in writing and mathematics [*abachum*].' His salary subsequently rose to 125 lire per year, and he always taught writing and mathematics, but never to more than half a dozen students. In an unusual case, on 30 December 1546, the MIA assigned the treasurer of the Ospedale Maggiore, Giovanni Pietro f. Baptista of Rovato, to Tiraboschi for a few months to receive instruction in reading and arithmetic. Tiraboschi was reconfirmed repeatedly from 1548 to 1555, but on 3 December 1556, a major quarrel broke out in the church of Santa Maria Maggiore, 'bringing shame and opprobrium to all concerned.' Paolo Tiraboschi, along with three chierici and a Jewish student, was held responsible and immediately fired.[67]

Reverend Alessandro Beroa, variously described as a *pedagogo*, a *hypodidascalas*, and a *ripetitore*, was initially appointed without a salary, but in 1556, shortly after Tiraboschi had been fired, the MIA voted to give Beroa forty-five lire per year. On 20 December 1557 three MIA deputies noted substantial improvement in his performance and praised his character, rewarding him with a raise of ten lire per year. Despite this praise, however, in 1560 Beroa informed the MIA that he had been offered a better job as chaplain and *praeceptor scolarium* by the confraternity of Sant'Alessandro in Colonna, whereupon the MIA granted him permission to leave. Beroa then taught for the confraternity of Sant'Alessandro in Colonna from at least 1560 to 1567.[68]

Lastly, senior students might also serve as *ripetitori*. For assisting Bono de Lulmo, Baptista de Mutio and Antonio de Licinis were exempted from their regular clerical responsibilities but received the standard stipend, plus a salary of twenty lire per year. Baptista de Mutio subsequently quit his job in August 1552. Antonio de Licinis, however, was promoted to the position of chaplain in May 1554, where he said Mass and served as an assistant to the head teacher for a salary of 110 lire per year plus two *brenta* of wine.[69] One year later (1555), de Licinis composed some verses in honour of Bergamo's first printer, Michele Gallo de' Galli, which appeared in the beginning of Francesco Bellafino's *Libro dell'origine et tempi de la nobile et antica città di Bergamo*.[70] These examples demonstrate that it was possible for students and teachers inside the MIA's school to move up the hierarchy if they were meritorious and attentive.

The minutes of the MIA council in the mid-sixteenth century reflect another intriguing shift of emphasis, as the confraternity began providing more money to boys who wished to learn a craft or take up an apprenticeship. Unfortunately, the precise trades are never mentioned in the minutes, but they probably included cobblers, tailors, carpenters, and the like. For example, beginning in 1538 and continuing until 1542, Joseph Sabatini was paid four sacks of grain and one *brenta* of wine per year in exchange for teaching his craft to selected students of the MIA. Pietro de Bordonia of Stezzano and Alberto Venitiano of Bergamo were awarded similar sums for teaching their (unspecified) profession to certain students. When ten-year-old Giovanni Antonio Portebello of Val Imagna wished to learn a trade, the MIA awarded him four sacks of flour to be given to his unnamed master.[71] In 1545 Francesco della Porta, resident in Milan, was authorized to receive twenty lire over two years so that he might continue to learn a craft.[72] Although the status of the boys was not listed, surely they must have been lay students rather than chierici. The MIA's apparent interest in underwriting vocational education again underscores its willingness to think creatively about promoting instruction for boys of the town.

By the mid-1540s the Misericordia Maggiore had once again refocused attention on its day school for chierici. The *terminazione* of 25 October 1547 provides an excellent example of a typical contract between the MIA and one of its teachers. Since all subsequent contracts for the MIA's school were virtually identical to this one, it merits a detailed summary. In addition, we have already met the instructor in question (Bono de Lulmo). The previous teacher, Giovanni Minoli, had elected to retire in mid-February 1547 because he was not permitted to have additional boarders in his house. The deputies used this occasion to draw up a formal list of expectations for the new teacher.[73] He had to be a priest of a reasonable age and praiseworthy character, an expert in literature who had led an exemplary life. He was required to teach forty adolescent boys assigned to him by the MIA in grammar, letters, and good habits, examining them every day to ensure that their mistakes were gently corrected. On Sundays and holidays he should teach the offices of the Roman Catholic Church and have all the students read a lesson from the Holy Scripture. Furthermore, he was expected to celebrate mass every day, and to participate in all of the Easter ceremonies. Although he was permitted to have a limited number of student boarders in his house, they had to be chosen from among the students supported by the confraternity. No outside students were allowed to attend his lectures, 'even if they stood behind the curtain.' The teacher had to report all student absences to the confraternity, just as he was expected to inform the MIA if he himself were ill for more than a day or two. Lastly, the teacher was expected to provide make-up lessons in the afternoon for those clerics who had to serve in the church in the morning.

The MIA decided to promote Bono de Lulmo to this job of *rector scolarium*, offering him an elevated salary of 350 lire per year, financed in part by the bequest of Giovanni Antonio de Biffi. Various *ripetitori* were hired to assist him with classroom teaching and supervision of the students. In the spring of 1552, however, Bono de Lulmo was fired from his position as rector after a squabble in the sacristy one Sunday with his colleague Paolo Tiraboschi (ironically, the same Paolo Tiraboschi fired four years later for an identical cause). The assistant teachers were asked to assume de Lulmo's responsibilities and to finish out the academic year.[74] During the summer of 1552, the MIA voted to recall

Giovanni Minoli, and offered him two hundred lire per year to return as rector of the school. He agreed to the same terms as had Bono de Lulmo, and taught without incident until the spring of 1555, when he retired on account of illness.[75]

Here we begin to see the MIA's tendency to re-employ teaching staff with whom it was already familiar. Of course such a tendency may reflect the reality that there were few other options in Bergamo and that the MIA had to make do with those teachers who were available. Yet the documents seem to suggest that the MIA also held a strong sense of loyalty to its staff, as well as to students and members. The MIA often disciplined a teacher or student by cutting off funds, for example, and then later reinstated that person.[76] Perhaps the MIA, which was fundamentally a group of laymen dedicated to helping others in need, saw forgiveness as a virtue to be not only preached but also practised.

Minoli's replacement, Julio Ascanio, came from the small town of Tucci, located between Turin and Genoa. When the number of students rose to sixty-three, his salary was accordingly raised to five hundred lire per year plus the boarding fees from his students. The house assigned to 'Magister Julius' suffered from a lack of heat, and the MIA repeatedly provided him with coal and wood so that classes could be held in the winters of 1556 and 1557. In February of 1557, Ascanio asked to leave Bergamo in order to move to the town of Crema, and the MIA responded that it never kept anybody against his will (*ideo si vult ire quod vadat in pace*).[77]

The last teacher hired for the MIA's school was the Reverend Michele Manili (Manilio, Monilio, Millio) of Val Camonica. In May of 1557 he agreed to teach sixty-three students for a salary of 450 lire per year and a house where he could lodge ten of his students. Giovanni Baptista Rota and his father, Ludovico, agreed once again to rent their house in the neighbourhood of Antescholis to the MIA's head teacher for fifteen scudi per year, as soon as the jurist Paolo Zambillo moved out. During the winter of 1558 Manili received permission to supplement his income with five or six outside boarders, provided that they were all citizens of Bergamo, of appropriate age, well behaved, eager to learn, and approved by the MIA ahead of time. Manili was also allowed to provide private instruction to these boys, but under no circumstances could he substitute them or increase their number. Manili was assisted by several senior chierici, including Francesco Rota and Benalio Benaglio, whose salaries were paid for by funds from the Apibus bequest.[78]

Michele Manili's tenure as rector of the MIA's school was interrupted by two Inquisitorial investigations. At some point in late 1558 or early 1559 four of his students lodged accusations of heresy, sodomy, and other evil actions with the Holy Office in Rome. Those accusations were repeated by another man, Ludovico Maccanello of the nearby village of Albano. After Manili had been incarcerated in the Inquisitor's prison in the episcopal palace, the students – Lorenzo [Lauro] Rota, Cristoforo Assonica (nicknamed Betarolo), Simone Terzi, and Hieronimo Federico – confessed to the MIA's council that the accusations were false. Condemned by the MIA on 14 March for participating in a 'diabolical conspiracy' against their master and for bearing false witness with wicked, criminal, and evil intentions, the students were immediately expelled and ordered to pay back their stipends. A fifth student, Camillo de Licinis, was also sacked for lying about this incident to the MIA. Cristoforo Assonica apparently tried to flee the city in the spring, after which he and the other students were transferred from the episcopal prison to that of the podestà, before being released on their own recognizance in mid-August. Their case dragged on for months with a series of depositions, investigations, and counter-accusations. As historian Andrea del Col has noted, the case is particularly interesting for what it reveals about the shifting boundaries of jurisdiction between the Inquisition, the bishop and his vicar, the city council, and the Venetian podestà and captain, all of whom were involved in this case. Nine months later (16 December) the students' calumny was confirmed by the archdeacon Marc Antonio Avinatri and they were sentenced to an unspecified 'severe' punishment which was then mitigated on 23 December. Ludovico Maccanello received a harsher punishment; the Inquisition opened a separate case against him in March 1559, confiscated his goods, and imprisoned him throughout the spring and summer. On 5 December the podestà of Bergamo, Lorenzo Bragadin, ordered that Maccanello be tortured. In the meantime, Manili had been quickly absolved of the charges, and continued to teach and receive praise from the confraternity for his superior instruction. In 1560 he was excused from attending morning services because he was teaching Holy Scripture to the chierici. However, in 1562 he was again investigated by Holy Office, presumably for heresy, and once again absolved. In a vote of confidence in their rector, the MIA in 1563 extended his contract for another six years. By this date the number of students had risen to seventy-three, and Manili's salary was increased yet again to 650 lire. Failing health forced him to restrict his activities during the harvest season of 1563, however, and in January 1564 he retired. He taught briefly in the new diocesan seminary in 1569 and died in January 1572.[79]

An inventory of Manili's personal property after his death not only reveals that he possessed an extraordinary number of books (about four hundred in all), but that the Inquisition (and his students) were justly concerned with his orthodoxy. In addition to the standard works of grammar, history, literature, linguistics, and theology that we might expect to find on his shelves, there appear about thirty prohibited or expurgated books. Even more surprising is that about a dozen of these works had previously appeared on the Roman and Venetian Index of Prohibited Books. About half of these suspect books had been published in Basel, with more coming from Lyon and Paris. They included two editions of the work of Lucan, edited by Erasmus; the Protestant theologian Johan Spangenberg's *Tabule in Evangelia*; Battista Folengo's *Commentary on the Psalms*; and even anti-clerical plates depicting the *danse macabre* designed by Hans Holbein and published in Venice in 1545.[80] It is difficult to understand how the pair of Inquisitorial investigations did not turn up these books, nor is it easy to explain how Manili might have justified the existence of these books to his superiors or to the MIA.

Three days after Manili's resignation, the MIA once again turned to Bono de Lulmo, citing his extensive knowledge and many worthy qualities. His contract was identical to the one offered to Manili six months earlier, and he remained the head teacher of the MIA's school until the foundation of the Academy of Clerics early in 1566. Since this new Academy would require all of the students to live under the direct supervision of the master(s), the MIA began to write to other cities in search of additional teachers.[81] Although both institutions were directed by the MIA and both were designed to train chierici for service in the church of Santa Maria Maggiore, the new Academy was quite different from its predecessor. Before examining the Academy of Clerics, however, it is necessary to consider the history of an educational initiative unlike anything the MIA had attempted before.

The Paduan College, 1531–circa 1542

During the sixteenth century, more than a hundred young men from Bergamo took degrees in law or medicine from the prestigious University of Padua.[82] Drawn from Bergamo's leading families, many of these students went on to illustrious careers as jurists, doctors, politicians, professors, or diplomats. Bergamo had a long history of sending students to Padua: their ranks included such subsequently illustrious men as the medieval jurist Alberico da Rosciate, the Protestant physician Guglielmo Gratarolo, and the Enlightenment pedagogue and scientist

Lorenzo Mascheroni.[83] Despite a number of works on foreign 'nations' at the University of Padua, no study exists to document the identity, experiences, and achievements of Bergamo's academic elite at university during the era of the late Renaissance and the Catholic Reformation. One important chapter of this story concerns the brief history of a residential college for Bergamasque students in Padua that opened in 1531.[84]

Founded by the Misericordia Maggiore to house five Bergamasque students in residence at the university, this Collegio Patavino continued a long tradition of confraternal support for education. Such a college, the MIA believed, would not only reduce the cost of obtaining a degree but would allow the confraternity to keep a closer eye on the students whom it was paying to educate. This concept of a residential college was common in sixteenth-century Padua: testamentary bequests and confraternal support funded colleges for students from other *terraferma* cities as well as from other regions of Italy and Europe.[85] The MIA's college was among the smallest and most ephemeral of Padua's residential student colleges. Despite its obscurity, it signified a critical initiative for the MIA as the confraternity sought to support education in ever more diverse ways. As we have seen earlier, primary and secondary education in Bergamo was usually directed by local authorities. Higher education, on the other hand, remained a jealously guarded monopoly of the Venetian state. When Bergamo submitted to Venice in 1428, the doge immediately declared that all Venetian subjects were required to take their degrees at Padua. While some Bergamasques went to study at Bologna, Perugia, or Pavia, it appears that most Venetian subjects did in fact attend the university at Padua. It was precisely during the period when the MIA founded the Collegio Patavino that the University of Padua's reputation began to improve, so that by the end of the sixteenth century it was more famous and well respected than its sister institution in Bologna.[86]

On 14 September 1531 the MIA's council of ministers read out and unanimously approved the founding charter of the Collegio Patavino.[87] Prepared by council deputies Pietro Passi, Ezekiel Solza, and Francesco Bellafino, this charter spelled out the objectives and rules for the new institution. Designed 'for care of both body and soul,' the college promised 'mutual peace, love, and harmony to the city and to the students.' The confraternity announced that it would elect five deserving students of good character and honest families to receive an annual stipend of one hundred lire for a maximum of seven years. It is notable that this sum was five times larger than the Apibus scholarship and lasted two years longer. The students, who had to be at least seventeen years old, could specialize in either civil and canon law, philosophy, or medicine. They were to be paid twice a year, in mid-October and at Easter. The MIA insisted that students must receive a diploma by the end of the seventh year and then return to Bergamo to have the degree officially recognized and inscribed in the records of the confraternity. If a student wished to repeat his seventh year, he was required to do so at his own expense, and his parents or relatives must make a public declaration of their willingness to support him financially. The MIA reserved the right to investigate secretly the behaviour and academic progress of its students at Padua and to dismiss them from the college if the results were unsatisfactory. A family could enrol only one student at a time in the college, and the MIA was constrained to elect the son with the greatest chance of success. The confraternity made a point of emphasizing that the election of students 'must be free of favouritism or hatred, based solely upon a student's honesty, poverty, character, and merit.'

At first glance it appears that the MIA simply transferred the funds of the Apibus legacy to pay for this Paduan college. After all, the objective was similar, and many recipients of the Apibus scholarship were attending university at Padua anyway. However, not one of the Apibus recipients was ever elected concurrently to the Collegio Patavino. Furthermore, one of the clauses in the founding charter stipulated that a student could not hold simultaneously an Apibus scholarship and a place in the college. This rule is confirmed by the case of Gian Anselmo Maffei, a student of law in the late 1520s; when he was elected to the first class of the residential college, his Apibus scholarship was accordingly withdrawn.[88] These examples suggest that the MIA saw the Paduan college as a new project, independent of the Apibus bequest.

The MIA paid close attention to the fortunes of the Collegio Patavino during its brief existence. The confraternity appointed three deputies annually to monitor the college and to conduct visitations as necessary. These deputies intervened in disciplinary affairs, assisted students in renting a house, and recorded the names of those who had obtained a degree. New students were regularly elected whenever a vacancy occurred, owing either to graduation from the university or expulsion from the college. The MIA instituted the position of 'prior' or 'prefect,' an advanced student charged with supervising other students and reporting misbehaviour. Correspondence between the confraternity and the students in Padua reveals the MIA's close interest in students' academic progress and its concern that they conduct themselves in a disciplined and appropriate manner. For example, the prior was instructed to report the name of any student who left the college without permission during the school term; a copy of this requirement was mailed to the students to ensure that they were aware of the rule.[89]

Student housing in Padua, then as now, was a critical issue for both the university and the city. Statutes about the matter date back to the early thirteenth century, when the commune of Padua offered subsidized housing to students and attempted to regulate an otherwise chaotic market. In 1551 the university published eleven ordinances governing student residences.[90] These rules were designed to protect students from unfair evictions, exorbitant rents, and lack of maintenance by unscrupulous landlords, but they also anticipated the problems of noise, violence, and trash often associated with student neighbourhoods. It was precisely to avoid these difficulties that the MIA decided to institute a residential college in Padua for deserving Bergamasque students. Although the college was always located in the centre of Padua, in response to student requests the MIA leased a series of different houses.

The first house, nicknamed *casa dei merli*,[91] was rented by the student Gian Anselmo Maffei in October 1531 with the assistance of a Paduan notary, Guglielmo di Ferrara. This house, occupied earlier in the decade by other Bergamasque students, was recommended both by the MIA and by the current students. Although Maffei's letter to the MIA deputy Francesco Bellafino did not specify the location of the house, he boasted that he had obtained it for a rent of just under twenty-eight scudi per year, the lowest possible price.[92] The rent was to be paid twice per year, half at Easter and half on the festival of Santa Giustina (7 October). Maffei signed a contract in the name of the MIA with an agent of the Venetian nobleman who owned the property, Giovanni Antonio Malipietro. Three years later (1534) the college moved into a 'more distinguished and comfortable house' owned by Francesco Bellafino's family, located in the quarter of Pozzo della Vacca in the neighbourhood of Sant'Antonio.[93] They remained there until the summer of 1538, when the students declared that they wished to move to another house. Bellafino wrote to the MIA that even though he had been offered more money by other tenants, he would never have rented the house to anyone else; now that the students wanted to live elsewhere, he remained ready to assist the students in any way that he could.[94]

In the fall of 1538, one of the students wrote to the MIA to say that he had rented a house in the quarter of Sant'Agata from Paolo Conti for twenty-eight scudi.[95] Located on Via Colombina, the house was very near the university. Bellafino made good on his promise to assist the students by providing a deposit of fourteen scudi to secure the rental. In the summer of 1541 the college moved yet again, back into Bellafino's house at a price of thirty-five scudi per year.[96] The MIA continued to rent this house until 1550, even though by that point, as we shall soon discover, the college (and Bellafino) had ceased to exist.[97]

The frequent relocation of the MIA's college is important for at least three reasons. First, it suggests that during the initial decade of the Collegio Patavino, the confraternity was not entirely committed to the concept of a distant residential college. Once the first cohort of students had successfully graduated from university, the MIA seemed more willing to sign a longer-term (i.e., nine-year) contract to ensure greater stability. Indeed, the later contract specified that the house was intended 'to house the present and future scholars of the MIA's college.' Second, the MIA's loyalty to its own members is once again evident in the favouritism shown to Francesco Bellafino. Last, the negotiations and contracts about housing imply a strong sense of cooperation between the confraternity and the students. Deputies were occasionally sent to visit or to bring funds, but the MIA appears to have placed a substantial amount of trust in the ability of the students to govern themselves and to conclude housing arrangements on behalf of the consortium.

Who were the students, and how were they elected? Although the MIA's college theoretically existed to aid poor students, in fact many of the residents were members of Bergamo's more important families. A parallel example of elitism can be found in Brescia's Collegio Lambertino, founded in 1509 for poor boys from Brescia who wished to study medicine at Padua. The Collegio Lambertino was first administered by deputies of the commune and after 1601 by the College of Physicians. The doctors emphasized nobility as the first prerequisite for admission and even stated that it was better to admit no noble boys at all than one poor or rural scholar![98]

In Bergamo, the criteria for a student's election, outlined in the founding charter, do not appear to have ever been altered. The first group of students was elected on 14 October 1531, exactly one month after the founding charter had been approved. Appearing before the council two days later, each student promised to observe all the rules of the college and to reimburse the MIA if he failed to do so. It is interesting to note that only one of the four boys had a living father: Viscardo Terzio promised to be the 'guarantor and principal debtor' of his son Gian

Andrea, while the other boys presumably provided guarantees from their extended families. A fifth student, Girolamo Adelasio, declared that he was too ill to accept a position at the college, and Maffeo Guarneri was immediately elected in his place.[99] These five scholars left for Padua to take up residence in the *casa dei merli* and began their studies in mid-November 1531.

The issues of curriculum, lodging, and student life at the University of Padua have already been examined in considerable depth by other scholars; thus we know a great deal about student activities, both licit and illicit, in the medieval and Renaissance eras.[100] From a variety of documents – notarial acts, correspondence, council minutes, testaments – we see that these Bergamasque students were like most students who go away to university. Although some studied diligently, a significant number failed to attend classes, took unannounced vacations, held parties without permission, and got involved in fights. They also spent money provided by their parents (and the MIA) on non-academic activities, or lamented the exorbitant fees, like Julio Agosti in 1540: 'those scholars spend 18 ducats to graduate in arts and medicine at Padua, and I have to spend 44 gold scudi to graduate only in civil law, and 64 scudi to graduate in both [civil and canon law]; while they spend 25 or 30 scudi on books, I spend no less than 60.'[101] The secondary literature on university life at Padua, as well as the relevant statutes, confirms that Bergamo's students were not unusual in this misbehaviour. It would be inaccurate to claim that they were all as unruly as Antonio Giordani, a Bergamasque student who terrorized his Paduan neighbourhood two centuries later and was cited for 'horrendous curses,' blasphemy, and routinely threatening anyone who spoke to him.[102] Nonetheless, the documents tell us that five Bergamasque students in particular were far from model scholars.

Their misbehaviour is of more than casual interest; by examining their missteps and the response of the MIA, we can better gauge the philosophy and attitude of the confraternity toward education. Prescriptive documents like the founding charter are useful, but – as historians of crime know very well – deviance and rule-breaking often reveal more about social mores and underlying values. To judge from the five cases presented here, the MIA was quite forgiving of student behaviour, even when it caused physical harm to others or risked a charge of heresy. These cases also suggest that the MIA was willing to bend the rules, its own as well as those imposed by the Venetian state, in order to help students obtain a *laurea* (university degree).

The first problem arose with Maffeo Guarneri, selected as an alternate for the initial group of Paduan scholars. Between 1531 and 1535, the MIA gave him three hundred lire for living expenses, plus free housing in the college. In the spring of 1534, however, the MIA demanded that he return the money because 'this Maffeus is not devoted to his studies as he is required to be.'[103] Two years later, after Guarneri had obtained a benefice from Luigi Vianova, a canon of the church of Santa Maria Maggiore, the MIA again demanded that he renounce his scholarship and repay his debts. Ten years after that, on 15 April 1547, Jacopo Guarneri drew up a will that disinherited his son Maffeo on account of the extravagant expenses that he had incurred in the previous two decades. Jacopo Guarneri's will provides a detailed accounting of the 3,620 lire that he had squandered on his son's sumptuous and dissolute lifestyle. Prior to Maffeo's departure for Padua, Jacopo Guarneri claimed, he had spent 250 lire to send his son to various mountain valleys with a tutor and plenty of spending money. Then he spent one hundred lire to hire a grammar teacher named Maestro Fedrigino [Taluino] to teach Maffeo in Bergamo, but his son sold all of his books and clothes in order to escape to Brescia. Despite the place that Maffeo had won in the MIA's college at Padua, Maffeo's father twice found him a furnished room there at a cost of two hundred lire. He paid additional sums to have Maffeo transported in style from Bergamo to Padua, and another thousand lire on books. The list of expenses continues for several pages: illicit expenses and sumptuous banquets (*spesa illicite et banchetti sumptuose*), living expenses for Matteo and a friend of his, food and medicine during a fever, horses and a velvet cloak for a trip to Marseilles, legal fees, and 'other expenses which for the sake of decency cannot be named here.'[104] Even the benefice had cost Maffeo's father 530 lire, and with interest and unspecified 'damages' the total came to 1000 lire. It need hardly be added that Maffeo Guarneri's name does not appear among the list of graduates from the University of Padua.

In response to Maffeo Guarneri's misadventures, the MIA appointed three deputies to review the rules of the college and to suggest appropriate changes. In June 1540 the MIA declared that henceforth any student expelled from the college for poor behaviour would have to repay immediately all expenses incurred at Padua. Furthermore, warned the MIA, the student's family shared responsibility for such a debt.[105] As we will see shortly, the MIA did not always enforce its own rule, but perhaps it wished to serve notice to candidates and their families not to expect a free ride.

In the same meeting of 4 June 1540, Ludovico dei Conti di Callepio was elected to the college. Two years later the MIA suspended his stipend for a minimum of two months because he had invited certain foreign students to sleep inside the college. Even worse, these students had organized a party where dancing occurred, and all this during the first week of Lent. The MIA lamented that the college had suffered a 'very serious scandal' as a result of these escapades. One month later, in an act of charity, the MIA revoked Callepio's suspension on account of the penitence he had demonstrated for his errors. In 1545, after the MIA had abolished its college, the MIA awarded seven ducats to Callepio so that he might pay rent to Francesco Bellafino. Still identified as a scholar of the confraternity's Collegio Patavino, he was encouraged to continue his studies as he had been elected to do.[106] This suggests that the MIA continued to look after the Bergamasque students in Padua even if it no longer managed a house for them.

Alessandro Roncalli, elected in 1539, was expelled in 1542 for unspecified violations of the rules of the Collegio Patavino (perhaps he too participated in the dance party). He appealed to the MIA to be readmitted, confessing that he had made mistakes and promising to reimburse the MIA for all of his expenses in the event of another expulsion. The MIA accepted his appeal; Roncalli's two brothers and father appeared before the council to provide surety. Yet just a few months later, Roncalli was involved in another unspecified scandal in Padua. This time the confraternity suspended his stipend and warned him that he was not permitted to re-enter the college while the MIA was deliberating his fate under pain of forfeiting all his benefits. When he nevertheless dared to move back in, the MIA did not hesitate to expel him (in the only unanimous vote that I have seen). A few months later, Gian Giacomo Roncalli successfully petitioned the MIA to excuse him from the debt incurred by his brother. Indeed, the MIA even went so far as to grant Gian Giacomo fifty lire 'for the love of God and so that his studies might be completed.'[107] Since in 1544 both Alessandro Roncalli and Gian Giacomo Roncalli were identified as law students, they apparently continued their studies despite the lack of housing provided by the MIA. Once again, this anecdote suggests that the MIA continued to support its students even as it enforced punishment and discipline upon them.

Yet another case of student misbehaviour concerns Lattanzio Marchese, who was elected to replace Julio Agosti in 1541. Given the companions with whom he was living, perhaps it is not surprising that he should quickly find himself in trouble. In any case, in September 1542 Marchese's stipend, like Alessandro Roncalli's, was suspended owing to a scandal perpetrated the previous summer. Excused by the MIA for that infraction, perhaps because his father Fantini lectured in moral philosophy at Padua, the following year he was involved in a brawl with foreign students at Padua. After one of the other students was wounded, Marchese was banished from Padua by the city authorities and threatened with a fine of three hundred lire. Therefore he asked the MIA to grant him special permission to finish his degree at the University of Bologna or another university. Surprisingly sympathetic to his plight, the MIA voted 7–5 to give him twenty-five gold scudi so that he might finish his studies. Marchese thanked the confraternity profusely, and the following year a payment was made to his brother Clemente, as Lattanzio Marchese was presumably away at school.[108] As noted earlier, it was unusual – indeed, illegal – for a subject of the Venetian Republic to study elsewhere than Padua. The MIA's records do not indicate why an exception was made in this case, but presumably the confraternity recognized that it was impossible for Lattanzio Marchese to continue studying in Padua.

The most intriguing case may be that of Guglielmo Gratarolo (1516–68), the famous medical doctor who converted to Protestantism, corresponded with Calvin, wrote influential religious and medical treatises, and fled to Basel in the 1550s.[109] Twenty years earlier, as a student at the MIA's Collegio Patavino, he was involved in a scandal concerning 'particular behaviour, speeches, and letters' (*certi suoi modi, verbis, et opibus* [*sic*]). The MIA immediately investigated, and Gratarolo's fellow students wrote a letter asking that he be pardoned and allowed to remain at the university.[110] Perhaps intentionally, neither the students' letter nor the MIA's minutes specify Gratarolo's misbehaviour. However, Orazio Bravi, who has studied Protestantism in Bergamo in considerable depth, is convinced that Gratarolo must have been experimenting with new religious ideas.[111] Padua was a recognized haven for those with Protestant sympathies, and their books circulated freely in Venetian territory. Gratarolo could easily have come into contact with German Protestants at Padua in the mid-1530s. Gratarolo received his doctorate from Venice in 1537, and within two years he was a member of the College of Physicians in Bergamo. In 1544 he was required by the Milanese inquisitor to abjure 'certain articles concerning which he was held suspect.' In 1548, the bishop of Bergamo, Vittore Soranzo, warned him to be more careful about his public statements. In 1550 the Venetian Inquisition accused him of numerous heresies, including those concerning purgatory, indulgences, papal authority, and veneration of the saints. Later that year he took refuge in the northern valley of Valtellina, pursued by claims that he was a *peste contra la fede* (plague upon the faith). In 1551 Bishop Soranzo and the Inquisitor in Bergamo declared him to be an obstinate and relapsed heretic, while later that year the Venetian authorities promised immediate decapitation if he were captured within the Republic. Not surprisingly, Gratarolo moved to Basil in 1552 where he later joined the College of Physicians; he continued to practice medicine, to travel widely, to publish astronomical and medical treatises, and to disseminate Calvin's ideas until his death in 1562.[112]

It seems unlikely that these five students represent a typical cohort of the young men selected for Bergamo's Collegio Patavino. Nearly a dozen other students, none of whom engaged in the kind of misbehaviour cited above, were members of the college between 1531 and 1541 and eventual graduates of the university. Gian Anselmo Maffei, for example, not only received an additional award of twenty-five gold scudi to study law as a reward for his diligent efforts but was praised as a model student and graduated on time.[113] Pietro Zanchi too was lauded for his virtue, his honour, and his 'wise and studious' ways while taking a degree in medicine.[114] Hieronymo Lulmi (also known as Girolamo di Olmo) graduated with a medical degree in October 1539 and pursued a successful medical career in Bergamo.[115] Julio Agosti corresponded regularly with the MIA about events in the college, and penned an oration in Latin giving thanks to the MIA for its financial support.[116] After earning a degree in law, he was elected to the College of Jurists and appointed to teach civil law in Bergamo in 1542.

Nevertheless, the MIA eventually decided that the negative aspects of the Collegio Patavino outweighed its positive benefits. In a decree of 17 April 1542, the confraternity declared that it intended to close the Paduan college in order to reallocate the money to a more profitable end. In a rather aggrieved tone, the MIA explained its reasoning:

> Whereas on 14 September 1531 a college for five poor scholars from Bergamo was founded and erected in the city of Padua by the magnificent ministers of this confraternity of the Misericordia for the purpose of studying the liberal arts, as explained in greater detail in the rules and regulations announced on that day. Whereas they created this pious and holy institution hoping that students would acquire the greatest virtue and glory

for themselves, their fatherland, their family, and their friends, from their daytime study and their nighttime reading. Whereas Pietro Andrea Zonca, the distinguished president of the aforementioned confraternity, considering the way that this pious organization has been cheated [of its hope], and that not all of the students have taken advantage of the benefits offered to them, as it was hoped, but have done very little; nor did they behave as they should have, nor are they behaving as they ought to, in an exemplary manner, [but] many of them have caused diverse complaints to reach the ears of the magnificent ministers of the confraternity, bringing scandal and displeasure to all of them, in contrast to the godly motives for which this institution was created. Considering the modest accomplishments of these students, and the scarcity of funds available to this confraternity owing to the many debts by which it is already oppressed and which can be paid off only with difficulty, [therefore] they judge that it would be better if the money allocated to this fruitless enterprise of the scholars were to be distributed in other works more beneficial to God and to the world.[117]

Henceforth, announced the MIA, no new scholars would be elected to the college in Padua, although those already in residence would be allowed to remain until they had finished their degree. The motion passed by a vote of 10–2.

As noted above, the MIA continued to rent a house in Padua from Francesco Bellafino for the benefit of Bergamasque students, but very few references to the initiative in Padua are to be found after 1542. Instead the MIA turned its focus back to Bergamo, and its day school there. Five years later (August 1547), while appointing a new teacher, the MIA emphasized that one of its principal objectives had always been to train boys and adolescents in letters and proper behaviour. Having learned from previous experience, it declared, it wished to educate clerics first and laymen second. Therefore the MIA wanted to hire a new schoolteacher, 'preferably a priest, who will diligently teach the boys to be erudite and respectful in all things.'[118] It seems probable that the confraternity's repeated mishaps with rebellious college boys played a significant role in this decision. Of course, 1547 was the year that Vittore Soranzo was appointed bishop of Bergamo, so the MIA may also have been eager to demonstrate its moral virtue and its commitment to educating chierici.

The MIA's commitment to education did not stop with the closure of the Collegio Patavino. To the contrary, this failure apparently taught the MIA how to manage its subsequent colleges in Bergamo more successfully. The Collegio Patavino stands as one example among many of the charitable actions of Bergamo's largest confraternity in its efforts to help improve the quality of education both inside and outside the city. The college is also important because it demonstrates Bergamo's effort to identify with the Venetian Republic. Despite its poverty and its location on the far western edge of the dominion, Bergamo sought to educate its youth in the same manner as the larger, wealthier cities of the *terraferma*. Although the MIA's ambitious effort to maintain the Collegio Patavino collapsed after only a few years, the mere fact that the confraternity wished to create such an institution reveals something of the ambitious sixteenth-century mindset in Bergamo. Lastly, the Paduan college demonstrates the considerable financial and administrative resources of the MIA in this period. No other confraternity in Bergamo possessed the means to orchestrate such an endeavour.

The MIA's Academy of Clerics, 1566–1610

The next important step in the development of education in Bergamo occurred with the foundation of an Academy of Clerics (Accademia dei Chierici) by the Misericordia Maggiore in the spring of 1566. In many ways this academy resembled the school founded by the MIA in 1506: both were designed for the education of chierici; both taught Latin grammar and catechism; both gave preference to boys who served in the church of Santa Maria Maggiore; and both were funded by the MIA. However, the new academy reflected a half-century of further experience and a heightened commitment to religious orthodoxy. The rigorous and austere vision of the Catholic faith following the Council of Trent led the Church to seek stricter control over lay confraternities, schools, texts, and teachers in the second half of the sixteenth century. The MIA's Academy of Clerics embodies this more rigid vision of a school. For example, the new academy was a boarding school, with much stricter rules and increased supervision. Dice-playing and other unseemly games were prohibited in the loggia of the MIA's church, Santa Maria Maggiore, and in the school itself. The character of the master teacher was now as important as his pedagogical skills: he must be *veramente cattolico* (very orthodox) with impeccable morality. In addition to required attendance at confession and Mass, students in the academy were prohibited from wandering around the town and from idle conversation with city residents. The MIA immediately expanded its palace on Via Arena, specifically to provide 'decent and honest'

housing for the preceptors and students of the academy.[119] The rebuilding was completed before the end of the first academic year, testifying
to the MIA's commitment to support its educational mission. A closer
look at the founding and subsequent operation of the Academy of Clerics, as well as the difficulties it faced, will illuminate the twin themes of
Catholic orthodoxy and confraternal support for education.

The Academy of Clerics was first proposed by the MIA's council on 9
January 1566. On 30 April the MIA declared its formal intention to create an academy for twenty-five young boys. Similar to the founding act
of the 1506 school, this declaration lays out the principal reasons for the
new school and the ways in which the MIA intended to achieve these
goals:

> The evil circumstances of recent times have created such a dearth of
> priests that only with difficulty can a sufficient number be found to carry
> out the bequests and obligations of this church; higher salaries and ad-
> ditional payments were offered to bring in priests from outside, many of
> whom have fled with the money provided for their sustenance, while oth-
> ers, mischievous and scandalous, had to be expelled on account of their
> behaviour. Additional funds were allocated to train clerics to serve in this
> church, but many of them left to travel about, while others, ungrateful, left
> without any recognition of the many benefits received from this vener-
> able consortium ... Considering once again the grandeur of this city and
> of the Republic, and that their preservation are [guaranteed by] literate,
> virtuous, and Catholic men, it has been decided to hire a reverend teacher
> of good learning, excellent character, and firm faith, with a respectable
> and appropriate salary to be paid completely by the consortium; he will
> teach good learning, perfect manners, [and] humane and sacred letters to
> twenty-five clerics, who will be under the governance and discipline of
> this reverend teacher both night and day, in the devoted and pious Acad-
> emy of the Misericordia Maggiore of Bergamo.[120]

The MIA then formulated more than two dozen articles (*capitoli*) to
govern the organization of the school, the responsibilities of teachers
and students, and miscellaneous aspects of school life.[121] In order to
be admitted, students had to be at least twelve years old, demonstrate
a desire to be a priest, and already know how to read. Preference was
given to chierici already serving in the church of Santa Maria Maggiore,
particularly those who were 'obedient, well-dressed, virtuous, intelligent, [and] catholic.' The MIA demanded an eight-year commitment

from each student, as well as a financial guarantee from the parent or guardian to assist as needed. In the event that the student was expelled, a penalty of fifteen scudi would be assessed for each year that the student had lived in the academy. Clearly, the MIA was tired of losing its students (and future priests) after investing a good deal of money in them. The confraternity declared itself responsible for providing housing, food, haircuts, and daily instruction in grammar, singing, and catechism. The confraternity further agreed to provide a light blue cloak, dark blue stockings, a hat, and twenty-four soldi for a pair of new shoes every five years. Each student was expected to provide the basic necessities for himself: four napkins, a pewter platter, two bowls, two plates, one glass, a knife, a bed with sheets, a pillow, and two blankets.[122]

The students lived a regimented lifestyle under the close supervision of their teachers. The day always began and ended with bedside prayer and a solemn trip to the chapel in Santa Maria Maggiore. Detailed instructions specified the order and number of prayers to be said on each occasion, even explaining how low a boy must kneel when visited by his teachers, the ministers of the MIA, or the bishop of Bergamo! Students were permitted to exit the academy only in the company of a teacher and were expected to march two by two according to age. Licentious books were forbidden, all meals were eaten in common, and recreation inside the academy was carefully regulated. Friendships with boys outside the academy were discouraged in an effort to reduce distractions and to promote cohesiveness among the chierici. With the exception of temporary visits by mothers and sisters, the presence of women was of course prohibited. The 1590 redaction of the students' *capitoli* contains a list of punishments for various infractions (for example, tardiness, swearing, skipping mass or meals, punching another student, failure to complete homework).[123] As we will see shortly, despite (or perhaps because of) these rigid guidelines, the MIA's academy suffered from recurrent disciplinary problems.

The MIA set the maximum number of students living within the academy at twenty-five. In addition, another twenty-five chierici were allowed to attend the grammar school and to serve in the church on special holidays. If a vacancy occurred, then this 'shadow academy' could provide an immediate replacement.[124] A few years later, in an attempt to increase the pool of eligible candidates – and perhaps spark competition among the students – the MIA created a third and a fourth group of students who received correspondingly fewer privileges. Each cohort wore a different colour cloak: light blue, black, dark blue, and red. Since chierici were regularly expelled for being 'depraved,' disrespectful, or incorrigible, it was not unlikely that a promising student might move up the academic ladder in a short period of time. Three members of the MIA's council were selected as deputies to manage the school; they were expected to visit the school once a week and to report to the council once a month. Clearly, the MIA intended to stay on top of this new project and to forestall any misbehaviour or misappropriation of funds.

In addition to a rigid daily schedule and precise instructions regarding the chierici's religious training, the Misericordia Maggiore spelled out the academic curriculum.[125] Every weekday morning, the head teacher read excerpts from Cicero's *Epistulae ad familiares* (Letters to his friends), first demonstrating the intention(s) of the author and then explaining the syntax and construction of each passage. Each student recited one or more passages aloud according to his ability. The master was further expected to explicate the appropriate grammar rules, to read a catechism lesson, and to teach a few lines from a poet of his own choosing. In the afternoon students translated a letter from Italian into Latin, which was then corrected individually by the master. Eloquence in Latin was a primary goal of the MIA's academy; boys who did not speak Latin in class were required to eat their next meal standing up.[126] To further encourage an effective speaking style, the MIA recommended an evening lesson of rhetoric.

Each day's lesson continued with more grammar and translation, followed by a review of the poem introduced the day before. In keeping with the guidelines of the 1523 treatise by Giovita Ravizza, Saturday morning was reserved for review and repetition of the week's lessons, often in the form of a general debate. Similar to the Caspi Academy, which we will examine in chapter 5, on Sunday afternoons one of the senior boys recited a passage from Cicero, followed by comments and questions from other students. Archbishop Carlo Borromeo's visitation in 1575 noted that in addition to reading Cicero, the students studied Horace, Virgil, and Aristotle's *Prior Analytics*.[127] Students were expected to write down the important passages in their notebooks and to review them, along with the translations, later in the week. Separate notebooks were required for Cicero, poetry, catechism, dictation, and the morning lectures. The youngest class had a more limited curriculum designed to teach them how to read, to decline nouns, and to write simple Latin phrases. Dictation in Latin and Italian, memorization of grammatical rules, and study of the most important glosses on classical texts rounded out the academic curriculum.[128]

Perhaps the most interesting pedagogical aspect of the MIA's academy, however, was its emphasis on peer teaching. The *capitoli* repeatedly refer to examples of older students tutoring younger ones in grammar and singing. Article nineteen of the 1566 *capitoli*, for example, stipulated: 'And in order that the head teacher is not overburdened with more obligations than he ought to be, and can best devote himself to school and to the aforementioned chierici of the academy, it is decreed that four or six chierici from the academy be elected, and that a portion of the twenty-five other chierici [outside the academy] be assigned to each of them according to the judgment of the head teacher, and they will teach them according to the instructions of the reverend head teacher.'[129] Occasionally, advanced students might be selected to do some teaching outside the academy too. In 1590, for example, Count Ludovico Secco Suardo wrote to the MIA to request the services of Pietro Rota as a tutor to three of his younger children living at home. Rota, who had completed four years of study in the academy, was permitted to leave with a promise to return and complete his obligations to the MIA at a later date.[130] In 1594 Hieronimo Pisenti was offered a teaching position in Cremona, and a year later Alessandro Terzi asked to go to Pavia to study law and theology.[131] The chierici thus sat on both sides of the desk, combining their academic and religious studies with practical teaching experience. The MIA did not intend to run a teacher-training school, but it did recognize the benefit of catering to local elites and to additional training for its own students.

In keeping with the nature of the academy, the head teacher was always a priest. The Reverend Pietro Bonacursio of Cremona appears to have been the first to hold this position. His contract, virtually identical to those signed by head teachers in the MIA's previous school, obligated him to teach fifty-two students in letters, grammar, and proper behaviour for a period of two years beginning in 1567. In order to assist Bonacursio, the confraternity hired two young chaplains from Pavia, Teodoro Calvi and Don Innocenzo. These young men each received a salary of two hundred lire per year and an eight-year contract in return for saying mass, being in residence, and teaching literature, grammar, or singing to ten younger students.[132] The academy experienced considerable turnover amongst the staff and students during the first decade of its existence, as was to be expected, but seems eventually to have settled into a steady routine of teaching and learning. No serious problems are recorded until 1574–5, when the combination of multiple expulsions, a new master teacher, and a visit by Carlo Borromeo shook up the academy.

On 15 February 1574 the MIA angrily denounced several of its students as disobedient and poor learners and voted to expel them immediately. Considerable soul-searching followed, as the confraternity considered whether to continue investing its resources in the academy.[133] By November of that same year, the consortium decided to hire a new master in conjunction with the city council of Bergamo. As explained in chapter 1, the city and the confraternity agreed to employ Nicolò Cologno for a period of five years to offer three general lectures per day and to supervise other teachers. Lessons for both clerical and lay students were held in the MIA's spacious school on Via Arena. The curriculum included prose, poetry, logic, rhetoric, and ethics, to be presented 'in a manner that was easily understandable by all who attended.' This more sophisticated list of academic subjects speaks to the caliber of Nicolò Cologno and his ability to teach such subjects.

As noted earlier, Cologno's job title of *maestro principale* was more akin to that of a master teacher than a mere classroom instructor; he visited public school teachers all over the city and supervised a large staff. Within the academy, the Reverend Antonio Lauretto Placchino taught grammar, supervised the servants of the academy, and ensured *totis viribus* (with all his might) that the clerics were appropriately dressed and behaved at all times.[134] Cologno was also assisted by Michelangelo Bello, hired in January 1576 as a *ripetitore* for 340 lire per year. Bello was instructed to review diligently the lessons of Cologno, to substitute for him in the event of illness, to read a lesson from the catechism in the evening, 'and above all to guide [his students] with pious examples and a Catholic conscience.'[135] A third member of the staff, identified only as Father Lorenzo, held the important position of *maestro di costume* (master of deportment). He was to walk the boys to and from choir, classes, and meals, administer punishment as necessary, read a page or two from the Bible in the evening, and sleep just outside the dormitory so that he could check on the students in the middle of the night. Lower-level assistant teachers known as *sottomaestri* or *coadjutori*, such as Battista Suardi or Giovanni Antonio Raimondi, earned a few dozen lire each year from conducting simple repetitions and drills.[136]

In the fall of 1575 Archbishop Carlo Borromeo arrived to conduct an apostolic visitation. In the space of three months, Borromeo and his staff visited almost every church, convent, and school in the diocese of Bergamo. The visitation records include not only Borromeo's own notes and decrees but a wide assortment of letters, statutes, reports, budgets, drawings, and membership lists collected by the archbishop and his staff.[137] On 24 September, only a few days after his arrival in the city, Borromeo visited the MIA's academy on Via Arena. The archbishop found the students of the academy divided into three levels, each supervised by an assistant teacher. His evaluation of the students was harsh:

First class
Francesco Foresto, 19 years old, studied seven years in the academy: not greatly accomplished in grammar, nor in the art of rhetoric and eloquence; mediocre intelligence; but he explains the catechism well enough.

Innocenzo Torri of Bergamo, 19 years old, sponsored for two years by this *luogo pio*: in grammar he knows little; he cannot easily recite that which he has learned from his teacher; hasty pronunciation, and he gives little hope of himself.

Paolo Corini of Bergamo, 24 years old, a deacon, educated four years in the academy: well-enough instructed in grammar; in other subjects he has progressed little; he explains the Roman catechism well; he does not offer great hope.

Bartolomeo Zanchi of the diocese of Bergamo, 19 years old, a student of the academy for six years; he has not made great progress in his letters because he is interested in many different activities; he has a quick mind.

Giacomo Suardi of the diocese of Bergamo, 18 years old, a student in the academy for three years; he has a good mind even if he has made little progress in his letters.

Pietro Locatelli of Bergamo, 23 years old, a deacon, in his fourth year as a student in the academy; he has not accomplished much in his studies, but he is eager to learn and industrious.

Giovan Battista Pizzoni of Bergamo, 19 years old, supported by the academy for three years; he has a good memory, and sometimes learns well.

Second class
In the second class there are 16 boys who study Virgil and Horace, but they are not yet adequately trained in grammar, and they have no texts to study.

Third class
In the third class there are 5 boys who know nothing at all of grammar.[138]

The archbishop's report highlighted the low level of academic achievement within the MIA's academy. Despite Borromeo's deserved reputation for doctrinal severity and discipline, his comments here suggest at least an equal interest in the quality of each student's mind. An apostolic visitation, by its very nature, was intended more to uncover shortcomings and deficiencies than to bestow praise. Furthermore, although this would have been little consolation to the governing fathers of the MIA, Borromeo criticized the seminary students in equally stern language. Borromeo ordered several changes to be made, including a stronger effort at teaching grammar to the youngest boys. Notably, he did not recommend closure of the academy.

Nevertheless, Borromeo's visitation foreshadowed darker days ahead for the academy. Shortly after his visit, the council again considered closing the academy. In the end they decided to persevere for three reasons: (1) Reverend Nicolò Cologno's loyalty, erudition, and excellent instruction; (2) the substantial investment already made in the academy; and (3) Carlo Borromeo's support and patronage.[139] The confraternity emphasized that the election of new chierici must be based strictly on merit and not on love, fear, or nepotism – thus perhaps offering a clue about why their previous performance had been so mediocre. But the situation did not improve. In 1576 Nicolò Cologno issued a decree to his staff and students concerning how the school was to be run.[140] Cologno's instructions not only revealed his decades of experience as a teacher but also echoed the guidelines of Giovita Ravizza a half-century earlier. Cologno's academic program, consistent with the one already described, went into even more detail about which days of the week were reserved for dictation, letter-writing, translation, and review of grammar rules.

Yet in 1577 the MIA complained bitterly that 'after great effort, exertion, and expense on the part of this consortium,' the students in the academy 'with a series of cunning and deceitful tricks have avoided the discipline of the teachers and have repeatedly skipped classes.' In response, the MIA reorganized and expanded the academy, both to increase competition among students and to ensure a sufficient number of students to serve in the cathedral. But only three years later the MIA denounced the 'disorder and difficulties that occur every day as a result of the poor behaviour of the academy students ... since many of these ungrateful wretches have profited from their study of grammar or music which should have benefited both the Academy and the Church.'[141] A letter from the music teacher Giovanni Florio in 1588 confirms the persistent lapses in student discipline: Florio found one of his students lounging on a dormitory bed instead of attending his class, but upon scolding the student he was 'seriously threatened by the student's brother with vile and slanderous words.'[142] Valeriano Guarguanti suggested that the school's difficulties were not caused by students alone. Guarguanti had been a student at the academy in 1585, but his teacher, Paolo Cordaro, had tormented him to such a degree that his mother sent him to Venice and then to Rome with the Bergamasque nobleman Giovanni Girolamo Grumelli until the teacher was replaced. Guarguanti cited instances of verbal abuse, argument, and insult on the part of Cordaro.[143] In 1590 the MIA's deputies once again issued a new set of *capitoli* stipulating the responsibilities of everyone from the head teacher to the cook to the chierici, but such action did little to ameliorate the situation.[144]

Faced with the prospect of increasing unrest, the MIA reacted by hiring back a familiar and trusted face, just as it had done when faced with a similar crisis in its day school a half century before. In the summer of 1590, Nicolò Cologno was asked to return for six months, for the academy 'had gone from bad to worse' in his absence. Cologno agreed, but would come only on his own terms: 'After much discussion, I responded [that] I would be happy to do this job again, but that I would not set foot there unless I were given absolute authority to run the school.'[145] Ensconced in the school by 1 November 1590, he exercised great effort in rousing the boys, teaching them grammar and rhetoric, and supervising the assistant teachers. However, his unlimited authority apparently rankled some members of the MIA's council, whereupon Cologno angrily declared his intention to step down as head of the school. By the beginning of the next academic year Cologno had been appointed as reader of moral philosophy at the University of Padua, where he ended his career, though not without more controversy.[146]

The MIA's academy survived for another two decades, beset by continuing problems. Giovanni Florio, whom we saw physically threatened by a student and his brother in 1588, complained that the number of students in his care continued to rise each semester, and even came to include 'public' students beyond those within the MIA's school.[147] He further complained that he and his music students were 'seriously inconvenienced' (*gravemente disturbati*) by the students studying letters next door, and vice versa. In 1590 the MIA investigated the alleged beating of the academy's cook by two chierici, Francesco Muzio and Cristoforo Romanello.[148] In 1592–3 Father Hiacinto Benza described new 'impediments' that imperiled the academy's mission and drove the students to live dishonestly and in mediocrity.[149] In 1595 the academy was rocked by the theft of twenty lire from the servants' quarters; the MIA was forced to investigate and interrogate each of the students in turn.[150] In contrast to the successful example of colleges and seminaries organized elsewhere by the Jesuits, the Somaschans, and Archbishop Borromeo, the MIA's academy continued to founder until it was finally closed in 1610.

Why did the MIA's Academy of Clerics finally shut its doors? Given the litany of troubles described above, it would be easy to blame student misbehaviour and teacher discontent. The MIA's records from 1610 are surprisingly terse in their description of the reasons behind the academy's closure. The documents allude to concerns that the MIA's money was not being well spent, but say little about specific issues. Later documents suggest that the MIA wished to emphasize musical instruction more heavily; for example, in hiring Giovanni Cavaccio in 1615, it insisted that he teach two full hours of singing to students.[151] Perhaps the MIA felt that it would be easier to simply close the school and start afresh.

Nearly two centuries later, the MIA issued a report explaining its view of the academy's failure. The confraternity did not mention student misbehaviour, as it had in earlier denunciations. Instead it offered three reasons. First, the Tridentine Seminary was providing too much competition and drawing the MIA's potential students away. Second, the financial burden on the MIA was too great. Third, the number of priests had increased substantially, hence the academy was not as urgently needed as a half-century earlier. [152] There is no reason to doubt the substance of the explanation offered by the MIA, even if it does appear to whitewash some of the difficulties that the school had encountered.

Our analysis of the MIA's Academy of Clerics would be incomplete without due consideration of its neighbour and presumed competitor, the diocesan seminary. Both institutions existed to train priests. The existence of two institutions with such similar goals, and in such close physical proximity, begs the question of why the MIA felt its school was necessary. In hindsight, as noted just above, the confraternity believed it could not compete with the seminary. Yet it soldiered on for nearly fifty years before closing its doors. In addition to the reasons offered by the MIA itself in 1566, two additional factors may explain the founding of this school. First, the MIA's school was opened one year prior to the seminary and thus there was no direct conflict with the seminary at the outset. Second, the academy was in many ways a continuation of the MIA's own day school, thus representing an extension rather than a true innovation. The academy's existence also illustrates the religious fervour of the later sixteenth century and the concomitant demand for more rigorous preparation of churchmen.

Then again, the MIA surely would have been aware of the bishop's intention to found a diocesan seminary. Even if the MIA did not see its academy as a rival to the seminary, it seems likely that the bishop or other residents of the city would have. Yet there is no evidence of which I am aware that portrays the seminary and the MIA's academy to be in competition. Even Carlo Borromeo, who visited the seminary and the MIA's academy within a few days of each other, did not comment upon a battle between them or even upon an overlap in their responsibilities. In his position as apostolic visitor, it was precisely his job to look out for weaknesses in the diocese or challenges to ecclesiastical authority. The *absence* of his condemnation is perhaps as strong as any other evidence that we have. Of course, it is possible that there were sufficient students, teaching staff, and resources to support two similar institutions, at least for a couple of decades. We must also remember that Bergamo in the mid-sixteenth century witnessed several joint ventures between different institutions in order to promote education, including that between bishop and commune, between commune and MIA, and between commune and Somaschans. In this era of apparent détente, perhaps the seminary and the Academy of Clerics agreed to ignore each other unless some serious conflict arose.

Another possible explanation for such cross-institutional cooperation might be found in the person of Nicolò Cologno. An instructor for the commune, the MIA, and the seminary at various points in his career, he may have provided the personal touch and means of communication necessary to avoid direct conflict. A third explanation might be found in Bergamo's divided allegiance between Venice and Milan. We know that the MIA was closely intertwined with Bergamo's civic government and had been so since the thirteenth century.[153] The MIA's responsibility for the upkeep of Santa Maria Maggiore, and its deep commitment to assist the disadvantaged residents of the city, would have reinforced this partnership with town government. The MIA's interest in training priests was chiefly to staff the basilica of Santa Maria Maggiore and other nearby churches. Thus its loyalty would have been to the town and its Venetian governors. Those governors were chiefly responsible for lay institutions and secular practices in Bergamo, including trade, taxes, bandits, and so forth.

By contrast, the seminary (as we shall see in chapter 3) always had to keep an eye on the powerful archdiocese of Milan to the south. Even though Venice steadfastly protected its right to nominate bishops within the borders of the Republic, and occasionally rejected the Vatican's candidates if they were not Venetian noblemen, the bishop of Bergamo found himself in an unusual position because part of his diocese was subject to the archbishop of Milan. It is certainly telling that Bishop Girolamo Ragazzoni wrote repeatedly to the archbishop of Milan when seeking advice about his seminary, rather than to a Venetian colleague. Thus Bergamo's bishop had to satisfy two masters. Perhaps the existence of a confraternal academy and a diocesan seminary was a compromise solution that allowed Bergamo and its bishop to satisfy both Venice and Milan. An additional explanation may lie in the goodwill and long tradition of the Misericordia Maggiore. During the early years of the seminary, Bishops Cornaro and Ragazzoni may have hesitated to take on a powerful and well-loved institution like the MIA, instead hoping that the MIA's Academy of Clerics might eventually crumble of its own accord.

In conclusion, it is difficult to say with certainty why Bergamo had two institutions for training priests in the second half of the sixteenth century. Prior to the destruction of the original cathedral of Sant'Alessandro in the 1560s as part of a Venetian building program to reinforce Bergamo's exterior walls, the city had enjoyed two cathedrals (S. Vincenzo and Sant'Alessandro).[154] This history, as much as the other reasons offered here, may explain why the bishop's diocesan seminary and the MIA's Academy of Clerics coexisted without apparent rancour for half a century.

Although the Academy of Clerics reflected the austere morality and rigid orthodoxy of the Catholic Reformation, the curriculum appears to have remained oriented toward the traditional works of Graeco-Roman philosophers, poets, and historians. This confirms Paul Grendler's conclusion that in Venice lay and religious boys studied virtually identical curricula.[155] Doubtless the chierici devoted substantial hours to learning their religious offices, but it would be inaccurate to conclude that they studied only catechism and religious texts. The MIA's Academy of Clerics reflected the overly optimistic view, shared by fifteenth-century humanists and sixteenth-century reformers alike, that the appropriate classical texts and a virtuous environment were certain to produce a class of wise and morally upright young men prepared to render service to Church and State. The reality of the MIA's chierici, and of several boys within the MIA's Collegio Patavino, as we have seen, turned out to be quite different, and the MIA ultimately had to admit that the Academy of Clerics was not succeeding. Yet the MIA's example did not discourage other institutions from throwing their hat(s) in the educational ring. Indeed, the commune, the seminary, and the smaller confraternities in Bergamo were inspired by the MIA and sought to replicate its success while avoiding its failure.

Other Confraternities in Bergamo, 1555–1615

Although the Misericordia Maggiore always remained the largest and most powerful confraternity in Bergamo, it was not the only one to promote education. Beginning in the mid-sixteenth century, several neighbourhood confraternities provided money, clothing, and teachers to instruct children of the parish. These 'neighbourhood' schools never rivalled the MIA's academy or the diocesan seminary. Insofar as they mixed religious instruction with elementary schooling and hired confraternal members as teachers, these confraternal schools resemble the Schools of Christian Doctrine (discussed in the next chapter). As with so many other aspects of the early modern period, it is difficult to draw a line between the sacred and the secular. Lay students and chierici might come from similar backgrounds, read similar texts, and learn from teachers trained in similar ways. Yet the neighbourhood confraternal schools offered classes at a more advanced level than the Schools of Christian Doctrine, and on a daily basis rather than once a week. Thus the schools sponsored by other confraternities appear to stand midway between the complex, hierarchical academies promoted by the MIA and the Church, and the local, less formal, catechetical lessons provided by the Schools of Christian Doctrine. A complete history of these parish-based institutions is beyond the scope of this book; instead, I shall sketch the broad outlines of the schooling provided by other confraternities and draw parallels with and distinctions from the Misericordia Maggiore. The local confraternities discussed here include Sant'Alessandro in Colonna, San Lorenzo, Santo Spirito/San Giovanni, and Sant'Alessandro della Croce.

The parish confraternities typically sponsored instruction for both chierici and lay boys. Elected in identical fashion, they sometimes shared the same master and classroom. When there were separate facilities, the confraternities held similar expectations for both (e.g., regular progress reports from the teachers, and monthly visitations of

classrooms by confraternal deputies). The number of chierici selected
ranged from three to twelve, each of whom was expected to serve in
his own parish church. Chierici from these 'neighbourhood' schools
were occasionally admitted to the MIA's Academy of Clerics to pursue further studies. In comparison with lay boys, the chierici typically
received more advanced training and their education required more
years of study. Toward the end of the sixteenth century, the education
of clerics was slowly separated from its lay counterpart. The diocesanal
seminary is perhaps the clearest example of this division between secular and religious education, but the MIA's Academy of Clerics and the
confraternal schools of Sant'Alessandro in Colonna, Sant'Alessandro
della Croce, and Santo Spirito confirm this tendency. The number of lay
students educated by a confraternity was usually between forty and
sixty, but the duration of their education was often abbreviated. It appears that the confraternities wished to equip lay boys with a minimum
degree of literacy in Latin or Italian, but no more.

The earliest and most well-documented example of a 'neighbourhood' school comes from the parish of Sant'Alessandro in Colonna, located just below the upper city on the west side of town.[156] Although the
confraternity of Sant'Alessandro in Colonna had traditionally provided
sustenance for the 'corporeal needs' of the poor in its parish, after 1556
it wished to provide intellectual and moral instruction for those boys
whose parents could not afford to maintain their children in school.
In a meeting on 29 May 1556 the consortium declared that it wished
to hire two teachers to instruct chierici in grammar and singing. The
confraternity authorized a maximum of fifty lire per year, with the expectation that the boys chosen would assist in the parish church. A year
later, on 11 April 1557, the confraternity voted to appoint either one or
two teachers to instruct thirty of the 'most poor and most able' boys of
the neighbourhood how to read, write, and be proficient in grammar.
The confraternity initially hired Nicolò Cologno to teach both groups,
but he quickly withdrew on account of his appointment to teach in the
city's public school. On 4 June 1557 the priest Sebastiano Pagani was
elected as chaplain and schoolmaster with an annual salary of 120 lire
and the stipulation – probably inspired by Cologno's hasty resignation
– that he was not to teach students anywhere else.[157] Pagani in turn
was succeeded by the Reverend Alessandro Beroa, who had previously
tutored students for the MIA and who remained with Sant'Alessandro
in Colonna until at least 1567.

The confraternity's sudden interest in sponsoring education can be traced to two events. First, the mid-1550s witnessed a revival of interest in schooling at the local level. In those years, the commune and the bishop jointly hired Nicolò Cologno, the Schools of Christian Doctrine arrived, and the MIA was busy hiring new teachers for its own school. More important to the confraternity of Sant'Alessandro in Colonna was the resolution of a festering dispute with another confraternity, the Scola di Corpo di Cristo, regarding the legacy of Amighino da Mariano, who had died more than three decades earlier. After repeated arguments in Venice and Rome, the governor of Bergamo intervened in 1553 and a final agreement was executed in 1557 giving control of the legacy to Sant'Alessandro. Apparently the Scola di Corpo di Christo had previously supported the education of three chierici, and Angelo Filogenio, rector of the church of Sant'Alessandro in Colonna, had also supported the education of three chierici; these different bequests were combined with the six supported by the consortium to make up the twelve students cited so frequently by the confraternity.[158]

The minutes of the confraternity's monthly meetings (*Libro delli Parti*) contain frequent references to the activities of students and teachers sponsored by the confraternity and its council of ministers. The detailed anecdotes reinforce the impression of a small-scale, local initiative seeking to benefit its parishioners while simultaneously responding to larger exterior influences such as the Council of Trent. On 19 May 1559, for example, the names of ten new lay students and four new chierici were listed, each identified by first name, surname, and family parish (the vast majority from Sant'Alessandro in Colonna). In March 1560 three new lay students were elected *ad ludum letterarium* (for the study of letters), while in January 1561 the council noted that because Paolo Stabello had refused to attend the lessons of Master Antonio Villa, his brother was permitted to attend in his place. New teachers were regularly appointed to replace or supplement those elected earlier, just as deputies were elected annually to visit the school, which expanded to reach sixty-seven students by February 1585. The confraternity even took measures to ascertain that its money was being well spent, announcing just after Christmas in 1565 that henceforth all teachers employed by the consortium must bring their students to a special meeting once a month to demonstrate what they had learned. Lay students who had reached the required level of competency in reading, writing, and mathematics were to be excused so that others might take their place; students who demonstrated a lack of ability and little promise were to be dismissed immediately.[159]

In 1568 Angelo Filogenio was charged with organizing a separate grammar school for twelve chierici, who were to be subdivided into different levels depending upon their ability.[160] (Filogenio was also involved with the creation of Bergamo's School of Christian Doctrine at this time, as we shall see in the next chapter.) Six years later, in an effort to clarify its expectations, the confraternity issued a list of requirements (*capitoli*) for its grammar master.[161] The primary function of this school was clearly specified: 'every time that the Most Reverend and Illustrious Bishop holds an ordination ceremony, the oldest chierici must be presented and ordained as needed.' Filogenio was commanded to teach Greek and Latin 'with great loyalty and devotion' for a period of three years to twelve students chosen by the confraternity. He was allowed to hire an assistant teacher (*ripetitore*) but could not dismiss his students without the express permission of the consortium. In return he received a handsome salary of forty gold scudi per year, the use of a house near the parish church, and some grain and wine at harvest time. Furthermore, the master was allowed to enrol an additional dozen students (presumably lay boys) and three boarders at a fee to be determined between him and the individual parents. As with schoolmasters hired by the commune and by the MIA, the admission of fee-paying students was clearly a way for the master to supplement his income. In a candid display of parochialism, however, the consortium required the master to admit boys from the neighbourhood before considering boys from other parts of the city. It also required the master to live inside the parish, and to teach the nephew of a local priest, Ludovico Cerane, at no additional cost. Thus far the school of Sant'Alessandro in Colonna resembles the schooling offered by the Misericordia Maggiore prior to 1566. The financial arrangements, the consortium's expectations of the teacher, and the intended audience, though by no means identical, were roughly similar.

The *Libro delli Parti* contain nearly two hundred references to the teaching of both lay boys and chierici through the end of the sixteenth century and into the beginning of the seventeenth century, only a sampling of which are discussed here. Many of these entries refer to the routine business of school life: the expulsion of lazy students, the selection of replacements, the debate over the amount of a new teacher's salary. There are occasional surprises, too: for example, the podestà in 1586 asked to send his son to the lectures of Maestro Giovanni Perlizolo on Aristotle's *Ethics*; and between 1575 and 1578 at least four students petitioned the confraternity to be excused from other lessons or services to attend the lessons of Nicolò Cologno.[162] Reading, writing, and mathematics were the focus for lay students, while chierici received additional instruction in Latin, singing, and the liturgy.[163] In addition to a professional grammar master, the confraternity also hired its own members to tutor students at a nominal fee. Unfortunately, the minutes reveal practically nothing about the specific texts or pedagogy adopted in this parish school, nor do they provide much detail about the identity or background of the students. It is clear, however, that the confraternity selected (and dismissed) the students while allowing the teacher to choose methodologies at his discretion.

The educational activities of this confraternity can also be examined through a different type of document, the *Regola* (Rule) of the consortium. Published in Bergamo by Comin Ventura in 1589, the *Regola* contains a brief history of the confraternity and a description of its principal goals as well as a more lengthy description of its individual responsibilities and officers. Page eight contains a summary of the consortium's actions regarding schools: '[The consortium] has at all times taught forty poor children to read and write. And furthermore twelve clerics are diligently trained in grammar, in music, and in ecclesiastical ceremonies in preparation for service in other churches ... and their teachers are members of this confraternity, to whom each child ... gives four lire per year ... To the aforementioned clerics a black cloth coat is to be given every third year.'[164] The *Regola* noted that this instruction served two complementary purposes: the poor children (who otherwise would not have had the means) learned to read and write, and the instructors earned a bit more money to support themselves. Lay students and chierici were to be elected simultaneously by the confraternity. The chierici were paid an additional fifteen lire per year for their service in the Church; the confraternity noted further that they could do their service in turn so as to permit more of them to study in the school. The chierici were expected to master a humanist curriculum, as seen in the *Regola's* instructions to all teachers: 'When it comes to [instruction in] letters, suggest to them that they imitate Cicero, the master of the art of writing and speaking; and make them (as much as possible) not only devour all of Cicero but also digest him and absorb him (if that is possible) into their own blood.'[165] This tradition of 'devouring' a text goes back to Ezekiel the prophet in the Hebrew tradition, and to Seneca's letter to Lucilius in the Latin tradition; the latter described the reading process as akin to a bee's consumption of marjoram and thyme to produce honey. This topos was picked up by Quintilian, then by Augustine, and later by humanists such as Petrarch, Erasmus, and Montaigne. The confraternity was probably influenced by Petrarch's comment that 'I ate in the morning what I would digest in the evening; I swallowed as a boy what I would ruminate upon as a man. These writings I have so thoroughly absorbed and fixed, not only in my memory, but in my very marrow, these have become such a part of myself, that even though I should never read them again they would cling in my spirit, deep-rooted in its inmost recesses.'[166]

The confraternity of Sant'Alessandro in Colonna assigned several of its members to serve as deputies and to conduct monthly visitations of the schools in order to determine 'whether the teachers are fulfilling their responsibility, and with the correct number of students,' and 'whether the students are lazy and might be occupying places better filled by more eager students.' The deputies were to report immediately any student who was disobedient, distracting, or obstinate, for which behaviour the ministers of the confraternity promised immediate expulsion from the school. Curiously, the confraternity emphasized that schooling for chierici was of much greater importance than schooling for poor boys, even though the *Regola* admitted there were only three chierici in contrast to forty lay boys.[167] The apostolic visitation of Carlo Borromeo in 1575 confirmed the interest of this confraternity in supporting clerical education, noting that the 1571 budget of twelve thousand lire was spent on alms for the poor, celebrations of the mass, upkeep of the church, and 'gifts on behalf of instructing clerics in grammar.'[168]

In 1611 the confraternity of Sant'Alessandro in Colonna declared that the number of teachers must always correspond to the number of students in a ratio of 1:16. Therefore the number of salaried teachers jumped to eight, with a corresponding decline in salary to only eighty lire per year. Salaries (and occasional honoraria) steadily increased, however, so that by 1630 the treasurer of the consortium noted that he had paid out sixteen hundred lire for educational expenses during the preceding year.[169] Sant'Alessandro in Colonna continued to follow the *Regola* and to support local instruction until the Napoleonic invasion and the subsequent suppression of the confraternity.

Sant'Alessandro in Colonna thus stands as our best example of a neighbourhood school within the parish. Its aims were admittedly modest but it seems to have avoided the frequent closures that plagued civic-sponsored schooling. It also represents both the broader desire of townspeople in the mid-sixteenth century to expand education, and the increasing preference to privilege religious over lay education.

The *disciplini* (members) of San Lorenzo, a small confraternity in the parish of Santa Caterina, also ran a neighbourhood school. In 1575 the members listed half a dozen goals for their *schola*, including the responsibility to ensure that 'the students, on whose behalf this consortium pays the school, are really there to learn how to read, write, and keep accounts, and that they recite the *De Profundis* every evening.'[170] The confraternity declared that it was carrying out the testament of one Girolamo Novelli. Unfortunately, the will has not been found and no further evidence survives regarding this confraternity's educational activities. This may reflect their transient nature; certainly, Borromeo's impression of the confraternity of San Lorenzo was less than flattering.[171] It is not clear whether the brothers of San Lorenzo organized their own school, or simply supported another school or schoolmaster. The reference to studying arithmetic and the implication that the lessons were at a basic level suggests that the confraternity of San Lorenzo supported lay students only.

Another example of educational activity concerns the lay confraternity of Santo Spirito and San Giovanni.[172] The result of a 1533 merger between two confraternities founded in the late medieval period, this confraternity remained true to its mission to the needy poor and the sick; they distributed bread and wine at Christmas, Easter, and on the feast day of Saint John the Baptist (24 June). Page six of this *Regola* makes clear that the confraternity was run entirely by laymen. This *Regola*, published in 1617 but consistent with those published in the later 1500s, is remarkably similar to that of Sant'Alessandro in Colonna.[173] Indeed, the parts on educational objectives are identical to that of its cross-town rival. Perhaps this imitation is simply flattery, or perhaps the two groups had common members or a common notary. Whatever the reason, the confraternity agreed in 1585 to hire a master to teach fifty poor students, an action 'of such importance and benefit to the poor that with much satisfaction and praise it has been continued ever since, and it is to be expected that it will continue into the future.'[174] These fifty students included three chierici who served in the church of Sant'Alessandro della Croce: they had to be at least nine years of age, enthusiastic, intelligent, and dedicated to the Church. Alessio Marentio was hired in May 1586 as a schoolmaster at an annual salary of 350 lire, a position he held for many years.[175] In 1593 the confraternity announced its intention to hire a (supplementary?) teacher of exemplary character and reputation to teach both types of students to read, write, and figure, as well as to provide instruction in morality and character. The teacher, to be reconfirmed every year, was expected to provide regular reports to the deputies.[176] In 1614, owing to the death of Alessio Marentio, the confraternity hired the Reverend Fermo Bressani as a schoolmaster for poor boys for 280 lire per year.

The *Regola* of Santo Spirito states clearly that chierici were to receive more advanced schooling 'in grammar and other humanistic letters according to their ability,' but in the sixteenth century they were still educated alongside lay boys.[177] Beginning in 1605, however, the confraternity hired individual priests to train the chierici separately from their lay counterparts. Once again we see the impact of Borromeo and the Council of Trent in their efforts to separate the sacred and the secular. The Reverend Giuseppe di Contro was elected to teach the three chierici who served in the church of Sant'Alessandro della Croce at a salary of sixty-three lire per year, and he was succeeded by a series of other priests.[178] The significantly lower salary suggests that this position may have been part time, or perhaps it was subsidized by the Church through a benefice.

The most intriguing aspect of this confraternity's approach to schools is the emphasis on the voluntary nature of its support. The *Regola* makes clear that the decision to support instruction was 'neither necessary nor perpetual nor obligatory ... but solely at the judgment and discretion of the consortium.'[179] No other *Regola* or *terminatione* that I have examined reflects this particular concern. Perhaps the confraternity of Santo Spirito was concerned that it did not possess the funds necessary to support such schools on a long-term basis. It may also have been reacting to the financial difficulties faced by the MIA in previous years as even this large and wealthy confraternity struggled to keep its school afloat. Or perhaps Santo Spirito wished to preserve a degree of flexibility for subsequent charitable donations, in the event that its priorities changed.

The confraternity of Sant'Alessandro della Croce, founded in 1272, had a long history of providing both spiritual and material nourishment to its members and neighbours. Like the Misericordia Maggiore and others, the consortium of Sant'Alessandro della Croce distributed wine, bread, and alms to the poor and the sick. The confraternity maintained the parish church, paid for masses in memory of deceased members, and hosted a feast for the community every year to celebrate the grape harvest.[180] Near the end of the sixteenth century, the confraternity declared that, in accordance with other confraternities, it too wished to provide instruction for neighbourhood children. On 8 June 1593 Sant'Alessandro della Croce's council of ministers noted the dearth of young priests-in-training (*una carestia di chierici*) in its own church, while admiring the accomplishment of the confraternities of Santo Spirito and San Sacramento, which had begun to school neighbourhood boys several years before. Therefore, declared the council, for the benefit of both the neighbourhood and the children themselves, two obedient and God-fearing local boys would hereafter be elected to serve in the church, and the council would hire a humanities teacher to instruct them in their letters. This *maestro di humanità* was to be paid a maximum of three scudi per student each year. The council expressly reserved the right to expel the students and to replace them with others at its discretion. Zo (Giovanni) Maria Chiodi and Prevario Terzo were promptly elected and awarded four lire each to buy a respectable cloak. Their education was entrusted to Augustino di Prestisio, *grammatice professore*.[181] Unfortunately, the documents from this first year tell us almost nothing about the curriculum or the results of the schooling provided to these two boys. The initial scope of this effort was decidedly modest, with only two students and a tiny financial outlay. Still, it appears to have been consciously designed as a pilot program, and that may account for its limited intentions.

This initial project had focused primarily on training boys to work in the parish church, but two years later the council decided to expand the educational opportunities in the neighbourhood and sought 'a master who will teach poor boys of this consortium to read, and at the appropriate time and proper age also to write and do arithmetic.'[182] Note that this latter effort, which continued through 1605, was directed at poor *lay* boys. The confraternity's efforts to train chierici were initially more sporadic but gained traction once the schooling of lay boys was suspended in 1605.

Alessandro Nigrone was hired in the summer of 1595 to teach lay boys, but only after the council had examined his handwriting and determined that he had previous teaching experience. This concern over the qualifications of teachers is echoed in other documents of this confraternity and in those of the MIA; the ministers of each confraternity were clearly concerned that their children receive a proper education from a qualified instructor. Nigrone's father, Gaspare, was also a teacher and had served as treasurer of the confraternity, so presumably young Alessandro was a known quantity. Nevertheless, the confraternity spelled out its expectations in no uncertain terms: Nigrone must accept the salary of twenty-two scudi and seven lire offered to him; the council retained the right to fire him at any time; and he must ask permission if he needed to be away on personal business. If Nigrone should stay away longer than he had requested, he must make up double the amount of time that he had missed with his students. Nigrone's contract contains an unusual clause that directly linked his salary to the number of students whom he taught. He was expected to teach a maximum of twenty-four lay students, but if the number should fall below fifteen, then his salary would be reduced by one scudo (seven lire) for each missing student. Such a clause is redolent of Italian commercial contracts with their sophisticated understanding of profit and loss. Nigrone was to offer instruction in the room currently being used by the council for its meetings, and the council promised to provide two more benches at its own expense. The names of twenty students approved by the council were listed in the minutes so that Messer Nigrone would know whom he was to begin teaching in August.[183]

The most intriguing part of the council's declaration comes at the very end, where it suggests that the confraternity wanted lay students to acquire only the minimum level of instruction before ceding their places to others. As noted in the minutes, 'And when these boys will have learned to read, write, and do accounts at a minimum level (*mediocramente*), they will be let go and other students will be elected by the Council.'[184] Such a statement implies once again the strong demand for basic education that existed in Bergamo in the late sixteenth century and the concomitant desire to instruct as many students as possible. Yet this desire to provide instruction was frequently balanced by an impulse to conserve funds. (The council's budget in February 1596 reveals a balance of only 782 lire, indicating that its prudence in husbanding funds was a wise choice.) Sant'Alessandro della Croce's desire to provide a minimum of training also seems at odds with the humanist tendencies earlier in the century to train boys in virtue and citizenship. Those humanists believed that the more classical learning, the better. Perhaps Sant'Alessandro della Croce simply sought a practical education, one that would help parish boys to find jobs more easily.

In the event, Nigrone returned to the council six months later to report that he had an overflow of students. The council denied his request for an increase in salary, responding that he must turn the extra students away and continue teaching at the same salary.[185] The council minutes imply that a waiting list existed for students who wished to attend the school; the deliberations of 31 December 1595 referred to five students as *supernumerarii* who were to be admitted to the school as soon as other students departed.[186] The council reiterated its position that the maximum number of twenty-four students must be respected and warned that students who skipped four consecutive days without a good reason would be reported by the teacher and subsequently expelled. The council made good on its threat just five weeks later, expelling Zo Maria Chiodi after he failed to show up for services in the church and electing Bartolomeo Marangon in his place. Bartolomeo's cousin, Domenico Marangon, took over the vacant spot in the school for poor boys.[187]

Nigrone continued to teach the neighbourhood lay boys of Sant'Alessandro della Croce until December 1596, when he was forced to quit in order to attend to his business interests. The council once again interviewed candidates, examined their handwriting, and discussed their previous teaching experience. Cornelio Tertio, a *chierico* from the parish of Sant'Alessandro della Croce, was hired to teach the same subjects at the same salary as his predecessor.[188] On 31 December the council presented a list of twenty-four lay boys for instruction and provided Tertio with an advance payment. Tertio received regular quarterly payments throughout 1596 and was confirmed in January 1597 for another year of teaching. Sometime during the fall of 1598, however, Tertio was fired for unknown reasons. The confraternity announced that it earnestly wished to continue its pious work and voted to hire Giovanni Battista Calcone from the neighbouring suburb of Boccaleone. Calcone had, in fact, been the runner-up candidate two years earlier, so his qualifications were well known to the council.[189] From 1598 to 1605 the documents say little about the school for poor boys other than to note the annual election of two deputies to visit the school, so we can assume that Calcone performed satisfactorily. On 16 January 1605, however, the council and deputies agreed to suspend the school 'for just and good cause.' In particular, the council was concerned that the confraternity was wasting its money. After extensive debate and careful reflection, the council voted to uphold the suspension, and no further mention is made of Sant'Alessandro della Croce's school for poor boys.[190]

During these two decades (1593–1613), the confraternity of Sant'Alessandro della Croce also maintained an active interest in the training of young chierici to serve in the parish church. In 1596, three years after the council had hired Augustino Prestisio to teach two young boys from the neighbourhood, it authorized the spending of six scudi in order to send two chierici to the school of Giovanni Jacomo Ligrigni. Ligrigni was ordered to begin tutoring the two within the month in his house on Via Pradello (only a few steps away from the parish church of Sant'Alessandro della Croce). The dual mission of the confraternity is evident in the council's observation that Ligrigni 'teaches not just the humanities, but out of respect for the profession in which they will be engaged, [he teaches] also the ceremonies to be officiated.'[191] It is not clear whether Ligrigni replaced Prestisio and ran his own school, or if he was a supplementary tutor. Just one month later the council agreed to hire another priest, Giovanni Giacomo Carrara, because two members of the confraternity were unable to send their sons to the school of Ligrigni. Little activity is recorded concerning clerical education from 1596 to 1604, probably because the focus was on lay boys at that time, but from 1605 to 1614 no fewer than six different priests were hired to teach chierici.[192] Since none of the dates directly overlap, it seems reasonable to conclude that the confraternity hired one teacher at a time for a maximum of three chierici. The small number of chierici suggests that the instruction provided was more akin to individual tutoring than to group instruction by an independent master.

The lopsided ratio of chierici and lay boys is consistent among all of the neighbourhood schools, implying that training boys for priestly careers was viewed as a more labour intensive process. Several of these confraternities, including Sant'Alessandro della Croce, clearly believed that poor lay boys required only a smattering of instruction whereas those destined for an ecclesiastical position required significantly more training. Nevertheless, the confraternities' commitment to education of both lay and religious boys is clearly evident.

Thus, while the MIA's activities in support of education began earlier and clearly influenced more students, other confraternities also promoted pre-university instruction. Reflecting their intention to serve as neighbourhood schools, these confraternity-run institutions were often restricted to children resident in the parish. These schools taught reading, writing, and mathematics to poor local boys, as well as providing more advanced instruction to a small number of clerics who wished to train for the priesthood. The primary emphasis was on providing a basic education to as many students as possible within limited financial constraints. Smaller confraternities simply did not possess the resources of the Misericordia Maggiore, nor did the parish churches require as many boys to assist with church services.

The larger significance of these previously unstudied confraternities may lie in what they reveal about the desire for education in the later sixteenth century. Clearly, the confraternities recognized a need for more instruction, and they moved to meet that need in several different ways. Most of the education provided by confraternities was local and basic in nature. I am not aware of any students from the schools in Sant'Alessandro in Colonna or Sant'Alessandro della Croce who later enrolled at the University of Padua. Yet the strong desire for instruction persisted. J.H. Hexter has observed a similar phenomenon in late sixteenth-century England, when instruction was no longer seen as 'clerkly' but as a necessary prerequisite to obtain a position in government, law, banking, or another profession.[193] The history of confraternally sponsored schooling also reflects the increasing clericalization of the later sixteenth century. The gradual separation of lay students from chierici reflects a deliberate attempt by the Church to isolate young acolytes and steep them in ecclesiastical tradition without the threat of outside 'contamination.' Ironically, this trend toward clericalization is seen here in confraternal associations that were resolutely lay in character.

The New Academy of Clerics (1617) and the Collegio Mariano

We have seen a variety of educational programs sponsored by Bergamasque confraternities. For the final portion of this chapter, we return once more to the Misericordia Maggiore. Despite the numerous problems associated with its Academy of Clerics, the MIA did not abandon training prospective priests. In 1611, one year after closing its residential academy, the MIA set up a day school for forty chierici to study music and grammar. Students were given twenty-five or thirty-five lire per year plus grain, wine, and a new cloak. Within six years, however, the MIA found that 'the chierici are wasting time coming and going from school, especially in winter when they just do not have time to attend to their letters and their music.'[194] Furthermore, 'because it is obvious that many outstanding professors of letters and of music have graduated from our academy, and because the church has benefited greatly in music and in other ways, and [because of] the edification of the public,' the MIA voted to open a new academy in August 1617. The new academy was to be strictly residential and focused exclusively on the preparation of young men for the priesthood. The two most important objectives were the development of 'good manners and character' and 'profit in the study of letters.' Although the new academy closely resembled its predecessor of 1566–1610, it was far better organized and much more financially sound. As Giuseppe Locatelli has pointed out, the new academy was not simply a boarding house for the clerics of Santa Maria Maggiore but nearly a full-fledged college, where many students paid tuition and expected instruction in a variety of subjects.

The new academy was designed for approximately sixty students, subdivided into three groups. Half of the students, called *accademici* (academics), paid fees of twenty scudi per year, lived in the dormitory, and studied full time. A smaller group of twenty students, usually referred to as chierici, was selected to serve on a weekly basis in the church of Santa Maria Maggiore, for which each *chierico* earned a salary of twenty lire plus six bushels of grain and two vats of wine. Although the chierici received an identical education, they lived in a residence separate from the *accademici* and were subject to even stricter rules. The third group of students, known as *accoliti* (acolytes), received neither housing nor a salary but only the right to attend the grammar school. It appears that the acolytes were younger students, often still living at home, who could be promoted if a vacancy occurred in one of the residential establishments. Dividing students into groups with different privileges and stipends obviously recalls the structure of the previous academy.

How did the MIA's new academy compare with the previous one? Both institutions emphasized an austere environment and a strict daily schedule in which students were isolated from the outside world. Both required boys to dress conservatively, to speak Latin as much as possible, and to provide some of their own utensils and furnishings. Both academics had a full-time teaching staff of four to six masters, including a rector, a *ripetitore* for grammar and humanities, and several music teachers, as well as a barber and a servant. Yet the new academy was not identical to its predecessor. In an effort to attract more students, it soon added classes in philosophy and logic. A generous donation from Guglielmo Beroa and the introduction of student fees led to higher salaries and a more robust balance sheet. The founding document of the new academy reiterated that the academy would not exclude poor boys, but indicated a clear preference for boys from noble and distinguished families:

> The students must be legitimate, without any physical handicap, between the ages of twelve and eighteen, inclined toward the ecclesiastical life, and in need of assistance; they must be descended from citizens who have been honoured in this city and who have achieved membership in the city council, the college of Jurists, the college of Doctors, or the college of Notaries. We believe that the nobility are more disposed toward distinguished actions, and that it is wise to raise children of a similar background together so that they can profit from their residence near the church of Santa Maria Maggiore, in compliance with the new regulations. Lacking students of this type, the sons of less-distinguished citizens may be admitted,

and six places are to be reserved for other boys who lack any kind of social
background, who will carry out other tasks.[195]

Along with the requirement of paying fees, this preference for noble
students indicates that the new academy was beginning to imitate the
Colleges of Nobles recently established in Milan and in Parma.[196] Note,
too, the explicit preference for raising elite boys together, which once
again underscores the trend toward aristocratization. The reference to
'other tasks' to be completed by boys without a social pedigree antici-
pates the 'scholarship boys' of modern schools and universities, and
once again emphasizes the emerging focus on class distinctions.

The new academy began on the eve of All Saint's Day (31 October)
and continued through the summer until the festival of the Virgin's
birth (8 September). The students' daily schedule was a gruelling one
in which every hour of the day was planned meticulously. A long list of
prohibitions underscores the sense of Tridentine morality that pervad-
ed such institutions. The MIA also established a weekly menu featuring meat, salad, soup, fruit, eggs, and, of course, fresh fish on Fridays
and during Lent. The teachers were granted an additional antipasto
of salami, liver, and cheese, along with additional portions of soup or
meat.[197] The *accademici* were expected to bring along most of their own
belongings, including a black cloak with modest sleeves approved by
the rector or deputies, and clerical clothes for summer and winter; a
wool mattress with a bolster, a pillow, a straw mattress, sheets, and a
cover to be changed monthly; a chest, desk, and bench; napkins, sufficient linens, two plates, two bowls, two platters of pewter, a knife and
a fork; the books necessary for school, a diurnal, an Office of Our Lady,
a rosary, a devotional book, and a small vase of holy water.[198] As under
the rules of the previous academy, students were prohibited from leaving school grounds unless accompanied by a master or another student, and then only with the written permission of the deputies or the
rector.

The MIA was deeply involved in the day-to-day operations of its new
academy. All aspects of the academy were discussed in the council's
weekly meetings, and numerous reports were commissioned to explore
specific issues in more detail. The MIA even created a separate index in
its archive in order to track decisions and documents pertaining to the
new Academy between 1617 and 1703.[199] Teachers and students were
regularly expelled from the academy for moral transgressions. In 1623,
recognizing that the required service in Santa Maria Maggiore was

distracting some of the chicrici from their studies, the MIA permitted seven of them to be excused from services in order to study full-time. The MIA's academy clearly impressed the members of the city council, who in 1628 voted that the academy did not need the supervision of city council deputies.[200]

Evaluating the academic quality of the new academy is difficult. No independent judgment of it exists from the seventeenth century, and practically no examples of student writing have survived. Although literacy, rhetorical ability, and a knowledge of the Scriptures were always important in the MIA's schools, it is clear that the ability to sing became increasingly important in the late sixteenth and early seventeenth centuries. The emphasis on musical ability reflects the desire of the Catholic Church to use more music in religious services, even as it questioned and sometimes prohibited the use of polyphony as a dangerous mutation. Nevertheless, we must remember that the MIA's academy was not intended to be a secular academic institution; it was designed to train boys for service in the Church, and as such respected contemporary values and priorities. In later years this academy would grow to become famous for the quality of its music program, culminating in the influential works of Simone Mayr and Gaetano Donizetti.

The academy closed for fourteen months in 1630–1 on account of a terrible plague and then reopened on 10 April 1631. In a 1635 oration, the new vice-rector, Carlo Francesco Ceresolo, referred to the academy as the Collegio Mariano (Marian College). During the course of the seventeenth century the academy slowly transformed itself into a college, attracting more and better students from a wider geographical range. The Barnabite order assumed control of the Collegio Mariano in 1700, followed by the Jesuits in 1711. The college included such notable Enlightenment thinkers among its teaching staff as Giovanni Marioni del Ponte, Lorenzo Mascheroni, and Pier Antonio Serassi. Its history from 1630 onward – amply documented in the MIA's own archive – has been studied by several Italian scholars and students.[201] These studies confirm the trajectory that we have already witnessed as the MIA continued to strengthen its commitment to training young men for suitable careers.

Conclusion

Bergamo's confraternities, then, played a decisive role in expanding opportunities for instruction of both lay and clerical boys. The Misericordia Maggiore and other smaller socio-religious associations offered scholarships, subsidies, housing, texts, and food to deserving young scholars from the city and countryside of Bergamo. My investigations suggest that the extensive support of education by Bergamo's confraternities was not unique to this city, but the perhaps fortuitous conservation of relevant documents has permitted this history to be reconstructed more fully in Bergamo than elsewhere. The experience of Treviso and its grand confraternity Santa Maria dei Battuti appears to be similar, but D'Andrea does not describe the presence of other confraternities that also contributed strongly to education. Nicholas Terpstra's excellent study of abandoned children in Bologna and Florence traces how various brotherhoods administered orphanages, which often included education as part of their mission, although those confraternities rarely sponsored independent schools. Robert Black's monumental study of Florentine education (albeit for a slightly earlier period, 1250–1500) as well as his previous study of educational curricula say nothing about confraternities.[202] Nor is the topic mentioned in Paul Grendler's *Schooling in Renaissance Italy*, which encompasses so much else about Italian education from 1300 to 1600.

The clericalization and aristocratization of education in the late sixteenth and early seventeenth centuries are two obvious themes that emerge in this chapter. These developments are most clearly evident in the gradual separation of noble, lay, and religious youths. By way of contrast, Jo Ann Hoeppner Moran's comprehensive book on education in the diocese of York points to a 'laicization' of education there, which prompted an explosion in educational options long before the English Reformation and the 'educational revolution' proposed by Lawrence Stone.[203] As seen in chapter 1, Bergamo's communal schooling reflects a transition from lay-dominated schooling to a more prominent role for Church-affiliated associations. Lay confraternities represent a similar, albeit slightly later, trend. The schooling sponsored by confraternities, especially that for lay boys, was less focused on religious orthodoxy than the alternative offered by the seminary or the MIA's Academy of Clerics. Nevertheless, the overall trend in the later sixteenth century, in confraternity-sponsored schooling as in other educational institutions, was toward greater control and influence by the Tridentine Church.

The level of assistance offered by Bergamo's confraternities varied widely, from a stick of firewood or a bag of grain to the establishment of a full-fledged residential academy and multi-year scholarships. The level of instruction also fluctuated substantially. Younger students began to study in confraternally supported schools as early as the age of nine, while others waited until the age of seventeen to utilize a confraternal scholarship for university study. Unfortunately, we cannot determine their precise academic attainments, nor can we always judge the degree of success they ultimately achieved. For example, the MIA's track record might be judged a series of failures and abrupt school closings. Yet the MIA's goals were consistently more ambitious than those of other confraternities, and despite repeated setbacks the confraternity continued in its quest to offer instruction and training. In comparison to the commune's efforts at public schooling between 1500 and 1650, the results achieved by the MIA and its fellow confraternities appear quite favourable.

3 *Catechismo*: Schooling and the Catholic Church

This chapter and the one that follows analyse education provided by institutions of the Roman Catholic Church to the youth of Bergamo between 1500 and 1650.[1] In medieval Europe, the Church had been the leading source of education, literacy, and knowledge. Mendicant friars, cloistered monks, and parish priests provided lessons in religion, reading, and (less often) writing and arithmetic. Cathedral schools and monastic libraries preserved the few books available and trained young acolytes for an ecclesiastical career. Beginning in the thirteenth century, however, the Church slowly lost its monopoly on education as independent masters and communal schools combined with broader intellectual changes and the later invention of the printing press to make instruction more widely available.[2] The Church's influence did not disappear, but its ability to dictate what was read, by whom, and to what purpose was increasingly curtailed from the thirteenth to the sixteenth century. Although the Italian Renaissance is no longer viewed by scholars as a pagan interlude hostile to all religious thought, the intellectual movement *ad fontes* (back to the sources) did encourage a different kind of education. Humanists continued the long tradition of reading Cicero, Virgil, and Augustine, but they emphasized different aspects of this literature to suit their interests and needs.[3] In addition, the humanists promoted a revival of Terence, Juvenal, Quintilian, and other Graeco-Roman philosophers, historians, and poets.

The Council of Trent (1545–63) was a critical milestone as the papacy sought to reclaim its primacy on a host of intellectual and moral issues, education among them. Both as an institution and through a series of passionate reformers, the Church began to promote education to a wider audience. Recognizing the need to instruct children, teenagers, and adults, the Church adopted or encouraged a multitude of educational alternatives. Occasionally these new approaches were coordinated by a central authority and followed a single plan (e.g., under the forceful leadership of Carlo Borromeo, or in the requirement to found seminaries in each diocese), but more often individual reformers developed their own model in response to local needs. New religious orders such as the Jesuits, the Ursulines, the Somaschans, and the Barnabites were founded to help defend the faith and to provide instruction at all social levels and to both sexes. Schools of Christian Doctrine sprang up by the hundreds in an effort to teach the rudiments of the faith along with simple reading and writing. Seminaries were created in order to provide more rigorous training to young men who wished to join the priesthood. 'Tridentine education' usually emphasized obedience, conformity, orthodoxy, and faith. As in the medieval era, a teacher had to possess not only the requisite knowledge of grammar, rhetoric, and catechism, but also to display *buoni costumi* (proper behaviour) and be *veramente cattolico* (very orthodox). As one sixteenth-century source put it, a teacher of Christian doctrine 'must not only be a good teacher of Christianity but also a good Christian.'[4]

Like other cities in northern Italy, Bergamo reflected the impact of the Catholic Reformation in many ways. Bergamasque bishops eagerly implemented Tridentine decrees, albeit with stiff resistance from their clergy and parishioners. The vigorous efforts of Archbishop Carlo Borromeo and Bishop Federico Cornaro, to name just two examples, resulted in significant reform among confraternities, churches, and other religious institutions. The Holy Office persecuted a number of Protestant sympathizers, most famously in the twin trials of Bishop Vittore Soranzo between 1550 and 1558. New religious orders arrived to preach, teach, and carry out charitable works. Although violated repeatedly by booksellers and owners of private libraries, by the 1570s the Index of Prohibited Books had been astonishingly effective in erasing 'heretical' ideas and enforcing orthodoxy. In sum, the different institutions and individuals that operated under the broad aegis of the 'the Catholic Church' permeated Bergamo's religious culture in myriad ways during the middle of the sixteenth century.[5]

Schools and academies were founded all over the city in response to ecclesiastical directives or the perceived need to shore up the faith. At times these initiatives were guided directly by the episcopate and the papacy, while at other times they were only tangentially related to the institutional Church. A specific example may be illustrative. The pas-

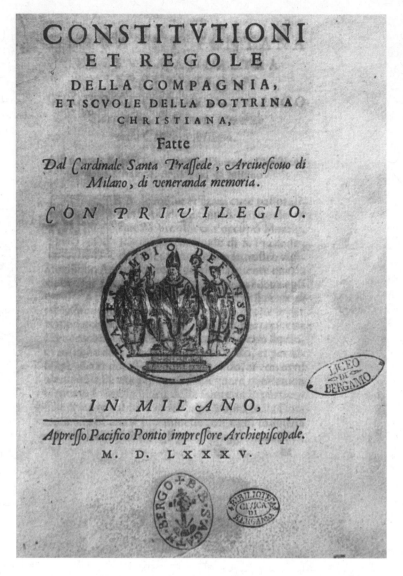

The Constitutions and Rules of the Company of Schools of Christian Doctrine
(Milan, 1585). This edition was approved by Milan's archbishop, S. Carlo
Borromeo. Given Borromeo's close friendship with the bishops of Bergamo,
this edition was likely to have been used frequently in Bergamo to organize
the teaching of the rudiments of the faith as well as elementary reading and
writing.

toral letters sent by Bergamo's bishops Federico Cornaro and Girolamo Ragazzoni exemplify the strict, top-down philosophy adopted after Trent: women and men must be strictly separated at Mass because otherwise the young men try to make love to the women; priests are forbidden to travel to multiple churches on feast days in an attempt to earn more money (*ivi celebrando per l'avidità del guadagno*); banquets after the Mass are forbidden for priests; the MIA was too generous (*troppo amorevole*) in distributing alms and wine and must instead follow the bishop's rules in this matter.[6] In contrast, the efforts of Girolamo Miani, founder of the Somaschans, to assist orphans was driven by local needs; only later did Miani and his followers seek episcopal and papal recognition for their efforts. Both cases, however, reflect the religious sentiment of the day and a resurgent Church.

Politically beholden to the Republic of Venice but ecclesiastically subject to the Duchy of Milan, Bergamo found itself the object of a politico-religious struggle between these two powerful regional states. As we will see in this chapter and later, such competition was often reflected in the educational arena. Despite repeated invasions in the sixteenth and seventeenth centuries, a lack of proximity to the lagoons, and a thriving (if illicit) commercial relationship with Milan, Bergamo remained loyal to Venice from its submission in 1428 to the Napoleonic conquest of 1797. For example, Bergamo respected Venetian decrees regarding the admission and expulsion of religious orders that wished to teach inside the city, and students seeking a university degree nearly always attended the University of Padua. Nevertheless, Bergamo could not avoid the strong ecclesiastical pressure coming from Milan, particularly when Carlo and Federico Borromeo served as archbishops. Although the appointments of Federico Cornaro and then Girolamo Ragazzoni as bishops of Bergamo were made by Venice, both men were close friends of Carlo Borromeo and actively sought his guidance during their tenure in the city. Carlo Borromeo's influence is to be found in numerous aspects of Bergamo's educational network: the curriculum and teaching staff of the seminary, the structure of the Schools of Christian Doctrine, and the catechisms chosen for distribution. Xenio Toscani has observed that the Spanish viceroys in Milan were indifferent about public education until the early seventeenth century, which may help to explain why the Milanese influence on Bergamo is chiefly in the area of religious instruction.[7] The twin examples mentioned above, of pastoral letters by Cornaro and Ragazzoni, and the care of orphans by Miani, exemplify the dichotomy between Venice and Milan. The bishops were loyal to Milan's archbishop and the Tridentine decrees, while Miani (a patrician born and raised in Venice) adopted a more practical, secular approach to charity. Out of necessity, Bergamo adapted to both approaches.

In vivid contrast to the modern, highly centralized educational system directed from Rome, schooling in Renaissance and early modern Italy was shaped by local prerogatives and privileges. Bergamo's split allegiance and status as a 'frontier city' may have permitted it even more freedom to govern its own schools. It is important not to overstate the case: Bergamo was never powerful or important enough to flaunt its authority or to make demands. Nevertheless, as observed in previous chapters, Bergamo's city fathers could exercise some independent judgment. We have just examined the plethora of educational options supported by Bergamo's confraternities in the sixteenth and early seventeenth centuries. The MIA and other neighbourhood consortia promoted both lay and religious education through a variety of means. While the efforts of these lay confraternities often paralleled the goals of the Church (e.g., both trained priests), the schools, scholarships, and other activities supported by lay confraternities were independent of pope and bishop.

In these two chapters, by contrast, I focus on schooling and schoolmasters promoted by institutions of the Church. The Schools of Christian Doctrine, founded in Bergamo in the mid-1550s, provided basic instruction in catechism and literacy. Bergamo's seminary, established a decade later (1567), was designed to instruct young chierici. These two topics offer an opportunity to examine Church-sponsored education circa 1550–1650 from two very different perspectives: one broadly inclusive, staffed by and oriented toward laypeople; the other exclusionary and focused on those dedicated to a life inside the Church. Although both sought the same broad goal of training youth in religious belief and practice, the methods, staff, and audience were starkly different.

The subsequent chapter looks closely at the history of two religious orders of men in order to understand their contribution (or lack thereof) to Bergamo's schooling. The rejection of the Jesuits in 1573 and 1591 is an intriguing tale whose mysteries may never be fully unravelled, but the story can tell us something about how Bergamo viewed education provided by this highly visible new order of the Catholic Reformation. The focal point is the late sixteenth century, but we will also consider later efforts and documents in order to gain a better perspective. The Jesuits' failure is contrasted with the educational efforts of another religious order, the Somaschans, in an orphanage and in a public school between 1532 and 1650. Each of the four cases illustrates a different aspect of the Catholic Reformation; taken together, they reveal some of the Church's priorities in educating the next generation.

Although education after Trent emphasized obedience and conformity, diverse methods and goals continued to proliferate. No broad agreement existed about exactly how to select and instruct young men for ecclesiastical careers, for example, nor about the extent to which girls should be taught to read and write. The Church recognized the need to improve the quality of its priests and to disseminate the faith more widely, yet its actions sometimes served to stifle academic enquiry in the name of orthodoxy. Ecclesiastic educators were torn, it seems to me, between a number of different objectives: training young men as priests; offering advanced instruction to elite boys; 'raising' lower-class students to be informed and obedient Catholics; promoting the religious faith, knowledge, and participation of the laity; and eliminating heterodox beliefs or actions, particularly those stemming from Protestant influence. The range of educational alternatives proposed by Church institutions reflects the divergent goals that they were trying to accomplish.

As we shall see, some of these educational efforts met with great success while others slid into oblivion. The papacy and the bishops devoted enormous resources to expanding the seminaries and to combating the spread of heresy. The Schools of Christian Doctrine continued to prosper in the late sixteenth and seventeenth centuries, but this was due largely to extensive lay participation rather than ecclesiastical involvement. The Jesuits developed a worldwide network of colleges, but they encountered fierce resistance, expulsion, and eventual suppression. The Somaschans continued to teach in Bergamo and in the Veneto for many years, although they too were ultimately suppressed by Napoleon. Thus the story of Church-sponsored schooling in Bergamo, as elsewhere, is neither one of unmitigated triumph nor one of abject failure. Rather, the Church succeeded in meeting many of its own goals but was also frustrated in its attempts to regain a dominant position in the education of early modern Italian youth.

Schools of Christian Doctrine

The Schools of Christian Doctrine represent an unusual compromise between lay and ecclesiastical instruction. Founded in 1536 in Milan to teach the rudiments of faith to poor boys and girls, the *Scuole della Dottrina Cristiana* (Schools of Christian Doctrine) grew rapidly to include tens of thousands of participants throughout Italy by the end of the sixteenth century. The vast majority of teachers were laymen and laywomen who met with the children of their parish on Sundays and holidays to provide simple instruction in religion, morality, reading, and writing.[8] It is important to understand at the outset that the Schools of Christian Doctrine were primarily interested in religious and ethical issues; instruction in reading and writing, while important, was merely a means to an end. Thus while the *Regole* (Rule) and other primary sources often allude to the acquisition of literacy or the ability to write, this was not the focus of the Schools. Nevertheless, Roman Catholic reformers believed that spiritual and physical charity must include not only alms and a place to live but also the teaching of literacy and some vocational skills.[9] The widespread participation of lay teachers is another phenomenon worthy of note; in the diocese of Bergamo there were nearly twelve hundred men and women teaching in the Schools, while in Milan there were more than seven thousand lay teachers.[10] Popes, bishops, and country priests were involved too, but despite Tridentine reform efforts, the Schools of Christian Doctrine remained an overwhelmingly lay enterprise well into the seventeenth century. Thus the Schools present an intriguing paradox: driven and staffed by laymen and laywomen, yet engaged in training boys and girls in catechism and rudiments of the faith.

The Schools of Christian Doctrine were rarely permanent or professional in character. With a few exceptions, both students and teachers attended voluntarily. Thus the Schools' enrolment fluctuated from year to year, as did the quality of instruction. While some lay parent-instructors may have been well educated or widely read in the religious and theological literature of the period, most probably had only a superficial knowledge of the catechism and Christian doctrine that they were teaching. One exception might be the Schools associated with other educational institutions, such as the seminary, the MIA's Academy of Clerics, or the various boarding houses/academies supervised by grammar teachers. Although we cannot speculate on the religious probity of teachers in these institutions, at a minimum they must have possessed some knowledge of the humanities and of leading religious texts. Most students in the Schools of Christian Doctrine, however, would have been taught by lay volunteers. The extensive and continued lay participation suggests that the students' needs for basic spiritual instruction were being met by the Schools of Christian Doctrine.

The Schools provide one of the few examples of early modern instruction in which, on occasion, we know the exact ratio of boys and girls. In the case of Bergamo, while we have figures for every one of the Schools in the diocese between 1609 and 1611, we can only guess at the ratio in other years. It is clear, however, that a substantial majority of the students and teachers in the Schools of Christian Doctrine were female. Girls attended the Schools in great numbers because they represented one of the few avenues for female education. Furthermore, early modern society often expected girls to be well versed in moral education not only in anticipation of motherhood but also to 'protect' their virtue. The 'spiritual' education offered in the Schools seemed appropriate to the private domain of the house, while boys – particularly in the elite classes – were trained in the public arts of grammar and rhetoric. In this chapter we follow the development of the Schools of Christian Doctrine in Bergamo from their humble beginnings in the mid-sixteenth century through their rapid expansion in the first half of the seventeenth century. Owing to the local, informal, parish-based nature of these 'Sunday schools,' we know little of the precise curriculum and even less about the individual teachers or students who attended. Nevertheless, enough documents survive to reconstruct at least a partial vision of the instruction provided.

As Paul Grendler has noted, prior to 1530 there is only scattered evidence of religious instruction.[11] In the drive to (re)establish a curriculum based on the classics and emphasizing Latin grammar and rhetoric, the Quattrocento humanists often ignored catechism and Christian doctrine. This is not to suggest that the humanists were vehemently opposed to religious instruction or the teaching of *buoni costumi* (good habits or proper behaviour), but rather that they perceived that such instruction could be gained informally in a culture suffused with Christian tradition. After 1530, however, several determined individuals sought to promote the spiritual education of young children in a more direct manner. For example, we will encounter Girolamo Miani and his early efforts to teach orphans the value of religion, grammar, and hard work, as well as Ignatius Loyola and the Jesuit approach to instruction. Angela Merici taught girls the fundamentals of Christianity in nearby Desenzano and in 1535 formed the Company of Saint Ursula, later a formal order of professed nuns dedicated to teaching girls. The Barnabites, the Theatines, and the Piarists all viewed moral education as a critical part of the free instruction that they provided in the later sixteenth century.[12] The most important initiative, however, was founded by Castellino da Castello in Milan in 1536.[13] Luring boys inside the church with a combination of entertaining stories and fresh apples, Castello taught them how to make the sign of the cross and recite the beginning of the Lord's Prayer. Ten years later he founded a lay confraternity known as the Compagnia dei Servi di Puttini in Carità (Company of the Servants of Children in Charity), whose members travelled two by two throughout Italy in order to found new chapters. The schools were known everywhere as the Schools of Christian Doctrine.

The exact date of the company's arrival in Bergamo remains unknown, but the venerable historian of the Schools of Christian Doctrine, Giambattista Castiglioni, argues that two members of the Milanese company arrived in 1554 to establish a branch in the church of San Pancrazio. The first conclusive proof comes from 1561, when Paolo Donadoni was elected Prior General of the Bergamasque company.[14] In the same year Federico Cornaro was appointed bishop of Bergamo, a post he would hold for sixteen years (1561–77). Cornaro worked actively to promote the Schools of Christian Doctrine as a tool for defeating religious ignorance and heresy. On 18 July and again on 4 November 1561 Cornaro authorized an indulgence of forty days for members of the company and for those who contributed to the acquisition of books for children's instruction. The following July, Cornaro again ordered forty days of indulgences to brothers and helpers (soccorritori) of the School of Christian Life, where 'boys are instructed and are taught to live in a religious and Christian manner according to divine precepts of Holy Mother Roman Church.' Andrea Magno suggested to Bishop Federico Cornaro that indulgences be published and nailed to church doors in Bergamo in order to whip up enthusiasm for the Schools of Christian Doctrine, a suggestion approved by the bishop's vicar general.[15]

Seven years later the bishop declared that a recent tour of the diocese had convinced him that parish priests must instruct the faithful in the primary elements of Christian doctrine 'so that barbarism can be avoided.' In 1570 Cornaro announced that he had invited Giovanni Francesco di Mazochi, a member of the Venetian company of Schools of Christian Doctrine, to come to Bergamo 'to plant and to cultivate these schools and to teach faithfully Christian morals and belief to children and other persons in our diocese of Bergamo.' Mazochi was permitted to recruit assistants from Bergamo or from among his own companions, each of whom would receive an indulgence of forty days.[16]

In the meantime, a flurry of letters between Bergamo and Milan reveals that – despite the bishop's fervent support – the Schools of Christian Doctrine were struggling. In 1563 Andrea Magno summarized the condition of the various Schools located in different areas of Bergamo:

> The reverend priest of Santa Caterina had a school in his church, but we doubt that it will survive if God does not intervene. In the suburb of Sant'Antonio, and especially at San Bernardino, the number of students has declined but the teachers have increased. In our suburb of the Maddalena the women who usually assist the school have disappeared but the school is continuing and there are enough male teachers to meet the need. In Santo Defende the school is getting along moderately well. In Sant'Antonio the number of students is no longer what it was. In San Bernardino there is an abundance of teachers and students; so many, in fact, that we must not forget to give thanks to the Lord for inspiring the minds of the faithful to embrace these necessary works.[17]

In response to Andrea Magno's description, the Prior General of the company in Milan wrote that the Bergamasques 'should not be disheartened just because you are few, for soon you will be many.' Early in 1564 the company of Milan wrote to Bishop Cornaro to enquire why the Bergamasque Schools were not flourishing: 'even if until now your Schools have declined, pick yourselves up, beloved brothers ... and seek to fill your city and all of the countryside with works so great and useful that the men of Bergamo are recognized to be men of great worth and value.' To help meet this objective, the Milanese company sent two members to assist Bergamo's bishop, and four months later the Schools of Christian Doctrine were restored in San Pancrazio, Santa Caterina, and Santa Maddalena. In 1567, however, the Prior General of Bergamo, Angelo Filogenio, criticized his 'tepid' companions and acknowledged that 'those of us here are apathetic, with the result that there are few teachers.'[18]

The company of Bergamo was not alone in encouraging the foundation of Schools of Christian Doctrine; local confraternities, the pope, and a series of Bergamasque bishops also supported them. In a letter of 18 June 1564, the Prior General of Bergamo remarked that 'the ruling officers of our local confraternity, that is the Minister and his colleagues, ordered that those who expect alms must send their children to the Schools [of Christian Doctrine] or else they will not receive anything.'[19] Chapter 20 of the *Regola* of the consortium of San Lorenzo required the chaplain of the confraternity to be present every Sunday during Lent to assist with the School of Christian Doctrine inside the church.[20] By the beginning of the seventeenth century, Schools of Christian Doctrine not only existed within every church but could also be found within the seminary, the MIA's Academy of Clerics, and various boarding houses for students.[21]

The Council of Trent decreed in 1563 that the rudiments of faith should be taught on holidays to young children. In *Ex debito* (1567), Pius V commanded that all bishops should institute this catechetical instruction and that confraternities might be granted indulgences to carry out this sacred work. The pontiff stated that children who were regularly nourished and instructed in Christian doctrine could avoid the spiritual ruin that had befallen others. In his 1575 apostolic visitation of Bergamo, Carlo Borromeo emphasized the importance of widespread religious instruction. For the company of Bergamo, he nominated a new Prior General and an assistant, promised to send regular visitors to verify progress, and encouraged Bishop Federico Cornaro to utilize the *Regole* that would soon be published in Milan.[22]

We have already seen that Bishop Cornaro wasted little time implementing the Schools during the 1560s. In 1574 Cornaro declared that all Schools of Christian Doctrine in Bergamo must follow the Milanese model set by his close friend Carlo Borromeo. Cornaro recognized that some parishes had already instituted the Schools and their attendant confraternities, but insisted that *all* parishes found one within thirty days. One year later, Carlo Borromeo surveyed 248 parishes during his visitation, but acknowledged Schools of Christian Doctrine in only 107 (45 per cent).[23] Two years after that, in 1577, Bishop Girolamo Ragazzoni sent a pastoral letter to all rural vicars insisting that they teach Christian Doctrine and expressing his 'infinite displeasure' about the prior indifference of many priests in this matter. He appointed Massimo Bonello to supervise the schools, demanded quarterly reports from the vicars, and threatened a fine of two scudi if his directives were not carried out within a month.[24] Two decades later Bishop Giambattista Milani addressed the issue both in his synodal decrees and in his triennial reports to the Holy See on the state of the diocese. For example, in 1593 Milani proclaimed that under pain of mortal sin, all ecclesiastics must teach Christian Doctrine. In 1594 Milani submitted a report to the pope that implicitly criticized his own priests while confirming the extensive lay participation in the Schools:

But the chief concern [of city residents] is that little boys and girls are edu-

cated in the principles of piety. To that end the tradition of Christian Doctrine has been developed with great care, and it would have even more
force and consistency if the chierici, who have not yet been promoted to
priestly orders, came to the church during the afternoon of feast days, and
if they assisted those who are teaching. In this manner two useful things
would be accomplished: we would be of use to the parishioners, and we
would accustom the *chierici* to ecclesiastical labours and train them in their
responsibilities.[25]

In 1603 Milani issued yet another decree, this one prohibiting games,
dances, or other distracting behaviour in the vicinity of the churches
when the Schools were meeting on Sunday afternoons.[26] In 1605 he
introduced the catechism of Robert Bellarmine, requiring that every
parish use this edition exclusively for instruction within the Schools.
The proliferation of episcopal decrees and threats suggests the bishops' frustration that the task was not being accomplished. For the next
several decades, Bishops Giovanni Emo, Agostino Priuli, and Luigi
Grimani continued the tradition of episcopal support for the Schools.[27]
By now it should be clear that the Schools of Christian Doctrine enjoyed
widespread support in Bergamo from both religious and lay institutions and individuals. This enthusiastic promotion helped the Schools
to expand their mission to teach the rudiments of faith and morality
to a wide audience of boys and girls. It also highlights the popularity
of the Schools of Christian Doctrine within the city and diocese of Bergamo, even if the Schools never reached every single parish.

How precisely did the Schools of Christian Doctrine contribute to
the instruction of Bergamo's youth? As noted above, these *scuole* taught
the basics of reading, writing, and religion to poor boys and girls who
might not have been able to obtain any other type of education. The
Schools would have met about eighty-five days per year, generally
in the parish church on Sunday and holiday afternoons for a total of
about three hours.[28] Although the primary task remained catechetical
instruction, the *Regole, Interrogatorio,* synodal decrees, and correspondence make it clear that learning to read and write was an important part
of the curriculum. The level of instruction was not particularly high;
repetition and memorization were the primary pedagogical techniques.
Students began by memorizing letters and syllables, then words and
phrases, and finally whole prayers. *Regole* printed in Milan and in
Brescia between 1558 and 1598 describe a typical schedule. (Bergamo
relied heavily upon works printed in these two towns until the late

sixteenth century.) The prior might teach a lesson from the *Interrogatorio* (a standard text) or engage in a Socratic dialogue to test the students' comprehension and recall. Students might be asked to give a little sermon, to engage in a disputation, or to recite hymns, psalms, or excerpts of a religious text. Younger students would be taught to count, to write their letters, and to read simple words.

A much more specific description of student activities can be found in the *Ordini e Regole per Formar ed Instruir le Scole della Dottrina Cristiana di Bergamo e sua Diocese*, published in 1711 but clearly based upon an early seventeenth-century predecessor. This large-format poster described responsibilities for each of the staff positions within the Schools (e.g., prior, subprior, secretary, silencer, doorkeeper), and then divided the students into five distinct levels. The first (elementary) class was to memorize the sign of the cross, recite the Pater Noster, Ave Maria, and Credo in Latin, and learn the Ten Commandments in Italian. The second and third classes were to study a little booklet by Robert Bellarmine called *Sete voi Christiano* [sic], while the fourth class recited a question-and-answer catechism also by Bellarmine. The fifth class, reserved for illiterate adults, met in a separate locale because 'men of that age are ashamed to be mixed together with boys while learning.' These newcomers to Christian faith were instructed in daily prayers, the rosary, the sacraments, the angelus, and how to raise one's child.[29] Clearly, the emphasis here is upon religious instruction and oral response rather than pure reading and writing.

Boys and girls were always taught separately but often studied identical curricula. The catechisms sometimes state explicitly that they were intended for both sexes. In Bergamo the boys and girls either met on separate sides of the church or, more frequently, in adjoining buildings.[30] By 1610 females constituted the majority of participants in the Schools of Christian Doctrine in Bergamo, with twice as many female teachers and thirteen hundred more girls enrolled than boys.[31] This discrepancy is surprising, since the Schools made a point of recruiting *all* children into their schools. However, given that boys had a wider range of schooling options, they may have seen it as superfluous. As noted earlier, Schools of Christian Doctrine existed in the seminary, in various 'academies,' and in boarding houses that catered to boys who were attending school. Furthermore, the Schools were designed primarily for poorer children; boys belonging to the elite and even the merchant class were more likely to be tutored at home or to attend schools where religious instruction might be part of the regular curriculum.[32]

The student-teacher ratio varied widely; in 1609, for example, the boys at the churches of Sant'Agata and Santa Caterina enjoyed a ratio of 4:1, while at Sant'Anna in Borgo Palazzo the ratio was 11:1.[33] In general the ratio for female teachers and female students was lower, in the range of 3:1. Given the large number of lay teachers, the ample space afforded by parish churches, and the desirability of individual instruction, it is not surprising that much of the teaching took place in small groups. Tutoring of younger students by more advanced pupils was common practice in the grammar schools of the sixteenth century. Giovita Ravizza had advocated this practice in his 1523 treatise, and the existence of a *decurio* (head boy) was an integral part of Jesuit pedagogy that permitted the Society of Jesus to teach classes of sixty or seventy students at a time.[34] Although no documentation of peer tutoring in Bergamo's Schools of Christian Doctrine has survived, it probably did exist.

Larger cities such as Milan and Venice often divided the students into multiple levels according to age and ability. The town of Albino, just a few kilometres north of Bergamo, divided its 190 students into eight distinct classes. Given the enormous numbers of participants, Bergamo too must have divided the students in a similar fashion. For the year 1609, out of a total population of approximately thirty thousand, about 18 per cent (5,372) participated in the Schools. The parish of Sant'Erasmo, for example, included 52 male teachers and 62 female teachers who taught 170 boys and 215 girls respectively.[35] My calculations indicate that every parish in the city of Bergamo had established a School of Christian Doctrine by 1609, although outlying parishes were slower to do so.

Despite the Council of Trent's expectation that such schools should always have an ecclesiastic in attendance, they continued to be dominated by the laity. Instruction was provided by laymen and laywomen of the parish, known as *operarii* and *operarie*. These *operarii* held different positions within the school: doorkeeper, scribe, head teacher, recruiter. The prior – who might be a priest or a canon of the church – taught children the fundamentals of Catholicism, while two other teachers usually taught reading and writing.[36] Carlo Borromeo's 1585 *Constitutioni et Regole* (Constitutions and Rules) described the responsibilities of the prior, the secretary, the peacekeepers, the head teachers, the instructors, and the assistants. For example, the *cancelliere* (secretary) of each company was required to teach some of his 'disciples' to write. In choosing texts for instruction, he was reminded to select those that would both teach his pupils how to write well and promote virtue and good behaviour. The doorkeeper was to set up the benches, keep out stray dogs, and monitor student arrivals or departures, while the recruiter (*pescatore*) was to 'fish' the streets for tardy or forgetful students. Borromeo's directives were surely the norm in Bergamo. While his instructions are obviously prescriptive, they provide a clear sense of the Schools' structure and the dominant values that he expected the Schools to espouse.[37]

Corporal punishment, for example, was discouraged. Instead, prizes and praise were recommended to reward students.[38] This lenient attitude contradicts the popular stereotype of harsh discipline that has sometimes characterized early modern education. Yet Borromeo was adamant that it was better 'to teach with love than with fear' and 'to use promises rather than threats.' Teaching was an important responsibility that must be taken seriously: 'it would be better for one who scandalized a boy to tie a rock around his neck and throw himself into the sea than to offend even one of the [other] boys.'[39] This attitude of tender concern forms an interesting contrast to the strict rules created for the seminary and the Academy of Clerics. Such a contrast reminds us of the voluntary nature of the Schools of Christian Doctrine; presumably, if the teachers were overly harsh, the students would vote with their feet. The contrast also underscores the low level of instruction: students who were younger or who were approaching this material for the first time might need to be coddled more than those who had definitively selected an ecclesiastical career. Or perhaps the *operarii*'s lack of pedagogical experience made it more important to emphasize the prohibition of corporal punishment.

The year 1609 was a watershed for the Schools of Christian Doctrine in Bergamo. Representatives of the Archconfraternity of Christian Doctrine arrived in Bergamo in mid-summer, and people throughout the diocese flocked to join. Founded in Rome on 7 October 1607 by Pope Paul V with *Ex credito nobis*, the archconfraternity sought to standardize the practices of diverse chapters under the centralized leadership of the Roman Curia. In return for subscribing to the archconfraternity, members in Bergamo were able to enjoy a variety of indulgences commensurate with their contribution to the Schools: one hundred days for parents who instructed their children or servants, two hundred days for mediating a dispute within the Schools, three years for assisting with services for the dead, and ten years for visiting rural villages to teach Christian doctrine. Formally known as 'The Congregation of Christian Doctrine under the name of Saints Vincent and Alexander of the cathedral church of the city of Bergamo,' this new confraternity was officially founded in Bergamo in October 1609. The arrival of the archconfraternity, however, occurred at 4:00 p.m. on 5 July 1609 with a formal procession of men through the upper city. After visiting each of the major churches, the procession returned to the cathedral and 'entered through the main doorway with the boys and the members of the said School singing holy litanies.'[40] Throughout the summer and for the next eighteen months, the representatives of the archconfraternity welcomed new members. For each new School an act of aggregation was drawn up, following a set formula which acknowledged the superiority of the archconfraternity and the spiritual blessings, favours, and indulgences conceded to new members. Although the lists of individual names have been lost, the number of *operarii* and new students was recorded in the margin of each act of aggregation.[41]

A few tantalizing clues exist about the position of women who wished to join this archconfraternity. The applications from Schools of Christian Doctrine consisting only of women were invariably represented by a procurator who signed the documents on behalf of the female *operarie*. It was a common, though far from universal, practice in early modern Italy that women had to be represented by men in legally binding agreements. Yet this example does not indicate that women were precluded from full membership. Despite the fact that only men were allowed to march in the parade and that in the case of Sant'Agata the word *sorelle* (sisters) was deleted from a description of who might enjoy the benefits of confraternity membership, it appears that women were full participants in this confraternity. We have already witnessed the extensive participation of women and girls in the Schools of the confraternity. The documents of aggregation from 1609 to 1610 repeatedly stated that the indulgences and remissions of sin were open to both sexes (*l'uno et l'altro sesso*).[42]

The applications for membership in the archconfraternity followed a logical order, beginning with parishes in the upper city, then those in the lower city, and finally those in the upland valleys. All of the male Schools in the city were approved first, followed by the female Schools in the city; then other institutions such as the seminary, followed by the Schools outside the city limits. A minor dispute broke out during the summer when both Sant'Agata and San Pancrazio claimed to be the oldest School of Christian Doctrine. In separate documents, the archconfraternity diplomatically agreed that each was the oldest,

and moved on to the next case. The archconfraternity was phenome-
nally successful; in 1609 it signed up 185 schools; in 1610 it signed up
an additional 122, totalling more than 300 new schools across 244 parishes.[43]

Perhaps the most intriguing aspect of this set of documents from
1609 concerns the foundation of Schools of Christian Doctrine in places
other than parish churches. The three orphanages founded by Girolamo Miani, for example, petitioned to join the archconfraternity, as did
the MIA's Academy of Clerics and the confraternal School of Clerics in
the parish of Sant'Alessandro in Colonna. The seminary declared that
it wished to be associated with the archconfraternity, and so did ten
private 'academies' or boarding houses. All of these institutions submitted their requests during the same week in mid-August 1609. All of
them had to demonstrate a link with a nearby church and the presence
of a teacher competent to instruct the students. All subscribed to the
formulaic contract used elsewhere to join the archconfraternity, and all
were accepted even if their numbers were fewer than in other churches.
Nevertheless, this eclectic group of academies, boarding houses, and
schools reflects some notable differences with the other institutions that
joined the Archconfraternity of Christian Doctrine. Such differences
can help us to peek beneath the surface and better understand how
schools and students functioned.

The Misericordia Maggiore petitioned to have a School of Christian
Doctrine founded within its Academy of Clerics. The rector, Troylo
Agosti, appeared before the archconfraternal deputies on behalf of the
twenty-three clerics living in the Academy and the fifty-seven external
students who enrolled in classes there. He reminded the deputies that
for a long time the MIA had taught Christian Doctrine to its chierici,
but without being subject to any external guidelines. Now, however,
the rector wished to found a 'well-regulated and legitimate School of
Christian Doctrine in order to take advantage of this opportunity and
to acquire the sacred treasures of indulgences.'[44] The indulgences were
clearly a major incentive to both institutions and individuals to participate in the Schools of Christian Doctrine.

The seminary, too, requested an affiliation with the Schools of Christian Doctrine. In addition to two teachers and an unspecified number
of students, the rector, Giovanni Maria Persico, promised that the seminary staff (*portinari, servi, et serve*) would also participate in the Schools
of Christian Doctrine. The confraternal school for chierici in the parish
of Sant'Alessandro della Croce followed the same formula closely, offering eleven boys and one maestro.

In addition to these three established institutions, nine others defined as 'academies' appear in the records of the archconfraternity. The term 'academy' is problematic because it is used in this context to refer to what appear to be independent secondary schools, whereas in documents of the later seventeenth century the term refers to an intellectual club for adult men (e.g., *Accademia degli Eccitati*, the predecessor of today's Ateneo delle Scienze). The first example is the academy of Pietro and Giovanni Andrea Pasta. These two brothers directed a public academy in Bergamo from 1609 to 1630 in order to provide instruction in good letters and philosophy. The Pasta brothers later authored a textbook for their students, the *Brevis collectio grammaticarum exercitationum*, and composed several opera librettos. In August 1609 they stated that they wished to found a 'donzina' (boarding house) and a School of Christian Doctrine for their students. The School of Christian Doctrine would meet in their own house on Via Santa Lucia Vecchia, in the neighbourhood of San Leonardo. The new School would be affiliated with another one already in existence at the parish church of Santa Lucia. The Pasta brothers promised that their school would have thirty-five students and two teachers (presumably themselves). Furthermore, they promised to send one or two of their best students to a *disputa generale* (general disputation) each year.[45]

A remarkably similar example concerns the request of Marc Antonio Lazzaroni, *dottore e professore di grammatica*.[46] He too wished to establish a School of Christian Doctrine for the forty-eight students whom he instructed and supervised in his *donzina*. Lazzaroni requested that 'for his own greater convenience' (*per sua maggior commodità*) he be allowed to provide instruction in his own house. He too promised to send one or two of his best students to compete in the public disputations when the officers of the confraternity organized such an event. Lazzaroni indicated that he would maintain an affiliation with the nearby church of San Pancrazio. The deputies of the archconfraternity approved his request, with the stipulation that the boys in his care must attend confession and communion once a month at San Pancrazio.

Eight other 'academies' petitioned to add Schools of Christian Doctrine to their institutions, with conditions similar to those outlined above.[47] Nearly all of these academies included a master teacher and a *ripetitore*, with the number of students ranging from ten to forty-eight. Usually named after the master who was in charge, these academies were distributed evenly around the upper city and the lower city. Several of the petitioners to join the archconfraternity described themselves as supervising *donzine* (boarding houses) rather than a more academic institution. It seems probable that these instances represented independent masters teaching boys in their own homes. Unfortunately, no other documents attest to the existence of these academies, so we cannot speculate as to their other activities or continued longevity. [48] The paucity of surviving information about these academies makes it difficult to judge which function a particular academy was fulfilling at any given time.

What conclusions can we draw from this unusual subset of petitions? It appears that Schools of Christian Doctrine were supposed to meet in a church, but that exceptions could be granted for valid reasons. If the Schools met in a private house, then an affiliation had to be maintained with a local church where boys could go to confess and receive communion (often the third Sunday of the month was reserved for this activity). Apparently the archconfraternity insisted that every School of Christian Doctrine be formally refounded in order to receive the benefits and indulgences. The emphasis upon obedience is not surprising, nor is the effort to establish greater clerical oversight of these potentially powerful lay confraternities. The Catholic hierarchy sought to provide education to a much wider audience in the late sixteenth and early seventeenth centuries, and to make that education more overtly religious. The Schools of Christian Doctrine helped to meet both of those goals.

It should be obvious from the discussion above that the number of Schools of Christian Doctrine skyrocketed in the period around 1609. By the end of 1611 there were 311 Schools of Christian Doctrine in the diocese of Bergamo, a threefold increase over 1575, when Borromeo had visited the city. Much less obvious is the type of instruction that occurred in these Schools. Presumably they continued to teach fundamental skills of reading, writing, and religion as they had during the previous half-century. One historian has referred to the early seventeenth century as the 'golden age' of the Schools of Christian Doctrine.[49] In Bergamo, at least, far fewer documents survive to describe the activities of the Schools after 1611.[50]

In conclusion, then, we have seen that the Schools of Christian Doctrine offered a means to impart reading, writing, and religion to thousands of boys and girls in Bergamo beginning in the mid-sixteenth century. Located in nearly every parish of the diocese by 1609, the Schools featured extensive lay participation complemented by increased attention from the pope, the bishop, and the archconfraternity based in Rome. While the emphasis always remained upon catechetical and moral instruction for poor children, the existence of Schools in the seminary and various 'academies' testify to its existence across class lines.

The development and structure of the Schools of Christian Doctrine merit attention for several larger historiographical reasons. Jean Delumeau has argued that Europe only became truly Christianized after Luther and the Council of Trent staked out opposing positions on a host of doctrinal issues. Only then, according to Delumeau, were the people of Europe consciously aware of what it meant to be 'Christian' or 'Catholic.'[51] The Schools of Christian Doctrine, which flourished in the middle of this contentious period, surely provided a means by which the laity could become more aware of their religious convictions. Unlike the Seminary or the sophisticated theological debates that raged among the elites, the Schools provided basic, fundamental religious instruction (or indoctrination) to the people.

A closer study of the Schools may also shed light on the thorny issue of popular literacy. Conventional wisdom has long held that the Protestant Reformation was a stimulus to literacy in northern Europe because people wished to read the vernacular Bible and broadsheets for themselves. Some years ago Gerald Strauss studied the catechism schools of Germany in an effort to assess the effectiveness of the spiritual education provided.[52] He concluded that the schools were largely ineffectual, although his results may have been biased by relying too heavily upon the episcopal visitations and their intrinsic bias to identify problems within the diocese. Xenio Toscani has studied popular literacy in Lombardy from 1500 to 1900 and come to the startling conclusion that literacy rates were *higher* in the mountain/valley region of Bergamo than they were in the fertile plains.[53] This contradicts the standard assumption that the wealthier flatlands enjoyed more schooling and a greater circulation of books and therefore possessed higher literacy. Toscani posits that the creation of Schools of Christian Doctrine in many of the small, isolated hamlets of the valleys may have increased literacy rates. In this way, the Schools of Christian Doctrine may have allowed those who otherwise would have been blocked from elementary schooling – poor boys, girls, and those in isolated areas – to receive at least the rudiments of an education.

The Seminary

The diocesan seminary in Bergamo reflects another aspect of the Catholic Church's efforts to educate its members and its officials in a more comprehensive and orthodox manner during the latter half of the sixteenth century. Founded just three years after the conclusion of the Council of Trent, Bergamo's seminary was among the earliest to be established in accordance with the new Tridentine decrees. It began in 1567 in exceedingly modest circumstances, with twenty-five students crammed into one building near the church of San Pancrazio. In 1573 it transferred to the church of San Matteo, but financial difficulties continued to bedevil the *seminarino*. The powerful archbishop of Milan, Carlo Borromeo, aided Bishops Federico Cornaro and Girolamo Ragazzoni as they struggled to bolster the financial and spiritual health of the young seminary in the 1570s and 1580s. The bishops remained preoccupied with increasing revenue and hiring staff, neither of which proved easy to do. Borromeo's 1575 apostolic visitation showed the weaknesses of the seminary but also marked a turning point in the right direction. Slowly the seminary expanded, adding several new students each year and continuing to train them in academic, ecclesiastical, musical, and liturgical subjects. By the seventeenth century the seminary was on stable ground; it moved to its current location on the hill of San Giovanni at the beginning of the nineteenth century, where it still looms over nearby buildings.

The history of Bergamo's seminary has received little scholarly attention. While the recent expansion of the seminary and its renaming in honour of Pope John XXIII has been extensively documented, the early history of the institution has been somewhat overlooked. Indeed, the only significant article on the history of Bergamo's seminary was written by Angelo Roncalli (later Pope John XXIII) when he was professor at the seminary in the early twentieth century.[54] Roncalli combed the seminary archive, the episcopal archive of Bergamo, and the Ambrosian Library in Milan in order to reconstruct the early history of the seminary, and all subsequent scholarship (including my own) has relied heavily upon his research.

The seminary is important in the history of education in Bergamo for several reasons. Clearly illustrating the pedagogy and curriculum favoured by the Catholic Church, it allows us to compare Bergamo's efforts and accomplishments with those of other Italian cities. Although Bergamo's seminary remained small in comparison with those erected in Milan or (later) in Padua, it was an important step forward in the establishment of diocesan seminaries across Italy. Comparisons can also be drawn with other educational institutions in the city: the MIA's

Academy of Clerics is the most obvious parallel, but contrasting the seminary with the communal school and the Somaschans is useful too. The history of the seminary also contributes to our understanding of related pedagogical issues in early modern Bergamo: for example, the growing distinction between lay and religious education, the contribution of the Jesuits, and the financial arrangements favoured by the Church to train aspiring priests. Most importantly, analysis of the early seminary reveals the concrete steps taken by the Church to shore up priestly education in an increasingly confessional era.

Bergamo's seminary was established in October 1567, in accordance with a declaration issued during session XXIII entitled *Cum adolescentium aetas*, whereby the Council of Trent announced its unanimous intention to establish a seminary in every diocese. Sometimes referred to as the 'magna carta' of seminaries around the world,[55] this document outlined their purpose, curriculum, financial resources, administrative organization, and entrance requirements. With the windfall from new taxes, every bishop was ordered to found a seminary as soon as possible. Boys of legitimate birth and twelve years of age who knew how to read and write and showed promise for an ecclesiastical career were to be admitted. The young seminarians would be trained in 'grammar, singing, ecclesiastical computation, and other useful arts ... Sacred Scripture, ecclesiastical books, the homilies of the Saints, the manner of administering the sacraments, and the rites and ceremonies.'[56] Subject to strict discipline and the threat of expulsion, they were expected to wear the clerical habit and tonsure and to assist at Mass. The Council of Trent required that a board of trustees be appointed for each seminary, to consist of two members of the cathedral chapter and two members of the council. Furthermore, urged the council fathers, any ecclesiastical official in possession of a benefice should teach free of charge. Although this decree was not the first discussion of the importance of seminaries to the Catholic Church, it became the guiding force behind the foundation of seminaries all over Catholic Europe.[57]

Bergamo's Bishop Federico Cornaro (1561–77) attended this twenty-third session, as did his future successor, Girolamo Ragazzoni (1577–91).[58] Cornaro immediately rushed back to Bergamo so that he could begin the work of reforming Bergamo's church. Gathering his clergy together on 5 September 1564 in the cathedral of San Vincenzo for his first diocesan synod, Cornaro read out *Cum adolescentium aetas* and then a declaration of his own, committing himself *totis viribus omnique diligentia* (with the greatest effort and care) to the foundation of a seminary.[59]

As instructed by the Council of Trent, Cornaro appointed two canons and two clergy to oversee the fund-raising and other administrative duties necessary to start up the seminary. In addition to Filippo Salvioni, Nicolò Azzonica,[60] and Giovanni Antonio Guarnero,[61] the bishop selected Nicolò Cologno, whom we have already met as a teacher of grammar and rhetoric at the MIA's academy and at the commune-sponsored school.

Throughout the academic year 1564–5 the deputies worked hard to raise money for the new seminary and to establish a budget. The combination of Bergamo's agricultural poverty and the reluctance of some monasteries to provide the requested sums proved a difficult hurdle to overcome. Cornaro wrote a revealing letter to Carlo Borromeo on 25 February 1565 concerning the financial difficulties that he was facing:

Up to now I have done my very best to carry out the orders of the sacred Council of Trent. Only one project remains to be done, the foundation of the seminary, and despite exploring many avenues I have been unable to get it under way. This diocese, your Reverence, is very poor, and with eight or ten of the monasteries and temporary benefices having been exempted, the rest of the benefice income is so little that it is hardly enough to support the rectors of the churches. In addition, with the Venetians' 10 per cent [to support the war against the Turks] and new taxes, I cannot possibly impose more financial burdens without a great outcry. It is true that the fruits of this bishopric might be used to give life to this holy work of the seminary, and that such action might inspire the clergy to support the seminary themselves; but the bishopric's income is divided into several parts, and my portion is only enough to support my own modest and temperate lifestyle for four months of the year. Even if Monsignor Morone [Cardinal Giovanni Morone, past president of the Legates of the Council of Trent] were to donate his income in support of the project, and even with the promised support of my brother, Cardinal Luigi Cornaro, to whom a portion of the bishopric's income goes, still I would not be encouraged ... I humbly kiss your hands and recommend myself to your kind grace, your most humble servant, the bishop of Bergamo.[62]

Cornaro's plea to Borromeo was justified; of the forty-five hundred gold scudi intended for the bishopric of Bergamo, Cornaro received only one thousand, with the balance going to Cardinals Morone and L. Cornaro. Nevertheless, Bishop Federico Cornaro promised to commit two hundred scudi in support of the seminary, the largest sum asked of any person or institution.

Monasteries in the diocese were asked for thirty to fifty scudi each, and a tax of 4–10 per cent was placed upon different types of benefices. However, several of the monasteries balked at such payments. In 1568 the Augustinians of the monastery of Santo Spirito refused to pay even a reduced tax, claiming that they had their own students and teachers to support inside the monastery. Cornaro wrote an angry letter to Borromeo's vicar on 8 March of that year, pointing out that Santo Spirito had only four novices and a total population of twenty-three, yet enjoyed a healthy income of more than two hundred scudi per year. Later that year the Vallombrosan monastery of Astino filed a similar complaint, and in 1570 Cornaro had to accept a list of exempt abbeys and monasteries. Cornaro also tried to have vacant benefices transferred to the benefit of his seminary, but here too he encountered resistance.[63]

Difficulties with fund-raising, however, did not end with the local religious. During the winter of 1566, the deputies of the seminary wrote to the Procurators of San Marco in Venice to ask for financial support. Since the Procurators regularly collected taxes from all ecclesiastical institutions within the diocese of Bergamo, such a request was not unusual. Pleading the poverty of the Bergamasque lands, inhabited by a 'very numerous and poor' population, the deputies noted that 'if any diocese truly has need of a seminary, this one needs it most of all, so that throughout the diocese spiritual food can be distributed by suitable people.'[64] But the Venetian administrators refused to contribute. Claiming that they needed the funds to support their own clerics in the basilica of San Marco, the Procurators repeatedly denied requests by the deputies, the bishop, and even the papal nuncio who attempted to intercede on Bergamo's behalf. Ultimately, Bishop Cornaro managed to extract a paltry payment of 620 lire, a pittance in comparison to the thousands of scudi that Venice collected from the Bergamasque clergy each year.

Despite such financial difficulties, the seminary lurched forward; on or around 1 October 1567 its doors opened to admit twenty-five young men.[65] The deputies rented a small house in the neighbourhood of San Pancrazio belonging to one Polidoro Agosti. The exact location of the house was not specified, but – in accordance with Tridentine guidelines – it would have been only steps away from the cathedral and the episcopal palace. The traditional home of goldsmiths and an active site for commerce as well as heretical ideas, the parish of San Pancrazio was located in the heart of the old city.

The deputies hired Gerolamo da Gromo, the parish priest of Colognola, to serve as *ludimagister* of the young seminary. No direct evidence exists of the seminary's curriculum during its first five years, but we can infer a few conclusions from extant documents. In keeping with the pedagogical tradition of the time, da Gromo was expected to do a great deal more than simply provide academic instruction for the boys in his care. As preceptor, he lived in the house with them, supervised their meals and activities, and inculcated the strict, orthodox piety favoured by the Catholic Reformation. Da Gromo trained the young men in their letters and tried to develop their character. Thus he would have taught the usual texts of Horace, Virgil, and Cicero as well as Latin grammar, rhetoric, and dialectic. Cicero's famous speech defending Milo for his assault on Clodius was known as a standard text in Bergamo's seminary. Roman catechism, saints' lives, and Christian doctrine constituted other crucial parts of the daily lesson.[66] Although no extant document testifies to it for this five-year period, the seminarians must have served in the cathedral on Sundays and other feast days as part of their ecclesiastical education. Such practice was standard for all clerical academies and seminaries in the second half of the sixteenth century.

Kathleen Comerford's study of Tuscan diocesan seminaries in the sixteenth and seventeenth centuries summarizes the curriculum for other newly founded seminaries. In Arezzo, for example, 'chant, writing, arithmetic, ethics, rituals, sacraments, sacred rhetoric, and scripture were taught.' In Siena, the list included grammar, humanities, logic, philosophy, and rhetoric; in Volterra, it was catechism, grammar, rituals, and singing. Lucca, the most independent, offered casuistry, Greek, music, and two kinds of rhetoric. Interestingly, only the Aretine seminary stressed 'disciplinary and moral foundations' although such topics surely suffused the informal curriculum in each seminary.[67]

The teachers and administrators struggled to define the traditions and rules of the new institution. Similar to the MIA's Academy of Clerics, the Bergamo seminary sought to restrict contact between its impressionable young men and the outside world. A redaction of the rules in 1575 specified that 'the house must be arranged in a proper manner: specifically, the second [inner?] door must be locked with a key so that outsiders cannot enter.' A servant was employed to assist with the preparation of food and with house cleaning; it was initially a woman, but Carlo Borromeo insisted that such a practice was not seemly and decreed that a man should be hired in her place. Although the financial situation had improved marginally, the seminary still charged fees to two-thirds of its students.[68] Required payment contrasted with the initial objective of the seminary in 1567 to provide an education to poor boys from the diocese who could not afford their own tutors. Perhaps the seminary felt a financial pinch from competition with the MIA's Academy of Clerics, or perhaps the vacant benefices did not come through as quickly as anticipated.

Nevertheless, the seminary seems to have enjoyed some modest success in these opening years. A statement by Bishop Cornaro at the end of the 1567–8 academic year reflects his pleasure with the progress of the seminary:

> With the assistance of those [deputies] who were elected in the previous synod, we have established a seminary for clerics. There are now twenty-five young men who are supported, clothed, and instructed in their letters and behaviour by a good teacher ... With the money collected from taxes and properly distributed, as you can see from the account books, the expenses of the seminary have been covered; and we remain optimistic that this institution will continue to grow and expand.[69]

In recognition of the demands upon da Gromo, who remained *magister principalis clericorum* (head teacher of the chierici), the seminary began to add staff. In September 1569 the Seminary hired Michele Manili – who had previously taught for the MIA and had retired in 1564 after two bouts with the Inquisition – to be the Seminary's maestro.[70] An additional teacher was hired with various titles: *gubernator seu minister* (governor or minister), *praefectus domus* (housemaster), and *rector seminarii* (rector of the seminary). Bonifacio Guerinoni, about whom we know little else, assumed this position in 1570 and remained at the seminary until at least 1575. A second sign of success can be unearthed in Bishop Cornaro's decree of 3 June 1573 informing da Gromo and Guerinoni that lay boys and non-boarding *chieirici* were no longer permitted to study in the seminary.[71] Given the array of other educational options in Bergamo in the 1570s, lessons that attracted boys from outside the seminary must have been popular indeed. The tighter admission standards suggest that the seminary could now afford to be more selective about its students and could survive without the fees paid by lay boys. Cornaro's decree also underscores the Tridentine insistence on separating secular and ecclesiastical functions as much as possible.

In considering the early years of the seminary, several contextual factors should be kept in mind. First, the existence of the MIA's day school, founded in 1506, and the Academy of Clerics, established in 1566, must have spurred the bishop to press ahead with the founding of the seminary. The MIA's Academy of Clerics reflected the spirit and the letter of *Cum adolescentium aetas*, for it sought to train the young men who would be serving in the church of Santa Maria Maggiore. While the bishop never specifically mentioned the MIA's academy as a competitor, he could hardly have avoided seeing it in this light. Indeed, the existence of two parallel institutions, both created expressly to train young men for the priesthood, exemplifies the drive to define and separate religious and lay education. Second, the major seminaries in Rome and Milan served as models for the seminary in Bergamo. The Milanese seminary was one of Carlo Borromeo's cherished projects, and – as we will see shortly – he regularly provided advice and resources to the Bergamasque seminary. The seminary represents one of the few examples of education in Bergamo where Milanese influence was stronger than Venetian. That balance would shift circa 1650 with bishop Barbarigo and his strong, pro-Venetian stance, but initially the seminary looked to Milan.

Furthermore, the construction of the enormous city walls around Bergamo, which resulted in the destruction of hundreds of private homes, monasteries, and churches, including the basilica of Sant'Alessandro, made it difficult for the young seminary to find an amenable location. Paradoxically, the walls made the Bergamasque residents more uneasy about their future by reminding them how much control Venice exercised over their city. Housing and land also became more scarce, and more expensive, just as the seminary sought to put down permanent roots. The decision to found a seminary and to ensure its location in the upper city may have stemmed in part from the bishop's desire to respond to Venetian pressure by staking a firm claim for Church property. Regardless of the precise reason(s) behind the seminary's foundation, it stood as a tangible symbol of the Catholic Church's renewed commitment to education.

After several years in San Pancrazio, the seminary was forced to move to a new location in 1573. One of the canons of the cathedral, Giovanni Paolo Ossa, offered to donate a benefice consisting of a house and five acres of land. The house was attached to the small church of San Matteo, located on the north side of the upper city and facing the gate of San Lorenzo. In return for the donation, valued at about one hundred scudi per year, Ossa asked the deputies for an annual payment of forty to forty-four scudi. The house was small and in poor condition, but a rescript from Pope Gregory XIII on 7 October 1573 and the continuing generosity of Giovanni Paolo Ossa permitted the renovations necessary to accommodate the seminary. On 16 and 17 September 1574, in an address to his third diocesan synod, Bishop Cornaro once again expressed his joy at the progress of the seminary:

> In this seminary of Bergamo twenty-five priests-in-training [chierici] are being instructed in letters and the proper traditions of a clerical life; they attend the chapel [of San Matteo] every day and participate on Sundays and holy days, and they are assiduous in observing the ecclesiastical ceremonies. The most teachable [dociliores] of the young men are selected by the deputies of the seminary. With the help of the Holy Spirit, this seminary is thus producing rich fruit. Not only are new priests emerging from here as we had hoped but others are quickly replacing them, in such a manner that soon there will be no shortage of good workers to cultivate the vineyard of the Lord.[72]

In the following year (12 November 1575) Cornaro boasted to Carlo Borromeo that 'I have taken responsibility for the founding of a clerical seminary in this city according to the decrees of the Council of Trent, and I have bestowed five benefices upon it.'[73] Thus he conveyed the impression that the seminary had overcome the financial obstacles that had hindered its early development and was now producing competent priests for the city and countryside of Bergamo. Cornaro even began recruiting students from throughout the diocese, instructing the rural vicars on 12 July 1575 to 'search for some boys of good character, of at least fourteen years of age, and with a good prospect for learning their letters, to be accepted into the seminary.'[74] A formal visit by Carlo Borromeo, however, calls this rosy picture into question and forces us to re-examine the true levels of success attained by the seminary in the first ten years of its existence.

One of the most important events in the religious history of Bergamo in the sixteenth century, the apostolic visitation by Carlo Borromeo in the fall of 1575 provides a remarkable snapshot of religious and secular life in the diocese of Bergamo. In his efforts to create a more orthodox religious environment, Borromeo left a trail of decrees and remonstrances behind him, as we have already seen with the MIA's Academy of Clerics. There can be little doubt that Borromeo strongly influenced the direction of education in those institutions directly sponsored by the Catholic Church. Chief among these institutions was the seminary of Bergamo.

Arriving in the city with great pomp and circumstance at the beginning of September 1575, Borromeo made a point of visiting the seminary within ten days' time. Given the keen interest he had displayed earlier, and the advice he had proffered to Bishop Cornaro, it is not surprising that Borromeo would wish to visit the seminary early in his tour. Several informants had submitted letters to Borromeo alleging that the benefices intended for the seminary had not been properly transferred. The anonymous letters criticized the resulting impoverishment of the clergy and noted further that the clothing of the *chieirici* was 'a long way from modesty and religious decency.'[75] These informants went on to say that the seminary was 'lacking discipline and very badly governed in both spiritual and temporal matters, and it is very poor, and also passive.'[76] Borromeo dutifully investigated these charges, but his final report did not include them – indeed, Roncalli has noted that the final redaction specifically excluded these comments with a line drawn vigorously through that part of the text, perhaps by the hand of Borromeo himself. Nevertheless, Borromeo's decrees and recommendations make pointed comments about reforming the financial controls and emphasizing the observance of ecclesiastical ceremonies more consistently.[77]

As part of his visitation, Borromeo interrogated each of the students about his studies. He recorded the names and individual results of the most advanced students, just as he had when visiting the MIA's academy. The nine students listed by name received a range of marks; most were adequate in Latin grammar and catechism, and a few were *optimi* (excellent) or *eruditi* (intelligent), but several 'offered little hope' or were even unable to write properly.[78] In striking contrast to Bishop Cornaro's optimistic statements of preceding years, Borromeo's observations reveal a streak of mediocrity among the students. Pietro Deleidio, for example, twenty-three years of age, had studied in the seminary for nine years, but Borromeo's conclusion was that he had made little progress in rhetoric, did not write well, and was not very bright. Several of the other students displayed similar results.

Why was their performance so lacklustre? One possible explanation was the inability of the bishop to recruit Jesuit teachers at the seminary on a regular basis. Given their activities elsewhere, the Jesuits likely would have imposed a more rigorous academic curriculum. The Jesuits had already made one unsuccessful attempt to establish themselves inside the city, and they would shortly make another; yet despite the support of Borromeo and the bishops of Bergamo, the city council refused to admit them. The staff at the seminary (da Gromo, Manili, Guerinoni) do not appear in other civil or ecclesiastical documents as important and influential men, suggesting that they may have been competent but not (like Cologno) exceptional. Nor can we discount the impact of the financial burdens that the seminary had recently faced. The shortage of funds, combined with Bergamo's economic fragility, may have hampered the seminary's ability to stock a library or to attract bright students on scholarship. The anonymous critics in Borromeo's documents had further warned about the school's passivity and lack of discipline, a charge perhaps borne out in a subsequent letter from Massimo Bonello. Lastly, by attracting talented students who otherwise would have attended the seminary, the MIA's Academy of Clerics may have lowered the quality of the seminary's student body. There is no firm evidence for these suppositions – Borromeo did not mention his views on the issue, and Cornaro would never have speculated about such sensitive matters in writing. Yet it seems likely that a combination of financial pressure, mediocre students, and too few staff hampered the seminary's performance. Or perhaps Bergamo's seminary was simply like so many others in early modern Italy that found a distinct lack of success in the early decades. In summarizing her research results on select Tuscan dioceses, for example, Kathleen Comerford observes that 'the process of reforming priests and pastors in Tuscany was, at least in the first century after the Council of Trent, less than successful.'[79]

As with other institutions that he found wanting, Borromeo did not simply accept poor performance; he legislated a list of changes to be instituted immediately. In the case of Bergamo's seminary, these mostly reiterated the essence of the Tridentine decrees of session XXIII. For example, the bishop had to redouble his efforts to collect outstanding tax pledges; he must work closely with the deputies elected annually to run the seminary; and he must ensure that the priests in training were properly educated in letters, behaviour, ceremonies, and care of religious relics.[80] In addition, a new set of rules for the seminarians offers a revealing glimpse into seminary life and the strict philosophy promulgated by Borromeo:

• First, that all solemnities are to be observed; that all vigils and holy days are to be marked by fasting; that every Saturday the seven psalms are to be said; that every Sunday all the offices of the dead are to be celebrated in honour of our benefactors.

- That one person shall read at the table in the morning and in the evening.
- That when any person goes outside, he shall observe silence, especially in the city and in the suburbs, so that he gives no cause for scandal, and everyone will walk two by two.
- That every night after the common prayer nobody shall speak to anyone else without permission.
- That nobody will enter anyone else's room by day or by night without permission of a superior.
- That nobody shall sing Neapolitan songs or other lascivious songs.
- That nobody shall write or receive letters without permission from his preceptor.
- That nobody shall buy or sell anything without permission.
- That nobody shall receive either his father or mother nor any other person inside the house.
- That nobody shall keep anything to eat within his locker.
- That Latin is to be spoken both within school and outside of school if that be the will of the teacher ...
- That everyone sitting at the table shall drink no more than three glasses [of wine, presumably] and having left the table, nobody shall be impudent enough to drink anything without permission.
- That no games shall be played except with a ball or with wooden pegs, and those always with permission.
- That upon being summoned in the morning everyone will immediately arise, and make his bed and wash himself in a quarter of an hour, and at the sound of the bell everyone will meet for daily assembly.[81]

To ensure that the new rules would be observed, Borromeo installed a new rector, Massimo Bonello, the parish priest of the church of Sant'Agata. It appears that Bonello was one of the informers who supplied Borromeo with information about the seminary, possibly including the negative comments about its poor governance and low level of achievement. Thus it comes as little surprise that Bonello encountered stiff opposition to the new reforms. Indeed, after only four months on the job, Bonello wrote an angry letter of resignation to Borromeo:

Most Illustrious and Reverend Monsignor,
It pains me greatly to inform your Reverence of new unpleasantness and more insupportable behaviour on the part of those men of the seminary, from whom I would have hoped to be aided, but everything has happened

in such a contrary fashion that I cannot and should not be expected to tolerate any more ... At the present moment I am not able to describe the malice and hatred that they have demonstrated [toward me] in so many ways ... And then the very scornful and arrogant responses of the clerics ... but in truth I finally realized that some of them are a long ways from wanting the reform and that they still wish to preserve their ingrained habits; understanding that I am not equal to the task, I hereby resign.

Your most humble servant, Massimo Bonello.[82]

Bonello would go on to a successful career as an administrator at the Collegio Elvetico (Swiss College) in Milan, and the seminary would find a more successful accommodation with the subsequent rector. Bonello's letter, while obviously biased, does suggest that the seminary staff wished to preserve its way of life, which may account for some of the previous poor performance.

In 1577 Bishop Cornaro was transferred to the more prestigious and profitable bishopric of Padua, and thence to a cardinalate, while Bergamo welcomed its new bishop, Girolamo Ragazzoni. A close friend of Carlo Borromeo and the former bishop of Famagusta (Cyprus), Girolamo Ragazzoni supervised the diocese of Bergamo from 1577 until his death in 1592.[83] He lavished attention upon the seminary and ultimately succeeded in solidifying its financial position. The correspondence between Ragazzoni and Borromeo provides some insight into the development of the seminary, but few other documents are extant. Ragazzoni does not appear to have discussed the seminary in his diocesan synods, for example, nor have many documents from his era survived in the seminary's archive. Nevertheless, it is possible to trace his assiduous efforts to hire teachers for the seminary as well as his endeavours to obtain more benefices.

Despite the city council's rejection of the Jesuits in 1573, Ragazzoni desperately wanted to hire the Jesuit fathers to teach in Bergamo's seminary.[84] Ragazzoni knew how successful the Milanese seminary had been with its large staff of Jesuit instructors, and he had visited other cities in the Veneto and Lombardy where the Jesuits had established successful schools. Thus, in 1578 Ragazzoni wrote to Borromeo to request that the archbishop send some young Jesuits from Milan to Bergamo. In the spring of 1579 Borromeo agreed to Ragazzoni's request and wrote a glowing letter of introduction for a young Jesuit about to graduate. This student – he remains anonymous, though circumstantial evidence suggests that his name was Sigismondo Pellegrino – was proficient in theology, letters, and philosophy, but Borromeo noted dryly that the young man needed to spend more time on his Latin.[85] Ragazzoni agreed to supervise the young man's exercises in Latin composition and style, in return for his assistance 'in the office of maestro' within the seminary. Pellegrino was scheduled to return to Milan to finish his studies in theology and Latin the following year, but it appears that he remained at Bergamo for a total of three years. Pellegrino's own letter of 7 November 1582 implied that he would have remained even longer at the seminary in Bergamo, but Borromeo appointed him as preceptor in the Milanese seminary.[86]

Despite (or perhaps because of) Pellegrino's presence, Ragazzoni continued to write to Borromeo to request more Jesuits to staff the seminary. In the fall of 1579 Ragazzoni implored Borromeo to send him another new teacher. Despite an exhaustive search, the bishop claimed, he had been unable to find even a mediocre teacher, and the school year was about to begin.

> I humbly remind your Grace of the need of my seminary, reassuring you that if I had found or were to find any other means of providing a teacher for the students, I would not have bothered you with this matter. But although I have made every effort and spared no expense, it has not been possible to find even a mediocre teacher for this job. And now the time to gather the boys together in school is drawing near. Wherefore I wish to send this letter as a testimony of my urgent need. I kiss your hand, etc.[87]

Borromeo responded quickly that he did not have any students to spare, as they were either too young or in the middle of finishing their own studies. Over the next decade Ragazzoni continued to request teachers from Borromeo's seminary, but with little success. A Jesuit did come to preach the Lenten sermons in 1585 and 1586, but in 1591, despite a lucrative benefice and the strong support of Bishop Ragazzoni, the Society of Jesus was once again turned away by the city council.

Ragazzoni had more success in convincing Borromeo to intercede on behalf of the seminary's financial needs. In 1578 and 1579 the bishop wrote several letters urging that the seminary be awarded more benefices, either from the abbey of Vallalta in Albino or from the chapel of San Bartolomeo in Trescore (both located on the outskirts of the city). Borromeo made a counter-offer that the remaining four benefices of the church of San Matteo might be consolidated for the exclusive use of the seminary. Ragazzoni immediately agreed. The benefices were worth approximately three hundred scudi per year, and owing to the small number of inhabitants who lived in the parish (many had been displaced by the construction of the new Venetian-built walls), it would not be necessary to maintain a full-time residential priest. Although it took another year or two for the benefices to be transferred, Ragazzoni soon wrote with glee that with this new financial stability guaranteed, 'the seminary is proceeding very well with regard to [teaching] letters and behaviour.'[88]

Given Ragazzoni's close friendship with Borromeo, it comes as no surprise that the bishop promoted the rigour of the Catholic Reformation. In addition to the strict rules we have already seen imposed in 1575, the bishop required one of the seminarians to prepare a reflection on the Gospels every Sunday, and he demanded frequent confession and private meditation. Furthermore, in order to encourage spiritual reflection among the laity and to rein in the temptations for his young charges, he asked the seminary students to put on a sacred play each year during the last days of Carnival.[89] Borromeo had instituted a similar program in Milan, which had brought him into bitter conflict with the civil authorities there, but there is no record of such a quarrel between Ragazzoni and Bergamo's city council.

Ragazzoni's successor, Bishop Giambattista Milani, continued to expand the seminary. In a report submitted to the pope on 16 October 1594, Milani noted that the seminary now enjoyed an annual income of more than seven hundred gold scudi from the many benefices that had been assigned to it. Enrolment had increased to thirty boys, who were being educated 'in the study of letters and of piety, in the acquisition of proper behaviour, in the knowledge of ecclesiastical music, and who serve in the cathedral church on holy days with correctness and devotion.'[90] Milani also rebuilt the chapel of San Matteo between 1595 and 1602.[91] The Venetian captain Giovanni da Lezze recorded forty seminarians in 1596, dressed in red cloaks and black berets. He wrote that the young men were governed and disciplined by their teachers in good letters, and that they would be eligible for ecclesiastical benefices and offices once they had completed their training.[92] Bergamo's next bishop, Giovanni Emo (1611–22), donated some of his personal property in order to found the Accademia Ema, designed to spur competition with the seminary. Bishop Agostino Priuli (1627–32) stiffened the requirements for entry into the seminary, but the number of seminarians still continued to increase slowly, reaching a high of fifty between 1625 and 1650.[93] The most significant physical changes to the seminary occurred under Bishop Luigi Grimani (1633–56), who completely redesigned the chapel and courtyard of San Matteo.

The seminary continued to grow under the care of subsequent bishops, particularly Gregorio Barbarigo, who used Bergamo's seminary as a training ground for the great seminary he would later establish at Padua. By 1700 the seminary had more than one hundred students, by 1800 it had grown to two hundred, and when it was transferred to the hill of San Giovanni in Bergamo, it would grow to over four hundred students.

With one short-lived exception in the late 1560s when the bishop allowed lay boys to be educated alongside the seminarians, the exclusive focus of Bergamo's seminary has always been to prepare young men for the priesthood. However, the students received an education that in many ways resembled that offered to lay boys in communal or confraternal schools. The seminarians read Virgil, Cicero, and Horace, studied Latin and rhetoric, and learned how to write properly in Latin and Italian. They also studied the Roman Catechism, learned how to perform ecclesiastical ceremonies, and were subjected to strict discipline and enclosure during their period of study. The seminary in Bergamo clearly illustrates the impact of the Catholic Reformation upon pedagogical theory. The boys were to be supervised at all times, were not to send or receive letters, were never to exit the seminary without a companion, were to dress modestly, and were to speak Latin at all times. Their physical and intellectual separation from other lay boys was not unusual for Church-sponsored education in the later sixteenth century.

Despite a rocky start, then, the seminary grew slowly to occupy a position of importance in the town. It exchanged students and teachers with other scholastic institutions in Bergamo (e.g., the Somaschans' school of San Giuseppe), and its reputation drew students from such neighbouring towns as Brescia and Clusone. Financial stability was gradually attained through the accumulation of benefices. The extent to which the seminary succeeded in its primary mission – to reduce ignorance, incompetence, and heresy by improving the discipline and knowledge of priests and parishioners alike – awaits further research in parish and episcopal archives. Even if Bergamo's seminary trained only a small percentage of the priests within the diocese, that surely made a difference. The best proof may lie in the fact that the seminary outlived its competitors, chiefly the MIA's Academy of Clerics, and for four centuries has continued to be one of the most important examples of Church-sponsored education in Bergamo.

Conclusion

In conclusion, although the methods and the audience diverged widely, both the Schools of Christian Doctrine and the diocesan seminary
were able to meet the Catholic Church's goal of expanding education
in the sixteenth and seventeenth centuries. Inspired by the Council of
Trent and assisted by Carlo Borromeo, these two institutions promoted
education to a wide audience. The role of Bergamo's bishops, particularly Federico Cornaro and Girolamo Ragazzoni, was fundamental in
encouraging these two initiatives. Both men recognized the importance
of reaching out to children and of instructing them in the Catholic faith.
Such instruction might be at the most elementary level for just two
hours per week in a country chapel, or it might be a decade of intensive
training in Latin grammar, rhetoric, music, liturgy, and cases of conscience. In both cases, the Church benefited from a more knowledgeable audience and more literate priests.

The resurgence in Church-sponsored education did not happen in
a vacuum, of course. Both the Schools of Christian Doctrine and the
seminary had to interact with the commune, and both had to contend
with Venetian and Milanese oversight. Even if there is no extant record
of enmity or rivalry, the seminary surely competed with the other institutions in town for students, teaching staff, and financial resources.
Yet the seminary and the Schools of Christian Doctrine are unusual in
that neither formed an explicit partnership with other institutions in
town. The Schools utilized lay teachers, of course, but made no contracts with the confraternities or the commune. Nor did the seminary
(with one exception) partner with other groups or associations. Such
isolation is in stark contrast with the approach adopted by the Somaschans, who sought to share responsibility for instructing boys with the
town and the MIA. In any case, the Church's goal remained the expansion of education and religious faith. That goal would be further met by
the achievements of new religious orders of men, especially the Somaschans and the Jesuits, to whom we turn next.

4 *Chiesa*: Schooling with Jesuits and Somaschans

Having examined the seminary and the Schools of Christian Doctrine, we turn now to the role of the Jesuits and the Somaschans in early modern Bergamo. These two religious orders were well known in northern Italy and enjoyed steady growth in membership and influence. Each 'company' reflected the particular interests of its respective founder: Ignatius Loyola of the Jesuits and Girolamo Miani of the Somaschans. Ironically, neither man considered education of youth to be a primary goal at the outset. Miani wished to provide charity to destitute children and reformed prostitutes, while Loyola sought to lead a small band of followers to the Holy Land. Spurred by specific requests from town councils, Loyola was the first to accept schooling as a vital function, and the Jesuits have remained schoolmasters *par excellence* for more than four centuries. Miani, too, soon recognized that teaching orphans was an effective way to preach the Gospel and to improve the virtue of the Christian faithful, although only well after his death did Miani's society agree to supervise actual schools. The Somaschans never enjoyed the spectacular growth nor the (in)famous reputation of their Jesuit brethren, and even today the Somaschans remain a modest organization in comparison with the high-profile universities and missionary work of the Society of Jesus. In the mid-sixteenth century, however, the two groups still resembled each other and were surrounded by a burgeoning number of other religious orders devoted to similar goals. We have already examined the Theatines and their contribution (albeit brief) to communal education in Bergamo. The Ursulines, the Piarists, and the Barnabites were not significant in Bergamo until the eighteenth century and thus do not appear in our analysis here.

The Somaschans arrived in Bergamo in 1532 to establish twin orphanages and a shelter for former prostitutes. For the next one hundred years the orphanages remained their primary focus. In 1632, following a devastating plague, the Somaschans agreed to supervise the communal school and continued to do so through the eighteenth century, albeit with some difficulty. The Jesuits' first contact with Bergamo occurred in 1569, and it intensified in 1573 when the fathers asked permission to establish a college in Bergamo. That request was rejected, as was a subsequent petition in 1591. Not until 1711 would the Jesuits finally arrive in Bergamo, and that experience, too, ended badly. On the surface, then, the Somaschans were more successful in Bergamo while the Jesuits encountered repeated failure.

As we consider the success and failure of Jesuits and Somaschans in Bergamo, however, it is important to analyse their achievements in light of what we already know. These two groups clearly represent the post-Tridentine resurgence of the Catholic Church, as well as the increasing importance of education across all segments of society. They will illustrate efforts at cooperation among diverse institutions on behalf of education, as we have seen previously with the MIA and the commune. This is not to suggest that such cooperative efforts were always successful; the Jesuits and the Somaschans sometimes quarrelled bitterly with other institutions in Bergamo and Venice. The power struggle between Milan and Venice is also evident in these two religious orders; the Somaschans were more closely associated with Venice, while the Jesuits blossomed in Lombardy. The chronic instability that we have seen in civic- and confraternal-sponsored schooling is, to some extent, evident in the experiences of Jesuits and Somaschans. Certainly, both orders found their achievements (or lack thereof) in Bergamo to be strongly influenced by Bergamo's economic fragility. It is more difficult to ascertain whether the Jesuits and Somaschans can be used to exemplify aristocratization. Both offered schooling free of charge to students, at least initially, and both declined extravagant buildings or large endowments. Both were targeted to assist with the communal schools of Bergamo and enjoined to assist poor boys. Such examples suggest that these two religious orders helped to promote a sort of 'democratization' of learning by making it more readily available. Yet the Jesuits were often associated with the education of princes and aristocrats at court, and elsewhere even became private confessors to European monarchs. The Somaschans, too, seem to have veered toward education of the nobility in the mid-seventeenth century. Here as in other areas, the example set by Bergamo is both representative and idiosyncratic.

Boethius, *Opere* (Venice, 1497). Sitting at his desk, this cleric copies a manuscript from a large volume propped on a stand by the window of his room. Another large volume, partially obscured by a bishop's mitre, stands on the shelf behind the column. The inscription on the base of his chair reads 'De Voragine' and probably indicates a reference to Jacopo de Voragine (1230–98), the Dominican friar and archbishop of Genoa best known for his compiling of the *Golden Legend*.

The Jesuits, 1571–1729

Despite a lucrative benefice, substantial political support, and repeated petitions, the Society of Jesus was unable to establish a permanent presence in Bergamo during the sixteenth and seventeenth centuries. This failure stands in marked contrast to the Jesuits' success in founding colleges elsewhere; by the turn of the seventeenth century, the Jesuits supervised forty-nine colleges in Italy and were recognized as the leading schoolmasters of Europe.[1] The Jesuits, who offered free instruction in Latin grammar, rhetoric, and humanities, were frequently hired by princes or communes to assume direction of local schools. Bergamo's poverty and inability to consistently support communal education would appear to make the city a perfect candidate for the Jesuits' assistance. Bergamo's city council boasted frequently of its devotion to the Catholic faith and repeatedly invited Jesuits to preach Lenten sermons. The archbishop of Milan and the bishops of Bergamo both supported the entry of the Jesuits, and the pope issued an apostolic letter in favour of their acceptance. Why, then, were the Jesuits repudiated in Bergamo?

No single motive suffices to explain the Jesuits' inability to establish a college in Bergamo for more than 150 years. Rather, we must examine a variety of reasons, some obvious and others less so. This search will require us to consider sources spread over three centuries and scattered in Bergamo, Rome, and Venice. Why does the *absence* of a school matter when so many others were present? First, an analysis of this issue brings into clear relief the relationship between Venice and her dominion cities. It shows that although Venice generally permitted cities in the *terraferma* a free hand in matters of local education, the Republic did not hesitate to intervene if it felt that its interests were threatened. Second, Bergamo's rejection of the Jesuits, contrasted with its acceptance of the Somaschans and the Theatines a few years later, helps to elucidate just what the city fathers were seeking from outside educators. This example of powerful institutions and individuals jockeying for position within Bergamo not only provides insight into the city's internal politics but once again underscores the importance of education in early modern Italy. In addition, the issue is intriguing from a methodological point of view. In order to illuminate the Jesuits' inability to establish a presence in Bergamo, I follow Marc Bloch's suggestion of 'reading history backwards,' or using documents from a later period to speculate about attitudes and beliefs of Bergamo's residents during an earlier period for which documentation is scarce.[2]

The analysis is divided in two parts. The first reconstructs the chronology of events from the initial contact in 1569 to the Jesuits' ignominious departure in 1729. The second proposes a number of explanations for the failure of the Jesuits to establish themselves in the city. The latter section is more speculative, as it attempts to uncover the motivations and prejudices of the principal individuals and institutions involved in these decisions. The reasons for the Jesuits' rejection were not tied to a particular year or a specific event; thus a full understanding of the sequence of events is necessary before turning to possible explanations.

The first indication of Jesuit interest in Bergamo comes from a letter written on 3 January 1569 from Bishop Federico Cornaro to the Jesuit Father General's secretary in Rome, Juan Polanco. In thanking Polanco for having sent Father Carlo Faraone to preach a series of sermons in Bergamo's cathedral, Cornaro noted the 'strong desire that has emerged not only in me but in all of the city to have a house of the [Jesuit] fathers here.' Cornaro indicated that he had already found an excellent site for the Jesuits to live, with a beautiful church and ample room for later expansion. In addition, he promised an income sufficient to support six or eight people. This benefice was almost certainly the one associated with the church of San Bartolomeo in Rasulo, about to be vacated by the Humiliati.[3] A bit later in the same letter, Cornaro states explicitly that 'I am ready to take any steps necessary in order to have a Jesuit house here, to which in time a college can be added. And furthermore I will ensure that this college will have the means to live comfortably, in such a way that the fathers can be sure that they will lack nothing.'[4] Cornaro added that the presence of a Jesuit college would serve many purposes, but he stressed assistance in the seminary and further expansion of Christian education for Bergamo's youth. Within a few days Polanco replied that the Jesuits' other obligations made it impossible for them to come to Bergamo. Disappointed, Cornaro promised to continue his search for benefices to support a Jesuit school in Bergamo 'so that a college can be introduced here to the honour of God and of this city.'

In 1573 the Jesuits changed their mind and submitted a formal request to Bergamo's city council to establish a house and college in Bergamo. In a deliberation of 14 August 1573, the council recognized the strong desire of the bishop to bring the Jesuits to Bergamo and promised to give the matter careful consideration. In an unusual parliamentary manoeuvre, the council proposed two similar motions in the same session: one to elect five deputies to consider the expediency of admitting the Jesuits to the city, and another to open negotiations with the

Jesuits and work out the details of their entry into the city. Both motions sparked fierce debate; while the arguments raised are not recorded in the minutes, the secretary noted that there was much discussion among the members of the council. The secretary even took the unusual step of noting that the decision would be made according to a majority of votes cast by the council. Subscribing to the will of the majority may seem self-evident to us, but it was probably an attempt to avoid any confusion over the procedures and ultimate resolution of such an important debate. The first proposal appears to be more cautious, in merely proposing a subcommittee to consider the issue, while the second called for more immediate negotiations with the Jesuits. In the event, both proposals were defeated, although the vote was quite close: 32–38 for the first motion, and 29–41 for the second.[5] The Jesuits' first attempt to enter Bergamo was thus rebuffed.

Six years later Bergamo's next bishop, Girolamo Ragazzoni, wrote to Carlo Borromeo to request some young Jesuits from Borromeo's own seminary in Milan.[6] His letter of 1579 implies that he had tried to solicit Jesuit teachers or preachers from elsewhere in Italy but had been unsuccessful. As we have seen in chapter 3, Borromeo agreed to Ragazzoni's request and sent Sigismondo Pellegrino to study Latin and to assist at the seminary.

Ragazzoni's interest in the Jesuits did not end with their activities at the seminary. He also wished to bring them to Bergamo to assist with evangelization in the mountain and valley regions of the diocese, an area notorious for witchcraft and Protestantism.[7] Perhaps Ragazzoni also hoped that the Jesuits would assist with the Schools of Christian Doctrine, or offer a few of the sermons and debates for which they were becoming famous. He almost certainly shared the desire of his predecessor Cornaro that the Jesuits might eventually open an independent college in Bergamo.

Carlo Borromeo himself had tried to recruit Jesuits to come to Bergamo. During his 1575 visitation, the archbishop indicated that he very much wished to open an Academy of Clerics similar to his own school in Milan. Within a few weeks, the Jesuit secretary had responded to Father Francesco Adorno in Milan to state that 'being unable to accept the offer, we shall send some [Jesuit] missionaries instead.'[8] Several months prior to Ragazzoni's first request of 1579, Borromeo had also written to his friend Monsignor Speciano at the papal court to enquire about the feasibility of a Jesuit house in Bergamo. Speciano replied to Borromeo on 26 November 1578 that 'the Society was inclined to accept the offer of a house.' Speciano pursued the matter with another cardinal in Rome, but in the event was unable to secure an agreement.[9] Thus it appears that the powerful support of Carlo Borromeo was firmly behind the plan to bring the Jesuits to Bergamo.

In September 1585 the city council's 'deputies of religion' wrote to the Jesuit Father General in Rome to request the services of Father Lodovico Gagliardi for the cycle of Lenten sermons. According to the effusive letter of the city council, Gagliardi had impressed the entire town with his eloquence during a brief visit, and the deputies wished to have him return for a more extended stay. Lacking a reply, the deputies wrote again to Rome to repeat their request for Father Gagliardi. Ironically, the deputies listed as one of their chief reasons the fact that 'this city has never had the opportunity in the past to demonstrate its loyalty to the most worthy Society of Jesus.' The Father General responded affirmatively to this request for a Jesuit preacher in Bergamo in 1585 and again in 1586. Thus it appears that the city council did not object to short-term visits by members of the Society. Indeed, the council actively recruited Jesuit preachers, even in the face of initial denials by the Father General.[10]

In addition to the above, the Jesuits had the enthusiastic support of aristocrat Cavalier Giovanni Girolamo Grumelli and his wife. According to a letter from Father Achille Gagliardi to Father General Claudio Acquaviva early in 1585, the Grumellis insisted that prior to the order's arrival in Bergamo, the Jesuits must have 'at least 1000 scudi as well as their own church and a furnished house.' The Grumellis promised to raise the necessary funds and even proposed a specific benefice that could be transferred to the Jesuits. Padre Achille Gagliardi's letter of 1585 further notes that 'all of these negotiations occur with the greatest of secrecy,' which may explain why there is no allusion to it in the city council records. By September of 1585, just as the city council was writing to request Father Lodovico Gagliardi, Grumelli and Acquaviva had come to an agreement, and Grumelli promised once again that he 'eagerly awaited the chance to do all that was needed to achieve a successful outcome.'[11]

The most important moment in this story, however, occurred in August 1591. On 15 August Pope Gregory XIV issued an apostolic letter, *Cathedram militantis Ecclesiae*, authorizing the foundation of a Jesuit college at Bergamo.[12] The Jesuits were granted the benefice of the church of Santa Maria in Misma, about ten kilometres east of Bergamo in the town of Cenate, which amounted to approximately 120 gold scudi per year.[13] With the support of the pope, the bishop, the archbishop, the deputies, and some of the populace, the admission of the Jesuits appeared to be a foregone conclusion. Acknowledging the assignment of the benefice in favour of the Jesuits and declaring their admission to be a matter of 'the greatest importance,' on 31 August 1591 the council promised to devote all of its attention and care to the matter. In an ominous foreshadowing, however, the council simultaneously pointed out the potential for 'extreme disorder' if caution were not exercised regarding this decision. Once again the council proposed two motions. The first was to elect five deputies charged with taking all steps necessary to avoid public disorder during and after this decision. The second motion was to elect another five deputies to 'advise, consult, and consider whether it would be expedient or not to introduce the Reverend Fathers into this magnificent city; and to gather diligently information about how the Reverend Fathers have been introduced into other cities of the Serene Republic; and having carefully considered and consulted the facts, to submit their opinion to this magnificent Council so that this affair can be wisely decided by the good government of this City.'[14] Although the first motion passed by a vote of 37–33, the second motion was defeated 29–41 (interestingly, a distribution of votes virtually identical to the decision taken twenty years earlier). Thus for a second time the Jesuits' bid to establish themselves in Bergamo was defeated. The council deliberations are maddeningly vague with regard to the precise reasons for the defeat of the motion.

Five months later, the Jesuit Father Maggio sent a letter to the Venetian ambassador withdrawing the Society's claim to the benefice of Santa Maria in Misma, effective immediately. Maggio noted that the Jesuits 'do not think it reasonable to enter into somebody else's house against his will.'[15] Maggio then went on to apologize for the apostolic letter of Gregory XIV, claiming that it had been issued without proper authorization by the Father Provincial, who wished to promote the Society's entry into the city. However, it appears that the Society did not entirely give up hope. Ten years later the captain of Bergamo, Almorò Nani, confirmed an order of the Venetian Senate denying the request of the Jesuits to occupy the church of Santa Maria in Misma.[16] This suggests that the Jesuits still hoped to convince the Bergamasque city council to grant them permission to enter.

Any hope of reaching an accord with Bergamo was dashed with the Interdict of April 1606 against Venice. Angered by the Venetian Senate's punishment of two clerics, Pope Paul V forbade the administration of the sacraments within the borders of the Venetian Republic, and instructed all religious orders to leave immediately. The Jesuits temporized for a short while but eventually abandoned their schools in Padua, Verona, and Brescia. Despite – or perhaps because of – their absence, the Jesuits spoke out vigorously against the Venetian government, and in return the Senate prohibited its subjects from any kind of oral or written contact with the Society. Conversation with the Jesuits, threatened the Senate, could result in permanent exile from all Venetian lands. This edict applied to all residents of Venetian territory, but it was directed particularly at noble parents, who were accustomed to sending their children to Jesuit schools.[17] In compensation, the Venetian Senate instructed the governors of Bergamo and other mainland towns to do everything possible to find 'good, brave, and learned men' to teach in the Schools of Christian Doctrine.[18] After protracted negotiations, the pope and the Venetians agreed on a compromise that permitted the return of all religious orders *except* the Society of Jesus.[19] Six years later, the Venetian governors in Bergamo confirmed to the Council of Ten that they had publicly announced the prohibition against sending children to the Jesuit schools.[20] For the next century there is virtually no news of the Jesuits in Bergamo. The Society was readmitted to the city of Venice in 1657 and returned to teach in Padua, Brescia, and other cities of the *terraferma*. In 1661 the Jesuits petitioned for the use of a house in the village of Borgo a Terzo, several miles northeast of Bergamo's upper city. Once again the city council refused to grant admission.[21]

The year 1711 marks a watershed in the history of the Jesuits at Bergamo. The Misericordia Maggiore called the Jesuits to succeed the Barnabites in administering the Collegio Mariano, and the city council voted promptly to approve their entry. Even more important than the approval of the MIA and of Bergamo's city council, however, was the agreement of Venice. In a request to the Senate dated 25 July 1711, Bergamo promised that there would be no more than ten Jesuits, that they would all be of Venetian origin or citizenship, and that they would come to Bergamo only to teach.[22] Clearly, Venice was determined to restrict appointments within the republic to her own citizens. Not only did Somaschan and Jesuit teachers have to be of Venetian origin, but in 1639 a Florentine nominated as abbot of the convent in Astino (Bergamo) was politely but firmly excused by the Venetian Senate.[23] The Jesuits were admitted to the city and immediately assumed direction of the Collegio Mariano.

In 1719, despite some apparent misgivings, the Society agreed to stay on for another ten years. Contemporary sources hint that by then there were already problems with low enrolment and steep tuition hikes. However, the greatest problem arose in 1720 from a most unlikely source: the testament of Count Giovanni Battista Bonometti, who left his house and twenty thousand scudi to the Society upon the condition that it maintain a college in his house. If the Jesuits were not able to found and maintain a college, the estate would pass to the control of the Ospedale della Maddalena, in support of its work caring for the insane and the disabled.[24] Naturally the Ospedale's director, Coriolano Brembati, immediately contested the validity of the will. The case became a *cause célèbre* in Bergamo from 1720 until 1729, when the city council finally ruled in favour of the Ospedale. In the same year that the City Council decided in favour of the Ospedale della Maddalena, the Jesuits were fired from their job by the MIA, and the Society left the city in disgust.

In contrast to the late sixteenth century, numerous extant sources from the early eighteenth century document the Jesuit experience in Bergamo. In addition to correspondence between the Jesuit fathers in Bergamo and Rome, the deliberations of the city council contain frequent entries concerning the Society. The deliberations often incorporate verbatim the reports submitted by council deputies or by the litigants. Two private epistolaries, Count Bonometti's testament, and ducal decrees from Venice each contribute to the documentary record. An anonymous manuscript from the late 1720s entitled 'Information concerning the introduction of the Jesuits to Bergamo' offers a polemical, anti-Jesuit interpretation of these events, while a nineteenth-century account by librarian Agostino Salvioni called 'Recollections of the Jesuits in Bergamo' offers a much more balanced view.[25]

These later documents, if used with caution and in combination with sixteenth-century sources, can shed light on the Jesuits' unpopularity in the sixteenth and seventeenth centuries. Although the historical context of early eighteenth-century Bergamo is quite different from that of a century earlier, the arguments presented by the friends and foes of the Jesuits are eerily similar. Perhaps both sides felt freer to speak out at the dawn of the Enlightenment than they had at the crest of the Catholic Reformation. Litigation and testaments also tend to generate more of a paper trail. And of course the Jesuits' bid to enter the city in the eighteenth century was successful, resulting in more documentation. The later documents occasionally comment on the reasons why the Jesuits were rejected in an earlier period, or draw explicit comparisons between the two eras.

As noted above, few sixteenth-century sources address the rejection of the Jesuits directly. Typical is the account reported by Monsignor Speciano, the Roman agent of the archbishop and cardinal Carlo Borromeo. When Speciano presented the idea of a Jesuit college in Bergamo to Cardinal Albano circa 1575, the latter replied only that 'a matter of such importance needs much more time to mature.'[26] Let us consider four possible rationales for the exclusion of the Jesuits, in greater detail than did Cardinal Albano. First, political fears and personal antipathy influenced powerful patrons in Bergamo and Venice against the Jesuits. Second, negative economic consequences (i.e., impoverishment of Bergamo's own schools and charitable organizations) appear to have fostered some opposition to the Jesuits. Third, the stance of the Misericordia Maggiore and its substantial influence on civic affairs must be considered. Lastly, several miscellaneous issues – including civic pride, the availability of alternate schools, and scandalous Jesuit behaviour – may have tipped the balance against the Jesuits. Categorization of this type is clearly artificial and obscures the natural overlap among the different factors, but it is a useful analytic tool.

Politics – on both a local and a regional level – played a critical role in the exclusion of the Jesuits from Bergamo. Despite their reputation as consummate insiders when it came to royal and ecclesiastical politics, the Jesuits blundered by not establishing relationships with Bergamo's city council. Agostino Salvioni, a nineteenth-century Bergamasque librarian and historian, noted that the Jesuits were not related to any of the sixteenth-century city council members by blood, and therefore the council had refused to consider the Society's request.[27] In an interesting twist, the anonymous author of a polemic written against the Jesuits in the 1720s claimed that the Jesuits were finally accepted at Bergamo in 1711 precisely because 'a copious number of relatives of the Jesuits, despite being specifically barred from voting on these matters ... [nevertheless] were blinded by their blood relationship with this order.'[28] In addition to concerns of nepotism or favouritism, the deputies of the city council complained in 1722 that the Jesuits had tried earlier to bypass the appropriate channels by appealing directly to Venice and to the neighbourhood of San Leonardo where the college would have been located.[29] It is not unlikely that the Jesuits might have wished to evade lower-level officials in an attempt to have their petition approved more quickly. Viewed in this light, the Jesuits' strong support from the archbishop of Milan and the pope in the late sixteenth century may have only antagonized the city council deputies.

A second political factor was fear of the disorder that might result from the admission of the Jesuits. Both of the sixteenth-century deliberations emphasize the fractious nature of the debate, just as accounts from the eighteenth century highlight the 'very tumultuous and bitter arguments in this communal council.'[30] One source lamented 'the chaos that has destroyed the harmony of the inhabitants and has divided them into enraged factions.'[31] While the Jesuits were recognized as excellent teachers, they were also controversial on account of their doctrinal rigidity. The Jesuits' allegiance to the pope, and their perceived orientation toward the Spanish monarchy, were both political liabilities in Bergamo. With the Duchy of Milan under Spanish control just a few kilometres to the south, Bergamo's city council was nervous about admitting such 'foreigners' into the city. Thus, for fear of civil discord and political repercussions, Bergamo's city council may have decided to decline the free schooling and stirring sermons that the Jesuits could have provided.

Venetian antipathy to the papacy, coupled with the perception that the Jesuits were *papalini* (papal disciples), constitute additional reasons why Bergamo might have distrusted the Jesuits. The Venetian Senate had closed the Jesuit school in Venice within six years of its founding in 1551. As we have seen, following the resolution of the Interdict crisis in 1606 all religious orders except the Jesuits were permitted to return, and the Senate continued to prohibit any kind of contact between Venetian subjects and the Jesuit fathers. When the Jesuits were finally admitted to Bergamo in 1711, the Venetian Senate insisted that all ten of them be Venetian subjects. In his 1592 *memoriale* to the Venetian ambassador, the Jesuit secretary Father Maggio pointed to regional politics as a key factor:

When your Excellency spoke to me some weeks ago with regard to the matter in Bergamo, letting me know that the Most Serene Signoria, with all due respect, did not look favourably upon the proposed college and would certainly prefer that we withdraw the idea, I responded to you in my own name and in the name of the Father General that your Excellency might assure the Signoria, as we have assured them, that we will immediately intervene in this affair and will not take any further action, for we do not think it reasonable to enter into somebody else's house against his will ... On account of the esteem and reverence that we hold for you, I assure you that we do not expect to found a college without your specific blessing.[32]

Although it is true that the deliberations of Bergamo's city council do not specifically mention Venetian influence, the Venetian podestà and capitano routinely chaired council meetings and their mere presence would have reminded council members of Venice's distrust of the Jesuits.

Additional pressure to exclude the Jesuits from Bergamo also came from an unlikely source: Pietro Alzano, the Bergamasque rector of the law faculty at the University of Padua. Resolutely anti-Jesuit, Alzano appears to have played an important role in guiding the opposition of law professors to a Jesuit college in Padua or Venice – and perhaps also in Bergamo. Elected rector in 1591 and assassinated just a year later, Alzano nevertheless influenced the composition of a deputation sent to present the law school's position to the Venetian Senate in 1591. Nor was Alzano alone – many of the professors in Padua banded together in 1591 to voice their opposition to a Jesuit college there. According to Maurizio Sangalli, who has studied the Jesuit presence in the Veneto with great care, Alzano's opposition to the Jesuits appears to have had its origins in a 'personal aversion' stemming from his Bergamasque roots. No firm documentation exists to support such a theory, but the bad blood between Bergamo and the Jesuits by 1591 must have influenced Alzano.[33]

Economic concerns appear to have been another of the chief reasons why the entry of the Jesuits was repeatedly rejected. Bergamo lacked both natural resources and trade, and the city fathers did not want to see Bergamo's limited assets drained in favour of the Society of Jesus. The sixteenth-century Venetian governors of Bergamo routinely declared that Bergamo could only produce enough grain to support itself four or five months out of the year. The governors also commented on the relative poverty of Bergamo's noble class, which in comparison to those of Brescia, Verona, Venice, or Milan possessed little land and less capital.[34] In a report dated 28 February 1722, the deputies of religion specifically referred to the events of 1573 and 1591 to sustain their claim that Bergamo's meagre resources (*tenue patrimonio*) could not support a new religious order.[35] The anonymous author of the 1720s commented that 'the introduction of that religious order [i.e., the Jesuits] would be too prejudicial to the economy of this poor and limited land.'[36] In particular, he mentioned the Society's habit of coming empty-handed to a new city even when it had possessed a well-furnished house in a previous location.

In its deliberations, the city council regularly displayed a preoccupation with minimizing expenses. When negotiating with the Somaschans or with individual teachers, for example, the council always made certain to specify its maximum contribution. The commune's joint project with Bishop Soranzo in 1556 was predicated upon specific cost controls. At times this tight-fisted attitude seems almost comical. But it also reflects the stark reality of a provincial city that often existed on a precarious edge between survival and starvation. The irony, of course, is that the Jesuits offered *free* education; indeed, this was one of their signature characteristics and a major cause of their rapid expansion. As Paul Grendler has noted, municipal governments intending to foster education usually saved money and time by bringing in a religious order.[37] Despite the Jesuits' promise to offer 'grammatica, rettorica, et humanità gratis,' Bergamo apparently remained nervous about the associated expenses and negative financial impact of accepting the Jesuits.

Aside from the capital outlay for a building in which instruction could take place, there were other ways in which a city's limited assets could be strained when a new religious order was introduced. These new groups would compete with other pious institutions in the city for testamentary gifts, and inevitably more potential recipients meant fewer bequests for each organization. The quarrel over the Bonometti legacy, for example, pitted the Jesuits against the Ospedale della Maddalena. The anonymous author of the treatise *Informazione* pointed out that if the Ospedale were granted the property, not only would the Ospedale and its patients benefit from the income, but current residents would not be displaced. In contrast, he claimed, the Jesuits would build a 'monument of stone' of little benefit to the city.[38] Among many alleged cases of Jesuit cupidity, this author described the case of Luigi Donatis, a Bergamasque who had supposedly planned to donate ten thousand scudi to his nephew but who was convinced on his deathbed by a Jesuit priest to alter his will. Some of the claims in this document are clearly exaggerated: for example, that the Jesuits had amassed ninety thousand scudi plus an untold number of testaments before even being admitted to Bergamo. Nevertheless, it seems reasonable to conclude that Bergamo's city council might have feared the Jesuits' potential to siphon away donations from other institutions. Venice apparently shared this fear, for a ducal letter of 1619 decreed that the Jesuits were no longer permitted to receive bequests within the republic.[39]

Protecting the *luoghi pii* (charitable organizations) of the city was particularly important because of their role as a social 'safety net' for the city and countryside of Bergamo. As our anonymous author noted early in his treatise, the arrival of the Jesuits could threaten their income: 'In our own time [early eighteenth century] various substantial legacies have not been distributed to poor families and pious institutions, but instead have been shifted to that religion; so that if that religion had not stuck out its hand, these benefices would have gone to the universal benefit of the city, the territory, and especially of the poor.'[40] Following a similar logic, this author concluded that opposition to the Jesuits was good not only for individual citizens but also for the general public. The city council may have feared that if the *luoghi pii* became impoverished, the city council might have to take up some of their charitable and educational responsibilities. In its final deliberation concerning the Jesuits in Bergamo, on 26 May 1729, the city council announced that it had decided to overturn its contract with the Jesuits 'not only because of inheritance issues but also for many other notorious consequences.'[41]

One of these 'consequences' may have been the Jesuits' poor management of the school. According to a contemporary source,

> even the supporters of the [Jesuit] fathers agree that the boarding college is a great detriment; whereas when the schools were governed by secular priests, the college counted more than 100 students because it cost only 35 or 36 scudi, at the present moment there are fewer than 20 students on account of the substantial increase in fees for lodging and other expenses demanded by the fathers, which amount to 100 or more scudi per student. This fact makes the families realize that it's better to send their children outside the city. And all this, despite an annual salary of 1000 scudi from the Misericordia, and a free house with furniture and tools.[42]

Given the polemical environment of the 1720s, such a claim must be examined with care. It appears to be true that fees increased and enrolment dropped during the Jesuits' tenure, although perhaps not to the extent claimed here.[43] Since the Jesuits were never admitted in the sixteenth century, however, we cannot assume that financial mismanagement was one of the reasons for their rejection.

A third factor in the exclusion of the Jesuits in the sixteenth century may be found in the conspicuous silence of the Misericordia Maggiore. As we have seen, the Misericordia was deeply involved in all aspects of education in Bergamo and contributed regularly to joint projects. When the Somaschans were assigned responsibility for running Bergamo's public schools in 1632, the MIA made an annual donation of fifty scudi; when the Somaschans proved unable to teach rhetoric, the MIA paid for an additional teacher. It was the express invitation of the MIA in 1711 that finally brought the Jesuits into Bergamo, and it was the MIA's termination of that contract that contributed to their expulsion twenty years later. Thus one might reasonably expect the MIA to have stated an opinion in 1573 or 1591; instead there is only silence. Perhaps the MIA, fearing competition with the Jesuits, worked quietly to deny their entry. Or perhaps the MIA's long-term relationship with the Dominicans in Bergamo prejudiced them against the Jesuits. Whatever the reason – and the sources are silent on this point – the MIA's attitude was surely crucial in influencing the outcome.

In addition, miscellaneous concerns about the Jesuits troubled the Bergamaschi. Parents may have seen the creation of a Jesuit college as unnecessary given the proximity of Jesuit colleges in Milan and Brescia. Furthermore, the extensive schooling network available in Bergamo did not leave much room for the Jesuits to establish a niche of their own. Civic pride and a reluctance to relinquish control of communal schools may also have motivated the council to look unfavourably upon the Jesuits. In looking back at the sixteenth century, Agostino Salvioni declared that Bergamo wished to run its own schools, and for this reason rejected the Jesuit bid: 'our old government itself attends to every branch of public instruction; it supports famous professors, it provides textbooks, it maintains discipline, it prescribes rules and ensures their execution.'[44] Salvioni's observation contains more than a grain of truth, but he is also romanticizing the city council's involvement by overstating their commitment to public education in the waning decades of the sixteenth century. Closely related to civic pride was Bergamo's sense of 'local religion,' a Catholicism centred around its own churches and pious organizations, which remained hostile to foreign influence.[45] To a certain extent this *campanilismo* (parochialism) is to be expected; every Italian city and village wished to defend its own institutions and protect its inhabitants. Bergamo was also following the example of Venice, which categorically refused to consider nominations for bishoprics in the Veneto if the candidates were not Venetian patricians. Bergamo's position as a 'frontier city,' caught between the politico-religious struggles of Milan and Venice, might have exacerbated its concern about admitting 'foreign' orders of men and women.

There is also the curious fact that the benefice of Cenate, intended to support the Jesuits in Bergamo, was offered simultaneously to a competing religious order. The holder of the benefice, Leone de Cucchi, had volunteered circa 1585 to surrender the benefice in favour of the Jesuits in return for a pension for himself and his nephew, and a promise that Cenate would never be left without a priest in residence. Apparently angered that the 'secret negotiations' with the Jesuits were not proceeding as planned, Leone de Cucchi offered the benefice to the Somaschans. In their general meeting on 12 April 1587 in Pavia, the Somaschans agreed to accept the offer of a benefice at the church of Santa Maria in Misma along with other conditions specified in the offer. One year later, on 1 May 1588, the Somaschans again announced their willingness to accept this benefice and the Somaschan fathers currently in Vicenza were ordered to move to Bergamo. Despite continued interest by the Somaschans, the benefice was never actually transferred. When word of this controversy leaked to Venice in 1591, it cast a poor light on the Jesuits, who were seen once again as rapacious and conniving. The Jesuits' position was worsened by the fact that the Somaschans were viewed as a 'local' religious order. This affair may also have influenced the rector Pietro Alzano in his opposition to the Jesuits.[46]

Lastly, a pair of scandals involving Jesuit fathers in Bergamo may have damaged the Society's reputation and thus hindered their entry. In 1577 Bergamo's bishop wrote to Father General Everard Mercurian concerning a certain Lorenzo Condivi, who had been living 'an irregular life' while teaching at the Milanese college. Condivi's errors were not specified, but he moved to Bergamo and begged the bishop to help him obtain release from the Society.[47] A more significant scandal concerned Francesco De Sanctis, who forged a letter of introduction to Bishop Ragazzoni in April 1583 which claimed that he was a secular priest from Macerata. Assigned by the bishop to a parish in the Bergamasque mountains, he was discovered four months later to have been a Jesuit for twelve years; he had left his position as vice-rector of the college in Siena under cover of night the previous May after stealing fifty scudi. Ragazzoni immediately wrote to the Jesuit fathers in Milan, who instructed him to hand over De Sanctis to the Jesuit authorities in Brescia for punishment. Ragazzoni explained that if the affair had been kept secret in Bergamo, he could have transferred De Sanctis with ease, 'but being that the news is already widespread, and that many serious crimes are committed in my own diocese each year by secular priests who are outside their cloister, I do not see how I can graciously fulfil your request without some prejudice to my own tribunal and without setting a bad example.'[48] Such scandals may well have contributed to the Jesuits' poor reputation in Bergamo just as the council was preparing to decide upon their application for entry. The reputation of the clergy during this period remains nearly impossible to ascertain with any certainty. However, a series of events in Bergamo from the sixteenth century indicates that a shortage of qualified priests was perceived as a problem. The primary reason for the foundation of the MIA's academy in 1506 and again in 1566 was to provide better-trained priests for the church of Santa Maria Maggiore. Carlo Borromeo's apostolic visitation in 1575 criticized the behaviour and education of quite a few ecclesiastics, while the triennial reports submitted to Rome by Bergamo's bishops contained numerous references to dissolute priests. The Jesuits present an interesting case in this regard: they had a positive reputation as learned, strict, and devoted to their work, but at the same time their obedience and strict observance made them unpopular with many laypersons and also with some elements of the Roman Curia.

In conclusion, what does the rejection of the Jesuit order tell us about education in Bergamo? It would be possible to interpret the rejection of the Jesuits as simply a rejection of the need for schooling, but such a conclusion would be misguided. As demonstrated above, political and economic factors, combined with a dash of xenophobia and the MIA's silence, clearly contributed to the city council's unease about admitting Jesuit teachers. Equally important, however, was the availability of other schooling options. Bergamo's educational network permitted parents to look beyond the possibility of a Jesuit college and to embrace the myriad options already available. This example also shows that while Venice did exercise control over a few educational matters in the *terraferma*, the city council was at liberty to make its own decision. The Jesuits enjoyed the support and cooperation of some – but not all – institutions in Bergamo. As the next example of the Somaschans illustrates, Bergamo's city council clearly preferred that local teachers educate the city's youth.

The Somaschans, 1532–1659

The Somaschan Fathers played an important role in the education of Bergamo's youth through their management of orphanages and public schools. Beginning in 1532, they provided instruction in reading, writing, catechism, and 'Christian living' to boys and girls from a range of social backgrounds. During the first century of their residence in Bergamo, the Somaschans concentrated exclusively on caring for orphans and reformed prostitutes. In 1632 they agreed to take charge of a public school in Bergamo and to found a 'College of Nobles' where Latin grammar, rhetoric, and humanities would be taught. Given the absence of the Jesuits and the Barnabites in Bergamo until the beginning of the eighteenth century, the Somaschans represented an important conduit for the dissemination of Tridentine ideas to students and parents alike. Furthermore, the Somaschans' experience clearly demonstrates the intricate network of schooling in Bergamo: the MIA, the seminary, the city council, and the Somaschans collaborated to educate Bergamo's youth. The Somaschans' experience in Bergamo was far from tranquil – the documents report arguments, litigation, and threats of expulsion – but their continued presence testifies to their positive contributions.

The history of the Somaschans begins with Girolamo Miani (or Emiliani), a Venetian nobleman who renounced his aristocratic background and responsibilities in order to dedicate himself to works of charity.[49] Influenced by Gaetano da Thiene and Gian Pietro Carafa (later Paul IV), as well as by the devastating combination of plague, famine, and war that swept through the Veneto in the 1520s, Miani founded a hospital and an orphanage in Venice in which he instructed the orphans in their ABCs and paid artisans to teach them a trade.[50] In 1531, despite the protests of his family, he donated all of his possessions to his nephews, donned rough and oversized peasant clothes, and set out to found orphanages elsewhere in the Veneto. After brief stays in Verona and Brescia, Miani arrived in Bergamo in the spring of 1532, whereupon he founded a boys' orphanage, a girls' orphanage, and a house for reformed prostitutes.[51]

Miani immediately received the enthusiastic support of Bergamo's bishop, Pietro Lippomano, who sent a circular letter to the diocese to announce Miani's intention to provide 'instruction, training, and tutelage, as well as spiritual and corporal nourishment to any poor, sick, or desperate person, male or female, and especially for widows and orphans.'[52] Bergamo's Hospital of San Marco provided the wood necessary to construct twenty beds for the orphans, and three years later offered space in its own building to the male orphans at a rent of twenty-nine lire per year. The female orphans and the reformed prostitutes (convertite) were housed in the parish of Pozzo Bianco and supervised by prudent noblewomen of good reputation.[53]

The female orphans and reformed prostitutes were always housed in a separate building from the male orphans. The presence of former prostitutes in such a fashionable part of town caused some consternation among the neighbours, and episcopal visitations document several cases of concubinage and public promiscuity involving Miani's wards.[54] Nevertheless, both groups lived in the parish of Pozzo Bianco until around 1547, when the *orfanelle* (orphans) moved to the Caserma Monteluogo on Via San Giovanni all'Ospedale, where they remained for centuries: the *convertite* (ex-prostitutes) moved to Borgo San Leonardo and later to Borgo Sant'Antonio near the church of Santo Spirito. Around 1556, with the support of some noble benefactors, the male orphanage acquired a building just below the fort of Santo Stefano, known as the 'orfanotrofio de San Martino vecchio' (old orphanage of St Martin). In 1599 the orphanage acquired a property from the Suardi family but as a result of squabbles with the city council and with the Benedictines, it subsequently moved in 1614 to a nearby residence owned by the Caspi family.

Miani wished to devote himself exclusively to the educational aspects of the orphanage but recognized quickly that he would need assistance. Therefore he established two groups of supporters who jointly administered the orphanage: the Company of Servants to the Poor, and the Deputies of the Company. The former were admirers of Miani who renounced all their worldly possessions in imitation of the apostles and dedicated themselves to charity. Holding various offices in turn (lieutenant, guardian, reader, nurse, etc.), the Company of Servants lived together in poverty with the orphans. Following Miani's death in the village of Somasca in 1537, the members of this Company called themselves the Somaschans and were officially recognized as a religious order in 1568 by Pope Pius V.[55]

In contrast, the Deputies of the Company – also known as the Company of Merchants and Nobles, and drawn largely from the lay confraternity of Santa Maria Maddalena – were all laymen. The deputies were responsible for administering the financial affairs of the orphanage, examining orphans about their studies, and placing them in appropriate jobs when they left the orphanage. The deputies held various positions in turn (president, treasurer, minister, secretary, etc.) and met weekly, plus three times per year (Pentecost, All Saints Day, and Annunciation) for formal meetings. The deputies supervised all three institutions, even though they were sometimes administered separately. While members included the bishop of Bergamo and representatives from Bergamo's most important families, the deputies also included such members of the artisan class as the tailor Girolamo Carminati and the swordmaker Angelo di Scanzo.[56] This dual system of governance worked well until 1597, when a quarrel between the deputies and the Somaschans forced the city council to assign a mediator to settle disputes.[57] Nevertheless, this system did allow Miani and the Somaschans to concentrate their efforts on the education of orphans and prostitutes in their care, and it was rapidly imitated by other Somaschan orphanages in Lombardy and the Veneto.

Who were the orphans? The answers might help us to compare these children with those we know from other sources in Bergamo, and thus learn more about who was likely to be educated. Unfortunately, no comprehensive list survives to document the names of those admitted to the orphanage(s) in Bergamo. We know the identity of certain orphans who were asked to write letters about Girolamo Miani in support of his canonization, but such letters reveal little about the orphans themselves.[58] Later admission requirements to the orphanage mandated that children be destitute of both parents, healthy, able to work, and between the ages of seven and thirteen. Children of the city were always preferred, but all had to provide a record of baptism and proof of legitimate birth, a health certificate attesting that they did not suffer from contagious diseases, and two letters of recommendation.[59] It seems unlikely that Bergamo's orphans came from the upper levels of society, a supposition confirmed by the type of education that they received and the jobs that they ultimately held.

Education in the Orphanages

The orphanages founded by Miani were intended to equip young boys and girls with the skills necessary to be productive members of society. As the *Regole* (Rule) of Bergamo's orphanage put it, orphans have 'training in religion and in other necessary skills provided to them, all in an effort to make them useful to themselves, to their homeland, and to the state.'[60] Recognizing that each child had different aptitudes, the Somaschans allowed and even encouraged orphans to pursue different types of training, 'in religion or in letters or in honest work,' according to the ability of the individual child.[61] In 1620 the Somaschans' *Ordini per educare li poveri orfanelli* (Instructions for educating poor orphans) reflected the same philosophy: 'for example, induct him into a religious order, or assign him to service in a church, or to work for a merchant, or for a famous, well-regarded artist.'[62] The historian Giuseppe Landini has viewed Miani's orphanages as 'a first attempt to dispense elementary education among the common people.'[63]

Religious instruction was of primary importance within the orphanage. Miani insisted upon daily prayer, catechetical instruction, and an

assembly (*udienza*) in which the orphans were lectured about morality and virtue. Silence was required at meals so that the reader of the
orphanage might read excerpts from religious texts. Orphans were required to recite a prayer upon rising from bed in the morning and just
before going to sleep at night. Miani drilled his orphans so that they
might visit the Bergamasque countryside to instruct peasants about the
life of Jesus Christ. All members of the orphanage participated in daily
lessons of Christian doctrine, in which students repeated their lessons
aloud to each other or recited dialogues by rote. A 1549 decree insisted
that 'the teaching of Christian doctrine to our children be attended to
with great seriousness.'[64]

A second fundamental aspect of Miani's philosophy was his insistence upon hard work. Vocational education was an integral part of his
vision for improving the life of his orphans. His letters make clear that
not only were the orphans expected to learn a trade, but the adults too
were expected to work diligently. Miani castigated any of his colleagues
who appeared to be loafing and introduced the simple rule, following
Saint Paul, that those who did not work should not eat. Orphans who
did not work quietly, carefully, and productively were to be sent to the
hospital or expelled from the orphanage. When the boys' orphanage
was forced to move several times at the end of the sixteenth century,
the Somaschans specifically looked for a house where the local artisans
would be willing to accept apprentices from the orphanage.[65] Each orphanage emphasized a different type of work, depending upon local
industries, available materials, and the abilities of the orphans. In Venice, for example, the orphans produced iron pitchers, in Brescia they
sewed berets, and in Bergamo they teaseled wool and plaited straw to
make hats.[66] Usually the work was supervised by one of the Somaschans, but occasionally an outside master would be hired to teach the
boys a particular trade. When the orphans reached eighteen years of
age and were ready to leave the Somaschans, they frequently accepted
one-month trial contracts with these local tradesmen.

Orphans were provided with basic instruction in reading, writing,
and arithmetic in order to improve their chances of obtaining a good
apprenticeship. These lessons were given within the orphanage by the
lay Deputies and by the Somaschans themselves. In a letter of 1536 to
Messer Ludovico Viscardi in Bergamo, Miani exhorted his companions
to be vigilant in teaching the boys to read. He wrote, 'Do not trust the
boys to read by themselves: supervise them, interrogate them, examine them, and pay careful attention to how often they read and recite.'

In the same letter Miani instructed Viscardi to identify boys who excelled at Latin grammar and to pass this information along to Alexander Besozzi, one of Miani's companions, presumably so that such boys could be tutored at a more advanced level. This letter underscores the importance of reading in the orphanage, as does Miani's injunction that the designated 'reader' of the orphanage was to read 'as frequently as possible during the course of the day.' An anonymous friend of Miani's from Venice recalled a visit to one of Miani's orphanages, where Miani proudly pointed out a group of eight-year-old boys 'who knew how to read well and to write.'[67] In a chapter meeting presided over by Miani in the mid-1530s, one of the rules for the orphanage was that 'one must [always] remember the reading lesson.'[68] The *gubernator et rector* (governor and rector) was responsible for visiting the orphans frequently to correct their mistakes and to ensure that they were reading diligently.[69] This strong emphasis upon the acquisition of literacy suggests that such a skill was not a luxury in sixteenth-century Italy, but rather a necessity. Miani and the Somaschans understood that some of their orphans would be limited to a career of manual labour, but they clearly saw the potential for others to use reading and writing to advance themselves. From such limited evidence we cannot draw conclusions about literacy rates, but it is significant that even penniless orphans in sixteenth-century Bergamo had an opportunity for education.

Although reading and writing instruction was occasionally combined with catechetical instruction, Giuseppe Bonacina has observed that one of the unusual aspects of the Somaschan orphanages was their tendency to separate primary schooling from religious instruction.[70] While it is probable that the majority of students never achieved anything more than basic literacy in the vernacular, this simple attainment could set them apart from their illiterate peers. Even if the level of instruction within the orphanages never equalled that in the public schools and colleges administered by the Somaschans, a minimal degree of literacy remained important.[71]

The Somaschans' orphanage possessed a library containing 134 texts, which served as a resource for both the Somaschans and the orphans.[72] An inventory prepared in February 1600 shows a preponderance of religious texts including sermons, catechisms, psalms, commentaries, and other 'spiritual' works. The medieval saints Aquinas, Bonaventura, and Bernard of Clairvaux are represented here along with Peter Lombard's *Sentences* and Thomas à Kempis's *De imitatione Christi*. Sixteenth-century works are present too, such as the *Summa doctrinae christianae* of Jesuit

Peter Canisius (1574) or the decrees from the Council of Trent. Clearly intended for the Somaschan fathers rather than the students was a trio of manuals about exorcism, including the *Flagellum demonum exorcismos terribiles* (1589), as well as Gerolamo Savonarola's 1517 manual on how to perform confession. Although few in number, several classical works appear in the library's collection including Ovid's *Metamorphoses*, Terence's *Six Comedies*, and Cicero's *On Offices*. Other works were clearly intended for the orphans: an introduction to literature by Gabriel Pedocha (1550) and a *Libro primo delle lettere* by Antonio di Guevara (1560). Half a dozen grammar books, a 1588 edition of *Vocabulista ecclesiastico latino e vulgar*, and a schoolbook on learning Latin by Juan Luis Vives serve as a reminder of the importance the Somaschans placed upon education of the orphans. Most of the books were published in Brescia or Venice, but several have a distinctly local flavour, including the 1586 *Methodus Grammatices* written by Nicoló Cologno and published in Bergamo by Comino Ventura, or the famous dictionary of Ambrogio Calepio that appeared in multiple editions during the sixteenth century. In short, while the library is modest in comparison with those of the Franciscans or Dominicans in Bergamo, it clearly reflected the religious and educational goals that the Somaschans had set for the orphanage.

Female orphans, although housed separately, were apparently provided with the same type of basic schooling as boys. The *Regole* for the girls' orphanage in Bergamo have been lost, but the earliest extant rules from the girls' orphanage in Milan (circa 1580) clearly indicate that attending school was an important part of the daily schedule. The woman in charge of the girls' orphanage divided the girls among the various women who volunteered at the orphanage for instruction in reading and catechism. She was to make sure that instruction began and ended promptly, that the girls were making progress, and that the teachers were performing their duties. Toward the end of the sixteenth century music was added to the girls' curriculum to complement lessons in reading and catechism.[73] Since female orphans were usually faced with the standard choice of *maritar o monacar* (marrying or becoming nuns), the deputies were prepared to provide small dowries when the girls left their care.

The rules and regulations adopted by Miani and the Somaschans confirm the importance of schooling for orphans. Miani himself left few letters and no written rule, perhaps because he was in such a rush to carry out charity with his own hands; as one of Bergamo's twentieth-century bishops observed, '[he] moved so quickly that we must call him a fire starter rather than a seed planter.'[74] The *Ordini* (Regulations) compiled in 1547 offer one of the first references to education in the orphanages: 'Then it was declared that all sites should be visited twice per year, and that the visitors should talk seriously with the well-behaved and intelligent students in order to persuade them to learn Latin.'[75] Furthermore, all orphans were expected to attend two hours of study, one in the morning and one in the afternoon; they had to recite their lessons at the table when called upon by the teacher so that each student said something every day. Among the earliest versions of the *Regole*, probably written between 1550 and 1555, chapter 7, 'On admitting the orphans to grammar [instruction] and orders,' directly addresses educational aims:

> All of the orphans who are competent must be taught to read and write. But those whom the priest and the director shall judge capable of learning and profiting from the study of grammar, with the approval of the visitor, shall be admitted to such study after they have learned to read well; however, they are not excused from manual labour beyond the time required for such study, nor from the rules that apply to the other orphans ... And after it has been determined that they are making progress in their letters and moral virtue, they can be relieved from their other labours and placed in a school of letters, with the goal of making them clerics.[76]

Like the schools run by the MIA, the orphanage wished to prepare some of its students to serve the religious needs of the larger community. It is not surprising that the Somaschan-run orphanages would designate some of their charges for the priesthood – indeed, what seems unusual is the Somaschans' willingness to prepare children for such a variety of careers, from ecclesiastical and domestic to vocational and academic.

An official statement of 1560 declared 'in all orphanages let the smart children be taught to read the alphabet, [to study] the Latin grammar of Donatus, and to write down the holidays.'[77] The 1568 *Regole* included a chapter that specifies the teaching of Latin grammar as one of the expected activities within a Somaschan orphanage.[78] A 1571 *Decreto* noted that 'the ministers can teach the orphans to read and learn good arts without sending them to work in shops.'[79] The *Constitutiones* declared that the teaching of reading and writing must occur daily: 'at least once during the day let the orphans read, and write according to their ability, encouraging and exhorting each one of them to increase his own knowledge so that he can leave with a good understanding.'[80]

The earliest *Regole* for Bergamo's orphanage date from 1597. Oddly, they do not specifically mention anything about schooling or instruction. However, we know that the Somaschans, like other religious orders of the Catholic Reformation, sought uniformity in their activities. Thus it seems probable that the decrees, rules, and practices observed in other Somaschan orphanages or houses would have been observed in Bergamo as well. In addition, we possess *Regole* for Bergamo's orphanages from the eighteenth century that describe in detail the type of instruction provided in the orphanage. Perhaps such instruction was a later innovation, but more likely these later *Regole* simply codify pre-existing practice. According to the eighteenth-century *Regole*, the orphans were taught by the rector and by the house treasurer (*Reverendo Economo*) to read, write, and do figures. Instruction was offered every night from the first of November until Easter. After Easter the lessons were reduced to once a week, and Sundays and holidays, until the end of October. Exceptional students were to be referred to the deputies, and, circumstances permitting, promoted to a more advanced Latin school. Interestingly, while the Somaschan fathers appear to have done most of the classroom teaching, it was the Deputies who actually examined the students, recorded their progress, and decided upon promotions. The deputies conducted examinations twice per year, at Easter and in August. At that time the orphans were asked to read aloud and to solve some arithmetic problems. The deputies examined the student notebooks, encouraged them to continue learning, and provided unspecified rewards for good performance.[81]

From Orphanages to Schools

Boys and girls in all Somaschan orphanages clearly received a mixture of spiritual, vocational, and academic instruction. In 1583 the Somaschans assumed control of a lay boarding college, the Collegio Gallio in Como, a development that persuaded them to open other schools, including the Collegio San Giuseppe in Bergamo. Before examining that institution, however, it will be useful to consider briefly three specific examples of Somaschan schooling in Somasca, Pavia, and Milan. These examples illustrate how the Somaschans began the transition from orphanage to school between the mid-sixteenth and the mid-seventeenth century.

In 1544 the Somaschans had transformed the orphanage founded at Somasca into a grammar school. For three years this school also admit-

ted elite local boys who wished to become priests. In 1547, however, the
Somaschans prohibited local boys from attending so that the orphans
might receive greater attention from their teachers.[82] The creation of
a grammar school dedicated to training future members of the order
was a response to the ever-increasing demand upon the Somaschans
to staff orphanages. The concept of a seminary in which young boys
could be trained in common in letters, morality, and the ecclesiastical
offices was not unique to the Somaschans, of course. Nevertheless, it
is worth noting that the Somaschans helped to pioneer this concept in
mid-sixteenth-century Italy.

The Somaschans' desire to open a separate, special grammar school
for their own orphans anticipated another sentiment of the Council of
Trent and the Catholic Reformation, namely, the desire to separate secular from ecclesiastical education. As archbishop of Milan and apostolic
visitor to Bergamo in the 1570s, Carlo Borromeo championed this concept, and as we have seen it was a general tenet of the Catholic Church
that seminary education should be distinct from 'public' schooling. In a
statement made by the Somaschan General Congregation of the Protec-
tors of the Orphans during the 1547 chapter meeting, this philosophy of
separation is abundantly clear: 'It was ordered again that steps be taken
to place the boys in good academies, or else to send them to lessons
with good teachers for the purpose of enlightening them, and not [to
send them] to the dangerous and public schools.'[83] Although this order
was issued during the general chapter meeting of the Somaschans, it
was a statement of the *lay* deputies. Thus both the deputies and the
Somaschans wished to offer a distinct and separate educational opportunity for boys intent on a career in the Church. Examples from Pavia
and Milan further illustrate the development of Somaschan pedagogical practice and offer some comparisons with Bergamo's orphanage.

Less than a year after the 1547 chapter meeting, the Somaschans
founded a 'mini-Seminary' in the university town of Pavia. Under the
direction of Angiolmarco Gambarana,[84] the Somaschans had been directing an orphanage known as the Colombina and a home for widows
in the parish of Santa Maria Maddalena. For several years the Somaschans had wished to establish a 'professed house' where members and
acolytes could 'attend to spiritual matters, to mortification, and to sacred studies.'[85] At the same time the city and the bishop of Pavia were
searching for a way to better instruct their own chierici. Therefore, on
9 April 1548 the city asked the Somaschans to send two of its members
to instruct both chierici and the sons of local gentlemen who had fallen

from good habits into bad.[86] The city praised the Somaschans' success as teachers in Milan and Somasca, and the Somaschans responded by sending a rector and several teachers to Pavia.[87]

Given the large number of orphans in and around Milan, the Somaschans quickly began searching for a place to establish a similar school. In 1561 the Congregation of Somasca resolved 'to accept the house of Signor Giacomo d'Adda in Triulzio ... in order to teach and train twelve or more poor orphans in reverence for the Lord and in letters, so that they can become priests and scholars.'[88] The donation included a two-storey house with a courtyard, a well, a vegetable garden, and the small church of Santa Croce di Triulzio, all located about four miles outside Milan's Porta Romana. A petition outlining the objectives and structure of the school, dated 26 February 1561, was accepted by King Philip II of Spain and in 1563 the school opened.[89] As elsewhere, the Somaschans taught the boys to read, and women were strictly forbidden inside the house gate. This school was essentially a branch of the Milanese orphanage, designed to tutor more advanced students. One of the first *maestri* to teach at Santa Croce di Triulzio was Giovannipaolo da Seriate, who had grown up in Bergamo's orphanage of San Martino. The school remained small and rather unimportant until it closed between 1625 and 1627, perhaps owing to its isolation or perhaps because of the deteriorating military situation around Milan.[90]

A similar but much more successful school known as the Colombara was founded in the 1560s through the generous donation of Girolamo Dugnani, one of the deputies of the Somaschans' Milanese orphanage. Dugnani offered 660 lire and the use of three houses 'in order to support the literary studies of ten orphans eager to undertake the religious life.' The house was sumptuous, with the furniture alone valued at six thousand lire. After selling most of the furniture in order to build a chapel dedicated to San Martino, the Somaschans constructed two dormitories, a classroom, and three storage rooms (*cantine*). Dugnani provided detailed and continuing direction regarding how his bequest ought to be administered. According to him, orphans might be accepted from Milan or the surrounding area at the discretion of the rector. Students were to be chosen 'with extraordinary care' in order to admit 'the most motivated and the most intelligent orphans.'[91] Although the exact curriculum remains something of a mystery, a seventeenth-century document entitled 'The Origins of the Orphans of San Martino [of Milan]' noted that 'beyond lessons in letters, they will have responsibility for sending them to lessons in Christian Doctrine.'[92] The boys probably followed a curriculum of study similar to that offered in other Somaschan orphanages, but with a greater emphasis upon Latin grammar and literature. Several of the orphans went on to become important professors, including Giovanni Mezzobarba of Pavia, professor of rhetoric at the University of Turin at the end of the sixteenth century.

Despite the substantial donation offered by Girolamo Dugnani, the Somaschans at the Colombara had trouble meeting their budget. The deputies therefore decided to accept seven boarding students at a fee of forty ducats per year, who would live and study in common with the seven orphans and two Somaschan fathers. The boarding students were usually the sons of noble families seeking a good education. Despite the deputies' admonition that the needs of the orphans must always take precedence, the school deteriorated to the point where only three orphans were in residence, resulting in temporary closure in 1635. Four years later the deputies agreed to give the house to the Somaschan order, which would pay an unspecified rent and teach orphans selected by the Deputies. Under the new arrangement, the deputies no longer bore official responsibility for the Colombara. Although the number of orphans in 1639 remained low, the number of noble boys jumped to between ten and twenty; all were there 'for their moral and religious education, and to receive instruction in letters suitable to their condition.'[93] The school continued in this fashion for approximately 150 years, until the building was sold in 1785 to the merchant Francesco Visconti.

This transition from orphanage to school was echoed in Bergamo too. The orphanage of San Martino in Bergamo moved repeatedly in the sixteenth and seventeenth centuries as a result of bequests, military construction, financial difficulties, and a bitter quarrel with the Benedictine nuns near the church of Matris Domini. Ample documentation exists about these transfers and relocations, but that material does not pertain directly to the question of education in Bergamo. One example will suffice to demonstrate that education continued to be important in Somaschan orphanages throughout the seventeenth century. An addendum to the 1776 *Regole* of Bergamo noted that 'having completed the competition among the students in grand style, it was decided on 3 December 1664 to require the maestro to teach sixty students, with an increase in salary of fifty-six lire.'[94] It should be clear by now that the Somaschans valued vocational, academic, and moral instruction. During the sixteenth century their primary activity was oriented towards orphanages and charitable works, but they would soon embrace other challenges.

The Collegio San Giuseppe in Bergamo

The Somaschans opened their first school in Como in 1583, followed by the Collegio Clementino in Rome in 1595.[95] Given Miani's Venetian origins and the strong presence that the order maintained in the Veneto during subsequent centuries, it is ironic that the Somaschans established their first two schools outside the Veneto. Fearing that it would compromise their other work or displease the pope, the Somaschans were initially reluctant to accept responsibility for administering communal schools. In 1596, for example, the chapter meeting responded to one Monsignor Ferreri that 'the Somaschan Fathers would gladly take on responsibility for the orphans in the city [of Biella] ... but recuse themselves from teaching school and running a dormitory, this being completely contrary to the will of his Holiness.'[96] Having overcome their initial hesitation, however, the Somaschans taught rich and poor students, ran day schools and boarding colleges, and administered both lay schools and clerical seminaries. They opened a boarding school in Padua (1606), a school for nobles in Brescia (1628), a communal school in Bergamo (1632), and still another school in Verona (1639). They even relented and agreed to open a school in Biella (1632). In response to Tridentine guidelines the Somaschans also agreed to manage selected seminaries in the late sixteenth century, but without a great deal of success.[97] Despite invitations to open orphanages in Germany, Austria, and Spain in the 1620s, the Somaschans chose to concentrate their efforts in Italy.[98] By 1650 the Somaschans were specializing in the teaching of poor and middle-class boys who could not pay the fees for a private college, but who instead attended public schools sponsored by the commune. The communes generally agreed to pay the minimal expenses necessary to sustain the Somaschan teachers and to procure a building for the school.

In Bergamo, despite the Somaschans' steady service in managing the orphanages, there is no record of them as schoolteachers until 1631. In December of that year, the city council recognized the desire of the Somaschans to manage the public schools of Bergamo and immediately elected three council members to conduct negotiations. The council selected the Somaschan order for several reasons. The order was a familiar presence in Bergamo; indeed, the council noted that the order 'had suckled its first milk' in Bergamo's territory and that Bergamo's countryside now provided a resting place for the glorious bones of Girolamo Miani.[99] Furthermore, the 'paternal zeal,' frugality, and good reputation of the Somaschans in other cities of the Veneto encouraged the council to accept them. The initial deliberation of 5 December 1631 is blunt about the other reason(s) why the city council rushed to hire the Somaschans to manage the city schools at this time: 'Recognizing the desire of the illustrious podestà to establish public schools where grammar and humanities can be taught by the Reverend Somaschan Fathers, and motivated furthermore by the desire to promote the public welfare, especially in these times when a majority of the schoolmasters have died of the plague.'[100] The great plague of 1630–2, chronicled by Bergamo's secretary Lorenzo Ghirardelli (whose account was later immortalized by Alessandro Manzoni's famous novel *I Promessi Sposi*), killed more than half the population, closed numerous schools, and substantially disrupted trade. It is significant to note that the three deputies elected by the council were empowered to negotiate with other religious orders or teachers if that seemed appropriate to the public interest. The Somaschans must have satisfied the deputies, however, for on 24 April 1632 the city council proposed a contract between the Somaschans and the city.

The contract spells out the responsibilities of the city and of the Somaschans in ten brief chapters.[101] The city promised to provide a house and a church inside the city walls where the Somaschans could live and teach. The church of San Pancrazio, 'third in beauty and second in age among the churches of Bergamo' and with an income estimated to be in the thousands of scudi every year, was designated for the Somaschans' use. The order was to receive 150 scudi per year plus additional fees from students. In return, the Somaschans were to instruct the youth of the city and territory of Bergamo in Latin grammar, humanities, and rhetoric. The city emphasized that, although the Somaschans did not have to accept total beginners or students who were not well dressed, the order should emphasize the instruction of poor boys. In addition, the city insisted that 'at their earliest convenience the Somaschans are required to erect a College of Nobles so that students of noble families and good breeding might be educated.' It is worth noting the distinction made by the city council here between the two social classes it desired to educate: poor boys and noble boys should both be educated, but not together. No clearer example of 'aristocratization' can be found than this explicit segregation by class. The city council also expressed confidence in the teaching ability of the Somaschans and hope that they would remain in the city for some time. The contract was weighted heavily in favour of the city: the deputies reserved the right to visit the schools, to review all cases of admission and expulsion, and to terminate the contract if the Somaschans were judged insufficient in any one of a number of ways.

The city council made it very clear that it did not wish to pay more than one hundred scudi per year for the management of these public schools. Indeed, the Somaschans were chosen in part because of their frugality. In order to demonstrate their commitment to minimizing the financial outlay by the city council, the deputies cited the example of the famous Athenian orator Lycurgus. Lycurgus had been criticized by his fellow citizens for providing too high a salary to the Athenian teachers of rhetoric, whereupon he offered to donate half of his own wealth to these teachers so that Athenian youth could still be well trained. The deputies claimed that while Bergamo's city council doubtless harboured this sort of generous sentiment, under no circumstances would the rent of the Somaschans' living quarters exceed forty scudi per year, nor the total salary exceed one hundred scudi per year.[102] The MIA volunteered an annual contribution of fifty scudi to make up the difference, though as we will see shortly, this payment became a bone of contention soon after the Somaschans began to teach.

In addition to the 150 scudi from the city and the MIA, the Somaschans were allowed to accept money from their students. These fees were to be paid in advance, and on a scheduled determined solely by the council.[103] While the council guaranteed a minimum of 150 scudi per year to the Somaschans, it also decreed a maximum annual income. If the Somaschans received a total of 200 scudi, they had to pay the rent for the house in which they were teaching; if they received 350 scudi, they had to refuse any further gifts from students. Although the initial contract required the Somaschans to teach extra lessons if they reached this maximum income limit, the final version of the contract excluded this clause.

The contract concentrated on delineating specific details of finance and administration as outlined above. Yet the deputies also took the opportunity to demonstrate their own classical education by including several rhetorical flourishes. The example of Lycurgus represented one allusion to the Graeco-Roman world. Another occurred at the very beginning of the contract, where the deputies describe two opposite views of schooling. In contrast to a Spartan mother who was more concerned with the physical appearance of her four sons than with their intellectual development, the people of Athens prized education of both mind and body. The deputies then praised the members of Bergamo's city council for similarly ensuring proper instruction for Bergamo's youth. A third example can be found in an oration given by one of the Somaschan fathers upon the opening of the school in Bergamo. Luigi Cerchiari offered numerous classical references and examples of the benefit of schooling to youth in earlier times. He focused particularly on the theme of *Cedant arma togae* (Let arms yield to civilian dress), an appropriate theme for 1632 given the bloody war in Mantua and the widespread pillaging in northern Italy by the German Landsknecht troops. In an effort to compliment his hosts, Cerchiari also cited such famous Bergamasque scholars as Alberico da Rosciate and Torquato Tasso.[104] Such classical references were common in the late fifteenth and early sixteenth centuries; their presence here in the seventeenth century not only demonstrates the continuing fascination with the Graeco-Roman world, but underscores the type of education both the deputies and the Somaschans sought to offer.

The contract was sent to the Somaschans' general chapter meeting in Cremona for approval in the beginning of May 1632. The Somaschans, finding parts of the contract to be 'excessive and prejudicial to the liberty of our Congregation,' suggested a number of changes regarding the amount of compensation, the location of the church, and the expectations for instruction.[105] The city council accepted a few of these changes and immediately wrote to Venice and Rome to request permission for the Somaschans to begin teaching in the fall of 1632. Pope Urban VIII responded on 15 May that the Somaschans might enter the city for the purpose of establishing a school.[106] Doge Francesco Erizzo also responded on 15 May that the Somaschans would be allowed to enter Bergamo, but only for the purpose of instructing children.[107] Thus they were not permitted to use the church of San Pancrazio and its attendant benefice, nor could they found a church or monastery elsewhere in the city. The doge further instructed the Venetian governors of Bergamo to inform him of the subsequent details regarding the entry of the Somaschan fathers in order to ensure that the wishes of Venice were being followed. (Direct parallels with the response to the Jesuit petitions of a half-century earlier are self-evident.) The doge's response reflected the concern of at least one member of the city council, Alessandro Adelasio, who complained that Bergamo had no business admitting new religious orders into the city when those already there were poverty-stricken and starving. Adelasio claimed that if the Somaschans were given the wealthy benefice of San Pancrazio, they would quickly lose interest in teaching. Curiously, Adelasio cited Philip II of Spain as a 'very great and most prudent monarch' who understood that it was better to have just a few well-run religious orders than many that were poorly run.[108]

The city council amended the contract to observe the wishes of Venice, and assigned the Somaschans a house in the parish of San Michele al Pozzo Bianco. The house belonged to the noble family of Giorgio and Alvise Passi, who asked a rent of forty scudi per year. A week later, however, the deputies discovered that the house had previously been rented to soldiers and as a result was practically uninhabitable. Since neither the city nor the Somaschans wished to invest a substantial amount of capital in rebuilding the house, the deputies were authorized to find another house in the same neighbourhood for a similar price. The exact location of the new house was never specified, but twenty-five years later the Somaschans were still teaching in a house owned by the Passi family in the same parish. The revised agreement was formally executed on 30 June 1632, and on that day the Somaschans entered the city.[109]

The Somaschans' public school was formally known as the Collegio San Giuseppe (College of Saint Joseph). It remained in the parish of Pozzo Bianco until 1659, when it was transferred to the lower city and renamed the Collegio San Leonardo after its new neighbourhood. The Collegio San Giuseppe was often referred to in the seventeenth century as the 'Somaschan public schools' (*scuole pubbliche dei Somaschi*). The use of the plural is a bit mysterious at first, because there was only one institution. Within the college, however, there were several 'schools' (i.e., a school of Latin grammar, a school of humanities, a school of rhetoric), a form of internal organization confirmed by subsequent visitations of council deputies.

In accordance with the instructions of Venice, the Collegio San Giuseppe was founded in 1632 as a day school. In 1633 the general chapter meeting prohibited the establishment of new boarding schools, while permitting those already in existence to remain. Nevertheless, in response to Bergamo's repeated requests of 1635, the Somaschan general chapter instructed Paolo Carrara to visit Bergamo to determine 'whether the necessary arrangements have been made so that this Congregation can safely erect a residential school (Collegio dei Convittori), in conformity with our own rules for the education of boarding students.'[110] Carrara's report does not survive, but shortly thereafter the Collegio San Giuseppe indicated an income of 110 scudi per year from its boarding students. It appears that the Collegio San Giuseppe simply added a residential facet to its pre-existing day school, rather than founding a separate College of Nobles. The absence of a College of Nobles in Bergamo is puzzling. Perhaps sufficient funds were not available for a second college, or perhaps local parents decided to try mixing different social classes after all.

The curriculum of the Collegio San Giuseppe reflected both the priorities of Miani and those of the city council of Bergamo. As noted above, Miani believed fervently that children needed training in religion, work, morality, and grammar if they were to succeed in life. The city council wished to prepare students for university study and a future career while simultaneously conserving its own financial resources. The precise curriculum was not specified during contract negotiations. Unlike the Jesuits, who published a *Ratio Studiorum* in 1599 outlining the subjects and methods to be followed and the various responsibilities of each teacher, the Somaschans did not compile a formal description of their pedagogy until the *Methodus Studiorum* of 1741.[111] The *Methodus* was intended to be a guide for teachers, a sort of recommended reading list for works of Latin grammar, history, geography, Greek, Italian, philosophy, logic, physics, geometry, and theology.

Despite the absence of a formal guide to Somaschan pedagogy prior to the eighteenth century, it is possible to reconstruct the curriculum and methods in use at the Collegio San Giuseppe in Bergamo. Visitation reports, contracts and correspondence, treatises on education, and comparisons with other colleges each help to illuminate the lessons taught by the Somaschans in the parish of Pozzo Bianco. The city expected the Somaschans to teach 'good letters,' 'Christian piety,' and 'proper behaviour.' More specifically, the 1632 contract called for instruction in grammar, humanities, and rhetoric. These were standard topics in Italian schools of this era. The Somaschans, the Jesuits, and the Barnabites, along with public and private schoolteachers everywhere in Italy, were generally expected to teach students to read, write, and figure, as well as to behave in a socially appropriate and Christian way.

Instruction in Latin grammar was fundamental for any student who wished to proceed to more advanced study. A number of different texts and horn-books existed with which students could enhance their knowledge of the classical language.[112] The Somaschans were fond of a grammar book entitled *De Institutione grammatica* by the Portuguese Jesuit Manoel Alvarez (1526–85), published in many editions and officially recommended for the Somaschan Collegio Clementino in Rome.[113] Students also read letters of Quintus Curius, Valerius Maximus, and Cicero. The founding bull of the Collegio Clementino contained a specific rule mandating the study of Latin grammar; such a rule would have applied also to the college in Bergamo. Students were expected to study the etymology of Latin verbs and nouns with the objective of conjugating and declining them, as well as being able to explain the rapport between Latin and Italian words. Students were further expected to be able to demonstrate knowledge of the topics discussed by the Latin authors, and to summarize in a few words the explanations offered by their teachers. This level of Latin instruction appeared to be fairly basic. Although a visitation in 1657 clearly showed the Somaschan fathers teaching elementary reading and writing at the Collegio San Giuseppe, such instruction was not part of their original contract. Indeed, the Collegio San Giuseppe was designed for students who had already mastered the basics of Latin grammar and who wished to study at a more advanced level. The 1632 contract with Bergamo specified that the Somaschans 'were not required to accept students in their school ... who do not know at least how to decline [nouns] and conjugate [verbs], match noun and adjective endings, and perform other simple tasks in Latin.'[114]

Once students had mastered the basics of Latin grammar and were able to translate the simple authors without the aid of a dictionary, they could proceed to the study of humanities and rhetoric. As we will see below, the Somaschans did not succeed in teaching rhetoric in Bergamo, at least not by 1650. Elsewhere, however, they did manage to teach a number of different subjects that comprised the study of *humaniores litterae*. Students in Verona and Como studied geography with the *Introductio in universam geographiam* of Phillipe Cluvier of Danzig (1580–1623).[115] This particular text was also favoured by Gregorio Barbarigo, bishop of Bergamo from 1659 to 1663, who prepared an edition that included 84 additional maps. The study of history was equally important, and here the Somaschans favoured the *Rationarium Temporum* of Dionysius Petau, first published in 1633.[116] This universal history, which appeared in many editions, was also favoured by Barbarigo. It could not have been adopted by the Somaschans during the first years of their college in Bergamo, but it seems probable that it was used in the following decades. The Somaschans obviously taught the principal Latin authors and poets: Cicero, Ovid, Sallust, Julius Caesar, Virgil, Horace, Quintilian. The *Methodus Studiorum* suggested that easier authors such as Terence or Phaedrus should be introduced first, and that students ought to read them 'not hastily but with the greatest of care, so that the purity and elegance of the work is noticed.'[117] Some Somaschan schools even taught Greek in order to improve students' eloquence.[118] In 1623 Father General Maurizio De Domis commissioned three other members of the order to write textbooks which would standardize the curriculum in Somaschan schools. De Domis requested a grammar text and a rhetoric primer, but they were not completed until the late 1630s.[119]

The 1632 contract also called for students to be well dressed and expected that they would contribute toward the cost of their education. Thus – despite the city council's call to teach 'poor boys' – the Somaschans were not required to teach just anyone who wandered in off the street. They offered a classical Latin curriculum intended for the children of middle- and upper-class Bergamasque families. Unfortunately, we do not possess a complete list of students for this school as we do for the MIA's Academy of Clerics or the Caspi Academy. A 1657 visitation lists the names of a few students whom the deputies encountered, and notarial acts provide scattered clues as to the identity of other students, but there is no way to determine conclusively the social background of the Somaschans' students. However, the Latin curriculum and the city's desire to have a College of Nobles indicates that they were not predominantly lower class.

In addition to the academic curriculum, the Collegio San Giuseppe offered lessons in morality, catechism, and 'Christian life.' Such subjects were a part of every school curriculum in early modern Italy. Girolamo Miani himself wrote a brief catechism to be used in orphanages, although the Somaschans generally relied upon the works of the Dominican Fra Reginaldo, or the Jesuits' Peter Canisius and Robert Bellarmine. After 1609 the Schools of Christian Doctrine had a branch in the Collegio San Giuseppe in which students would have learned the catechism and simple prayers of the Catholic faith.

An undated letter from one Somaschan teacher to another, entitled *Consigli ad un maestro* (Advice to a teacher), explained how to integrate moral and academic subjects.[120] The author, Paolo Caresana, insisted that students must be taught to tell truth from falsehood, and right from wrong. Students must acquire a 'love of reading' and seek 'an understanding of truth'; specifically, he admonished his fellow teacher to make sure that his students realized the corruption, deceit, and trickery that abound in the world of the nobility.[121] How was this to be accomplished? The teacher must point out examples of virtue in the literature being studied and must model honest comportment at all times (e.g., during meals, games, visitations, and lessons). Children must always be kept busy with the study of history, geography, sciences, and other subjects, including physical education. Clearly, Caresana placed more faith in reading canonical texts than in listening to contemporary interpretations or glosses.[122] Caresana's overarching point was that a student must learn to develop his own faculties of judgment. As an example, he said that he preferred a student who could read a text and judge its value to one who could translate or recite Virgil from memory.

Three months after the Somaschans began teaching in Bergamo, the city council noted its satisfaction with the progress of the school. In a deliberation of 28 December 1632, the council congratulated itself for its wise choice in selecting the Somaschan fathers, and in particular praised the diligent labour of the three deputies assigned to this matter. To signal its approval, the council authorized additional funds for the purchase of more benches and the publication of school ordinances.[123] This decree implies that the Somaschans were having considerable success in attracting students and thus required additional space for instruction.

At the beginning of the next academic year, the council noted that the Somaschans had already been employed for a year in the city 'with no small profit to the youth of Bergamo.' Believing that students could benefit from additional instruction in more advanced subjects, the council voted an additional subsidy of 350 lire to found a new school of rhetoric. The money was intended to purchase still more benches and to reconfigure the walls of the existing school to provide a separate space where students could practise reading aloud the classical works of rhetoric (Cicero, Quintilian, et al.).[124]

The council's satisfaction was further demonstrated by repeated attempts to transfer a benefice specifically for support of the Somaschan schools. With a value of 120 gold ducats, this benefice was worth approximately 910 lire, or 142 scudi, almost exactly the amount that the city council and the Misericordia had agreed to pay the Somaschans each year. This benefice was linked to the church of Santa Maria in Misma in the community of Cenate, about ten kilometres east of Bergamo.[125] As noted above, it had been awarded by Paul III in 1546 to eighteen-year-old Leone de Cucchi, who tried to transfer it to the Jesuits and then to the Somaschans in the 1580s. The benefice subsequently passed to his nephew, the Reverend Father Fabrizio Personeni (or Personè), who held it until his death circa 1634. In its efforts to have this benefice transferred in 1634, the city council offered several justifications. First, it would fulfil the wishes of Pope Gregory XIV, who had expressly decreed that this benefice be transferred from priests to regulars for the benefit of public schooling. Second, the fruits of this benefice would be shared by many Venetian subjects, not just the individual recipient or the people of Cenate. Third, the city council would be relieved of the burden of paying one hundred scudi per year, and could dedicate such funds to other activities. Thus a combination of self-interest and public benefit pushed the council to pursue this particular benefice on behalf of the Somaschans.[126]

On 3 September 1633 the city council instructed the *provveditore* (representative) of Bergamo, Giorgio Zorzi, to request an audience with Doge Francesco Erizzo in order to broach this issue. The doge could then order the Venetian ambassador in Rome to intercede with the pope to effect a transfer of the benefice in favour of the Somaschans. Zorzi duly wrote to the doge on 26 November 1633 and on 18 March of the following year received a positive response. The doge confirmed that the Venetian ambassador Contarini and the pope had agreed to the transfer of the benefice in favour of the Somaschans, effective immediately.[127] He added that 'for matters of this nature, it is of the first importance to remove any contradictions' which might hinder the transfer. He was referring to the fact that during the interval between Zorzi's initial letter and his response, the community of Cenate had written to protest the transfer of the benefice. Cenate had benefited from this income for many years and was loath to surrender it to someone else. For example, the income from the benefice of Santa Maria in Misma had been used to build the church of San Leone, a project recommended by Carlo Borromeo during his apostolic visitation of 1575. Therefore the representative of Cenate, Prospero Leone, wrote to the doge to request that the transfer be cancelled. The doge sided with Bergamo, however, and instructed that Cenate's representative should immediately come to Venice to present his arguments. Realizing the futility of Cenate's request, that commune's secretary, the Reverend Paolo Trebuchino, responded that 'in obedience to your wishes, next Saturday I will write to our procurator in Rome and instruct him to cease all action in this case, without claiming any further benefit, and as if this matter had never happened.'[128]

Trebuchino must have dragged his heels on this matter, however, for on 6 May 1634 the doge again wrote to Zorzi to say that the matter of the benefice had to be settled soon. The doge threatened to suspend the transfer of the benefice temporarily and instructed both Bergamo and Cenate to submit their arguments within fifteen days. If Cenate failed to comply, he warned, he would allow the transfer to the Somaschans to proceed. A week later Zorzi wrote an irate letter to the doge claiming that 'the commune of Cenate is trying to block this process without any good reason.' Zorzi submitted a 'most humble request at the feet of your Serenity ... to prevent these extravagant attempts by Cenate' to impede justice. Zorzi's letter must have had a positive effect, for on 28 July he again wrote to the doge to say that he had just delivered the doge's ultimatum to Cenate. Although the documents do not record the final outcome of this case, the Somaschans' continued presence as schoolteachers in Bergamo suggests that they obtained this benefice.[129]

The income derived from the benefice, combined with the MIA's annual contribution and with student fees, was enough to support five Somaschan teachers plus a lay servant. In 1634 the rector of the college was Giovanni Calta; other teaching staff included Giovanni Luigi Cerchiari (whom we have already met), Pier Paolo Piovene, Verginio Gamba, and Giovanni Bernardino Suallino. Cerchiari had delivered the opening oration in 1632, and in 1634 the Somaschan general chapter commissioned him 'to write a rhetorical handbook for use in our schools' and to publish a book of poetry. He died in 1636, however, whereupon Paolo Carrara was requested to publish the book of poetry while Michelangelo Botti was asked to finish the book on rhetoric. In 1635 only three teaching staff were listed: Calta continued as rector, and Paolo Zuintano was appointed as maestro along with Pier Paolo Piovene.[130] By 1645 the number of teaching staff had again risen to five and it remained so through 1650, although, as we shall see shortly, the school was enduring a difficult period.

Despite the fact that the city council and the MIA had both earmarked funding for a school of rhetoric in 1633, the Somaschans never added this component to their curriculum. In light of the demand for this particular subject, such an omission is surprising. The MIA had at least half a dozen young chierici every year who wished to study rhetoric or the humanities in the Somaschans' school. These students could not be sent to the Somaschan school, however, because there was no teacher capable of instructing them. As a result, in 1635 the MIA was forced to hire its own rhetoric teacher, Carlo Francesco Ceresolo, an oblate from Milan who assumed the position of vice-rector.

Ceresolo demonstrated his rhetorical skills by delivering a panegyric in honour of the podestà Giorgio Mariano in 1636. He was reconfirmed in 1637 but subsequently called to Milan in 1638 by Cardinal Monti.[131] Shortly before Christmas of 1639, the MIA voted to send a delegation to appear before Bergamo's city council; the minutes of the MIA's meeting summarize the essential complaint:

> Monday, 5 December 1639 in the magnificent council of the venerable con-
> fraternity of the Misericordia Maggiore ...
>
> After reviewing the actions taken in this council on 19 April and 12
> August of 1632 in favour of the schools run by the Reverend Somaschan
> Fathers, and having read the contract of 29 August 1632 drawn up by the
> commune's secretary Lorenzo Ghirardelli, by which this *pio luogo* prom-
> ised to pay fifty scudi to the city in support of public schools, with certain
> conditions as outlined in the contract, it should be noted that this *pio luogo*
> received no benefit from the said schools. Indeed, instead of sending our
> students to the Somaschans' schools, as one would expect from the agree-
> ment described above, suddenly our own schools are full of students who
> have recently abandoned the Somaschans' schools. In order to respond, it
> has been necessary to hire a third teacher. For this and for other reasons,
> a complaint and petition for relief must be lodged with the city. Therefore
> it is decided that our school deputies should present a resolution to the
> city in the name of this confraternity in order to obtain relief from the
> aforementioned obligation, with the freedom to do, say, and respond in
> whatever manner they deem expedient to achieve the desired result.[132]

The MIA's petition was unsuccessful, and in desperation the confraternity sent twelve chierici to the diocesan seminary for further instruction. Fortunately, Ceresolo returned to Bergamo in 1641–2 and resumed
his teaching responsibilities, but always within the MIA's school rather
than that of the Somaschans.[133]

This conflict with the MIA presaged other negative reports about
the Somaschan school. In September of 1642 the city council's deputies wrote to the Father General of the Somaschans in Pavia to express
their dissatisfaction with the state of the Collegio San Giuseppe.[134] The
deputies criticized the poor quality of the Somaschan teachers in Bergamo, who gave the impression that they did not care whether classes
in the college were well organized or not. Such sloppy behaviour not
only reflected poorly upon the reputation of noble students and their
families, noted the deputies, but even more upon the teachers themselves. 'With strong emotion and little satisfaction have we watched
the transfer of Father Pier Paolo Piovene,' they wrote, dismissing the
replacement teachers who followed Piovene as far less competent. The

deputies demanded that in order to overcome this disgraceful state of affairs, it was 'most necessary' to hire new teachers who were not only competent but willing to pull their own weight (*non solo atto ma che anche voglia portare il peso*). In particular, the deputies suggested that Somaschans born and educated in Bergamo should be appointed to the college because they would be willing to remain there and would provide the greatest benefit to the area. In this regard, Bergamo's city council was following the lead of the Venetian Senate, which strongly preferred its own citizens over outsiders.

The Somaschans' own correspondence confirms the sad state of affairs in Bergamo. In early January 1645 the rector, Bartolomeo Cerchiari, wrote to the General Procurator in Rome concerning 'the poverty and continuing misery of this house.' The college had very little money, Cerchiari explained; furthermore, 'we have no students, only eight boarders, and still I have to feed and clothe six of our own; I leave it to your Most Reverend Father Master to imagine how it is possible to survive.'[135] Cerchiari begged that the college be released from saying some of the nine hundred masses it had agreed to perform, and asked for confirmation of the indulgence of San Giuseppe.

Nor was the earlier squabble with the MIA to be easily resolved. On 11 December 1642 the president of the Misericordia Maggiore, Girolamo Agnelli, announced unequivocally that the MIA would no longer contribute its annual payment to the Somaschan fathers. The MIA complained again that the Somaschans were not meeting the conditions that had been set in their contract; more specifically, that 'they do not now, and did not in the past, teach rhetoric in their schools.'[136] Furthermore, Agnelli alleged, the MIA's own school was becoming increasingly crowded because the Somaschans' students were leaving in order to enrol at the MIA's academy. (This may explain Cerchiari's lament above about the absence of students in the Somaschans' school.) As a result, the MIA was forced to hire a third maestro to assist the regular two teachers. Not only did the MIA have to pay the salary of this third instructor, but the number of students requesting admission continued to increase, and the MIA was constrained to turn away promising disciples because there was no more room in the school. Therefore Agnelli requested that the podestà cancel the MIA's obligation. This bureaucratic squabble continued until 1650 with accusations and petitions circulating amongst the podestà, the city council, the MIA, the Somaschans, and the bishop.[137] The final document in this case, dated 12

February 1650, was yet another request by the MIA to be freed from this obligation; no evidence exists to indicate whether they were ultimately successful or not.[138]

In the same year the Somaschan Father General, following the command of Innocent X, ordered all seminaries and schools administered by the Somaschans to submit a report describing their financial status.[139] The rector of the school in Bergamo, Bonifatio Albano, included a brief budget which showed that over half of the Somaschans' income was collected from boarders and 'foreign students.'[140] The balance of their income was derived from a vegetable garden, rent from two small shops, alms, and masses. Despite the Somaschans' pleas of poverty, by 1650 the college included five teachers, each with a salary of 55 scudi per year. All of the teachers, including four priests and one layman, were housed in the 'comfortable palace' offered by the city. However the college still sustained a debt of one hundred scudi and appeared to be struggling financially.[141]

The Somaschans' woes were confirmed with a formal visitation by three members of Bergamo's city council on 14 December 1657. These three deputies and the city's secretary arrived in the parish of Pozzo Bianco early in the morning to investigate complaints that had been made by some local citizens. They were met by two Somaschan fathers who served as teachers, Girolamo Toriglia and Francesco Maria Pomodoro. The deputies entered into a large room with a considerable number of benches, which served as the Scola Maggiore (Upper School) for the teaching of grammar. However, only four students, two of whom were absent, were enrolled in that class. The deputies then visited an adjoining room of equal size where eleven younger students were being taught the fundamentals of reading and writing.

After their visit the deputies wrote a highly critical report of the Somaschan school: 'the schools of the Somaschan fathers have very few students because the fathers are unable to teach them, just as the town residents have claimed.'[142] The deputies then reviewed the ten chapters of the 1632 contract between the city and the Somaschans, listing the various ways in which the Somaschans had violated their agreement. They did not teach rhetoric; they had not been visited regularly by the deputies; they did not seek approval for the admission of new students; and they accepted gifts from their students without the advice and consent of the deputies. Therefore, the deputies concluded, since the Somaschans had not honoured their obligations, the city should not be obligated to pay the rent of the Passi house where the fathers lived and taught. The extant records do not specify whether the Somaschans were ultimately forced to pay their own rent or not.

It is telling, however, that two years later the Somaschan school was moved to the convent of San Leonardo, which had been vacated by Pope Alexander VII's suppression of the Padri Crociferi. The Somaschans paid a total of six thousand lire for the convent, assuming formal possession on 9 October 1659. Donato Calvi provides a detailed description of the buildings, which included a hospital, a garden, and a church 'with a very beautiful portrait of Girolamo Miani.'[143] The Somaschans would remain at this location until the general suppression of 1810. According to historian Giovanni Alcaini, the Somaschans had never been satisfied with their location in the parish of Pozzo Bianco, but it took thirty years before their request for a transfer would finally be granted by Bishop Barbarigo.[144] While it is possible that the Somaschans initiated the request for their transfer to a different location, it seems far more likely that the city council and the MIA worked together to expel the order from the upper city. Thus even a religious order that had amassed as much goodwill as the Somaschans could be turned out by a series of unfortunate events.

Conclusion

It should be clear that ecclesiastical institutions did not limit themselves exclusively to religious education. Indeed, the majority of examples cited reflect efforts to teach grammar, rhetoric, humanities, and other subjects typical of a practical, lay education. 'Moral' education was no doubt an indispensable part of this instruction, but it was only a part of a larger mission. In a similar fashion, the confraternally sponsored schools described earlier were administered by lay organizations, but they did not limit instruction to the secular realm. The confraternities of the MIA, Sant'Alessandro in Colonna, and Sant'Alessandro della Croce each sponsored schools for lay boys and for young priests in training. The curricula and the student body described in all schools thus far bear many striking resemblances.

Yet at least one critical difference emerges clearly in both this chapter and the previous one: the effort to define and separate the education of lay boys from the instruction provided to future ecclesiastics. Encouraged by zealous reformers such as Carlo Borromeo of Milan and Bishop Gian Matteo Giberti of Verona, and following the guidelines set forth by the Council of Trent, ecclesiastics all over Italy sought to keep these two groups of students distinct. The seminary is the most obvious example of this drive to isolate future priests and to protect them from outside influence. Bergamo's seminary, for example, flirted briefly with admitting lay boys, but almost immediately changed course and soon thereafter instituted new rules that severely limited contact with the outside world, including parental visits and letters from friends and family. The orphanages governed by Miani and his companions sought to provide a 'mini-seminary' in Somasca and in Pavia that would protect those orphans planning to join the order from the 'dangerous' public schools. Even the Schools of Christian Doctrine reflect this 'isolationist' tendency: when the Archconfraternity of Christian Doctrine arrived in the summer of 1609, the seminary, the MIA's Academy of Clerics, and the clerical schools sponsored by the confraternities of Sant'Alessandro in Colonna and Sant'Alessandro della Croce all wished to found Schools of Christian Doctrine inside the pre-existing schools. No doubt this was in part, as the documents claim, for the greater convenience of the maestro. But it was also presumably an attempt to ensure that the boys in the academies or seminaries would not mingle regularly with other children. In the case of the Somaschans (and presumably the Jesuits, had they been admitted), they were only teaching lay boys. Both orders did sometimes teach in local seminaries, but in the Collegio San Giuseppe there was a strict separation and the focus remained exclusively on lay education.

A second important conclusion emerges from these two chapters: namely, the fortunes of the Church-sponsored schools and schoolmasters fluctuated, sometimes dramatically, and without any predictable pattern. The Jesuits' experience in Bergamo was a disaster: they were rejected three times, the Collegio Mariano nearly closed under their leadership, and they were abruptly fired by the MIA in 1729. In contrast, the Somaschans were able to remain in Bergamo and continued to operate their school and orphanage for centuries (albeit with some bumps in the road). It seems likely that the Somaschans profited from the rejection of the Jesuits, not only because a niche remained open for them to fill in 1632, but also because they avoided the mistakes of the Society. While the Jesuits had a reputation for acquisitiveness, the Somaschans emphasized their frugality to a penurious city council. The Jesuits did not campaign ahead of time for their acceptance in 1573, whereas the Somaschans 'solicited a favourable public opinion with all their might and with every weapon at their disposal,' and their supporters publicized the Somaschans' charitable work elsewhere.[145] While the Jesuits were seen as a 'foreign' presence, the Somaschans identified themselves with the Venetian *terraferma*. The Somaschans escaped neither harsh criticism nor a financial crisis, but they endured the difficulties of the mid-seventeenth century before moving to San Leonardo in 1659.

The seminary's fortunes also fluctuated substantially during the first century of its existence. In one year the bishop might write proudly of the success that the seminary was enjoying, and the next year a financial emergency or a negative assessment of the students' ability would paint a very different picture of the seminary's achievements. Contemporary sources also disagreed about the well-being of the seminary. There is little doubt that the seminary provided a more comprehensive, more consistent, and more orthodox education to aspiring priests than had generally been available prior to the Council of Trent. The Schools of Christian Doctrine, too, reflect these vagaries of fortune. The Schools struggled early on in Bergamo, requiring the repeated intervention of the Milanese company. Yet the Schools grew steadily and by 1609 the number of participants had more than tripled to what it was three decades earlier.

It remains difficult to calculate the 'success' of these institutions in any meaningful way. The Jesuits' experience clearly represents one end of the continuum (an almost total lack of success), while the others had more mixed results. Even an attempt to judge the relative success of each by the number of people affected or by the extent of influence is an exercise in frustration. The Schools of Christian Doctrine surely affected the largest number of individuals, but at such a basic level that no discernible effect can be perceived. In the long run the seminary probably had the greatest impact, as its graduates preached to thousands every year in an effort to increase the faith of the people and the strength of the Roman Catholic Church. The Somaschans received mixed reviews at different times, and despite the plethora of documentation on their activities after 1632, it remains difficult to draw conclusions about their success or failure.

A third conclusion is that the type and extent of education promoted by the ecclesiastical institutions were strongly influenced by Bergamo's split allegiance between Milan and Venice. The curriculum, texts, and structure of the seminary and the Schools of Christian Doctrine clearly illustrate the impact of the Milanese archbishops and ecclesiastics. The Somaschans' Collegio San Giuseppe, on the other hand, had little to do with Milan but was closely bound to Venice. Given the focus of the Collegio San Giuseppe on lay education, and the small number of Somaschan colleges and orphanages in Lombardy as compared to the Veneto, it is not surprising that the Somaschans would be more oriented towards Venice. Furthermore, the Somaschans had frequent interaction with Bergamo's city council (chaired by two Venetian governors, let us remember), while the seminary and Schools of Christian Doctrine rarely followed a specifically Venetian model. Bergamo's communal and confraternal schools operated with a good deal of autonomy, but the schooling sponsored by ecclesiastical institutions was more strongly influenced by Bergamo's powerful neighbours.

Lastly, it is important to keep in mind the diverse and often contradictory aims of these ecclesiastical educators. Just as there was no single monolithic 'State' in early modern Italy to direct public education, the 'Church' included a multitude of diverse educational philosophies and practices. To some extent these disparate aims were unified by the Council of Trent. After 1563 the principal beliefs of the Roman Catholic Church were clarified and codified. In education, this standardization resulted in a common administrative structure for all diocesan seminaries, and an effort to unify the catechisms utilized in the Schools of Christian Doctrine. Much more common, however, was a diversity of pedagogical theory and action under the aegis of church-sponsored schooling.

5 *Genitori*: Schooling, Parents, and Tutors

The best-known examples of Italian Renaissance education are the private tutors hired by princes and patriarchs to train children in Latin, letters, and etiquette. Epitomized by Vittorino da Feltre and Guarino da Verona in the fifteenth century, and idealized by Baldassare Castiglione in *The Courtier* during the sixteenth century, the tutor was frequently a humanist scholar who travelled from one city to the next in search of a wealthy patron. The subjects to be studied varied according to the competency of the teacher, the desire of the parent, and (perhaps) the aptitude of the child. The curriculum might include hawking and horsemanship, real-life lessons in diplomacy and statecraft, and more conventional academic subjects such as grammar, rhetoric, and literature. The schooling provided to children of such great families as the Medici, the Gonzaga, and the Este has been carefully studied, and we know a good deal about royal courts, illustrious pedagogues, and famous pupils. Private education in provincial cities like Bergamo, on the other hand, remains something of a mystery. In contrast to the institutionally sponsored instruction examined thus far, parents who hired private tutors were involved directly in the financial, intellectual, and moral decisions to be made about their children's education. In addition to paying the full cost of private lessons, parents often provided housing or other benefits to private teachers. An examination of schooling sponsored by parents thus allows us to study the values and skills that were most important to parents, without the 'filter' of an institution.

In comparison with their peers in other Italian cities, Bergamasque parents were not very wealthy. This may explain the low number of independent masters and private tutors who lived in Bergamo. Bergamasque parents relied instead on the network of civic, ecclesiastical, and confraternal schooling described in previous chapters. To be sure, powerful families like the Suardi and the Passi utilized private tutors, but children from these and other important families were regularly listed in the matriculation rolls of institutionally sponsored schools, too. The small number of tutors in Bergamo may also reflect the documentary sources used in this study. Private tutors most often appear in tax returns or notarial documents (e.g., contracts and wills); although notarial cartularies are utilized for this study, I have not relied upon them as heavily as have other historians of education.[1] The delayed introduction of a printing press and a perception of the city as a cultural backwater constitute other reasons for the low number of independent masters.[2] In addition, the opposition of the Misericordia Maggiore probably inhibited private teachers from opening up small schools or soliciting private students. In 1538, for example, the MIA prohibited instruction in letters, dance, and music in all of its buildings in the neighbourhood of Sant'Agata, apparently to prevent competition from outside masters.[3]

Yet Bergamo offers an unusual, perhaps even a unique, pair of examples in sixteenth-century Italy of how parents assumed control of their children's education. In 1547 a group of sixteen local parents founded a small residential academy intended to educate a select group of their own children in a classical curriculum. Approximately twenty boys ages five to fourteen were instructed by two teachers in Greek, Latin, religion, and proper behaviour. Located just outside the city walls in a large house next to the Hospital of San Marco and near the monastery of Matris Domini, the Caspi Academy (Accademia dei Caspi) included a dormitory where students and teachers lived together. With the exception of a small donation by the bishop to help start the school, the academy was financed entirely by parents whose sons were enrolled there. Nor did the bishop play any significant role in the subsequent history of the Caspi Academy.[4] Parents governed all aspects of the academy: selection of teachers, admission of students, supervision of new construction, even the management of periodic inventories. Thus, despite the nominal presence of the bishop, the academy was clearly under the control of this small group of elite lay fathers. Indeed, the founding charter of the academy specified that all decisions were to be taken by majority vote of the fathers. Such a resolutely lay school is especially interesting in light of the mid-century drift toward religiously influenced schooling that we have seen thus far.

Immediately upon the closure of the Caspi Academy circa 1557, another academy was founded with nearly identical goals, structure, and

View of Bergamo in the fifteenth century. From *Vita di S. Benedetto*, ms. 239 (B. IV. 13), f. 15r, Biblioteca Comunale Teresiana of Mantua. This perspective shows a group of nuns talking to a monk in the meadow of Sant'Alessandro, with the upper city of Bergamo in the background. Note the gate of S. Agostino to the upper right, and the gate of S. Giacomo to the left, with the cupola of S. Maria Maggiore and the Palazzo della Ragione in the middle. Also depicted are the fortress of the Rocca, the Civic Tower, the Citadel, and the convent of S. Stefano. The name 'Bergamum' appears in the centre of the wall.

staff. We know much less about this second academy – even its name remains a mystery. Yet it invoked the Caspi Academy as a model of what it planned to accomplish and hired teaching staff with similar qualifications. It appears that this second academy might have been founded by a group of parents linked to the initial Caspi Academy, perhaps after the first cohort of children had grown up.

Parental involvement in a child's education is, of course, a common feature of schooling around the globe and across the centuries. Giacomo Chizola's academy in sixteenth-century Brescia (discussed later in this chapter) recognized that mothers and fathers would want to visit frequently and made provision for them to do so. Rebecca Bushnell has analysed the intricate relationship between parents and teachers in humanist pedagogical theory and practice in Tudor-Stuart England.[5] Parent-teacher associations and volunteer 'teacher's helpers' in the classroom have long taken advantage of parental willingness to assist with instruction. The burgeoning popularity of home schooling and of charter schools in recent years underscores the contemporary interest and direct participation of parents in their children's schooling. Although parental involvement may have been common in early modern Europe, documentary evidence of such activity remains difficult to recover. Bergamo's Caspi Academy and its anonymous successor represent an exception, one that allows us to look more clearly at what parents sought to accomplish by creating their own school.

This chapter considers the intriguing, albeit brief, history of the Caspi Academy from 1547 to 1557, and its successor institution from 1559 to circa 1569. Like so many other schools in Bergamo, both opened with great optimism and closed after just a few years. To the extent permitted by the survival of the documents, we will consider the teaching staff, students, texts, administration, location, and legacy of these two unusual schools. Other notarial documents, including the library of one private tutor (Bonino de Mauris), provide hints of other arrangements between parents and teachers. Despite the nuggets to be unearthed here and there, we must confront the reality that we know much less about private tutors and parental involvement than we do about the institutional governance of schooling in Bergamo.

The Caspi Academy

The Caspi Academy demonstrates that schooling existed beyond the confines of the major institutions that promoted education in Bergamo (i.e., the commune, ecclesiastical institutions, and the confraternities). Wealthy parents sometimes hired private tutors to teach their children in-house for a year or two, but the Caspi Academy reflects a more extensive, cooperative effort by a private group of parents. This academy also embodies an interesting compromise between religious and secular education. While the bishop and the archdeacon were consulted about the first important decisions of the academy and the curriculum naturally required catechism and regular attendance at Mass, the teachers, texts, and governance of the school were firmly under the control of lay parents. The Caspi Academy's first instructor, Andrea Cato, was a well-known humanist who vehemently defended the study of letters as the path to virtue and knowledge. Yet this academy necessarily reflected the strict morality of Tridentine reform with its eventual prohibition of the presence of women and girls. In contrast to other 'academies' in Bergamo about which we know very little, the Caspi Academy was clearly a functioning school for young children. The records of the Caspi Academy also shed light on other little-known academies and schools in sixteenth-century Bergamo. Lastly, the variety and number of documents about the Caspi Academy permit a careful look at some little-studied aspects of sixteenth-century school life. For example, more than a dozen inventories of the furniture and utensils owned by this academy are extant, as well as a list of books owned by individual students, a detailed testament by the housemaster, and a series of letters to and from the master teachers. Thus we learn that teachers were permitted to enrol their own children in the school; that the kitchens of the Caspi Academy were well stocked; and that parental visitations were strongly encouraged to motivate both students and teachers.

Previous scholarship on the Caspi Academy has been superficial and limited in scope. Barnaba Vaerini mentioned it in passing in 1874. In 1910 Giuseppe Locatelli published the founding charter and three letters about the opening of the academy, but his investigations were limited to the year 1547. Locatelli did not place the Caspi Academy in any kind of historical context, nor did he investigate related documents from other archives. All subsequent references recycle the comments of Vaerini or Locatelli.[6] One notable exception is the recent study of Massimo Firpo, who links the Caspi Academy with his analysis of Bishop Vittore Soranzo. Based upon his archival investigations, Firpo emphasizes the important role of the bishop and the religious character of the Caspi Academy as well as the heretical leanings of several teachers.[7] The primary source of information about the Caspi Academy remains a collection of documents maintained by the academy itself and later preserved amongst the financial records of the bishop. Notarial cartularies in Bergamo's State Archive and a family archive in Bergamo's Civic Library provide further source material.[8]

The earliest reference to the Caspi Academy is found in a letter addressed to Bergamo's Bishop Vittore Soranzo, dated 15 March 1547.[9] Written by Giacomo Chizola (also Chizzola), a schoolmaster who had recently founded an academy in the neighbouring city of Brescia, the letter provided suggestions to the bishop on how to organize a school.[10] It remains unclear whether the bishop requested this information or if Chizola was trying to spark interest in a new school. Chizola described the physical location and structure of his school, faculty and staff positions, the daily schedule of lessons and meals, and the clothing worn by students. Chizola also described the curriculum in some detail: Cicero, Virgil, Terence, Horace, Isocrates, Homer, and the Gospel of Saint Luke. On Sunday afternoons, continued Chizola, one of the older boys read an excerpt from Cicero, followed by a disputation with the other boys. A recurring concern throughout Chizola's letter is the moral value of his lessons. According to Chizola, students must be taught the worthwhile parts of these texts, whether classical literature, catechism, or other sacred writings, leaving aside the unseemly and distracting portions. This concern with the ethical substance of lessons is a common humanist refrain in pedagogical treatises. Chizola uses the words *putti, figliuoli, tutti,* and *essi* to describe the students, which implies that they were boys, but could conceivably refer to a mixed group of boys and girls. Since there are no other references to girls in the Caspi Academy, except for the daughters of the maestro, it seems reasonable that the students were all boys.

Chizola also emphasized the important role of parents, especially fathers, whose presence he viewed as critical for motivating both students and teachers. In describing the benefits of a parental visit, Chizola demonstrated shrewd psychological insight for improving academic performance: 'This motivates [students] more than all the blows that the teachers might give them. Parental visits are also necessary to increase the profit that students obtain from studying their letters; because if students know that they will be examined in the presence of their fathers, they will do all they can to avoid failure, and in the same way the teachers will be more diligent if they know that they will regularly be called to account.' Chizola recounted that he had chosen a site for his school that was 'not so far from the city that fathers cannot visit their sons in the academy, but not so close that mothers and nurses can arrive there too easily.' A further comment revealed his bias for the male parent: 'I have found nothing else helps the students more than to be visited frequently by their fathers.'[11]

This letter clearly piqued the bishop's interest, and he wrote to Chizola asking for further information. Chizola responded immediately with more details about the teachers' salary, the desired number and age of students, and the best method for collecting money from parents.[12] Chizola's advice strongly influenced the organization of the Caspi Academy: as we shall see, many of the decisions taken by the bishop and the academy fathers follow the suggestions of the Brescian schoolmaster. This positive reaction must have pleased Chizola, for in the following year he wrote several long letters to other pedagogues in Rome outlining his ideas for organizing a school.[13]

Chizola's letters contained little pedagogical theory and no sense of long-range vision for the future development of the school. In this way they differ markedly from the treatises of Pier Paolo Vergerio, Maffeo Vegio, and other Italian humanists. Instead, Chizola's missives were replete with practical information derived from his own experience. He explained to Bishop Soranzo, for example, that he had forbidden the use of a warming pan (schaldaletto) by the students, and that 'while the concept nearly incited the mothers to mutiny, they adapted to the idea when they say how ruddy and healthy their boys had become.'[14] Yet Chizola's practical insights often touched on important pedagogical principles. He advocated organizing the boys by skill rather than by age, a concept soon adopted by the Jesuits in their own colleges. He advised that boys be given ample time for recreation after meals, and suggested appropriate games to keep them entertained without introducing improper thoughts. Chizola's promotion of parental involvement – which included disciplinary action – was unusual for a boarding school but sensible given the young age of the students. Chizola's letters bear no obvious sign of influence from Giovita Ravizza's 1523 treatise, even though they both came from the area around Brescia and their writings often discuss similar issues.

Just a week after Chizola's second letter had been written, the bishop and sixteen fathers met in the episcopal palace and agreed to establish a scuola ovvero accademia de putti (school or academy for young boys). In a charter containing the signatures of all the fathers, each member of the Magnificent Company of the Academy promised to obey the thirty clauses of an agreement signed some days before, and to support one *putto*.[15] The prior agreement remains lost, but it surely included many of the details that Giacomo Chizola had provided to the bishop. Presumably those details included an explanation of how the parents planned to organize themselves (i.e., an executive board, an overseer, or a series of subcommittees with deputies for specific tasks). The extant charter contained almost no details about how the actual academy would be organized; it was rather a promise by all the founding fathers that they would support the school financially. The charter does set out the principle of majority rule for all future decisions, an important statement of independence from the bishop and the Roman Curia.

The fathers represented many of the noble families of Bergamo: Marcantonio Bolis, Bartolomeo Barili, Giovanni Andrea Della Valle, Pietro Passi, Scipione Boselli, Ludovico Alessandri, Girolamo Longo, Giovan Giacomo Terzi, Lattanzio Maffei, Castello Benaglio, Girolamo Poncini, Gabriele Albani, Pietro Spino, Giovan Giacomo Tassi, Alessandro Allegri, Ventura Foresti.[16] Their names appear frequently in the civic and episcopal documents of mid-century Bergamo as holders of important offices. For example, the *iuris pontificii peritus* (expert in papal law) Marcantonio Bolis was archdeacon of the cathedral and a canon for more than thirty years, during which time he sometimes served as the bishop's vicar and accompanied him on pastoral visitations.[17] Bartolomeo Barili was secretary to the commune and a fellow canon, subsequently imputed for heresy in 1557.[18] Pietro Passi, whose family would later assist the Somaschans to find a house for the school of S. Giuseppe, served on the city council intermittently from 1528 to 1550 and was one of 'two pre-eminent doctors' (*doi dottori primarii*) appointed in 1548 to the Inquisitorial commission to represent Venetian interests (*congregatio dominorum deputatorum ad interessendum in causis fidei iuxta partem excellentissimi Consilii Decem*).[19] Pietro Spino – an orphan who studied with Giovita Ravizza after that teacher's departure from Bergamo in 1523 – also served on the city council from 1546 to 1589 and was treasurer for the commune as well as a poet, historian, and man of letters whose work was published by Comin Ventura in 1580 and 1587.[20] The nobleman Giovan Giacomo Tassi, the communal and Inquisitorial notary Alessandro Allegri, the poet Ventura Foresti: all of these men held public office in Bergamo and contributed to the civic culture of the city.[21] Several also appear in Soranzo's trial records as witnesses, notaries, and occasionally as subjects of investigation in their own right. In short, it was a very distinguished group that gathered in 1547 to launch this new school, one which possessed the intellectual and financial capital to ensure a strong start.

The first step was to hire a *primo maestro* (head teacher) responsible for providing instruction, directing the *ripetitore* (assistant teacher), and supervising students in the classroom and the dormitory. The bishop and the fathers appointed three deputies to negotiate a contract with Andrea Cato of Romano, a noted humanist who would later teach for the commune of Bergamo. Signed on 4 May 1547 in the episcopal palace, the contract promised an annual salary of four hundred lire, paid in quarterly installments, in addition to food and lodging for Cato and his family.[22] Unlike many other teachers in sixteenth-century Bergamo, Cato was not allowed to accept gifts from either students or parents unless intended for the benefit of the entire academy. He was required to treat all students equally, and to observe the enumerated clauses of the founding decree. More specifically, for three years 'he must renounce all other commitments, whether related to his family or to business, and dedicate himself diligently and assiduously to his job of encouraging, instructing, and teaching the boys assigned to him.'[23] Fines ranging from ten to twenty-five scudi were threatened if Cato failed to observe or enforce these stipulations of the contract. The deputies encouraged him to relocate as soon as possible and reminded him that his salary would not begin until his arrival in the city.

With the exception of prohibiting gifts and payments by individual students, most of these terms were standard elements of sixteenth-century teaching contracts in Bergamo. All subsequent contracts for the Caspi Academy followed this model. Obviously, the salary varied from one teacher to another, but the first three were each paid four hundred lire annually. Each contract contained minor modifications: for example, Cato was allowed to enrol up to three of his own children, including a daughter, at the expense of the academy until they reached the age of seven, but he had to pay for their clothing, beds, and meals. The founders clearly did not want Cato to hold another job during his tenure at the Caspi Academy, nor even to have family commitments that might distract him from teaching. Although by today's standards the restrictions upon a teacher's 'private' life might seem excessive, such limitations were common in an era when the teacher's moral guidance (and physical presence) was at least as important as his practical knowledge of literature, philosophy, history, and mathematics. A virtuous teacher was especially important in a boarding school for impressionable young children.

As we have seen, ethics constituted an increasingly important aspect of a teacher's résumé in the later sixteenth century. The teaching contracts offered by the parents of the Caspi Academy closely resemble those drawn up by the MIA and by the commune for their own teachers. Unlike the MIA's Academy of Clerics and the Paduan College, the Caspi Academy appears to have escaped violence, theft, and student pranks. Granted, the Caspi Academy enrolled much younger students, and we would expect an elementary or middle school to have far fewer disciplinary incidents than a high-school classroom or college-age dormitory. Still, we must ask if direct parental involvement might have played a role in avoiding trouble at the Caspi Academy.

Owing to the survival of nearly a dozen of his letters, orations, and poems, we know more about Andrea Cato than about other teachers employed by the Caspi Academy. He was the author of a short entry entitled *Descrittione et destruttione di valle Brembilla* (Description and Destruction of the Bremba Valley) which appeared in Celestino Colleoni's *Dell'historia quadripartita di Bergamo* (History of Bergamo in Four Parts), first published in Bergamo in 1617.[24] Not surprisingly, Cato's writing displays an excellent Latin style and a profound knowledge of classical sources. Cato's letters also permit us to reconstruct his negotiations with the academy. Even before he signed his employment contract, Cato sent a formal letter to the academy fathers, agreeing to their request for a public lecture and asking time to prepare.[25] In early June 1547 Cato wrote to his cousin, the notary and co-founder of the Caspi Academy Alessandro Allegri, to explain that his trip had been postponed because of flooding rivers and a near-fatal pleurisy, but that he wished to reassure the academy of his intention to arrive soon.[26]

The Italian school year traditionally began after the feast of Saint Luke (18 October), as it still does for many Italian universities today. In response to parental pressure, however, the Caspi Academy began classes in June. In mid-June all patrons (or 'fathers') of the Caspi Academy were invited to attend an opening Mass and an oration by the academy's head teacher (Cato), as well as a business meeting to review the academy's status. These meetings, plus the fact that teaching contracts were always signed in May, confirm the early summer start for instruction in the Caspi Academy. There are also hints that many families went on holiday in the countryside in September; thus earlier classes may have been a way to compensate for these vacations around harvest season.

After just two months of instruction, Cato asked the patrons and parents of the academy to convene so that his disciples might recite excerpts from the *Eclogues* of Giovanni Pontano. A prolific Italian humanist and poet, as well as an astrologer and a historian, Pontano

(1422/6?–1503) had served as advisor to the king of Naples and tutor to his son. He also became the head of an academy of letters, soon known as the Accademia Pontaniana in his honour.[27] Pontano's *Eclogues*, always in Latin, celebrated family life and often honoured his deceased wife and son. Although Cato's letter does not specify which of the *Eclogues* his students would study, it was an inspired – if somewhat curious – choice to inaugurate the Caspi Academy. Pontano represented the ideal well-rounded man who was both a courtier and a scholar with works on history, philosophy, ethics, astrology, and even erotic poetry. Cato promised that while the students might begin in a timid, modest manner, they would soon benefit from these recitations and learn to speak with passion and precision.[28] Cato's choice of the date of 24 August, the feast day of San Bartolomeo, was similarly inspired. Cato knew that a large crowd would assemble in Bergamo on the following day (25 August) to honour Sant'Alessandro, patron saint of Bergamo. Thus a public Latin recital on the eve of Bergamo's largest annual fair would provide an excellent means to advertise his school and to show off what his students had already learned.

Two weeks later, Cato sent a note to Giovanni Maria Rota, secretary of the commune, explaining that he had just written a little oration (*orationcella*) in praise and defence of the study of letters against those ignorant people who speak badly of them. If Rota, the bishop, and the academy fathers approved, Cato promised to deliver his oration publicly as well as to require his students to study it in their lessons.[29] Cato sent copies of the same oration to his friend (and co-founder of the academy) Giovanni Andrea della Valle and to the Reverend Jacomo da Codogno, a schoolmaster at the church of San Domenico in Lodi.[30] The oration discussed the texts that Cato hoped to teach, the grammars he was planning to use, and the different types of pedagogy he expected to employ. It was, as promised, a vigorous defence of humanist schooling, in which Cato praised the benefits of reading Virgil, Cicero, Saint Paul, Donatus, and Guarino of Verona.[31]

Before Cato could begin teaching, however, the founding fathers needed to identify and acquire a suitable house for the fledgling school. In late May a deputy of the academy, Ludovico Alexandri, had signed a three-year contract with Antonio Colleoni for a house and garden called 'of the Caspi' (*domus Casporum*), probably a reference to a previous owner. The house was located midway between the monastery of Matris Domini and the open field that housed the annual fair of Sant'Alessandro, close to the Ospedale Grande of Sant'Antonio. The

Caspi Academy agreed to pay twenty gold scudi per year for the use of the house, the furniture, and the orchard. The contract prohibited a refund in the event of war or plague but permitted the academy to make structural changes as needed to accommodate a school. The academy renewed the lease every three years and remained in this house for the duration of its existence. Regular inventories conducted by the academy reveal that the house possessed a substantial amount of furniture and very well-stocked kitchens.[32] The house contained at least two kitchens, four bedrooms, a large living room, and a cellar. An open porch was enclosed in 1547 in order to provide additional living space for students.

The Caspi Academy included a small staff responsible for preparing food, managing the budget, and teaching students. Giacomo Chizola had explained that his academy in Brescia included two teachers, a housemaster, a purchaser, a handyman, a cook, and an errand boy.[33] Furthermore, the treasurer, whose job was to collect money from other parents and distribute it to the house staff as necessary, was always selected from among the parents of the academy. We will return shortly to a consideration of the Caspi Academy's support staff, but the academy really revolved around the *primo maestro*.

As holder of the most visible and well-paid position, the head teacher assumed responsibility for instructing the students and for managing other staff. He decided what the *ripetitore* ought to teach in class, ensured that the rules of the academy were observed by everyone, and, as we have seen above, occasionally delivered public speeches to promote the academy. The Caspi Academy expected the *primo maestro* to devote himself exclusively to his job within the academy. He was generally allowed to choose the texts and methods with which he wished to teach, so long as these conformed to the sixteenth-century canon. In addition to teaching the Greek and Latin works previously cited by Andrea Cato, the head teacher provided instruction in good Christian behaviour and proper public manners (*buoni costumi christiani et politici*).[34] No doubt the public recitations favoured by Cato helped to promote both these goals.

A letter from the mid-1550s outlines the qualities of a *primo maestro* sought by the Caspi Academy: 'a mature man learned in both Greek and Latin, having a pure and lucid style in our vernacular as in Latin, and of such an upright and Christian lifestyle, to whom one would happily entrust such an academy.'[35] Here again we perceive parents' concern with both the intellectual and the moral development of their children. Cato appears to have recognized this apprehension, for his public oration sought to reassure parents that he would 'avoid corruption of the mind through excessive leisure.' In other words, he would ensure that even the youngest of students was engaged in memorizing appropriate epigrams and moral exemplars.[36]

At the conclusion of the first school year, Andrea Cato declared himself unable to teach on account of illness (*propter stomachi et capitis indispositionem*).[37] Within a few months, however, he had begun teaching for the commune of Bergamo, a position he held from 1548 to 1551. In 1551 he informed the city council of his intention to retire to Tirano.[38] However, it appears that Cato's departure was probably triggered by an anonymous denunciation of 7 May 1551 in which he was accused of being a Lutheran and a follower of Vittore Soranzo. Addressed to the Inquisitor Michele Ghislieri, this denunciation attacked Cato and his staff in no uncertain terms:

> Reverend Inquisitor, I know that your lordship is here to investigate the affairs of the bishop of Bergamo and also of others ... I wish to advise you that the teacher of the Academy [located] in the meadow [of Sant'Alessandro] was completely loyal to the bishop, and that he was – according to what is said – one of your brothers(?); and he [Soranzo] put him [Cato] in that place, and he exalted and maintained him there against the wishes of many. I have him for a Lutheran, and one cannot find anyone who has seen him at Mass or other offices; it cannot be otherwise that he is Lutheran, being that he is so close to the bishop. Therefore you can do an investigation of him as you know how to do, in order to find out the truth of what I write. The priest that usually acts as his assistant [Battista] da Ghisalba and the priest Maifredo, who has also been his assistant, will be able to give you additional information, in addition to those who are in his house, both servants and staff who have been there in the past and who are there at the moment.[39]

In the same month of May 1551, Cato was identified in a separate case as a participant in a book-smuggling ring to import heretical texts from Switzerland to Bergamo, together with Guglielmo Gratarolo and Cristino del Botto.[40] These facts put his departure to Tirano in a very different light. While Cato's academic credentials remain unquestioned, his possible heresy points to one of the potential hazards that institutions and individuals had to consider when hiring a schoolmaster. As we will see shortly, Cato was not the only teacher at the Caspi Academy to fall under suspicion of heresy. It must be noted, however, that in 1556–7 Cato appears once again in the ledger of the Caspi Academy as a teacher, drawing an annual salary of about ninety lire.[41] The absence of any formal contract, and the fact that his salary was only 25 per cent of what it had been a decade earlier, suggests that his return to the Caspi Academy was only a part-time position.

Upon Cato's initial resignation from the Caspi Academy, he was quickly replaced by Angelo Caliano of Tuscany. After interviewing Caliano in his palace, the bishop opined that he was a good man, able to teach both Greek and Latin, with a knowledge of mathematics and a superior mastery of philosophy, complemented by a virtuous character, dignified manners, and a firm faith. The bishop's involvement here is curious, for otherwise he had little to do with the Caspi Academy. Perhaps the bishop desired to review the candidate to ensure his moral suitability. However, there is no documentation to support the bishop's interviews of subsequent candidates – indeed, the bishop largely disappears from the schools' records after 1549. A few days later Caliano obtained the requisite licence to teach from Torquato Brembate, an official whose precise function remains unknown. An example from a neighbouring valley suggests that this licence was connected to the prior episcopal interview, and that it was intended to guarantee Caliano's morality and good standing within the Church.[42] Offered a salary of four hundred lire per year plus a place in the school for his nephew Cesare, Caliano agreed to arrive by 1 June for a period of two years, with the possibility of a three-year extension at a higher salary. He promised to introduce new and more efficient methods of teaching and to share all of his ideas with the academy fathers.[43] Caliano remained at the school for four years, apparently without incident. Occasional references to his name between 1548 and 1552 (e.g., acknowledged as *primo maestro* or asked to confirm the number of students) confirm his presence, but no record exists of his 'new' teaching methods, nor have his promised reports to the academy patrons been preserved.

In June 1552 the academy replaced Caliano with 'the excellent professor of grammar Julio Terzi' on a five-year contract at the usual salary of four hundred lire per year. Terzi's wife and three children accompanied him, and his eldest son, Silvio, was hired to assist his father in the classroom. Two years later, Terzi's two younger children, Dario and Sulpizia, were admitted to study with the other students at the expense of the academy.[44] The only occasion on which girls appear to have been admitted to the Caspi Academy is when they were the teacher's own children (e.g., Sulpizia Terzi and Andrea Cato's anonymous daughter).

Terzi was an established if rather unimportant figure in the ecclesiastical world of Bergamo. Curate (*viceparroco*) of San Salvatore di Almenno from 1537 to 1543, he was later promoted to be parish priest of Curno, a post he held until at least 1557. According to pastoral visitations, he seems to have been appreciated by his parishioners even if the conditions of his church were sub par. In 1552, contemporaneous with his appointment to the Caspi Academy, Terzi was designated by Bishop Soranzo as confessor for the nuns of Matris Domini. He left the Caspi Academy after three years (1555). Thereafter he experienced several problems. In 1557 he was investigated by the vicar Giovan Battista Brugnatelli for suspected heresy and close association with Bishop Soranzo. In a face-to-face encounter, Soranzo defended Terzi as 'a good man and a good Catholic' (*huomo da bene e buon catholico*) but Brugnatelli was not convinced: 'Afterward I examined three other witnesses against him [Terzi], from which I concluded and am certain that he is a heretic, both because of the opinions he is said to have held and because of prohibited books that he has read and owned and tried to share with others.' Brugnatelli subsequently barred Terzi from visiting any monasteries, although the vicar did not feel he had enough evidence to formally charge Terzi. One year later, however, Brugnatelli did open an investigation in April 1558 of Terzi's habitual practice of strolling around town in lay clothes. In 1575 Terzi's multiple benefices and poor administration of his responsibilities landed him in trouble with the strict decrees of Carlo Borromeo.[45] Thus none of the first three teachers hired by the Caspi Academy finished out the full term of their respective contracts. Such instability was all too familiar to those trying to organize schools in Bergamo.

The last teacher hired by the Caspi Academy, Teodoro Vannio, arrived in the summer of 1555 on the strength of a recommendation by the notary Giovanni Maria Rota.[46] Lauded for his character, his erudition, and his teaching ability, Vannio signed a contract for one hundred scudi (= 600–700 lire) per year, almost double the salary of his predecessors. The deputies of the academy remarked upon this increase explicitly in his letter of appointment, noting that his salary was 'far more than we have ever paid anyone else.'[47] In all other respects, however, his contract was similar to those of the academy's other head teachers, including meals and housing for the entire family. Vannio taught in the

Caspi Academy for at least two years, following a curriculum consistent with that of his predecessors.

All four of the principal *maestri* employed by the Caspi Academy appear to have been accomplished teachers. While we know much more about Cato's extracurricular activities, scattered references imply that his successors also sought to bolster the public image of the academy through civic participation. Three of the four head teachers arrived with a family in tow and enrolled their children at the academy. Their status as fathers in their own right may have reassured other parents that these men could be trusted with the education of such young students. In this light, Giacomo Chizola's comment about the strategic placement of his school in Brescia to facilitate parental visits takes on added significance; the Caspi Academy's head teachers had to provide a delicate balance of academic rigour, physical safety, and moral guidance.

The Caspi Academy regularly hired an assistant teacher, usually called the *secondo maestro* or sometimes the *ripetitore*. He conducted grammar drills, organized a review of the day's lessons, and provided general support to the head teacher. He might be either a priest or a layman. In 1548, for example, the priest Manfredo Bescio was hired to assist Andrea Cato in the classroom, but the final clause of his contract permitted him to continue celebrating Mass for the nuns at the nearby monastery of San Benedetto so long as it did not interfere with his teaching responsibilities.[48] Chizola pointed out that a second teacher was indispensible 'both for teaching and for governing the boys, because they are never allowed to go out without one of the teachers, and having only one, he could not always be there.'[49] The assistant's salary was generally a fraction of his superior's: Chizola suggested a range of eight to twenty-five ducats, while in Bergamo the second teacher usually earned around eighty lire per year.[50] A 1554 letter from Alvise Malipiero of Vicenza provides part of a curious story about an assistant teacher at the Caspi Academy. Acknowledging the 'unreasonableness' of his behaviour and claiming that he was 'not the type to gain a private profit with a public insult,' Malipiero begged the forgiveness of the academy's deputies for slurs he had uttered against an anonymous second teacher. Malipiero justified his behaviour by claiming that he had simply wished to increase the likelihood of his friend Giuseppe being hired as the new assistant teacher.[51] The eventual outcome of the case remains lost but the anecdote suggests that the job of *ripetitore* was a desirable one. The priest Bartolomeo Zanchi was hired circa 1556 as an assistant teacher, presumably to assist Teodoro Vannio. Just two years earlier (1554) Zanchi had been a procurator for Cristoforo Oldofredi, who was subsequently investigated for heresy. Zanchi, too, was the subject of discussion by the Bergamasque inquisitor in July 1557 about whether it would be necessary for him to abjure. It is possible that Battista da Ghisalba, whom we have already met as *ripetitore* for Andrea Cato in 1548, still held this position in 1556–7 when he was investigated for possession of suspicious books.[52]

The house staff of the Caspi Academy included Zuanne (Giovanni) Todescho of Padua, who served as housemaster (*maestro della casa, dispensatore*) from the founding of the academy until his death on 24 July 1550.[53] Todescho lived in the house with the boys and was responsible for providing food to students and teachers. His last will and testament distributed money and goods to other members of the academy. Shortly after the academy opened, the bishop had received a letter from an Augustinian friar in Milan who wished to recommend the bearer of the letter for a position as an accountant (*ragionere*). The friar noted that if the academy did not need an accountant, this person could also teach writing to the students.[54] In June of 1548 Giovanni Bonghi applied for the job of bursar (*spenditore*) at the academy, and was hired with the condition that Guglielmo Gratarolo provide a surety of twenty-five scudi.[55] The academy asked for a deposit because of the financial risks and the public nature of the job. Some time later the Bergamasque canon Antonio Pighetti (Pigretti) was appointed treasurer. Pighetti had worked on behalf of the Roman curia in Trent, Bologna, and Rome and possessed a notable collection of benefices within the diocese of Bergamo which supplemented his meager salary from the academy.[56]

Other individuals, each of whom earned a paltry salary, are mentioned occasionally as house servants, laundry washers, cooks, and the like. Chizola had reminded the bishop in 1547 that the presence of support staff was important 'because one does not want the teachers to have any responsibilities in this area that might distract them from their job.'[57]

Who were the students of the Caspi Academy? Aside from the children of various *maestri*, nearly all the others were scions of prominent Bergamasque families. Bishop Soranzo's reference to the noble parentage of the students and a reference to the *ripetitore* in 1548 as the riding master (*hippodidascalum* [*sic*]) emphasize the elite character of the academy.[58] The stress on Latin grammar and literature and lack of any mention of a vernacular curriculum further suggest the noble background of the students. The boys started as young as five and were expected to leave school no later than age thirteen or fourteen. Thus the Caspi Academy was the equivalent of an elementary and middle school; by contrast, the MIA's school and the confraternal schools usually had a minimum of between nine and eleven years of age. A number of Caspi Academy students went on to graduate from the University of Padua later in the century. One undated document surviving among the papers of the Caspi Academy lists eighteen students by name; like the founding charter of 1547, this document includes the names of numerous prominent Bergamasque families.[59] Once again we see the creeping trend toward an elitist education and the concept of separate instruction for boys who were wealthier or more religiously oriented than their peers.

The texts possessed by the boys were standard ones for a Renaissance classroom.[60] Seventy-two per cent (13/18) of the students owned a '*Regola*,' almost certainly the *Regulae Grammaticales* of Guarino da Verona. Guarino's grammar manual enjoyed tremendous popularity owing to its brevity and clarity, advantages that would have been particularly important in an elementary/middle school like the one in Bergamo.[61] Over half of the students declared that they owned a 'Donato,' which would have been one of several variants of the famous fourth-century manual, *Ars Donatis*. Paul Grendler has demonstrated that almost all sixteenth-century Italian pedagogues used a variant of the *Ars Donatis* commonly called the *Ianua*, created in the late medieval period, or else a bilingual fifteenth-century version known as *Donato al senno*.[62] Robert Black's exhaustive study of school manuscripts confirms that an abbreviated *Ianua* was used frequently in fourteenth- and fifteenth-century Italy to teach basic reading.[63] This simplified text would have been ideal for the younger students of the Caspi Academy. No grammar manuals were published in Bergamo during the sixteenth century, although manuals published in Brescia, Verona, Venice, and Milan were surely available. One-third of the students in the Caspi Academy owned an 'alphabeto,' a simple booklet showing how to form and join different letters.

Four students declared that they had a copy of Pier Paolo Vergerio's *De ingenuis moribus et liberalibus studiis adulescentiae* (On noble customs and liberal studies of adolescents), the most frequently copied pedagogical treatise in Europe prior to Erasmus.[64] Vergerio's treatise celebrated the *studia humanitatis* and the benefits conferred by the study of history, philosophy, and eloquence in preparation for a civic life. First published in Padua, Vergerio's work was both an important transition from the medieval tradition and a dramatic break with the past. One student (Battista Boselli) stated that he had a 'carta greca' (table of Greek letters?), an intriguing clue but one about which no further information is available. In sum, the students at the Caspi Academy possessed the texts one would expect to find in a Renaissance school.[65] The omission of any vernacular texts (e.g., *Aesop's Fables*, or Vives's *Colloquia*) might reflect the vagaries of chance, but more likely it underscores the Latinate nature of instruction.

The exact closing date of the Caspi Academy remains unknown, but it probably shut its doors in 1557–8. An inventory lists twenty-three items bought from the Caspi Academy and transferred to a new school located at the gate of Sant'Antonio in late autumn of 1556.[66] On 20 May 1557 the academy recorded an inventory of 'old stuff' (*robbe vecchie*) found in the house, and three months later the academy produced a balance sheet with its final debts and credits.[67] The last dated document of the Caspi Academy is a notice addressed to all of the fathers dated 26 May 1558, reminding them to pay the instalment of thirty lire per student that had been due two weeks earlier.[68] On the eve of All Saints Day in 1558, Antonio Colleoni rented the Caspi property to a new tenant, Antonio de Prata, for ninety-five lire per year.[69] Given the lack of other references to the Caspi Academy after this date, it seems reasonable to conclude that it ceased to exist.

The reasons behind the closure of the Caspi Academy remain something of a mystery. Since the final balance sheet of 1556–7 indicates a positive credit balance, the academy did not simply collapse on account of bankruptcy or poor financial management. There is no record of frustration or disappointment with the performance of students and teachers. To the contrary, this school seems to have avoided the controversies that plagued so many of the other schools in Bergamo. It is always possible that the founding fathers no longer had young children to send to the academy and that other parents were not interested in continuing the school. Yet the evidence suggests an ever-increasing demand for instruction precisely in the decade when the Caspi Academy closed down: the Schools of Christian Doctrine opened in 1554, the school of the confraternity of Sant'Alessandro in Colonna in 1556, an anonymous academy in 1559, the seminary in 1564, and the MIA's Academy of Clerics in 1566. On the other hand, none of these schools would have served the same pool of younger, elite students that the Caspi Academy did.

Massimo Firpo suggests that the academy's closure is directly linked to the beginning of Soranzo's second trial in Rome in 1557.[70] Not only would the bishop be absent, but many of the founding fathers would be busy defending him or avoiding their own persecutions. Furthermore, Firpo's research indicates that a substantial number of the men affiliated with the academy – teachers Andrea Cato, Julio Terzi, Battista da Ghisalba, and Bartolomeo Zanchi, as well as 'patrons' Marcantonio Bolis and Giovan Giacomo Tassi – were tainted by the whiff of heresy during the 1550s. Perhaps the Caspi Academy simply could not withstand the repeated accusations of heresy against its principal members, especially when the moral component of education was seen as so important. Certainly the inquisitors in Bergamo saw these men of the academy as close allies of the bishop: for example, Giovan Battista Brugnatelli described Julio Terzi as 'the body and soul of the bishop' (*corpo et anima di esso monsignore*).[71] Given that the academy, at least initially, was Soranzo's brainchild, his downfall and subsequent death in 1558 may well have forced the Caspi Academy to shut down too.

An intriguing set of clues from the years immediately after the closure of the Caspi Academy suggests that the desire of parents to found their own academy had not dimmed entirely. During the summer of 1559 the 'professor of good arts' Ubaldo di Gherardo of Milan was hired by four deputies representing the 'Magnificent Fathers of the Academy in Bergamo.'[72] That academy remains anonymous throughout the contract, but Gherardo's responsibilities are virtually identical to those of the previous maestro at the Caspi Academy: to teach Greek and Latin to twenty-five boys in residence, to supervise their meals and walks, and to live with his family within the academy. Gherardo received the impressive salary of 150 scudi per year and the opportunity for additional private lessons, plus food, drink, and lodging for himself and his family. Gherardo was also allowed to maintain five boarding students in his own quarters; these five boys were permitted to fraternize and to study with the boys within the academy proper. Again this suggests a parallel with the socially exclusive nature of the Caspi Academy. It also implies that the 'Magnificent Fathers' were willing to relax the stipulation about private boarding arrangements within a teacher's house. Such a concession probably represents a nod to the financial realities of what was needed to induce someone to come teach in this school.

The deputies who signed the contract again represent some of the most important families of Bergamasque society (Barillo, Benaglio, Poncino, Zambello), and three of the four were drawn from the same families that had founded the Caspi Academy. The notary who recorded the contract, Alessandro Allegri, had also been one of the founding fathers of the Caspi Academy. Although it is clear that the deputies were acting on behalf of a larger group of men, the precise identity of that group was never specified beyond the vague term 'congregation.' It seems unlikely that this academy was sponsored by the commune, the MIA, or another confraternity. Each of those institutions had their own priorities at this time, and none ever displayed an interest in an elite residential academy targeted at younger students. Nor is there any record of such an academy for children within the respective archives of those institutions. Given the similarity between this anonymous academy and the Caspi Academy, the former was probably the direct successor of the latter.

Additional evidence comes from a subsequent contract in 1566 between the same anonymous fathers of the academy and the familiar figure of Nicolò Cologno. Once again drawn up by the notary Alessandro Allegri, the preface to Cologno's agreement made explicit reference to the Caspi Academy:

> In the name of Christ, amen. Everyone knows that the parents who had their children in the Caspi Academy for the purpose of being educated, had exercised every diligence to ensure the presence of a teacher from whom their children could learn good letters and good behaviour. For they knew that a parent's most important job is to never let a child slip into vice through neglect; and therefore [they knew that] the highest parental responsibility and the most precious inheritance, is to educate their children in a Christian manner and to provide them with those gifts that can never be lost.[73]

The contract noted further that Ubaldo Gherardo, who 'had taught in this academy since 1559,' wished to retire in his native city of Milan, and therefore the deputies of this academy were seeking a new instructor. Impressed by Nicolò Cologno's reputation, devout character, and pedagogical ability, the deputies nominated him to teach identical subjects to the same number of students. The only important differences in Cologno's contract were a salary increase to two hundred scudi per year and the presence of a *ripetitore* to assist him. If he fulfilled his contract – a prospect which seems somewhat doubtful – he would have remained at this academy until 1569. I have found no record of Cologno teaching elsewhere until 1574, so conceivably he could have remained five more years, until he was jointly hired by the MIA and the commune. Files in the episcopal archive and in the state archive, however, make no further reference to this 'shadow' academy.

Thus, even though the Caspi Academy had closed its doors in 1556–7, a remarkably similar school was immediately resurrected to replace it. The significance of this anonymous academy lies not in whether it represented an extension of a previous institution, but rather in what it reveals about the pattern of education in Bergamo. The Caspi Academy, and its anonymous successor, may simply represent one more example of the fragility of Bergamo's commitment to schooling. Other attempts to establish new schools had begun with a burst of enthusiasm, only to wither away after a decade or two (e.g., the MIA's Paduan College, the commune's lessons in civil law, and the bishop's attempt to open a Jesuit college). Even the more successful initiatives, such as the MIA's Academy of Clerics or the confraternal schools of Sant'Alessandro della Croce, closed after several decades. The Caspi Academy may simply be part of this larger pattern. Such an interpretation is not necessarily negative. Although one could view such school closings as a string of failures, one could also point to Bergamo's willingness to be innovative, accompanied by resilience and a determination to find better solutions for the children.

Given the brief life of the Caspi Academy and its successor, it is difficult to trace any substantial changes in their character, organization, or objectives. For about a decade, each trained young boys (and the occasional teacher's daughter) in a humanist Latin curriculum that emphasized the study of Greek, Latin, rhetoric, religion, and 'noble' behaviour. Despite the titular presence of the bishop, each school remained firmly under the control of the lay fathers who had founded it. The schools' small size, Latin curriculum, and distinguished participants strongly suggest its elite orientation.

In at least one respect, however, these two academies reflected the changing attitudes of the day. A decree preserved among the papers of the Caspi Academy stated that, in order to avoid scandal and to respect the new rules, henceforth no more women were to be permitted in the academy or on its grounds. This prohibition included servants and members of the students' extended family. Unfortunately, the document lacks a date, but it is placed between two others written circa 1557–8. Thus the prohibition could have come at the conclusion of the Caspi Academy or at the opening of its successor school. It does not appear from other sources that the Caspi Academy had any specific problem with women inside the academy. Instead, this decree suggests that the moral imperatives of the Tridentine Church trickled down even to this level and even at this relatively early date. In the Caspi Academy and in other sites of schooling around Bergamo, the prohibition of women, the constant supervision of students, and the importance of a devout teacher all reflected the Church's effort to reinvigorate the faith. The Caspi Academy thus represents a microcosm of the larger movements that were shaping Italy in the sixteenth century: Renaissance humanism, Tridentine Catholicism, aristocratization, the gradual laicization of education, and the strong desire of parents to obtain an education for their children.

Private Tutors

As noted at the outset of this chapter, few private tutors seem to have resided in Bergamo. The isolated references that exist can still be taken as representative, even if we do not possess the evidence to evaluate fully the status, responsibilities, and careers of teachers who taught privately in Bergamo. In some cases these private tutors also taught at other institutions in Bergamo, and thus we know something of their concurrent activities. For example, Nicolò Cologno tutored students privately in his house for several years in between his appointments to the communal school and the MIA's Academy of Clerics. Most of the teachers employed by the commune or by a confraternity in sixteenth-century Bergamo had the opportunity to teach students privately at the same time that they were teaching larger classes in an institution. Since the experiences of those teachers have been examined elsewhere in this study, and since the documents reveal virtually nothing new about the details of such private tutoring, let us turn to the instruction provided by purely private masters.

One example illustrates that while Bergamo's elite may have been poor relative to the Milanese or Venetian nobility, they nevertheless maintained some similar traditions when it came to providing a tutor. In 1535 Hieronymo Agosto was appointed as guardian of seven-year-old Alessandro Passi. For a salary of sixty scudi per year, Agosto managed Alessandro's property, dressed him appropriately, supervised his behaviour, and maintained a grammar teacher to instruct him.[74] Agosto's contract does not reveal other specific responsibilities in terms of 'educating' his young charge, but it probably included the gentlemanly arts of hunting, horseback riding, and dance. Agosto was not an academic instructor, as Giovanni Battista Pio had been to Isabella d'Este at the end of the fifteenth century, responsible for tutoring his pupil in grammar and literature. Instead, Agosto was expected to be a companion and to serve *in loco parentis* if necessary. Agosto's example reminds us that not all tutors were academicians; as with apprentices in a workshop or acolytes in a church, instruction could often occur outside a formal classroom.

Several other examples from sixteenth-century Bergamo confirm the practice of hiring a live-in tutor. Ludovico Suardi's tax return of 1526 noted the presence of a salaried teacher residing in his house for the purpose of instructing his children.[75] Antonio Sale, a ten-year-old orphan from a wealthy noble family, had a *ripetitore* to teach him lessons at home in 1525.[76] Alessandro Offlaga, usually referred to simply as Alessandro di Brescia *rector scolarum*, appeared frequently as a witness and an instructor in notarial documents between 1508 and 1545.[77] For example, from 1518 to 1524 he lived as a tutor in the house of the medical doctor Guido Carrara.[78] Later he lived with several other well-off Bergamasque families, including a stint with the Marenzi family beginning in 1534.[79] Another example concerns Pietro Rota, a young man studying at the MIA's Academy of Clerics, who was hired in 1590 by Count Ludovico Secco Suardo to tutor three children at home.[80] Rota remained as an in-house tutor until the summer of 1592. At least a dozen other teachers appear briefly in contracts, tax returns, and other financial documents; since none of them worked for the schools of the commune, the confraternities, or the bishop, it seems reasonable that some of them must have taught privately.[81] Not all of these private tutors would have lived in residence, of course, but clearly a substantial number of them were housed with a family.

As members of one of the few professions that necessitated literacy, notaries sometimes served as private tutors, too. In 1453 Marino Fogaccia, a notary originally from the village of Osio, opened both a notarial workshop and a small school in Borgo San Leonardo to teach reading and writing. His son Giovanni Fogaccia, nicknamed Zinino, continued the family tradition, working as both a notary and a grammar teacher; three boys in the successive generation also entered the notarial profession. Giovanni Fogaccia's notarial register of 1488–1502 contains a fascicle filled with materials for teaching basic Latin: short sentences to be translated from Italian to Latin, verses and epigrams, grammatical rules, lists of adjectives, and so forth. Yet no other references have survived to document the teaching careers of the Fogaccia family. Giovanni Marsilio Zanchi exercised the notarial profession in Bergamo in the beginning of the sixteenth century and also served as a tutor for a small group of boys and girls. Inside the back cover of a personal notebook, Zanchi listed the names of his students, but he did not specify whether he was training apprentices in the notarial arts or teaching reading and writing to local children.[82] The presence of several girls among his students suggests the latter. Neither the names of Zanchi's students nor Zanchi himself have appeared in any other reference to Bergamasque schooling.

Lastly, we come to the example of Bonino de Mauris, a grammar professor who amassed a substantial teaching library prior to his death in 1542.[83] Like the tutors listed above, de Mauris remains a one-dimensional figure, known only indistinctly through fleeting appearances in notarial contracts. We do not even know for certain that he was a tutor, although the circumstantial evidence is strong. Analysis of the works that he possessed can reveal the balance in his teaching between Renaissance humanism and Tridentine Catholicism, between vernacular and Latin texts, or between classical and contemporary works. His library thus helps us to imagine the collections of other anonymous tutors in Bergamo.

The library owned by de Mauris at his death consisted of 111 books, a sizable collection for any Renaissance pedagogue, particularly in a smaller city like Bergamo. Humanist Adriano da Spilimbergo (1511–41) possessed nearly two hundred volumes, while the master teacher of Canobio, Bartolomeo Luato, owned ninety-seven books. More typical, however, are the Milanese *maestri* like Battista Crespo (thirty-three books), Reverend Nicolai of San Michele al Gallo (twenty-eight books), and Giovanni Cressino (twenty-six books).[84] The posthumous inventory of de Mauris's texts was primarily to establish the value of the books, and thus they are grouped by size and type of binding, often providing only the name of the author or a fraction of the full title. Despite the fact that we can only be certain of about half of the titles, it is possible to reconstruct the outlines of a 'working library' for a private tutor in Bergamo.

In the case of de Mauris, nearly one-quarter of his collection consisted of the great Latin authors, including poets (Virgil, Juvenal, Ovid, Claudius, Lucan), playwrights (Terence, Plautus), philosophers (Seneca), and orators (Cicero). Half a dozen Greek authors are present, too, including Plutarch, Diogenes of Halicarnassus, and Aesop. These books formed the core of the curriculum favoured by Renaissance humanists, with its focus on the acquisition of virtue and eloquence. Approximately 15 per cent of de Mauris's library consisted of grammar texts, lexicographies, and dictionaries (including the first Latin dictionary of the late fifteenth century, the *Calepino*, edited by the Augustinian monk Ambrogio da Calepio). Most of these reference works would have been in Latin. Clearly, such works were used for didactic purposes, whether at home or in the classroom, and there is some overlap with the texts owned by students of the Caspi Academy. An additional 10 per cent were books penned by fifteenth-century Italian humanists (Angelo Poliziano, Cristoforo Landini, Francesco Filelfo, Pier Paolo Vergerio), which discussed philology, linguistics, and poetry.

It is worth noting the types of books that did *not* appear in de Mauris's library. Bonino de Mauris did not appear to own any works by Petrarch, even though these were widely published in the sixteenth century. Nor are there works by Ariosto and Boccaccio; nor is there evidence of romances or poetry (*romanzi cavallereschi*) in the vernacular. This absence of recent vernacular works suggests that the library was intended to be primarily a scholarly resource for de Mauris and his students. Interestingly, de Mauris had virtually no interest in mathematics, natural science, astronomy, or theology (only four books deal with theology). Nor did his interests run to philosophy: just one copy of Plato and two copies of Aristotle appear in this collection. Despite some obvious gaps, we can see the strongly humanistic orientation of this provincial library, with its emphasis upon the humanist program of Latin grammar followed by direct study of the classics. It is, in short, a teacher's library, albeit a teacher with limited interests or a limited budget. It remains true that we cannot know which texts he assigned to or shared with students, and which he kept for personal use. Nevertheless, de Mauris's library can inform us about his pedagogical ideas even when we lack firm knowledge about exactly when, where, and whom he taught.

Conclusion

Our lack of knowledge about Bonino de Mauris and the other tutors in Bergamo underscores the fortuitous survival of so much information about the Caspi Academy. Although the extant documents tell us quite a bit about this school, they do not speak directly to the issue of why parents sought to create their own lay schools. It must have required enormous energy to start up and to maintain such a school, particularly in light of the frequent turnover of the head teachers. The wealthiest of parents could simply have hired a live-in tutor, and evidence exists to show that some did so. Perhaps these parents of the Caspi Academy and its successor school were searching for something more. They apparently did not want their sons to attend either the MIA's school or the public school sponsored by the commune. Nor did they wish to send them to Brescia for instruction, where more private tutors were available. One possible conclusion is that the parents wished to maintain a certain degree of social exclusivity regarding the education of their young sons. The Colleges of Nobles that the Jesuits were just beginning to establish elsewhere in Italy would have provided such a social buffer. In addition, parents probably sought greater control over the curriculum and costs of their sons' schooling. Lastly, given the very young age at which students couldenrol in the Caspi Academy, it is likely that no equivalent school existed for those aged five to nine.

The purpose of the Caspi Academy and its successor is at once obvious and elusive. Together with the bishop, these parents wanted a classical education for their children. They hired highly qualified humanists and provided the material support necessary so that students and teachers alike could focus on their lessons. This thirst for education parallels that which is visible in other contexts in Bergamo. Yet it is not entirely clear whether the education sought by these parents was intended to be practical or ornamental. Reciting the *Eclogues* of Giovanni Pontano was certainly good for a student's command of Latin and rhetoric, and was also in line with contemporary pedagogical practice. It marked the student as a member of the elite classes, confirming his status in the social hierarchy. Yet the Caspi Academy is something of an enigma because of its unusually young student body and its curious balance between religious and secular motivation. While we cannot be certain of Bishop Vittore Soranzo's motivation in co-founding the Caspi Academy, he clearly wished (together with the parents) to promote lessons in morality and catechism. Soranzo's reforming tendencies from 1544 to 1554, most evident in his injunctions to the clergy to read beyond traditional Catholic works and to embrace some of the new literature from the north, suggest that he maintained a more open mind about education and its purpose in Bergamo. That openness, of course, ultimately landed Soranzo, along with several of the teachers within the Caspi Academy, in trouble with the Holy Office.

The evidence from Bergamo suggests that there was no uniform pattern for schooling sponsored by parents. Some wealthy parents in Bergamo imitated their peers elsewhere by hiring private tutors to instruct and accompany their children. Bergamo apparently had fewer private tutors than other Italian cities of comparable size. Perhaps in compensation for the lack of private instructors, and for other reasons outlined above, Bergamasque parents founded the Caspi Academy in 1547, and a successive academy in 1559, to meet their needs. Nearly all of the examples cited in this chapter describe the activities of Bergamo's social elite. Schooling was available to those further down the social scale, but private tutoring – or its cooperative equivalent, as in the Caspi Academy – remained the province of the wealthy and privileged classes.

6 *Fuori le mura*: Schooling beyond Bergamo

In his 1553 compendium of Italian cities and their inhabitants, the Bolognese Dominican Leandro Alberti lauded Bergamo for its high level of education: 'The residents of this city are very civilized, even if they speak roughly, and they possess a subtle craftiness, being as good at the art of letters as they are with trade. Indeed, the people of Bergamo are so well-educated that they have no need of foreign physicians, nor lawyers, nor notaries, and least of all do they need grammar teachers, as the city is abundantly provided with excellent schoolmasters in every generation.'[1] Two hundred years earlier, the poet Petrarch had made a nearly identical comment about the 'abundance of teachers' that Bergamo enjoyed.[2] Such positive comments stand in stark contrast to the stereotype of Bergamo as a home of illiterate hillbillies whose dialect was considered incomprehensible. This stereotype, nurtured through the stock characters in Italy's commedia dell'arte, also appears in other examples of literature.[3] Which image of Bergamo's schooling is closer to the truth? Equally important, we must understand the extent to which Bergamo's experience represented either the exception or the rule within the Venetian Republic.

To put it another way, was schooling in Bergamo unique, or was it more broadly representative of other towns and cities? As we have seen, Bergamo offered a wide, if sometimes sporadic, array of possibilities to those seeking an education. Certain aspects of this schooling were idiosyncratic and distinctive to Bergamo alone, but much of Bergamo's experience with education parallels that of its neighbours. In my view, the myriad opportunities for instruction in Bergamo were not unusual, but exemplify the desire of institutions and individuals to promote education between the fifteenth and the seventeenth century.

COMMENTARIORVM IVI

ALBERICVS DE ROSATE.

Frontispiece from Alberico da Rosciate, *Commentariorum Iuris* (Lyon, 1545). Recognized throughout Italy for his achievements in law and diplomacy, Rosciate served a series of cardinals, popes, and princes in Rome, Bologna, and Bergamo. He also served on the executive council of the Misericordia Maggiore confraternity and wrote numerous books on law, history, mythology, grammar, and rhetoric. This scene shows an active debate between two men, each gesticulating toward the other. A small crowd surrounds the men, but several of them seem to be distracted by events outside the frame. It is not clear if this scene represents a classroom or (more likely) an animated discussion about jurisprudence. The men depicted are clearly more mature than the students in earlier images.

Throughout central and northern Italy, schools were opened and lessons were offered in greater numbers than ever before. The desire for education is attested to by the meteoric rise of Jesuit schools; by the burgeoning number of diocesan seminaries; by the growing presence of universities; and by the increasing participation of confraternities and communes in support of schooling. In all of these areas, Bergamo's example illustrates a larger reality about the increasing role of education in early modern Italy.

A comparative analysis with neighbouring towns permits us to assess exactly how Bergamo's success (and failure) was replicated elsewhere. Other municipalities might have chosen different routes to educate their children or taken advantage of unique resources available only in certain locales, but nearly all of them shared commonalities with Bergamo's educational network. Similarly, these neighbouring cities and towns often illustrate the same broader themes that have emerged in Bergamo: for example, the popularity of humanism, the resurgence of Catholic-led education, the balance between centre and periphery, the debate over aristocratization, and so forth.

To begin, a brief snapshot of education in Renaissance Venice draws some important parallels with the Serenissima. Of course, Venice was more affluent and more international; nevertheless, Bergamo and Venice shared some fundamental characteristics in how pedagogy was organized. Next we turn to Brescia, Verona, and Vicenza, the other 'jewels' in Venice's *terraferma* crown. This trio of cities demonstrates numerous parallels with Bergamo, and the remaining differences are instructive in establishing a pattern of education on the Venetian mainland. By virtue of its proximity to Bergamo, Brescia receives a more detailed analysis than the other two cities. Lastly, we consider the five small towns of Lovere, Alzano Maggiore, Clusone, Gandino, and Romano di Lombardia, all located within the diocese of Bergamo but well beyond the city's immediate influence. Their respective histories, although considered only briefly here, echo yet again the themes already observed in Bergamo and its sister cities. In contrast to the rest of the book, which relies heavily upon archival research, in this chapter we evaluate schooling through a synthesis of primary sources and previous scholarship.

Venice

On account of their size, wealth, and cosmopolitanism, the large urban centres of Italy featured an educational network substantially differ-

Northern Italy, ca 1575

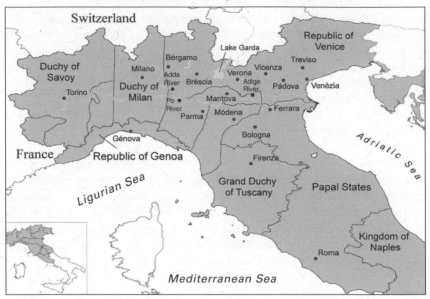

Cities	States	Bodies of Water
Venice	Republic of Venice	Po River
Treviso	Duchy of Milan	Adda River
Padua	Duchy of Savoy	Adige River
Vicenza	Republic of Genoa	Lake Garda
Verona	Grand Duchy of Tuscany	Adriatic Sea
Brescia	Papal States	Ligurian Sea
Bergamo	Kingdom of Naples	Mediterranean Sea
Milan	Switzerland	
Turin	France	
Genoa		
Parma		
Modena		
Mantua		
Bologna		
Ferrara		
Florence		
Rome		

ent from that of the smaller cities and towns. While provincial cities like Bergàmo, Treviso, Arezzo, and Pistoia relied heavily on civic-sponsored education, larger cities like Venice and Florence relied more upon independent masters. Paul Grendler has estimated that in Renaissance Italy nearly 90 per cent of the teachers in large cities were independent masters; such men could look to the numerous wealthy elites for employment as tutors, and in addition might expect to find work as copyists, translators, or speechwriters. Larger cities frequently sponsored a university, boasted more printed books, and offered more opportunities to attract scholars and teachers.

Nevertheless, significant parallels existed between the schooling offered in major urban centres and that available in their smaller counterparts. Schooling everywhere reflected the dominant contributions of parents and communes in the fifteenth and early sixteenth centuries as they replaced the weakened Church. Nearly all schools displayed the impact of humanist educators, with their promotion of classical literature, Latin grammar, and virtuous wisdom obtained through study. Low-level instruction, often based on religious and charitable motives, was of little interest to secular and ecclesiastical rulers alike until the Protestant and Catholic Reformations. After the middle of the sixteenth century, on the other hand, princes, popes, and bishops attempted to obtain control of schools from towns, parents, and confraternities.

Given Bergàmo's location and history, Venice is a natural comparison to understand Bergàmo's case in a wider context. The history of schooling in Venice has been studied in some detail by both Italian and Anglo-American scholars.[4] J.B. Ross focused attention upon the Scuola di San Marco and its efforts to teach rhetoric in the fifteenth and sixteenth centuries.[5] The survival of more than 250 *professioni di fede* (professions of faith) from 1587, published by Vittorio Baldo in 1977, provides an extraordinary opportunity for scholars to reconstruct the texts, teachers, and students in late sixteenth-century Venice.[6] Paul Grendler devoted a chapter to Venetian schools in the Renaissance, and Gherardo Ortalli has written a useful overview of late medieval Venetian schools.[7]

Research to date indicates that approximately half of the instruction in Venice concerned Latin grammar and literature. As in Bergàmo, students would have utilized grammar manuals, elementary Latin readers, and the famous works of classical antiquity. A few teachers declared that they offered additional lessons in Greek, philosophy, or logic. Latin schools were generally small, with a student-teacher ratio of 12:1, and enrolled mainly middle-class and noble boys. Larger vernacular schools taught reading, writing, and arithmetic to students destined for careers as clerks, bookkeepers, or merchants.

Similar to Bergamo, Venice offered schooling for both aspiring priests and for lay boys. During the course of the sixteenth century, in response to Tridentine reforms, these two tracks were increasingly separated in both cities. Yet Paul Grendler has argued that, even if physically separated, boys intending to become clergymen (*zaghi*) 'followed exactly the same humanistic lay curriculum as did lay students.'[8] Just as in Bergamo, the future priests would have received additional instruction in singing, liturgy, and administration of the sacraments. As Grendler notes, the Church often viewed these boys as apprentices to clerical life, who studied in school and assisted parish priests in their duties. We have seen identical practices in Bergamo, whether in parish-sponsored schools or in confraternity-sponsored schools. Other aspects of Church-sponsored schooling, such as the seminary or Schools of Christian Doctrine, follow the same broad trajectory in Venice as in Bergamo.

One essential difference between Venice and Bergamo was the preponderance of independent masters; as noted above, nine out of ten Venetian students studied in such independent schools, with the balance in church- or communal-sponsored schools. One obvious consequence was that the Venetian government was less involved in directly supporting communal schools than its counterpart in Bergamo, especially prior to the sixteenth century. After 1551, perhaps spurred by publication of Ravizza's treatise, the Venetian government became more involved with communal schooling and – like Bergamo – worked with confraternities and religious orders of men to offer more options.

Given its importance in medieval and Renaissance Europe, Venice naturally attracted a series of prominent humanists to teach both publicly and privately: George of Trebizond, Giorgio Valla, and Giovita Ravizza, to name only a few. It was not uncommon for such men to begin their careers in provincial cities like Bergamo and later 'graduate' to an appointment in Venice. Part of the attraction for both Italian and international humanists was the plethora of Venetian bookmen who published and sold a variety of texts. The University of Padua, too, would have been a significant draw for teachers and students alike. Bergamo (like Brescia, Verona, etc.) had few or none of these ancillary attractions with which to recruit teachers, scholars, and students. Nevertheless, as we have seen, Bergamo and provincial cities could still offer a substantial, if sometimes inconsistent, array of educational opportunities for such humanists and their pupils.

Obviously, Venice's student population far exceeded that of Berga-mo, but there are other important differences, too. According to the *pro-fessioni di fede*, 62 per cent of Venetian teachers belonged to the clergy, a percentage substantially higher than that estimated for Bergamo.[9] Venice's reputation for tolerance, while perhaps not entirely deserved, nevertheless resulted in a much more diverse population that included Jews, Germans, Turks, and other 'foreigners'. The impact of such out-siders on Venetian education has not yet been studied, but presumably it offered more opportunities for language training and exposure to for-eign cultures.

The importance of the Jesuits and Somaschans has already been discussed at length in the context of Bergamo, and will be consid-ered shortly for selected cities of the Venetian empire. Clearly, Venice harboured significant antipathy to the Jesuits, closely regulating the fathers' college in Padua and exiling the Jesuits on several occasions. Bergamo's reluctance to invite the Jesuit fathers within the city walls is noticeably similar to that of Venice. As we have seen, the Somaschans received more favourable treatment in Bergamo, and in Venice too they were well received even if they never established a formal college there. In broad strokes, the role of these two religious orders in Venetian edu-cation offers some parallels with that found in Bergamo.

It should come as little surprise that Bergamo and Venice shared as-pects of their educational program. Their political and economic for-tunes were already intertwined, their statutes were often comparable, and they perceived similar enemies and external threats. The expansion of a Latin and vernacular curriculum, the competing (and sometimes complementary) institutional sponsorship of education, the central role of education in civic and ecclesiastical life – all of these issues were fundamental in Venice and its dominion cities from the fifteenth to the seventeenth century.

The Veneto

One historian has likened the placement of dominion cities around Venice to a series of jewels set in a crown – each valuable in its own right, but clustered together primarily to glorify the ruler.[10] Venice cer-tainly viewed its *terraferma* lands in this proprietary fashion: as a source for raw materials, as a buffer against foreign invasion, and as a training ground for young Venetian nobles to hone their administrative skills in service to the republic.[11] The Venetian government struggled to subdue the great feudal families and to limit the privileges of peasant communes. At the same time, however, Venice ruled its mainland empire with a light hand. It sought to preserve many local institutions and encouraged its governors to respect local traditions wherever possible. Nowhere is this laissez-faire attitude more noticeable than in education. With the exception of two issues – higher education in Padua and the admission of Jesuits and Somaschans into individual cities – the Venetians followed a policy of 'salutary neglect' with regard to schooling in the mainland cities. Thus the cities of Brescia, Verona, and Vicenza were free to hire teachers, administer schools, provide scholarships, train priests, and engage in other educational activities as they saw fit.

Brescia

Located less than thirty miles from Bergamo and possessing equivalent resources and population, Brescia has often been viewed as the sister city of Bergamo. The political, economic, and artistic history of the two cities is closely intertwined, and frequent exchange occurred between students, scholars, and merchants. Like Bergamo, Brescia was the capital city of its diocese and was ruled by a pair of Venetian governors. Brescia, too, served as an important military outpost against the Milanese, and – like Bergamo – has been little studied by Anglo-American historians.[12] During the Renaissance, Brescia established itself as an early centre of printing; until the third quarter of the sixteenth century, in fact, many of the works written in Bergamo had to be printed in Brescia.[13] The city produced a number of important humanists in the Quattrocento and Cinquecento, including Giovan Francesco Boccardo, Giovanni Calfurnio, Marino Becichemo, Cristoforo Barzizza, and Giovita Ravizza.[14] Although the city was occasionally attacked by disgruntled scholars, such as the professor of grammar Gabriele da Concoreggio, who called the city 'an enemy of letters' (*litteris inimica*), or the poet Ubertino Posculo, who lamented the lack of interest displayed by the commune in the institution of schools and insisted that students attend his classes on holidays, Brescia did boast a significant number of schools and academies.[15]

As in Bergamo, schooling in Brescia was sponsored by a number of institutions, individuals, and associations. The commune and the Church played leading roles in providing instruction, but with the commune once again unable (or unwilling) to offer consistent backing to public education. Episcopal support for the Schools of Christian Doctrine, the orphanages, and the seminary closely resembled that in Bergamo. Also like Bergamo, the commune of Brescia opened its own college and began providing regular instruction in law during the second decade of the seventeenth century. Several generous bequests permitted the formation of residential colleges in Brescia, Padua, and Bologna for the benefit of Brescian students. Yet Brescia was not identical to Bergamo. The role of confraternities in Brescia appears to have been less important than in Bergamo, while the number and influence of private teachers was significantly greater. The Jesuits were able to gain a foothold in Brescia in 1564. Although surviving records are scarce, it appears that instruction at home by parents was a crucial aspect of Brescian education. Since a complete history of early modern education in Brescia is not practical here, what follows are selected topics that highlight relevant comparisons with Bergamo.

The early history of education in Brescia is similar to that of Bergamo, with scattered references to teachers, the predominance of the cathedral school, and no civic expenditure for public education. The late Trecento and early Quattrocento in Brescia conform to the picture drawn by Paul Grendler for much of Italy: instruction was dominated by private teachers hired by parents to educate small groups of elite boys, and by ecclesiastical schools for future priests. Still, it must be noted that by the 1450s, twenty-eight masters taught grammar and rhetoric inside the city.[16]

Brescia's city council took tentative steps in favour of public education toward the end of the Quattrocento. As in Bergamo, Brescia's council granted tax exemptions to teachers, agreed to found a school of rhetoric and philosophy, and allocated one hundred ducats to hire a master 'of distinguished character and proper wisdom' to teach two or three daily lessons in either philosophy or Latin and Greek.[17] In 1500 Rafaello Regio of Bergamo was nominated for the job, but after six months of waiting he quit in disgust, and the job was given to Giovanni Taberio. Taberio's stature as a humanist scholar is confirmed by a laudatory preface written by the Venetian printer Aldo Manuzio, complimenting Taberio for his intellectual accomplishments. Two years later the city council awarded Marino Becichemo the chair of Greek and Latin with a salary of 112 scudi. Becichemo's career is astonishingly similar to that of Pio, Ravizza, and Cologno in Bergamo. He taught in several Italian cities before settling down in Brescia, lured no doubt by the unusually high salary. In 1508 he quarrelled with the city council when it refused to pay a portion of his salary, departed for Rome with one of his students, and eventually accepted a professorship at the University of Padua. Brescia's city council wasted no time in hiring Francesco Arigoni that same year to teach Greek and Latin to the sons of the patriciate and to anyone else who wished to attend.[18]

From 1508 to 1516 Brescia suffered through the War of the League of Cambrai, and the documents speak primarily of military matters and widespread famine. In September 1519, however, Brescia's city council issued a ringing declaration of its support for education and promised an outlay of four hundred ducats per year. Yet eight years would pass before the council began a detailed discussion of the conditions under which four new teachers would be hired to teach rhetoric, humanities, civil law, philosophy, and logic. The contracts were never finished, and the new school remained only a dream.[19]

Although Brescia's commune mouthed enthusiastic support for public education, it was unable to sustain any kind of long-term institutional support for public instruction. Despite a strong push by the rising middle class and an environment that witnessed great strides in literature, art, and architecture, the commune could not get beyond isolated actions *ad personam* in its efforts to promote communal schooling. This is not to suggest that Brescia's city council totally neglected its responsibilities. It helped to establish a chair in civil law, oversaw a residential college for students, recruited outside teachers, and negotiated repeatedly with the Dominicans and Franciscans to provide lessons in theology, reading, and writing. In 1542 the city council devoted several meetings to establishing a grammar school for infant paupers, and as late as 1554 there are indications that this school continued to function. In 1545, in 1563, and again in 1586 the council reiterated its desire to hire one or more worthy citizens to publicly teach humanities and rhetoric within the city, for the benefit of both the city and the youths receiving instruction.[20] Yet these efforts almost never lasted longer than a year or two. Like Bergamo, for much of the sixteenth century Brescia preferred to rely upon the charisma and organizational ability of one maestro rather than creating an institutional framework for education.

Several parallels between Bergamo and Brescia demand further reflection. Both cities began tentative efforts to hire a public teacher around 1480, just as both tried to hire famous humanists from outside the city during the first two decades of the sixteenth century. When it became clear a century later that the Jesuits and the Theatines were not going to assume direction of the public schools, both city councils tried to institute a public college. Bergamo's attempt ended in ignominious failure less than a year later, but Brescia was more successful. Combining the income from Jesuit properties with bequests from Carlo Bornato and Altobello Averoldi, Brescia's city council authorized the expenditure of eight hundred lire per year for three years to hire five teachers.[21] Detailed contracts were once again drawn up, and written and oral examinations were administered to applicants. After three years the contracts were renewed, and the city council expressed its satisfaction with the results to date. The commune held high expectations for the professors, and rewarded them with equally high salaries and benefits.

The city of Brescia was so pleased with the results, in fact, that it voted to spend an additional four hundred lire so that public lessons of civil law might be offered: 'Realizing the good fruit and notable benefits that have resulted and are still now resulting from the public lectures ... not only must they be continued but if at all possible expanded, for the universal advantage of everyone.'[22] The council even voted to hire a doorman and a porter to assist with lessons. The timing of this decision to add instruction in jurisprudence was virtually identical to that in Bergamo. In 1621, however, the harmonious accord broke down, and the head of the city council proposed that all teachers currently employed must be re-evaluated before contract renewals. It is not clear why a faction of the council pursued this course; it may have been out of concern over the teachers' religious orthodoxy, or it may simply reflect political skirmishing. In any event, the proposal failed, and the school survived until the return of the Jesuits in 1657, when the fathers resumed direction of the city's public college.

While it remains true that the northwestern edge of the Venetian empire was commonly considered to be the poorest of its territories, and that its residents were famous for their parsimonious habits, a lack of arable farmland or the absence of a major trade route cannot explain the fragility of the communal commitment to public schooling in Bergamo and Brescia. Both cities had a strong tradition in literature and the arts, as well as a significant number of wealthy patrons and institutions to support education. Despite popular stereotypes of the Bergamasques and the Brescians as foolish hicks who lacked refinement, these two cities did value literacy, humanism, and intellectual life. And yet both cities, while claiming to support public instruction, resisted making a sustained institutional commitment to communal education. The presence of other institutions – confraternities, Schools of Christian Doctrine, seminaries – may have persuaded the communes that they did not need to provide schooling consistently. It is also possible that the communes were simply satisfied with their own actions, or at least that the elites who governed the councils felt that their civic commitment to education was sufficient.

In the seventeenth century, particularly in Brescia, both communes adopted a more active role in determining what kinds of education should be offered. Perhaps by that time a sufficient number of schools had been established elsewhere to serve as models, or perhaps the local economy improved, or maybe the demands of the citizenry finally became too loud to ignore. It seems likely that the absence of the Jesuits and the Theatines in the seventeenth century forced each city to accept responsibility for an area that it had traditionally ignored. It is also possible, as shown by the case of Giacomo Carrara Benaglio in Bergamo and Alessandro Luzzago in Brescia, that the leadership of an exceptional teacher could make a vital difference.

The relationship between religious orders of men and the commune provides another lens to examine the extent of civic commitment to instruction. In fifteenth-century Bergamo, the Dominicans ran a school of theology at the church of Santo Stefano, described by one modern historian as offering 'philosophical studies for aspiring clerics, open lessons for lay boys, and a library so amply endowed that it was counted among the best in Europe.'[23] In the following century the convent of Santo Spirito offered education to aspiring monks and, perhaps, also to lay boys. Yet Bergamo's city council never sought to develop any kind of pedagogical relationship between the religious and the city's youth. The Dominican prior certainly worked with the MIA to disburse scholarships, and the Dominican convent was located close to city hall. No obvious enmity existed between the friars and the town. The Dominicans, along with the Franciscans and the Benedictines, appear to have had sufficient funds to have run a school. Thus the reason for the lack of interaction between Bergamo and its early religious orders remains a mystery.

In contrast, recognizing that local friars often represented some of the most well-educated men in the city, the commune of Brescia sought to utilize this potential educational resource from an early date. In 1471 Brescia gave twenty-five ducats to the Dominicans to provide a public reader in logic and philosophy.[24] In 1508 the commune elected three deputies to negotiate with the Franciscans about admitting lay students to their famous school of theology and belles-lettres. (The Franciscan school had been founded years before by Father Francesco Sanson with the idea that it would serve both Franciscan novices and lay boys simultaneously.) The outcome of this negotiation remains unknown, but the mere attempt illustrates Brescia's early efforts to take advantage of ecclesiastical education for public benefit.

The role of the newer religious orders, founded during the Catholic Reformation, also reveals something of the civic commitment to public instruction. As we have seen, Bergamo permitted Girolamo Miani and his companions to establish orphanages that cared for abandoned children and provided basic education in reading, writing, and mathematics. As noted in chapter 4, at the commune's request and after a terrible plague in 1630–1, the Somaschans eventually assumed responsibility for managing the public schools in Bergamo. The chronology in Brescia is practically identical; Miani founded an orphanage there in 1532, and ninety-six years later the commune granted the monastery of San Bartolomeo to the Somaschans so that they might open a residential college. Interestingly, Brescia (like Bergamo) never gave the Somaschans official permission to settle in the city, ostensibly because it feared that the order might inherit too much valuable property.[25] The important point in both cities remains the same: after a century of ineffectual management, the commune slowly came to realize that other institutions were better equipped to provide education. The Somaschans' success as teachers in both cities surely owed something to their Venetian origin and to their positive reputation.

The case of the Jesuits provides a richer and more complex example. While the Jesuits' bid to enter Bergamo was turned down twice by Bergamo's city council, in Brescia the Jesuits moved into the convent of Sant'Antonio and opened a college of nobles between 1560 and 1567.[26] The Society's entry into Brescia was clearly facilitated by the presence of Angelo Paradisi, a Brescian citizen who was the only Italian member of Ignatius Loyola's original band of followers. Upon his return to Brescia in the 1560s, Paradisi created a congregation of priests and clerics in the monastery of Sant'Antonio known as the Company of Fathers of Peace (Compagnia dei Padri della Pace). Although this congregation had no formal pedagogical obligations, within two years it had begun teaching twelve pupils, and was considering the foundation of a school of rhetoric and *studia humanitatis*. Its primary activity was teaching Christian doctrine, but as the congregation gradually accepted more professed Jesuits, it began to resemble an ordinary Jesuit college. By 1601 the staff consisted primarily of Jesuit fathers.[27]

The College of Sant'Antonio's identity as a Jesuit institution resulted in its closure during the Interdict crisis of 1606; the Jesuits did not return to Brescia until 1657, when their school was reopened as the Brescian

College of Nobles.[28] The Brescian case is interesting for two reasons. First, the Jesuits were never perceived as an 'outside' group in Brescia and thus were able to establish a beachhead in Venetian territory. Second, during the half-century between 1607 and 1657, the commune does not appear to have negotiated with the Jesuits as it had (and would in the future) with other religious orders about running a public school. The Jesuits' activities elsewhere indicated that they certainly were not averse to running a school for the commune, yet in this case they did not do so until 1657. Perhaps this hiatus simply meant that Brescia was respecting the wishes of Venice to keep the Jesuits out of the *terraferma*.

One of the most distinctive features about the educational network in Bergamo was the decisive role played by the Misericordia Maggiore confraternity. As discussed in chapter 2, the MIA granted scholarships, administered schools, recruited teachers, founded colleges, and contributed in innumerable ways to the development of education. In Brescia, on the other hand, confraternities appear to have focused their efforts on charity, religious devotion, and community involvement. The only confraternity that supported young students, the Congregation of Santa Caterina, was founded in 1592 by Alessandro Luzzago.[29] It seems probable that several of the local parish confraternities helped boys from their neighbourhood to attend local schools or the seminary, but no organized pattern of instruction has emerged. Given the importance of the MIA in Bergamo, of Santa Maria dei Battuti in Treviso, and of the *scuole grandi* in Venice, the absence of a 'maxi-confraternity' in Brescia is puzzling. On the other hand, the lack of a major charitable organization in Brescia may help to explain the plethora of individuals who supported both lay and religious education in the city.

Brescia boasted an extraordinary number of men and women who contributed to the instruction and training of Brescian youth during the sixteenth century.[30] Although most were laypeople, they often worked closely with the Catholic Church in their efforts to teach catechism, literacy, and proper manners. Angela Merici, for example, pioneered the idea that young women should be taught not only morality and the rudiments of faith, but also the ability to read. She founded the Company of Ursulines at Brescia in 1535 to promote her vision of non-cloistered women teaching and ministering to the poor and to young girls.[31] Merici's efforts can be viewed in the same light as those of her male contemporaries Ignatius Loyola, Girolamo Miani, Castellino da Castello, and José Calasanz.[32] Francesco Cabrino, a provocative preacher at Brescia early in the Cinquecento, laboured for many years to promote the study of Christian doctrine as a pre-Tridentine reformer.[33] Angelo Paradisi and Alessandro Luzzago worked closely with the Jesuits and the College of Sant'Antonio, but they also established lay parochial schools for the poor. The latter were not ecclesiastical schools, but free schools open to any who wished to enrol.[34]

Giacomo Chizola, a Brescian nobleman who served Cardinal Pole for decades as a diplomat, worked closely with Angela Merici, Girolamo Miani, Gaetano Thiene, and the priest Bartolomeo Stella in his efforts to encourage schooling in Brescia. As noted in the previous chapter, Chizola founded an academy in Brescia in 1547 intended for young boys who wished to acquire a secular education, and Cardinal Pole agreed to serve as its 'protector' in 1550.[35] Correspondence between Chizola and Stella provides an astonishing range of detail about the student body, schedules, and even sleeping arrangements of the new school. Nor did Chizola's influence remain limited to Brescia; his 1547 letter to Bergamo's bishop provided the impetus for the founding of the Caspi Academy in Bergamo later that year.

Brescia's Bishop Domenico Bollani (1559–79) implemented many of the new Tridentine decrees, including expansion of the Schools of Christian Doctrine and foundation of a new seminary in 1563. Although Brescia too was a border town, it did not exhibit as strong a Milanese influence as did Bergamo in the arena of religious education. Broadly speaking, the history of the Schools of Christian Doctrine and of the seminary bear a strong resemblance to that of their sister institutions in Bergamo.

Equally impressive were the bequests made in favour of schooling by Brescian citizens during the sixteenth and seventeenth centuries. Whereas in Bergamo nearly all of these bequests were channelled through the Misericordia Maggiore (e.g., the Apibus and Biffi scholarships), in Brescia such donations were handled in a variety of ways. Three examples are particularly instructive. The earliest bequest was that of Girolamo Lamberti, 'the deaf doctor,' who left his Paduan residence to the commune of Brescia so that it might house Brescian medical students at the university. The subsequent history of this college is of particular interest for understanding changes in attitude toward the issue of schooling. Lamberti's will was dated 27 June 1509. A protracted legal dispute with Lamberti's remaining family delayed the opening of the college for a number of years, but eventually the commune began to select deserving students who wished to attend the university. In 1601 responsibility for selecting students was transferred to the College of

Physicians (of which Lamberti had been a member). The medical doctors declared that noble descent was the first prerequisite for admission, and that it would be better to admit no noble boys at all than even one poor or rural scholar! This example illustrates yet again the tendency of communes to back away from the sponsorship of public education in the late sixteenth century, and the gradual aristocratization that afflicted Italian society in the same period. A half-century later, the Brescian College of Nobles would display an identical attitude about social exclusivity and the privilege of advanced intellectual training. The Collegio Lambertino remained active in Padua until 1772, when it was incorporated into the College of San Marco and the doctor's original house was sold.[36]

Another doctor, Girolamo Fantoni of the village of Salò, directed that the income from his estate should be used for the benefit of poor students who wished to study philosophy, theology, law, and medicine. His will, dated 1587, created a commission specifically to administer this rich legacy. The Fantoni bequest continued for more than two centuries, and in 1796 supported sixteen students.[37] The third example concerns the Collegio Peroni, established in 1634 by doctor Francesco Peroni for the benefit of boys from impoverished noble families of Brescia. Peroni's will of 27 April 1634 named the rector of the orphanage and the senior member of the Peroni family as directors of his bequest. Peroni wanted a college bearing his name to be established in his former home, and the students living there to be instructed in grammar and philosophy. Peroni's college also lasted until at least 1796, at which time it housed twelve young boys who received instruction and training free of charge.[38]

What does the history of these three bequests-cum-colleges reveal about education in early modern Brescia? Bequests promoting instruction were not unusual in northern Italy. Such bequests were usually administered by confraternities or other groups designated by the testator, and not by the commune or the Venetian state.[39] It seems likely that these testators realized that the commune was not as successful as other institutions in maintaining a commitment to long-term schooling arrangements. Confraternities or orphanages, or even the college of medical doctors, were less likely than city governments to siphon the money off into other projects only tangentially related to the testator's original intention. The long duration of these bequests and colleges is also worthy of note; as we have seen, Bergamo had few educational programs that lasted beyond two or three decades, while those in Brescia seem to have enjoyed more stability and longevity.

Other bequests in Brescia illustrate the widespread desire of the citizens to promote schooling in different ways. In 1531 Altobello Averoldi left the enormous sum of eleven hundred ducats to the College of Jurists of Brescia to create a chair in civil and canon law for the benefit of aspiring legal students.[40] As in Bergamo, the professor was to be chosen from among the ranks of the College of Jurists. Several decades later, Carlo Bornato left money to the Ospedale Maggiore expressly for the creation of public schools.[41] Centuries prior to the creation of the Collegio Lambertino, the papal physician and university professor Guglielmo Corvi of Brescia founded a residential college for Brescian students in Bologna.[42]

In short, Brescia enjoyed a wealth of educational opportunity for its youth in the sixteenth and early seventeenth centuries. Many of the schooling options bore a close resemblance to those available in Bergamo, while a few were substantially different. Overall, however, Brescia's example largely confirms that Bergamo's experience with schooling seems to have been quite typical for a small to medium-sized town subject to Venice in the early modern period. Further confirmation may be found by examining, albeit in less detail, the history of two other Venetian cities.

Verona

Nestled along the Adige River and astride the major north-south and east-west trade routes, Verona enjoyed a thriving commercial and intellectual exchange with other European cities. Dante and Petrarch visited Verona, Guarino da Verona grew up and later taught there, and numerous printers and booksellers called the city home in the late fifteenth and sixteenth centuries. In 1407, 'out of regard for the traffic and commerce that this city has with the lands of Germany,' Verona's city council allocated funds to hire a certain Master Nicholas to teach boys the German language.[43] Artists, merchants, scholars, and students flocked to Verona, making it the third-largest city in northern Italy after Venice and Milan. It is not surprising, therefore, to find a surplus of schooling arrangements within the city. Despite rich archival holdings and the obvious importance that the Veronese assigned to schooling, the history of education in Verona has been studied carefully but never systematically.[44] Many aspects of its educational history mirror those we have seen already in Bergamo and Brescia: tax exemptions for teachers, communal statutes requiring a law professor, public lessons in grammar and arithmetic, the later presence of Jesuits and Somaschans. Other aspects of Veronese schooling are unique to this city: for example, the continuing presence of a school devoted to mathematics and surveying, a school established by the College of Notaries, and lessons in German, logic, and medicine. The early date at which the commune addressed educational issues is also important; statutes as far back as 1276 call for a *magister* to instruct boys in appropriate subjects.

The 1276 statutes, commonly referred to as the Albertini, devoted half a dozen paragraphs to subjects that should be taught and salaries that should be paid.[45] The professor of civil law, who received the enormous sum of five hundred lire plus the use of a free house for his family, was clearly *primus inter pares* (first among equals). The commune also declared its desire to hire a professor of canon law, a professor of medicine, a professor of logic, and a professor of mathematics (specifically, algorithms and arithmetic), each at a salary of fifty lire per year. All of the teachers were expected to participate in one public debate per month during the academic year. The Albertini statutes also called for a grammar master to be hired, but the low annual salary of twenty-five lire and his exemption from the debates signalled his initial inferiority relative to the other pedagogues.[46] According to the statutes, full-time students were exempted from military service (although they still needed to hire someone to serve in their place). By 1328 Verona – like Bergamo – had passed under the control of a powerful *signore*, in this case Cangrande della Scala, who arrogated to himself the right to appoint teachers, and awarded them tax exemptions so long as they continued to teach effectively.

In 1450, after more than two decades under the Venetian Republic, the statutes were again reissued.[47] This redaction assigned specific institutions the responsibility to select, and pay, the various kinds of teachers. Thus the commune of Verona had to hire the grammar and rhetoric teachers; the civil law and medicine professors were to be selected by the Venetian Senate; the Merchants' Association (Domus mercatorum) designated a mathematics teacher; and the podestà, with the advice and consent of the bishop, selected a professor of canon law. Even the College of Notaries participated, passing a motion in 1469 that established a two-year course of free study and mandated the hiring of a judge to teach the necessary legal precepts.

Such a complex system sounds inefficient, and extant evidence suggests that it often broke down or resulted in litigation. For example, Venice was unlikely to pay for a teacher outside the lagoons, and indeed the city council minutes show no record of anyone being hired for the chair in medicine after 1450. The motivation must have been to avoid concentrating power in the hands of one individual or institution, or perhaps to ensure that some form of schooling would always be available even if one of the sponsors went bankrupt. Fifteenth-century statutes in Bergamo and Brescia were much less detailed, devoting only one or two paragraphs to the necessity of hiring a teacher of law or grammar. It is probable that Bergamo's bishops, confraternities, and college of notaries supported education in the fifteenth century, but such cooperation, if it existed, must have been more informal than in Verona.

Teaching mathematics in Renaissance Italy was not unusual, particularly in the busy commercial centres of the Italian peninsula. Richard Goldthwaite has analysed the teaching of commercial arithmetic in Florence while Paul Grendler summarizes the practice in various Italian towns. Robert Black carefully considers how *abbaco* (arithmetic) was taught in Florence and in several Tuscan towns, concluding that it was more popular within fifteenth-century Florence than the traditional Latin grammar curriculum. Teachers in Bergamo often had 'mathematics' or 'arithmetic' included in their contracts, but the subject never seems to have been a priority for the commune or confraternities. Rarely was a teacher hired specifically to teach arithmetic in Bergamo; it was usually included in a list of desirable subjects but never do we find speeches or statements about its utility as we do with the humanities or the law.

Verona's lessons in abbaco stand out, however, because of their longevity and rich documentation.[48] The first reference, to Master Loto da Firenze, comes from the thirteenth-century Albertini statutes. A succession of men – curiously, all from Tuscany – continued teaching mathematics until 1437, when Master Baldassare of Verona began a family tradition of teaching mathematics in the city. His sons Battista, Cristoforo, and Bernardino each succeeded him as teachers, and Battista was further cited in 1478 as a land surveyor for local farmers and artists. The most famous mathematician in Verona was certainly Nicolò Tartaglia, who arrived from Brescia as a private tutor to the Mazzanti family in 1520 and subsequently published his opus on engineering and mathematics, *Quesiti e inventioni diverse*.[49] Other arithmetic teachers were hired regularly until the end of the sixteenth century, including Giovan Maria Fanice of Rovigo, whose petition to the city council of Verona beautifully illustrates the practical applications of his subject:

After travelling through many cities in Italy, I decided to establish myself in Verona, for the public honour and for the utility of anyone who wished to train himself in the subject that I teach; instruction in how to read and record every type and variation of money and arithmetic, in theory and in practice, that exists in Italy, and especially to keep a single and double-entry account book in the Venetian fashion ... and also to measure and estimate, via theoretical and practical geometry, lands of various shapes, [as well as] mountains, hills, valleys, pasture, grain, forests, vats, wells, drains, [and] cisterns; to gauge the depth of [bodies of] water, to make square walls, pyramids, columns, towers, palaces, and foundations both above and below ground, just as a surveyor is expected to do.[50]

Abbaco books typically explained multiplication and division, fractions and whole numbers, and mathematical business problems. The emphasis in abbaco schools was upon the commercial applications of mathematical skills, with illustrations and vernacular text to underscore this practical orientation. Fanice's petition confirms that abbaco teachers emphasized the practical side of mathematics. Paul Grendler has noted that abbaco treatises 'tacitly assumed the moral acceptability of interest-bearing loans by repeatedly presenting problems in which the student calculated the payment of principal and interest due as a result of the loan.'[51] Robert Black comes to a different conclusion, namely, that the 'small number of *libri di abaco* indicates that these theoretical treatments were not used directly by the pupils.'[52] Although such treatises have not been found in Bergamo, the practical aspects of instruction, exemplified by the moral dilemma over usury, must surely have been present in all *terraferma* cities.

Gian Paolo Marchi's research on fourteenth- and fifteenth-century Veronese schooling confirms that while grammar teachers may have received little respect in Verona's early statutes, during the Renaissance their situation improved dramatically.[53] Not all of them enjoyed the popularity or remuneration of Guarino Guarini, or the adulation that Vittorino da Feltre received from the Gonzaga princes, but many achieved success and recognition. In 1451, for example, fourteen grammar masters were listed as participants in a Corpus Domini parade in Verona.[54] As late as 1499, Gregorio Amaseo wrote to his brother Leonardo about the reputation enjoyed by an entire generation of humanists (e.g., Aretino, Valla, Poliziano, Guarino, Filelfo, Beraldo). Like other cities of the *terraferma*, including Bergamo, Verona regularly recruited famous humanists to teach grammar and rhetoric in its public schools.

In 1467 the city council hired the son of Francesco Filelfo, Gian Mario, to teach three daily lessons on the classics, in addition to a Sunday lecture on Dante. Gian Mario lasted less than a year before transferring to Bergamo, where he encountered an equal lack of success. More typical in Verona was the performance of Martino Rizzoni, Bernardino Donato, and Matteo Del Bue, each of whom taught grammar for several years. Yet Verona's city council treated public schooling much like Bergamo's council: both paid lip service to the importance of education but were unable to provide institutional leadership and support to ensure the long-term success of public schooling. Donato's success in Verona – as an editor, orator, and teacher – came in part because he had the bishop's unfailing support even when the commune failed to increase his salary.

Verona's city council minutes, which regularly discuss the appointment of public teachers prior to 1550, do not contain a single reference to this topic after mid-century. Part of this absence can be explained by the arrival of the Jesuits in Verona in the late 1570s and by the substantial number of private teachers who appear on the tax rolls.[55] Economic woes may have played a part, too; like Bergamo, Verona was surely affected by the gradual decline of Venetian shipping and the rise of competition in Spain and northern Europe in the later sixteenth century. Marchi cites the intermittent attention paid to schooling and the 'vain ambitions' (*velleitarismo*) of Verona's council as contributing to the decline of Veronese public schooling. It is worth remembering that in 1551 Giovita Ravizza's treatise, calling upon the Venetian government to intervene more actively in schooling, had been published in Venice. Presumably Ravizza perceived a need for the Venetian Senate to intercede more directly in educational matters. Two generations later a nearly identical perception surfaced in Verona, as captured in Orlando Pescetti's *Orazione dietro al modo dell'istituire la gioventù* (An oration on how to instruct children).[56] Pescetti believed fervently that communal education should be a first priority for the city, and he urged the council to limit both private tutoring and the introduction of religious men and women as instructors. In yet another sign of creeping aristocratization, Pescetti also criticized elite families who isolated their children in country villas. He called for the election of four wise deputies to draw up a list enumerating which teachers might be authorized to teach in Verona. Pescetti's other proposals – a public library, performance-based salaries for teachers, more tax revenue for schools – while not explicitly favouring the improvement of public education, would have contributed strongly to that cause. In Pescetti's opinion at least, the public schools in Verona were not doing their job; and the city council minutes stand silent witness in agreement.

Verona's relationship with religious orders of men appears to have been rather typical. On 14 December 1576, Bishop Agostino Valier submitted a request to Verona's city council that the Jesuits be called into the city to open a college. The bishop's petition pointedly noted that the foundation of peace and tranquillity within the city was the discipline provided to children, and yet Verona's city fathers had done and were doing little in support of schooling for their sons. The motion passed by a vote of 34–20, and six months later the pope issued a bull transferring the church of San Sebastian to the Society of Jesus. The Jesuits were granted permission to open three schools for a maximum of two hundred students, but the actual beginnings were much more modest: six Jesuits and four lay teachers provided instruction to just ten students. In 1577 the seminarians in Verona were transferred *en masse* to the Jesuit college after financial difficulty and a homemade bomb threatened the seminary's main building.[57] According to reports mailed to the Father General in Rome, the Jesuit college in Verona enjoyed three decades of modest success until it was forced to close in 1607 owing to the Interdict.[58]

The records do not indicate how Verona coped with the sudden departure of the Jesuits in the early seventeenth century. Unlike Bergamo and Brescia, Verona does not appear to have reacted by founding a public college. Perhaps the Veronese elite sent their sons to Jesuit colleges in Lombardy, which were unaffected by the Interdict crisis. In 1637, probably in reaction to the plague six years earlier, Verona's city council belatedly asked the Somaschans to open a public school in the neighbourhood of Sant'Anastasia. In 1654 the Somaschans moved to the neighbourhood of San Vitale and opened a small boarding college, followed by yet another transfer in 1669 to the convent of San Zeno in Monte. In the same year, the Venetian Senate called for the creation of a new academy for the instruction of noble young boys, and selected the Veronese Somaschans to administer it.

Once again we see the commune relinquishing its role in supervising public education to the Church or other institutions, as well as the trend toward aristocratization with another College of Nobles. Verona's history of schooling thus shows both similarities and differences to Bergamo's. Its abbaco school, for example, had no counterpart in Bergamo, nor did Bergamasque statutes address schooling as early as did Verona's. In general, however, with the notable exception of confraternities, the portrait of schooling is a similar one. The example of Vicenza offers a final opportunity to assess the schooling of another city on the Venetian mainland.

Vicenza

Although Vicenza is famous primarily for its profusion of Palladian villas and neoclassical buildings, the city boasts a significant and well-documented history of schooling.[59] Given that Vicenza's population and economy were similar to Bergamo's, it is not surprising that numerous similarities existed between the two towns. Yet they were hardly identical. Both cities used tax exemptions, high salaries, and free housing to attract humanist 'superstars' from out of town to teach grammar, rhetoric, and humanities to town boys in the fifteenth and sixteenth centuries. Among these imported teachers was Giovita Ravizza, who taught public lessons in both Bergamo (1508–23) and in Vicenza (1524–33). City councils in both cities prohibited judges from practising their profession while teaching, took little advantage of the educated religious who lived close to town, and demonstrated inconsistent support for public education. With two notable exceptions, both cities displayed considerable autonomy in designing their educational networks. Both towns witnessed a serious decline in public schooling toward the end of the Cinquecento, driven by a combination of factors that included the reeemergence of the Church, the new character of humanism, the relative decline of the Veneto's economy, and larger social changes in early modern society. Yet the two cities were far from identical: humanism enjoyed greater success and diffusion in Vicenza than in Bergamo; and Vicenza (like Verona) appears to have been committed to public education from a much earlier date than was Bergamo. Perhaps on account of the Vicentines' greater per capita wealth, private tutors were employed more frequently. Lastly, while Vicenza boasted a 'prodigious flowering' of social initiatives headed by confraternities and religious orders beginning in the thirteenth century, very few of these associations appears to have offered instruction to lay or secular boys.

The first immediate and substantial difference to note between Vicenza and Bergamo was the presence of a 'university' (*studio*) at Vicenza in the early thirteenth century. Founded in the convent of San Vito by academic exiles from Bologna, and designed to teach law and perhaps also letters, it closed after only five years. Attempts to reopen a university in the early fifteenth century, when Vicenza submitted to Venice, were initially encouraged but soon rebuffed as the republic sought to guarantee the primacy of Padua. The memory of this Vicentine *studio* and the inability to re-establish it may have pushed the Vicentine elites to support their public secondary schools instead. Several scholars have suggested that the inability of Vicenza's elite to enter the Venetian patriciate after the *serratura* (closing) of the Great Council in 1297, combined with the city's lack of a royal court, may have encouraged Vicentine nobles to expand educational opportunities for their children.[60]

Vicenza displayed an early and enduring interest in its public schools. A decree of 1261 awarded five hundred lire to Arnoldo di Guascogna with the obligation to instruct at least twenty students in canon law. Statutes governing the salary and conduct of public school teachers appeared in 1264, 1311, 1339, and 1406; the 1339 statute specifically declared that the commune must hire two masters biannually to teach medicine and law.[61] In the fifteenth century Vicenza boasted an extraordinary succession of famous humanists, including Gian Mario Filelfo, George of Trebizond, and Francesco Maturanzio.[62] Bartolomeo Borfoni, hired away from Verona in 1406, taught in Vicenza for forty years, while Ognibene Leoniceno received praise not only for his pedagogy, but also for his devotion to noble, clerical, and poor students alike. Although Vicenza never again enjoyed the concentration of scholars and intellectuals that it did during the first half of the Quattrocento, its emphasis on public education continued into the sixteenth century.

One example of that commitment can be found in the commune's hiring of Giovita Ravizza to give public lectures beginning in 1524. Reappointed in April 1527, Ravizza was granted Vicentine citizenship less than a month later, with the right to extend such citizenship to his sons and descendants. Coupled with the salary boosts that the city council awarded him on a regular basis, this evidence suggests that Ravizza was a popular figure with Vicenza's city council. Like Giovanni Battista Pio in Bergamo, Ravizza occasionally engaged in non-curricular activity on behalf of the city, including a funeral oration in honour of Polissena Attendi in 1526. In 1533 Ravizza moved on again, this time to Venice, where he would once again be awarded citizenship while teaching lessons both public and private.[63] He was followed by Fulvio Peregrino Morato, father of female humanist Olimpia Morata, and then by Jacopo Grifoli, Francesco Machiavelli, Leonardo Fusco, and a series of other grammar professors into the 1570s. A declaration by Vicenza's city council in 1556 noted that Vicenza had always tried to hire two lecturers at public expense because of the importance of instilling proper manners and good letters.[64]

Most 'public' education, like that offered by Ravizza and his fifteenth-century predecessors, was in fact intended for a relatively limited circle of noble boys who intended to go on to university.[65] Further down the social scale, private teachers and *ripetitori* provided lessons in vernacular grammar and functional literacy. Although texts, treatises, and inventories authored by teachers do occasionally survive, insufficient evidence exists to reconstruct the curriculum adopted by public and private teachers in Vicenza. Extensive notarial cartularies make it possible to identify teachers and their involvement in contracts or other official correspondence, but again this evidence tells us little about actual instruction.

The substantial number of charitable associations in Vicenza provided assistance to the poor and the destitute of the city. One such example was the Hospital of Mercy (Ospedale della Misericordia), founded in 1309 and governed by a succession of confraternities whose membership represented the cream of Vicentine society. In 1565, at the urging of the city council, the hospital imitated the work of Girolamo Miani in creating an orphanage where a large number of male and female orphans were instructed in letters, morality, and civic responsibility. The organization of the orphanage, and the skills imparted to its young residents, were quite similar to those found in Bergamo. Perhaps more notable, however, is the apparent lack of involvement by Vicentine confraternities in supporting education. Unlike their counterparts in Bergamo, they did not grant scholarships and hire teachers.[66]

Another important distinction between Bergamo and Vicenza was the latter's high number of private teachers. Many of them were notaries who taught reading and writing as private tutors to wealthy families.[67] Some of them also served as copyists. Vicenza was a wealthier town than Bergamo, and its proximity to Venice and Verona may have encouraged more private masters to try their luck. Teaching private students was not easy; a late fifteenth-century teacher named Serpe D'Arzignano complained in the preface to his *Libellus grammaticus* (1492) that private teaching was a necessary burden to be endured because it put bread on the table. Master Lorenzi of Vicenza wrote to his friend Paolo Bissari in 1622 that he felt chained to his students and his pedagogical responsibilities. These responsibilities included two daily lessons of poetry and rhetoric, plus occasional lessons in other subjects.

Nevertheless, to judge from marriage records and testaments, Vicenza's teachers were reasonably well off and enjoyed considerable social mobility. Many of them were allied with the great families of the city, and their intellectual prowess was respected by merchants and nobles.

A further difference between Bergamo and Vicenza is the role of the College of Notaries in providing instruction. The Vicentine College of Notaries had rented its large meeting room to public grammar teachers since the beginning of the fifteenth century, but in 1443 it established a school of its own that taught elementary grammar, civil law, and the formulae necessary to be a notary.[68] The school was intended for current members who wished to educate themselves, aspiring members who desired to improve their chances of admission to the college, and young boys who sought to read and write. Scattered references to this school can be found until 1533, but it appears that during many of the intervening years the school lay dormant. It is worth noting, however, that the commune never had any formal involvement with the school of the College of Notaries. This suggests that – like the Caspi Academy in Bergamo – private interests were both capable and desirous of supporting instruction.

According to Giovanni Pellizzari, the abundance of private school teachers and the efforts of the commune should not obscure the fact that most of the instruction offered in fifteenth-century Vicenza was intended for future priests. Toward the end of the Quattrocento, the humanist movement introduced an expanded number of secular texts and temporarily wrested education out of the hands of the Church. As in Bergamo and other cities of the Veneto, by the late fifteenth and early sixteenth centuries civic institutions and confraternities had stepped in to fill the gap. By the middle of the sixteenth century the Church realized the necessity of religious instruction that was both more diffused and of higher quality. In Vicenza as elsewhere, the Jesuit order provided highly trained educators; the seminary offered an education for boys who desired a life in the Church; and the bishop provided the resources necessary to promote instruction in the city.

In vivid contrast to Bergamo, where the Society had few contacts, the Jesuits in Vicenza had numerous cousins and in-laws to promote their cause, including several connections among the city council deputies responsible for selecting new teachers.[69] A bequest from Cornelia Loschi, donating half of her property to the Society for the specific purpose of opening a school in Vicenza, no doubt helped to lure the Jesuits into town. Nevertheless, the concern of the Venetian Senate was sufficient to delay the actual arrival of the Jesuits by almost twenty years, and in 1606 they were exiled for another fifty years on account of the Interdict crisis. Gian Paolo Brizzi's research on Jesuit colleges in Lombardy has indicated that the Vicentine nobility sent a higher proportion of their children to Jesuit schools than any other city in the Venetian Republic.[70] The boarding colleges staffed by the Jesuits provided a balance of rigorous intellectual education and proper social behaviour, just the sort of training that provincial nobility thought to be critical to success.

The Jesuits' arrival contributed to the decline of Vicenza's public schools, but the symptoms of deterioration were present considerably earlier. The precarious military situation during the battles of the War of the League of Cambrai (1508–16), an investigation of the *magister* Pellegrino Morato by the Holy Office in the 1540s, and an oration by Vicenza's public master in 1557 criticizing venality all signalled dark times for public schooling.[71] By 1586 the public school classrooms were virtually empty. In that year the city council deputies noted with frustration that 'the public lectures have become superfluous and of little use, for the lack of audience means that the lessons are rarely held; but in the private school(s) the competition is so fierce that a single teacher, even if he is talented and diligent, and even with the help of assistants, cannot keep up with the demand.'[72] The reasons for the decline in communal education were in many cases identical to those in Bergamo. The vast growth in printed works, especially those written in or translated into the vernacular, made books and broadsheets more available to the average reader. New educational alternatives, close to home and sometimes even free of charge, were suddenly available. The decline of Venetian shipping and the steady inflation of the long sixteenth century impoverished many *terraferma* towns. In addition, the humanist program had lost its allure. During the fifteenth century, in an attempt to improve their own social position, the humanists had argued for meritocracy and social mobility, but political and religious developments in the latter half of the sixteenth century discouraged such ideas by favouring hierarchy. Aided by the forced departure of the Jesuits in 1606, Vicenza's public schools revived themselves until 1657, when the Jesuits returned and the public schools once again collapsed.

Bergamo, Brescia, Verona, and Vicenza all displayed important parallel achievements in late medieval and Renaissance education. Each has isolated references to education in the twelfth or thirteenth century, and each later subscribed to the humanist movement by offering lessons in grammar and humanities as well as related subjects. Each of these provincial Venetian cities offered passionate rhetoric but only inconsistent support by the commune for public education. Each eventually turned to the new religious orders of men to assume control of a college or a school on behalf of the town, especially in the seventeenth century. Each introduced a seminary shortly after the Council of Trent and each witnessed the rise of the Schools of Christian Doctrine to teach rudimentary classes. Yet as we have seen, there were important distinctions too. Proximity to the urban poles of Milan or Venice influenced schooling at all levels. The presence or absence of wealth made a substantial difference, especially in private tutoring. The role of confraternities apparently varied quite a bit, with Bergamo's Misericordia adopting a role that was not replicated elsewhere. In short, this regional comparison helps us to see that Bergamo's experience, while certainly not identical, is broadly representative of other cities within the Venetian Republic.

The *Bergamasco*

The extent to which instruction was available in Bergamo's small towns and villages presents a paradox. In order to avoid starvation, these settlements – often isolated by mountainous ridges and cursed with rocky soil – needed the labour of every man, woman, and child. Yet whereas we might expect education to have been a low priority for these outlying areas, many small towns developed a surprisingly vigorous tradition of education. Such schooling may have been public, private, religious, or – most often – an amalgam of the three. Even more than in Bergamo, these local schools depended heavily upon the ability and continuity of a singular maestro to provide instruction. Although scattered examples of cooperation between towns are evident, it is clear that no organized 'system' of education ever existed. Locally published civic histories often speak proudly of early efforts at schooling in these small towns, but extant documents are scarce.[73] A sampling of cases from half a dozen towns scattered through the *bergamasco* (Bergamo's countryside) shows how education was administered in the valleys and plains.

Lovere and Alzano Maggiore

An intriguing first example comes from the town of Lovere, located at the northern end of Lake Iseo. Between 1450 and 1520 more than a dozen men were identified in notarial cartularies as teachers or 'rectors of the school.'[74] Frequent references to the 'schools of Lovere' suggest that these rectors were administering some type of public school and not just teaching privately (although they may well have done some private tutoring, too). Like their counterparts elsewhere, Lovere's teachers benefited from the use of a house and an assistant teacher. About half of these men had emigrated from the countryside, while the remaining half were from established urban families. More importantly, Lovere's teachers exercised the notarial profession simultaneously. It is not surprising that notaries occasionally tutored students who wished to train for the profession, or even took on young boys as apprentices. The documents in Lovere, however, suggest that notaries regularly served as teachers for town boys. This phenomenon of notary-cum-teacher is documented in Verona, but only isolated cases have emerged in Bergamo. It seems reasonable that smaller towns or villages might expect their more literate residents to serve in a dual capacity, and the extra income certainly would have been advantageous to a teacher-notary. Although judges and lawyers were routinely prohibited from arguing cases while employed as public teachers, no such prohibition existed for notaries.

In late fifteenth-century Alzano Maggiore, the nobleman Bernardino Adobati left an enormous legacy of nearly twenty-five thousand lire to the local church of San Pietro. One portion of the bequest was to be used for a daily Mass in honour of the testator; the balance was to institute a school with three salaried instructors who would teach students, gratis, to read, write, do figures, dance, and ride horses.[75] One hundred and fifty years later, Bishop Luigi Grimani noted the presence of two public schools in Alzano Maggiore. A small school for girls was administered by a widow and a couple of female tertiaries, while three priests provided instruction at the school of Saint Peter Martyr. According to the bishop's report, the school's only income was derived from the income of Bernardino Adobati's bequest, which had been intended to provide education to local boys. The Reverend Defendo Bidasio was listed as having a salary of fifty scudi per year in exchange for teaching regular lessons.[76] Two decades later Bishop Gregorio Barbarigo also noted three priests teaching grammar and humanities to the boys of Alzano Maggiore, as well as lessons by Sister Chiara Maria for girls desirous to read, write, and sew.[77] Adobati's bequest therefore lasted at least 250 years and conceivably supported the education of dozens, even hundreds, of children. Such an achievement would be on a par with the long-term success of the MIA's Apibus scholarships in Bergamo. Yet further evidence exists to suggest that these two long-lasting scholarships may not have been as unusual as initially thought.

Clusone

The town of Clusone, at the foot of the Val Seriana, never included public schooling as part of its annual civic budget, nor do civic records include many references to teachers or students.[78] Nevertheless, there is
evidence of private support for schooling as well as legal statutes that
comment on the *maestri* to be employed. The 1461 statutes of the Upper Val Seriana, drafted by an association of towns scattered along the
Serio River a few miles north of Clusone and Bergamo, attempted to
regulate a wide variety of issues that affected life in the valley.[79] Article
169 declared that within one month of the end of instruction, grammar teachers in the valley were to be paid a maximum of twenty soldi.
The teachers were required to provide a written declaration attesting
to their receipt of funds from the appropriate civic official. The statute
does not actually require individual towns to engage a master teacher,
but only specifies an upper limit for his salary (presumably to avoid
sparking competition among the various towns that were members of
the association). By requiring payment to be made at the conclusion
of the school year, the statute sought to avoid the embarrassing (and
costly) spectacle of teachers running off midway through the academic
year. A lack of supporting documents makes it impossible to know the
extent to which this statute actually influenced schooling in the Upper
Val Seriana.

   One hundred and seventy years later we encounter the testamentary
gift of Ventura Fanzago, who left money to the Misericordia confraternity of Clusone in support of education. In a will redacted by the notary Marco Antonio Bonicelli on 16 November 1630, Fanzago explained
his wishes: 'Item [he] requires this confraternity to provide 43 scudi to
three poor and eager boys from distinguished families of good reputation, so that each of them may study the liberal arts; this will be for a
period of three years, and the students wishing to study will be selected
as explained below.'[80] The students were responsible for enrolling in
an appropriate course of study and for informing the confraternity of
their choice(s). The will did not indicate a required area of study, nor
did it specify any post-award obligations of the scholarship recipients.
The only obligation of the students during their tenure at school was to
recite the Office of the Blessed Virgin Mary six days a week. During the
seventeenth century, students on a Fanzago scholarship specialized in
medicine, civil and canon law, music, and rhetoric.

   Ventura Fanzago's will did not specify that the bequest was to favour students from his own family, but extant documents indicate

that family members were often selected ahead of other candidates. A 1659 letter from Antonio Fanzago explicitly requested a scholarship to Padua for his son Bartolomeo because of his lineage, and a 1779 memorandum from Bergamo's Bishop Gian Paolo Dolfin confirmed both the bequest and the tradition of favouring family members. This preference continued for centuries: in a letter dated 18 July 1937, Mario Fanzago noted that from 1892 to 1895 he had enjoyed a scholarship from the Fanzago bequest because he was descended from the original Fanzago family.[81] Thus the Fanzago bequest, like the Apibus scholarship of Bergamo and the Adobati legacy of Alzano Maggiore, endured for more than 250 years. Such longevity is particularly impressive in a small provincial town.

The Fanzago bequest also appears to have adapted to the changing needs of the recipients. For example, in the early eighteenth century, the bequest was used in support of a public school in Clusone. These students met daily with three teachers in the Fanzago family house. Parts of the bequest were also used to maintain a chaplain and to endow the saying of masses. Since the amount of money from the bequest remained fixed, however, the actual value slowly diminished. By 1736 it was no longer possible for the bequest to support both instruction and masses. The bishop was asked to clarify which of these obligations the bequest should continue to support in the future. No record appears of the bishop's response, but Mario Fanzago's letter of 1937, coupled with Bishop Dolfin's memo, suggests that education remained a principal focus of the Fanzago bequest.[82] Unfortunately, since very few documents concerning this bequest have been preserved for the eighteenth and nineteenth centuries, it is impossible to determine how regularly the scholarship was awarded. Nevertheless, the very fact of its existence in the early seventeenth and early twentieth centuries testifies to the desire of private citizens to support education even in remote and rural locations. This example also echoes aspects of bequests entrusted to the Bergamasque confraternities of the Misericordia Maggiore, of San Lorenzo, and of Sant'Alessandro in Colonna, just as the Val Seriana statutes echo the decrees of Bergamo's city council in the late fifteenth century.

Gandino

The town of Gandino boasted fewer than three hundred residents in the early modern period, and even today it remains a small village perched on the side of the Val Seriana. Yet the town's inhabitants were praised repeatedly in the fifteenth and sixteenth centuries 'for their love of letters and because among them there is almost nobody who does not possess the language of the Romans.'[83] In his *Grammatices fundamenta*, published in Verona in 1520, Marco Antonio Moro praised Gasparino Barzizza, Marco Antonio Sabellico, and other learned gentlemen of Gandino for having established the foundations of the new humanistic culture in the area around Bergamo. Perhaps this penchant for humanistic studies in Gandino came from the Barzizza family, which produced several generations of humanistic scholars during the late Trecento and early Quattrocento. Tiny Gandino once again reminds us that schooling and humanism were never monopolized by large towns.

Romano di Lombardia

A final example comes from the town of Romano di Lombardia. Unlike Gandino, Clusone, and Lovere, Romano di Lombardia is located a few miles south of Bergamo, where agriculture and trade were generally more lucrative. Romano enjoyed the distinction of having its own Venetian governor and thus some degree of autonomy from Bergamo. Similar to Bergamo, during the late Quattrocento and the early Cinquecento Romano experimented with several approaches to public education. It sought to hire prominent humanists; it awarded tax exemptions and housing to teachers; and it proposed joint appointments with the Misericordia confraternity of Romano. Also similar to Bergamo, Romano expected parents to pay the master directly, according to the number of children and the amount of schooling provided. Schooling in Romano was almost certainly limited to the scions of noble and wealthy families.

Evidence from the first three decades of the Quattrocento suggests that public schooling was a very low priority for the commune of Romano.[84] Teachers were poorly paid, sometimes receiving only a bed frame or some firewood; one teacher even had to put a garnish on the property of parents who had not paid him on time. In 1494, however, worried by the lack of public instruction, the podestà and the commune proposed hiring a master teacher to instruct 'boys and people of every age in the art of grammar.' The wording of this motion suggests that the council wished to improve the literacy rate of adolescent boys and of other town residents. The timing, too, is remarkably similar to that found in the actions of Bergamo's city council. By a vote of 21–3, the communal council approved the motion, and awarded Giovanni Carminati of Lodi not only the post of *magistro da schola* but also a monopoly on the right to teach within the city limits of Romano. This monopoly was subsequently enforced in 1497, when the city council ordered two priests and a layman to cease teaching local chierici and the sons of wealthy families. Carminati's contract also called for the commune to provide him with a decent house, a garden, and four loads of wood, while the parents were expected to pay one ducat per student and the students were asked to provide their own paper. The renewal of Carminati's contract in 1497 was contingent upon his agreeing to teach a small number of poor boys from the town along with his paying students. This later amendment appears to represent the commune's effort to ensure that schooling remained available even to those who were poverty-stricken.

In 1499 the commune and the Misericordia confraternity of Romano agreed to split the cost of hiring Francino de Allegreno from Venice to teach good letters and customs. Allegreno taught three classes, in literature, grammar, and catechism; in addition, twice per month he was expected to read Juvenal or another author 'for the benefit of the community.'[85] This example of joint support for schooling clearly precedes any examples from the city of Bergamo; not until the second half of the sixteenth century did the Misericordia Maggiore and the commune of Bergamo work together to hire a teacher. The emphasis upon reading aloud for the benefit of the community also echoes the concern of Bergamo's city council (and later the MIA) that at least some lessons be freely available to anyone who wished to listen.

From 1502 to 1507 Romano hired a native son, the priest Antonio Lallio, to instruct fifty boys in grammar and letters. Evidently Lallio was a successful teacher, for he went on to teach in Bergamo at the Misericordia Maggiore's school for chierici from 1508 to 1514. Called out of retirement in 1529, Lallio taught in Romano for one additional year before his death in 1530. In a resolution shortly after Lallio's death, the deputies of Romano's city council unanimously declared that their school must be continued at all costs, and promised a generous salary of one hundred ducats plus the use of a house and permission to have nineteen boarders. Yet in the same way that Bergamo's city council favoured rhetoric over substance, Romano's city council failed to take action on this promise for at least the next two decades.[86] In the second half of the sixteenth century, Romano appears to have experienced a resurgent Catholic Church and an expansion of educational opportunities with the bishop, confraternities, and other religious institutions.[87]

Examples from Romano, Lovere, Clusone, and other small towns of the *bergamasco* thus confirm the general impression of instruction derived from the case of Bergamo. Although the extant evidence is much more scarce, these outlying areas offered civic support, private scholarships, and joint ventures to promote education. Rural towns sometimes had to cobble together whatever form of instruction they could manage, and demonstrated considerable flexibility by assigning notaries or local priests to provide education. Parents everywhere had to absorb part of the cost of their children's education. These outlying cases, then, confirm the principal trends visible in Bergamo's network of educational options.

Further research may help to provide answers to three important questions: Why was literacy higher in Bergamo's valleys than in the plains? To what extent was this higher literacy connected with schooling? And how did literacy rates influence the development of Protestantism in northern Italy? Orazio Bravi has suggested that the Protestant Reformation had much greater success in the upper valleys north of Bergamo than in the flatlands, and he makes an explicit connection to literacy rates. Citing the towns of Gromo and Ardesio as examples, he points to their institution of schools in the Quattrocento as a fundamental factor in their turn to heresy.[88] Inquisition records for the diocese of Bergamo focus upon the city rather than the country, and nearly all of the men investigated for heresy possessed a university degree and were clearly literate. Xenio Toscani's research on literacy in Lombardy has confirmed that in the seventeenth and eighteenth centuries literacy rates were substantially higher in the mountain valleys than in the flatlands to the south, which is exactly the opposite of what one might expect. Toscani touches only briefly upon the situation in the sixteenth century, but it seems clear that the phenomenon he describes was present in the Cinquecento too.[89]

Conclusion

In a 1990 review article on pre-university education, Paul Grendler argued that the Latin schools of the Renaissance provided a common foundation for European elites.[90] According to Grendler, this intellectual bond linked the upper echelons of European society even as religious schism and political differences threatened to tear the Continent apart.

> The great achievement of Renaissance humanistic education was to impart a standard classical Latin education to the upper ranks of European society.

By the middle of the sixteenth century the Venetian noble, the Spanish bish-op, the French judge, and the German prince had all memorized some of Virgil's poetry and shared a common rhetoric. So did the civil servants, cler-gymen, and lawyers who made the machinery of government and church function ... The humanistic curriculum unified the Renaissance, an intellec-tual unity that endured beyond the shattering of religious unity.

It is clear that the humanistic educational movement, which began in Italy and then spread through most of Europe in the sixteenth century, exerted an enormous influence upon the types of schooling offered to students at all levels. The similarities in pan-European schooling em-phasize the connections among the many principalities, kingdoms, re-publics, and ecclesiastical states that populated early modern Europe, while the variations confirm their individuality and the importance of local conditions. The example of Bergamo is one small piece in this larger jigsaw puzzle, and its schooling confirms many patterns visible elsewhere.

In conclusion, then, a case study of Bergamo offers an extraordinary opportunity to peer closely at how education was designed and deliv-ered in one specific context, while a comparative analysis with other areas – from tiny, isolated Gandino to an urban metropolis like Venice – suggests several common educational patterns. Nearly everywhere public education flourished from the late fifteenth to the mid-sixteenth century, driven by a confluence of factors that included humanism, eco-nomic growth, and printing. The communal commitment to education, however, was frequently unstable, and more evident in words than in deeds. Again and again throughout northern Italy we see civic gov-ernments fail to follow through on their promises to support public schooling. Secondly, towns in the Venetian Republic exercised a good deal of freedom in their choices about whom to hire, what to teach, and how to pay for it. By and large, Venice was content to allow local lead-ers to govern their own schooling systems. Third, the Catholic Church returned in force in the second half of the sixteenth century with a va-riety of methods to instruct young men and women. From grandiose seminaries and imposing Jesuit colleges to humble chapels and Sunday sermons, the Church used myriad approaches to spread its message, to instruct the faithful, and to train its officials. Lastly, examples from Brescia, Verona, Vicenza, and elsewhere confirm the presence of a mul-tiplicity of options for schooling, keyed to the particular context of each city. From small villages to major metropoli, the desire for education in these centuries was a powerful one indeed.

Conclusion

As documented in the preceding chapters, a surprisingly large array of educational options was available to Bergamasque students from the fifteenth to the seventeenth century. Students – both lay and religious – could study Latin grammar and literature, rhetoric and poetry, philosophy and logic, catechism and theology. Scholarships and subsidies were available to assist those who could not afford to pay for schooling on their own. University-level courses in law were offered and could count toward a degree from the University of Padua. Nor were such options restricted to the urban center, for students could find schooling even in the isolated valleys and small towns of the *bergamasco*. A similar – but not identical – range of schooling alternatives existed in the neighbouring cities of the *terraferma* such as Brescia, Verona, and Vicenza.

The pluralism evident in Bergamo's scholastic offerings extended to the different institutions that sponsored instruction. The commune, the confraternities, and the Church all offered schooling that reflected their particular agendas and resources. The cooperation among various institutions traditionally assumed to be at cross-purposes constitutes one of the most surprising and important conclusions of this book. Joint appointment of teachers and shared classrooms constitute just two examples of how the city, the episcopate, and the MIA could work together in Bergamo to promote education. The commune's repeated interactions with the Somaschans, the Theatines, and the Jesuits also demonstrate how different groups could work together, albeit with some serious conflict. Even when competing for the same pool of students and teachers, institutions like the diocesan seminary and the MIA's Academy of Clerics appear to have coexisted harmoniously. Taken together, the institutions and individuals of sixteenth-century

Bergamo offered an impressive collection of choices for young men who wished to be educated.

The examples from Bergamo and elsewhere also make the clear the fundamentally *ad hoc* nature of schooling in this time period. Schools were founded by a wide variety of individuals and institutions but rarely lasted more than a few decades. In contrast to modern universities or high schools, whose institutional permanence encourages students to shape their educational goals around the mission of the institution, in the Renaissance the demands of students and their parents often shaped the curriculum to a much larger degree. Thus schooling in Bergamo and its sister cities was in many ways more impermanent and more fluid than our modern educational systems. This instability is particularly noticeable for civic-sponsored schools; by contrast, schools run directly by the Catholic Church (e.g., seminaries) tended to endure longer and to preserve their identity more forcefully.

The nearly total absence of female students and teachers in this study may offend our modern sensibilities, but it reflects the historical reality that had for two millennia separated men and women into public and private spheres. Certainly, there were exceptions to this gendered division in education. Heloise, Christine de Pizan, Isotta Nogarola, Cassandra Fedele, and Laura Cereta all demonstrated the ability to learn and to write eloquently for a public audience. Yet their very exceptionalism underscores the lack of women to be found in the archives that document the history of education in Bergamo and its sister cities.

Bergamo's educational network possessed a number of idiosyncrasies that are difficult to find elsewhere in Italy. The extensive involvement of the Misericordia Maggiore, for example, seems to have been a special feature of Bergamasque history. The many positive consequences of the MIA's involvement with schooling have already been discussed at length; it is sufficient to note here that the MIA's actions offered opportunities to Bergamo that otherwise would have been unattainable. A residential school with a classical curriculum for elementary students like the Caspi Academy, while not unique, was certainly rare in the sixteenth century. Equally unusual was Bergamo's repeated rejection of the Society of Jesus. Nevertheless, Bergamo's experience with education also parallels that of other provincial cities and villages. The creation of a seminary, the role of the new religious orders of men, and the inconsistent support provided to public education are examples replicated outside of Bergamo. Thus in many ways Bergamo's history of schooling exemplifies patterns and trends throughout the Venetian Republic.

Albertus Magnus, *Liber aggregationis: De mirabilibus mundi* (Venice, 1490).
Resting his weary head upon his left hand, this scholar reads an open text
while grasping a second text in his right hand. The shelf below the desk
contains an inkpot and other necessary tools for writing. The 'Marvels of the
World' by Albertus Magnus was an enormously popular text in early modern
Europe, featuring discussion of gems, herbs, birds, and related topics. The
precise identity of this scholar remains unknown.

Several broad changes are visible in schooling between 1500 and 1650. The number of institutions and organizations involved with education increased steadily. For example, in the late fifteenth century there was very little opportunity to gain an education in Bergamo, aside from apprenticeships, ecclesiastical training, and the occasional independent master. By the beginning of the seventeenth century, half a dozen confraternities were each paying teachers to instruct children from the parish, and an ever-growing number of private academies were being founded by parents, bishops, and others. Numerous religious orders of men and women followed the example of the Jesuits and added school teaching of lay children to their ministries. Testamentary bequests resulted in the creation of more residential colleges and endowed scholarships, with such gifts often administered by charitable or civic organizations. The city, too, recognized the importance of supporting education for its young citizens. In short, more and more people – as individuals and as members of larger institutions – were involved with schooling in this crucial era.

These increasing levels of support for education in Bergamo and the Venetian Republic were neither linear nor consistent. As examples from the commune, the confraternities, and the Church suggest, support peaked (and dropped) at different times. The city of Bergamo, for example, was most deeply involved with schooling in the early sixteenth century, while its later participation waxed and waned. The major neighbourhood confraternities there demonstrated greater commitment to schooling in the latter half of the sixteenth century. The bishops and religious orders of men tried to support instruction for clerics and lay boys from 1550 onward, but they too demonstrated erratic commitment. Yet the singular example of the Misericordia Maggiore confraternity demonstrates that an institution could be involved with education in a variety of ways for hundreds of years. The sources make clear that even one zealous teacher or patron could make a substantial difference in creating and sustaining a vibrant school. Similar variations can be seen in other cities of the *terraferma*; Vicenza promoted civic education much earlier, but its confraternities never became involved with schooling, while instruction in Brescia generally parallels the patterns described in Bergamo. Thus it is difficult to lay out an overarching chronology that applies to all facets of education in Bergamo and the Veneto between 1500 and 1650, for individual variation was significant.

The expansion of instructional possibilities, albeit with some gaps, suggests more broad-based support of, and desire for, education. The ability to read, write, and figure was no longer viewed as a privilege reserved to an elite few, but as a basic skill necessary for participation in civic and religious life. The professors of the twelfth and thirteenth centuries had emphasized a utilitarian, pre-professional training for doctors, lawyers, and scholars based on texts in logic, law, and theology. As Craig Kallendorf has observed, 'Renaissance humanists, in contrast with medieval university professors, aimed to educate an entire social and political elite.'[1] The humanists' stated goal was to imbue all youth with moral virtue and eloquence, and they eagerly sought to spread the 'new education' across Europe. This is not to suggest that the humanists or the cities of the Venetian Republic had any concept of universal education; the idea of free, public education for all boys and girls was never considered seriously prior to the nineteenth century. Education in these cities, particularly at the university level, remained the preserve of the socio-economic elite. Nor would be it accurate to accept the humanists' other claims at face value, for they often wrote prescriptive or propagandistic treatises. Nevertheless, instruction was certainly more available in 1650 than it had been in 1500.

The purpose of education, from a student's perspective, does not appear to have altered much during the one and a half centuries considered here. Many students attended school in order to become priests; many more sought instruction to become successful merchants or bureaucrats. Some probably wished to take advantage of scholarships or to postpone a career decision. Nor does the family's perspective on the purpose of education seem to have changed much. Schooling then, as now, usually represented a major capital expense for most families. A young man's education was viewed as an investment in a potential higher return, designed to offset the loss of labour while in school. Parents also viewed schooling as a means to socialization and self-discipline for their children, even if they rarely framed it in such modern terms, preferring instead to describe the development of 'character' and 'virtue' in their offspring. Developing a sense of moral judgment, too, had long been a central purpose of education, and it continued to be so during this era.

From the perspective of institutions, however, the purpose of education did shift, sometimes dramatically so. Church-affiliated institutions realized that education had to be both more orthodox and more inclusive. Seminaries and clerical academies adopted an insular mentality, attempting to shield their pupils from the potential 'contamination' of the outside world. Schools of Christian Doctrine, in contrast, sought to educate a wider range of people and to incorporate reading as part of the catechism. The purpose of religious education remained, as always, the defence and propagation of the faith, but there was a growing recognition that diverse means were necessary to achieve that goal.

Confraternities in Bergamo saw the purpose of education as twofold: to improve the knowledge and virtue of lay members along with their children, and to train future priests for service in the local church. The Misericordia Maggiore, Sant'Alessandro in Colonna, and Sant'Alessandro della Croce each pursued these twin goals with vigour. With the exception of the MIA's long-standing Apibus scholarship program that dated back to the fourteenth century, no confraternity in Bergamo was committed to education prior to 1500. For Bergamo's confraternities, then, while the purpose of education may have been the same, the degree of their involvement jumped substantially in the sixteenth century. Confraternities in other Venetian towns were often involved in promoting charitable activities, but with certain exceptions (e.g., Treviso's Santa Maria dei Battuti), they focused much less on schooling than did their *confratelli* (confraternal brothers) in Bergamo.

Throughout the sixteenth and seventeenth centuries, Bergamo's city council – like those of its sister cities in the Veneto – continued to reiterate the numerous benefits of an education. Adopting the flowery rhetoric of the Quattrocento humanists, the city councils declared that the purpose of education was to instil virtue in the city's youth, to guarantee the safety of the republic, and to bring honour to the city. On a more prosaic level, the city councils wished to ensure a competent pool of notaries and civic bureaucrats. The stated objectives of the communes do not appear to have changed much between 1500 and 1650. Their willingness to provide financial support to public education, however, did gradually wane during the course of the sixteenth century.

In conclusion, what does the story of 150 years of Bergamo's schooling reveal? The wide array of schooling options in Bergamo, and the unexpected cooperation among institutions, requires us to reconsider outdated stereotypes about who taught what to whom and why. The relative autonomy enjoyed by Bergamo in many areas of education also speaks to a new understanding of the balance between centre and periphery in the early modern Venetian state. The impact of Tridentine reform upon schooling has already been discussed at some length and needs no further explication here. It is sufficient to note the orthodoxy and rigidity of education in seminaries and academies affiliated with the Church. The impact of humanism has been similarly considered, and its effect was at least as profound. Certain fundamental texts were read throughout the medieval period, and the humanists continued this scholastic tradition, while simultaneously introducing new texts and innovative pedagogical methods. Schooling in Bergamo and the cities of the Venetian Republic exemplified all of these critical trends as it sought to train children for the tasks of tomorrow.

Appendix 1: Teachers in Late Medieval and Early Modern Bergamo, by Institution

Institution	Name of Teacher	Date(s) of Service	Title of Teacher
Commune – Grammar	Bonifacio da Osio	1291–1311	n/a
	Lorenzo de Apibus	1298–1337	maestro di grammatica
	Jacopo de Apibus	1322–61	'maestro Crotto'
	Gasparino Barzizza	1396	n/a
	Spiclarus de Grandinis	1431	n/a
	Gian Mario Filelfo	1471	maestro d'umanità
	Paolo Terzi	1475–87	rettore delle scuole
	Marco Solza	1487	n/a
	Francesco Romano	1491	n/a
	Giovanni de Lulmo	1497	lectore logicam
	Viviano Morzenti	1502	rettore delle scuole
	Giovanni Battista Pio	1505–7	professore di grammatica
	Demetrio Calcondilla	1507–8	n/a
	Giovita Ravizza	1508–23	rettore della scuola
	Nicolò Cologno	1539–41	rettore della scuola
	Baptista Benevolo	1545–8(?)	professore di grammatica
	Andrea Cato	1549–51	n/a
	Nicolò Cologno (same as above)	1556–64(?), 1574–79(?)	maestro di grammatica
	Padre Crescenzio	1615	n/a
	Lorenzo Biffi	1615	n/a
Commune – Law	Giovanni Carlo Tiraboschi	1476	iuresperito
	Jacopo Agazzi	1482	iuresperito
	Gio. Agostino Colleoni	1483	iuresperito
	Guglielmo Suardi	1493	iuresperito
	Bartolomeo Caleppio	1494	iuresperito
	Leonardo Comenduno	1497	lector Institutiones

Institution	Name of Teacher	Date(s) of Service	Title of Teacher
	Baptista Botani	1539	lector Institutum
	Francesco Suardi	1540	lector Institutum
	Girolamo Zanchi	1541	lector Institutum
	Julio Agosti	1542	lector Institutum
	Giacomo Carrara Benaglio	1625–48	lector Institutum
	Ludovico Cursino Petrobello	1648–50(?)	lector Institutum
Misericordia Maggiore (MIA's) School	Bernardino Fogaccia di Alzano	1506	rector scolarium
	Marco da Brignano	1506	rector scolarium
	Antonio Lallio da Romano	1507–14	rector scolarium
	Fedrighino da Taliuno	1515–27	rector scolarium
	Giovanni Zanchi	1525(?)–6(?)	ripetitore
	Nicolas de Capitanei de Scalve	1529–?	rector scolarium
	Giovanni Minoli	1537(?)–47, 1552–5	rector scolarium
	Alessandro da Brescia [Alessandro Offlaga]	1538–?	pedagogo
	[Baptista?] Bonini	1541	n/a
	Bono de Lulmo [Bono da Olmo]	1543–6, 1547–52, 1564–?	rector scolarium
	Paolo Tiraboschi	1546–1556	'ad docere scribendum'
	Pietro de Bracha	1548–9	ripetitore
	Julius de Val Camonica	1550	ripetitore
	Baptista de Muzio	1551–2	ripetitore
	Antonio de Licinis	1551–4	ripetitore
	Julio Ascanio de Tucci	1555–7	rector scolarium
	Alessandro Beroa	1556–60	ripetitore
	Michele Manili	1557–64	rector scolarium
	Francesco Rota	1560–2	ripetitore
	Benalio Benaglio	1562–?	ripetitore
	Paolo Zafferro	1564	ripetitore
	Pietro de Poncio	1564	maestro di capella
	Francesco Cribello	1564	maestro di capella
	Lodovico Sonzonio	1565	maestro di capella
MIA's Academy of Clerics[1]	Don Innocenzo	1566	ripetitore
	Teodoro Calvo	1566	ripetitore
	Pietro Bonacursio	1567–9	precettore
	Nicolò Cologno	1574–9	preceptor scolarium
	Antonio Lauretto Placchino	1575	rector clericorum acad.
	Padre Lorenzo	1575	magister morum
	Michelangelo Bello	1575–6	ripetitore, precettore
	Battista Suardi	1575–6	ripetitore, precettore
	Battista Pelandi	1592–1617	maestro principale d. scola

Institution	Name of Teacher	Date(s) of Service	Title of Teacher
MIA's New Academy of Clerics	Felice Osio	1617	rettore e maestro principale
	Alessandro Carrara	1617	prefetto degli studii
	Annibale Solza	1617	ministro ed economo
	Pietro Rota	1617	prefetto della disciplina
	Donato Facagno	1618	prefetto
	Giovan Antonio Rossetti	1620	rettore
	Hieronimyo Zanchi	1623	pro lectura casum
	Giuseppe Laurenzi	1625	rettore
	Rev. Donati	1628	rettore
S. Alessandro in Colonna[2]	Nicolò Cologno (Rev.)	1557	[never taught]
	Sebastiano Pagani	1557	capellano e maestro di scuola
	Alessandro Beroa	1560–7	ripetitore
	Antonio Villa	1561–7	capellanus et preceptor consortij
	Ludovico Corono	1564–7	n/a
	Maestro' Lamberti	1566	maestro
	Piero Mutio	1566	n/a
	Angelo Filogenio	1566	parocchiano
	Tommaso d. Nic. D. Caravaggio	1567–8	capellanus et preceptore
	Jacopo Munio	1568	n/a
	Pietro Ponte	1569	maestro di capella/ organo/canto
	Orlando de Rumano	1571	maestro di grammatica
	Francesco Prechio [Pechij?]	1573–4	n/a
	Giov. Petrengo	1573, 1574, 1579	maestro di grammatica
	Gio. Antonio Cavalli	1574–7	maestro di grammatica
	Gio. Maria Piatti	1575–7	maestro di leggere e scrivere
	Andrea de Borleri	1575	maestro di leggere e abbaco
	Giovanni Antonio Agazio	1575–6	maestro di leggere e abbaco
	Ludovico Ceroni	1575–9	n/a
	Francesco Mazone	1576	maestro di leggere e scrivere
	Pietro de Medici	1577–8	maestro di grammatica
	Nicolò Cologno	1578	n/a [assisted w/ exams]
	Giov. Plizoli	1579–?, 1584–9	maestro di grammatica
	Domenico de Lallio	1579	n/a
	Battista Capoferro	1584	maestro di grammatica/ canto

Institution	Name of Teacher	Date(s) of Service	Title of Teacher
	Paolo Isabello	1585	Rev. di grammatica
S. Spirito	Alessio Marentio	1586–1614	maestro di sc[u]ola
	Fermo Bressani	1614	Rev. maestro di scuole dei poveri
	Giosetto(?) di Contro	1605	maestro di chierici
S. Alessandro della Croce	Augustino de Prestisio	1593–5	grammatice professore
	Alessandro f. Gasp. Nigrone	1595–6	grammatice professore
	Gio. Jacomo Ligrigni	1596	maestro sacerdote
	Gio. Jacomo Carrara	1596–?	maestro sacerdote
	Cornellio Tertio	1597–8	maestro dei filioli poveri
	Battista Calcone di Boccaleone	1599–?	maestro dei filioli poveri
	Alessandro	1605	reverendo
	Stephano d. Nic. Benaglio	1606	maestro dei chierici
	Paolo Foresti	1607	maestro dei chierici
	Eduardo Michaele	1612	maestro dei chierici
	Pietro [Paolo?] Foresti	1614	maestro dei chierici
Diocesan Seminary	Gerolamo da Gromo	1567–?	ludimagister, magister principalis clericorum
	Michele Manili	1569–70	preceptoris seminarium
	Bonifacio Guerinoni	1570–5	praefaectus domus, rector seminarii
	Massimo Bonello	1575	rector seminarii
	Sigismondo Pellegrino	1579–82(?)	maestro del seminario
Somaschans: College of St Joseph	Giovanni Calta	1634–5(?)	rettore del collegio di S. Giuseppe
	Giov. Luigi Cerchiari	1632(?)–6	n/a
	Pier Paolo Piovene	1634–5(?)	n/a
	Verginio Gamba	1634	n/a
	Giov. Bernardino Suallino	1634	n/a
	Paolo Zuintano	1635	n/a
	Bartolomeo Cerchiari	1645–?	rettore
	Bonifatio Albano	1650–?	rettore
	Girolamo Toriglia	1657–?	insegnante
	Francesco Maria Pomodoro	1657–?	insegnante
Caspi Academy	Andrea Cato [Catto]	1547	primo maestro
	Manfredo Bescio [Manfredo Pasti?]	1548–51?	secondo maestro, ripetitore
	Battista da Ghisalba	1551–7	ripetitore
	Julio Terzi [Giulio da Terzo]	1552–5	grammatice prof. magister
	Teodoro Vannio	1555–?	primo maestro
	Antonio de Gritti	1549–?	secondo maestro
	Bartolomeo Zanchi	1556–?	secondo maestro

Institution	Name of Teacher	Date(s) of Service	Title of Teacher
[Anonymous] Academy	Ubaldo di Gherardo	1559–66	professore delle belle arti
	Nicolò Cologno	1556–59(?)	maestro, reverendissimo
Miscellaneous [Flemish]	Herrico Farnese	ca 1570	prof. di lettere umane
	Silvestro Castelliono	1578	maestro dell'Accademia di Borgo Canale
	Bartolomeo di Grigno	1603	maestro dell'Accademia di Borgo Pignolo
	Nicolo Benaglio	1603	ripetitore dell'Accademia di Borgo Pignolo
	Andrea Pasta	1610	maestro dell'Accademia Pasta
	Marino Garzino	1604	maestro dell'Accademia

Appendix 2: Distribution of Teachers and Students in Bergamo's Schools of Christian Doctrine, 1609[3]

ACVBg, Archivio Capitolare, CAP 872, *Fundatio Scholae Generalis Doctrinae Christiane in Cath. Ecclesia Bergomensis ... de anno 1609.*

N.B. The table below includes only the parishes within the city of Bergamo. Records for the entire diocese are extant in the ACVBg. The Academies were generally named after the teacher who supervised them.

Total number of male teachers:	377
Total number of male students:	1466

Total number of female teachers:	810
Total number of female students:	2719

Total number of participants in the Diocese of Bergamo:	5372

Area of City	Indiv. Church/ School	Date of Aggregation	Male Tchrs. / Studs.	Female Tchrs. / Studs.
Città Alta	S. Agata	5 July 1609	30 / 127	
Città Alta	S. Caterina	5 July 1609	23 / 108	
Città Alta	S. Pancrazio	5 July 1609	23 / 111	
Città Alta	S. Michele al Pozzo Bianco	5 July 1609	8 / 43	
Città Alta	S. Erasmo in Borgo Canale[4]	5 July 1609	52 / 70	
S. Ales. d. Croce	SS. Trinità	5 July 1609	27 / 101	
S. Ales. d. Croce	Sch. of Clerics	5 July 1609	1 / 11	
Città Alta	S. Lorenzo	12 July 1609	14 / 40	19 / 34

Area of City	Indiv. Church/ School	Date of Aggregation	Male Tchrs. / Studs.	Female Tchrs. / Studs.
Borgo S. Antonio	S. Giov. Battista	12 July 1609	28 / 54	
S. Ales. d. Croce	S. Pietro	12 July 1609	11 / 14	
S. Caterina	S. Tommaso	12 July 1609	17 / 43	
Borgo Palazzo	S. Anna di B.Pal.	12 July 1609	8 / 96	
Borgo S. Antonio	S. Bernardino	19 July 1609	19 / 93	
S. Ales. d. Colon.	S. Lazzaro	19 July 1609	24 / 80	
S. Ales. d. Colon.	S. Leonardo	19 July 1609	22 / 50	
S. Ales. d. Colon.	S. Lucia & Agata	19 July 1609	19 / 10	
S. Ales. d. Colon.	S. Rocco	19 July 1609	17 / 92	
S. Ales. d. Colon.	S. Antonio	2 August 1609		48 / 193
S. Ales. d. Colon	S. Pietro	2 August 1609		24 / 51
Daste	S. Brigida	2 August 1609	14 / 23	
Città Alta	S. Michele al Pozzo Bianco	2 August 1609		19 / 43
S. Ales. d. Croce	S. Elisabetta	2 August 1609		31 / 91
S. Ales. d. Croce	School of BVM	2 August 1609		28 / 164
Città Alta	S. Andrea	2 August 1609		44 / 66
Città Alta	S. Caterina	2 August 1609		59 / 177
Città Alta	S. Cassiano	2 August 1609		45 / 92
Borgo S. Leonardo	S. Bernardino	2 August 1609		32 / 166
Borgo S. Antonio	S. Bernardino	2 August 1609		64 / 162
S. Ales. d. Colon.	S. Rocco	2 August 1609		44 / 160
S. Ales. d. Colon.	S. Lazzaro	2 August 1609		28 / 124
S. Ales. d. Colon.	S. Defendente	2 August 1609		37 / 170
Città Alta	S. Eufemia	2 August 1609		? / ?
Città Bassa	S. Maria dello Spasimo	2 August 1609		43 / 144
S. Ales. d. Colon.	S. Maria Maddal.	2 August 1609		? / ?
Città Alta	S. Erasmo in Borgo Canale	2 August 1609		43 / 203
Città Alta	Seminary	15 August 1609	2 / ?	
Città Alta	Lazzaroni Academy	15 August 1609	1 / 48	
Borgo S. Tommaso	Mariani Academy	15 August 1609	1 / 20	
Città Alta	S. Salvatore Academy	15 August 1609	2 / 48	
Città Alta	MIA's Academy of Clerics	15 August 1609	? / 57	
Borgo S. Leonardo	Valerio Benis Academy	15 August 1609	2 / 22	
Borgo S. Leonardo	Pasta brothers' Academy	15 August 1609	2 / 35	
S. Lorenzo	Terzi-Assolari Academy	16 August 1609	2 / 31	
Borgo Canale	P. Deleidi Academy	16 August 1609	1 / 10	
S. Andrea	Caratte-Consoli Academy	16 August 1609	2 / 29	
Borgo Canale	Camerata-Metis Academy	16 August 1609	2 / 14	

Area of City	Indiv. Church/ School	Date of Aggregation	Male Tchrs. / Studs.	Female Tchrs. / Studs.
Città Alta	Boys' Orphanage	20 August 1609	4 / 36	
Città Alta	'Convertite'	23 August 1609		? / 46
Città Alta	Girls' Orphanage	23 August 1609		? / 51

Notes

Front Matter

1 Peter Spufford, *Handbook of Medieval Exchange* (London: Royal Historical Society, 1986), 96–9.

Introduction

1 The stereotype of Bergamasque stupidity, illiteracy, and lack of education probably has its roots in several different places. Bergamo was historically poor, particularly in the stony valleys to the north of the city. Many of Bergamo's residents had to leave the region in order to make a living, often as porters in Venice where brawn was more important than brains. The dialect of Bergamo was (and remains) famously unintelligible, lending credence to the belief that the people of Bergamo and the surrounding valleys could neither speak nor think clearly. Furthermore, Bergamo was a border town on the edge of the Venetian empire, and thus literally as well as figuratively far away from the cosmopolitan, cultured capital. Most importantly, Bergamo's reputation as a backward 'hillbilly' town was created through the stock characters of the *commedia dell'arte*, the Italian theatrical tradition born in the fifteenth century. The characters of Arlecchino and Brighella are most closely associated with Bergamo: poor and illiterate yet also crafty. Pierre Louis Duchartre observes: 'It is said that the lower town produces nothing but fools and dullards, whereas the upper town was the home of nimble-wits.' See Duchartre, *The Italian Comedy* (New York: Dover, 1966), 123–60 and 161–78, here at 124. See also Alberto Castoldi, *L'altra Bergamo* (Bergamo: Lubrina Editore, 1997) for analysis of how dozens of writers have characterized Bergamo through the centuries.

2 For a general history of Bergamo, see Belotti, *Storia di Bergamo*, cited below in note 11; the only substantive article on education is Locatelli, 'L'istruzione a Bergamo,' also cited in note 11. A more recent analysis of Bergamo's history is the series *Storia economica e sociale di Bergamo*, in multiple volumes published 1994–present, but it says little about education.

3 Robert Black, *Education and Society in Florentine Tuscany: Teachers, Pupils, and Schools, c. 1250–1550* (Boston and Leiden: Brill, 2007), 164–72 and 321–6; see also Paul Grendler, *Schooling in Renaissance Italy: Literacy and Learning, 1300–1600* (Baltimore and London: Johns Hopkins University Press, 1989), 71.

4 Robert Black's publication of excerpts from eighty-seven *ricordanze* (out of more than seven hundred in Florentine archives) shows that such sources can be very valuable: Black, *Education and Society*, 613–724 (Appendix 5).

5 David A. Lines, *Aristotle's Ethics in the Italian Universities (ca. 1300–1650): The Universities and the Problem of Moral Education* (Leiden: Brill, 2002).

6 Giovanni Vezzoli, 'Il collegio dei giuristi a Bergamo nel XVI secolo,' *tesi di laurea* Univ. degli Studi di Milano, a.a. 1986–7, 130–1.

7 James Grubb, 'When Myths Lose Power: Four Decades of Venetian Historiography,' *Journal of Modern History* 58, no. 1 (March 1986): 43–94; John J. Martin and Dennis Romano, eds., *Venice Reconsidered: The History and Civilization of an Italian City-State, 1297–1797*(Baltimore and London: Johns Hopkins University Press, 2000), esp. 1–38; Elena Fasano Guarini, 'Center and Periphery,' *Journal of Modern History*, 67, Supplement: The Origins of the State in Italy, 1300–1600 (December 1995): S74–S96.

8 For general studies, see Harvey Graff, *Legacies of Literacy: Continuities and Contradictions in Western Society and Culture* (Bloomington: Indiana University Press, 1987); idem, *Literacy and Historical Development* (Carbondale: Southern Illinois University Press, 2007); and R.A. Houston, *Literacy in Early Modern Europe* (London: Longman, 1988). For England, David Cressy, *Literacy and the Social Order: Reading and Writing in Tudor and Stuart England* (Cambridge: Cambridge University Press, 1985), and John S. Pendergast, *Religion, Allegory, and Literacy in Early Modern England, 1560–1640* (Aldershot, UK: Ashgate, 2006); for Central Europe, Istvan Gyorgy Toth, *Literacy and Written Culture in Early Modern Central Europe* (Budapest: Central European University Press, 2000); for Spain, Sara T. Nalle, 'Literacy and Culture in Early Modern Castile,' *Past and Present* 125 (1989): 65–96; for medieval Italy, Armando Petrucci, *Writers and Readers in Medieval Italy* (New Haven, CT: Yale University Press, 1995); for early modern Italy, Peter Burke, 'The Uses of Literacy in Early Modern Italy,' in *The Social History of Language*, ed. P. Burke and R. Porter (Cambridge: Cambridge University Press, 1987), 21–42.

9 Black, *Education and Society*, 1–42, estimating an adult male literacy rate of 70 per cent and supporting Giovanni Villani's figures of 9500–11,000 students for 1338; Grendler, *Schooling*, 72–4, estimates only one-third the number of students and a correspondingly lower literacy rate more in line with Venice.

10 Robert Black, 'Italian Renaissance Education: Changing Perspectives and Continuing Controversies,' *Journal of the History of Ideas* 52, no. 2 (April 1991): 315–34, esp. 315–16. For more historiographical analysis of Italian Renaissance education, see idem, *Humanism and Education*, 12–33; and Lines, 7–21.

11 William H. Woodward, *Vittorino da Feltre and Other Humanist Educators* (New York: Columbia University Press, 1908); idem, *Studies in Education during the Age of the Renaissance* (Cambridge: Cambridge University Press, 1906); Giuseppe Locatelli, 'L'istruzione a Bergamo e la Misericordia Maggiore,' *Bergomum* 4, no. 4 (1910): 57–169; and no. 5 (1911) no. 1: 21–100; Giuseppe Manacorda, *Storia della scuola in Italia: il medio evo.* 2 vols. (Milan, Palermo and Naples: R. Sandron, 1913; rpt. Florence: Le Lettere, 1980). On education in Bergamo, see the following: Bortolo Belotti, *La storia di Bergamo e dei Bergamaschi,* 9 vols (Bergamo: Bolis, 1989); Locatelli, 'L'istruzione,' cited earlier in this note; Angelo G. Roncalli (later John XXIII), *Gli inizi del Seminario di Bergamo e S. Carlo Borromeo* (Bergamo: SESA, 1939); Paola Valota, 'Il Collegio Mariano di Bergamo nella seconda metà del Settecento,' *Bergomum* 89, no. 2 (1994): 99–221; Luisa Boroni, 'Maestri e scolari a Bergamo nei secoli XIV e XV: Ricerche sull'attività assistenziale del consorzio della Misericordia Maggiore,' tesi di perfezionamento, Università Cattolica del Sacro Cuore di Milano, Facoltà di Lettere e Filosofia, relatore Giuseppe Billanovich, 1969–70; Omar Capoferri, 'La pedagogia a Bergamo nel Settecento e il caso del Collegio Mariano,' tesi di laurea, Università degli Studi di Milano, Facoltà di Lettere e Filosofia, relatore Marco Todeschini, 1993–94; Francesco Lo Monaco, 'Civitati autem illi magistrorum copia semper fuit (Appunti su maestri, scuole, e biblioteche a Bergamo fra i secoli XIII e XIV),' in *Maestri e traddutori bergamaschi fra Medioevo e Rinascimento*, ed. Claudio Villa and Francesco Lo Monaco (Bergamo: Civica Biblioteca Angelo Mai, 1998), 27–50.

12 Eugenio Garin, *L'educazione in Europa (1400–1600)* (Bari: Laterza, 1957); idem, *Educazione umanistica in Italia* (Bari: Laterza, 1966).

13 Grendler, *Schooling*; idem, The *Universities of the Italian Renaissance* (Baltimore and London: Johns Hopkins University Press, 2002).

14 Anthony Grafton and Lisa Jardine, *From Humanism to the Humanities: Education and the Liberal Arts in Fifteenth- and Sixteenth-Century Europe* (Cambridge, MA: Harvard University Press, 1986).

15 Robert Black, 'Humanism and Education in Renaissance Arezzo,' *I Tatti Studies* 2 (1987): 171–237; idem, *Studio e Scuola in Arezzo durante il medioevo e Rinascimento* (1996); idem, *Humanism and Education in Medieval and Renaissance Italy: Tradition and Innovation in Latin Schools from the Twelfth to the Fifteenth Century* (Cambridge: Cambridge University Press, 2001); idem, *Education and Society* (Leiden and Boston: Brill, 2007), second volume forthcoming. Other research includes: Piero Lucchi, 'La Santacroce, il Salterio, e il Babuino: Libri per imparare a leggere nel primo secolo della stampa,' *Quaderni storici* 38 (1978): 593–630; Maurizio Sangalli, 'Università, scuole private, collegi d'educazione, accademie a Padova tra Cinque e Seicento: alcuni spunti per una storia'integrata' delle istituzioni scolastiche,' *Annali di storia dell'educazione* (1996): 93–118; idem, '"Venezia non è tera di studi"? Educazione e politica nel secondo Cinquecento. I gesuiti e i procuratori di San Marco de supra,' *Studi Veneziani* 34 (1996): 97–163; Arie S. Zmora, 'Schooling in Renaissance Pistoia: Community and Civic Humanism in Small-Town Tuscany,' *Sixteenth Century Journal* 34 (2003): 761–77; idem, 'The Pia Casa di Sapienza of Pistoia: A Charitable Foundation and the Promise of Education in a Late Renaissance Community' (PhD dissertation, University of Maryland College Park, 1995).
16 Lines, *Aristotle's* Ethics 3n10; Charles Schmitt, 'Towards a Reassessment of Renaissance Aristotelianism,' *History of Science* 11 (1973): 159–93, and in many of his later essays.
17 George Huppert, *Public Schools in Renaissance France* (Urbana, IL: University of Chicago Press, 1984); Karen E. Carter, 'Creating Catholics: Catechism and Primary Education in Early Modern France' (PhD dissertation, Georgetown University, 2006); Susan Karant-Nunn, 'Alas, a Lack: Trends in the Historiography of Pre-University Education in Early Modern Germany,' *Renaissance Quarterly* 43 (1990): 788–98; Amy Leonard, *Nails in the Wall: Catholic Nuns in Reformation Germany* (Chicago: University of Chicago Press, 2005); Gerald Strauss and Richard Gawthrop, 'Protestantism and Literacy in Early Modern Germany,' *Past and Present* 104 (1984): 31–55; Nicholas Orme, *Medieval Schools: From Roman Britain to Tudor England* (New Haven, CT: Yale University Press, 2006); idem, *Education and Society in Medieval and Renaissance England* (London and Ronceverte, WV: Hambledon Press, 1989).
18 Jo Ann Hoeppner Moran, T*he Growth of English Schooling, 1340–1548: Learning, Literacy, and Laicization in Pre-Reformation York Diocese* (Princeton, NJ: Princeton University Press, 1985); Joan Simon, *Education and Society in Tudor England* (Cambridge: Cambridge University Press, 1966).
19 For a defence of the term 'Renaissance,' see Paul Grendler, 'The Italian

Renaissance in the Past Seventy Years: Humanism, Social History, and
Early Modern in Anglo-American and Italian scholarship,' in *The Italian
Renaissance in the Twentieth Century*, ed. Allan J. Grieco, Michael Rocke, and
Fiorella Gioffredi Superbi (Florence: Leo S. Olschki, 2002), 3–23; for an erudite review of the issue, see Randolph Starn, 'A Postmodern Renaissance'
Renaissance Quarterly 60, no. 1 (2007): 1–24; for a thoughtful overview of
the historiography of humanism, with emphasis on the medieval period,
see Glenn W. Olsen, 'Humanism: The Struggle to Possess a Word' *Logos* 7,
no. 7 (Winter 2004): 97–116.
20 Grendler, *Schooling in Italy*, 274–331.
21 Grendler, *Schooling*, 182–94; Black, *Education and Society*, 45.
22 See Black's *Humanism and Education* as well as Grendler's *Schooling* for
comprehensive discussion of the different parts of the curriculum in late
medieval and Renaissance Italy.
23 Black, *Education and Society*, 44–60; Black, *Humanism and Education*, 82–172;
Grendler, *Schooling*, 111–274.

1. *Comune*: Schooling and the City

1 I use the terms 'commune,' 'city,' and 'city council' interchangeably to refer
to the civic government of Bergamo. The City Council consisted of two
distinct bodies: the Consiglio Maggiore (Great Council) of one hundred
citizens who served one-year terms and were elected by members of the
outgoing council, and the Bina (Executive Council) of twelve Anziani
(Elders) who were elected from the Consiglio Maggiore to serve a two-
month term. The *Bina* generally met twice a week to propose legislation,
approve spending, and debate pending issues. In this chapter I often refer
to the two groups collectively as the 'city council.' After 1428 the city was
supervised by two Venetian governors, the *podestà* (governor) and the
capitano (captain), who met regularly with the city council and served as
a link with the Venetian government. The Venetian governors supervised
areas of direct interest to the republic – criminal justice, taxes, military
matters – while the city council managed many of the day-to-day affairs
of the city, including public education. On the Venetian governors (*rettori*),
see Bruno Polese's introduction in *Relazioni dei Rettori Veneti XII: Podestaria
e Capitanato di Bergamo*, ed. Amelio Tagliaferri (Milan: A Giuffrè, 1973–9);
on the composition and function of the city council, see Roberto Galati,
'Il patriziato bergamasco alla vigilia di Agnadello,' tesi di laurea, Università di Venezia, Facoltà di Lettere e Filosofia, relatore Marino Berengo,
1978–9.

2 Surprisingly little information exists about the history of public schooling in Bergamo. Bortolo Belotti, *La storia di Bergamo e dei Bergamaschi*, 9
vols. (Bergamo: Bolis, 1989), vol. 4, 224–45, provides a partial overview.
See also Giuseppe Locatelli, 'L'istruzione a Bergamo e la Misericordia
Maggiore,' *Bergomum* 4, no. 4 (1910): 57–169, and idem, *Bergomum* 5, no. 1
(1911): 21–100 (the 1911 volume contains all of the endnotes and transcriptions). Locatelli himself relied in part upon an annual Bergamo publication
entitled *Bergamo o sia notizie patrie, almanacco scientifico-artistico-letterario per
l'anno 1858* (Bergamo: Tip. Pagnoncelli, n.d. [1859]), 64–104, herafter *Notizie
Patrie*, but the latter contains no specific citations and freely mixes myth
with fact.
3 George Huppert, *Public Schools in Renaissance France* (Urbana, IL: University of Chicago Press, 1984), 116–29.
4 On inscriptions in Augustan Bergamo, see Belotti, vol. 1, 213. On Bishop
Ambrogio, see BCBg, Mario Lupi, *Codex Diplomaticus*, tom. II, 310, 'Dona-
tio Ambrosii Episcopi nonnulorum prediorum facta magistris grammaticae et cantus cathedralis ecclesie, anno 973,' cited by Locatelli (1910), 60.
5 Locatelli (1910), 60–1, and idem (1911), 24–5. See also BCBg, *Notizie Patrie*
(1858), 71–2; and Francesco Lo Monaco, 'Civitati autem illi magistrorum
copia semper fuit (Appunti su maestri, scuole, e biblioteche a Bergamo
fra i secoli XIII e XIV),' in *Maestri e traddutori bergamaschi fra Medioevo e
Rinascimento*, ed. Claudio Villa and Francesco Lo Monaco (Bergamo: Civica
Biblioteca Angelo Mai, 1998), 27–50.
6 Paul Grendler, *Schooling in Renaissance Italy: Learning and Literacy, 1300–
1600* (London and Baltimore: Johns Hopkins University Press, 1989),
6–10. Grendler argues that cathedral schools dominated the educational
landscape from 1000 to 1300, but then gradually disappeared with the rise
of independent masters.
7 On Bonifacio, see Belotti, vol. 2, 337; Vaerini, *Gli Scrittori de Bergamo*,
214–22; Girolamo Tiraboschi, *Storia della letteratura italiana* (Venice, 1796),
vol. 4, 424–5; Luigi Chiodi, 'Note brevi di cose bergamasche ignote o quasi:
Maestro Bonacio da Osio' *Bergomum* 61, no. 3–4 (1967): 106–15 (reprinted in
idem, *Note brevi di cose Bergamaschi ignote o quasi* [Verdello: Comune di Verdello, 1988], 65–73). Tiraboschi, vol. 4, 425, observes that Bonifacio 'taught
to such acclaim that nobody in his lifetime could equal him in honours
or in praise.' For an entertaining summary of the letters written both to
Bonifacio and to the podestà of Bergamo, pleading for Bonifacio's return,
see Tiraboschi, 424.
8 Identified as a *doctor in grammaticalibus et logicalibus*, Lorenzo probably
graduated from the University of Padua between 1270 and 1285. In a

notarial document of 13 December 1287 (BCBg, Arch. MIA, Perg. no. 7078), he swore to execute faithfully the art of being a notary. See Luisa Boroni, 'Maestri e scolari a Bergamo nei secoli XIV e XV: Ricerche sull'attività assistenziale del consorzio della Misericordia Maggiore,' tesi di perfezionamento, Università Cattolica del Sacro Cuore di Milano, Facoltà di Lettere e Filosofia, relatore Giuseppe Billanovich, 1969–70, 14–22; Belotti, vol. 2, 337, and vol. 3, 169–70. On Lorenzo's son Venturino, a famous Dominican preacher referred to as 'the Savonarola of the fourteenth century,' see Angelo Mazzi, *Il beato Venturino da Bergamo* (Bergamo: Fratelli Bolis, 1905); Giuseppe Clementi, *Il Beato Venturino da Bergamo, dell'ordine de' Predicatori (1304–1346)* (Rome: Tip. Vaticano, 1904), 1–29; and a dozen other works cited by Boroni, 19n16. For information about his other son Jacopo, and the scholarships endowed by the Apibus family and subsequently administered by the MIA, see the following chapter.

9 On being nominated by the MIA, see BCBg, Arch. MIA, Perg. no. 6618, cited by Boroni, 18. On the destroyed house, see Locatelli (1910), 83, and idem (1911), 49–50. Lorenzo de Apibus's original will is in ASBg, *Atti Notarili* di Gerardo Soiario, busta 13, ff. 184–92 (16 Jul. 1361); a copy of the will also exists in BCBg, Arch MIA, Perg. no. 2966; excerpts of it were published by Clementi, 146, and by Boroni, 20–2.

10 Boroni, 23, citing BCBg, Arch. MIA, Perg. no. 2973, V (anno 1347); no. 2974, I (a. 1350); no. 2974, III; no. 2975 (a. 1350); and no. 2978 (a. 1358).

11 Boroni, 27–9, citing BCBg, Ms. Ψ, 4, 34 (now MA 144). This grammar book subsequently passed to the MIA, which used it to instruct *chierici* (priests-in-training) beginning in the mid-fifteenth century, as illustrated by a note of possession dated 1468.

12 Boroni, 25–6; Locatelli (1910), 83. The two met when Petrarch visited Bergamo on 13 Oct. 1359. See Arnaldo Foresti, 'La gita del Petrarca a Bergamo il 13 ottobre 1359,' *Bergomum* 17, no. 2 (1923):, 45–65, esp. 55–6. Note that Belotti's reference (in vol. 3, 170–1 and 184) incorrectly cites the letters of Petrarch; the proper references are Petrarch, *Letters on Familiar Matters (Rerum familiarum libri)*, Book 18, letters 13 & 14; see also Book 21, Letter 11.

13 *Letters on Familiar Matters*, trans. Aldo S. Bernardo (Baltimore: Johns Hopkins University Press, 1985), 65.

14 BCBg, Arch. MIA, Perg. no. 6975; recopied in BCBg, Angelo Mazzoleni, *Zibaldone, Libro'B' (Liber rerum extravagantium)*, f. 47, and published by Locatelli (1911), 50: 'quod ipse magister sicut est notorium actu legit et docet scolares grammaticam, dialecticam, et rhetoricam.'

15 Tommaso Ghighliazza, 'Curiosando tra gli antichi Statuti dei Medici di Bergamo,' *L'Eco di Bergamo* (26 May 1948), 3.

16 Locatelli (1911), 50. De Apibus's petition referred to the 1336 act of Lucchino Visconti, in which he exempted Bergamasque teachers from the *estimo* in order to encourage them to teach more students: see *Notizie Patrie (1858)*, 75. On tax exemptions for each profession in Renaissance Bergamo, see Roberto Taschini, 'Popolazione e classi sociali a Bergamo tra XV e XVI secolo,' tesi di laurea, Università di Padova, Facoltà di Economia e Commercio, relatore Gino Barbieri, 1970–1, esp. 187–8.

17 BCBg, Arch. Storico del Comune, *Estimo del 1430*, f. 82, cited by Taschini, 54n18.

18 BCBg, Arch. Storico del Comune, *Azioni del Consiglio* (hereafter *Azioni*), v. 98, f. 12r (16 Dec. 1468), and v. 98, f. 12v (31 Apr. 1470), published in Locatelli (1911), 52–3. N.B. both citations come from the *Index decretorum Mag. Civitatis Bergomi ab anno 1428* (v. 98); the original *Azioni* for these years have not survived.

19 BCBg, *Azioni*, v. 2, f. 37v (15 Sep. 1475). 'In consilio praefati magnifici domini Rectores proposuerunt quod pro bono et utilitate huius rei publice, et etiam attentis modis estimi super hanc materiam disponentibus et meritis magistri Pauli de Tertio rectoris scolarum in hac urbe, bonum eis videretur quod firmiter statuatur quod omnes magistri scolarum civitatis et burgorum Pergami publice regentes scolas exempti sint ab omnibus oneribus realibus personalibus et mixtis, datiis dumtaxat exemptis.'

20 BCBg, *Statuta Bergomi, Brixie per Angelum et Jacobum fratres de Britannicis*, 1491 XV kl. Jan. [18 Dec.], Coll. I, Cap. 54, 'De non solvendo per scolares pro antecedente.' An identical version was reprinted much later, the *Statuta magnificae civitatis bergomi* (Bergamo: Typographia Joannis Santini, 1727). Locatelli (1911), 55, reprints chap. 54.

21 BCBg, Arch. MIA no. 1263, *Terminazioni,* f. 167v (4 Aug. 1547). Ironically, Giovanni Francesco Minoli was a nephew of the powerful canon Antonio Minoli, described by Firpo as a collector (and distributor) of multiple benefices and titles. See Massimo Firpo, *I Processi Inquisitoriali de Vittore Soranzo* (Vatican City: Archivio Segreto Vaticano, 2004), 379n1, 380–1.

22 Grendler, *Schooling*, 29–33.

23 The literature on the Barzizza family is extensive. The first to collect and publish Gasparino Barzizza's works was Cardinal Alessandro Furietti: *Gasparini Barsizii et Guiniforti Opera* (Rome, 1723). The most recent study is Carla Frova, 'Una dinastia di professori nel Quattrocento: I Barizza,' in Villa and Lo Monaco, 85–95; also helpful is R.G.G. Mercer, *The Teaching of Gasparino Barzizza with special reference to his place in Paduan Humanism* (London: Modern Humanities Research Assocation, 1979). On Barzizza at Bergamo, see Belotti, vol. 3, 176–7, and vol. 4, 247; idem, *Gli Eccellenti Bergamaschi*, 3 vols. (Bergamo: Ediz. Orobiche, 1956), vol. 1, 25–37; and

Boroni, Appendix I, 1–31. Each of these works contains more bibliography.
24 Locatelli (1910), 90–1, and idem (1911), 52.
25 Belotti, vol. 4, 337.
26 *Mafei Vegij, Laudensis de educatione liberorum [et] eo[rum] claris moribus liber primus* (Milan: Leonardo Pachel, 1491), was the first printing, followed by others in Paris (1508, 1511) and Tübingen (1511, 1513). Vegio died in 1458. Belotti, vol. 4, 248–9, offers an introduction and more bibliography. See also Vincent J. Horkan's thesis, published as *Educational Theories and Principles of Maffeo Vegio* (Washington, DC: Catholic University Press, 1953).
27 F. Pignatti, 'Filelfo, Gian Mario,' in *Dizionario Biografico degli Italiani (DBI)* (Rome: Istituto della Enciclopedia Italiana, 1997), vol. 47, 626–31; Diana Robin, *Filelfo in Milan: Writings, 1451–1477* (Princeton, NJ: Princeton University Press, 1991); *Francesco Filelfo nel Quinto Centenario della Morte* (Padua: Editrice Antenore, 1986). Pietro Frassica, 'I Filelfo: Due generazioni di umanisti,' in *Francesco Filelfo nel Quinto Centenario della Morte*, 515–27, discusses the relationship between F. Filelfo and his sons Gian Mario and Xenophon. On Gian Mario's poor scholarship and frivolous teaching, see Pignatti's entry in the *DBI*, and F. Patetta, 'Sulla "Glychephile" di Mario Filelfo ...,' *Atti della Reale Accademia d'Italia* 7 (1941), no. 2, 275–341, esp. 281; and Lucia Gualdo Rosa, 'Una prolusione inedita di Francesco Filelfo, rielaborata dal figlio Gian Mario nel 1467,' in *Francesco Filelfo nel Quinto Centenario della Morte*, 299–301. Belotti, vol. 4, 358, briefly discusses Filelfo in Bergamo.
28 BCBg, *Azioni*, v. 3, f. 62r (7 Jan. 1482). Locatelli (1911), 53–4, publishes the complete text of the 1482 motion. On Terzi, see BCBg, *Azioni*, v. 3, f. 162r (8 Apr. 1483), and ibid., v. 4, f. 115r (28 Jun. 1486). On Soltia, see BCBg, *Azioni*, v. 4, f. 217v (7 Jul. 1487).
29 BCBg, *Azioni*, v. 5, f. 259v (25 May 1491), published in Locatelli (1911), 56–7.
30 BCBg, *Azioni*, v. 5, ff. 265v–266r (10 Jun. 1491); Locatelli (1911), 56–7, publishes the complete text. See also BCBg, *Azioni*, v. 5, f. 259v (25 May 1491). My thanks to Paul Grendler for this observation about the word 'contubernium.'
31 BCBg, *Azioni*, v. 7, f. 68r (30 Dec. 1496).
32 BCBg, *Azioni*, v. 7, f. 255r–v (8 Jan. 1498), published in Locatelli (1911), 57. It is not clear whether this teacher was to replace Giovanni de Lolmo or to share teaching duties.
33 No scholarly biography of Pio exists. On Pio's experience in Bergamo, see Christopher Carlsmith, 'A Peripatetic Pedagogue: G.B. Pio in Bergamo, 1505–1507,' in *Ritratti: La dimensione individuale nella storia (secoli XV–XX)*,

ed. Robert Pierce and Silvana Seidel Menchi, 45–55 (Rome: Edizioni di Storia e Letteratura, 2008). Carlo Dionisotti's *Gli umanisti e il volgare fra Quattro e Cinquecento* (Florence: Le Monnier, 1968), 78–130, does an excellent job of situating Pio in the historical context, although it devotes only one sentence to Pio's time in Bergamo. Tiraboschi's *Storia della letteratura italiana*, vol. 7, pt. 4, 1475–8, offers a brief overview of Pio's life and works, as does Giovanni Fantuzzi, *Notizie degli scrittori bolognesi* (Bologna, 1789), vol. 7. Valerio Del Nero, 'Note sulla vita di Giovan Battista Pio (con alcune lettere inedite)' *Rinascimento* 21 (1981): 247–63, briefly reviews what is known and includes previously unpublished correspondence between Giovanni Garzoni and Pio. See also Paul F. Grendler, *Universities of the Italian Renaissance* (Baltimore and London: Johns Hopkins University Press, 2002), 218–21.

Pio's first important work was his edition of Plautus, *Plautus integer cum interpretazione Io. Bap. Pio* (Milan, 1500), followed by the *Apologia Plautum* (Bologna, 1508). He wrote a poem in hexameter called *De pace* and a collection of various poems known as the *Elegidia* (Bologna, 1509). Among the numerous commentaries and editions, he edited *De rerum natura* of Lucretius (Bologna, 1511), *Argonautica* of Flaccus (Venice, 1523), and the *Comedies* of Plautus (Venice, 1511).

34 Tiraboschi, vol. 7, pt. 4, 1478; Del Nero, 255. On Pio and humanism in Bergamo and Brescia, see Cortesi-Bosco, 5–42; and Belotti, vol. 4, 224–313.

35 Dionisotti, 94–8; Robin, 3–10. See also John F. D'Amico, 'The Progress of Renaissance Latin Prose: The Case of Apuleianism' *Renaissance Quarterly* 37 (1984), 351–92, esp. 362–3.

36 BCBg, *Azioni*, v. 9, f. 56v (31 Mar. 1505).

37 BCBg, *Corrispondenza di Paulo Zanchi (1497–1509)*, f. 272 (29 Aug. 1505), 'Pacta inita inter Magnificam Communitatem Bergomi, et excellentem utriusque lingue professorem D. Jo. Baptistam Pium Bonon. Binas quotidie lectiones publico in audiotorio promat. Privatas scholas erigat, et qua decet cura regat; a discipulis condignam mercedem recipiens. Centenar [*sic*] aureos quotannis, menstrua, sive quae sibi magis placuerit, partitione, publico exare percipiat, eosque nulla ex parte diminuitos. Commoda in usus suos domus gratis praestabitur. Ad duos, sive maluerit, tres annos, faedera isthaec feriantur.' Zanchi's epistolary is in Rome's Biblioteca Alessandrina, ms. 103, ff. 260r–283v; I consulted the microfilm at the BCBg, Micr. 505. My thanks to Francesca Cortesi-Bosco for this reference. Cortesi-Bosco (17n31) notes that in the spring of 1505, after the council's action but before Pio had been selected, Girolamo Suardi wrote to his former teacher in Brescia, Giovanni Britannico, to enquire about finding a suitable teacher on behalf of the city of Bergamo.

38 BCBg, *Azioni*, v. 9, f. 121r–v (25 Aug. 1505). The *Azione* of 29 Oct. 1507 (v. 10, f. 59r) records that Pio lived in a house owned by Nicolò Bonghi, an important member of the city council. On Pio's acceptance, see BCBg, *Corrispondenza di Paulo Zanchi*, f. 272 (29 Sept. 1505). On Pio's arrival, see BCBg, MMB 323, Marco Beretta, *Memoriale*, f. 63; BCBg, *Azioni*, v. 9, f. 146r (14 Nov. 1505); Donato Calvi, *Effemeride sacro profana di quanto di memorabile sia successo in Bergamo*, 3 vols. (Milan: Francesco Vigoni, 1676), vol. 3, 302, notes the enthusiastic popular reception accorded to Pio upon his arrival to direct 'the public schools of Humanities and Rhetoric.'

39 BCBg, *Azioni*, v. 9, f. 211v (20 Apr. 1506), and Luigi Chiodi, '1508 – Police de Fr. Catana massarolo,' *Bergomum* 52, no. 1 (1958) 63–144, especially 69–70, 90, 92, 124.

40 BCBg, *Azioni*, v. 9, f. 227r (12 Jun. 1506), *Azioni*, v. 9, ff. 258r–v (20 Nov. 1506); *Azioni*, v. 9, f. 260r (27 Nov. 1506); *Azioni*, v. 9, f. 288v (29 Jan. 1507); *Azioni*, v. 10, f. 15v (7 May 1507); *Azioni*, v. 10, f. 16v (15 May 1507), and f. 19r (29 May 1507). Cortesi-Bosco, 17n31, cites Pio's correspondence with Suardi. The appointment at Bologna is noted by Del Nero, 252–3; Pio's resignation appears in BCBg, *Azioni*, v. 10, f. 54v (27 Oct. 1507). The council accepted Pio's departure and on 29 Oct. agreed to send him the remainder of his salary, but by 31 October he was *jam recessit* (already gone): ibid., f. 57r (29 Oct. 1507), f. 59r. (5 Nov. 1507). Luigi Chiodi suggests that Pio's long absence and hasty departure implies a falling out between Bergamo and the Bolognese humanist, and I am inclined to agree. Chiodi, '1508 – Police de Fr. Catana massarolo,' 70.

41 Del Nero, 252–3.

42 Del Nero, 253.

43 The best work on Ravizza is Luigi Boldrini, *Della vita e degli scritti di Messer Giovita Rapicio* (Verona: Tip. Annichini, 1903). Grendler, *Schooling*, 64–6, offers a brief analysis of Ravizza and his most important pedagogical treatise in the context of Venetian schooling in the 1550s. Both rely upon Lodovico Ricci, *Notizie intorno alla vita ed alle opere di M[esser] Giovita Rapicio* (Pavia, 1790). On the Vicentine period, see Giovanni Mantese, *Memorie storiche della chiesa vicentina*, vol. 3, pt. 2 (*Dal 1404 al 1563*) (Vicenza: Neri Pozza, 1964), 758–9. I have not seen the *tesi di laurea* of Anna Maria Menicocci, 'Giovita Rapicio, 1476–1553,' Università Cattolica del Sacro Cuore di Milano, Facoltà di Magistero di Brescia, 1975–6.

44 Boldrini, 24–8.

45 On reappointment, see BCBg, *Azioni*, v. 11, f. 104v (1 Jun. 1511); and *Azioni*, v. 15, f. 134r–v (30 Dec. 1519); Boldrini, 26n3, provides the full text. On location of classes, see BCBg, *Azioni*, v. 15, f. 219v (20 Nov. 1519); and *Azioni*,

v. 17, ff. 77v–78r (7 May 1524). On his raise, see BCBg, *Azioni*, v. 16, f. 24v (12 Oct. 1520), f. 106r (13 Dec. 1521). On his resignation and replacement, see BCBg, *Azioni*, v. 17, f. 79r (31 May 1524) and *Azioni*, v. 17, ff. 77v–78r (7 May 1524).

46 Boldrini, 30–2, lists a dozen pupils, including Ravizza's two sons, Eleuterio and Giulio. On Gratarolo, see the following chapter for his involvement with the MIA's Collegio Patavino. On Pellegrino, see 314n70.

47 Giovanni (Panfilo?) Zanchi , *De origine Orobiorum sive Cenomanorum ad Petrum Bembus libri tres* (Venice, 1531), vol. 3, 67; cited by Boldrini, 31. 'Cum praesertim memoria teneam, non ita pridem haec vobis commonstrata fuisse atque ostenta a Jovita illo Rapicio, homine et summo dicendi studio et peracri prorsus ingenio ac singulari doctrina praedito: quem scire omnes facile potestis tum multis civibus nostris, tum nobis praesertim et ad suscipienda et ad ingredienda istaec politioris humanitatis atque ingenuarum artium studia principem et auctorem et magistrum exstitisse.'

48 Jovita Rapicius, *Oratio in funere Pauli Zanchi Bergomatis* (Venice, 1561).

49 Boldrini, 37–8, and Calvi, *Effemeride*, vol. 3, 272–3.

50 The letters to the Suardi family are in BCBg, *Epistolario di Girolamo Suardi* [Micr. 500]. I am grateful to Francesca Cortesi-Bosco for this reference. The letters to Arrone Battaglia, as well as letters to Paolo Ramusio, Francesco Bellafino, and other literary friends, in BCBg, Mss. 67 R 10 (2), *Miscellanea dell'abate Pierantonio Serassi*, are briefly discussed in Erminio Gennaro, 'Arrone Battaglia de Butinoni,' *Bergomum* 73, no. 1–2 (1979): 145–64.

51 Boldrini, 38.

52 BCBg, *Azioni*, v. 17, f. 12r (19 Jun. 1523). This manuscript has a complicated history. It was presented in ms. to Bergamo's city council in 1523 with the title *De modo in scholis servando*. In June 1551 it was published in Venice, probably at the behest of Ravizza's friend and former pupil Paolo Ramnusio, under the title *De liberis publice ad humanitatem informandis* with a dedication to the doge Francisco Donato. In 1790 it was edited by Lodovico Ricci and published in 'Ticinii' [Pavia] under the title *De scholarum instauratione* with a dedication to Prof. Francesco Zola of the University of Pavia. The original manuscript of 21 pages is now housed in the Fondazione Biblioteca Morcelliana of Chiari (BS): Armadio mss. D.I.05. The 1551 version is preserved in Venice: Biblioteca Marciana, Fondo Antichi, Misc. 1719.6, ff. 1–9. The 1790 version is also preserved in the Biblioteca Marciana: Fondo Antichi, Misc. 1718.19, ff. 1–41. The 1790 version includes the original dedication *Magnificis rectoribus et decurionibus Bergomensis*, but the 1551 edition does not. The 1790 version has been divided into many smaller chapters and subchapters with headings. The text of the two editions is similar but not identical.

It is not known when or how the original manuscript left the Archive of the Commune of the BCBg. Boldrini (40n 2) and the editor of *Bergomum* (1909), 159, note that the manuscript passed to the canons of S. Afra in Brescia, and from there to a shopkeeper in Brescia who acquired it along with other books. The son of this anonymous shopkeeper noticed the beautiful calligraphy of the manuscript and gave it to his teacher, Don Gian Jacopo Barachetti, who in turn presumably donated it to the Fondazione Biblioteca Morcelli.

Boldrini, 40–2, demonstrates that other historians have erred in their interpretation of this history, usually because they assumed that Ravizza had written more than one pedagogical treatise. It is true that Ravizza published other pedagogical works – for example, his inaugural academic address in Venice in 1543–4, *De praestantia earum artium quae ad recti loquendi, subtiliter disputandi et bene dicendi rationem pertinent* (On the excellence of those arts which lead to correct speech, subtle disputation, and good pleading) – but none of his other works presents the systematic approach to organizing a school evident in *De modo in scholis servando*. I follow the 1790 edition of Ricci because it is more accessible, and because it includes the dedication to the Rectors of Bergamo.

53 Giuseppe Gullino, 'La politica scolastica veneziana nell'età delle Riforme,' in *Miscellanea di Studi e Memorie*, vol. 15 (Venice: Deputazione di Storia Patria per le Venezie, 1973), 1–183, esp. 73n92.
54 Gullino, 73.
55 Grendler, *Schooling*, 65.
56 Obviously I have rendered these terms in contemporary English. Ravizza wrote that he wished to follow the example of Pythagoras by dividing his treatise into four sections: time, place, people, and things. As noted above, the 1790 edition includes many chapter and subheadings (e.g., *De Auditorio, De Bibliotheca, De Moribus et vita magistrorum*).
57 *De Scholarum instauratione*, 8–11, 'De loco' and 'De partibus loco.'
58 *De Scholarum instauratione*, 12: 'quod facile consequetur, si plurimus ei de honesto ac bono sermo sit; nam quo saepius monuerit, hoc rarius castigabit.'
59 *De Scholarum instauratione*, 16–20 ('De tempore'), 21 ('De Feriis').
60 *De Scholarum instauratione*, 11–15 ('De moribus et vita magistrorum,' 'De doctrina magistri universalis,' 'De magistris peculiaribus').
61 *De Scholarum instauratione*, 42 ('De officio parentum').
62 *De Scholarum instauratione*, 39–42 ('De officio parentum'); the 1551 version includes an additional chapter at the end ('De officio praesidum').
63 Locatelli (1910), 93. Locatelli offers no evidence to support his conjecture. Furthermore, the two pages that Locatelli wrote on public schools in

Bergamo represent the weakest part of his article and are riddled with errors.

64 BCBg, *Azioni*, v. 19, f. 127v (10 Dec. 1533). 'Ritrovandosi al presente in questa città rari et pochi magistri de grammatica respetto al bon numero della gioventù qual ha bisogno di esser disciplinata et erudita in boni costumi et lettere, et essendo necessario per tal bisogno de magistri mandar in donzene [dozzina] fori della terra con incomodo et spesa impo[nente], et ben al proposito prender che essa gioventù non si nutrisca in otio et che si dia fomento de vitij et altre male qualità, ma in dottrina et laudevoli exercitij; l'andava adunque parte che siano eletti cinque probi cittadini experti in similibus quali habbiano ad inquirer qualche preceptor de grammatica de costumi probi, cosa che in primis in il preceptor si debba desiderar, et simile in dottrina et scientia.'

65 BCBg, *Azioni*, v. 19, f. 156r (27 Jan. 1534). The teacher remains anonymous.

66 The identity of Nicolò Cologno remains problematic for several reasons, including the absence of definitive paternity, the presence of several eponymous men in Bergamo, and disagreement among previous historians about his contributions. In sixteenth-century Bergamo, Nicolò f. Gerolamo Cologni (active 1565–1601) and Nicolò f. Paolo Cologni (active 1545–74), as well as the similarly named Nicolò f. Gio. Pietro Colleoni (active 1540–97) were all notaries in the city (see ASBg, *Indice dei Notai*, *s.v.* 'Cologni' and 'Colleoni'). To the best of my knowledge, none of these three men ever worked as a schoolteacher. More troubling is the possibility put forth by Locatelli (1910), 93–4, Belotti, v. 4, 281 and Firpo, *I Processi Inquisitoriali*, 996n140 that there were two schoolteachers with the name Nicolò Cologno, both active in sixteenth-century Bergamo. My own archival research has never revealed explicit reference to two separate schoolteachers with this name; therefore I treat him as one person with an admittedly varied and prolonged teaching career. I plan to publish elsewhere an article exploring the identity and contributions of Nicolò Cologno in more depth than is possible here.

67 BCBg, *Azioni*, v. 20, f. 131v–132v (3 May 1539) and *Azioni*, v. 21, f. 12r (16 Jul. 1541).

68 BCBg, *Azioni*, v. 21, f. 275r (12 Jan. 1545); *Azioni*, v. 21, f. 302r (27 May 1545); *Azioni*, v. 22, f. 76r (22 Feb. 1546).

69 BCBg, *Azioni*, v. 24, ff. 148r–149r (7 Feb. 1551), and f. 157v (6 Mar. 1551). For more on Cato, see chapter 5.

70 On Cato's encomium, see BCBg, *Azioni*, v. 24, ff. 33v–34r, 39r (9 Nov. 1550); for more on Pellegrino and the context of this encomium, see Firpo, *Vittore Soranzo*, 3–8. On the accusations against Cato from an anonymous denun-

ciation to the Inquisition on 7 May 1551, see Firpo, *I Processi Inquisitoriali,* 641–2, esp. note 4; and Firpo, *Vittore Soranzo vescovo ed eretico* (Rome: Laterza, 2006), 387. On the City Council's regret about Cato's 1551 resignation, see BCBg, *Azioni,* v. 24, f. 157v (6 Mar. 1551), transcribed in Firpo, *Vittore Soranzo,* 287n294.

71 BCBg, *Azioni,* v. 25, f. 223r (1 Jun. 1556).

72 ASBg, *Atti Notarili* di Gio Maria fu Andrea Rota, b. 2239 (anni 1538–1561) (23 June 1556). An identical copy appears in BCBg, Arch. Storico del Comune, *Instrumenti* (1538–1610), ff. 100v–101r. See also Locatelli (1910) 94, and Belotti, vol. 4, 241. On the problem of identifying Nicolò Cologno, see note 66.

73 BCBg, *Azioni,* v. 29, f. 257r (6 Dec. 1564). 'Essendo non solo utile ma sommamente necessario l'havere uno magistro dotto et sufficiente nella professione d'humanità per universal comodo et benefitio della gioventù di questa città, non si deve manchare di far ogni provisione perchè ne venga ritrovato et condotto uno sí come anche altra volta, e sta per gli antecessori nostri condutto et eletto a fine si dia occasione alla gioventù di fuggire l'otio et indirizzare la mente a studij lodevoli et virtuosi.'

74 BCBg, *Azioni,* v. 35, ff. 46r–49r (30 Nov. 1574). 'havendo noi … molte volte discorso, et con esperienza provato, che con molta difficoltà si trovano persone atte a satisfare al desiderio comune, essendo rarissimi e di molta stima gl'huomini che si giudicarebbero a proposito et appresso che puoco giovani lo rifiuta.'

75 Ibid. A nearly identical contract appears in BCBg, Arch. MIA no. 1519, *Liber Capitulorum,* ff. 71r–72v. (18 Jun. 1576). 'Et giudicando a tal impresa d'ogni parte idoneo il Reverendo Messer Nicolo Collonio nostra compatriota per bontà di vita et di costumi, per eccellenza di dottrina et per ottima maniera d'insegnare, conosciuto, amato, et venerito da tutti.'

76 BCBg, *Azioni,* v. 35, ff. 46r–49r (30 Nov. 1574). 'et che possa esser abbraciata per tutti a tempi futuri; la qual essere debba di tanto maggior beneficio et lauda a questa Magnifica Città quanto più comune et più comoda sarà l'opera del maestro, a ricchi et poveri et universalmente a tutti.'

77 Ibid. 'non solo i figlioli siano essercitati per buona via et in buone lettere, ma si allevino in buona copia maestri buoni per il bisogno della città senza haver cura d'andarli mendicando in paesi alieni.'

78 Ibid. 'Li quali lettioni non si leggerono a pompa ma a utilità d'ascoltanti, talmente che ciaschuno possa esserne capace.'

79 BCBg, Arch. Storico del Comune, *Relazioni ai consigli,* vol. 6 (1569–86), f. 465 (n.d.) 'che quanto alla persona del lettore non si può opponersi cosa alcuna ma da un tempo in qua sono mancati assai li auditori di maniera che

pare che questa lettura publica serva più per i chierici della Misericordia che per altri ... riputiamo che altramente la Mag.[nifica] Com.[unita] potria sparagnare questi cento scudi al'anno, spendendoli in altro migliore et più necessario uso.' My thanks to Sandro Buzzetti of the BCBg, who alerted me to the existence of this document.

80 On the seminary and the Pasta brothers' academy, see chapter 3; on the MIA and the other confraternal schools, see chapter 2; on private tutoring, see chapter 5; Calvi, *Effemeride*, vol. 1, 443, describes the Accademia Ema, founded inside the seminary by Bishop Giovanni Emo on 15 April 1617 and in existence until the beginning of the eighteenth century, but Belotti, vol. 4, 87, notes that 'rather than an academy per se, this was more an arena for seminarians and theologians to learn about Church dogma.' Calvi further notes the brief existence of a 'celebrated and glorious' academy founded in 1604 by Bergamo's treasurer, Marino Garzoni, which closed with the coming of winter (ibid., vol. 2, 653).

   The most intriguing example of late sixteenth-century instruction concerns Henrico Farnese, a Flemish professor of humane letters who married an Italian woman and came to Bergamo after a successful academic career elsewhere. In Bergamo he ran an academy 'with great distinction,' and circa 1581 he was called to Pavia as a professor of humanities where he contributed to the appendices of the 1622 edition of a *calepino*. The reference to Farnese appears in a letter of Cardinal Giovanni Gerolamo Albani, dated 17 February 1582 from Rome, and addressed to the archbishop of Milan, Carlo Borromeo; Albani was asking Borromeo for assistance in placing one of Farnese's many daughters in the Collegio della Guastalla in Milan until she could decide whether to marry or become a nun. A secular boarding school for girls founded by Countess Ludovica Torelli of Guastalla (1500–69) in 1565, the Collegio della Guastalla accepted twenty-five poor, noble girls to study reading, writing, and the domestic arts; as Paul Grendler has noted, 'such a school was extremely rare in Counter-Reformation Italy, and without the institutional strength of an order of professed nuns, Torelli could not recruit others to perpetuate and expand her initiative.' Grendler, *Schooling*, 393. The letter is in BCBg, Registro Albani, f. 404r, and is cited by Luigi Chiodi, *Note breve*, 76.

81 The Theatines arrived in Bergamo on 24 Feb. 1590, and settled first in the church of S. Michele all'Arco and later in the church of S. Agata. On 1 April 1599 and again on 23 January 1600 the city council awarded them a subsidy of 100 scudi to rebuild part of S. Agata, but in 1610 a bitter argument erupted between the Theatines and their next-door neighbour, the Pio Luogo Colleoni, over the dimensions of the new church. For details, some

documents, and more bibliography, see Ermenegildo Camozzi, *Le istituzioni monastiche e religiose a Bergamo nel Seicento*, 2 vols. (Bergamo: Tip. Vescovile Secomandi, 1982); see also BCBg, *Azioni*, v. 52, f. 53r (22 May 1610).

82 BCBg, *Azioni*, v. 52, ff. 40r-v (17 Apr. 1610); *Relazioni* (1606–12), vol. 9, f. 180r ('ibis 24 aprile lecta in cons. Minori'); *Azioni*, v. 52, f. 41v (24 Apr. 1610); and f. 79r (24 Jul. 1610).

83 The *Azioni* of 19 Feb. 1611 and 24 Feb. 1611 (v. 52, ff. 166v–168v) nominated a new deputy to replace Scipione Boselli but no other action is mentioned. On 24 March 1612 (v. 53, ff. 16v–17r) the Executive Council urged the deputies to overcome past delays and complete the agreement with the Theatines to teach 'logic, philosophy, and other important lower-level subjects in a manner that will be beneficial and easy for all concerned.'

84 Grendler, *Universities*, 140–2 on 'paper' universities.

85 BCBg, *Azioni*, v. 54, ff. 159v–161r (19 Jun. 1615). '[Dopo] longa e matura consideratione a questo negotio, havendo prima veduto li ordini et capitoli delli collegij di Milano et Parma, quali a questi giorni tengono il primo luogo in Italia, et havendo havuto riguardo alle accademie e donzene di questa città, et esser nostra opinione che sia eretto un collegio publico in questa città, al quale ogni tre anni siano deputati tre Provedditori da esser eletti nel magnifico Maggior Consiglio, tra quali almeno sia un dottor legista.' The original report is in BCBg, *Relazioni (1613–1627)*, vol. 10, f. 100 (n.d.), 'Per il collegio de giovani nobili.'

86 On colleges, see Gian Paolo Brizzi, 'I collegi per borsisti e lo Studio bolognese. Caratteri ed evoluzione di un'istituzione educativeo-assistenziale fra XIII e XVIII secolo,' in *Studi e Memorie per la storia dell'Universita di Bologna*, n.s., IV (1984): 9–51; Peter Denley, 'The Collegiate Movement in Italian Universities in the Late Middle Ages,' *History of Universities* 10 (1991)· 29–91; Piero del Negro, *I collegi per studenti dell'Universita di Padova: una storia plurisecolare* (Padova: Signum, 2003).

87 Archivio di Stato di Venezia (hereafter ASVe), Senato, 'Lettere dei Rettori di Bergamo,' busta 10 (26 Sep. 1615); cited by Belotti, vol. 5, 87.

88 Lorenzo Ghirardelli, *Storia della peste del 1630* (Bergamo: Fratelli Rossi, 1681), 353–6 (*libro ottavo*).

89 BCBg, *Azioni*, v. 60, f. 210v (5 Dec. 1631). 'Inteso l'amorevole ricordo dato dall'Illustr. Sig. Podestà d'instituire pubbliche Scuole, dove si legga Grammatica & Umanità col mezzo delli RR. Padri Sommaschini, che pare si siano offerti a far quest'opera pia, li Magnif. Signori Anziani desiderosi non solo di'incontrare la soddisfazione di Sua Signoria Illustr., ma d'introdurre ancora quelle Scuole per pubblico benefizio, massime in questi tempi, che sono morti il più delli Maestri da Scuola.'

90 The only substantive scholarship on Bergamo's College of Jurists is Giovanni Vezzoli, 'Il collegio dei giuristi a Bergamo nel XVI secolo,' tesi di laurea, Università degli Studi di Milano, Facoltà di Giurisprudenza, relatore Antonio Padoa Schioppa, 1986–7. Founded in 1301, Bergamo's College of Jurists supervised various aspects of justice to ensure consistency and to preserve a monopoly for its members as judges, attorneys, and legal advisors. The collegio routinely supplied members to investigate and regulate commercial transactions (*mercatura*), foodstuffs (*vettovaglie*), public works (roads and bridges), as well as the teaching of law. Elsewhere see Marco Boscarelli, *Il collegio dei giuristi di Piacenza: dall sue origini alla fine del sec. XVI* (Padua: CEDAM, 1989); Ileana DelBagno, *Il collegio napoletano dei giuristi: privilegi, decreti, decisioni* (Naples: Jovene, 2000).

91 On Rivola, and Marc Antonio Michiel's *Agri et Urbis Bergomatis Descriptio* (Venice, 1523), see *Notizie Patrie* (1858), 80; on Alberico da Rosciate, see Emanuele Roncalli, *I Grandi di Bergamo* (Bergamo: Burgo Editore, 1991), vol. 1, 23–9; and vol. 3, 21–6, 170–6; on Bonghi, Albani, and Calepio, see Belotti, vol. 4, 269–70; on Alzano, see Tullia Franzi, 'La famiglia degli "Alzani,"' *Bergomum* 43, no. 1–2 (1949): 3–4 of the insert 'Atti dell'Ateneo.' The jurist Ambrogio da Calepio (1618–22), author of *Praxis ecclesiastica criminalis*, not to be confused with the eponymous Calepio (1440–1510) in 327n43.

92 On the 1301 statutes, see BCBg, Angelo Mazzoleni, *Zibaldone*, f. 97. (The 1301 statutes of the College of Jurists, which have not survived, were transcribed in the eighteenth century by Angelo Mazzoleni.) On Visconti decrees, see Belotti, vol. 3, 170. On Venetian decrees, see Donato Calvi, *Effemeride*, vol. 1, 178, and vol. 3, 94. See also Belotti, vol. 4, 245, and vol. 5, 87; and Giovanni Vezzoli, 'Il collegio dei giuristi a Bergamo nel XVI secolo,' 45–6; and Locatelli (1910), 96.

93 The *Acta Graduum Academicorum Universitatis Patavinae* (Padua: Antenore, 1970–), 5 vols. to date, contain references to more than a hundred Bergamasque graduates in the sixteenth century alone. See also chapter 2 on the 'Collegio Patavino.'

94 BCBg, *Azioni*, v. 2, f. 104r (11 Oct. 1476). BCBg, *Azioni*, v. 3, f. 62r (7 Jan. 1482), published in Locatelli (1911), 53–4. On the election controversies, about questions of pluralism and citizenship, see Locatelli (1911), 54–5. For the proposal to teach the 'true spirit of the law,' Locatelli (1910), 94, cites BCBg, *Azioni* (18 Jan. 1487), but no such entry exists on this date, nor have I been able to find it.

95 BCBg, *Statuta Bergomi*, Coll. I, Cap. 67, 'De uno bono jurisperito.' Locatelli (1911), 55, publishes chapter 67.

96 On Suardi, BCBg, *Azioni*, v. 6, ff. 146v (18 Apr. 1493). Locatelli (1910), 94, gives a date of 26 Jan. 1494 for Caleppio, but no council meeting occurred

on that date, nor does Caleppio's name appear in any subsequent meetings for two years.

97 BCBg, *Azioni*, v. 7, f. 93v (27 Apr. 1496).

98 BCBg, *Azioni*, v. 7, ff. 67v–68r (30 Dec. 1496) and f. 280v (11 May 1498); see also Belotti, vol. 4, 35, 38, 43, 44, and 62.

99 Vezzoli, 49–56, drawn from the *Acta Graduum*.

100 Belotti, vol. 4, 195–7.

101 Vezzoli, esp. chapter 2. See also Grendler, *Universities*, 21–40; and *The Oxford Companion to Law*, ed. David M. Walker (Oxford: Clarendon Press, 1980).

102 BCBg, *Azioni*, v. 20, f. 100r (28 Dec. 1538), and f. 101r (29 Dec. 1538): 'Quanto utile et necessario sia ad una ben instituta Republica il studio et scientia legale.'

103 On Francesco Suardi's appointment, see BCBg, *Azioni*, v. 20, f. 212v (27 Feb. 1540).

104 On Girolamo Zanchi, see Calvi, *Scena letteraria*, v. 1, 283–4; idem, *Effemeride*, v. 3, 110; Firpo *I Processi Inquisitoriali*, 966n48. For his appointment, see BCBg, *Azioni*, v. 20, f. 273v (14 Jan. 1541). The *Inforziato* (*Infortiatum*) is what the late medieval Bolognese jurists called the 2nd volume of the *Digest*.

105 On Julio Agosti see the admirable research of Firpo, *I Processi Inquisitoriali*, especially 947n1 and 162n1, which contain numerous citations, transcriptions, and additional bibliography; see also the briefer entry of Mario Rosa in *DBI*, v. 1, 454–5. For Agosti's appointment, see BCBg, *Azioni*, v. 21, f. 34r (19 Dec. 1542). For the city council's remarks, see BCBg, *Azioni*, v. 26, ff. 20v–30r, transcribed in Firpo, 162n1.

106 BCBg, *Azioni*, v. 21, f. 125v (26 Feb. 1543).

107 BCBg, *Historiae Patriae Monumenta* (Turin: Frat. Bocca, 1876), tom. 16, vol. 2 (Leges municipales), 'Statuta civitatis Pergami circa consules iustitiae (1416–1557),' 2070–86, esp. 2085; cited by Vezzoli, 129–30.

108 BCBg, *Azioni*, v. 51, ff. 234v–235r (14 Dec. 1609).

109 BCBg, *Azioni*, v. 58, ff. 133r–134r (24 May 1625). 'Connobero li nostri maggiori che al ben publico e primato di questa Città nessun altra cosa può esser altretanto necessaria, quanto la virtuosa educatione de figliuoli, onde ... che si debba elegger un giureconsulto collegiato, che pubblicamente legge le ragioni civili, le scienze delle quali è principalissimo sostegno di ogni ben regolato governo.'

110 See BCBg, *Stampe per il Sig. dott. Franco Farina contro il Collegio dei Giuristi* [Sala 1 Loggia E 6 27 (4)], 14–18, which includes an excerpt from the 9 Dec. 1627 meeting of the College of Jurists in which conditions for admission to the college were specified.

111 BCBg, *Azioni*, v. 58, ff. 153r–154r (6 Sept. 1625). 'Capitoli et ordini da esser osservati dall'Eccelente Sig. Lettore delle ragioni civili, che doverà eleggersi in virtù della parte del magnifico maggior Consiglio sotti dì 24 maggio 1625.' 'Che sia tenuto ogni giorno che non sia festa di Palazzo far una lettione sopra l'instituta che dura per il spatio d'un hora in circa in lingua latina con buono et approbato methodo secondo il stile dei buoni legisti nella sale delle Bine del palazzo novo sopra una cathedra magistrale da esserle fatta a spese del publico in quel hora che sarà ordinato dalli magnifici Signori Regolatori; la lettura debba principiarsi nelle Calende di Novembre et debba esser continuato sin alla metà del mese d'Agosto.' Today this room is known as the *Sala Tassiana*, in the Biblioteca Civica 'Angelo Mai.'

112 BCBg, Arch. Storico del Comune, *Sindaci del Palazzo*, v. 152, ff. 117–18.

113 BCBg, *Relazioni* (1628–1643), v. 11, f. 366 (n.d., but read aloud in the *Azione* of 6 Feb. 1642, [v. 64, ff. 74r–v]). 'Noi infrascritti deputati dalle Vostra Signoria Illustrissima [governors] e Magnifici Illustrissimi [council members] alla regolatione delle schole dell'Instituta, riverentemente le riferiamo che veduta la frequenza de molti degni soggetti, che giornalmente concorrono a tal lettione, et conosciuta la diligente e sollecita cura dell'eccellentissimo Sig. Giacomo Carara Benaglio Dottore eletto a questa carica con riguardevole profitto dei studenti, stimiamo, attesa la disposizione dei statuti, la continuatione di essa lettura essere attione non solo honorevole al Pubblico ma com[odo] et profittevole a non pochi cittadini, quanti in questo studio si vanno avanzando come anco la confirmatione di esso eccellentissimo Sig. Carrara ben degno et atto sogetto a tal fontione.'

114 BCBg, *Azioni*, v. 59, f. 271v (30 Aug. 1629); see also BCBg, *Relazioni* (1606–1612), v. 9, f. 36. Classes did not meet in the following periods: neither Thusday nor Saturday, all public holidays, Christmas Eve, New Year's Day, the eight days of Carnival, and Easter week.

115 BCBg, *Azioni*, v. 62, ff. 70v–71v (5 Jun. 1635).

116 BCBg, *Azioni*, v. 62, ff. 175r–176r (23 Dec. 1636). Bergamo was also reacting to a Senate decree of 24 Oct. 1635, reminding the cities of the *terraferma* that five years of study in Padua were required before a degree could be granted. The Venetian response is unknown, but Bergamo's actions of 1643–5 imply Venetian approval of the two-year exemption.

117 BCBg, *Azioni*, v. 65, ff. 81r–82v (8 Apr. 1645). See also BCBg, *Azioni*, v. 64, ff. 249r–v (20 Dec. 1643). 'Che siccome questa ultima condotta di essa Ecc. mo Sig. Lettore è stata fatta per un anno solo principiando da Natale a Natale, sia essa lettura et condotta fatta di due anni in due anni, acciò in

detto biennio possa il lettore compartire e dividere tutto il corpo dell'Instituta e li scolari intieramente sentirla. Qual lettura debba principiare
secondo già soleva all'entrare di Novembre acciò leggendosi il Novembre
e Decembre possano et i scolari guadagnare il tempo di quei due mesi
et i loro Padri consolarsene con l'impiego. Che la elettione che di tempo
in tempo occorresse rinnovarsi, debba essere fatta per sei mesi almeno
anticipatamente al Novembre susseguente, acciò [nel] caso si mutasse la
persona dell'ecc.mo lettore possa quello eletto haver tempo congruo a
preparare le lettioni, et i padri di figli sapendo anticipatmente di havere,
o non havere la lettura nella Patria, possano provedere d'impiego in altro
Studio mancando quello.'
118 BCBg, *Azioni*, v. 66, ff. 23v–24r (16 Mar. 1648), and ff. 28v–29r (6 Apr. 1648).
119 ASVe, Fondo *Riformatori dello studio di Padova*, b. 510: 'Scuole e collegi nella
    terraferma,' fald. 1, 'Bergamo: Processo circa il Collegio dei Leggisti.' The
    earliest dated document is a copy of the minutes from the college's meet-
    ing of 6 September 1638, in Latin, which lists all the members of the college
    and explains their complaint. This file also contains numerous letters, sum-
    maries, affidavits, and excerpts of statutes and meetings that pertain to this
    debate; all subsequent citations in this section are from this folder.
120 Ibid., a letter signed by Alvise Valle, n.p., n.d. 'Alquanti Procuratori sono
    state per qualche tempo a Padova seben per povertà non hanno potuto
    continuare le studij.' A similar idea is expressed in the 11 July 1648 letter
    of Giovanni Andrea Locatello, who wrote 'essendosi molti Procuratori,
    che hanno studiato nel predetto studio, come si vede comprobato per il
    sesto capitolo. Et perche ve ne sono molti, li quali per la loro impotenza et
    debole fortuna non possono conferirsi al studio di Padoa, resta perciò [s]
    pro[v]visto per li statuti di questa Città alla Collegio, in Cap. 67 confir-
    mato dalla Maestà del Principe, che la Città debba ellegere ogni anno
    un Dottore del Collegio dei soprascripti Dottori, il qual debba leggere
    publicamente le leggi Civili, acciochè la Città produceva sempre persone
    prudenti, literate, et virtuose.'
121 Ibid., n.p., (31 Dec. 1647), no title.
122 Ibid., n.p. (25 Jul. 1648), 'Bergamo informatione sopra la supplica di Dot-
    tori di Collegio.'
123 Ibid., n.p. (11 Jul. 1648), letter of Giovanni Andrea Locatello. 'A così pre-
    cipitosa deliberatione sono stati li Signori Dottori indotti, non da puro zelo
    del bene, ma da' messo interesse borsale, mediante la qual supplica pre-
    tendono persuadere alla publica sapienza, che per reputazione del studio
    di Padoa, per ornamento della Città di Bergamo, per tutela de litiganti.'
124 Ibid., letter of Alvise Valle, n.d.

2. *Misericordia*: Schooling and Confraternities

1 Amelio Tagliaferri, ed., *Relazioni dei Rettori Veneti, XII: Podestaria e Capi-tanato di Bergamo* (Milan: A. Giuffrè, 1973–9), 19 and 33. See also Amelio Tagliaferri, ed., *Atti del Convegno: Venezia e la terrafirma attraverso le Relazioni dei Rettori (Trieste, 23–24 Ottobre 1980)* (Milan: A. Giuffrè, 1981).
2 Lester K. Little, *Liberty, Charity, Fraternity: Lay Confraternities at Bergamo in the Age of the Commune* (Northampton, MA: Smith College Press, 1988). Other works on medieval confraternities in Bergamo include Roisin Cossar, *The Transformation of the Laity in Bergamo, 1265–c.1400* (Leiden and Boston: Brill, 2006); Maria Teresa Brolis, 'Confraternite bergamasche bassomedievali: nuove fonti e prospettive di ricerca,' *Rivista di Storia della Chiesa in Italia* 49 (1995): 337–54; idem, 'A Thousand and More Women: A Register of Women for the Confraternity of Misericordia Maggiore in Bergamo, 1265–1339,' *Catholic Historical Review* 88, no. 2 (April 2002): 230–46; Giuseppe Locatelli, 'La Casa della Misericordia di Bergamo,' *Bergomum* 25 (1931): 124–48; idem, 'L'istruzione in Bergamo e la Misericordia Maggiore' *Bergomum* 4, no. 4 (1910): 19–113 and 5, no. 1 (1911): 21–99.
3 Christopher Black, *Italian Confraternities in the Sixteenth Century* (Cambridge: Cambridge University Press, 1989), 1, 23–4.
4 Little, 13.
5 Black, 17–21.
6 Adriano Prosperi, 'Clerics and Laymen in the World of Carlo Borromeo,' in *San Carlo Borromeo: Catholic Reform and Ecclesiastical Politics in the Second Half of the Sixteenth Century*, ed. John M. Headley and John B. Tomaro (London: Associated University Presses, 1988), 133.
7 Brian S. Pullan, *Rich and Poor in Renaissance Venice: The Social Institutions of a Catholic State to 1620* (Cambridge, MA: Harvard University Press, 1971); Ronald F. Weissman, *Ritual Brotherhood in Renaissance Florence* (New York: Academic Press, 1982); idem, 'Brothers and Strangers: Confraternal Charity in Renaissance Florence,' *Historical Reflections* 15, no. 1 (Spring 1988): 27–45; Richard C. Trexler, *Public Life in Renaissance Florence* (New York: Academic Press, 1980); idem, ed., *Persons in Groups: Social Behavior as Identity Formation in Medieval and Renaissance Europe* (Binghamton, NY: Medieval and Renaissance Texts and Studies, 1985); Konrad Eisenbichler, *The Boys of the Archangel Raphael: A Youth Confraternity in Florence, 1411–1787* (Toronto: University of Toronto Press, 1998); idem, ed., *Crossing the Boundaries: Christian Piety and the Arts in Italian Medieval and Renaissance Confraternities* (Kalamazoo, MI: Medieval Institute Publications, 1991);

Lorenzo Polizzotto, *Children of the Promise: the confraternity of the purification and the socialization of youths in Florence, 1427–1785* (New York: Oxford University Press, 2004); Nicholas Terpstra, 'Apprenticeship in Social Welfare: From confraternal charity to municipal poor relief in early modern Italy,' *Sixteenth Century Journal* 25 (Spring 1994), 101–20; idem, 'Catechizing in Prison and on the Gallows in Renaissance Italy: The Politics of Comforting the Condemned,' in idem, ed., *The Renaissance in the Streets, Schools, and Studies: Essays in Honour of Paul F. Grendler* (Toronto: Centre for Reformation and Renaissance Studies, 2008), 157–82; idem, ed., *The Act of Executing Well: Rituals of Execution in Renaissance Italy* (Kirksville, MO: Truman State University Press, 2008), esp. 118–56, 183–292; idem, *Lay Confraternities and Civic Religion in Renaissance Bologna* (Cambridge: Cambridge University Press, 1995); idem, *The Politics of Ritual Kinship: Confraternities and Social Order in Early Modern Italy* (Cambridge: Cambridge University Press, 1999); Lance Lazar, *Working in the Vineyard of the Lord: Jesuit Confraternities in Early Modern Italy* (Toronto: University of Toronto Press, 2005); David M. D'Andrea, *Civic Christianity in Renaissance Italy: The Hospital of Treviso, 1400–1530* (Rochester: University of Rochester Press, 2007). The classic work in Italian, which unfortunately covers only the medieval period, is G.G. Meersseman, *Ordo Fraternitas: Confraternite e pietà nel medioevo*, 3 vols. (Rome: Herder, 1977). See also Giancarlo Angelozzi, *Le confraternite laicali: un'esperienza cristiana tra Medioevo e età moderna* (Brescia: Queriniana, 1978), and the quarterly journal *Confraternitas* published by University of Toronto. On confraternities in Bergamo, see note 2 above.

8 Cossar, *Transformation of the Laity*, cited in note 2 above.
9 Little, 66 (describing thirteenth-century Bergamo, but his phrase remains accurate into the seventeenth century).
10 Roisin Cossar has found numerous links between the government of Bergamo and the Misericordia Maggiore confraternity in the thirteenth and fourteenth centuries: 'The Quality of Mercy: Confraternities and Public Power in Medieval Bergamo,' *Journal of Medieval History* 27 (2001): 139–57; idem, *Transformation of the Laity*, 52–7.
11 *Chierici* were young men training for the priesthood. Usually they had taken minor orders and the tonsure, and assisted with religious services on Sundays and holidays. I use the term *chierici* rather than 'cleric' in order to distinguish between young men in training and those who were already priests.
12 Cossar, *Transformation of the Laity*, 48–51, 51–7, 114–16, and 206–10 for examples.

13 Locatelli, 'L'istruzione a Bergamo' (1910): 58, noted that 'in Bergamo the
history of schooling *is* the history of the MIA' (emphasis in the original).
Margherita Pizzighella's thesis maintained that the MIA's extraordinary
wealth and influence inhibited the development of schools sponsored
by other institutions. (M. Pizzighella, 'Progetti di riforme scholastiche a
Bergamo nella seconda metà del'700,' tesi di laurea, Università Cattolica
del Sacro Cuore di Milano, Facoltà di Magistero, relatore Aldo Agazzi,
1968–9.) I do not agree; a comprehensive look at confraternities and education in Bergamo must include these other associations and their important
contributions.
14 Jacopo's will is in the Archivio di Stato di Bergamo (hereafter ASBg), *Atti
Notarili* di Gerardo Soiario, busta 13, anno 1360–1, ff. 184–92 (16 July 1361).
On the MIA and education, see Luisa Boroni, 'Maestri e scolari a Bergamo
nei secoli XIV e XV: Ricerche sull'attività assistenziale del consorzio della
Misericordia Maggiore,' tesi di perfezionamento, Università Cattolica del
Sacro Cuore di Milano, Facoltà di Lettere e Filosofia, relatore Giuseppe Billanovich, 1969–70, esp. 33–4 for the will and 34–47 for the legal description
of each piece of land near the Adda River.
15 BCBg, Arch. MIA no. 1259, f. 55r–v (26 Feb. 1528).
16 Roberto Cessi and Antonio Favaro, *L'università di Padova: Notizie Raccolte*
(Padua: Zanocco, 1946) contains a list of major bequests to the university
beginning in the late medieval era, including those of Salinguerro and
Lamberti. On the Salinguerro bequest, see Luciano Gargan, 'Studenti
trevigiani a Padova tra Tre e Quattrocento: Il lascito di Tommaso Salinguerra,' *Quaderni della storia della Università di Padova* 13 (1980): 1–35. On
the Lamberti bequest, see Paolo Guerrini, 'Il Collegio Lambertino,' *Archivio
Veneto-Tridentino* 1 (1922): 93–108; idem, 'Il legato Lambertino,' *Bollettino
municipale di Brescia* 11 (1922): 307–13; Giovanni Fabris, 'Quale fu la sede
del "Collegio Lambertino" per gli scolari Bresciani in Padova,' *Atti e Memorie della Regia Accademia di Scienze, Lettere, ed Arti in Padova* 46 (1929–30):
435. On the Cerasoli bequest, created in 1640 to benefit six Bergamasque
students in Rome by the creation of a small college, see Belotti, vol. 6,
18. Even as late as 1540, the scholarship was almost always calculated in
imperial lire rather than Venetian ducats.
17 Boroni, 74, calculates the rate to 1956; my later estimates rely upon
www.x-rates.com and *International Financial Statistics*, with a conversion
rate of 1 USD = Lire 1,328.
18 For scholarship recipients, see Boroni, 51–73 for the period 1361–1510;
Locatelli (1910), 86–9, for 1491–1510; Carlsmith, 'Schooling and Society,'
295–301 (appendix 2) extends the list through 1540. Boroni and Locatelli

relied exclusively upon the *Terminazioni* of the MIA to gather this information; even more useful are the MIA's account books, which record each of the payments made to students in that period: BCBg, Arch. MIA no. 734, *Liber Onerum (1498–1533)*; and Arch. MIA no. 735, *Liber Onerum (1522–1546)*.

19 For examples, see BCBg, Arch. MIA no. 1256, *Term.*, f. 123v (10 Jul. 1510), f. 147v (20 Feb. 1511) and f. 229r (7 Jan. 1513); Arch. MIA no. 1257, *Term.*, f. 1v. (12 Feb. 1515); Arch. MIA no. 1258, *Term.*, f. 77r (26 Nov. 1522) and f. 93v (9 Apr. 1523).

20 Carlsmith, 'Schooling and Society,' 297–9 (appendix 3). The Grignanos began receiving scholarships on 30 Dec. 1501, 27 June 1505, and 14 Aug. 1510; the Della Valle family received scholarships on 26 Feb. 1511, 29 Dec. 1512 (twice), and 7 Jan. 1513 (twice).

21 D'Andrea, *Civic Christianity*, 125; Paul Trio, 'Financing of University Students in the Middle Ages: A New Orientation,' in *History of Universities*, vol. 4, ed. Charles B. Schmitt (Oxford: Oxford University Press, 1984), 1–24; *A History of the University in Europe*, vol. 2, *Universities in Early Modern Europe (1500–1800)*, ed. H. De Ridder-Symoens (Cambridge: Cambridge University Press, 1996), 363–6.

22 On Pesenti, BCBg, Arch. MIA no. 1256 *Term.*, f. 205v (3 Apr. 1512): 'Si costituisce Vincenzo di G. Antonio Pesenti che dichiara di essere uno studente di belle lettere e grammatica nella scuola del prete Marco de Valotis. Egli desidererebbe vivere 'de lucro scientie' ma non ha modo di mantenersi agli studi, essendo gravato da famiglia numerosa. Con la massima riverenza egli supplica quindi che gli venga conferito un legato di L. 18 all'anno per scolari di buona indole che vogliano applicarsi nella grammatica e diritto canonico.' On Pellegrino, see BCBg, Arch. MIA, *Liber Onerum* f. 52v: 'Jo. Sebastianus de S. Pellegrino, scolaris, f.q. magister Jo. Christofori, beretarij …' Pellegrino died the next year on 10 Nov. 1529, thus receiving only L. 29 s. 20.

23 Boroni, 83–4.

24 Boroni, 98.

25 Francesco L. Maschietto, *Elena Lucrezia Cornaro Piscopia, 1646–1684: prima donna laureata nel mondo* (Padua: Antenore, 1978), 119–32; *s.v.* 'Cornaro Piscopia, Elena' in *Encyclopedia of the Renaissance*, ed. Paul Grendler (New York: Charles Scribner's Sons, 1999), vol. 6, 189–93.

26 BCBg, Arch. MIA no. 1264, *Term.*, f. 93v (25 Feb. 1553). An additional problem in reconstructing the story of the Apibus scholarships results from the transfer of record-keeping about Apibus recipients, from the *Terminazioni* and the *Liber Onerum* to another account book described as the *Liber Sco-*

laribus, which has not survived. The *Liber Scolaribus* appears to have been a register devoted exclusively to recording all payments, bequests, and obligations of the MIA that concerned education.

27 BCBg, Arch. MIA no. 1519, *Liber Capitulorum,* f. 49v (30 Apr. 1566).

28 Marco Antonio Benaglio, *Compendium onerum Ven. Consor. Misericordiae* (Bergamo, 1612), 14–15, in BCBg, Arch. MIA no. 738. Benaglio claims a date of 7 June 1611, based on the *Terminazioni*: BCBg, Arch. MIA no. 1279, f. 70r.

29 Benaglio, 61–2.

30 BCBg, Arch. MIA, *Term.,* f. 111v–112r (10 Oct. 1533); Arch. MIA no. 1261, *Term.,* f. 90v (2 Sep. 1535); Arch. MIA no. 1263, *Term.,* f. 195r (8 Jan. 1549); Arch. MIA no. 1264, *Term.,* f. 111v–112r (18 Dec. 1553). Arch. MIA no. 1263, *Term.,* f. 195r (8 Jan. 1549) makes reference to the bequest of Giovanni Leonardo de Capetanio de Mozzo, who on 21 Aug. 1531 left money to the MIA to support future scholars in his family.

31 BCBg, Archivio MIA no. 1279, *Term.* f. 155r (2 Dec. 1613). I have been unable to locate the original will. In this *terminazione* the brother of Marco Antonio Benaglio, Giovanni Jacopo, received forty scudi to study in Milan or elsewhere. There is no indication of why someone outside the Cannelli family received the scholarship.

32 BCBg, Arch. MIA no. 1263, *Term.,* f. 176r (30 Jan. 1548), f. 176v (bis) (6 Feb. 1548).

33 A detailed examination of these activities would be stultifying; therefore I have chosen to offer just a few representative examples. Boroni, 89–103, has compiled a table of similar actions for the years 1421–1502, as has Locatelli (1910), 109–10, for the period 1496–1512.

34 Boroni, 101, citing Arch. MIA *Term* (17 May 1498), 'due pani al giorno per un periodo indeterminato.'

35 BCBg, Arch. MIA no. 1262, *Term.,* f. 52v (9 Mar. 1534), f. 193v (22 Jul. 1538).

36 BCBg, Arch. MIA, no. 1263, *Term.,* f. 184r (4 Mar. 1548).

37 Boroni, 102.

38 BCBg, Arch. MIA no. 1265, *Term.,* f. 44r (12 Dec. 1555).

39 One notable exception exists: In 1553 Hieronymo Cataneo da Val Scalve demonstrated his poverty and his oratorical skills in front of the MIA's council, which granted him an annual scholarship of one hundred lire for a period of five years so that he might study medicine. In return he was required to return to Bergamo upon completion of his degree and to freely render his services to all families which belonged to the confraternity. According to the MIA, this special scholarship was approved because the funds from the Apibus testament were no longer available. See BCBg, Arch. MIA no. 1264, *Term.,* f. 93v (25 Feb. 1553). Students paid little or

nothing to attend university lectures, but sitting for examinations and graduating from the university as well as day-to-day living costs could involve significant expense. Most of the MIA's grants do not specify the exact purpose or level of study they were intended to support.

40 BCBg, Arch. MIA no. 1255, *Term.*, f. 110r (10 Apr. 1505), f. 180r (12 Oct. 1506); Arch. MIA no. 1256, *Term.*, f. 93r (5 Jan. 1512); Arch. MIA no. 1258, *Term.*, f. 106v (12 Oct. 1523). In 1544 Paolo Melioratti's petition for alms was approved with a subsidy of 150 lire: Arch. MIA no. 1263, *Term.* f. 97r (25 Feb. 1544).

41 On Terzi, see BCBg, Arch. MIA no. 1447, *Scritture/Suppliche*, f. 126r (ca 1588); on Locatello, Arch. MIA no. 1448, *Scritture/Suppliche*, f. 365r (ca 1597). On Capodiferro, Arch. MIA no. 1447, *Scritture/Suppliche*, f. 282r (ca 1590).

42 See note 46 below re: inventories of the MIA.

43 A *calepino* is the generic name for a Latin dictionary or vocabulary in-tended for school use. It was devised by Ambrogio da Calepio (1440–1510), an Augustinian monk in Bergamo, and published repeatedly, with twenty-four editions between 1502 and 1520, including translations into French, Spanish, and Portuguese, and ultimately in a seven-language edition, the *Calepinus septem linguarum*. See Bortolo Belotti, *La storia di Bergamo e dei Bergamaschi*, 9 vols.(Bergamo: Bolis, 1989), vol. 4, 255–8.; and Carlo Battisti and Giovanni Alessio, *Dizionario Etimologico Italiano*, vol. 1, 679–80.

44 BCBg, Arch. MIA no. 1264, *Term.*, f. 3v (13 Jan. 1550).

45 BCBg, Arch. MIA no. 1264, *Term.*, f. 27v (24 Nov. 1550), f. 28r (1 Dec. 1550) Valerius Maximus was a professional rhetorician who lived during the reign of Augustus and Tiberius. His *Nine Books of Memorable Deeds and Say-ings* was intended as a commonplace book of historical anecdotes for use in schools of rhetoric; it utilized extravagant and artificial language along with highly coloured epithets to teach virtue and vice through historical examples.

46 For an inventory of literary texts and treatises owned by the Misericordia Maggiore at the end of the fifteenth century, see Boroni, 111–16; Locatelli (1910), 98–101, has published an inventory of texts owned by the MIA in 1536; Maria Mencaroni Zoppetti graciously shared with me a portion of the MIA's 1626 inventory of the Academy of Clerics, which includes more than two dozen religious books and an equal number of 'libri de Human-ità' grouped by the size of the book: BCBg, Arch. MIA no. 3597, 'Inventario dei mobili dell'Accademia.' See also BCBg, Arch. MIA no. 1517, 'Inventario dei mobili dell'Accademia, 1633.' The general inventories of the MIA are

328   Notes to pages 86–93

enormous: that of 1526 is six hundred pages long. For book inventories of two teachers in 1543 and 1572, see also Rodofo Vittori, 'Le biblioteche di due maestri bergamaschi del Cinquecento,' *Bergomum* 96, no. 2 (2001): 23–56.

47 BCBg, Arch. MIA no. 26, *Liber proprietarum … hereditatis Antonij de Mafeis doctoris*, ff. 11r–v (18 Sep. 1497), cited by Boroni, 110n119.

48 D'Andrea, *Civic Christianity*, 109–32.

49 BCBg, Arch. MIA no. 1255, *Term.*, ff. 144v–145v (26 Jan. 1506). For the Latin text, see Locatelli (1911), 66–8; for additional information, see Locatelli (1910), 123–4.

50 Ibid.

51 BCBg, Arch. MIA no. 1255, *Term.*, f. 148r (16 Feb. 1507), and f. 149v (23 Feb. 1507); and Locatelli (1910), 123–7, for the period 1506–14.

52 BCBg, Arch. MIA no. 1255, *Term.*, f. 176v (7 Sep. 1506) and f. 177r (13 Sep. 1506) for Brignano's appointment. For the list of scholars and the necessity of an assistant, see ibid., ff. 183v–184r (18 Sep. 1506).

53 BCBg, Arch. MIA no. 1256, *Term.*, f. 25r (1 Nov. 1507) and f. 29r (13 Dec. 1507). For the story of the house, see ibid., f. 34v (20 Jan. 1508), f. 35v (27 Jan. 1508), and f. 61v (1 Dec. 1508).

54 BCBg, Arch. MIA no. 1256, *Term.*, f. 102v (14 Jan. 1510), f. 104v (28 Jan. 1510), f. 106v (11 Feb. 1510).

55 BCBg, Arch. MIA no. 1256, *Term.*, f. 108r (14 Feb. 1510), and f. 159r (30 Mar. 1511).

56 BCBg, Arch. MIA no. 1256, *Term.*, f. 288v (20 Jul. 1514) for the request to go to the baths at Trescore. For more information on Lallio, see Luigi Michelato, 'Il maestro romanese Antonio de Lallio,' *L'Eco di Bergamo* (6 Feb. 1935).

57 BCBg, Arch. MIA no. 1256, f. 298v (29 Jan. 1515) records his initial appointment.

58 BCBg, Arch. MIA no. 1257, *Term.*, f. 92r (1 Feb. 1518) and Arch. MIA no. 1258, *Term.*. f. 39v (12 Dec. 1521).

59 BCBg, Arch. MIA no. 1258, *Term.*, f. 81r (4 Jan. 1523).

60 BCBg, Arch. MIA no. 1258, *Term.*, f. 155v (21 Aug. 1525), f. 186r (23 Jul. 1526).

61 BCBg, Arch. MIA no. 1259, *Term.*, f. 33r (15 Mar. 1529) (repeated in Arch. MIA no. 1260, f. 101v, same date) for the motion to find *unum indoneum preceptorem*; Arch. MIA no. 1260, f. 101v (22 Mar. 1529) (repeated in Arch. MIA no. 1259, f. 34r, same date) for the election of Nicolò Capitani. On 22 April and 30 April 1529 (Arch. MIA no. 1260, ff. 104v, 106v, and 107r), the deputies elected the thirty-eight students to be taught by Capitani.

62 BCBg, Arch. MIA no. 2322, *Lettere varie sec. XVI* (12 Jan. 1530); Arch. MIA

no. 1259, *Term.*, f. 47v (10 Jul. 1530), repeated in Arch. MIA no. 1260, f. 122v (10 Feb. 1530); Arch. MIA no. 1260, *Term.*, f. 153r (19 Dec. 1530).

63 BCBg, Arch. MIA no. 1263, *Term.*, f. 45r (11 Apr. 1541).

64 Ibid., f. 77v (31 Jan. 1543), f. 169v–170r (25 Oct. 1547).

65 On Bono de Lulmo, see Firpo, *I Processi Inquisitoriali*, 94–5 and 806 for de Lulmo's two depositions of 1550, as well as 94n1 for citations to the information in this paragraph.

66 On *maestri di capella* (music teachers), see BCBG, Arch. MIA no. 1264 for 10 March 1544, 26 February 1545, 14 March 1546, and 28 February 1547.

67 BCBg, Arch. MIA, *Term. no.* 1263, f. 150r [appointment]; f. 153v [tutoring the treasurer]; f. 177v (13 Feb. 1548) [reconfirmation], f. 179r (18 Feb. 1548); idem, *Term.* no. 1264, f. 40r (30 Apr. 1551); f. 55r (3 Mar. 1552) [which included the *capitoli* he must observe], f. 103v (23 Jun. 1553); idem, no. 1265, *Term.*, f. 38v (26 Sep. 1555); f. 84r (3 Dec. 1556) [quarrel].

68 BCBg, Arch. MIA no. 1265, *Term.*, f. 53v (11 Feb. 1556) [appointment]; f. 133v (20 Dec. 1557) [raise]; idem, no. 1266, *Term.*, f. 47v (29 Apr. 1560) [resignation].

69 BCBg, Arch. MIA no. 1264, *Term.*, f. 42r (1 Jun. 1551) [Mutio] and ff. 63r–64v (13 May 1552) [Licinis]; f. 69r (4 Aug. 1552) [Mutio quits]; f. 138r (10 May 1554) [Licinis's promotion].

70 Firpo, *I Processi Inquisitoriali*, 324n19, who quotes four lines of the verse.

71 BCBg, Arch. MIA no. 1262, *Term.*, f. 193r (4 Jul. 1538), f. 202r (9 Dec. 1538); Arch. MIA no. 1263, *Term.*, f. 3v (14 Nov. 1539), f. 34r (14 Jul. 1540).

72 BCBg, Arch. MIA no. 1263, *Term.*, f. 126v (13 May 1545).

73 Ibid., ff. 169v–170r (25 Oct. 1547), see also f. 172v (1 Dec. 1547); f. 173r (14 Dec. 1547); f. 176v (6 Feb. 1548).

74 BCBg, Arch. MIA no. 1264, *Term.*, f. 58v (24 Mar. 1552). See Firpo, *I Processi Inquisitoriali*, 94n1 for a long list of judicial squabbles in which de Lulmo was involved during the 1540s and 1550s, as well as incidents of pluralism and absenteeism. See also Firpo, *Vittore Soranzo,* 137–303 for a clear demonstration that de Lulmo's misbehaviour was not atypical for the clergy in Bergamo or elsewhere in northern Italy, a point made by Anne J. Schutte in her review of Firpo's 2006 work, in *Sixteenth Century Journal* 39 no. 1 (Spring 2008): 229–31, at 230.

75 Ibid., f. 68r (21 Jul. 1552) and f. 69v (18 Aug. 1552); Arch. MIA no. 1265, f. 23v (9 May 1555) and f. 32v (11 Jul. 1555). See also BCBg, Arch. Storico del Comune, *Instrumenti*, vol. 1 (1538–1610), ff. 48v–49r (26 Jun. 1551).

76 In addition to Bono de Lulmo and Giovanni Minoli in this section, see the stories of Ludovico dei Conti di Callepio and Lattanzio Marchese in the next section, and of course the figure of Nicolò Cologno.

77 BCBg, Arch. MIA no. 1265, *Term.*, ff. 25r–v (16 May 1555) for the *capitoli*, which were delivered to Ascanio on 28 June (f. 31v).; on heating issues, f. 44r (12 Dec. 1555); f. 53v (11 Feb. 1556); f. 77v (30 Jul. 1556); on his resignation, f. 95r (1 Feb. 1557).

78 On the initial agreement, BCBg, Arch. MIA no. 1265, ff. 113v–114r (10 May 1557) and ff. 120v–121r (bis) (14 Jun. 1557). On house rental, BCBg, Arch. MIA no. 1265, *Term.*, f. 125r (5 Aug. 1557); and Arch. MIA no. 1267, *Term.*, f. 34v (22 Apr. 1563). On supplemental income, BCBg, Arch. MIA no. 1265, *Term.*, f. 135v (20 Jan. 1558) for the request; ff. 142v–143r (3 Feb. 1558) for the response. For Rota, see BCBg, Arch. MIA no. 1266, *Term.*, f. 162v (30 Jul. 1562). For Benaglio, see f. 163r (30 Jul. 1562).

79 On the case against Manili in 1559 as recorded by the Misericordia Maggiore, see BCBg, Arch. MIA, no. 1265, *Term.*, ff. 202v–203r (20 Mar. 1559), which identifies him as 'Michele Millio' and does not specify the charges. The trial of 1559 is one of very few that have survived in the archives of the Holy Office in Rome (ACDF, *Stanza storica*, R 4-f, *ultimo fascicolo*); I have not seen it but a brief summary appears in Andrea del Col, *L'Inquisizione nel Patriarcato e Diocesi di Aquileia, 1557–1559* (Trieste: Edizioni Università di Trieste, 1998), 130–1. Firpo, *I Processi Inquisitoriali*, 94n1, notes that Bono de Lulmo testified in Manili's 1562 trial, but until Del Col's promised volume on the trials of 1560–2 is published, to the best of my knowledge nothing else is known of that trial. On Manili's teaching Holy Scripture, see BCBg, Arch. MIA no. 1266, *Term.*, f. 71r (11 Nov. 1560); on his contract renewal, Arch. MIA no. 1267, *Term.*, f. 34r (19 Apr. 1563); on Manili's retirement, ibid., f. 52v (12 Aug. 1563); f. 103v (5 Jan 1564). His death date was kindly provided to me by Rodolfo Vittori. Note that Locatelli (1910) 128, identifies this priest as 'Michele Millio' based on the entry in the MIA's records per above, while Del Col calls him 'Michele Monilio'. I follow Vittori and Firpo in calling him 'Manili.'

80 Rodolfo Vittori, 'Le biblioteche di due maestri bergamaschi del Cinquecento,' *Bergomum* 96 no. 2 (2001), 23–44. Vittori is currently researching other private libraries in sixteenth-century Bergamo, including those of the canons Ludovico Terzi and Marco Moroni. My thanks to him for sharing his research with me in advance of its publication.

81 BCBg, Arch. MIA no. 1267, *Term.*, f. 187v (7 Feb. 1566).

82 For graduation acts from Padua, see the *Acta Graduum Academicorum Universitatis Patavinae* (Padua: Antenore, 1970–); for a comparison, see Richard Palmer, *The Studio of Venice and its Graduates in the Sixteenth Century* (Trieste and Padua: Edizioni LINT, 1983); for a list of thirty-five Bergamasques who graduated with law degrees from Padua betwen 1501

and 1535, see Giovanni Vezzoli, 'Il collegio dei giuristi a Bergamo nel XVI secolo,' tesi di laurea, Università degli Studi di Milano, Facoltà di Giurisprudenza, relatore Antonio Padoa Schioppa, 1986–87. For brief references to Bergamasque students in Padua, see Angelo Pinetti, 'Ricordi bergamaschi all'università di Padova,' *Rivista di Bergamo* vol. 1, no. 5 (1992) 236–8; and Tancredo Torri, 'Artisti e studiosi bergamaschi all'Ateneo di Padova nei secoli,' *Giornale del Popolo* (Feb. 10 & 14, 1953), 3. On student groups at Padua, see Jonathan Woolfson, *Padua and the Tudors: English Students in Italy, 1485–1603* (Toronto: University of Toronto Press, 1998); Biagio Brugi, 'La Nazione tedesca dello studio di Padova nel sec. XVII,' in *Memorie Storiche sullo Studio di Padova: Contributo del Regio Istituto Veneto alla celebrazione del VII centenario dell'Università* (Venice: C. Ferrari, 1922); Adriana de Lazari Bumbaca, 'Schede per scolari francesi a Padova (1532 36),' *Quaderni per la storia della Università di Padova* (1970), 137–44; Enrico Besta, 'Gli studenti valtellenesi e la Università di Padova,' *Archivio Veneto* 9 (1895), 179–219.

83 On Alberico da Rosciate, see Emanuele Roncalli, *I Grandi di Bergamo* (Bergamo: Burgo Editore, 1991), vol. 1, 23–9; Belotti, vol. 3, 21–6, 170–6; on Guglielmo Gratarolo, see later in this chapter; on Lorenzo Mascheroni and other distinguished scholars and intellectuals from Bergamo, see Belotti per above.

84 Some of this material was previously published in Christopher Carlsmith, 'Il Collegio Patavino della Misericordia Maggiore di Bergamo, 1531– ca. 1550,' *Bergomum* 93, no. 1–2 (1998): 75–98.

85 The best study of Paduan colleges is Piero del Negro, 'L'età moderna,' in idem, ed., *I collegi per studenti dell'Università di Padova. una storia plurisecolare*, 97–161 (Padova: Signum, 2003); also useful is Peter Denley, 'The Collegiate Movement in Italian Universities in the Late Middle Ages,' *History of Universities* 10 (1991): 29–91, which offers an overview of all late medieval Italian colleges as well as finding lists for various archives.

86 Paul Grendler, *Universities of the Italian Renaissance*, 38–40.

87 BCBg, Arch. MIA no. 1260, *Term,* f. 173r–75r (14 Sep. 1531).

88 BCBg, Arch. MIA no. 735, *Liber Onerum (1522–1546),* f. 52v & f. 106r (31 Dec. 1528). Maffei was selected for an Apibus scholarship on 31 Dec. 1528, which paid him a total of 64 lire and 10 soldi. The final Apibus payment recognized his election as a scholar at the MIA's Paduan college: BCBg, Arch. MIA no. 1260, *Term.,* f. 170r (31 Jul. 1531). Cf. Bernardo Licinus, identified as *juris scolaris in presentiorum patavij studentes* (student of law at Padua), who received a total of sixty lire from the MIA after he was elected as an Apibus scholar, but *not* to the MIA's college, on 19 Feb. 1529: BCBg, Arch. MIA no. 735, *Liber Onerum (1522–1546),* f. 71r, f. 82v.

89 On prefects, see BCBg, Arch. MIA no. 1261, *Term.*, ff. 75r–v (15 Feb. 1535). On deputies, BCBg, Arch. MIA no. 1260, *Term.*, f. 171r (21 Aug. 1531) records the election of three deputies to draw up the *capitula et ordines* (rules and regulations) of the college. On 15 Feb. 1535 (Arch. MIA no. 1261, f. 75r), there is specific mention of the the *deputatos ad scolares tam padue quam Bergomi*. On 4 Mar. 1536 (Arch. MIA no. 1261, f. 105r) deputy Lodovico Agosti was sent to investigate whether the students were living and studying in an honest manner; the officers of Treviso's largest confraternity also regularly visited their scholarship students to ascertain proper behaviour (D'Andrea, *Civic Christianity*, 125).

90 Oliviero Ronchi, 'Alloggi di Scolari a Padova nei secoli XIII–XVII,' *Bollettino della Associazione dei laureati dell' Università di Padova* 9, no. 2 (1932): 8–22, republished in idem, *Vecchia Padova* (Padua: Museo Civico, 1967), 293–320, which is the edition I cite, here 294–5. See also *Statuta Spectabilis et Almae Universitatis Juristarum Patavini Gymnasii* (Venetiis: per Jo. Patavinum, 1551), ff. 124–8, cited by Ronchi, 295–7. An identical set of rules existed for the students in Arts and Sciences.

91 'Merli' can mean either blackbirds or rooftop crenellations.

92 BCBg, Arch. MIA no. 2339, 'Lettere varie del sec. XVI,' ff. 1r–v (20 Oct. 1531).

93 BCBg, Arch. MIA no. 2312, f. 2 (1 Sep. 1534) is a letter from Bellafino to one of the MIA's notaries, Hieronymo S. Pellegrino, confirming rental of the house; f. 3 (10 Oct. 1537) is a receipt of payment of 15 ducats from S. Pellegrino to Bellafino for rental of his house; f. 1 (7 Jul. 1538) is a letter from Bellafino to Ezekiel Solza confirming cancellation of the contract. See also Archivio di Stato di Padova (hereafter ASPd), *Atti Notarili* di Guglielmo Ferrara, no. 5196 (12 May 1534) for a contract between Bellafino and the MIA.

94 BCBg, Arch. MIA no. 2312, f. 1r (7 Jul. 1538). On Francesco Bellafino, see the account of Renzo Negri in *DBI*, vol. 7, 588; Calvi, *Scena letteraria* v. 1, 158–9; Tiraboschi, 921. Bellafino became secretary of the city council beginning in 1504; he carried out several diplomatic missions during the War of the League of Cambrai (1508–16), one of which resulted in his imprisonment ca 1512 when the French took control of the city. Although he edited Marc Antonio Michiel's well known *Agri et urbis bergomatis descriptio* (1532), Bellafino's only published work is *De origine et temporibus urbis Bergomi*, which was translated into Italian (1555) and has received attention both because of its objectivity in recording events of his own day and because of its polemical tone toward the increasing diffusion of the vernacular. As is evident from his work on behalf of the Collegio Patavino,

Bellafino's family was based in Padua and his son Giovan Paolo continued to honour his father's commitment to the MIA after Francesco's death on 13 Feb. 1543.

95 BCBg, Arch. MIA no. 2306, f. 2v (10 Sep. 1538) is a copy of a one-year lease for a house on Via Colombina (today Via Papafava). See also f. 2r (18 Oct. 1538) for a letter from Julio Agosti regarding rent.

96 BCBg, Arch. MIA no. 1263, *Term.*, f. 52r (21 Jul. 1541), and f. 52v. (28 Jul. 1541). See ASBg, *Atti Notarili* di Girolamo di San Pellegrino, b. 1278, protcollo III (1530–45), ff. 68r–v (5 Feb. 1542) for the actual contract. A summary of the notarial act act exists in BCBg, *Carte Angelo Meli*, 23–V-15, 'Collegium Patavinum.'

97 See ASBg, *Atti Notarili* di Girolamo di San Pellegrino, no. 1279, ff. 119r–v (30 May 1550) for the acknowledgment of the end of the lease, and the rental of the property to Marino Lamberto of Treviso, 'post recessum scolarium collegij.' An identical document appears in ibid., b. 1278, f. 55r–v (30 May 1550). A summary of the act may be found in BCBg, *Carte Angelo Meli*, 23–V-15, 'Collegium Patavinum.'

98 Paolo Guerrini, 'Il Collegio Lambertino,' passim, cited above in 324n16.

99 On the initial election, BCBg, Arch. MIA no. 1260, *Term.*, f. 176v (14 Oct. 1531). On Maffeo, ibid., f. 177v (30 Oct. 1531). See also BCBg, Arch. MIA no. 1644, 'Processo consortij contra Rev. D. Mapheum De Guarneris Canonicum Bergomensem' (1551), which contains a copy of the contract between the MIA and Jacopo Guarneri (Maffeo's father) as well as an excerpt from the MIA Council meeting electing him, a record of payments to Maffeo from 1531 to 1535, and a denunciation dated 21 Feb. 1551.

100 The scholarship on Italian university life is vast. The most recent survey is Paul Grendler, *Universities in the Italian Renaissance*. An excellent overview of the University of Padua is Piero del Negro, ed., *L'università di Padova: otto secoli di storia* (Padua: Signum, 2001). On Padua, in addition to the works of Woolfson, Ronchi, and Favaro and Cessi cited above in 324n16, 331n82, and 332n90, see Biagio Brugi, *Gli scolari dello Studio di Padova nel'500* (Padua: Drucker, 1905); Emilio Lovarini, ed., *Un allegro convito di studenti a Padova nel'500: epistola* (Padua: L. Crescini, 1889). Also useful, although focused on the medieval period, are Andrea Gloria, *Monumenti dell' Università di Padova, 1318–1405*, vol. 2 (Padua: Tipografia del Seminario, 1888; reprinted 1972], and Nancy Siraisi, *Arts and Sciences at Padua* (Toronto: Pontifical Institute of Mediaeval Studies, 1973). The consortium CISUI (Centro Interuniversitario per lo Studio delle Università Italiane) has a number of fine books and a good journal dedicated to university history.

101 BCBg, Arch. MIA no. 2306, f. 4 (25 Nov. 1540). 'Essi dotti spendino in

dottorarsi in artes et medicina in padoa 18 ducati mozzi, a me converà
spendere 44 scudi d'oro dotorandomi in civili solamente, et in utroque 64;
essi doti si stimano di 25 o 30 scudi io non meno di 60 scudi in libri.' Agosti was writing to request additional money from the MIA for an eighth
year of study at Padua, so it is possible that he overstated his expenses.

102 Ronchi 313–14, citing AAUP, *Processi*, vol. 610. 'Costui ogni mattina
"levato dal letto va a S. Lorenzo al Trucho e sta sino il doppo sonato mezo
giorno; subito mangiato torna al loco solito; non va a scola da nissun;"
usa "parole improprie con biasteme orrendissime;" ma come l'acqua
va alla china, così egli non arresta la sua corsa lungo la via del male e,
armata mano, osa minacciare seriamente l'uomo che lo ospita.'

103 BCBg, Arch. MIA no. 1644, 'Processo consortij contra Rev. D. Mapheum De
Guarneris Canonicum Bergomensem' (1551), ff. 1v–7r: 'Item terminave-
runt quod pecunie date Domino Jo. Jacobo de Guarneris et eius filio scolari
ellecto in Gymnasio patavino repetantur attento maxime quod ipse (Maffeus) non est deditus studiis prout tenetur.' On Maffeo's lack of dedication,
BCBg, Arch MIA no. 1261, *Term.*, f. 54v (30 Mar. 1534), and Arch. MIA no.
1644, 'Processo,' ff. 1–2. On renouncing the scholarship, BCBg, Arch. MIA
no. 1261, *Term.*, f. 105r–v (4 Mar. 1536), repeated in Arch. MIA no. 1262,
Term., ff. 117v–118r (4 Mar. 1536); see also ff. 129r–v (16 June 1536).

104 ASBg, *Atti Notarili* di Giuseppe Gritti, b. 2254 (15 Apr. 1547): 'altre spese
occorse quae non sono licite esser nominate per bon respetto.' My thanks
to Giovanni Bonacina for this reference.

105 BCBg, Arch. MIA no. 1263, *Term.*, f. 2r (29 May 1539) and f. 32r (4 Jun.
1540).

106 BCBg, Arch. MIA no. 1263, *Term.*; on Callepio's suspension, f. 64v (20
Mar. 1542); 'In quo quidem consilio posita fuit pars quod suspendatur
salarium collegij Padue domino Ludovico de Comitibus [de Callepio]
scolari predicti Collegij per dues mense proxime fut. et ultra ad benepla-
citum pro eo quod ausus est accomodare domum collegij Padue certis
scolaribus forensibus pro in ea tripudiari faciendo in tempore carnisprivij
proxime passati ex quo secuta fuit rixa in ipsa domo cum gravi scandalo:
Et posito partito ad bussolas et balottas pars ipsa capta fuit per suffragia
undecim pro parte et duo tm. contra.' On his pardon, f. 66r (17 Apr. 1542);
124r (13 Apr. 1545).

107 BCBg, Arch. MIA no. 1263, *Term.*; on Alessanro Roncalli's election and
expulsion, f. 7v (29 May 1539), and f. 64r (16 Mar. 1542); for his appeal,
f. 66r (17 Apr. 1542); for his second expulsion, f. 71r (1 Sep. 1542) and f.
84v (27 May 1543); for Gian Giacomo's petition and the MIA's response,
f. 89r (19 Nov. 1543) and f. 102r (19 May 1544).

108 BCBg, Arch. MIA no. 1263, *Term.*; for Marchese's election, f. 41v (3 Mar. 1541); for his suspension, f. 71r (1 Sep. 1542); for his reinstatement, f. 88v (19 Nov. 1543).

109 On Gratarolo (also Gratarolus, Grataroli), see Alessandro Pastore's entry in *DBI*, v. 63, 731–5; Firpo, *I Processi Inquisitoriali*, 60n17; Frederic C. Church, *The Italian Reformers 1534–64* (New York: Columbia University Press, 1932), 194–201; Lynn Thorndike, *History of Magic and Experimental Science*, 8 vols. (New York: Columbia University Press, 1923–58), vol. 5, 600–16; Giovanni Battista Gallizoli, *Della vita, degli studi, e degli scritti di Guglielmo Grataroli, filosofo e medico* (Bergamo, 1788); and Belotti, vol. 4, 260–6.

110 BCBg, Arch. MIA no. 2306, 'Lettere varie del XVI secolo' (3 May 1538), n.p.

111 Personal communication to C. Carlsmith from G. O. Bravi, June 1997.

112 Church, 196–9.

113 On Maffei: BCBg, Arch. MIA no. 1261, *Term.*, f. 64v (17 Sep. 1534) and Arch. MIA no. 2306, f. 4 (25 Nov. 1540); and *Acta Graduum*, no. 2062 (3 Oct. 1534).

114 On Zanchi: BCBg, Arch. MIA no. 2328, f. 1r (9 Apr. 1536); and *Acta Graduum*, no. 2710 (5 May 1540).

115 On Lulmi: *Acta Graduum*, no. 2640 (23 Oct. 1539).

116 On Agosti: BCBg, Arch. MIA no. 2306, 'Lettere varie del sec. XVI,' n.d.; BCBg, Arch. Storico del Comune, *Azioni*, v. 21, f. 34r (19 Dec. 1541), and *Acta Graduum*, no. 2769 (19 Jan. 1541). N.B. it required ten years for Julio Agosti to graduate. For more on Julio Agosti, see p. 65 above.

117 BCBg, Arch. MIAn. 1263, *Term.*, f. 66v–67r (17 Apr. 1542).
   'Quum sit quod die 14 septembris 1531 per magnificos dominos tunc regentes consortium misericordie Bergomi institutum et erectum fuerit in urbe Padue collegium quinque scolarium pauperum et Civium Bergomi, liberalium artium et doctrinarum studiosorum, ut latius in Institutione et capitulis superinde confectis continetur, quod quidem pie et Sancte fecerunt sperantes scolares ipsos ex eorum studio et lucubrationibus, sibi ipsis, Patrie, agnatis, et amicis ex tam pia et laudabili Institutione maximas virtutes et gloriam reportaturos:
   Considerans modo Spettabilis domine Petrus Andreas dela Zoncha honoratus presidens prefati Consortij iam doctorum magnificorum dominorum tunc regentium piam mentem defraudatam esse; et quod non omnes scolares ipsi qui hactenus beneficio dicte Institutionis gavisi sunt, ut sperabatur, sed perpauci quidem perfectum fecerunt, nec se ut debuerunt et debent exemplariter gesserunt et gerunt, quinimo multe et

diverse de eis querimonie per tempora retroacta et in dies ad aures prefa-
torum magnificorum d. Regentium cum non mediocri eorum et totius
Civitatis scandalo et displicentia ac contra piam mentem magnificorum
qui huiusmodi Institutionem sanxerunt, pervenerunt et perveniunt:

   Consideransque modicum ipsorum scolariium fructum, ac pecuniarum
inopiam qua consortium multis debitis aggravatum opprimitur ut vix
mercenarijs satisfieri possit, Judicant melius esse si pecunie huiusmodi
Infructuose iam dictis scolaribus deputate, in alias magis necessarias, et
coram summo Deo et mundo laudabiliores operas dispensentur:

   Ideo non animo tamen aliquam Iniuriam Inferendi magnificis preces-
soribus qui Institutionem hanc ordinaverunt, certo credens quod si ipsi
nunc Curam dicti Consortij gererent, consideratis diligenter prenarratis,
partem profecto hanc [f. 67r.] retractationis ponerent:

   Idem spettabile domine Petrus Andreas partem istam posuit vz:

   Quod de cetero nullus alius scolaris sit qui esse velit, eligatur nec
admittatur ad beneficium dicte Institutionis collegij, sed collegium ipsum
et numerus collegiatorum in eo nunc degentium per eorum cessationem
prout de tempore in tempus acciderit diminuatus, et tandem retractetur,
ut finito numero in eo nunc degentium pro retractato habeatur.'

118 Ibid., ff 169v–170r (25 Oct. 1547). 'qui totam in ipsorum puerorum eruditione et omnem operam dilligenter impendat.'

119 On dice-playing, etc., see BCBg, Arch. MIA no. 1267, *Term.*, f. 61v (30 Nov.
1563), and f. 64r (16 Dec. 1563); and Locatelli (1910), 134. On the MIA's
house, see Gianni Barachetti, 'La "Domus Magna" della MIA,' *Bergomum*
59, no. 1 (1965): 63–86, esp. 71–2. The rebuilding was completed on 9 June
1567.

120 On the initial proposal, BCBg, Arch. MIA no. 1267, *Term.*, f. 180r (9 Jan.
1566); on Theodoldo, f. 187v (7 Feb. 1566); for the founding declaration,
BCBg, Arch. MIA no. 1519, *Liber Capitulorum Salariatorum Consortij*, f. 48r–
v (30 Apr. 1566). Locatelli (1910) publishes the text on 133–5.

121 BCBg, Arch. MIA no. 1519, *Liber Capitulorum*, ff. 48r–52r (30 Apr. 1566),
'Capitoli statuiti circa il governo dei chierici della Accademia.' F. 1r is an
index of the other *capitoli* for clerics, students, teachers, and staff: e.g., 'Ca-
pituli agiunti alli clerici di S.ta Maria Maggiore di Bergamo,' ff. 42r–46v (7
Dec. 1565) [identical to BCBg, Arch. MIA no. 1385, *Spese*, ff. 114r–v (1566)],
which describes in extensive detail the obligatory prayers, masses, and
other religious exercises; ff. 104r–113r contain the *capitoli* for all members
of the academy staff (i.e., master, assistant teachers, cook, steward) for
1590, plus later additions from 1592 and 1597; ff. 19r–v, ff. 55r–56r, ff.
60v–61r, ff. 71r–72v, and f. 75v are the *capitoli* concerning individual teachers in the academy. For a comparsion from another city, see BCBg, Arch.

MIA no. 1384, *Spese*, ff. 101r–106r, 'Capitoli portati della città di Verona,' which describe how grammar, choir and church offices should be taught to *chierici* in the cathedral of Verona. The MIA must have requested the Veronese *capitoli* just prior to redacting its own.

122 BCBg, Arch. MIA no. 1519, *Liber Capitulorum*, ff. 48r–52r (30 Apr. 1566).

123 BCBg, Arch. MIA no. 1519, *Liber Capitulorum*, ff. 48r–52r (30 Apr. 1566); ff. 107v–108v for punishments.

124 Locatelli (1910), 137.

125 BCBg, Arch. MIA no. 1519, *Liber Capitulorum*, ff. 105v–107r (18 Jan. 1590) describes the MIA's expectations of teaching staff in the academy.

126 BCBg, Arch. MIA no. 1519, *Liber Capitulorum*, f. 108r (18 Jan. 1590).

127 Angelo G. Roncalli, *Gli Atti della Visita Apostolica di S. Carlo Borromeo a Bergamo (1575)* (hereafter *AVASC*), 5 vols., (Firenze: Olschki, 1936), v. 1, pt. 1, 372.

128 BCBg, Arch. MIA no. 1519, *Liber Capitulorum*, f. 76r–78r (18 Jan. 1576). Robert Black (1989), 275–330, argues that manuscript glosses were primarily philological rather than moral; the MIA's archive has preserved so few glosses that it is impossible to determine the teachers' or students' intent. See the Introduction for more discussion of this issue.

129 Ibid., f. 51r (art. 19) (30 Apr. 1566). 'Et perche il principal maestro non habba occupationi più di quello porta il dovere, et possa benissimo attender alla scola, et alli sudetti clerici dell'accademia, sia statuito che siano elletti quattro sive sei dei clerici dell'accademia, quali al arbitrio del Reverendo precettore d'essa accademia gli sia assignato a ciaschun di loro la portione d'essi altri clerici venticinque extraordinarij, et altri scolari alla scola, ai quali siano tenuti insegnar secondo gli sarà ordinato per il Reverendo maestro.' See also f. 49r (art. 5).

130 BCBg, Arch. MIA no. 1447, *Scritture/Suppliche*, f. 239 (ca 1590). Cf. Arch. MIA no. 1448, *Scritture/Suppliche*, f. 547r (ca 1598–9), a request from Pietro Rota to go study in Turin.

131 BCBg, Arch. MIA no. 1448, *Scritture/Suppliche*, f. 5r (ca 1594), f. 525r (ca 1595).

132 On Bonacursio, BCBg, Arch. MIA no. 1519, *Liber Capitulorum*, ff. 55r–56r (14 Feb. 1567). A list of his students, 25 'in Accademia' and 25 'extra ordinarij,' is in Arch. MIA no. 1385, *Spese*, f. 244r–v (16 Feb. 1567). On his retirement, Arch. MIA no. 1386, *Spese*, f. 6r (20 Jun. 1569). On Calvi and Innocenzo, BCBg, Arch. MIA no. 1385, *Spese*, ff. 156r–v (1 Jun. 1566).

133 BCBg, Arch. MIA no. 1270, *Term.*, ff. 91v–92r (15 Feb. 1574); see also BCBg, Arch. MIA no. 1385, *Spese*, ff. 145r–v (n.d., but clearly post-1575), discussed below.

134 On Placchino: BCBg, Arch. MIA no. 1386, *Spese*, f. 15r (1570) lists the cler-

ics assigned to Placchino in this year. BCBg, Arch. MIA no. 1384, *Spese*, ff. 75r–76v (12 Jan. 1575) are the *capitoli* of his renewed appointment and describe his responsibilities in detail.

135 On Bello: BCBg, Arch. MIA no. 1384, *Spese*, ff. 116r–v (n.d.), identical to BCBg, Arch. MIA no. 1519, *Liber Capitulorum*, f. 75v (23 Jan. 1576). 'Sia tenuto con ogni cura ingegno et diligentia insegnare tutti quelli scolari che li saranno assignati di tempo in tempo per li Magnifici Deputati alla Achademia et a quelli leger lectioni dar epistole o datte dal Rev. Monsignor Colonio, principal maiestro a essi scolari rivederli et essi scolari instruere, interrogare, et fare tutto quello deve far uno diligente et fidele maiestro, et sopratutto con boni essempij et catholici costumi amaiestrarli, et la sera sia tenuto leger a essi scolari una lectione di cathechismo.' See also BCBg, Arch. MIA no. 1519, *Liber Capitulorum*, f. 76r (18 Jan. 1576).

136 On Father Lorenzo, BCBg, Arch. MIA no. 1384, *Spese*, ff. 81r–v. On *sottomaestri*, BCBg, Arch. MIA no. 1386, *Spese*, f. 78r (1576), Arch. MIA no. 1384, *Spese*, f. 117r (1576).

137 The original documents are preserved in twenty volumes at the Biblioteca Ambrosiana in Milan. Angelo G. Roncalli has edited and published many of the documents in *AVASC*, cited in 337n127 above. Volume 1, Parts 1 & 2, describe the city, while the three later volumes describe the diocese.

138 *AVASC*, v. 1, pt. 1, 372–4, for the original Latin; Locatelli (1910), 136, provides an Italian translation.

139 BCBg, Arch. MIA no. 1385, *Spese*, ff. 145r–v (n.d., but post-1575).

140 BCBg, Arch. MIA no. 1519, *Liber Capitulorum*, ff. 76r–78r (18 Jun. 1576), 'Capitoli statuiti et ordinati dal molto Reverendo et Excellentissimo Maestro dell'Accademia della Misericordia Maggiore di Bergamo, il Rev. Nicolò Collonio [*sic*] ... del mese di Giugno 1576 da esser osservati et adempiti dalli sotto maestri et scolari di essa accademia.' I will publish elsewhere a more detailed analysis of this document and its pedagogical implications.

141 BCBg, Arch. MIA no. 1271, *Term.*, ff. 82v–83v (24 Feb. 1577); 'Acciò con il tempo dopo tante fatiche, sudori, et spese ... con molte astuzie et inganni sotto pretesto di qualche loro ben colora a occasione cercano di subterfugere alla disciplina de' maestri et absentarsi molte volte da essa Accademia.' BCBg, Arch. MIA no. 1272, *Term.*, ff. 9v–10r (30 Apr. 1580): '[G]li disordini et inconvenienti quali ogni giorno seguir si veggono per li mali portamenti dei chierici ed allievi dell'Accademia ... Poichè molti di essi ingrati e scordevoli dei benefici avendo fatto qualche profitto o

nella grammatica o nella musica con il quale potrebbero render servizio e all'Accademia e alla Chiesa se ne vanno altrove.' See also Angelo G. Roncalli, *La MIA di Bergamo e le altre istituzioni di Beneficenza amministrate dalla Congregazione di Carità* (Bergamo: Tip. S. Alessandro, 1912), 66.

142 On Florio: BCBg, Arch. MIA no. 1447, *Scritture/Suppliche*, f. 64r (ca 1588): '[c]he non venendo alcuni di loro li andai cercando, et havendo ritrovato nel dormitorio gettato sopra il letto Ludovico figliuolo del Basso, gli dissi, che hora era quella di perder tempo, et altre cose, et havendolo ripreso et dattogli anchora due bosetti (?), venne suo fratello, et minacciò di volermi amazzare con biasteme et molte parole ingiuriose.'

143 On Guarguanti, ibid., ff. 373r–v (ca 1591).

144 BCBg, Arch. MIA no. 1519, *Liber Capitulorum*, ff. 104r–113r (various dates).

145 BCBg, Arch. MIA no. 1447, *Scritture/Suppliche*, ff. 226r–227r (31 Aug. 1590). 'Questa Academia, la quale dopo che io cessai de leggere era sempre caduta di mal in peggio. Dopo molte parole fra noi così risposi: son contento di far questo anchora, ma non vi metterei il piede se non mi fosse data la potesta assoluta di quel governo.'

146 ASVe, Fondo *Riformatori dello Studio di Padova* [vol. 348], 'Lettori nello Studio di Padova,' *s.v.* Cologno, Nicolò [p. 13]. Cologno (d. 1602) is listed as a 'lettore di filosofia morale in Padova' (6 May 1591) who earned two hundred florins per year, although he was rarely there after 1592. Part of the reason for Cologno's absence from Padua may have been his involvement in a fierce dispute over how to read Horace's *Ars Poetica*. In 1587 Cologno had proposed an alternative method to reading this important classical work, one which was attacked by Antonio Riccoboni out of pique because the more obscure Cologno had been offered a professorship in 1591 ahead of Riccoboni. See Bernard Frischer, 'Rezeptionsgeschichte and Interpretation: The Quarrel of Antonio Riccoboni and Nicolò Cologno about the Structure of Horace's "Ars Poetica"' in Helmut Krasser, Ernst A. Schmidt, eds.,'Zeitgenosse Horaz' (Tübingen, 1996), 68–116, and the brief description of Riccoboni's book online at International League of Antiquarian Booksellers [http://www.ilab.org/db/book849_19565.html] (accessed 9/26/2008). Also helpful is David A. Lines, *Aristotle's 'Ethics' in the Italian Renaissance (ca. 1300–1650)* (Leiden: Brill, 2002), *ad indicem s.v.* 'Colonio, Niccolo,' esp. 440, which provides much context about university teaching, and evidence for Cologno's 'lost' prolusion of 1592. See also Antonio Poppi, 'Il problema della filosofia morale nella scuola padovana del Rinascimento: Platonismo e Aristotelismo nella definizione del metodo dell'Etica,' in *Platon et Aristote à la Renaissance* (De Pétrarque à Descartes, XXXII) (Paris, 1976), 103–46; rpt. in idem, *L'etica del Rinascimento tra*

Platone e Aristotele (Naples, 1997), 11–87. My forthcoming article, 'Maestro dei Maestri: Nicolò Cologno in the Sixteenth Century,' explores Cologno's career in more detail.

147 BCBg, Arch. MIA no. 1447, *Scritture/Suppliche*, f. 64r (ca 1588).

148 BCBg, Arch. MIA no. 2045, ff. 1–8 (17–23 Jan. 1590).

149 BCBg, Arch. MIA no. 1447, *Scritture/Suppliche*, f. 459r, n.d.

150 BCBg, Arch. MIA no. 1148, 'Furto nell'Accademia' (4 Nov. 1595 – 13 Feb. 1596). The file includes interviews, summaries of fact, and other documents, but many are illegible.

151 Locatelli, 139.

152 BCBg, Arch. MIA no. 1334, *Relazioni*, fald. 20, f. 3r (22 Jul. 1795), cited by Locatelli (1911), 78.

153 Cossar, *Transformation of the Laity*, 51–7.

154 Ibid., 6–7.

155 Grendler, *Schooling*, 60–1.

156 Archivio Parrocchiale di S. Alessandro in Colonna (hereafter APSACol), *Libro delli Parti* (or *Libro delle Terminationi*) for the following volumes: 1549–67, 1567–73, 1573–84, 1584–91, 1607–14. For a (sometimes erroneous) history based on these documents, see Mario Lumina, *S. Alessandro in Colonna* (Bergamo: Greppi, 1977).

157 APSACol, *Libro delli Parti (1549–1567)*, f. 127r (29 May 1556), and f. 128v (19 Jun. 1556); f. 146v (11 Apr. 1557); on Pagani, f. 148v (4 Jun. 1557).

158 *Regola del Ven. Consortio di Santo Alessandro in Colonna, ove oltre gli Ordini, si contengono anche l'Origine, l'Antichità, e i Confini suoi* (Bergamo: Comin Ventura, 1589), 11–13. I cite from an identical version published in Bergamo in 1767 by Francesco Locatelli.

159 APSACol, *Libro delli Parti (1549–1567)*, f. 179v (19 May 1559); f. 193v (10 Mar. 1560); f. 205r (24 Jan. 1561); f. 274r–v (28 Dec. 1565).

160 Ibid., *Libro delli Parti* (1567–1573), f. 20v–21r (21 Nov. 1568).

161 Ibid., *Libro delle Terminationi* (1574–1584), ff. 32v–33r (2 Apr. 1574). 'Prima che il detto Magistro debba insegnar con ogni fideltà et diligenza boni costumi, boni lettere lattine et greche alli dodici chierici che dai Reggenti d'esso Consortio gli saranno consegnati, si come conviene et si può sperare da bon christiano et grammatico, et questo per anni treij, et oltra beneplacito delle parti quali treij anni cominciaranno.

Item sia tenuto ad habitar in questo borgo di S.to Leonardo nella casa che'esso potrà ritrovar più comoda alla chiesa.

Item sia tenuto ad insegnar oltra li detti dodici chierici al chierico nipote del R.do messer p. Ludovico Cerane nel infrascripto salario, over uno altro in logo suo talchè in tutto siano tredisi.

Item che detto maestro habba per suo salario all'anno et a raggion d'anno scudi quaranta d'oro in quattro page al'anno, doi somi di frumento et uno carro de vino; il frumento una soma ogni seij mesi, et il vino al tempo della vendemmia.

Item sia tenuto tutte le volte che Monsignor R.mo et Ill.mo vescovo tenerà ordinatione presentar detti chierici et farli ordinar como sarà bisogno.

Item che il detto Maestro possa nella medesima scola tener et insegnar sino ad altri dodici figlioli et non più tre donzananti et scolari per il prezio che tra lui et li parti converanno tra quali figlioli si comprendano sino a [blank] donzananti et in logo di quelli mancaranno nel avenir delli detti donzananti et scolari sia sempre obligato ad anteporre li figlioli delli habitanti del borgo chi gli ne voranno dare in donzena o a scola mentre gli pagino il pretio trovarà da altri.

Item che il detto Maestro tenendo uno idoneo ripetitore possa anchora tener sino al numero de dodisi altri scolari massime di quelli voranno imparare gli principij, et sempre intendendo che li vinticinque privati non habbino a patir per questa concessione.

Item che il detto maestro non possa dar vacantia alle detti chierici senza la licentia del Mag.co consiglio nè per il segande ne per la vendemmia.'

162 On Perlizolo, ibid. (1584–1591) ff. 68v–69r (21 Feb. 1586); on Cologno, ibid. (1573–1584), f. 48r (10 Dec. 1574), f. 54r (21 Jan. 1575), f. 61r (20 May 1575), f. 130r (7 Feb. 1578), and ff. 148v–149r (6 Feb. 1579).

163 Reading, writing, and singing appear frequently; references to *abbaco* appear in ibid. (1573–1584), f. 56r (19 Feb. 1575), f. 68v (15 Oct. 1575); f. 79 v (20 Jan. 1576). Although the *capitolo* of 1574 called for instruction in Greek, the council waived the requirement for grammar master Giovanni Antonio Cavalli on 18 April 1574 (f. 34r), noting that he only had to teach Latin letters and not Greek as specified in his contract. It seems unlikely that Greek would have been taught with any regularity in this school.

164 *Regola … di S. Alessandro in Colonna*, 8. Excerpts are also published in *AVASC*, v. 1, pt. 2, 262.

165 Ibid., 8v and 36.

166 Michel Jeanneret, 'The Renaissance and its Ancients: Dismembering and Devouring,' *MLN* 110, no. 5 (1995): 1043–53, esp. 1049–51. The translation from Petrarch is Jeanneret's.

167 *Regola … di S. Alessandro in Colonna*, 35.

168 *AVASC*, v. 1, pt. 2, 147–8: 'in mercede pro eruditione clericorum in tribus grammaticalibus.'

169 Lumina, 263, citing the ratio of 1:16 found in APSACol, *Libro delli Parti* (14 Jan. 1611).

170 The *Regola* of S. Lorenzo has been lost, but Borromeo and his staff compiled a 'Breve riassunto della regola del Consorzio di S. Lorenzo' (Brief summary of the Rule of the Consortium of S. Lorenzo), based upon the original rule submitted to them. See *AVASC*, vol. 1, pt. 2, 85.

171 *AVASC*, vol. 1, pt. 2, 76–7. Borromeo cited the 'rude and impertinent' behaviour of some members.

172 For a brief history of the confraternity, the church, and its art, see Andreina Franco-Lorii Locatelli, *Borgo Pignolo in Bergamo: Arte e storia delle sue chiese* (Gorle: Istituto Grafica Litostamp, 1994), 63–6; see also the 1995 *Inventario* of the Archivio Parrocchiale di S. Alessandro della Croce (hereafter APSACro) for a very brief introduction.

173 *Regola del Ven. Consortio di S. Spirito e S. Giovanni dell'Ospedale* (Bergamo: Lodovico Monza, 1617), in APSACro, no. 2423; also preserved in the BCBg, Salone Cassapanca I H I 2 (10). The chapter describing the responsibilities of the deputies to visit the schools and supervise the teachers also strongly resembles that of S. Alessandro in Colonna.

174 Ibid., 35–7.

175 APSACro, no. 2501, *Libro Maestro 'B' (1571–1617)* lists all expenses of the confraternity for this period of time, including medical doctors, surgeons, teachers, and the saying of masses.

176 APSACro no. 2423, *Regola di S. Spirito*, 36.

177 Ibid. 'si ellegerà un'huomo da bene … il qual insegni a detti scolari leggere, scrivere, & abacco, siccome alli Chierici la Grammatica, & altre lettere di Humanità secondo la capacità loro.'

178 APSACro, no. 2501, *Libro Maestro 'B,'* ff. 92–3.

179 APSACro, no. 2423, *Regola di S. Spirito,* 35. 'Se bene ne necessario, ne perpetuo, ne di obligo è il condurre Maestro per instruttione delli poveri scolari del Consortio, ma ad arbitrio, e beneplacito del Consiglio.'

180 APSACro, no. 1047, *Ordini del governo del consorzio di S. Alessandro della Croce in Bergamo: Statuti … alli 30 Decembre dell' Anno 1595*, 4–8, 8–10. An identical copy is in the BCBg, Sal. Loggia U IX 40 (5). See also Andreina Locatelli, *Borgo Pignolo in Bergamo*, 29.

181 Ibid., ff. 28r–29v (8 Jun. 1593).

182 Ibid., f. 35v (17 Jan. 1595); and APSACro, no. 1047, *Ordini*, 9: 'Che sia eletto & accordato un Maestro, che insegni a leggere, & al debito tempo, & conveniente età a scrivere, & Aritmetica alli figliuoli pover di detto Consortio.'

183 APSACro, no. 1050, *Libro delli Parti*, ff. 39r–40v (6 Jul. 1595).

184 Ibid. 'Et quando questi figliuoli haveranno mediocramente imparato a leggere, scrivere, e a far conti, talmente, che si possino valere della virtù imparata, siano licentiati, & fattone sotto entrare de gli altri a ballottatione del Consiglio.'

185 APSACro, no. 1050, *Libro delli Parti*, f. 43v (31 Dec. 1595).

186 APSACro, no. 1050, *Libro delli Parti*, ff. 43v–44v (31 Dec. 1595).

187 Ibid., f. 46r (11 Feb. 1596) for Chiodi's expulsion; f. 49r (17 Mar. 1596) for Domenico Marangon's election.

188 Ibid., ff. 52 r–v (16 Dec. 1596).

189 Ibid., f. 55r (31 Dec. 1596); f. 56r (28 Mar. 1596); f. 59r (10 Jan. 1597); and ff. 60r–v (12 Dec. 1597) for the appointment of Calcone.

190 For election of deputies, see APSACro, *Libro delli Parti*, f. 68r (10 Jan. 1600), f. 74r (6 Jan. 1602); f. 76v (2 Feb. 1603). For suspension of the school, see f. 80v–81r (16 Jan. 1605).

191 Ibid., f. 48r (10 Mar. 1596). 'Fu posta parte di mandar li duo chierici già elletti ... alla scola di Rx.do sacerdote che gli insegni non solo humanità ma ancora per rispetto della professione in che si hanno da esercitare gli insegni anco le cerimonie del officiare.'

192 On Ligrigni: ibid., f. 48r (10 Mar. 1596); on Carrara: f. 49v (17 Apr. 1596) and f. 50v (22 Apr. 1596); on subsequent teachers, ff. 80v–81r (16 Jan. 1605); f. 83v (21 Dec. 1606); f. 84v (6 Jan. 1607); ff. 88v–89r (28 Dec. 1607); f. 96r (8 Jan. 1612); f. 102r (7 Jan. 1614).

193 J.H. Hexter, 'The Education of the Aristocracy in the Renaissance,' 45–70, here at 49–50, in idem, *Reappraisals in History: New Views on History and Society in Early Modern Europe*, 2nd ed. (Chicago: University of Chicago Press, 1979).

194 BCBg, Arch. MIA no. 1280, *Term.*, ff. 60v–61v (20 Jan. 1617) and ff. 95 (12 Jan. 1618), quoted in Locatelli (1910), 139–44. Locatelli does an excellent job of exploring the history of this new academy from 1617 to 1630. For what follows I rely substantially upon his analysis.

195 Locatelli (1910), 140, citing BCBg, Arch. MIA no. 1280, *Term.*, f. 64r (3 Feb. 1617).

196 Gian Paolo Brizzi, *La formazione della classe dirigente nel Sei-Settecento: I seminaria nobilium nell'Italia centro-settentrionale* (Bologna: Il Mulino, 1976); idem, *Principe,Università, e Gesuiti: La politica farnesina dell'istruzione a Parma e Piacenza (1545–1622)* (Rome: Bulzone, 1980); Maurizio Sangalli, 'Università, scuole private, collegi d'educazione, accademie a Padova tra Cinque e Seicento: alcuni spunti per una storia'integrata' delle istituzioni scolastiche,' *Annali di storia dell'educazione* (1996), no. 3, 93–118.

197 Locatelli (1910), 143–4, publishes the schedule hour-by-hour and the weekly menu.
198 Locatelli (1910), 141, citing the BCBg, Arch. MIA no. 1280, *Term..* ff. 64r–66r (3 Feb. 1617).
199 See Locatelli (1910), 145–9, for sample reports. For the index of separate Academy affairs, see BCBg, Arch. MIA no. 2317, 'Partes pro Ecclesia – Accademia,' ff. 11–13 (n.d.).
200 Locatelli (1910), 148, citing BCBg, *Azioni*, ff. 148r–v (19 Aug. 1628).
201 See Locatelli (1910), 149–69, for a history of the new academy and the Collegio Mariano; see also the articles and the *tesi di laurea* of Paola Valota, Omar Capoferri, and Margherita Pizzighella.
202 D'Andrea, *Civic Christianity*; Terpstra, *Abandoned Children*; Black, *Education and Society*; idem, *Humanism and Education*; Grendler, *Schooling*.
203 Jo Ann Hoeppner Moran, *The Growth of English Schooling, 1340–1548: Learning, Literacy, and Laicization in Pre-Reformation York Diocese* (Princeton, NJ: Princeton University Press, 1985); Lawrence Stone, 'The Educational Revolution in England, 1580–1640,' *Past and Present* 28 (1964): 41–80.

3. *Catechismo*: Schooling and the Catholic Church

1 In general, when I refer to 'the Church' I mean the institution and its ecclesiastical officials (i.e., the Curia, cardinals, bishops, vicars, religious orders) rather than the body of the Church (i.e., lay believers). The word 'church' (lower-case) refers to a specific building (e.g., the church of San Pancrazio).
2 Black, *Education and Society*, 173–243; Grendler, *Schooling*, 6–11.
3 James Hankins, *Plato in the Italian Renaissance* (Leiden: Brill, 1990); *The Cambridge Companion to Renaissance Humanism*, ed. Jill Kraye (Cambridge: Cambridge University Press, 1996); for primary sources, *Humanist Educational Treatises*, ed. and trans. Craig Kallendorf; I Tatti Renaissance Library 5 (Cambridge, MA.: Harvard University Press, 2002); *The Earthly Republic: Italian Humanists on government and society*, ed. Benjamin G. Kohl and Ronald G. Witt (Philadelphia: University of Pennsylvania Press, 1978).
4 Miriam Turrini, '"Riformare il mondo a vera vita christiana": Le scuole di catechismo nell'Italia del '500,' *Annali del Istituto Storico Italo-Germanico di Trento* 8 (1982), 407–89, at 408.
5 For an overview of the religious history of Bergamo, see: Goffredo Zanchi, 'Dagli inizi del Cinquecento all'attuazione del Concilio di Trento,' and idem, 'L'età post-Tridentina e il consolidarsi della tradizione bergamasca,' in *Diocesi di Bergamo*, ed. A. Caprioli, A. Rimoldi, and L. Vaccaro (Brescia: La Scuola, 1988), 161–80, 181–200; Ermenegildo Camozzi, *Le istituzioni monastiche e religiose a Bergamo nel Seicento*, 2 vols. (Bergamo: Tipografia Vesco-

vile Secomandi, 1982), also published in *Bergomum* no. 1–4 (1981): 1–502; *Chiesa, Istituzioni, e Territorio*, ed. Lelio Pagani and Vincenzo Marchetti (Bergamo: Stamperia Editrice Commerciale, 1991), especially the essays by Antonio Pesenti, 'Fonti per la consoscenza della chiesa di Bergamo,' 233–44; and by Vincenzo Marchetti, 'Panorama degli studi sulla Chiesa a Bergamo,' 245–58, which reviews the 'classic' works in Bergamo's religious history from the sixteenth to the twentieth century; and of course Bortolo Belotti, *La storia di Bergamo e dei Bergamaschi* (Bergamo: Bolis, 1989). On the various religious orders in Bergamo, see the bibliography in the works cited above. On the Index in Bergamo, see Gianni Barachetti and Carmen Palamini, 'La Stampa a Bergamo nel Cinquecento,' *Bergomum* 84, no. 4 (1989): 1–147, esp. 11–15, reprinted with same title in Bergamo in 1990 by Tipografia Secomandi.

The studies of Massimo Firpo (*Vittore Soranzo Vescovo ed Eretico* and *I Processi Inquisitoriali di Vittore Soranzo: edizione critica*) and Andrea del Col (*L'Inquisizione nel Patriarcato e Diocesi di Aquileia*) have revealed the extent to which heresy was embedded in both the city and the countryside of Bergamo in the mid-sixteenth century. While Bishop Soranzo was the focal point for Firpo, as he was for the Inquisitor of Bergamo, both found extensive evidence of heretical ideas, books, and conversations, a conclusion affirmed by Del Col's earlier study. In Firpo's view, the activities of the Inquisition in Bergamo (and elsewhere) were primarily responsible for changing the 'hearts and minds' of the city's inhabitants. Although the Inquisition did not intervene directly in the schools studied here, the teachers of Bergamo were – as we shall see – sometimes targets or witnesses. In addtion, the multiple examples of heresy are important because they speak directly to efforts to instruct, catechize, and train Bergamo's youth.

The first notable example is the case of Giorgio Vavassori, known as 'Il Medolago,' who in October 1536 declared that he believed 'that which the Catholic Church proclaimed, but not the ideas of the Roman Church', thus rejecting the authority of the pope, the mass, and purgatory as 'tricks' to cajole money from parishioners (Firpo, *I Processi Inquisitoriali*, 475n5; idem, *Vittore Soranzo*, 308–9). Vittore Soranzo, bishop of Bergamo from 1544 to 1558, underwent a five-year investigation in the early 1550s before being reinstated in Bergamo, only to have a second trial commence in 1557. Soranzo's case – one of the few for which the entire dossier has survived in the Vatican Archives – illustrates how his intellectual and spiritual interests ran afoul of traditional Catholic belief. He is particularly important in our analysis because of his support of various educational enterprises, including the Caspi Academy (1547), the joint appointment of Nicolò

Cologno (1556), and the Schools of Christian Doctrine (1554). As noted above on 107–8, Guglielmo Gratarolo was investigated by the MIA in 1536 for behaviour that may well have been heretical while he was a student at Padua; even after his flight to the Valtellina, he continued to mail heretical books back to Bergamo. Firpo documents numerous other colorful cases, such as that of Giovan Francesco Bottigisi (il Medeghetto), which lasted for many years (Firpo, *Vittore Soranzo, ad indicem*). On 4 July 1563 the Company of Milan (the group administering the Schools of Christian Doctrine in Milan) wrote to Bergamo specifically to warn about the 'poison' of Lutheranism and to urge the foundation of more Schools (Tamborini, 146, cited in 346n8). In addition to the studies of Firpo and Del Col noted above, see also Gabriele Medolago, 'Inquisitori, eretici e streghe nelle valli bergamasche sottoposte all'arcidiocesi di Milano nei secoli XVI e XVII,' *Ricerche Storiche sulla Chiesa Ambrosiana* 20 (2002): 83–145; Giulio Orazio Bravi, 'Note e documenti per la storia della Riforma a Bergamo (1536–44),' *Archivio Storico Bergamasco* 11 (1987), 185–228, and idem, 'Girolamo Zanchi, da Lucca a Strasburgo,' *Archivio Storico Bergamasco* 1 (1981), 35–64. See also Francesco Rota, 'Vittore Soranzo, Vescovo di Bergamo (1547–1558),' *Archivio Storico Brembatese* (1974), 9–123; Pio Paschini, 'Un vescovo disgraziato nel Cinquecento' in idem, *Tre ricerche sulla storia della Chiesa nel Cinquecento* (Rome: Edizioni liturgiche, 1945), 89–151; Luigi Chiodi, 'Eresia protestante a Bergamo nella prima metà del Cinquecento e il vescovo Vittore Soranzo,' *Rivista di Storia della Chiesa in Italia* 35 (1981), 456–85.

6 ACVBg, *Lett. Pastorali, 1538–77*, v. 2: on misbheavior at Mass, f. 5r (4 Aug. 1558); on travelling priests and banquets, f. 107r (3 June 1578), on the MIA's generosity, f. 112r (14 Feb. 1579).

7 Xenio Toscani, *Scuole e alfabetismo nello Stato di Milano da Carlo Borromeo alla Rivoluzione* (Milan: La Scuola, 1992), 94, citing E. Chinea, 'Le scuole elementari del Ducato di Milano nel primo Settecento,' *Rivista pedagogica* (1928): 321–43.

8 The fundamental study is G.B. Castiglioni, *Istoria delle scuole della Dottrina Cristiana*, 2 vols. (Milan: C. Orena, 1800); an updated treatment is Alessandro Tamborini, *La compagnia e le scuole della Dottrina Cristiana* (Milan: Tipografia Arcivescovile Giovanni Daverio, 1939). More scholarly is Miriam Turrini's comprehensive thesis, 'La scuola di catechismo nell'Italia del Cinquecento: catechesi,"buoni costumi" ed alfabetizzazione,' Università degli Studi di Bologna, Facoltà di Lettere e Filosofia, relatore Ottavia Niccoli, 1980–1. Xenio Toscani's stimulating article has helped me enormously: X. Toscani, 'Le "Scuole della Dottrina Cristiana" come fattore di alfabetizzazione,' *Società e Storia* 7 (1984): 757–81, as has Daniele Montanari's book

Disciplinamento in terra veneta (Bologna: Il Mulino, 1987), especially 134–56. Paul Grendler devotes chapter 12 of *Schooling in Renaissance Italy* (London and Baltimore: Johns Hopkins University Press, 1989) to the Schools; see also idem, 'Borromeo and the Schools of Christian Doctrine,' in *San Carlo Borromeo: Catholic Reform and Ecclesiastical Politics in the Second Half of the Sixteenth Century*, ed. John M. Headley and John B. Tomaro (Washington, DC: Folger Shakespeare Library; London: Associated University Presses, 1988), 158–71; and idem, 'Schools, Seminaries, and Catechetical Instruction,' in *Catholicism in Early Modern History: A Research Guide*, ed. John W. O'Malley (St Louis: Center for Reformation Research, 1988), 315–30.

9 The 1561 decree of Bishop Federico Cornaro that 'those who teach grammar must persuade the pupils to [religious] devotion' captures the balance between these two objectives: 'Ancora s'esorta et ordina a tutti li curati ovvero altri che insegnano grammatica siano obligati di indure a qualche devotione li loro scolari et fare che ogni giorno lo osservino, dichiarando li dodici articoli de la fede et i dodici [*sic*] comandamenti, et altre cose poi de la santa scrittura a questi che ne saranno capaci.' ACVBg, *Lettere Pastorali*, vol. 2, f. 15r (19 Jul. 1561), no. 21.

10 For Milan, see Grendler, *Schooling*, 337. For Bergamo, see ACVBg, Archivio Capitolare, CAP 872, *Fundatio Scholae Generalis Doctrinae Christiane in Cath. Ecclesia Bergomensis ... de anno 1609*. This folder contains the act of foundation and subsequent aggregations, including the exact number of participants for each School of Christian Doctrine in Bergamo in 1609–11. See also appendix 2.

11 Grendler, *Schooling*, 333–5.

12 On Merici: see Teresa Ledochowska, 'Angela Merici,' in *DIP*, vol. 1, cols. 631–4; Francesco De Vivo, 'Indirizzi pedagogici ed istituzioni educative di ordini e congregazioni religiose nei secoli XVI e XVII,' *Rassegna di Pedagogia* 18 (1960): 326–33; Grendler, *Schooling*, 335, 392. On Theatines: see 316n81. On Barnabites: see the dated but still useful studies of Orazio Premoli, *Storia dei Barnabiti nel Cinquecento* (Rome: Desclee, 1913); and idem, *Storia dei Barnabiti nel Seicento* (Rome: Desclee, 1922). See also *Le Scuole dei Barnabiti nel IV centenario dell'approvazione dell'ordine, 1533–1933*, special issue of *Vita Nostra* (Florence: Collegio alla Querce, 1933); Angelo Bianchi, *L'istruzione secondaria tra barocco et età dei Lumi* (Milan: Vita e Pensiero, 1993); Francesco De Vivo, 'Indirizzi pedagogici ed istituzioni educative di ordini e congregazioni religiose nei secoli XVI e XVII,' *Rassegna di Pedagogia* 17 (1959): 22–57, 255–62. On Piarists (Scuole Pie): see the fascinating if sometimes sensationalist account of Karen Lieberich, *Fallen Order: Intrigue, Heresy, and Scandal in the Rome of Galileo and Caravaggio*

(New York: Grove Atlantic, 2004); Grendler, *Schooling*, 381–90; *Il Pensiero Pedagogico della Controriforma*, ed. Luigi Volpicelli (Florence: Giulio Sansoni, 1960), 561–85, for primary documents.

13 On Castello: see Luigi Cajani, 'Castellino da Castello,' in *DBI*, vol. 21, 786–7; and Castiglioni, chap. 1.

14 Castiglioni, 187; ACVBg, *Licentiae 1560–66*, f. 51v (4 November 1561).

15 ACVBg, *Licentiae 1560–66*, f. 15v; *Licentiae 1558–60*, f. 68v, and ACVBg, *Lettere Pastorali*, vol. 2, f. 32r (18 Jul. 1562) and f. 68: 'cum itaque intelleximus dudum in presenti urbe scholam seu confrraternitatem vitae christianae nuncupatam erectam fuisse in qua in diversis locis pueri instruuntur et edocentur religiose et christiane vivere secundum divina praecepta Catholice S. Matris Romanae Ecclesiae, unde … pro pueris instruendi quoties id fecerint quadraginta dies de vera indulgentia de iniunctis eis poenitentiis.' See also Castiglioni, 188.

16 Tamborini, 147, citing Cornaro's statement at his second synod on 10 May 1568; see ACVBg, *Acta Synodalia Bergomensis Ecclesiae* (hereafter *ASBE*) (Bergamo: Fratres Rubeos, 1737), 51, chap. 7I, for the phrase 'absque tot barbarismis.' On Mazochi: ACVBg, *Lettere Pastorali*, vol. 2, f. 54 (22 Jun. 1570): '[M]esser Gio Francesco di Mazochi da Civedal de Belù [Cividale di Belluno], uno delli fratelli delle Compagnie delle Scuole della Dottrina Christiana di Venetia ... debba continuare ad erigere et piantare di queste Scole et diligentemente insegnar a fanciulli et altre persone nella nostra diocesi di Bergamo la vita et Dottrina Christiana.'

17 Castiglioni, 188, and Tamborini, 145, citing a letter dated 15 Jun. 1563 in the Archivio di S. Dalm[atius] in Milan.

18 Castiglioni, 189–92, and Tamborini, 146–7, citing letters of 4 July 1563 and 13 Feb. 1564. For Filogenio's statement, see Castiglioni, 194.

19 Letter from Bergamo's Prior General to Milan's Prior General, dated 18 June 1564, cited by Castiglioni, 193. The confraternity is probably the MIA, or possibly S. Alessandro in Colonna.

20 BCBg, *Regola* del Consorzio S. Lorenzo (Bergamo: Fratelli Rossi, 1717), chap. 20, 'Del Capellano del Consorzio.'

21 ACVBg, Archivio Capitolare, CAP 872, 'Fundatio,' passim. See also appendix 2.

22 Council of Trent, Session XXIV, 11 Nov. 1563; on Pius V, see 'Ex debito pastorali officii,' 6 Oct. 1567, cited by Grendler, *Schooling*, 359–60; on Borromeo's recommendations, *AVASC*, vol. 2, pt. 3, 465–6, 'Ammonimento del Cardinale Borromeo al Vescovo circa la scuola della Dottrina Cristiana.' Borromeo had made a similar statement to all bishops at the 1572 Provincial Council (see Balini, 29, cited in the following note).

23 ACVBg, *ASBE*, 'Synodus Cornelio III' (25 Sep. 1574), chap. 8, 'De Scholis,
    & Sodalitatibus Doctrinae Christiane,' 70–2. On Borromeo's estimate, see
    Suor Melania Balini, 'Fondazione delle Scuole della Dottrina Cristiana a
    Bergamo,' 2, unpublished notes; some of this material has been published
    in an article in the exhibition catalogue, 'Sulle orme di Gregorio Barbarigo.
    La chiesa di Bergamo nel '600–'700: arte, cultura, fede (15 settembre-16 no-
    vembre 1997),' *Echi di Papa Giovanni* 18, no. 5, (Sept.-Oct. 1997): 24–35, here
    at 28. My thanks to Suor Melania for generously sharing this information
    with me ahead of publication.
24 ACVBg, *Lettere Pastorali, 1557–77*, vol. 2, f. 95r (22 Nov. 1577).
25 *Le Visite 'ad Limina Apostolorum' dei Vescovi di Bergamo, 1590–1697*, ed. Er-
    ménegildo Camozzi (Bergamo: Provincia di Bergamo, 1992), 150n28.
26 ACVBg, *ASBE*, 'Sinodo Milana' (4 Sep. 1603) 'Della Dottrina Christiana,'
    108.
27 See Castiglioni, 196n1, for brief citations to the actions of individual
    bishops. This includes Giovanni Emo's 1613 decree requiring *all* teachers
    to submit a declaration of faith, and Agostino Priuli's 15-article decree of
    24 March 1628 regarding expansion of the Schools in response to concerns
    about heresy. See also ACVBg, *Lettere Pastorali* vol. 3 (26 Mar. 1647) for a
    letter concerning Luigi Grimani's intended visits to examine Schools of
    Christian Doctrine. On Bishop Gregorio Barbarigo, see Montanari, *Disci-
    plinamento, ad indicem*.
28 Grendler, *Schooling*, 338.
29 *Ordini e Regole per Formar ed Instruir le Scole della Dottrina Cristiana di
    Bergamo e sua Diocese* (Bergamo: Fratelli Rossi, 1711), Col. B, summarized
    by Balini, 32 and available in ACVBg, 'Insegnamenti parrocchiale Dottrina
    Cristiana.' 'Questa quinta Classe sarà ben farla in luogo separato, se v'è
    commodità perchè uomini di tempo si vergonano mescolarsi con putti ad
    imparare.'
30 For an example in the commune of Solto, in Zorzino: ACVBg, CAP 872,
    'Fundatio,' f. 38v (28 Aug. 1609); see ibid. f. 43r for the town of Colognola.
31 ACVBg, CAP 872, 'Fundatio,' ff. 1–48v. In 1609 there were 377 male teach-
    ers and 1466 male students; 810 female teachers and 2719 female students.
32 See Grendler, *Schooling*, 356–9, for comments on 'High and Low in Cat-
    echism Schools.'
33 ACVBg, CAP 872, 'Fundatio.' Sant'Agata: 30 teachers, 127 boys; Santa
    Caterina: 23 teachers, 108 boys; Sant'Anna di Borgo Palazzo, 8 teachers,
    96 boys. For girls: San Pietro in Sant' Alessandro della Croce: 24 teachers,
    51 girls; Sant'Andrea: 44 teachers, 66 girls; certainly the most favourable
    ratio was in Santa Grata Inter Vites, with 19 teachers and 22 girls (perhaps

owing to the plethora of convents in that parish). See appendix 2.

34 On the *decurio*, see Allan Farrell, *The Jesuit Code of Liberal Education* (Milwaukee, WI: Bruce, 1938), 119–21, 291–6; and Grendler, *Schooling*, 380.

35 ACVBg, CAP 872, 'Fundatio,' f. 39r (29 Aug. 1609).

36 *Regole* of 1555 and 1566, as cited by Grendler, *Schooling*, 339.

37 Carlo Borromeo, *Constitutioni et Regole della Compagnia et Scuole della Dottrina Christiana* (Milan: Pacifico Pontio, 1585), ff. 30r–31v; in BCBg, 'Cinquecentini 3.3.'

38 Grendler (*Schooling*, 341) cites the *Regola* of 1555 and the *Constitutioni* of 1611 as examples of the prohibition of corporal punishment and the emphasis on making schools joyful. On corporal punishment in early modern humanist classrooms in England, see Rebecca Bushnell, *A Culture of Teaching* (Ithaca, NY: Cornell University Press, 1996), especially chap. 2.

39 Borromeo, *Constitutioni et Regole*, f. 38v and 39r.

40 ACVBg, CAP 872, 'Fundatio,' ff. 3v–6r, for nearly two dozen indulgences. Ibid., f. 1r–v. for the parade; f. 8r for the ceremony. 'Una solenne processione delli maschi habitanti dentro la fortezza, et anche nel borgo Canale, la quale è incominciata a dì ditto dopo le sedici hore in Santa Maria Maggiore et incaminatasi verso Santa Grata, il Salvecchio, Piazza Vecchia, Mercato delle Scarpe et quello del lino, e entrata in duomo per la porta maggiore cantando li figlioli et operarii de dette scuole le littanie Santi, e vi erano l'infrascripte scuole di S. Agata, S. Pancrazio, S. Andrea, S. Michele del Pozzo, S. Lorenzo, S. Erasmo.'

41 Ibid., f. 8r. For example: 'S. Michele al Pozzo Bianco: operarij, n[umero] 8; figlioli, n[umero] 43.' [in the left margin] See appendix 2.

42 ACVBg, CAP 872, 'Fundatio,' f. 4r for 'sorelle'. On the role of gender in medieval Bergamo's MIA confraternity, see Cossar, *Transformation of Laity*, 44–8, 108–11.

43 Balini, 28.

44 ACVBg, CAP 872, 'Fundatio,' ff. 29r–v.

45 ACVBg, CAP 872, 'Fundatio,' f. 26v. For brief references, see Belotti, vol. 5, 87; and vol. 6, 17, 27, 30. See also *Bergamo o sia Notizie Patrie, almanacco scientifico-artistico-letterario per l'anno 1858* (Bergamo: Tip. Pagnoncelli, n.d. [1858]), 82; Giulio Scotti, *Bergamo nel Seicento* (Bergamo: Bolis, 1897), 72; Locatelli (1910), 139; Luigi Volpi, *Tre secoli di cultura bergamasca* (Bergamo: Ediz. Orobiche, 1952), 16.

46 ACVBg, CAP 872, 'Fundatio.' No further information exists about Marc Antonio Lazzaroni, but there is a reference in the depositions of Martino and Gabriele Lazzaroni of 27 Sep. 1550 to their father 'Iohannis de Lazaronibus scolarium rectoris in praesenti urbe Bergomi' in the neighborhood

of S. Pancrazio. See Firpo, *I Processi Inquisitoriali*, 818–19. Note also that in Firpo, *Vittore Soranzo*, 4, the same Giovanni Lazzaroni is identified as 'maestro di grammatica' when on 14 June 1545 he presented an encomium to the city council on behalf of Bartolomeo Pellegrini.

47 See appendix 2 for the names and locations of these institutions.

48 No good study exists of the various seventeenth-century academies in Bergamo, but see Tancredo Torri, *Dalle antiche Accademie all'Ateneo* (Bergamo: Stamperia di Gorle, 1975), chap. 1; and Volpi and Scotti, cited above in 350n45.

49 Balini, 25.

50 ACVBg, CAP 872, 'Fundatio,' esp. Bishop Priuli's 1628 decree, and the *Registro* of S. Agata (1623–88). See also Bishop Gregorio Barbarigo's pastoral visitation to Martinengo of 21 Sep. 1659, in ACVBg, *Visita pastorale*, v. 49, f. 235, and to Fara Gera D'Adda in the same year (ibid., vol. 50, ff. 38v–40r).

51 Jean Delumeau, *Catholicism between Luther and Voltaire: A New View of the Counter-Reformation* (Philadelphia: Westminster Press, 1977).

52 Gerald Strauss, *Luther's House of Learning: Indoctrination of the Young in the German Reformation* (Baltimore: Johns Hopkins University Press, 1978).

53 Toscani, *Scuole e alfabetismo*, 34–37, 269–70.

54 Angelo Roncalli, 'Le origini del Seminario di Bergamo e S. Carlo Borromeo,' *Vita Diocesana* (Bergamo, 1910), 458–95. Thirty years later, Roncalli delivered a more scholarly address on the same topic to an audience at the seminary, entitled 'Gli inizi del Seminario in Bergamo e S. Carlo Borromeo,' subsequently published in *Humiltas: Miscellanea Storica dei Seminari Milanesi* 25 (1938), 988–1014; reprinted in Bergamo in 1939 by SESA, 1–85, which is the edition I cite, and in *Il Colle di S. Giovanni: Omaggio a Papa Giovanni*, ed. Ezio Agazzi, Luigi Pagnoni, and Santo Pesenti (Gorle: SESAAB, 1996–97), vol. 4, 21–44.

Roncalli's principal sources were three, as he explains on 31n3: a faldone in the Seminary archive containing early correspondence, decrees, and information about taxes on behalf of the seminary (Archivio Storico del Seminario Vescovile Giovanni XXIII di Bergamo, Sezione Patrimonio, b. 1, vol. 2, 'Venerando Seminario. Tasse antiche. Principio et incremento del Seminario stesso'); another faldone in the episcopal archive (ACVBg, no. 24, 'Seminario: carte antiche', fasc. A; [previously ACVBg, sala 2, f. 3]); and the apostolic visitation of Carlo Borromeo, preserved in Milan's Biblioteca Ambrosiana, and subsequently edited and published by him in *Gli Atti della Visita Apostolica di San Carlo Borromeo a Bergamo, 1575* (hereafter *AVASC*) 5 vols., ed. Angelo G. Roncalli (Florence: Olschki, 1936–57). My investigation of these primary sources confirms that Roncalli was accurate and thorough in his analysis and transcription of the documents. Belotti and Locatelli mention the seminary only in passing. Other works include: Carlo Ulietti, *Notizie storiche intorno al Seminario di Bergamo* (Bergamo: Tip. Sonzogni, 1831), which is careless and riddled with factual errors; Cesare Patelli, 'Uomini e vicende del Seminario di Bergamo dal 1576 al 1921,' *Studi e Memorie* (Bergamo: Seminario di Bergamo, 1972), 1–117, which relies upon Roncalli for the early decades but provides a useful overview of the seminary's later history; and Luigi Chiodi, 'In uno stabile della vicinia di S. Pancrazio il seminario trovò la prima sistemazione,' *L'Eco di Bergamo* (9 Nov. 1962), 3, which (despite the title) focuses largely on events at the seminary in 1774. *Il Colle di S. Giovanni* features beautiful historic maps, drawings, and photographs, but little text; F. Vistalli, *Il Cardinale Cavagnis* (Bergamo: Istituto Italiano d'Arti Grafiche, 1913), Appendix 1, 'Il Seminario di Bergamo, origini e vicende,' 463–78, plagiarizes huge chunks of Roncalli, Ulietti, and Locatelli.

55 The expression is Roncalli's, 'Gli inizi,' 11.

56 H.J. Schroeder, ed. *Canons and Decrees of the Council of Trent* (St Louis: Herder, 1941), 169.

57 Useful articles on Italian seminaries outside of Bergamo include: Kathleen Comerford, 'Italian Tridentine Diocesan Seminaries: A Historiographical Study,' *Sixteenth Century Journal* 29, no. 4 (Winter 1998): 999–1022, as well as her more recent book *Reforming Priests and Parishes: Tuscan Dioceses in the First Century of Seminary Education* (Leiden and Boston: Brill, 2006); Xenio Toscani, 'Recenti studi sui seminari italiani in età moderna,' *Annali di storia dell'educazione e delle istituzione scolastiche* 7 (2000): 281–307; Thomas Deutscher, 'From Cicero to Tasso: Humanism and the Education of the Novarese Parish Clergy (1565–1663),' *Renaissance Quarterly* 55 (2002): 1005–27; idem, 'Seminaries and the Education of Novarese Parish Priests, 1593–1627,' *Journal of Ecclesiastical History* 32 (1981): 303–19; and idem, 'The Growth of the Secular Clergy and the Development of Educational Institutions in the Diocese of Novara (1563–1772),' *Journal of Ecclesiastical History* 40 (1989): 381–97; Maurilio Guasco, 'La formazione del clero: i seminari,' in *Storia d'Italia, Annali 9: La chiesa ed il potere politico dal medioevo all'età contemporanea,* ed. Giorgio Chittolini and Giovanni Miccoli (Turin: Einaudi, 1986), vol. 9, 631–715; Paolo Preto, 'Il vescovo Gerolamo Vielmi e gli inizi della riforma tridentina a Padova,' *Rivista della Storia della Chiesa in Italia* 20, no. 1 (1966): 18–33; Silvio Tramontin, 'Gli inizi dei due seminari di Venezia,' *Studi veneziani* 7 (1965): 363–77; Rizieri Zanocco, 'Le origini del seminario di Padova,' *Bollettino diocesano* 12 (1927): 349–55.

58 Ragazzoni, in fact, delivered a famous closing speech to the Council of

Trent in December 1563, entitled *Audite hoc, omnes gentes: auribus percipite omnes qui habitatis orbem.* See *Sacrosanctum Concilium Tridentium* (Venice, 1746), 267–74.

59 ACVBg, *ASBE*, 'Synodus Cornelia 1' (8 Aug. 1564), 27; and ACVBg, *Sinodi Diocesi*, faldone 1, vol. 3, 'Ordines ceremoniarum in cathedra ecclesiae Bergomensis,' f. 50r.

60 On Nicolò Azzonica (also Niccolò Assonica), born 1505 and *iuris utriusque doctor*, provost of the cathedral of S. Alessandro since 1525 and vicar to several bishops, see Firpo, *I Processi Inquisitoriali*, 222n48. Azzonica was praised in 1544 as a 'gentiluomo di buona conditione et bene accommodato, et serve senza alcun premio et con qualche discommodo della sua quiete; è poi di buone lettere et di bonissimi costume et persona molto honorata' (ibid.). Fiercely loyal to Soranzo, Azzonica was investigated for heresy after the Bergamo Inquisitor claimed that Azzonica supported Soranzo's view of *sola fide.*

61 On Guarnero, see Pier Maria Soglian, '*Otia* humanistica in Val Calepio,' *La Rivista di Bergamo* 18 (Summer 1999), 56–61.

62 *AVASC*, vol. 1, pt. 1, 281–2.

63 On the Augustinians, see *AVASC*, vol. 1, pt. 1, 285–6, and Roncalli, 'Gli inizi,' 47–8; on the Vallombrosans and on benefices, see Camozzi, *Visite 'ad limina,'* 152n29. Comerford, *Reforming Priests and Parishes,* 135–6 notes that in Tuscany 'even the wealthy regions faced difficulties of funding' because the majority of bequests were traditionally given to monasteries or abbeys, not to bishops or seminaries.

64 *AVASC*, vol. 1, pt. 1, 284, and Roncalli, 'Gli inizi, 38–9.

65 Donato Calvi, *Effemeride*, vol. 3, 130.

66 *AVASC*, vol. 1, pt. 1, 288–9, and Roncalli, 'Gli inizi,' 46, 58–60, listed subjects like 'studiis catechismi, Virgilii, Horatii, et orationis Milonianae,' 'grammaticae praecepta,' and 'rethoricam.'

67 Kathleen Comerford, *Reforming Priests and Parishes,* 133.

68 For the 1575 redaction, see *AVASC*, vol. 1, pt. 1, 290–1, and Roncalli, 'Gli inizi,' 56–8; on student fees, see *AVASC*, vol. 1, pt. 1, 102. For example, Borromeo's visitation in 1575 notes that six students lived at the expense of the seminary, while the other fourteen each paid two sacks of grain, a cask of wine, and eleven or twelve scudi every year *pro victu.*

69 ACVBg, *ASBE*, 'Synodus Cornelia II' (May 1568), 47; cited and transcribed in Roncalli, 'Gli inizi,' 46–7.

70 Vittori, 25. My thanks to Rodolfo Vittori for sharing with me his unpublished research about Manili.

71 ACVBg, *Lettere Pastorali*, vol. 2, f. 56 (3 Jun. 1573).

72 Roncalli, 'Gli inizi,' 49–52, here at 52; *Acta Synodalia Bergomensis Ecclesiae*
   … (Bergamo: Filios Marci Antonii Rubei, 1661): 'In Seminario Bergomi 25
   clerici instituuntur in litteris et moribus vitae clericali decentibus, qui, cum
   quotidie in ecclesia versantur et festis diebus divinis intersunt, ecclesia-
   sticas quoque caeremonias discuntur. Dociliores in Seminario accipiuntur
   judicio et arbitrato regentium et institutorum. Ex hoc Seminario nimirum,
   suggerente Spiritu Sancto, uberes fructus Ecclesia perceptura est. Profi-
   ciunt certe multi et usque proficient, et certa effulget spes eos, non solum
   quales desiderantur evasuros, sed et alios quoque ita instituturos ut brevi
   colendae apud nos Dominciae vinea boni operarii non deficiant.'
73 Roncall, 'Gli inizi,' 53.
74 ACVBg, *Lettere Pastorali*, vol. 2, f. 64 (12 Jul. 1575). 'se vi è qualche figliuolo
   di buona indole, e di buona speranza di imparare lettere, che siano di età
   almeno di 14 anni, che se ne accetteranno nel Seminario.'
75 *AVASC*, vol. 1, pt. 1, 290, and Roncalli, 'Gli inizi,' 58. 'Circa la reforma-
   tione degli abiti et vestimenti i quali sono lontani dalla modestia et
   decentia religiosa.' This letter is anonymous, and undated, but probably
   came from Borromeo's hand-picked choice to run the seminary, Massimo
   Bonello.
76 *AVASC*, vol. 1, pt. 1, 223. 'Il Seminario è senza disciplina, et molto mal
   governato et nelle cose temporali, et spirituali, et è passivo, dandosi i bene-
   ficii, che se gli potrebbono applicare, a servitori del card. Cornaro et del
   vescovo.'
77 See *AVASC*, vol. 1, pt. 1: 102 (*verbali*), 164 (*decreti*), and 290–3 (*regole*) for
   the text of Borromeo's pronouncements; and Roncalli, 'Gli inizi,' 54–71,
   for a general discussion of Borromeo's visit based upon these same
   documents.
78 *AVASC*, vol. 1, pt. 1, 288–9, and Roncalli, 'Gli inizi,' 58–60.
79 Comerford, 137.
80 *AVASC*, vol. 1, pt. 1, 164, and Roncalli, 'Gli inizi,' 61.
81 *AVASC*, vol. 1, pt. 1, 290–3, and Roncalli, 'Gli inizi,' 63–4. 'Neapolitan'
   songs may refer to polyphony, which was sometimes forbidden by the
   Church in an effort to return to chant: *Norton-Grove Encyclopedia of Music*
   (New York: W.W. Norton, 1988), *s.v.* 'Neapolitan' and 'Naples.'
82 Roncalli, 'Gli inizi,' 68. In 1577 Bonello was appointed to supervise Bergamo's School of Christian Doctrine by Bishop Girolamo Ragazzoni, as noted
   above on 150.
83 On Ragazzoni's career, see Tarcisio Bottoni, *Girolamo Ragazzoni, Vescovo di
   Bergamo* (Bergamo: Edizione Corponove, 1994), especially chapters 6 and 7
   on his interaction with the seminary; Lorenzo Dentella, *I Vescovi di Bergamo*

(Bergamo: SESA, 1939), 341–7; Belotti, vol. 4, 144, 182, 266–7. On Ragazzoni's career and correspondence as papal nuncio to France (1583–6),
including transcriptions of hundreds of his letters, see *Girolamo Ragazzoni,
Èvêque de Bergamo, Nonce en France*, ed. Angelo Roncalli (later John XXIII)
(Rome and Paris: Presses de l'Université Grégorienne, 1962).

84 The Jesuits' attempt to enter Bergamo is discussed more fully in chapter 4;
here I describe Bergamo's interaction with the Jesuits only as it pertains to
the seminary.

85 Roncalli, 'Gli inizi,' 76.

86 Ibid., 78.

87 Ibid., 76–7.

88 Ibid., 79–81.

89 Bottani, 57.

90 Camozzi, *Visite 'ad limina,'* 151.

91 *Il Colle di S. Giovanni*, vol. 4, 145.

92 Giovanni da Lezze, *Descrizione di Bergamo e il suo territorio 1596*, ed. Vincenzo Marchetti and Lelio Pagani (Bergamo: Lucchetti, 1988), 168.

93 *Il Colle di S. Giovanni*, vol. 4, 145.

4. *Chiesa*: Schooling with Jesuits and Somaschans

1 Grendler, *Schooling*, 371; John O'Malley, *The First Jesuits* (Cambridge,
MA: Harvard University Press, 1993), 202–8. Across Europe, the Jesuits
had founded approximately 144 schools by 1580, nearly 250 schools by
1600, and more than 800 universities, seminaries, primary, and secondary
schools by 1773.

   For studies of specific Jesuit colleges, see Gian Paolo Brizzi (Parma,
Siena, Modena), Flavio Rurale (Milan), John Patrick Donnelly (Padua)
and Maurizio Sangalli (Padua), as well as Marina Roggero (Parma) and
Gaetano Capasso (Parma). On the Jesuits in Venice, see the many excellent
contributions in *I Gesuiti e Venezia*, ed. Mario Zanardi (Padua: Gregoriana,
1994). For more general studies of Jesuit education in English, see John
Donohue, Allan Farrell, William McGucken, John O'Malley, and Robert
Schwickerath. For explicit comparison of Jesuit and Somaschan efforts at
schooling in the Veneto, see Maurizio Sangalli, *Cultura, Politica, Religone
nella Repubblica di Venezia tra Cinque e Seicento* (Venice: Istituto Veneto di
Scienze, Lettere ed Arte, 1999), 363–85. For Jesuit sources, see the comprehensive *Monumenta Historica Societatis Iesu* (ca 160 volumes as of 2008),
which includes *Monumenta Paedagogica Societatis Iesu* (7 volumes on education, especially the *Ratio Studiorum*).

The historiography of Jesuit education tends to foucs on rapid expansion and pedagogical innovations while glossing over obstacles and difficulties. Two exceptions are Farrell, 98–106, and O'Malley, *The First Jesuits*, 227–32; even here, however, the attention given to 'failures, frustrations, and crises' is overwhelmed by the positive interpretation in the remainder of the work. For a more detailed consideration of difficulties encountered by the Jesuits in sixteenth-century Italy, see Christopher Carlsmith, 'Struggling Toward Success: Opposition to Jesuit Education, 1540–1600,' *History of Education Quarterly*, 42, no. 2 (2002): 215–46. The most relevant comparison to Bergamo's situation is certainly that analysed by John Patrick Donnelly, 'The Jesuit College at Padua: Growth, Suppression, Attempts at Restoration: 1552–1606,' *Archivium Historicum Societatis Iesu* 56 (1982): 45–79.

2   Marc Bloch, *The Historian's Craft*, trans. Peter Putnam (New York: Vintage Books, 1964), 45.

3   On the Humiliati, suppressed on 7 Feb. 1570 by Pius V, see Belotti, vol. 4, 122, citing Calvi, *Effemeride*, vol. 1, 185, and vol. 2, 577. The bishop instead awarded San Bartolomeo to the Dominicans, who have remained there for more than four centuries.

4   For Cornaro's letter, see Archivio Romanum Societatis Iesu (ARSI), *Epp. Ext.*, 11, ff. 217r–218v; published in Camozzi, *Le istituzioni*, vol. 2, 74.

5   BCBg, Arch. Storico del Comune, *Azioni dei Consigli*, v. 34, ff. 158v–159r (14 Aug. 1573).

6   Roncalli, 'Gli inizi,' esp. 74–8; and see chap. 3 above.

7   Bottani, 58.

8   ARSI, *Ven. 1*, f. 118v (18 Nov. 1575), quoted in Sangalli, *Cultura, Politica, Religione*, 223.

9   Roncalli, 'Gli inizi,' 74–5. The house considered was a villa owned by Cardinal Albano, in what is today Via Masone.

10   For Bergamo's initial requests for Gagliardi: ARSI, *Epp. Ext.*, 24, ff. 273r–274v (12 Sep. 1585); ff. 295r–296v (10 May 1586); published in Camozzi, *Le istituzioni*, vol. 2, 82–4. For Jesuit replies: ARSI, Ven. 3, vol. 1, *Epistolae Gen.*, ff. 84r–v (26 Oct. 1585); f. 112v (19 Apr. 1586); these are cited but not explained by Camozzi, *Le istituzioni*, vol. 1, 107n260. For a third request by Bergamo for Gagliardi: ARSI, Ven. 3, vol. 2, *Epistolae Gen.*, ff. 325r–v (31 Mar. 1590); ff. 334r–v (23 Jun. 1590).

11   ARSI, Ital. 160, f. 11r–v, letter on 24 Jan. 1585 from Achille Gagliardi in Milan to Claudio Acquaviva in Rome; and ARSI Ital. 160, f. 139r, letter on 11 Sept. 1585 from Cav. Grumelli in Bergamo to Claudio Acquaviva in Rome, both cited in Sangalli, *Cultura, Politica, Religione*, 223–4. Count Giovan

Girolamo Grumelli graduated in law from Padua in 1554, after which he
carried out numerous diplomatic missions for Venice in the Grison canton
of Switzerland. In contrast to his enthusiastic support of the Jesuits in
1585, thirty-five years earlier Giovanni Antonio Bolis's deposition of 9
Nov. 1550 identified 'il cavaliero Zoan Hieronimo Grumello' as being in
the house of Antonio Benaglio in the village of Boltiere when others were
discussing 'un libro volgare grando come saria uno psalterio'; according to
Bolis, the book spoke badly of popes and cardinals, even naming the pope
as the Antichrist. See Firpo, *I Processi Inquisitoriali*, 817–18.

12 ARSI, Ven. 111, *Fundationes Coll A-B*, ff. 386r–389v; published in Camozzi,
Le istituzioni, vol. 2, 76–80.

13 Camozzi, *Le istituzioni*, vol. 1, 108n261.

14 BCBg, *Azioni*, v. 43, ff. 156v–157r (31 Aug. 1591). 'Mandano parte che siano
eletti cinque idonei et honorati cittadini, li quali habbino a consigliar, trattar, et considerar se è espediente opur no a questa m[agnifi]ca città l'haver
di R.[everendi] Padri Gesuiti; et prender information diligentemente come
siano statti introdotti d[et]ti R.di nelle altre Città di questo Ser[inissi]mo
Dominio, et del tutto ben istrutti et consultati debbano rifferir l'opinione
loro in questo m.co consilio acciò pos[s]a maturamente et prudentemente
deliberar questio negocio come riesca il bon governo di questa Città.'

15 ARSI, Ven. 111, *Fundatio Collegi, A-B*, ff. 384r–385v (11 Jan. 1592); published
in Camozzi, *Le istituzioni*, vol. 2, 81–2.

16 ASV, Senato, 'Lettere dei rettori di Bergamo,' busta 1, n.p. (7 Aug. 1602)
and ibid. (8 Feb. 1603), as cited by Belotti, vol. 5, 4 4.

17 ASV, Senato 'Deliberazioni, Roma ordinaria,' registro 15, ff. 110v–11r (18
Aug. 1606). Maurizio Sangalli argues that after the Interdict many Venetian parents simply sent their children elsewhere, especially to the Jesuit
College of Nobles in Parma. Maurizio Sangalli, 'Università, scuole private,
collegi d'educazione, accademie a Padova tra Cinque e Seicento: alcuni
spunti per una storia'integrata' delle istituzioni scolastiche,' *Annali di storia
dell'educazione* 3 (1996): 93–118.

18 ASV, Senato, 'Deliberazioni, Roma ordinaria,' registro 15, f. 126 (9 Sep.
1606); described in Belotti, vol. 5, 53–4.

19 Felix Gilbert, *The Pope, His Banker, and Venice* (Cambridge, MA: Harvard
University Press, 1980) describes the negotiations and their larger signifi-
cance, as does Pietro Pirri, *L'interdetto di Venezia del 1606 e i Gesuiti* (Rome:
Institutum Historicum S.I., 1959); Belotti, v. 5, 47–9, describes how the
Interdict affected Bergamo. See also the many excellent essays in Zanardi,
I Gesuiti e Venezia, which consider numerous perspectives and related
issues.

20 ASV, Fondo *Consilio dei X,* 'Lettere dei Rettori di Bergamo (1582–1619),' busta 3, f. 206 (27 Jun. 1612).
21 Belotti, vol. 5, 171; Camozzi, *Le istituzioni,* vol. 1, 111.
22 Locatelli (1910), 157 ff.
23 Belotti, vol. 5, 171.
24 Bonometti's will is dated 13 March 1720; the original is in ASBg, *Atti Notarili* di Pietro Secchi, b. 8089 (13 Mar. 1720). For a transcription, see 'Testamento Bonometti' in BCBg, *Miscellanea bergomense ecclesiastica,* ff. 1r–4v [Salone Cassapanca 1 G 2 35 (1)]. A briefer summary of the will also exists in BCBg, AB 398, number 60, f. 1v. The story is related in considerable detail by Locatelli (1910), 157–63.
25 The following manuscripts are all held in the BCBg: Agostino Salvioni, 'Memorie Storiche delle vicende dei Gesuiti in Bergamo,' Salone N. 9 8/10 (6); 'Informazione sull'introduzione dei Gesuiti in Bergamo,' AB 225 (6); 'Memoriale presentato al Ser. Principe perchè non vengono introdotti i PP. Gesuiti in Bergamo,' AB 398, number 53; 'Ducale veneta relativa al memoriale della città di Bergamo all'introduzione dei Gesuiti [1721],' AB 374.
26 Roncalli, 'Gli inizi,' 75.
27 BCBg, Salvioni, 'Memorie Storiche' (dated 1842), ff. 1r–v.
28 BCBg, 'Informazione,' f. 2v. 'Certamente un numero copioso dei Padri Fratelli, Cognati, ed Agnati dei soggetti del corpo di questa religione, specialmente proibiti per lo statuto di Bergamo a votare, e quantunque siasi ballottata la religione, e non personalmente alcuno di Padri, è però innegabile ... che se non fossero stati acciecati i votanti da riguardi del sangue, e del privato interesse, non si sarebbero sovvertite le buone massime di tenere lontana questa religione, come consta dalle parti antiche e recente del Consiglio di Bergamo.' See also Roberto Galati, 'Il patriziato bergamasco alla vigilia di Agnadello,' tesi di laurea, Università di Milano, Facoltà di Lettere e Filosofia, relatore Marino Berengo, 1979, which is briefly summarized in idem, *Archivio Storico Bergamasco* 3 (1982): 251–6.
29 Locatelli (1910), 159.
30 BCBg, 'Memorie Storiche,' f. 2r. 'Tumultuoso assai fu questo comunale Congresso, ed acerbe ne furono le disputazioni.'
31 BCBg, 'Informatione,' f. 2. 'ed ecco il Turbine, che ha distrutta la quiete de' Cittadini divisi in rabbiose fazioni.'
32 ARSI, Ven. 111, *Fundatio Coll. A-B,* ff. 384r–385v; published in Camozzi, *Le istituzioni,* vol. 2, 81–2.
33 Sangalli, *Cultura, Politica, Religione,* 223–7.
34 *Relazioni dei Rettori Veneti, Podestaria e Capitanato di Bergamo XII*; see the reports of Pietro Sanudo (1549), Pietro Barbarigo (1555), and Catarino Zen

(1591) regarding the poverty of Bergamo's countryside; see also ASVe, *Fondo Consilio dei X*, 'Dispacci dei Rettori,' b. 1, f. 209 (1533) and f. 274 (1545).

35 BCBg, *Azioni*, v. 81, f. 225 (28 Feb. 1722).

36 BCBg, 'Informazione,' f. 1r. 'L'introduzione di quel ordine sarebbe troppo pregiudiciale all'economia di questo povero, e ristretto Paese.'

37 Grendler, *Schooling*, 395–6.

38 BCBg, 'Informazione,' f. 1v. 'una montagna di pietra.'

39 Ibid.

40 Ibid., f. 1r. 'In questo tempo sono succeduti varij considerabili legati in pregiudizio delle povere famiglie e Luoghi Pii per il più sostituiti alla med[esim]a religione; sic[c]he se questa non gl' avesse tolsa la mano sarebbero essi stati i beneficati a vantaggio universale della Città, e Territorio, e specialmente de' poveri.'

41 BCBg, 'Memorie Storiche,' f. 3r, referring to the city council's deliberations of 28 Feb. 1723. 'Riflettendo che l'assenso prestato a Reverendi Padri Gesuiti in un precedente Consiglio, si è ricongiuto sempre più pregiudievole a questa nostra Patria, non tanto per le eredità, quanto per le altre notorie conseguenze ... si propone che sia decretata la sospensione di quanto venne stabilito riguardo ai Gesuiti nel Consiglio 28 Febbraio 1723.'

42 BCBg, 'Informazione,' f. 1r. 'Viene accordato anco da' fautori de' medesimi padri che le scuole e collegio sono un forte e totale discapito, poichè nei tempi passati, nei quali venivano governate le scuole da preti secolari il collegio contava sopra cento collegiali per il vantaggio che si aveva di non pagare che scudi 35 o 36 al più, e di presente sono al minor numero di 20 a causa del pesante accrescimento di dozzina ed altre spese che essi padri esigono per la somma di cento o più scudi per cadauno convittore; il che fa conoscere ai parenti che tanto vale il mandarli fuori di paese, e tutto ciò, oltre l'avere dalla Misericordia lo stipendio di scudi mille all'anno, con la casa *gratis*, e tutta sorta d' utensili.' I have not found confirmation of the MIA's payment of 1000 scudi.

43 Paola Valota, 'Il Collegio Mariano di Bergamo nella seconda metà del Settecento,' *Bergomum* 89, no. 2 (1994): 99–221, here at 100.

44 BCBg, 'Memorie Storiche,' f. 5v. 'Il paterno nostro governo intende ovunque egli stesso ad ogni ramo di pubblica istruzione; la provvede di egregi professori, assegna libri di testo, stabilisce opportune discipline, ne prescrive la osservanza e ne invigila l'esequimento.'

45 William A. Christian, Jr, *Local Religion in Sixteenth-Century Spain* (Princeton, NJ: Princeton University Press, 1988) coined the phrase 'local religion' for his studies of Counter-Reformation Spain. In my opinion a similar phenomenon existed in Bergamo.

46 Sangalli, *Cultura, Politica, Religione*, 222–7, tells the story.
47 ARSI, Epp. Ext., 13, ff. 316r–317v (23 Dec. 1577); published in Camozzi, *Le istituzioni*, vol. 2, 144–5.
48 Camozzi, *Le istituzioni*, vol. 2, 145–6. The resolution of the case is unknown to me.
49 For information on the life of Miani, see Carlo Pellegrini, *San Girolamo Miani: Profilo* (Casale Monferrato: Tip. operaia artigiana, 1962); *Storia di Girolamo Miani, vagabondo di Dio*, ed. Lorenzo Netto (Milan: Istituto Propaganda Libreria, 1985); for earlier works, see *I Somaschi*, ed. Luigi Mascilli Migliorini (Rome: Edizioni di Storia e Letteratura, 1992), 9n2. I have not been able to see 'Acta e Processus integratis vitae, et miraculorum Hieronimi Aemiliani patritii veneti orphanorum et pauperum derelictorum Patris et congregationis de somasca fundatoris' (1615) in the Museo Correr of Venice.
50 Turrini, 'La scuola di catechismo,' 309, citing Pio Paschini, *Le Compagnie del Divino Amore*, 75.
51 For more about the history of the orphanages in Bergamo, see Camozzi, *Le istituzioni*, vol. I, 290–8, and vol. 2, 41–7, 244–54; Giuseppe Bonacina, 'L'orfanotrofio della Maddalena di Bergamo e le origini della Compagnia dei Servi dei Poveri,' *Somascha* no. 2/3 (1993): 88–169; Adriano Bernareggi, 'A ricordo della celebrazione del IV centenario di fondazione dell'Orfanatrofio maschile di Bergamo,' *Rivista della Congregazione di Somasca* 10 (1934): 141–59; Marco Tentorio, 'Saggio storico sullo sviluppo dell'ordine Somasco dal 1569 al 1650,' tesi di laurea, Università Cattolica di Milano, Facoltà di Lettere e Filosofia, 2 vols., relatore Giovanni Soranzo, 1941, 60–2, 446–53; Gianfranco Alessandretti, 'Il Fondo degli istituti educativi nel ASBg,' *Archivio Storico Bergamasco* 12 (1987): 125–56; Ettore Sornaga, 'Quattro secoli e mezzo ... le opere di S. Girolamo Miani a Bergamo,' *Atti del Ateneo di Bergamo* 43 (1982–3): 203–38; Alessandro Chiesa, 'Forme di pedagogia degli orfanotrofi Somaschi nel secolo XVI,' tesi di laurea, Università degli Studi di Torino, Facoltà di Lettere e Filosofia, relatore Luigi Pareyson, 1958–9, especially Appendix III, 'Deposizioni di ex-orfani di S. Martino di Bergamo,' 274–7; Ugo Finazzi, 'L'orfanotrofio di S. Martino dalle origine alla soppressione napoleonica,' tesi di laurea, Università Cattolica di Milano, 1969–70. Surprisingly, the 'Vecchio Archivio degli Orfanotrofi di Bergamo' at the BCBg contains little of interest.
52 BMC, Codice Correr 1350/2, ff. 48–9; a transcription appears in Camozzi, *Le istituzioni*, vol. 2, 41–6.
53 On male orphans, see Bonacina, 'L'orfantrofio,' 111, citing ASBg, *Atti Notarili* di Martino Benaglia, b. 3955, 18 Oct. 1535; and on female orphans, Bonacina, 'L'orfanotrofio,' 119–22.

54 ACVBg, *Visite Pastorali*, v. 4, f. 20r (20 Sep. 1536) and f. 28r (1 May 1536), as cited by Bonacina, 'L'orfanotrofio,' 120–2, 125–7, and in a personal communication of 28 April 1996 from Bonacina to the author.

55 On the Somaschans, formally known as the *Chierici Regolari Somaschi* (CRS), see *DIP*, vol. 2, cols. 975–8, and vol. 4, cols. 1108–10; *San Girolamo Miani e Venezia nel V. centenario della nascita: Atti del Convegno, 29–31 gennaio 1987* (Venice: Istituto di recovero e educazione, 1986); Francesco de Vivo, 'I Somaschi,' in *Nuove questioni di storia della pedagogia* (Brescia: La Scuola, 1977), vol. 1, 663–90; Marco Tentorio, 'Somaschi,' in *Ordini e congregazioni religiose*, ed. M. Escobar (Turin, 1951), 609–30; Maurizio Sangalli, *Cultura, Politica, e Religione*, 363–446; and Luigi Mascilli Migliorini, *I Somaschi* (Rome: Edizioni di storia e letteratura, 1992), 9–63. Miani and his followers usually called themselves the 'Company' during the early years of their existence, but in order to avoid confusion I refer to them as 'the Somaschans' throughout this chapter. One of Miani's early followers was Vincenzo Gambarana, who (like Miani) abandoned military life to perform charitable work. After working in Somasca and Como, he settled in Bergamo where he devoted himself to the orphans prior to his death on 27 Jan. 1561. Interestingly, he gave a deposition on 9 Dec. 1550 in which he declared that Soranzo 'not only does not pursue heretics, but he even favours them.' See Firpo, *I Processi Inquisitoriali*, 119n2, 130–4; and idem, *Vittore Soranzo*, 364. Also interesting is the account of Agostino Barili (1505–66), who succeeded Miani as General of the Somaschans in 1537 and later directed the boys' orphanage in Bergamo. Barili also criticized Soranzo (25 Sep. 1550) for excessive leniency toward former prostitutes and for giving prohibited books to the Benedictine nuns in Bergamo. See Firpo, *I Processi Inquisitoriali*, 81–3 for additional biographical information and bibliography on A. Barili.

56 Bonacina, 'L'orfantrofio,' 122–5. See also BCBg, *Stampa della Città di Bergamo, e Reggenza del Pio Luogo degli Orfanelli*, compiled in 1792 to gather the most important documents relating to the Orphanage of S. Martino of Bergamo.

57 Camozzi, *Le istituzioni*, vol. 2, 41–7, 244–54, and 7–9 of *Stampa ... degli Orfanelli* include the documents regarding this quarrel.

58 For orphans' letters, see Chiesa, 'Forme di pedagogia ...,' Appendix 3 (cited above in 360n51).

59 BCBg, *Regole per il pio luogo degli orfani di S. Martino in Bergamo* (Bergamo: Francesco Locatelli, 1776), ch. 3–4, pp. 10–13, 'De Requisiti per l'acettazione degli Orfani, o Dozzinanti.'

60 BCBg, *Regole per il pio luogo degli orfani di S. Martino*, 7. 'ammaestramenti

alla Religione, e all'arti necessari li provede, e tutto impiega per rendere i
loro costumi, e i loro ingegni utili a se stessi, alla Patria, e allo Stato.'

61 'Ordini dei signori protettori [di Ferrara]' (1 Jan. 1563), in *Fonti per la Storia
dei Somaschi* 7 (Rome, 1978), 45. 'Venuto l'orfano in età adulta, si conosca
l'animo et vocatione sua, et secondo il giuditio de protettori, ma massi-
mamente di chi l'ha praticato, si collochi a quella banda ove sarà più in
proposito: o religione, o lettere, o ad essercito honesto, donde possino
sostentar la loro vita.'

62 *Ordini per educare li poveri orfanelli*, 18, cited by Carlo Pellegrini, 'San Girolamo Miani e i Somaschi,' in *Esperienze di pedagogia cristiana nella storia*,
ed. Pietro Braido (Rome: LAS, 1981), vol. 1, 45–74. I cite from p. 21 of an
extract of Pellegrini's article printed separately in Rapallo in 1982, with the
title 'San Girolamo Emiliani, i Somaschi, e la cura degli orfani' (hereafter,
'La cura').

63 Giuseppe Landini, *L'opera sociale di S. Girolamo* (Rapallo, 1937), 25–30, cited
by Chiesa, 135.

64 'Bonacina, 'L'orfanotrofio,' 137–9; Pellegrini, 'La cura,' 11–22. 'Ordini e decreti capitolari dal 1547 al 1568,' in *Fonti per la storia dei Somaschi* 8 (Rome,
1979), 14, as cited by Pellegrini, 'La cura,' 17. ·

65 Bonacina, 'L'orfanotrofio,' 139–41; and in the 1789 reprint of *Regole per il pio
luogo degli Orfani di S. Martino*, chap. 7, 21.

66 Pellegrini, 'La cura,' 20n61, and 22; Bernareggi, 23–4; Bonacina,
'L'orfanotrofio,' 141, for a description of employment contracts between
the orphans of San Martino and a cobbler and a hatmaker in Bergamo
during the 1530s. See also the 'Ordini dei Signori Protettori' of 1563, which
encouraged the Somaschans to hire tailors or other artisans as necessary to
teach the boys.

67 For Miani's 1536 letter: 'Le lettere di S. Girolamo Miani,' in *Fonti per la
storia dei Somaschi*, 3 (Rapallo, 1975), 16. On the 'reader': Bonacina, 'L'orfanotrofio,' 137. On eight-year-old boys: *Vita del clarissimo signor Girolamo
Miani, gentil huomo Venetiano* (anonymous), in BMC, Correr ms. 1350,
ff. 22r–29v; published in *Fonti per la storia dei Somaschi* 1 (Manchester, NH,
1970), 12.

68 *Fonti per la storia dei Somaschi* 4 (Rome, 1978), 16.

69 BCBg, *Regole per il pio luogo degli orfani di S. Martino di Bergamo*, chap. 5,
p 14.

70 Giuseppe Bonacina, 'Note non pubblicate per una storia dei Somaschi,' 12.
In April 1997 Giuseppe Bonacina gave me a copy of a lecture he had delivered recently on the history of the Somaschans. The lecture summarized
his many years of research but contained no documentation.

71 Silvio Tramontin, 'Ordini e Congregazioni Religiosi,' in *Storia della Cultura*

Veneta (Vicenza: Neri Pozza, 1980), vol. 4, part 1, p. 46. On the importance of literacy in Lombardy from the sixteenth to the eighteenth century, see . Xenio Toscani, *Scuole e alfabetismo nello Stato di Milano da Carlo Borromeo alla Rivoluzione* (Milan: La Scuola, 1992); and Carlo Albertini, 'L'alfabetismo a Bergamo e nelle montagne bergamasche all'inizio del Ottocento,' tesi di laurea, Università di Pavia, Facoltà di Storia moderna, relatore Xenio Toscani, 1985–6.

72 Ermenegildo Camozzi, *Cultura e Storia Letteraria a Bergamo nei secoli XV– XVI: Dai Codici Vaticani Latini un Inventario delle Biblioteche Conventuali di Bergamo* (Bergamo: Civica Biblioteca A. Mai, 2004), 133–47.

73 Pellegrini, 'La cura,' 27–8.

74 Bernareggi, 19–20.

75 ASPSGe, B-59, *Acta congregationis*, 36; cited by Chiesa, 153. 'Restò decretato che tutte le opere si visitino due volte l'anno e che li visitatori faccian riflesso ai figlioli di buona indole ed ingegno persuadendo loro di imparare grammatica.'

76 'Ordini generali per le opere,' in *Fonti per la storia dei Somaschi*, 7 (Rome, 1978), 28.

77 On the 1560 declaration: ASPSGe, B-59, *Acta Congregationes*, 36, cited by Chiesa, 153–4.

78 On the 1568 *Regole*, see Marco Tentorio, 'La'Methodus studiorum' dei Somaschi nel 1741,' in *Il Cardinale Tomoloeo Gallio e il suo Collegio, nel quarto centenario della sua fondazione, 1583–1983*, 89–100 (Como: Opera Pia Collegio Gallio, 1983), 91.

79 Tentorio, 'Saggio Storico,' 289n18, citing the 'Decreto che nell'accettazione dei luoghi si osservino inviolabilmente gli infrascritti capitoli' of the Capitolo Generale of 1571, esp. chap. 18, '[C]he li ministri possano insegnare agli orfani a leggere e le buone arti senza mandarli a botteghe.' Also found in ASPSGe, B-59, *Acta Congregationes*, 92.

80 *Delle Constituzioni de RR.PP. Somaschi, libro IV, cap. 20*, n.d., cited by Turrini, 'La scuola,' 310 and 416.

81 BCBg, *Regole per il pio luogo degli orfani di Bergamo* (1789), 22 and 26.

82 Mario Tagliabue, *Seminari Milanesi in terra bergamasca* (Milan: Tip. S. Lega Eucaristica, 1931), 7–33, especially 13; see also Chiesa, 139–40.

83 Chiesa, 144 (he does not cite a specific source for the quotation).

84 Scion of an illustrious family from the area of Pavia, Angiolmarco Gambarana became General of the Somaschan order in 1563.

85 ASPSGe, *Acta congregationis*, B-52, 33. 'un luogo dove ritirarsi potessero i fratelli della Compagnia dei Poveri per attendere allo spirito, alla mortificazione e agli studi sacri.'

86 For the 1548 letter, see Chiesa, 142–3.

87 For the Somaschans' delayed response, Chiesa, 143–4, citing Luigi Valle, *Il Seminario di Pavia dalla dua fondazione all'anno 1902* (Pavia: Artigianelli, 1907), 23. The chronology and order of events here are very similar to the Jesuits' intial foray into teaching for the commune of Messina in the late 1540s.

88 ASPSGe, *Mil. 143*, 'Atto di accettazione, 12 May 1561,' cited by Chiesa, 147.

89 For the petition, Chiesa, 142–3. Gabriele Scotti, 'Contributo alla storia della carità a Milano nel secolo XVI,' tesi di laurea, Università Cattolica di Milano, 2 vols., relatore Luigi Prosdocimi, 1973–4, analyses the few extant primary sources on 513–48.

90 Scotti, 536–8, 542–50, 562.

91 Scotti, 551–67, here at 562, citing Archivio di Stato di Milano, Fondo *Religione*, parte antica, 'Cause Pie,' cart. 514, no. 1–4, dated Jan.-Dec. 1566: 'per mantenere agli studi letterari dieci orfani desiderosi d'intraprendere la vita religiosa'; and 'i più spiritosi e più habili alle lettere che siano tra loro.'

92 *Origini delli orfani di S. Martino* [di Milano], 134, cited by Scotti, 561. 'che oltre le lettere haveranno cura che si mandino alla Dottrina Cristiana.'

93 Scotti, 579. 'per la loro educazione morale e religiosa e per l'struzione nelle lettere confacente alla loro condizione.'

94 BCBg, *Regole per il pio luogo degli orfanelli di Bergamo* (1776). 'Essendosi poi anco fatto ben grande il concorso de' figliuoli alla scuola, fu con parte presa 3 Dicembre 1664 obligato il Maestro ad insegnare al numero di sessanta scolare, e le furono perciò accresciute al salario, che se la dava, altre lire cinquantasei.'

95 Grendler, *Schooling*, 391–7, offers a brief overview of the Somaschans' schools.

96 Bonacina, 'Per una storia dei Somaschi,' 19.

97 Tagliabue, 7–33, describes the seminary in Somasca and in Celana. Except as outlined below, I have found no evidence that the Somaschans were involved with Bergamo's seminary or the MIA's Academy of Clerics.

98 Bonacina, 'Per una storia dei Somaschi,' 19–21. One exception was the college of S. Antonio in Lugano (Switzerland).

99 BCBg, Archivio del Comune, *Azioni del Consiglio*, v. 60, ff. 269r–273v (24 April 1632), here at 269v–270r: 'già che la religione loro ha succhiato (si può quasi dire) il primo latte in questa città, e che il nostro territorio pure ha concesso grato et honorato riposo alle Gloriose ossa del suo Beato fondatore, mostrano ancora grata corrispondenza delli ricevuti favori et offrendosi d'insegnare con pubbliche lettioni, e d'istruire con paterno zelo nella pietà Christiana [f. 270r.] li figli nostri.'

100 BCBg, Archivio del Comune, *Azioni*, v. 60, ff. 210v–211r (5 Dec. 1631):
  'Inteso l'amorevole ricordo dato dall' Illustr[issimo] Sig[nor] Podestà
  d'instituire pubbliche Scuole, dove si legga Grammatica, & Umanità col
  mezzo delli RR. [Reverendissimi] Padri Sommaschini, che pare si siano
  offerti a far quest' opera pia, li Magnif. Sign. Anziani desiderosi non solo
  d'incontrare la soddisfazione di Sua Signoria Illustr., ma d'introdurre
  ancora quelle Scuole per pubblico benefizio, massime in questi tempi, che
  sono morti il più delli Maestri da Scuola.'

101 ASPSGe, Berg. 281–C, *Convenzioni da stabilirsi tra la città e i PP. Somaschi;*
  and again in BCBg, *Azioni*, v. 60, f. 270r (24 Apr. 1632).

  Quella generosa matrona di Sparta, mostrando quattro suoi figli d'ho-
  noratissimi costumi ben creati a quella Jonica donna, che vanamente si
  gloriava di certo suo tessuto come bello, e prezioso, ne volse insegnare
  nessun opera essere più eccelente, quanto, che l'ammaestrare i figli nei
  buoni costumi adornandosi con questi assai meglio la Patria, che con le
  tappezerie [f. 269v.] e riguardevole seppellettile. Onde di lode infinita si
  mostrano degne le VV. [Vostre] SS. [Serenissime] Ill[ustrissi]me et Ill[ust]
  ri col haver incaricato a noi di ritrovar il modo, co'l quale si puossa rendere egualmente instrutta, e nelle buone lettere, e nella pietà Christiana,
  la gioventù della Patria nostra; e doveranno conseguire commendation
  maggiore per haver somministrata la maniera di poter ben vivere, che per
  haver dati l'essere a proprij figlij, perché senza paragone sono molti più
  degni d'honore quelli Padri, che gli hanno procurata buona educatione
  che quelli li quali gli hanno solamente generati.

  In esecutione perciò de gli ordini delle VV. SS. Illustrissimi e molto
  Illustri, reverentemente riferiamo d'esserci ristretti con li Molti Reverendi
  Padri di Somasca, nei quali (non degenerando ponto da loro primi Insti-
  tutori) ritroviamo hereditaria inclinatione di giovar al pubblico nostro, e
  già che la religione loro ha succhiato (si può quasi dire) il primo latte in
  questa città, e che il nostro territorio pure ha concesso grato et honorato
  riposo alle Gloriose ossa del suo Beato fondatore, mostrano ancora grata
  corrispondenza delli ricevuti favori e offrendosi d'insegnare con pubbliche lettioni, e d'istruire con paterno zelo nella pietà Christiana [f. 270r.] li
  figli nostri, non ricercano altra ricompensa, che tenue salario da gl' istetti
  scholari, tale a punto, che basti per somministrare ai Maestri il modo di
  potere con religiosa frugalità vivere. Parendo a noi adonque: honesta
  l'instanza de sudetti Padri, et adattata ai tempi, e bisogni nostri, si hanno
  affatticati per ritrovare luogho atto alla loro habitatione, e tralasciando
  di riferire li trattati, che ne sono riusciti senza effetto per non tediarle, le
  diciamo solamente d'havere operato et in maniera tale, che rimaneranno

patroni della Chiesa e Cura di S. Pancratio, quando dalle VV. SS. Ill.me et molto Ill.ri venga aggradito il trattato nostro. Ma perchè meglio possano maturare le importante deliberationi le rappresentiamo ancora li capitoli particolari, ciò quali pensiamo di poter stabilire d'accordo da noi sin a quest' hora, solamente abbozzato, che sono gli infrascripti:

(1) Prima, Che la Magnifica Città di Bergamo s'adopri, e procuri con ogni più efficace et affetuosa instanza appresso Sua Serenità perchè sia effetuata l'instrumento di permute e renuncia del luogho di S. Pancratio a benef[icenza] delli Magnifici Reverendi Padri di Somasca, conforme all'appuntamento già stabilito.

(2) Che la Città ritrova casa ch'habbia a servire per le schole o a livello perpetuo, o in altro modo, la quale sia non solo capace per le dette schuole, ma ancora alli Padri commoda, e vicina, acciò che del canonico [?] possano a quelle assistere.

(3) Che li Padri siano perpetuamente tenuti ad allevare la gioventù [f. 270v.] di Bergamo et suo Territorio nel timor d'Iddio, insegnarla, e educarla nei buoni costumi, et a ciò fare si obbligaranno nel loro Generale Capitolo a stringendosi ad osservar queste con pubblico giuramento. Et se tralasciaranno mai in qualsivoglia tempo, e per qualsivoglia occasione questo essercitio, debbano esser licentiati dalla Magnifica Città, che non procura la loro introduttione per altro che per l'educatione de' giovani.

(4) Che habbino a leggere Grammatica minore, e maggiore, Humanità, et anco Rhetorica, quando vi sia numero competente di scolari habili et sufficienti.

(5) Che li Deputati che dalla Magnifica Città saranno eletto habbiano la soprain[ten]denza delle scuole, a quali s'aspetti la decisione d'ogni controversia nato per interesse di quelle, da quali ancora insieme coi Padri si doveranno stabilire le capitolari particolari, che s'haveranno di'osservare nel tenere le Scuole, nel leggere le lettioni, et in altre simili occorenze.

(6) Che li Padri non accettino, ne licenziano, alcun scholare senza il consenso e placito delli Illustrissimi Deputati, dovendo prima esser approvati dal P. Prefetto de Studij per habile alle Scuole, e di poi confermato per poliza sottoscritta dalla maggior parte di essi Signori.

(7) Che li Padri all'incontro non sono tenuti ad accettare alle loro scuole alcuno, che non sia decentemente vestito col mantello, e che non sappia almeno [f. 271r.] declinare, coniugare, fare le concordanze, e lattina[re] sopra gli attivi semplici.

(8) Che li Padri possano ricevere dalli scholari quella mercede che da

deputati della città sarà giudiziata convenirsi che doverà esser pa-
gata anticipatamente, o in altro miglior modo, che dai suddetti SS.
Deputati sarà stabiliti, non dovendone però sentire aggravio alcuno
la Città, e li Padri essere sicuri di non venir defraudata della loro
mercede.

(9)   Che se li Padri conseguiranno in qualsivoglia modo assegnamento
certo di scudi duecento all'hora sono tenuti insegnare senza mercede alcuna, e se l'assegnamento sarà maggior del sopradetto, debbano sollevar la Città dal livello, o da qualsivoglia altra spesa che
havesse sopradette per la fondazione, o mantenimento delle scuole,
et essendo ancora di maggior somma siano obligati ad assistere
quelle letioni che più saranno stimati necessarie dalli deputati della
Magnifica Città.

(10)   Che li Padri sono con prima comodità tenuti ad eriger un Collegio
de Nobili affine che in questo possano esser educati figli di buona
indole, di costumi, e di famiglie nobili; qual Collegio governarsi
debba con quei capitoli et ordini che saranno prescritti dalli detti SS.
Deputati alle Scuole.

Et acciò meglio rimangono le VV. SS. Ill.me e molto Ill.ri d'ogni partico-
lare informate, le aggiungiamo di non haver stabilita la Casa nella quale
li haveranno ad' aprire le pubbliche scuole, perche siam ancora perplessi
nell'ellettione di [f. 271v.] quella; tuttavia le assicuriamo che l'affitto e annua ricompensa sarà solamente, e non eccederà scudi quaranta, e sebbene
sappiamo, che non risiede minor generosità che nei loro petti di quella
di Lycurego oratore famoso della Città d' Athene, il quale rinfacciato,
che concedesse troppo grossa mercede alli Maestri di Rethorica, professò
di'esser disposte di donare la metà delle sue richezze a chi volesse affatti-
carsi per rendere migliori li suoi figli; tuttavia non lascieremo di ricordare
che il dispendio della Magnifica Città in riguardo della sublimità del'opera e del benef. che raggionevelmente ne doverà conseguire, è tenue e
debole, del quale ancora sarà del tutto nel corso di breve tempo sollevata,
dovendo in oltre essere molto tenue il salario, del quale habbiamo stimato
bene a sollievo del publico aggravarne li particolari come dal contenuti
de capitoli, chiaramente si vede. Le spese, che si ricercano per la permuta
o rinuncia delle cure saranno fatte dalli Padri, che in questo modo si sono
convenuti nell' Instromento celebrato dal Sig. Cancelliere del Vescovado.
In quanto alla perpetuità delle schuole in oltre a quello che habbiamo
spiegato nel capitolo 3, si doverà procurare, che l'approvatione che ne
concederà il Serenissimo Principe nostro sia con patto espresso della
continuatione [f. 272r.] di quelle, dal tener le quale cessando s'inten-

dano licentiare dalla Città nostra. In oltre, che se sarà consigliato, che si possa ottenere a Roma si potrà esprimere nel'Instromento di permuta, o rinuncia, che vengono fatte con questa intentione, che li Padri siano perpetuamente obbligati a tener le pubbliche schuole, a che mancando s'intendano privi, e deceduti dal luogho di S. Pancrazio. Sebbene, se habbiamo a dirne il nostro senso, teniamo che non debba succeder simil caso, perché l'allenare et insegnare la gioventù è il loro proprio essercitio co'l quale pretendono di mantener e accrescer la loro Religione, come osservano in ogni altra Città, ove si ritrovano. Quest' è quello, che per hora riferire le dobbiamo per iscarico delle commissioni imposteci, e per sentimento nostro, e co'l farle humile riverenza sottoponiamo il nostro parere alla censura della loro infinita prudenza.

Io. Marc Antonio Grumello, così riferisco et giuro.

Io. Guido Benaglio, ' ' ' .

Io. Gio. Fran. Barilli, ' ' ' .

Questa relatione lecta per Mag.cos Dominos. Antianos posita fuit, etc.

Letta la relatione dei SS. Deputati a trattar con li RR.di Padri di Somasca con li capitoli in essa contenuta stimandosi, che tutti si debbano esseguire fuorchè il primo, secondo, et ultimo che restano alterati per li [f. 272v.] motivi fatti da gl' Ill.mi Rettori, ai quali si deve omaggio, e piena reverenza, li M.ci Ill.ri Antiani mandano Parte:

Che la relatione et capitoli hora letti debban esser approvati secondo il primo, secondo et ultimo, assegnandosi delli RR. Padri sud. di Somasca la Casa de Fratelli Passi, heredi del Cav. Giorgio et Alvise Passi appresso il Pozzo Bianco hora tenuta dall Città per alloggio dei Soldati, acciò che in essa tengano le scuole, et facciano le lezioni come in essi capitoli con condicione espressa, che la Città non espenda più di scudi cento all'anno, oltre li 50 assegnati dalla MIA, moderando il capitolo nono in questa maniera:

Che se li Padri conseguiranno assegnamento certo di scudi duecento, debbano sollevar la Città, et la MIA del suddetto livello, o spesa annua, e se conseguiranno assegnamento che sia di scudi trecentocinquanta siano obligati insegnare, e farle scuole senza mercede restando fermo il rimanente del capitolo, che si approvato..

Et perche tutto ciò consegna (?) il desideratio effetto in commesso alli tre Signori Marc'Antonio Grumello Conte Cavaliere, Guido Benaglio Conte Dottore, et Fran. Giov. Barilla, già Deputati a trattar con essi Padri, che debbano a nome della Città stabilire il tratto con firme mutua, e reciproca obligatione, e procurarne [f. 273r] quanto prossima l'effetuatione, intendendosi a loro impartita ogni facoltà necessaria per la dovuta essecutione di quanto è stato espresso di sopra.

I quali tre Signori Deputati habbino a durare in questa carica di mode-
rare le scuole per tre anni continui, i quali finiti uno di loro dovrà esser
confermato et altri duoi eletti da questa M.co Consilio, che successiva-
mente havranno da servire il tempo, e con gl' obblighi come sopra.

Quo pars, auditis partes qua dicta et allegata fuese(?) ex publica
concorsie, ballottata exegit suffragia sexaginta quiinque favorabile, et
quatuordecim contrarie, et sic captos fuit et pubblicata.

In Consilio fuit resto tenoris seguentis, etc:

Ill.mi Rettori

M.ci Deputati del Consilio

102 Ibid., f. 271v (24 Apr. 1632).

103 ASPSGe, Berg. 281–C, *Convenzioni*.

104 Giovanni Luigi Cerchiari, *Orationes* (Bergamo: Antonium Rebeumis, 1645), 1–20.

105 ASPSGe, B-44, *Atti del Capitolo Generale, 1581–1663*, f. 159r; and ASPSGe, Berg. 281–C, *Convenzioni*. See also Tentorio, 'Saggio Storico,' 663–71, and Camozzi, *Le Instituzioni*, vol. 1, 296n2. The Somaschans wished to ensure that the city would pay all expenses associated with their house and that they were not obliged to move out if the number of students fell through no fault of their own. Recognizing that S. Pancrazio might not be avail- able, the Somaschans declared that they would be willing to accept the church of S. Michele (all'Arco? al Pozzo Bianco?) and the benefice previ- ously earmarked for the Jesuits.

106 Camozzi, *Le istituzioni*, vol. 1, 296n2.

107 The ducal letter is reprinted in BCBg, *Stampa della Città di Bergamo*, 12–13.

108 Ghirardelli, 355. Adelasio's personal history, and potential relationship to Philip II, remain unknown to me.

109 BCBg, *Azioni*, v. 60, f. 272v (24 Apr. 1632), and f. 278r–v (22 May 1632). Calvi, *Effemeride* vol. 3, 7 (dated 2 Sept. 1659); for the Somaschan's entry into Bergamo, ibid., vol. 2, 371. On the Passi family house on Via Porta Dipinta, see Maria Mencaroni Zoppetti, 'Echi e Modelli: un omaggio a Bartolomeo Colleoni negli affreschi di casa Passi in Bergamo,' 137–60, in *Bartolomeo Colleoni e il territorio bergamasco*, ed. Lelio Pagani (Bergamo: Edizioni dell' Ateneo, 2000).

110 ASPSGe, B-60, *Riassunto degli Atti del Capitolo Generale, 1603–62*, 'Collegio per Convittori (1633)'; and ibid., B-44, *Atti del Capitolo Generale*, f. 174v (10 May 1635). 'Fu determinato che alla domanda che fanno i Signori di Bergamo ... il Rev. Padre Paolo Carrara acciò vada colà e sul fatto vegga, se sono pronte le comodità e circostanze necessarie a poter erigere senza detrimento della Congregatione il Collegio dei Convittori, e se le condi- tioni ... siano conformi all'Istituto nostro nell'educar convittori.'

111 *Methodus studiorum ad usum Congregationis de Somascha per rei literariae moderatores deputatos exhibita atque anno 1741 Dom. Joannis Baptistae Riva, Praepositi Generalis auctoritate insinuata.* A copy is preserved in AsPSGe as Ms. B-114. The best study of this document is Tentorio's 'La "Methodus Studiorum" dei Somaschi nel 1741,' cited above at 363n78. The Jesuit *Ratio Studiorum*, officially published by Claudio Acquaviva in 1599, described a plan of studies for both lay students and novices. It combined the humanities with philosophy and theology, and became a benchmark for similar works that sought to describe educational ideals and practical methods. See 355–6n1 and Allan Farrell, *The Jesuit Code of Liberal Education: Development and Scope of the Ratio Studiorum* (Milwaukee, 1938); more recently, John Atteberry and John Russell, eds., *Ratio Studiorum: Jesuit Education, 1540–1773* [Exhibition Catalog] (Chestnut Hill, MA.: Boston College, 1999).

112 On grammar instruction in medieval and Renaissance Italy, see Paul Grendler, *Schooling*, 162–202; Robert Black, *Humanism and Education*, 34–172; Paul Gehl, *A Moral Art: Grammar, Society, and Culture in Trecento Florence* (Ithaca, NY: Cornell University Press, 1993), 55–7, 95–102. On the Somaschans' curriculum at the Collegio Gallio in Como, see Tentorio, *Il Cardinale Gallio*.

113 Tentorio, *Il Cardinale Gallio*, 93n16; and also citing the *Bollo di fondazione* (1595), in ASPSGe, *Como Coll. Gallio Co. I*. For more bibliography on Alvarez, see Grendler, *Schooling*, 192n98.

114 BCBg, *Azioni*, v. 60, f. 270v–271r (24 Apr. 1632). 'Che li Padri all'incontro non sono tenuti ad accettare alle loro scuole alcuno, che non sia decentemente vestito col mantello, e che non sappia almeno declinare, coniugare, fare le concordanze, e lattina[re] sopra gli attivi semplici.'

115 Tentorio, *Il Cardinale Gallio*, 95–6.

116 Ibid.

117 Ibid., 97.

118 Marco Tentorio, 'Lo studio del greco nell'ordine somasco nel sec. XVIII,' in *Rivista dell'ordine dei Padri Somaschi* 36 (1961): 24–31.

119 ASPSGe, *Atti del Capitolo Generale*, v. 1, 124, cited by Tentorio, 'Saggio Storico,' 860–1. Pietro Moro completed a grammar for Latin and Greek in 1639 for which all Somaschan colleges and schools were taxed four Milanese scudi.

120 BMC, ms. 3271–25, Paolo Caresana, 'Consigli ad un maestro,' n.d. I cite from a typed transcription of the original, preserved in ASPSGe, 13–15 Ms.

121 Ibid. 'Formare il giuditio di una persona non é altro che darli ... il conos-

cimento del vero' (3); 'la lettura dei libri é la più dolce e la più utile di tutte le occupationil' (10).

122 Ibid., 10–11: 'ben spesso più si approfitta in una hora della conversatione di questi morti maestri, che in molti giorni dalla viva voce dei precettori sopra le cattedre.'

123 BCBg, *Azioni*, v. 61, f. 45r–v (28 Dec. 1632).

124 BCBg, *Azioni*, v. 61, ff. 218r–v (3 Sep. 1633): 'essi Padri Somaschi già impiegati all'essercitio delle scuole con non poco profitto della gioventù.'

125 Camozzi, *Le istituzioni*, vol. 1, 108n261, for the history of this benefice; see also Sangalli, *Cultura politica religione*, 223–7.

126 The petitions, contracts, letters, and other documents are found in BCBg, Archivio del Comune, *Processi*, D427, 'Pro Mag.ca Civitate contra Comunem de Cenate et eius Preposita in Causa Coram in Pleno Collegio,' fasc. A & B, (hereafter 'Causa'). I am grateful to Francesca Giupponi at the BCBg for alerting me to the existence of these documents.

127 BCBg, 'Causa,' fasc. A, Doc. 10 (18 Mar. 1634) and ASPSGe, *Bergamo 281*, 'Lettere ducali per l'unione della cura di Misma ai Somaschi' (8 Mar. 1634), cited by Camozzi, *Le Instituzioni*, vol. 1, 296n2.

128 BCBg, 'Causa,' fasc. A, Doc. 10 (17 Mar. 1634) 'Il qual Reverendo [Trebuchino] rispose che obedisca et che sabato prossimo scriverà al suo Procuratore a Roma che a nome suo debba rimoversi d'ogni contraditione et atto fatto nella medesima materia, senza pretenderne più alcun beneficio come se non fosse mai stato fatto, che il tutto debba restar annullato et cessato, etc.'

129 BCBg, 'Causa,' fasc. A, doc. 4 (15 May 1634). 'Questa gratia perché pretenda di impedire il commun di Cenate, senza alcuna ragione; onde ricorre humilissimo a piedi di V[ost]ra Ser[eni]tà il Nuntio della medesima Città supplicandola che si degni licentiar esso comune da così stravaganti tentativi, qualsicome non apporta alcun pregiudicio ad esso comune, così ridonda ad universal beneficio di tutta la Città, et territorio insieme.' But cf. Camozzi, *Le istituzioni*, vol. I, 261n2, who is dubious that the benefice was ever actually transferred, based upon Ghirardelli (326) who notes that despite the vigorous attempts of Bergamo to transfer the benefice, 'non si fece altro di tal affare.'

130 On the staff: ASPSGe, *Bergamo 281*, n.p. (3 May 1634) and *Bergamo 283*, ca 1635. On classroom texts: ASPSGe, B-44, *Atti del Capitolo Generale*, f. 175r, cited by Tentorio, 'Saggio Storico,' 860–1.

131 Locatelli (1910), 150–1.

132 BCBg, Arch. MIA no. 1096, 'Processi della MIA contro la Città di Bergamo per le scuole Somasche (1643).' (5 Dec. 1639). 'Lunedì, Adì 5 Dec. 1639.

Nel Mag[nifi]co Consiglio del V[enerabile] Consortio della Misericordia
Maggiore di Bergamo è stata presa la parte del tenor che segue essendo
detto M.co Consiglio in legitimo numero congregato, cioè: Considerate
le parti de 19 April, et 12 Agosto 1632 prese in questo Consiglio a favor
de R.R. [Reverendissimi] Padri di Somasca per occasione delle pubbliche
scole, et l'Instrumento de 29 Agosto 1632 rogato dal Lorenzo Ghirardello
Cancelliere della M.ca Città ivi letto; per la quale si è obbligato questo Pio
Luogo di pagar ogni anno alla detta M.ca Città scudi cinquanta per occasione delle dette scole somasche con certe conditioni, come nelle dette
parti si vede, et ricordato che [a] esso pio luogo non viene alcun beneficio
dalle dette scole; anzi che in luogo di mandarli nostri scolari alle dette
scole somasche, come vien supposto nelle sopradette parti, hora si trovano piene le nostre scole di scolari partiti novamente dalle scole Somasche; onde per supplir al bisogno, si è convenuto eligger un terzo Maestro;
et che per le medesime et altre ragioni ivi considerate si deve procurare
dalla Mag.ca Citta la reclamatione et discarico dello obligo. Però si è porto
che sia commesso alli Sig. Deputati alle Nostre scole, che porgano memoriale alla Mag.ca Citta per nome di questo pio luogo per ottener da quella
la relassatione, discarico, e sollievo dalla detta obligatione, con libertà di
fare, dire, et operare quello che stimeranno espediente per conseguire l'effetto di tal sollievo. La quale parte ballottata è stata presa con tutti i voti.'

133 Ibid., ff. 1r–5r. See also ACVBg, *Congregazione religiose – Somaschi, carte
antiche (1579–1851)*, 'Varie relative ai Somaschi' (busta no. 1).

134 BCBg, Arch. MIA no. 1096, f. 17 (24 Sep. 1642). 'Deve perciò ella sapere
che con molto sentimento et poca sodisfattione habbiamo vista ora la
tramuta del Rx.do P[io] P[adre] Piovene, si come pur l'altre seguite tutti
questi anni adietro nella persona de' Padri cambiatici bene spesso in altri
men atti a tal ministero; onde questa nostra Patria ha formato concetto
che la loro Religione si curri poco che le cose del Collegio passino con
buon ordine, et che quel luogo si mantenga in quella riputatione che si
ritrova con danno non solo dei figli della prima Nobilità di Bergamo, ma
con vilipendio ancora de medesimi Padri che vi assistano.'

135 ASPSGe, *Bergamo 287* contains a typed transcription of this letter of 4 January 1645 from Bartolomeo Cerchiari to P. Petrignani, Proc. Gen., Roma,
S. Biagio. The original citation is to Archivio Vaticano [Fondo Somasco?],
pacco 12. 'Scolari non ne habbiamo, convittori solo otto et bisogna che io
mantenga sei bocche de nostri on le provisioni necessari e de vestito et
viatichi; onde lascio pensare a V.P.M.R. [Vostro Padre Molto Reverendo?]
come è posibile vivere.'

136 ACVBg, *Congregazione religiose – Somaschi, carte antiche*, 'Varie relative ai

Somaschi,' f. 5r. 'Che i padri Somaschi nel tempo della bona condotta non
hanno fatto ne continuato a legere ne al presente leggono Rettorica nelle
loro scole pubbliche di Bergamo.'

137 BCBg, Arch. MIA, no. 1096, f. 37 (31 Jan. 1643); f. 1 (26 Feb. 1643); f. 2 (7
Mar. 1643); f. 20 (9 Mar. 1643); ff. 6r–7v (12 Jun. 1643); f. 8 (21 Jul. 1643);
f. 11 (31 Aug. 1643). See also ACVBg, *Congregazione religose – Somaschi*,
ff. 1r–5v.

138 Ibid., f. 13 (20 Mar. 1645), and ff. 14–15 (12 Feb. 1650). I do not know how
the matter of the fifty scudi was eventually resolved. Bergamo's city
council steadfastly refused to go beyond the one-hundred-scudi limit that
it had decided upon a decade earlier. The city council threatened legal
action against the MIA or the Passi family if it had to pay the extra costs,
but there is no record that such legal action ever occurred. Perhaps the
Passi family agreed to a lower rent, or maybe the Somaschans were able
to make up the difference by collecting larger student fees.

139 The reports are in ASPSGe, B-62, 'Stato del Ordine compilato nel 1650';
they appear in Luigi Mascilli Migliorini, *I Somaschi*, and those pertaining to Bergamo are on 147 and 167–8. Many were published in *Somascha*
(1990), no. 2, including that of the Orphanage of S. Martino (94–6) and
the Collegio S. Giuseppe (124–5). The latter report was also published by
Camozzi in *Bergomum* (1981): 295–8.

140 Camozzi, *Le istituzioni*, vol. 1, 297. The single largest contribution came
from alms collected at 'manual' Mass (120 scudi), but boarding students
paid 110 scudi while *scolari forestieri* (external students) paid 80 scudi.
Other income came from the rent of two workshops (6 scudi), a garden
(15 scudi), and the saying of daily masses (38 scudi). The budget does
not include expenses for the boarding students, but the meals for the five
Somaschans plus one lay servant came to 240 scudi per year, in addition
to other miscellaneous expenses (laundry, sacristy, outside guests, maintenance of the house, medicines, etc.)

141 The *Riassunto* of the *Atti del Capitolo Generale* notes that in 1650 the Venetian Houses (*Case Venete*) paid one hundred scudi to the Collegio di S.
Giuseppe, presumably to discharge this debt. ASPSGe, B-60, *Riassunto*,
anno 1650.

142 BCBg, *Azioni*, v. 69, ff. 150v–151v (17 Dec. 1657); reprinted in BCBg, *Stampa della Città di Bergamo*, 16–19, here at p. 17: 'Questo è il stato, nel quale
sono declinate le Scole de' Padri Somaschi destitute de Scolari per non
esservi Maestri abili ad insegnarli, appunto corrispondente alle esclama-
zioni fatte da diversi Cittadini.'

143 Calvi, *Effemeride*, vol. 3, 161–2.

144 Giovanni Alcaini, 'Origini e progressi degli istituti tenuti e diretti dai
Padri Somaschi,' *Somascha*, no. 2/3 (1979): 70–174, especially 78–83.
145 Ghirardelli, 355.

5. *Genitori*: Schooling, Parents, and Tutors

1 For example, Jo Ann Hoeppner Moran's study of education in the diocese
of York, *The Growth of English Schooling, 1340–1548: Learning, Literacy,
and Laicization in Pre-Reformation York Diocese* (Princeton, NJ: Princeton
University Press, 1985) relied upon a careful examination of 15,000 wills.
Nor have I used tax returns and the *catasto*, as Robert Black has done for
Florence: Robert Black, *Education and Society in Florentine Tuscany: Teachers,
Pupils, and Schools, c. 1250–1450* (Boston and Leiden: Brill, 2007).
2 Bergamo lagged well behind Venice, Brescia, and other Italian cities
in printing. Although Luigi Chiodi argues that a liturgical calendar
was printed in Bergamo ca 1520, Giuseppe Nova presents convincing
evidence that Michele Gallo de' Galli introduced rudimentary printing to Bergamo from 1555 to 1569. Vincenzo de Sabbio was hired away
from Brescia by Bergamo's city council in 1577 and promptly printed
the statutes of the College of Physicians. However, the most important
Bergamasque printer was clearly Comino Ventura, who printed three
hundred volumes over thirty-eight years (1579–1617), including some
with Hebrew characters; he was declared to be the city's 'official printer'
(*urbis impressor*) and granted honorary citizenship. The most recent study
is Gianmaria Savoldelli, *Appunti per una storia della stampa a Bergamo*
(Bergamo: Poligrafici Artigiani Bergamaschi [PAB], 2006; he is currently
preparing a study of the more than 500 editions of Comino Ventura in the
period from 1570 to 1617. See Luigi Chiodi, 'I primi passi della stampa a
Bergamo,' *L'Eco di Bergamo* (17 Aug. 1976); Giuseppe Nova, *Stampatori,
librai, ed editori bresciani in Italia nel Cinquecento* (Brescia: Fondazione civili-
tà Bresciana, 2000), 82–6; see also Gianni Barachetti and Carmen Palamini,
'La Stampa a Bergamo nel Cinquecento,' *Bergomum* 84, no. 4 (1989): 1–147;
Luigi Pelandi, 'Stampa e stampatori bergamaschi' *Atti dell'Ateneo di Bergamo* 29 (1955–6): 319–69; and Belotti, vol. 4, 230–1. On the stereotype of
Bergamo's cultural illiteracy, see note 1 in the introduction.
3 ASBg, *Atti Notarili* di Giacomo Solari, b. 2344, f. 184v (19 Mar. 1538).
4 Massimo Firpo takes a different view, crediting Soranzo as the inspiration for the Caspi Academy in 1547 and linking its closure in 1557 to the
reopening of Soranzo's second trial. Firpo is probably right that Soranzo
was very much involved with the founding of the academy, but I maintain that the subsequent administration of the academy was handled

largely by the fathers (who were, admittedly, often close friends of the bishop). For example, there are no references to the Caspi Academy in Soranzo's pastoral visitations or pastoral letters. Firpo provides precious information about the identity of the academy fathers, for which I am grateful. See Firpo, *Vittore Soranzo*, 385–8.

5 Rebecca Bushnell, *A Culture of Teaching* (Ithaca, NY: Cornell University Press, 1996), 40–3.

6 Barnaba Vaerini, *Scrittori di Bergamo vescovi e cardinali* (Bergamo: Tipografia Pagnoncelli, 1874), 86; Giuseppe Locatelli, 'L'istruzione a Bergamo e la Misericordia Maggiore,' *Bergomum* 4, no. 4 (1910): 128–33. Works by B. Belotti, G. Scotti, and T. Torri offer nothing new. My preliminary analysis of this topic appeared in Christopher Carlsmith, 'Una scuola dei putti: L'Accademia dei Caspi a Bergamo' *Atti del Ateneo di Scienze, Lettere, ed Arti di Bergamo* 61 (1997–8): 291–302.

7 Firpo, *Vittore Soranzo*, 385–8.

8 ACVBg, Mensa Vescovile 68/1, '1547 e seguenti, Academia dei [Caspi]', ff. 1–76, hereafter 'MV.' Note that this *faldone* has subsequently been renamed 'Archivio Mensa Vescovile, *Amministrazione*, 22/1 (1547–1557).' I am grateful to the former archivist, Vincenzo Marchetti, for his assistance in locating and studying these documents. Notarial cartularies relative to the Caspi Academy are cited individually below. The BCBg holds one archive with related material: Archivio Silvestri, *Carte Stella-Chizola*, Scat. 40, no. 75 (prev. no. 92) (2 June 1548). On the latter, see Firpo, *Vittore Soranzo*, 385–6; Giuseppe Bonelli, 'Un archivio privato del Cinquecento: Le carte Stella,' *Archivio Storico Lombardo* 16 (1907), 3–57; and Irma Gipponi, 'Momenti di storia religiosa e culturale del Cinquecento nell'Archivio Stella,' *Archivio Storico Bergamasco* 4 (1984): 259–64, esp. 261. Calvi, *Effemeride* v. 1, 499, briefly describes the founding meeting of the Caspi Academy on 27 April 1547.

9 ACVBg, MV, f. 6v (15 Mar. 1547).

10 In addition to directing his own school, Chizola also worked closely with Girolamo Miani to found an orphanage in 1532; he cooperated with Angela Merici to found the Brescian Hospital for Incurables ca 1535; he served on a city council subcommittee in 1545 and again in 1554 to identify a suitable humanities teacher for the commune of Brescia; and in 1548 he founded an academy of agronomy in the town of Rezzato. See *Storia di Brescia*, ed. Giovanni Treccani degli Alfieri (Brescia: Fondazione Morcelli, 1961), vol 2, 511; vol 3, 307; and ASBs, Archivio Storico del Comune, 'Provvisioni' no. 538, ff. 28v–29r (18 Apr. 1545) and ibid., no. 542, f. 144r (9 Jun. 1554). Curiously, Chizola does not appear in Paolo Guerrini's article on Brescian schoolmasters.

11 ACVBg, MV, ff. 6r–v (15 Mar. 1547). 'Havemo eletto una abitatione, non tanto lontana dalla Citade che gli Padri quali hanno gli suoi figliuoli nella accademia non gli possino spesso visitare, ma nanco [neanche] tanto vicina che le madri et le nutrici vi possino andare così facilmente ... Questo [parental visits] giova più che tutte le botte, che gli possono dare gli maestri. È anche necessario il visitargli per intendere il profitto [che] fanno nelle lettere et fargli interrogare in sua presentia; perchè se li figlioli sanno dovere essere interrogati in presenza de' loro padri fanno ogni cosa, per non restare confusi, ed anche i maestri sapendo di dovere spesso rendere conto, gli mettono maggiore diligenza. Però [Perciò] io non trovo cosa che più gli giovi, che l'essere spesso visitati dalli padri.'

12 Ibid., ff. 4r–5v (15 Apr. 1547).

13 BCBg, Archivio Silvestri, *Carte Stella-Chizola*, Scat. 40, no. 75 (prev. no. 92) (2 June 1548). For example, a letter to the Reverend Bartolomeo Stella in Rome, dated 2 June 1548, is nearly identical to the letters from Chizola to Vittore Soranzo in Bergamo. For additional analysis of this letter see Firpo, *Vittore Soranzo*, 385.

14 ACVBg, MV, f. 6v (15 Mar. 1547). 'Havemmo bandito il schaldaletto, et questa cosa nel principio fece quasi mutinare le madri, pure avendo veduto come per questo modo di vivere sonno devenuti gli suoi figliuoli belli coloriti et grassi et che non si amalano mai, se sono agetate [sic].'

15 ACVBg, MV, ff. 2r–v (22 Apr. 1547).

16 Locatelli (1910), 132, maintains archaic spelling of the names; Firpo, *Vittore Soranzo*, 386–7, offers the same list with modern spelling, as do I.

17 On Marcantonio Bolis, see Firpo, *I Processi Inquisitoriali*, 205n29, which includes an accusation in 1536 against Bolis for keeping Maria, the wife of notary Giovanni Francesco Verdobbio, as his concubine; it also includes a clamorous case of assault in 1541 against two other canons.

18 On Bartolomeo Barili, see Firpo, *Vittore Soranzo*, 386, 400.

19 On Pietro Passi, see Firpo, *I Processi Inquisitoriali*, 814n174, and Calvi, *Effemeride*, v. 2, 603–4; the latter praised Passi's generosity and open-door policy toward the poor and the miserable of Bergamo. On the composition of the commission, see Firpo, *I Processi Inquisitoriali*, 206n32.

20 On Pietro Spino, see Firpo, *I Processi Inquisitoriali*, 768n7, containing much more bibliography.

21 On Tassi, see Firpo, *I Processi Inquisitoriali*, 810n156 and the deposition against Tassi on 810–14; on Allegri, idem, 676n43 for more bibliography.

22 ASBg, *Atti Notarili* di Giov. Maria di Rota, b. 2259, 'Conductio Mag[ist]ri Andrea Cato primi praeceptoris Academie quibus in domo Casporum' (4 May 1547). See also ASBg, *Atti Notarili* di Ottolino Rota, b. 2953 (13 May

1548) re partial payment of Cato's salary. On Cato, in addition to chapter 1, see Locatelli (1910), 93.

23 ASBg, *Atti Notarili* di Giov. Maria di Rota, b. 2259, 'Conductio' (4 May 1547). 'Item quod predictus Mag.r Andreas teneat et debeat vacare ab omnibus curis tam familiaribus suis particularibus quod mercantilibus seu alijo quibuscumque sed solum diligente et assidue habere curam ex officium studendi, instruendi, & docendi pueros eidem designandos per dictum temporem annorum.'

24 Cato's contribution appears in vol. 1, 353–6 of *Dell'historia quadripartita*; on the Capuchin historian Celestino da Bergamo (descended from the Martinengo Colleoni family), see the entry of Marco Palma *s.v.* 'Celestino da Bergamo' in *DBI* vol. 23, 415–16.

25 ACVBg, MV, ff. 11r–v (23 Mar. 1547). See Locatelli (1910), 133, for the text of the letter.

26 ACVBg, MV, ff. 12r–13v (3 Jun. 1547).

27 On Pontano's biography, see *Enciclopedia Italiana* (Rome, 1949), v. 27, 850–3; and Carol Kidwell, *Pontano: poet and prime minister* (London: Duckworth, 1991); on Pontano as a historian, Francesco Senatore, 'Pontano storico,' *Studi Storici* 39, no. 1 (1998): 291–6; on Pontano's political treatises, Claudio Finzi, *Re, baroni, popolo: la politica di Giovanni Pontano* (Rimini: Il Cerchio Iniziative Editoriali, 2004); for broader context, see Jerry Bentley, *Politics and Culture in Renaissance Naples* (Princeton, NJ: Princeton University Press, 1987), esp. 127–8. Pontano's works (*Pontani Opera*) were published in five volumes in Venice between 1505 and 1518; numerous editions of specific works have been published recently, often with facing translations and critical commentary.

28 ACVBg, MV, f. 18r–v (n.d.).

29 ACVBg, MV, f. 16r (7 Sep. 1547).

30 ACVBg, MV, ff. 14r–15v (7 Sep. 1547).

31 ACVBg, MV, f. 20r (n.d.).

32 Luigi Pelandi graciously shared with me an undated (18th century?) map from his private collection (Raccolta Pelandi-Bergamo) that identifies a house at the corner of Via Masone and Via Matris Domini as *olim Casa de Caspii*. Today it houses the offices of the postal service. My thanks to Paolo Oskar for identifying the existence of this map and providing a digitized image of it. On Pelandi's map, the house also bears the title 'Ospizio dei Poveri di S. Martino'; its use as an orphanage in 1614 is confirmed by Ermenegildo Camozzi, *Cultura e Storia*, 133n2, and by the 1680 map of Stefano Scolari (BCBg, *Bergamo Illustrata*, Fald. 1, c. 19, 20; reproduced in BCBg, *Antiche Stampe di Bergamo*, n.p.) which indicates this same house as

'San Martino mendicanti.' See also Firpo, *I Processi Inquisitoriali*, 641, for an anonymous denunciation against Andrea Cato, 'el mastro de la Achademia di Prato' (the teacher at the Academy in the meadow [of Sant'Alessandro]); the Caspi Academy was just on the edge of the meadow that hosted the annual Fair of Sant'Alessandro.

On the initial contract for the Caspi house, see ACVBg, MV, ff. 8r–v (24 May 1547). Renewals of the housing contract occurred on 24 Nov. 1549 (ff. 24r–v), 20 July 1553 (ff. 35r–v), and 26 June 1557 (ff. 45r–v). A final accounting of the academy's debts and credits on 2 Sept. 1557 (f. 68r) does not mention Colleoni or the rent in either category. For sample inventories, see ACVBg, MV, ff. 50r–51r (n.d.), ff. 54r–55r (26 Sept. 1549), f. 57r (13 Feb. 1550), ff. 62r–v (30 Aug. 1556), f. 64r (12 Nov. 1556), and ff. 64r–65r (20 May 1557).

33 ACVBg, MV, ff. 6r–7r (15 Mar. 1547).
34 ACVBg, MV, f. 39r–v (25 May 1555); see also the employment contracts cited below.
35 ACVBg, MV, f. 41r (n.d.). 'Un huomo ... greve d'età, dotto nelle lettere latine et greche, et ch'havesse un puro et candido stile così nel nostro volgare come ancora nel Latino; di vita integra, et christiana, al quale esseno darebbero volentieri il carico d'una accademia così.'
36 ACVBg, MV, f. 20r (n.d.).
37 ASBg, *Atti Notarili* di Ottolino f.q. Giovanni Maria Rota, b. 2953 (13 May 1548); ibid. (15 May 1548).
38 BCBg, Archivio del Comune, *Azioni*, v. 24, ff. 148r–149r (7 Feb. 1551), and f. 157v (6 Mar. 1551).
39 Quoted in Firpo, *I Processi Inquisitoriali* 641–2. Firpo (641n6) identifies don Battista da Ghisalba as probably the same man who was processed for heresy in 1557 after a suspicious manuscript and a booklet entitled *Thesauro de la sapientia evangelica* (Thesaurus of Evangelical Wisdom) were found among his possessions in his house in San Pancrazio on 22 Dec. 1556. I found no mention of Ghisalba in the records of the Caspi Academy. Firpo (641n7) further identifies 'fra Maifredo' as Manfredo Pasti, a parish priest of Santa Maria a Vilminore; I read the name as Manfredo Bescio but I have been unable to find additional information about him.
40 Firpo, *I Processi Inquisitoriali*, 641n4.
41 ACVBg, MV, ff. 62r–v (30 Aug. 1556), and f. 68r (2 Sept. 1557).
42 For the bishop's opinion, see ASBg, *Atti Notarili* di Ottolino Rota, b. 2953 (15 May 1548), 'Conductio magistri Angeli Caliani pro magistro Academie casporum.' For the licence, see ACVBg, MV, ff. 74r–v (27 Nov. 1592). A 1592 letter from the mayor of Lenna (Val Brembana), Rufino Rufinoni, to Valen-

tino Calvi in Bergamo asked that the bishop grant a teaching licence to one Giovanni Antonio Bertramelli so that he could open a school for reading, writing, and mathematics. Bertramelli had previously taught elsewhere in the Val Brembana, and in the neighbouring valley of Valsassina; the licence was soon granted on the condition that Bertramelli attend confession and communion in Lenna within two months.

43 ASBg, *Atti Notarili* di Ottolino Rota, b. 2953 (15 May 1548).

44 ACVBg, MV, ff. 33r–34r (6 Jun. 1552) is the employment contract; f. 36r (21 Aug. 1554) is the agreement to admit his own children.

45 On Julio Terzi [Giulio da Terzo], see Firpo, *I Processi Inquisitoriali*, 985–6 for Brugnatelli's account of 1557, and 985n109 for biographical information and further archival citations.

46 Giovanni Maria Rota was a powerful and well-respected lawyer, city council member, and secretary of the commune, as well as notary for the cathedral chapter of S. Vincenzo and a member of the Inquisitorial commissions of Bergamo. In the documents of the Caspi Academy he is described as a 'very shrewd and diligent' man; see Firpo, *I Processi Inquisitoriali*, 777n7.

47 ACVBg, MV, ff. 39r–v (25 May 1555). 'Et all'incontro noi si siamo mossi alle persuasioni di esso messer Gio. Maria di darvi per vostra provisione scudi cento all'anno, summa in vero di gran lunga maggiore di quella [che] habbiamo sin hora ad alcun altro nostro Maestro data, et oltre ciò haverete le spese di boccha et vi sarà provisto al letto per il vostro dormire.'

48 ACVBg, MV, ff. 23r–v (13 Jun. 1548).

49 ACVBg, MV, f. 6r (15 Mar. 1547), published in Locatelli, 128–9: 'Ci sono due maestri, il primo è di più dotti et acostumati che abbiamo potuto avere … Il secondo è suo coadiutore et repetitore. Non si può fare con mancho di due cossi per l'insegnare come ancho per il governo de' putti, perchè non si lasciano mai andare a solazo, nè in altro luogo senza uno de' maestri, et havendone uno solo non potrebbe essergli sempre.'

50 It is probably not a coincidence that Andrea Cato was paid 99 and 83 lire respectively in 1556 and 1557. Chizola's suggestion re. salary is found in his second letter to the bishop, in ACVBg, MV, f. 4r (15 Apr. 1547).

51 ACVBg, MV, ff. 37r–38v (1 Nov. 1554). 'Non sieda nel animo nostro alcuna fatta presuntuoso di me, ch'io habbi irragionevolmente deviato il secondo nostro maestro del Accademia, il che non farei, sì per non parere ingratto a quel honorato luogo, dal quale ricevei tanto utile, sì anche perché non sono di tal natura ch'io volessi l'util privato con il danno publico, il che sarà irragionevole e chiunche lo facesse farà indegno d'esser chiamato homo civil et discreto.'

52 On the investigation of Bartolomeo Zanchi, see Firpo, *Vittore Soranzo*,

387–8, and idem, *I Processi Inquisitoriali*, 993; on his position in the Caspi Academy, see ACVBg, MV 68/1; on Battista da Ghisalba, see Firpo, *I Processi Inquisitoriali*, 642n6 and 993.

53 ACVBg, MV, f. 31r (ca Aug. 1550) records bimonthly payment records in his hand for 1549 and 1550. A six-page description of his last actions and testamentary wishes is found on ff. 26r–30r (25 Jul. 1550).

54 ACVBg, MV, f. 10r (4 Sep. 1547).

55 ASBg, *Atti Notarili* di Ottolino Rota, b. 2953 (13 Jul. 1548). Note the irony of Gratarolo's subsequent flight to Switzerland on charges of heresy.

56 On Antonio Pighetti, see Firpo, *I Processi Inquisitoriali*, 380n43.

57 ACVBg, MV, f. 6r (15 Mar. 1547). 'Gli è uno servitore quale è il maestro di casa et dispensatore, et ha la cura di provvedere al vivere di tutta la famiglia, perchè non si v[u]ole che li maestri habbiano cura alchuna in questa parte per non distraherli dal suo esercitio.'

58 ASBg, *Atti Notarili* di Lattanzio Maffei, b. 2747, 12 June 1547. The reference to the horsemaster is in ASBg, *Atti Notarili* di Ottolino Rota, b. 2953, 15 May 1548.

59 ACVBg, MV, f. 47r (n.d.). Student names include: Redopho, Battista Boselli, MarcAntonio Allegri, Giorgio Passi, Martino Antonio, Camillo Passi, Andrea da Terzo [Terzi], Ventura Barili, Piligrino Spino, Cornellio della Valle, Nicolaus Bongo, Giovan Piero Mapheo [Maffei], Leonardo Mapheo, Carlo Boselli, Zoan Jacum del Follo, Zoan Domenec Cornello [Tassi, cavaliere del Cornello], [?] Poncini, and Silvio(a?) Cato. Of the nineteen student names, fourteen (73 per cent) correspond with the surnames of the founding fathers.

60 Ibid. The books are listed next to each boy's name.

61 Guarino and his pedagogical accomplishments have been studied extensively. See Grendler, *Schooling*, 167–9, for a brief overview of Guarino's *Regulae*; and Black, *Humanism and Education*, 124–9, for a more technical discussion. See also Remigio Sabbadini, *La scuola e gli studi di Guarino Garini Veronese* (Catania: F. Galati, 1896); idem, *Guariniana. La scuola e gli studi di Guarino Veronese*, ed. Mario Sancipriano (Turin: Bottega d'Erasmo, 1964), 38–58; Eugenio Garin, *Ritratti di umanisti* (Florence: Sansoni, 1967), 69–106; William H. Woodward, *Studies in Education during the Age of the Renaissance* (Cambridge: Cambridge University Press, 1906; rpt. New York: Russell & Russell, 1965).

62 Grendler, *Schooling*, 162–202. See also the numerous works of Keith Percival. For a definition of 'Donato,' see Carlo Battisti and Giovanni Alessio, *Dizionario etimologico italiano*, 5 vols. (Florence: Barbera, 1951), vol. 2, 1380; and *Grande dizionario della lingua italiana* (Turin: UTET, 1961–86), vol. 4, 943.

63 Black, *Humanism and Education*, 55–69.
64 Grendler, *Schooling*, 117–19. See also John McManamon, *Pierpaolo Vergerio the Elder: the Humanist as Orator*, Medieval and Renaissance Texts and Studies, 163 (Binghamton: MRTS, 1996).
65 In broad outline, these statistics about textbooks agree with those presented by Grendler, *Schooling*, and Vittorio Baldo, *Alunni, maestri e scuole in Venezia alla fine del xvi secolo* (Como: New Press, 1977).
66 ACVBg, MV, f. 64r–65r (12 Nov. 1556). The list included wooden furniture and iron kitchen tools. The goods were transferred 'nella nova Accademia alla porta de Santo Antonio adí 12 Novembre 1556' – perhaps to the MIA's Academy of Clerics, or perhaps to the anonymous successor of the Caspi Academy. The Porta Sant'Antonio is located not far to the southeast of the Caspi Academy, and was probably the closest gate to exit the city from the *domus Casporum*.
67 ACVBg, MV, ff. 64r–65r (20 May 1557), 'Inventario delle robbe vecchie si trovano in casa adì 20 maggio 1557,' which came to a paltry total of only ninety-eight lire. See also f. 68r (2 Sep. 1557), 'Credito della Accademia,' which listed a credit of 405 lire (furniture, outstanding payments, tuition), versus a debt of 336 lire (rent, salary of teachers and staff, flour, firewood, and laundry). The balance of sixty-nine lire was to be divided up equally among all of the academy parents. This certainly suggests that the school continued to function through the spring or summer of 1557.
68 ACVBg, MV, f. 46r (26 May 1558).
69 ASBg, *Atti Notarili* di Ottolino Rota, b. 2953 (31 Oct. 1558).
70 Firpo, *Vittore Soranzo*, 387.
71 Firpo, *I Processi Inquisitoriali*, 985.
72 ASBg, *Atti Notarili* di Alessandro Allegri, b. 1506 (1 Jul. 1559), 'Pro praeceptore Academie Bergomi.' My thanks to Marino Paganini of Bergamo, who generously shared with me his transcription of these documents.
73 ASBg, *Atti Notarili* di Alessandro Allegri, b. 1508, ff. 59r–v (6 Feb. 1566). 'In Christi nomine, amen. Neminem latet eos cives qui liberos suos in Academia, quae in domo Casporum exercetur, erudiendos pro tempore tenuerunt, omnem semper diligentiam adhibuisse ut praeceptorem haberent a quo filii bonis literis et moribus ornarentur, non ignorantes id potissimum parentibus imputari, si neglecta educatione adolescentes in vitia prolabuntur; parentes vero ipsos ullum officium erga filios exercere posse paterna pietate dignius, aut quicquam illis vel preciosius vel conducibilius relinquere quam si curaverint eos christiane institui et eis virtutibus exornari quae amitti non possunt.'
74 ASBg, *Atti Notarili* di Lattanzio Maffei, b. 2747 (20 Mar. 1547). Maffei refers

to the original contract, which should be in *Atti Notarili* di Jo. Angelo d. Bartolomeo Finardi, b. 1202, fald. 5 (4 Mar. 1535), but it is not there.

75 BCBg, *Estimi Veneti* no. 149, vicinia di S. Agata, f. 196 (1526). 'Item ha uno magistro per suoi fioli salariato.' My thanks to Gian Mario Petrò of Bergamo, who in May 1998 generously shared with me this citation and those that follow in this paragraph.

76 BCBg, *Estimi Veneti* no. 167, vicinia di S. Giovanni dell'Ospedale, f. 196 (1525).

77. ASBg, *Atti Notarili* di Giovanni Battista Donaselli, b. 933 (18 Sep. 1508); ASBg, *Atti Notarili* di Antonio Spini, b. 970, f. 274v (21 May 1524); ASBg, *Atti Notarili* di Bernardino Barili, b. 932 (21 Apr. 1545).

78 ASBg, *Atti Notarili* di Agostino Scarpa, busta 1090 (a. 1518–24).

79 Ibid., b. 1091 (20 Aug. 1533).

80 BCBg, Arch. MIA no. 1447, *Scritture/Suppliche*, f. 239r (ca 1590), and f. 443r (3 Jul. 1592).

81 For example, Andrea q. Gentile de Averara *rector scolarum*, in ASBg, *Atti Notarili* di Bernardino Barili, b. 931 (2 Jan. 1507); Domenico f. di Franceschino Barili *professor in artium humanitatis*, in ASBg, *Atti Notarili* di Fioravante Suardi, b. 549, f. 234v (4 Mar. 1484); Giuseppe di Bernardo Bononomine of Lecco *grammatice professor*, in ASBg, *Atti Notarili* di Daniele Terzi, b. 2553, f. 61 (1 Sept. 1565); Antonio q. Giovanni Deleidi of Cenate *gramatice doctore* and *Humanitatis professor*, in ASBg, *Atti Notarili* di Bartolomeo Facheris, b. 2880, no. 191 (8 Dec. 1569), and in ASBg, *Atti Notarili* di Gabriele Lazzaroni, b. 3715, no. 362 (8 Dec. 1581), and his testament in ASBg, *Atti Notarili* di Giuseppe Bresciani, b. 2983 (23 Sept. 1604). Antonio Deleidi may have been related to P[ietro?] Deleidi, identified as *maestro* to ten students in a private academy in the neighbourhood of Borgo Canale; see ACVBg, Archivio Capitolare, CAP 872, 'Fundatio...' (16 Aug. 1609).

82 For Fogaccia, see Boroni, 94n105, and ASBg, *Atti Notarili* di Giovanni Fogaccia, no. 308 (anni 1478–1511). Marsilio fu Gio. Zanchi was a notary active in Bergamo from 1500 to 1556 (see ASBg, *Atti Notarili*, b. 1144–1152); for this reference see BCBg, Arch. MIA no. 1868, 'Libro dei conti della famiglia Balanza' (1506–38), n.p. The inventory of the Arch. MIA lists Marsilio q. Gio Zanchi as 'notaio e insegnante.' My thanks to Maria Mencaroni Zoppetti for this reference.

83 For de Mauris's testament, which includes the inventory of his library, see ASBg, *Atti Notarili di Gerolamo Cologno*, b. 1914 (anni 1539–49), 28 May 1543; incisive analysis is found in Rodolfo Vittori, 'Le biblioteche di due maestri bergamaschi del Cinquecento,' *Bergomum* 96, no. 2 (2001): 23–44, on which I rely here. To the best of my knowledge, no copies of these

books with de Mauris's signature or nameplate are preserved in the libraries and archives of Bergamo.
84 Vittori, 27n7, citing Angelo Turchini and Ugo Rozzo.

6. *Fuori le mura*: Schooling beyond Bergamo

1 Leandro Alberti, *Descrittione di tutta l'Italia* (Venice: 1553), repr. Bergamo:
   Leading Edizioni, 2003, ed. Adriano Agnati, at 410v.: 'Il popolo di questa
   città [è] molto civile, & rozzo di parlare, ma d'ingegno molto sottile, & di-
   sposto tanto alle lettere quanto alla mercatantie [*sic*]. Talmente sono I Bergamaschi disposti alle lettere che non hanno bisogno di Medici stranieri,
   nè di Dottori di Legge, nè di Procuratori, nè di Notari, e meno di Maestri
   di Grammatica, conciossiache in essa città abbondantemente vi si trovano
   eccelenti.'
2 Petrarch, *Letters on Familiar Matters* (book XXI, letter 11), trans. Aldo S.
   Bernardo (Baltimore: Johns Hopkins University Press, 1985), 189–90.
3 Alberto Castoldi, *L'altra Bergamo* (Bergamo: Lubrina Editore, 1997).
4 On pre-university schooling in Venice, see the works of Paul Grendler, J.B.
   Ross, Piero Lucchi, Giuseppe Gullino, Vittorio Baldo, Gherardo Ortalli,
   Maurizio Sangalli, and essays by Manlio Pastore Stocchi and Fernando
   Leponi in *Storia della cultura Veneta*, as well as Gian Paolo Brizzi's previou-
   sly cited essay in Zanardi, *I Gesuiti e Venezia*, and Gilberto Pizzomiglio,
   'La'Repubblica dei letterari e i gesuiti nel primo Settecento veneto,' also
   in Zanardi, 513–28. The history of the University of Padua is a field unto
   itself; overviews are available in several of the multi-volume histories of
   Venice and in Paul Grendler's *Universities in the Italian Renaissance*. Richard
   Palmer's book on the *Studio* of Venice is an excellent analysis of a little-
   known aspect of education in Venice.
5 J.B. Ross, 'Venetian Schools and Teachers, Fourteenth to Early Sixteenth
   Century: A Survey and a Study of Giovanni Battista Egnazio,' *Renaissance
   Quarterly* 29 (Winter 1976): 521–65.
6 Vittorio Baldo, *Alunni, maestri e scuole in Venezia alla fine del xvi secolo*
   (Como: New Press, 1977).
7 Grendler, *Schooling*, 42–70; Ortalli, *Scuole, maestri, e istruzione di base tra
   Medioevo e Rinascimento: Il caso veneziano* (Vicenza: Neri Pozza, 1993).
8 Grendler, *Schooling*, 59.
9 Grendler, *Schooling*, 55.
10 Amelio Tagliaferri, 'Ordinamento Amministrativo dello Stato di Terraferma,' in *Atti del Convegno Venezia e la Terraferma attraverso le Relazione dei
   Rettori*, ed. idem (Milan: A. Giuffrè, 1981), 25.

11 On the relationship between Venice and Bergamo, see Ivana Pederzani, *Venezia e lo 'Stato de Terraferma': il governo delle comunità nel territorio bergamasco (sec. XV–XVIII)* (Milan: Vita e Pensiero, 1992); idem, 'L'organizzazione amministrativa del territorio: Venezia e la Bergamasca' in *Storia Economica e Sociale: Il Tempo della Serenissima, Il Lungo Cinquecento* (Bergamo: Fondazione per la Storia Economica e Sociale di Bergamo, 1998), 145–73; Gino Benzoni, 'Venezia e Bergamo: implicanze di un dominio,' *Studi Veneziani* 20 (1990): 15–58; more generally, see *Dentro lo 'Stado Italico': Venezia e la Terraferma fra Quattro e Seicento*, ed. Michael Knapton and Giorgio Cracco (Trent: Gruppo Culturale Civis, 1984); John Martin and Dennis Romano, introduction in *Venice Reconsidered: The History and Civilization of an Italian City-State, 1297–1897*, ed. idem (Baltimore: Johns Hopkins University Press, 2000), 1–35, esp. 8–12; for a bibliographic overview, Michael Knapton, 'Nobilità e popolo e un trentennio di storiografia veneta,' *Nuova Rivista Storica* 82 (1998): 167–92; Silvia Rota, *Per una storia del rapporto tra Venezia e Bergamo (sec. XV–XVIII): Rassegna Bibliografica* (Bergamo: Assessorato alla Cultura, 1987). Rota's book was the first of four in the series 'Terra di San Marco' to explore institutions, culture, economy, and society in mainland cities of the Venetian Republic.
12 Exceptions include Stephen D. Bowd, ed., *Vainglorious Death: A Funerary Fracas in Renaissance Brescia*, trans. J. Donald Cullington (Tempe: Arizona Center for Medieval and Renaissance Studies, 2006); Joanne Ferraro, *Family and Public Life in Brescia, 1580–1650* (Cambridge: Cambridge University Press, 1993); and Robert A. Peddie, *Printing at Brescia in the Fifteenth Century* (London: William & Norgate, 1905).
13 Giuseppe Nova, *Stampatori, librai, ed editori bresciani in Italia nel Cinquecento.* (Brescia: Fondazione Civiltà bresciana, 2000); Ennio Sandal, *La stampa a Brescia: notizie storiche e annali tipografici (1501–1553)* (Baden-Baden: Valentin Koverner, 1999).
14 Each is discussed in *Storia di Brescia*, ed. Giovanni Treccani degli Alfieri, 4 vols. (Brescia: Morcelliana Editrice, 1961–4). On Pilade, vol. 2, 538–42; on Calfurnio, ibid., 542–7; on Becichemo, ibid., 553–7 and *DBI*, vol. 7, 511–15; on Barzizza, *Storia di Brescia* vol. 2, 547–8 and *DBI* vol. 7, 33; on Ravizza, see citations in chapter 1.
15 On Concoreggio *DBI*, vol. 27, 743–6; Agostino Zanelli, 'Gabriele da Concoreggio e il Comune di Brescia,' *Archivio Storico Lombardo* 26 (1899), 60–8; *Storia di Brescia*, vol. 2, 568–9; and Girolamo Tiraboschi, *Storia della letteratura italiana*, vol. 6, pt. 3, 1589. On Posculo, see Paolo Guerrini, 'Un umanista bagnolese prigioniero dei Turchi a Costantinopoli e a Rodi,' *Brixia Sacra* 6, no. 4–5 (1915): 261–71; *Storia di Brescia*, vol. 2, 497, 568–9; U[golino?]

Ugolini, *Di una pretesa cattedra pliniana a Brescia nei primi anni del secolo XVI* (Brescia, 1923), 32. Posculo excepted only Christmas Day and Easter.

On schools in Brescia: the most comprehensive account appears in *Storia di Brescia,* vol. 2, pt. 3, 497–512, and pt. 4, 539–95; and vol. 3, pt. 4, 212–16, and pt. 5, 285–322. The best account of Brescian education in the early modern period is Agostino Zanelli, 'Del pubblico insegnamento in Brescia nei secoli XVI e XVII,' *Commentari dell'Ateneo di Brescia per l'anno 1896,* 24–53. The most prolific scholar, though unfortunately not always the most precise, is Paolo Guerrini; see in particular P. Guerrini, 'Scuole e maestri bresciani del '500,' *Commentari dell'Ateneo di Brescia per l'anno 1921,* 73–127. Other sources of marginal utility include: Teodoro Pertusati, *Dell'istruzione in Brescia* (Brescia, 1882); Luigi Francesco Fè D'Ostiani, *Sulle lettere intorno all'istruzione in Brescia del prof. T. Petrusati: osservazioni* (Brescia, 1882); Carlo Cocchetti, *Del movimento intellettuale nella provincia di Brescia dai tempi antichi ai nostri* (Brescia, 1880).

16 Grendler, *Schooling,* 3–13; *Storia di Brescia,* vol. 2, 501n2.
17 *Storia di Brescia,* vol. 2, 501–2.
18 Archivio di Stato di Brescia (hereafter ASBs), Archivio Storico Comunale, *Provvisioni del Consiglio comunale,* no. 517, ff. 173v–174v (13 Aug. 1500); f. 177r (22 Aug. 1500); on Bechichemo, *Provvisioni,* no. 521, ff. 22v–23r (18 Dec. 1508); Zanelli, 'Del pubblico insegnamento,' 28–38. Regio never taught in Bergamo, but on his courses at Padua, see Tiraboschi, vol. 6, pt. 3, 1573–8.
19 Zanelli, 'Del pubblico insegnamento,' 34–8.
20 ASBs, *Provvisioni,* no. 536, f. 147r (4 Apr. 1542), f. 162v (5 May 1542); ibid., no. 538, f. 102v (27 Oct. 1545); ibid., no. 539, f. 204v (13 Jul. 1548); ibid., no. 542, f. 112r–v (20 Mar. 1554). Zanelli, 'Del pubblico insegnamento,' 38 43.
21 Zanelli, 44–50.
22 ASBs, *Provvisioni,* no. 574, f. 148v (31 May 1618).
23 Tullia Franzi, 'La famiglia degli'Alzani,' *Bergomum* 43, no. 1–2 (1949): 'Atti dell'Ateneo,' 1–7, here 4–5, appears to exaggerate the role of the Dominican school. To my knowledge, no scholarly account of the educational role played by Dominicans, Franciscans, or Benedictines in Renaissance Bergamo exists; for the little that is known, see Locatelli (1910), 81–2, and Giulio Orazio Bravi, 'Girolamo Zanchi, da Lucca a Strasburgo,' *Archivio Storico Bergamasco* 1 (1981): 35–64, especially 39. Vanni Zanella, *Il Monastero Matris Domini in Bergamo,* 2 vols. (Bergamo: Monumenta Bergomensia, 1980) does not discuss education by the nuns at Matris Domini; nor is education considered by Mario Locatelli, *Bergamo nei suoi monasteri: storia e arte nei cenobi benedittini della Diocesi di Bergamo* (Bergamo, 1986). Ermenegildo

Camozzi's publication of the inventories of seven conventual libraries in Bergamo should help scholars to resolve this mystery: Camozzi, *Cultura e Storia*, passim.

24 *Storia di Brescia*, vol. 2, 502n2.

25 On the Somaschan college, see *Storia di Brescia*, vol. 3, 167–8, 212–13; Luigi Fè d'Ostiani, *Storia, tradizione, arte nelle vie di Brescia* (Brescia: Edit. Queriniana, 1927), 185–8. This prohibition against settlement probably reflected Ventian sentiment.

26 Antonio Cistellini, *Il Padre Angelo Paradisi e i padri gesuiti in Brescia* (Brescia: Scuola tipografica Opera Pavoniana, 1955) includes many archival transcriptions from ASBs and ARSI; see also Zanelli, 42–6; Fè d'Ostiani, *Storia, tradizione, arte*, 47.

27 *Storia di Brescia*, vol. 3, 153n2.

28 *Storia di Brescia*, vol. 3, 320 ff.

29 *Storia di Brescia*, vol. 2, 472.

30 Paolo Guerrini lists 135 public and private school teachers in sixteenth-century Brescia: P. Guerrini, 'Scuole e maestri Bresciani,' 95–127. My own research counts 91 public and private school teachers in sixteenth-century Bergamo, nearly all of whom were employed by the institutions described in this book.

31 On Merici, see *Storia di Brescia*, vol. 3, 308–11; Teresa Ledochowska, 'Angela Merici,' in *Dizionario degli Istituti di Perfezione* (DIP), vol. 1, cols. 631–4, includes all of the relevant bibliography, except for the recent study by Querciolo Mazzonis, *Spirituality, Gender, and the self in Renaissance Italy: Angela Merici and the Company of S. Ursula (1474–1540)* (Washington, DC: Catholic University of America Press, 2007).

32 Between 1530 and 1540, Loyola founded the Society of Jesus (Jesuits), Miani established the precursor to the Somaschan order, and Castello created the Schools of Christian Doctrine; in 1597 Calasanz instituted the Scuole Pie.

33 *Storia di Brescia*, vol. 3, 312–13.

34 *Storia di Brescia*, vol. 3, 313–16.

35 *Storia di Brescia*, vol. 2, 455.

36 See Paolo Guerrini, 'Il Collegio Lambertino,' *Archivio Veneto-Tridentino* 1 (1922): 93–108; idem, 'Il legato Lambertino,' *Bollettino municipale di Brescia* 11 (1922): 307–13.

37 *Storia di Brescia*, vol. 3, 334.

38 *Storia di Brescia*, vol. 3, 334; Fè d'Ostiani, 52–3.

39 D'Andrea, *Civic Christianity*, 119–27; Piero del Negro, ed., *I collegi per studenti dell'Universita di Padova: una storia plurisecolare* (Padova: Signum, 2003), 97–161.

40 Zanelli, 'Del pubblico insegnamento,' 45n1, citing ASBs, *Provvisioni*, no.
    531, f. 4r (17 Apr. 1531) and (28 Apr. 1531).
41 *Storia di Brescia*, vol. 2, 505.
42 Ibid. For Corvi's biography and some of the important documents, see
    Paolo Guerrini, 'Guglielmo Corvi da Brescia e il collegio bresciano in Bolo-
    gna,' *Studi e memorie per la storia dell'Università di Bologna* 7 (1922): 55–116.
    In 1286 Guglielmo Corvi was described in Bologna as a *magister in phisica*;
    by 1298 he was papal physician to Boniface VIII, and on 7 May 1326, just
    six months prior to his death, he created this institute to benefit poor
    students in Bologna so that they could attend the university and learn a
    profession.
43 Archivio di Stato di Verona (hereafter ASVr), Archivio del Comune,
    Registro no. 56, f. 91v (15 Sep. 1407). 'Facta propositione in dicto Consilio
    quantum foret expediens huic civitati Verone, habito respectu ad trafficum
    et comertium quod habet ista civitas cum partibus Allamanie, habere hic
    magistrum theotonicum qui sciret docere pueros linguam allamanicam,
    et ad talem actum commemorato ibidem magistro Nicolao de [blank]
    theotonico qui in civitate Verone artem huiusmodi bene et utiliter consue-
    vit exercere, datum fuit partitum ad ballotas, et captum fuit quod dictus
    magister Nicolaus docendo linguam theutonicam in civitate Verone habeat
    pro mercede et salario suo centum libras in anno recuperandas in Commu-
    ni de aliquo augmento faciendo contratis ultra expensarum suarum taxas
    consuetas.'
44 The best overview of Veronese schooling is Gian Paolo Marchi, 'Per una
    storia delle istituzioni scolastiche pubbliche dall'epoca comunale all'unifi-
    cazione del Veneto all'Italia,' in idem, *Cultura e vita civile a Verona: Uomini
    e istituzioni dall'epoca carolingia al Risorgimento* (Verona: Banca Popolare di
    Verona, 1979), 1–98, which includes an appendix of thirty-nine archival
    documents about schools. In the same volume, see Don Angelo Orlandi,
    'Scuole ecclesiastiche dall'Umanesimo all'Ottocento,' 271–318. Earlier
    sources include Eloisa Garibotto, 'Le scuole d'abbaco a Verona,' *Atti
    dell'Accademia d'agricoltura, scienze e lettere di Verona*, ser. 4, vol. 24 (1922),
    and Celestino Garibotto, 'I maestri di grammatica a Verona dal'200 a tutto
    il'500' (Verona: Tip. Veronese, n.d. [1921]); the latter includes a detailed
    list of all the grammar teachers who appeared in Verona's tax records, but
    no analysis or interpretation. See also Antonio Avena, 'Per la storia dei
    maestri di grammatica nel contado veronese durante il secolo XV: Maestro
    Onofrio da Rieti a Torri sul Garda,' *Giornale storico della letteratura italiana*
    60 (1912): 377–82; Giuseppe Biadego, 'Alberico da Marcellise maestro di
    grammatica e cancelliere scaligero,' *Atti del Regio Istituto Veneto di scienze,
    lettere e arti* 63, no. 2 (1903–4): 587–603; idem, 'Il grammatico Bartolomeo

Borfoni da Cremona, maestro a Verona e a Vicenza nel secolo XV,' *Archivio Storico Lombardo* ser. 4, 33 (1906): 353–7; idem, *Bernardino Donato grecista veronese del secolo XVI* (Verona, 1905). On musical and literary academies in Verona, see Marchi, ibid., 517–96.

45 Marchi, 'Per una storia,' 14–15. On 67–9, Marchi publishes the text of the Albertini statutes, as does G. Sandri, *Gli Statuti Veronesi del 1276 colle correzioni e aggiunte fino al 1323* (Venice, 1940), 123–7.

46 In 1277 the grammar teacher was awarded his own *cattedra* and by 1284 his salary was raised to fifty lire.

47 Marchi, 'Per una storia,' 24–9 and 78–80.

48 For Verona, see E. Garibotto, passim, and Marchi, 'Per una storia,' 29–32. See also Richard Goldthwaite, 'Schools and Teachers of Commercial Arithmetic in Renaissance Florence,' *Journal of European Economic History* 1 (1972): 418–33; Grendler, *Schooling*, 22–3 and 311–19; Black, *Education and Society*, 52–4, 162–3, 226–41, 274–8 , and 362–84 offers much detail on individual teachers.

49 See *Storia di Brescia*, v. 2, 599–617.

50 E. Garibotto cites the original document as being in ASVr, Arch. Storico del Comune, *Atti Consiliare* K K, f. 39r. 'Avendo, dopo molte peregrinazioni per molte città d'Italia, deliberato di stabilirmi in Verona, ad onor publico et utile di chiunque vorrà disciplinarsi nelle scienze ch'io professo, insegnando a leggere e scrivere d'ogni sorta e variazioni di lira e di abbaco per ragioni e pratiche a molti modi d'Italia, e specialmente di tener un libro semplice e doppio all'uso di Venezia, col modo di viaggi, fattoraggi, viaggi raccomandati, viaggi in persone et compagnie con facilità et aperta strada, et appresso anche di misurar et perticar, per Geometria teorica et pratica, terrreni di diverse forme, monti, colli, valli, campagne, grani, feni, legnami, veze, tine, pozzi, fossi, cisterne, livellar acque, quadrar muri, piramide, colonne, torri, palazzi et fondamenti sotto et sopra la terra, siccome spetta ad un agrimensore e geometra.'

51 Grendler, *Schooling*, 319.

52 Black, *Education and Society*, 53n47.

53 Marchi, 32–54. This is confirmed by, among others, Carlo Dionisotti, *Geografia e storia della letteratura italiana* (Turin: Einaudi, 1967), 65–6.

54 Marchi, 44.

55 C. Garibotto, passim, and Marchi, 'Per una storia,' 53.

56 Orlando Pescetti, *Orazione dietro al modo dell'instituire la gioventù alla magnifica et inclita città di Verona* (Venice, 1592), summarized in Marchi, 'Per una storia,' 49–53.

57 Orlandi, 282, 293.

58 Marchi, 'Per una storia,' 53–4; and Gian Paolo Brizzi, 'Scuole e collegi nell'antica Provincia Veneta,' 467–511.
59 The fundamental study is Ignazio Savi, *Memorie antiche e moderne intorno alle pubbliche scuole in Vicenza* (Vicenza, 1815). More recent studies of Vicentine schooling include Giovanni Pellizzari's dense but fruitful article, 'Continuità e trasformazioni di un sistema scolastico cittadino,' in *Storia di Vicenza*, ed. Franco Barbieri and Paolo Preto (Vicenza: Neri Pozza, 1990), vol. 3, pt. 2, 69–87; and Vincenza Sansonetti, 'Le pubbliche scuole in Vicenza durante il Medioevo e l'Umanesimo,' *Aevum* 26 (1952): 156–79. Although it tends to be biographical rather than analytical when discussing schooling, another indispensable source for general Vicentine history is Giovanni Mantese, *Memorie storiche della Chiesa vicentina* (Vicenza: Accademia Olimpica, 1974); see especially vol. 4, pt. 6, 793–910. Emilio Franzina's *Vicenza: Storia di una città (1404–1866)* (Vicenza: Neri Pozza, 1980) offers a one-volume, left-wing interpretation intended to counterbalance Mantese; see 395–407 for a few observations about schooling. James Grubb has written an excellent study of Vicenza's political history during the Quattrocento: J. Grubb, *Firstborn of Venice: Vicenza and the Early Renaissance State* (Baltimore: Johns Hopkins University Press, 1988). Also useful is Antonio Marco Dalla Pozza, *La cultura vicentina nel primo cinquantesimo della dominazione veneziana* (Vicenza: Accademia Olimpica, 1970). Several studies have been published about schooling in Vicenza's surrounding towns: e.g., G. Chiuppani, *Storia di una scuola di Grammatica dal Medioevo fino all'600* (Venice, 1915); A. Schiavo, *Notizie storiche intorno alle pubbliche scuole di Belluno* (Belluno, 1844).
60 Sansonetti, 167; Pellizzari, 71
61 Sansonetti, 163, citing Savi, p.115.
62 On Vicentine humanists, see Mantese and Sansonetti, passim.
63 Mantese, 758–9.
64 Mantese, 762–71.
65 Pellizzari, 72.
66 Ermenegildo Reato, 'Carità e assistenza in sette secoli di storia vicentina,' in *La Carità a Vicenza*, ed. Chiara Rigoni (Venice: Marsilio, 2001), 3–12.
67 See Pellizzari, 71, 73–4, 79 for these examples.
68 Sansonetti, 177–8.
69 Pellizzarri, 83–4, and Mantese, vol. 4, pt. 1, 815.
70 Gian Paolo Brizzi, *La formazione della classe dirigente nel Sei-Settecento: I seminari nobilium nell'Italia centrosettentrionale* (Bologna: Il Mulino, 1976), 155, table 7. See also idem, 'Scuole e collegi nell'antica Provincia Veneta della Compagnia di Gesù (1542–1773),' in Mario Zanardi, ed., *I Gesuiti e Venezia:*

Momenti e problemi di storia veneziana della Compagnia di Gesù (Padua: Gregoriana, 1994), 467–511.

71 Franzina, 460–88, discusses the Calvinists and Anabaptists in Vicenza; Pellizzari, 80–1, reviews the various crises in public instruction.

72 Savi, 87. 'le lettura pubblicata divenuta era cosa superflua e di niuna utilità, atteso che per mancanza di uditori rarissime volte potevasi leggere, quando invece alla scuola privata era sì grande il concorso, che un maestro solo, per diligente e famoso ch'ei fosse, sebbene aiutato dai ripetitori, non poteva supplire a tanto impegno.'

73 For example: Francesco Galbiati, *La comunità di Romano (1427–1429)* (Romano: Tip. Rottigni, 1895), 15–16; Bruno Cassinelli, Antonio Maltempi, and Marco Pozzoni, *La comunità di Romano in epoca viscontea e veneta* (Romano: Tip. Ghisleri, 1978), 49–50; Riccardo Caproni, Lidia Gamba Persiani, and Luigi Pagnoni, *Martinengo nella storia civile ed ecclesiale* (Bergamo: Bolis, 1992), 138–40; Paolo Manzoni, *Lemina dalle origini al XVII secolo* (Bergamo: Bolis, 1988); Giovanni Bergamelli, *Storia della parrocchia di Nembro* (Nembro: Bolis, 1992); Giulio Orazio Bravi and Pier Maria Soglian, *Storia delle terre d'Albino* (Bergamo: Grafo, 1996). Local newspapers, historical journals and commemorative volumes sometimes include reports of education in this period: e.g., L[uigi] Michelato, 'Scuole e maestri nel '400 a Romano di Lombardia,' *L'Eco di Bergamo* (24 Jan. 1935); idem, 'Il maestro romanese Antonio de Lallio,' *L'Eco di Bergamo* (6 Feb. 1935); Alvise Michiel, 'A Parigi nel '400 gli studenti della Sorbona appresero il Latino dal libro di un Bergamasco,' *L'Eco di Bergamo* (31 Oct. 1962), 3; Giovanni Silini, 'Appunti sulle scuole di Lovere nei secoli XV e XVI,' in *Convitto Nazionale 'Cesare Battisti' a Lovere, 1891–1991* (Lovere: Ferrari, 1991), 151–4.

74 Silini, 151–4 for details. The first reference is to Giovanni del fu Bertolino Bazzini detto Batalia, identified as a *magister* in a notarial act of 7 July 1454.

75 Cesare Patelli, *Alzano Maggiore e la Basilica di San Martino* (Bergamo: Bolis, 1978), p 46. My thanks to Roberto Rossi for references to Alzano Maggiore and Clusone in the diocesan archives, particularly in the *Visite pastorali*.

76 ACVBg, *Visite pastorali di Vescovo Grimani*, vol. 45, f. 234 (2 Feb. 1642). It is not clear when or how girls' education was included as part of the bequest.

77 ACVBg, *Visite pastorali di Vescovo Barbarigo*, vol. 52: 25, 51, & 383 (2 Feb. 1660).

78 No trace of public schooling appears in the statutes, notarial acts, or financial records preserved in the Archivio Storico del Comune di Clusone, nor in Luigi Olmo, *Memorie Storiche di Clusone e della Valle Seriana superiore* (Bergamo: Tipografia S. Alessandro, 1906).

79 Giovanni Silini graciously provided me with the citation and transcription to these statues, held in a private collection: *Statuti della Valle Seriana superiore,* 'De fine adhibenda magistris scolarum gramatice,' rubrica 169: 'Item quod cuique magistro scolarum gramatice detur fides per dominum Vicarium de eo quod iuraverit habere debere pro mercede sua, pro eo quod docuisset aliquem qui ivisset ad suas scollas, usque ad soldos viginti imperialium et non plus, dummodo iuraverit infra mensem postquam talis scolaris recesisset a scolis suis.' For more on late medieval rural statutes, see Mariarosa Cortesi, *Statuti rurali e statuti di valle: La provincia di Bergamo nei secoli XIII–XVIII, Atti del Convegno a Bergamo 5 Marzo 1983* (Bergamo: Provincia di Bergamo, 1984).

80 Archivio Storico del Comune di Clusone (hereafter ASCClusone), Serie II, *Legati (1614–1630),* fasc. 8–10; here fasc. 9, ff. 1–3 (16 Nov. 1630). '1630 16 Novembre. Punto di Testamento del Qu: [quondam] Ventura Fanzago.': 'Item obligavit dictum Consortium ad dandum, & solvendum tribus Filijs volentibus studere artes liberales pauperibus & de familijs honestis, & sine titulo infamie, Scuta 43 de Libris septem pro scuto pro quoque eorum, dantibus Fideiiussionem de cum effectus studendi per annos tres, qui eludere volentes ellegi debeant ut infra, & transactis dictis tribus Annis iterum detur dicta Elemosina dictorum Scutorum 43 cum dicta fideiussione, & sic semper in perpetuum servari debeat, quos tres obligavit ad dicendum Offitium Beate Marie Virginis omni die dictorum Annorum trium relaxante uno die omni hebdomada fine dicto onere.' A brief summary of the Fanzago bequest can be found in Antonio Previtali's 1986 *Inventario dell'Archivio della Congregazione di Carità di Clusone,* 34.

81 Ibid., fasc. 8, f. 5r–v (6 Jan. 1659); ibid., fasc. 8 (18 Jul. 1937). See also ACVBg, *Visite pastorali di Vescovo Dolfin,* vol. 100: 41, 45, & 393 (7 July 1779).

82 ACVBg, *Visite pastorali di Vescovo Redetti,* vol. 93, f. 119 (23 Jun. 1736).

83 Giuseppe Locatelli, 'L'istruzione a Bergamo e la Misericordia Maggiore,' *Bergomum* 4, no. 4, (1910): 95–6, paraphrasing Marco Antonio Moro's *Grammatices fundamenta* (Verona: Girolamo Legnano, 1520).

84 Michelato, 'Scuole e maestri,' cites examples of poorly paid teachers from 1402, 1421, 1422, and 1426.

85 Archivio Storico del Comune di Romano di Lombardia (hereafter ASCRomano), Serie 4, *Provvisioni,* no. 100 (anni 1489–1505), f. 91r (27 Dec. 1494). Ibid., f. 96v (13 May 1495); f. 127r (17 May 1497); f. 129v (6 Aug. 1497), f. 132v (21 Sep. 1497), ff. 138v–139r (27 Dec. 1497), and f. 139r (28 Dec. 1497); f. 96v (13 May 1495); on Allegreno, ff. 167r–v (21 May 1499). Michelato, 'Scuole e maestri' summarizes the story.

86 ASCRomano, *Provvisioni,* no. 101 (anni 1529–1546), ff. 5v–6r (11 Feb. 1529),

ff. 26r–v (28 Sep. 1530); Michelato, 'Il maestro romanese Antonio de Lallio,' 3; Locatelli (1910), 126–7.

87 Michelato, 'Il maestro romanese,' passim.

88 Giulio Orazio Bravi, 'Note e documenti per la storia della Riforma a Bergamo (1536–1544),' *Archivio Storico Bergamasco* 6, no. 2 (1986): 185–228.

89 Xenio Toscani, *Scuole e alfabetismo nello Stato di Milano da Carlo Borromeo alla Rivoluzione* (Milan: La Scuola, 1992).

90 Paul Grendler, 'Schooling in Western Europe,' *Renaissance Quarterly* 43 (1990): 774–87, here p. 783.

Conclusion

1 'Introduction' in *Humanist Educational Treatises*, ed. and trans. Craig Kallendorf; I Tatti Renaissance Library 5 (Cambridge, MA.: Harvard University Press, 2002), viii.

Appendices

1 The records of the MIA's Academy of Clerics (1566–1611) and the MIA's New Academy of Clerics (1617–1700) include dozens of references to *maestri di capella*. Although music was an important part of the curriculum for the young *chierici*, I have not included an analysis of that topic in this work, and I do not include the names of the music teachers for these two academies.

2 I include the names of all teachers hired by this confraternity from 1557 to 1585; additional teachers are referred to sporadically from 1585 to 1617, but are not included here.

3 My thanks to Suor Melania Balini of the Suore Orsoline of Bergamo, who generously shared her research results with me and confirmed my initial impressions about the Schools of Christian Doctrine in Bergamo. This list was prepared by her for an exhibit at the Archivio della Curia Vescovile di Bergamo in Fall 1997, and appears here with her permission. Note that it includes only those Schools in the immediate vicinity of Bergamo, not in the entire diocese.

4 The church of S. Erasmo in Borgo Canale included the following satellite churches, which were grouped together in the report of 5 July 1609: S. Vigilio, S. Sebastiano alla Botta, S. Maria di Astino, S. Matteo di Longuelo, S. Maria di Sudorno, S. Rocco di Castagneta, S. Roco di Fontana, S. Martino della Pigrizia.

Bibliography

Archives and Manuscripts

Bergamo, Biblioteca Civica 'A. Mai'
  Archivio Storico del Comune
    Azioni
    Instrumenti
    Processi
    Relazioni
    Sindaci del Palazzo
  Archivio del Consorzio della Misericordia Maggiore (MIA)
    Liber Capitulorum
    Liber Onerum
    Scritture/Suppliche
    Spese
    Terminazioni
  Archivio Silvestri
    Carte Chizola-Stella

INDIVIDUAL MANUSCRIPTS:
- Beretta, Marco. *Memoriale*. MMB 323
- Cesare Camozzi Vertova de Gherardi, *Rappresentanza comunale della città di Bergamo dal 1433 ad oggi*. AB 352.
- *Ducale veneta relativa al memoriale della città di Bergamo all'introduzione dei Gesuiti* [1721]. AB 374
- *Grammatica latina*. MA 144
- *Informazione sull'introduzione dei Gesuiti in Bergamo*. AB 225 (6)
- Mazzoleni, Angelo. *Zibaldone, Libro 'B' (Liber rerum extravagantium)*. Sala 1 N 10 2

– *Memoriale presentato al Ser. Principe perché non vengono introdotti I PP. Gesuiti in Bergamo.* AB 398, doc. 53.
– *Miscellanea dell'abate Pierantonio Serassi.* Mss. 6 7 R 10 (2)
– Salvioni, Agostino. *Memorie Storiche delle vicende dei Gesuiti in Bergamo.* Salone N 9 8/10 (6)
– *Stampa per il Sig. Dott. Franco Farina contro il collegio dei Giuristi.* Sala 1 Loggia E 6 27 (4)
– Suardi, Gerolamo. *Epistolario.* Micr. 500
– *Miscellanea bergomense ecclesiastica,* 'Testamento Bonometti'. Salone cassapanca 1 G 2 35 (1)
– Zanchi, Paolo. *Corrispondenza (1497–1509).* Micr. 505
Bergamo, Archivio di Stato
   Atti Notarili
Bergamo, Archivio della Curia Vescovile [now called Archivio Storico Diocesano de Bergamo]
   Lettere Pastorali
   Licentiae
   Seminario – carte antiche
   Congregazione religiose – Somaschi
      Carte antiche
   Mensa Vescovile
      1547 e seguenti, Accademia dei [Caspi], Fald. 68/1
   Archivio Capitolare
      Fundatio Scholae Generalis Doctrinae Christiane … de anno 1609.
Bergamo, Archivio Storico del Seminario Vescovile Giovanni XXIII di Bergamo
   Sezione Patrimonio
Bergamo, Parrocchia di S. Alessandro in Colonna
   Archivio Storico
      Libro delle Parti
Bergamo, Parrocchia di S. Alessandro della Croce
   Archivio Storico
      Libro delle Parti
      Libro Maestro
Brescia, Archivio di Stato
   Archivio Storico Comunale
      Provvisioni
Chiari, Biblioteca Morcelli
   Ravizza, Giovita. *De modo in scholis servando*
Clusone, Palazzo Marinoni-Barcha
   Archivio Storico del Comune
      Legati (1614–1630)

Genoa, Archivio Storico dei Padri Somaschi
  Acta Congregationes
  Atti del Capitolo Generale
  Bergamo 218–283–287
  Como Collegio Gallio
  Milano 143
  Riassunto degli Atti del Capitolo Generale
Padua, Archivio di Stato
  Atti Notarili
Padua, Archivio Antico dell'Università di Padova
  Acta Graduum Academicorum Universitatis Patavinae
Romano di Lombardia, Palazzo Municipale
  Archivio Storico del Comune
    Provvisioni
Rome, Archivum Romanum Societatis Iesu
  Epistolae Gen.
  Epistolae Ext.
  Ven. 111, Fundatio Coll. A-B
Venice, Archivio di Stato
  Consilio dei X
    Lettere dei Rettori di Bergamo
  Riformatori dello studio di Padova
    Scuole e collegi nella terraferma
  Senato
    Lettere dei Rettori di Bergamo
    Deliberazioni, Roma ordinaria
Venice, Biblioteca Museo Correr
  Caresana, Paolo. *Consigli ad un maestro*. Ms. 3721–25
  Codice Correr 1350/2

Printed Sources

The bibliography includes works cited in the notes and other works consulted during preparation of the book. It does not include manuscripts or printed sources mentioned only in passing in the text or the notes. Primary sources cited by others but not seen by me are not listed here.

Primary Works

Acta Graduum Academicorum Universitatis Patavinae. 5 vols. Padua: Antenore, 1970– .

Acta Synodalia Bergomensis Ecclesiae (ASBE). Bergamo: Apud Filios Marci Antonij Rubei, 1661.

Alberti, Leandro. *Descrittione di tutta l'Italia*. Venice: 1553. Reprint Bergamo: Leading Edizioni, 2003. Edited by Adriano Agnati.

Benaglio, Marco Antonio. *Compendium onerum Ven. Consor. Misericordiae*. Bergamo, 1612.

Borromeo, Carlo. *Costitutioni et Regole della Compagnia et Scuole della Dottrina Christiana*. Milan: Pacifico Pontio, 1585.

Calvi, Donato. *Effemeride sacro profana di quanto di memorabile sia successo in Bergamo*. Milan: Francesco Vigoni, 1767.

– *Scena letteraria degli scrittori Bergamaschi*. Bergamo: Per i figliuoli di Marc'Antonio Rossi, 1664.

Camozzi, Ermenegildo, ed. *Le visite 'ad limina Apostolorum' dei Vescovi di Bergamo, 1590–1697*. Bergamo: Provincia di Bergamo, 1992.

Cerchiari, Giovanni Luigi. *Orationes*. Bergamo: Antonium Rebeumis, 1645.

Da Lezze, Giovanni. *Descrizione di Bergamo e suo territorio, 1596*. Edited by Vincenzo Marchetti and Lelio Pagani. Fonti per lo studio del territorio bergamasco, 7. Bergamo: Luccheti, 1988.

Ghirardelli, Lorenzo. *Storia della peste del 1630*. Bergamo: Fratelli Rossi, 1681.

Historiae Patriae Monumenta. Turin: Frat. Bocca, 1876. Tome 16, vol. 2.

Mafei Vegij, Laudensis de educatione liberorum [et] eo[rum] claris moribus liber primus. Milan: Leonardo Pachel, 1491.

Methodus studiorum ad usum Congregationis de Somascha per rei literariae moderatores deputatos exhibita atque anno 1741 Dom. Joannis Baptistae Riva, Praepositi Generalis auctoritate insinuata. 1741.

Michiel, Marc Antonio. *Agri et Urbis Bergomatis Descriptio*. Venice, 1523. In *Bergamo 1516: città et territorio nella* Descriptio *di Marcantonio Michiel*, edited by Maria Luisa Scalvini and Gian Piero Calza. Padua: Centro grafica editoriale, 1983.

Petrarch (Petrarca, Francesco). *Letters on Familiar Matters*. Translated by Aldo S. Bernardo. Baltimore: Johns Hopkins University Press, 1985.

Ravizza, Giovita [Rapicius, Jovita]. *Oratio in funere Pauli Zanchi Bergomatis*. Venice, 1561.

– *De liberis publice ad humanitatem informandis*. Venice, 1551.

– *De scholarum instauratione*. Pavia, 1790.

Regola del Consorzio S. Lorenzo. Bergamo: Fratelli Rossi, 1717.

Regola del Ven. Consortio di S. Spirito e S. Giovanni dell'Ospedale. Bergamo: Lodovico Monza, 1617.

Regola del Ven. Consortio di Santo Alessandro in Colonna. Bergamo: Comin Ventura, 1589.

Regole per il pio luogo degli orfani di S. Martino di Bergamo. Bergamo: Francesco
Locatelli, 1776. Reprint Bergamo, 1789.
Relazione dei Rettori Veneti XII: Podestaria e Capitanato di Bergamo. Edited by
Amelio Tagliaferri. Milan: A. Giuffrè, 1973–9.
Roncalli, Angelo G. (later John XXIII), ed. *Gli Atti della Visita Apostolica di San
Carlo Borromeo a Bergamo, 1575 (AVASC).* 5 vols. Florence: Olschki, 1936–57.
Sacrosanctum Concilium Tridentium. Venice, 1746.
Stampa della Città di Bergamo, e Reggenza del Pio Luogo degli Orfanelli. Bergamo,
1792.
Statuta Bergomi. Brescia: Angelus & Jacobus Brittanicus, 18 Dec. 1491. Reprint
Bergamo: Joannis Santini, 1727.
*Vita del clarissimo signor Girolamo Miani gentil huomo venetiano. Life of Jerome
Emiliani, most distinguished Venetian nobleman.* Introduction by Carlo Pel-
legrini. *Fonti per la Storia dei Somaschi.* Manchester, NH: Somaschan Publish-
ers, 1973.
Zanchi, Giovanni. *De origine Orobiorum sive Cenomanorum ad Petrum Bembus
libri tres.* 3 vols. Venice, 1531.

Secondary Works

Agazzi, Ezio, Luigi Pagnoni, and Santo Pesenti, eds. *Il Colle di S. Giovanni:
Omaggio a Papa Giovanni.* 4 vols. Gorle: SESAAB, 1996–7.
Albertini, Chiaretta. 'L'alfabetismo a Bergamo e nelle montagne bergamasche
all'inizio dell'Ottocento.' Tesi di laurea. Università di Pavia, Facoltà di
Storia Moderna, relatore Xenio Toscani, 1985–6.
Alcaini, Giovanni. 'Origini e progressi degli istituti tenuti e diretti dai Padri
Somaschi.' *Somascha* (1979): 70 171.
Alessandretti, Gianfranco. 'Il Fondo degli istituti educativi nel ASBg.' *Archivio
Storico Bergamasco* 12 (1987): 125–56.
Angelozzi, Giancarlo. *Le confraternite laicali: Un'esperienza cristiana tra Medioevo
e età moderna.* Brescia: Queriniana, 1978.
Avena, Antonio. 'Per la storia dei maestri di grammatica nel contado veronese
durante il secolo XV: Maestro Onofrio da Rieti a Torri sul Garda.' *Giornale
storico della letteratura italiana* 60 (1912): 377–82.
Baldo, Vittorio. *Alunni, maestri e scuole in Venezia alla fine del XVI secolo.* Como:
New Press, 1977.
Balini, Melania. 'La scuola della Dottrina Cristiana.' In 'Sulle orme di Gregorio
Barbarigo. La chiesa di Bergamo nel' 600–'700: arte, cultura, fede (15 settem-
bre–16 novembre 1997),' *Echi di Papa Giovanni* 18, no. 5 (Sep.–Oct. 1997):
24–35.

Barachetti, Gianni. 'La'Domus Magna' della MIA.' *Bergomum* 59, no. 1 (1965): 63–86.

Barachetti, Gianni, and Carmen Palamini. 'La Stampa a Bergamo nel Cinquecento.' *Bergomum* 84, no. 4 (1989): 1–147.

Barsanti, Paolo. *Il pubblico insegnamento in Lucca dal secolo XIV alla fine del secolo XVIII.* Lucca, 1905. Reprint Bologna: Forni, 1980.

Battaglia, Felice, ed. *Il Pensiero Pedagogico del Rinascimento.* Florence: Sansoni, 1960.

Battisti, Carlo, and Giovanni Alessio, eds. *Dizionario Etimologico Italiano.* 5 vols. Florence: Barbera, 1951.

Belotti, Bortolo. *Gli Eccellenti Bergamaschi.* 2 vols. Bergamo: Bolis, 1956.

– *La storia di Bergamo e dei Bergamaschi.* 9 vols. Bergamo: Bolis, 1989.

Bentley, Jerry. *Politics and Culture in Renaissance Naples.* Princeton, NJ: Princeton University Press, 1987.

Benzoni, Gino. 'Venezia e Bergamo: implicanze di un dominio.' *Studi Veneziani* 20 (1990): 15–58.

Bergamelli, Giovanni. *Storia della Parrocchia di Nembro.* Nembro: Bolis, 1992.

Bergamo o sia Notizie Patrie, almanacco scientifico-artistico-letterario per l'anno 1858. Bergamo: Tip. Pagnoncelli, n.d. [1859].

Bernareggi, Adriano. 'A ricordo della celebrazione del IV centenario di fondazione dell'orfanotrofio maschile di Bergamo.' *Rivista della Congregazione di Somasca* 19 (1934): 141–59.

Besta, Enrico. 'Gli studenti Valtellenesi e l'Università di Padova.' *Archivio Veneto* 9 (1895): 179–219.

Biadego, Giuseppe. 'Alberico da Marcellise maestro di grammatica e cancelliere scaligero.' *Atti del Regio Istituto Veneto di scienze, lettere e arti* 63, no. 2 (1903–4): 587–603.

– *Bernardino Donato grecista veronese del secolo XVI.* Verona, 1905.

– 'Il grammatico Bartolomeo Borfoni da Cremona, maestro a Verona e a Vicenza nel secolo XV.' *Archivio Storico Lombardo* ser. 4, 33 (1906): 353–65.

Bianchi, Angelo. *L'istruzione secondaria tra barocco et età dei Lumi.* Milan: Vita e Pensiero, 1993.

Black, Christopher. *Italian Confraternities in the Sixteenth Century.* Cambridge: Cambridge University Press, 1989.

Black, Robert. *Education and Society in Florentine Tuscany: Teachers, Pupils, and Schools, c. 1250–1450.* Boston and Leiden: Brill, 2007.

– *Humanism and Education in Medieval and Renaissance Italy: Tradition and Innovation in Latin Schools from the Twelfth to the Fifteenth Century.* Cambridge: University of Cambridge Press, 2001.

– 'Humanism and Education in Renaissance Arezzo.' *I Tatti Studies* 2 (1987): 171–237.

– 'Italian Renaissance Education: Changing Perspectives and Continuing Controversies.' *Journal of the History of Ideas* 52, no. 2 (April 1991): 315–34.
– *Studio e Scuola in Arezzo durante il medioevo e Rinascimento*. Arezzo: Accademia Petrarca, 1996.
Bloch, Marc. *The Historian's Craft*. Translated by Peter Putnam. New York: Vintage Books, 1964.
Boldrini, Luigi. *Della vita e degli scritti di Messer Giovita Rapicio*. Verona: Tipografia Annichini, 1903.
Bonacina, Giuseppe. 'L'orfanotrofio della Maddalena di Bergamo e le origini della Compagnia dei Servi dei Poveri.' *Somascha* 18, no. 2/3 (1993): 88–169.
Bonelli, Giuseppe. 'Un archivio privato del Cinquecento: Le carte Stella.' *Archivio Storico Lombardo* 16 (1907): 3–57.
Boroni, Luisa. 'Maestri e scolari a Bergamo nei secoli XIV e XV: Ricerche sull'attività assistenziale del consorzio della Misericordia Maggiore.' Tesi di perfezionamento. Università Cattolica del Sacro Cuore di Milano, Facoltà di Lettere e Filosofia, relatore Giuseppe Billanovich, 1969–70.
Bottani, Tarcisio. *Girolamo Ragazzoni, Vescovo di Bergamo*. Bergamo: Edizione Corponove, 1994.
Bravi, Giulio Orazio. 'Girolamo Zanchi, da Lucca a Strasburgo.' *Archivio Storico Bergamasco* 1 (1981): 35–64.
– 'Note e documenti per la storia della Riforma a Bergamo (1536–44).' *Archivio Storico Bergamasco* 11 (1987): 185–228.
Bravi, Giulio Orazio, and Pier Maria Soglian, eds. *Storia delle Terre di Albino*. 2 vols. Brescia: Grafo, 1996.
Brizzi, Gian Paolo. 'I collegi per borsisti e lo Studio bolognese. Caratteri ed evoluzione di un'istituzione educativo-assistenziale fra XIII e XVIII secolo.' *Studi e Memorie per la storia dell'Universita di Bologna*, n.s., IV (1984): 9–51.
– *Il catechismo e la grammatica*. Bologna: Il Mulino, 1985.
– *La formazione della classe dirigente nel Sei-Settecento: I seminaria nobilium nell'Italia centro-settentrionale*. Bologna: Il Mulino, 1976.
– *Principe, Università, e Gesuiti: La politica farnesina dell'istruzione a Parma e Piacenza (1545–1622)*. Rome: Bulzone, 1980.
– 'Scuole e collegi nell'antica Provincia Veneta.' In Mario Zanardi, *I Gesuiti e Venezia*, 467–511. Padua: Editrice Gregoriana, 1994.
Brugi, Biagio. 'La Nazione tedesca dello studio di Padova nel sec. XVII.' In *Memorie Storiche sullo Studio di Padova: Contributo del Regio Istituto Veneto alla celebrazione del VII centenario dell'Università*. Venice: C. Ferrari, 1922.
– *Gli scolari dello Studio di Padova nel'500*. Padua: Drucker, 1905.
Bumbaca de Lazari, Adriana. 'Schede per scolari francesi a Padova (1532–36).' *Quaderni per la storia della Università di Padova* 3 (1970): 137–44.
Burke, Peter. 'The Uses of Literacy in Early Modern Italy.' In *The Social History*

of Language, edited by Peter Burke and Roy Porter, 21–42. Cambridge: Cambridge University Press, 1987.

Bushnell, Rebecca. *A Culture of Teaching: Early Modern Humanism in Theory and Practice*. Ithaca, NY: Cornell University Press, 1996.

Cajani, Luigi. 'Castellino da Castello.' In *DBI*, vol. 21: 786–7.

Camozzi, Ermenegildo. *Cultura e Storia Letteraria a Bergamo nei secoli XV–XVI: Dai Codici Vaticani Latini un Inventario delle Biblioteche Conventuali di Bergamo*. Bergamo: Civica Biblioteca A. Mai, 2004.

Capoferri, Omar. 'La pedagogia a Bergamo nel Settecento e il caso del Collegio Mariano.' Tesi di laurea, Università degli Studi di Milano, Facoltà di Lettere e Filosofia, relatore Marco Todeschini, 1993–4.

Caproni, Riccardo, Lidia Gamba Persiani, and Luigi Pagnoni. *Martinengo nella Storia Civile ed Ecclesiale*. Bergamo: Bolis, 1992.

Carlsmith, Christopher. 'Il *Collegio Patavino* della Misericordia Maggiore di Bergamo, 1531–c. 1550.' *Bergomum* 93 (1998): 75–98.

– 'The Jesuits in Bergamo, 1570–1729.' *Archivum Historicum Societatis Iesu* 70, no. 139 (Jan.-Jun. 2001): 71–93.

– 'Le *scholae* e la scuola: l'istruzione *amore dei* a Bergamo tra'500 e'600.' *Atti del Ateneo di Scienze, Lettere, ed Arti di Bergamo* 60 (1996–7): 235–56.

– 'Schooling and Society in Bergamo, 1500–1650.' PhD dissertation, University of Virginia, 1999.

– 'Struggling Toward Success: Jesuit Education in Italy, 1540–1600.' *History of Education Quarterly* 42, no. 2 (Summer 2002): 215–46.

Cassinelli, Bruno, Antonio Maltempi, and Marco Pozzoni. *La comunità di Romano in epoca viscontea e veneta*. Romano: Tipografia Ghisleri, 1978.

Castiglioni, Giovan Battista. *Istoria delle scuole della Dottrina Cristiana*. 2 vols. Milan: C. Orena, 1800.

Castoldi, Alberto. *L'altra Bergamo*. Bergamo: Lubrina Editore, 1997.

Cessi, Roberto, and Antonio Favaro. *L'università di Padova: Notizie Raccolte*. Padua: Zanocco, 1946.

Cherubini, Paolo. *Roma e lo studium urbis: spazio urbano e cultura dal Quattro al Seicento*. Rome: Ministero per i beni culturali e ambientali, 1992.

Chiesa, Alessandro. 'Forme di pedagogia degli orfanotrofi Somaschi nel secolo XVI.' Tesi di laurea. Università degli Studi di Torino, Facoltà di Lettere e Filosofia, relatore Luigi Pareyson, 1958–9.

Chiodi, Luigi. '1508 – Police de Fr. Catana massarolo.' *Bergomum* 52, no. 1 (1958): 63–144.

– 'Eresia protestante a Bergamo nella prima metà del Cinquecento e il vescovo Vittore Soranzo.' *Rivista di Storia della Chiesa in Italia* 35 (1981): 456–85.

– 'In uno stabile della vicinia di S. Pancrazio il seminario trovò la prima sistemazione.' *L'Eco di Bergamo* (9 November 1962), 3.
– 'Note brevi di cose bergamasche ignote o quasi: Maestro Bonacio da Osio.' *Bergomum* 61, no. 3/4 (1967): 106–15.
– *Note brevi di cose Bergamasche ignote o quasi.* Verdello: Comune di Verdello, 1988.
– 'I primi passi della stampa a Bergamo.' *L'Eco di Bergamo* (17 Aug. 1976), 3.
Chiuppani, Giovanni. *Storia di una scuola di Grammatica dal Medioevo fino all'600.* Venice, 1915.
Christian, William A., Jr. *Local Religion in Sixteenth-Century Spain.* Princeton, NJ: Princeton University Press, 1981.
Church, Frederic Corss. *The Italian Reformers 1534–64.* New York: Columbia University Press, 1932.
Cistellini, Antonio. *Il Padre Angelo Paradisi e i padri Gesuiti in Brescia.* Brescia: Scuola tipografica Opera Pavoniana, 1955.
Clementi, Giuseppe. *Il Beato Venturino da Bergamo, dell'ordine de' Predicatori (1304–1346).* Rome: Tipografia Vaticano, 1904.
Cocchetti, Carlo. *Del movimento intellettuale nella provincia di Brescia dai tempi antichi ai nostri.* Brescia, 1880. Reprint Bologna: Atesa, 1989.
Comerford, Kathleen. 'Italian Tridentine Diocesan Seminaries: A Historiographical Study.' *Sixteenth Century Journal* 29, no. 4 (Winter 1998): 999–1022.
– *Ordaining the Catholic Reformation: Priests and Seminary Pedagogy in Fiesole, 1575–1675.* Florence: Olschki, 2001.
– *Reforming Priests and Parishes: Tuscan Dioceses in the First Century of Seminary Education.* Leiden: E.J. Brill, 2006.
Contini, Gianfranco. 'Reliquie volgari dalla scuola bergamasca dell'umanesimo.' *L'Italia dialettale* 10 (1934). 223–40.
Cortesi, Mariarosa. *Statuti rurali e statuti di valle: La provincia di Bergamo nei secoli XIII-XVIII, Atti del Convegno a Bergamo 5 marzo 1983.* Bergamo: Provincia di Bergamo, 1984.
Cortesi-Bosco, Francesca. 'Sulle tracce della committenza di Lotto a Bergamo: un epistolario e un codice di alchimia.' *Bergomum* 90, no. 1 (1995): 5–42.
Cossar, Roissin. 'For the Good of the Poor: The Misericordia Maggiore of Bergamo, 1265–1365.' PhD dissertation, University of Toronto, 1999.
– 'The Quality of Mercy: Confraternities and Public Power in Medieval Bergamo.' *Journal of Medieval History* 27 (2001): 139–57.
– *The Transformation of the Laity in Bergamo, 1265–c.1400.* Leiden and Boston: Brill, 2006.
Cressy, David. *Literacy and the Social Order: Reading and Writing in Tudor and Stuart England.* Cambridge: Cambridge University Press, 1985.

D'Amico, John F. 'The Progress of Renaissance Latin Prose: The Case of Apu-
   leianism.' *Renaissance Quarterly* 37 (1984): 351–92.
– *Renaissance Humanism in Papal Rome.* Baltimore and London: Johns Hopkins
   University Press, 1983.
D'Andrea, David M. 'Charity and the Reformation in Italy: The Case of
   Treviso.' In *A Reformation of Charity: The Secular and Sacred in Early Modern
   Poor Relief*, edited by Thomas Max Safley, 30–46. Leiden: Brill, 2003.
– *Civic Christianity in Renaissance Italy: The Hospital of Treviso, 1400–1530.* Ro-
   chester: University of Rochester Press, 2007.
Dalla Pozza, Antonio Marco. *La cultura vicentina nel primo cinquantesimo della
   dominazione veneziana.* Vicenza: Accademia Olimpica, 1970.
Del Col, Andrea. *L'Inquisizione nel Patriarcato e Diocesi di Aquileia, 1557–1559.*
   Trieste: Edizioni Università di Trieste, 1998.
Del Nero, Valerio. 'Note sulla vita di Giovan Battista Pio (con alcune lettere
   inedite).' *Rinascimento* 21 (1981): 247–63.
Denley, Peter. 'Governments and Schools in Late Medieval Italy.' In *City and
   Countryside in Late Medieval and Renaissance Italy: Essays presented to Phillip
   Jones*, edited by Trevor Dean and Chris Wickham, 93–108. London: Hamble-
   don Press, 1990.
– 'The Collegiate Movement in Italian Universities in the Late Middle Ages.'
   History of Universities 10 (1991): 29–91.
Dentella, Lorenzo. *I Vescovi di Bergamo.* Bergamo: Editrice S. Alessandro, 1939.
Deutscher, Thomas. 'The Growth of the Secular Clergy and the Development
   of Educational Institutions in the Diocese of Novara (1563–1772).' *Journal of
   Ecclesiastical History* 40 (1989): 381–9.
– 'Seminaries and the Education of Novarese Parish Priests, 1593–1627.' *Jour-
   nal of Ecclesiastical History* 32 (1981): 303–19.
De Vivo, Francesco. 'Indirizzi pedagogici ed istituzioni educative di ordini
   e congregazioni religiose nei secoli XVI e XVII.' *Rassegna di Pedagogia* 17
   (1959): 22–57, 255–62; 18 (1960): 326–33.
– 'I Somaschi.' *Nuove Questioni di Storia della Pedagogia.* Brescia: La Scuola:
   1977.
Dionisotti, Carlo. *Geografia e storia della letteratura italiana.* 2nd ed. Turin:
   Einaudi, 1977.
– *Gli umanisti e il volgare fra Quattro e Cinquecento.* Florence: Le Monnier, 1968.
Dizionario Biografico degli Italiani (DBI). 71 vols. Rome: Istituto della Enciclo-
   pedia Italiana, 1960–pres.
Dizionario degli istituti di perfezione (DIP). 10 vols. Rome: Edizione Paoline,
   1974–2003.
Donnelly, John Patrick. 'The Jesuit College at Padua: Growth, Suppression,

Attempts at Restoration: 1552–1606.' *Archivium Historicum Societatis Iesu* 56 (1982): 45–79.

Duchartre, Pierre Louis. *The Italian Comedy*. New York: Dover, 1966.

Eisenbichler, Konrad. *The Boys of the Archangel Raphael: A Youth Confraternity in Florence, 1411–1787*. Toronto: University of Toronto Press, 1998.

– ed. *Crossing the Boundaries: Christian Piety and the Arts in Italian Medieval and Renaissance Confraternities*. Kalamazoo, MI: Medieval Institute Publications, 1991.

Fabris, Giovanni. 'Quale fu la sede del 'Collegio Lambertino' per gli scolari Bresciani in Padova?' *Atti e Memorie della Regia Accademia di Scienze, Lettere, ed Arti in Padova* 46 (1929–30): 435–57.

Fantuzzi, Giovanni. *Notizie degli scrittori bolognesi*. 9 vols. Bologna: 1789. Reprint Bologna: A. Forni, 1965.

Farrell, Allan. *The Jesuit Code of Liberal Education: Development and Scope of the* Ratio Studiorum. Milwaukee, WI: Bruce, 1938.

Fè D'Ostiani, Luigi Francesco. *Storia, tradizione, arte nelle vie di Brescia*. Brescia: Queriniana, 1927. Reprint Brescia: Moretto [1982].

Ferraro, Joanne. *Family and Public Life in Brescia, 1580–1650*. Cambridge: Cambridge University Press, 1993.

Finazzi, Ugo. 'L'orfanotrofio di S. Martino dalle origine alla soppressione napoleonica.' Tesi di laurea. Università Cattolica del Sacro Cuore di Milano, 1969–70.

Firpo, Massimo. *Artisti, gioelleri, eretici: il mondo di Lorenzo Lotto tra Riforma e Controriforma*. Rome: Laterza, 2001.

– *Vittore Soranzo Vescovo ed Eretico: Riforma della Chiesa e Inquisizione nell'Italia del Cinquecento*. Rome: Laterza, 2006.

Firpo, Massimo, and Sergio Pagano. *I Processi Inquisitoriali di Vittore Soranzo (1550–1558): edizione critica*. 2 vol. Collectanea Archivi Vaticani, 53. Vatican City: Archivio Segreto Vaticano, 2004.

Foresti, Arnaldo. 'La gita del Petrarca a Bergamo il 13 ottobre 1359.' *Bergomum* 17, no. 2 (1923): 45–65.

Francesco Filelfo nel Quinto Centenario della Morte. Padua: Antenore, 1986.

Franzi, Tullia. 'La famiglia degli 'Alzani.' *Bergomum* 43, no. 1–2 (1949): insert of 'Atti dell'Ateneo,' 1–7.

Franzina, Emilio. *Vicenza: Storia di una città (1404–1866)*. Vicenza: Neri Pozza, 1980.

Frassica, Pietro. 'I Filelfo: Due generazioni di umanisti.' In *Francesco Filelfo nel Quinto Centenario della Morte*, 515–27.

Frova, Carla. 'La scuola nella città tardomedievale: un impegno pedagogico e organizzativo.' In *La città in Italia e in Germania nel Medioevo: cultura, istitu-*

zioni, vita religiosa, edited by Reinhard Elze and Gina Fasoli. *Annali* del Istituto Storico Italo-Germanico, 8. Bologna: Il Mulino, 1981.

– 'Una dinastia di professori nel Quattrocento: I Barizza.' In *Maestri e traduttori bergamaschi fra Medioevo e Rinascimento,* edited by Claudio Villa and
Francesco Lo Monaco, 85–95. Bergamo: Civica Biblioteca Angelo Mai, 1998.

Furietti, Alessandro. *Gasparini Barsizii et Guinforti Opera.* Rome: 1723.

Galati, Roberto. 'Il patriziato bergamasco alla vigilia di Agnadello.' Tesi di
laurea. Università di Venezia, Facoltà di Lettere e Filosofia, relatore Marino
Berengo, 1978–9.

Galbiati, Francesco. *La comunità di Romano (1427–1429).* Romano: Tipografia
Rottigni, 1895.

Gallizoli, Giovanni Battista. *Della vita, degli studi, e degli scritti di Guglielmo
Grataroli, filosofo e medico.* Bergamo, 1788.

Gargan, Luciano. 'Studenti trevigiani a Padova tra Tre e Quattrocento: Il lascito di Tommaso Salinguerra.' *Quaderni della storia dell'Università di Padova*
13 (1980): 1–35.

Garibotto, Celestino. *I maestri di grammatica a Verona dal'200 a tutto il'500.*
Verona: Tipografia Veronese, [1921].

Garibotto, Eloisa. 'Le scuole d'abbaco a Verona.' *Atti e Memorie dell'Accademia
d'agricoltura, scienze e lettere di Verona,* ser. 4, 24 (1922): 315–28.

Garin, Eugenio. *L'educazione in Europa (1400–1600).* Bari: Laterza, 1957.

– *Il pensiero pedagogico dello Umanesimo.* Florence: Sansoni, 1958.

– *Ritratti di umanisti.* Florence: Sansoni, 1967.

– *Educazione umanistica in Italia.* Bari: Laterza, 1966.

Gehl, Paul. *A Moral Art: Grammar, Society, and Culture in Trecento Florence.* Ithaca, NY: Cornell University Press, 1993.

Gennaro, Erminio. 'Arrone Battaglia de Butinoni.' *Bergomum* 73, no. 1–2 (1979):
145–64.

Ghighliazza, Tommaso. 'Curiosando tra gli antichi Statuti dei Medici di Bergamo.' *L'Eco di Bergamo* (26 May 1948), 3.

Giannetto, Nella, ed. *Vittorino da Feltre e la sua scuola: Umanesimo, pedagogia,
arti.* Florence: Olschki, 1981.

Gilbert, Felix. *The Pope, His Banker, and Venice.* Cambridge, MA: Harvard University Press, 1980.

Gipponi, Irma. 'Momenti di storia religiosa e culturale del Cinquecento
nell'Archivio Stella.' *Archivio Storico Bergamasco* 4 (1984): 259–64.

Gloria, Andrea. *Monumenti della Università di Padova, 1318–1405.* 2 vols. Padua:
Tipografia del Seminario, 1888. Reprint Padua, 1972.

Goldthwaite, Richard. 'Schools and Teachers of Commercial Arithmetic in
Renaissance Florence.' *Journal of European Economic History* 1 (1972): 418–33.

Graff, Harvey J. *Legacies of Literacy: Continuities and Contradictions in Western Society and Culture.* Bloomington: Indiana University Press, 1987.
- *Literacy and Historical Development.* Carbondale: Southern Illinois University Press, 2007.
Grafton, Anthony, and Lisa Jardine. *From Humanism to the Humanities: Education and the Liberal Arts in Fifteenth- and Sixteenth-Century Europe.* Cambridge, MA: Harvard University Press, 1986.
Grendler, Paul. 'Borromeo and the Schools of Christian Doctrine.' In *San Carlo Borromeo: Catholic Reform and Ecclesiastical Politics in the Second Half of the Sixteenth Century*, edited by John M. Headley and John B. Tomaro, 158–71. Washington, DC: Folger Shakespeare Library; London: Associated University Presses, 1988.
- 'The Italian Renaissance in the Past Seventy Years: Humanism, Social History, and Early Modern in Anglo-American and Italian Scholarship.' In *The Italian Renaissance in the Twentieth Century*, edited by Allan J. Grieco, Michael Rocke, and Fiorella Gioffredi Superbi, 3–23. Florence: Leo S. Olschki, 2002.
- *Schooling in Renaissance Italy: Literacy and Learning, 1300–1600.* Baltimore and London: Johns Hopkins University Press, 1989.
- 'Schooling in Western Europe.' *Renaissance Quarterly* 43 (1990): 774–87.
- 'Schools, Seminaries, and Catechetical Instruction.' In *Catholicism in Early Modern History: A Research Guide*, edited by John W. O'Malley, 315–30. St Louis: Center for Reformation Research, 1988.
- *The Universities of the Italian Renaissance.* Baltimore and London: Johns Hopkins University Press, 2002.
Grendler, Paul, ed. *Encyclopedia of the Renaissance.* 6 vols. New York: Charles Scribner's Sons, 1999.
Grubb, James. *Firstborn of Venice: Vicenza and the Early Renaissance State.* Baltimore: Johns Hopkins University Press, 1988.
- 'When Myths Lose Power: Four Decades of Venetian Historiography.' *Journal of Modern History* 58, no. 1 (March 1986): 49–94.
Guasco, Maurilio. 'La formazione del clero: i seminari.' In *Storia d'Italia, Annali 9: La chiesa ed il potere politico dal medioevo all'età contemporanea*, edited by Giorgio Chittolini and Giovanni Miccoli, 631–715. Turin: Einaudi, 1986.
Guarini, Elena Fasano. 'Center and Periphery.' *Journal of Modern History* 67 (December 1995): S74–S96.
Guerrini, Paolo. 'Il Collegio Lambertino.' *Archivio Veneto-Tridentino* 1 (1922): 93–108.
- 'Guglielmo Corvi da Brescia e il collegio bresciano in Bologna.' *Studi e memorie per la storia dell'Università di Bologna* 7 (1922): 55–116.
- 'Il legato Lambertino.' *Bollettino municipale di Brescia* 11 (1922): 307–13.

- 'Scuole e maestri bresciani del'500.' *Commentari dell'Ateneo di Brescia per l'anno 1921*: 73–127.
- 'Un umanista bagnolese prigionero dei Turchi a Costantinopoli e a Rodi.' *Brixia Sacra* 6, no. 4–5 (1915): 261–71.

Gullino, Giuseppe. 'La politica scolastica veneziana nell'età delle Riforme.' *Miscellanea di Studi e Memorie*. Vol. 15. Venice: Deputazione di Storia Patria per le Venezie, 1973.

Hankins, James. *Plato in the Italian Renaissance*. Leiden: Brill, 1990.

Henderson, John. *Piety and Charity in Late Medieval Florence*. Oxford: Clarendon Press; New York: Oxford University Press, 1994.

Hexter, J. H. 'The Education of the Aristocracy in the Renaissance.' In idem, *Reappraisals in History: New Views on History and Society in Early Modern Europe*. 2nd ed. Chicago: University of Chicago Press, 1979.

Horkan, Vincent. *Educational Theories and Principles of Maffeo Vegio*. Washington, DC: Catholic University Press, 1953.

Houston, Rab. A. *Literacy in Early Modern Europe, 1500–1800*. London: Longman, 1988.

Huppert, George. *Public Schools in Renaissance France*. Urbana, IL: University of Chicago Press, 1984.

In onore di G. G. Pontano nel V. centenario della sua nascita. Naples: F. Sangiovanni e figlio, 1926.

Le istituzioni monastiche e religiose a Bergamo nel Seicento. 2 vols. Edited by Ermenegildo Camozzi. Bergamo: Tipografia Vescovile Secomandi, 1982.

Jardine, Lisa. 'O *decus italiae virgo*, or, The Myth of the Learned Lady in the Renaissance.' *The Historical Journal* 28 (December 1985): 799–819.

Jeanneret, Michel. 'The Renaissance and its Ancients: Dismembering and Devouring.' *MLN* 110.5 (1995): 1043–53.

Jedin, Hubert. *A History of the Council of Trent*. 2 vols. Translated by Ernest Graf. London: Thomas Nelson and Sons, 1957.

Kallendorf, Craig, ed. and trans. *Humanist Educational Treatises*. I Tatti Renaissance Library 5. Cambridge, MA: Harvard University Press, 2001.

Karant-Nunn, Susan. 'Alas, a Lack: Trends in the Historiography of Pre-University Education in Early Modern Germany.' *Renaissance Quarterly* 43 (1990): 788–98.

Kelso, Ruth. *Doctrine for the Lady of the Renaissance*. Urbana: University of Illinois Press, 1956.

Kibre, Pearl. *The Nations in the Mediaeval Universities*. Cambridge, MA: Mediaeval Academy of America, 1948.

- *Scholarly Privileges in the Middle Ages*. Cambridge, MA: Mediaeval Academy of America, 1962.

King, Margaret L. 'Concepts of Childhood: What We Know and Where We Might Go.' *Renaissance Quarterly* 60, no. 2 (2007): 371–407.
– *The Death of the Child Valerio Marcello*. Chicago: University of Chicago Press, 2003.
– *Women of the Renaissance*. Chicago: University of Chicago Press, 1991.
King, Margaret L., and Albert Rabil, Jr, eds. *Her Immaculate Hand: Selected Works by and about Women Humanists of Quattrocento Italy*. Binghamton, NY: Center for Medieval and Renaissance Studies, 1983.
Knapton, Michael and Giorgio Cracco, eds. *Dentro lo 'Stado Italico' Venezia e la Terraferma fra Quattro e Seicento*. Trent: Gruppo Culturale Civis, 1984.
– 'Nobiltà e popolo e un trentennio di storiografia veneta.' *Nuova Rivista Storica* 82 (1998): 167–92.
Kohl, Benjamin G. and Ronald G. Witt, eds. *The Earthly Republic: Italian Humanists on government and society*. Philadelphia: University of Pennsylvania Press, 1978.
Kraye, Jill, ed. *The Cambridge Companion to Renaissance Humanism*. Cambridge: Cambridge University Press, 1996.
Kristeller, Paul Oskar. *Iter Italicum: A Finding List of Uncatalogued or Incompletely Catalogued Humanistic Manuscripts of the Renaissance in Italian and Other Libraries*. London: Warburg Institute, 1963–97.
Labalme, Patricia H., ed. *Beyond Their Sex: Learned Women of the European Past*. New York: New York University Press, 1980.
Landini, Giuseppe. *L'opera sociale di S. Girolamo*. Rapallo: Scuola tipografia orfanotrofio, 1937.
Lazar, Lance. *Working in the Vineyard of the Lord: Jesuit Confraternities in Early Modern Italy*. Toronto: University of Toronto Press, 2005.
Ledóchowska, Teresa. 'Angela Merici.' In *DIP*, vol. 1, cols. 631–4.
Leonard, Amy. *Nails in the Wall: Catholic Nuns in Reformation Germany*. Chicago: University of Chicago Press, 2005.
Liebreich, Karen. *Fallen Order: Intrigue, Heresy, and Scandal in the Rome of Galileo and Caravaggio*. New York: Grove/Atlantic, 2004.
Lines, David A. *Aristotle's Ethics in the Italian Universities (ca. 1300–1650): The Universities and the Problem of Moral Education*. Leiden and Boston: E.J. Brill, 2002.
Little, Lester. *Liberty, Charity, Fraternity: Lay Confraternities at Bergamo in the Age of the Commune*. Northampton, MA: Smith College Press, 1988.
Locatelli, Andreina Franco-Lorii. *Borgo Pignolo in Bergamo: Arte e storie dele sue chiese*. Gorle: Istituto Grafica, 1994.
Locatelli, Giuseppe. 'L'istruzione a Bergamo e la Misericordia Maggiore.' *Bergomum* 4, no. 4 (1910): 57–169; and 5, no. 1 (1911): 21–100.

Lo Monaco, Francesco. 'Civitati autem illi magistrorum copia semper fuit (Appunti su maestri, scuole, e biblioteche a Bergamo fra i secoli XIII e XIV).' In *Maestri e traduttori bergamaschi fra Medioevo e Rinascimento*, edited by Claudio Villa and Francesco Lo Monaco, 27–50. Bergamo: Civica Biblioteca Angelo Mai, 1998.

Lovarini, Emilio, ed. *Un allegro convito di studenti a Padova nel'500: epistola.* Padua: L. Crescini, 1889.

Lucchi, Piero. 'La Santacroce, il Salterio, e il Babuino: Libri per imparare a leggere nel primo secolo della stampa.' *Quaderni storici* 38 (1978): 593–630.

Lumina, Mario. *S. Alessandro in Colonna.* Bergamo: Greppi, 1977.

Manacorda, Giuseppe. *Storia della scuola in Italia: Il medio evo.* 2 vols. Milan, Palermo and Naples: R. Sandron, 1913. Reprint Florence: Le Lettere, 1980.

Mantese, Giovanni. *Memorie storiche della chiesa vicentina.* 5 vols. Vicenza: Neri Pozza and Accademia Olimpica, 1952–74.

Manzoni, Paolo. *Lemina dalle origine al XVII secolo.* Bergamo: Bolis, 1988.

Marchetti, Vincenzo, and Lelio Pagani, eds. *Chiesa, Istituzioni, et Territorio.* Bergamo: Stamperia Editrice Commerciale, 1991.

Marchi, Gian Paolo. 'Il dottore, l'ignorante.' In *Palladio e Verona*, edited by Paolo Marini, 9–18. Vicenza: Neri Pozza, 1980.

– 'L'orazione di Guarino … e l'insegnamento della lingua tedesca a Verona nel' 400.' In *Università degli studi di Padova, Annali della Facoltà di economia e commercio in Verona* 3 (1967–8): 203–12.

– 'Per una storia delle istituzioni scolastiche pubbliche dall'epoca comunale all'unificazione del Veneto all'Italia.' In *Cultura e vita civile a Verona: Uomini e istituzioni dall'epoca carolingia al Risorgimento*, 1–98. Verona: Banca Popolare di Verona, 1979.

Martin, John and Dennis Romano, eds. *Venice Reconsidered: The History and Civilization of an Italian City-State, 1297–1897.* Baltimore: Johns Hopkins University Press, 2000.

Maschietto, Francesco L. *Elena Lucrezia Cornaro Piscopia, 1614–1684: prima donna laureata nel mondo.* Padua: Antenore, 1978.

Mazzi, Angelo. *Il beato Venturino da Bergamo.* Bergamo: Fratelli Bolis, 1905.

McGinness, Frederick. 'The Collegio Romano, the University of Rome, and the Decline and Rise of Rhetoric in the Late Cinquecento.' *Roma Moderna e Contemporanea* 3, no. 3 (1995): 601–24.

McManamon, John. *Pierpaolo Vergerio the Elder: the Humanist as Orator.* Medieval and Renaissance Texts and Studies, 163. Binghamton, NY: MRTS, 1996.

Medolago, Gabriele. 'Inquisitori, eretici e streghe nelle valli bergamasche sottoposte all'arcidiocesi di Milano nei secoli XVI e XVII.' *Ricerche Storiche sulla Chiesa Ambrosiana* 20 (2002): 83–145.

Meersseman, G.G. *Ordo Fraternitas: Confraternite e pietà nel medioevo*. 3 vols. Rome: Herder, 1977.

Michiel, Alvise. 'A Parigi nel' 400 gli studenti della Sorbona appresero il Latino dal libro di un Bergamasco.' *L'Eco di Bergamo* (31 Oct. 1962), 3.

Michelato, Luigi. 'Il maestro romanese Antonio de Lallio.' *L'Eco di Bergamo* (6 Feb. 1935), 3.

– 'Scuole e maestri nel' 400 a Romano di Lombardia.' *L'Eco di Bergamo* (24 Jan. 1935), 2.

Migliorini, Luigi Mascilli. *I Somaschi*. Rome: Edizioni di Storia e Letteratura, 1992.

Montanari, Daniele. *Disciplinamento in terra veneta*. Bologna: Il Mulino, 1987.

Moran, Jo Ann Hoeppner. *The Growth of English Schooling, 1340–1548: Learning, Literacy, and Laicization in Pre-Reformation York Diocese*. Princeton, NJ: Princeton University Press, 1985.

Nalle, Sara T. 'Literacy and Culture in Early Modern Castile.' *Past and Present* 25 (Nov. 1989): 65–96.

Netto, Lorenzo, ed. *Storia di Girolamo Miani, vagabondo di Dio*. Milan: Istituto Propaganda Libreria, 1985.

Nova, Giuseppe. *Stampatori, librai, ed editori bresciani in Italia nel Cinquecento*. Brescia: Fondazione civiltà Bresciana, 2000.

O'Malley, John W. *The First Jesuits*. Cambridge, MA: Harvard University Press, 1993.

– *Trent and All That: Renaming Catholicism in the Early Modern Era*. Cambridge, MA: Harvard University Press, 2000.

Olmo, Luigi. *Memorie Storiche di Clusone e della Valle Seriana superiore*. Bergamo: Tipografia S. Alessandro, 1906.

Olsen, Glenn W. 'Humanism: The Struggle to Possess a Word.' *Logos* 7, no. 1 (Winter 2004): 97–116.

Orlandi, Angelo. 'Scuole ecclesiastiche dall'Umanesimo all'Ottocento.' In *Cultura e vita civile a Verona: Uomini e istituzioni dall'epoca carolingia al Risorgimento*, edited by Gian Paolo Marchi, 273–320. Verona: Banca Popolare di Verona, 1979.

Orme, Nicholas. *Childhood in Medieval Europe*. New Haven, CT: Yale University Press, 2003.

– *Education and Society in Medieval and Renaissance England*. London and Ronceverte, WV: Hambledon Press, 1989.

– *Education in the West of England, 1066–1548*. Exeter, UK: University of Exeter Press, 1976.

– *Medieval Schools: From Roman Britain to Tudor England*. New Haven, CT: Yale University Press, 2006.

Ortalli, Gherardo. *Scuole, maestri, e istruzione di base tra Medioevo e Rinascimento. Il caso veneziano.* Vicenza: Neri Pozza, 1993.

Pagani, Lelio. *Bergamo e S. Alessandro: storia, culto, luoghi.* Bergamo: Edizioni dell'Ateneo, 1999.

Palmer, Richard. *The Studio of Venice and Its Graduates in the Sixteenth Century.* Padua: Edizioni LINT, 1983.

Paschini, Pio. *Tre ricerche sulla Chiesa del Cinquecento.* Rome: Edizioni liturgiche, 1945.

Pastore Stocchi, Manlio. 'Scuola e cultura umanistica fra due secoli.' In *Storia della Cultura Veneta*, vol. 3, pt. 1, 93–121. Vicenza: Neri Pozza, 1980.

Patelli, Cesare. 'Uomini e vicende del Seminario di Bergamo dal 1576 al 1921.' *Studi e Memorie*, 1–117. Bergamo: Seminario di Bergamo, 1972.

– *Alzano Maggiore e la Basilica di San Martino.* Bergamo: Bolis, 1978.

Patteta, F. 'Sulla "Glychephile" di Mario Filelfo ...' *Atti della Reale Accademia d'Italia* 7 (1941): 275–341.

Peddie, Robert A. *Printing at Brescia in the Fifteenth Century.* London: William & Norgate, 1905.

Pederzani, Ivana. *Venezia e lo 'Stato de Terraferma': il governo delle comunità nel territorio bergamasco (sec. XV–XVIII).* Milan: Vita e Pensiero, 1992.

Pelandi, Luigi. 'Stampa e stampatori bergamaschi.' *Atti dell'Ateneo di Bergamo* 29 (1955–6): 319–69.

Pellegrini, Carlo. 'San Girolamo Miani e i Somaschi.' In *Esperienze di pedagogia cristiana nella storia*, edited by Pietro Braido. Rome: LAS, 1981.

– *Fonti per la Storia dei Somaschi* 1 (1970); 3 (1975); 4 (1978); 7 (1978); 8 (1979).

– *San Girolamo Miani: profilo.* Casale Monferrato: Tip. operaia artigiana, 1962.

Pellizzari, Giovanni. 'Continuità e trasformazioni di un sistema scolastico cittadino.' *Storia di Vicenza*, edited by Franco Barbieri and Paolo Preto, vol. 3, pt. 2, 69–87. Vicenza: Neri Pozza, 1990.

Pendergast, John S. *Religion, Allegory, and Literacy in Early Modern England, 1560–1640.* Aldershot, UK: Ashgate, 2006.

Petrucci, Armando. *Readers and Writers in Medieval Italy.* New Haven, CT: Yale University Press, 1995.

Pignatti, Franco. 'Filelfo, Gian Mario.' In DBI (1997), vol. 47: 626–31.

Pinetti, Angelo. 'Ricordi bergamaschi all'università di Padova.' *Rivista di Bergamo* 1, no. 5 (1992): 236–8.

Pirri, Pietro. *L'interdetto di Venezia del 1606 e I Gesuiti.* Rome: Institutum Historicum Societatis Iesu, 1959.

Pizzighella, Margherita. 'Progetti di riforme scholastiche a Bergamo nella seconda metà del'700.' Tesi di laurea. Università Cattolica del Sacro Cuore di Milano, Facoltà di Magistero, relatore Aldo Agazzi, 1968–9.

Premoli, Orazio. *Storia dei Barnabiti nel Cinquecento*. Rome: Desclee, 1913.
– *Storia dei Barnabiti nel Seicento*. Rome: Desclee, 1922.
Preto, Paolo. 'Il vescovo Gerolamo Vielmi e gli inizi della riforma tridentina a Padova.' *Rivista della Storia della Chiesa in Italia* 20 (1966): 18–33.
Prosperi, Adriano. 'Clerics and Laymen in the World of Carlo Borromeo.' In *San Carlo Borromeo: Catholic Reform and Ecclesiastical Politics in the Second Half of the Sixteenth Century*, edited by John M. Headley and John B. Tomaro, 112–38. Washington, DC: Folger Shakespeare Library; London: Associated University Presses, 1988.
Pullan, Brian S. *Rich and Poor in Renaissance Venice: The Social Institutions of a Catholic State to 1620*. Cambridge, MA: Harvard University Press, 1971.
– 'Town Poor, Country Poor: The Province of Bergamo from the Sixteenth to the Eighteenth Century.' In *Medieval and Renaissance Venice*, edited by Ellen E. Kittel and Thomas F. Madden, 213–36. Urbana, IL: University of Illinois Press, 1999.
Rashdall, Hastings. *The Universities of Europe in the Middle Ages*. Edited by F.M. Powicke and A.B. Emden. 2 vols. London: Oxford University Press, 1936.
Ricci, Lodovico. *Notizie intorno alla vita ed alle opere di M[esser] Giovita Rapicio*. Pavia: 1790.
Reato, Ermengildo. 'Carità e assistenza in sette secoli di storia vicentina.' In *La Carità a Vicenza*, edited by Chiara Rigoni, 3–12. Venice: Marsilio, 2001.
Robey, David. 'Humanism and Education in the Early Quattrocento: The *De ingenuis moribus* of P.P. Vergerio.' *Bibliotheque d'humanisme et renaissance* 42 (1980): 27–58.
Robin, Diana. *Filelfo in Milan: Writings, 1451–1477*. Princeton, NJ: Princeton University Press, 1991.
Roggero, Marina. 'L'educazione delle classi dirigenti: il modello gesuitico.' In *La Storia: I grandi problemi dal Medioevo all'età contemporanea*, edited by Massimo Firpo and Nicola Tranfaglia, 359–78. Turin: UTET, 1986.
– *Insegnar lettere: Ricerche di storia dell'istruzione in età moderna*. Turin: Edizioni dell'Orso, 1992.
– and Donatella Balani. *La scuola in Italia dalla Controriforma al secolo dei lumi*. Turin: Loescher: 1976.
Roncalli, Angelo G. (later John XXIII). *Gli inizi del Seminario di Bergamo e S. Carlo Borromeo*. Bergamo: SESA, 1939.
– *La MIA di Bergamo e le altre istituzioni di Beneficenza amministrate dalla Congregazione di Carità*. Bergamo: Tip. S. Alessandro, 1912.
Roncalli, Emanuele. *I Grandi di Bergamo*. 2 vols. Bergamo: Burgo Editore, 1991.
Ronchi, Oliviero. 'Alloggi di scolari a Padova nei secoli XIII-XVII.' In *Vecchia Padova*. Padua: Museo Civico, 1967.

Rosa, Lucia Gualdo. 'Una prolusione inedita di Francesco Filelfo, rielaborata dal figlio Gian Mario nel 1467.' In *Francesco Filelfo nel Quinto Centenario della Morte*, 274–324. Padua: Antenore, 1986.

Rosmini, Carlo de. *Vita di Francesco Filelfo da Tolentino*. 3 vols. Milan: Presso L. Mussi, 1808.

Ross, J.B. 'Venetian Schools and Teachers, Fourteenth to Early Sixteenth Century: a Survey and a Study of Giovanni Battista Egnazio.' *Renaissance Quarterly* 29 (Winter 1976): 521–65.

Rossi, Francesco. *Bergamo, l'altra Venezia*. Milan: Skira, 2001.

Rota, Francesco. 'Vittore Soranzo, Vescovo di Bergamo.' *Archivio Storico Brembatese* (1974): 9–123.

Rota, Silvia. *Per una storia del rapporto tra Venezia e Bergamo (sec. XV–XVIII): Rassegna Bibliografica*. Bergamo: Assessorato alla Cultura, 1987.

Sabbadini, Remigio. *Guariniana: La scuola e gli studi di Guarino Veronese*. Edited by Mario Sancipriano. Catania: F. Galati, 1896. Reprint Turin: Bottega d'Erasmo, 1964.

Savoldelli, Gianmaria. *Appunti per una storia della stampa a Bergamo*. Bergamo: Poligrafici Artigiani Bergamaschi (PAB), 2006.

San Girolamo Miani e Venezia nel V. centenario della nascita: Atti del Convegno, 29–31 gennaio 1987. Venice: Istituto di recovero e educazione, 1986.

Sandal, Ennio. *La stampa a Brescia: notizie storiche e annali tipografici (1501–1553)*. Baden-Baden: Valentin Koverner, 1999.

Sandri, Gino. *Gli Statuti Veronesi del 1276 colle correzioni e aggiunte fino al 1323*. Verona: La Tipografica Veronese, 1940.

Sangalli, Maurizio. *Cultura, Politica, e Religione nella Repubblica di Venezia tra Cinque e Seicento*. Venice: Istituto Veneto di scienze, lettere, ed arti, 1999.

– *Università, Accademie, Gesuiti: Cultura e religione a Padova tra Cinque e Seicento*. Padua: LINT, 2001.

– 'Università, scuole private, collegi d'educazione, accademie a Padova tra Cinque e Seicento: alcuni spunti per una storia "integrata" delle istituzioni scolastiche.' *Annali di storia dell'educazione* (1996): 93–118.

– 'Venezia non è tera di studi'? Educazione e politica nel secondo Cinquecento. I gesuiti e i procuratori di San Marco de supra.' *Studi Veneziani* 34 (1996): 97–163.

Sansonetti, Vincenza. 'Le pubbliche scuole in Vicenza durante il Medioevo e l'Umanesimo.' *Aevum* 26 (1952): 156–79.

Savi, Ignazio. *Memorie antiche e moderne intorno alle pubbliche scuole in Vicenza*. Vicenza, 1815.

Schiavo, A. *Notizie storiche intorno alle pubbliche scuole di Belluno*. Belluno, 1844.

Scotti, Giulio. *Bergamo nel Seicento*. Bergamo: Bolis, 1897.

Scotti, Gabriele. 'Contributo alla storia della carità a Milano nel secolo XVI.' Tesi di laurea. 2 vols. Università Cattolica del Sacro Cuore di Milano, Facoltà di Lettere, relatore Luigi Prosdocimi, 1973–4.

Le scuole dei Barnabiti nel IV centenario dell'approvazione dell'ordine, 1533–1933. Special issue of *Vita Nostra*. Florence: Collegio alla Querce, 1933.

Secco, Luigi. *La pedagogia della Contrariforma*. Brescia: La Scuola, 1973.

Silini, Giovanni. 'Appunti sulle scuole di Lovere nei secoli XV e XVI.' In *Convitto Nazionale 'Cesare Battisti' a Lovere, 1891–1991*. Lovere: Ferrari, 1991.

Simon, Joan. *Education and Society in Tudor England*. Cambridge: Cambridge University Press, 1966.

Siraisi, Nancy. *Arts and Sciences at Padua*. Toronto: Pontifical Institute of Mediaeval Studies, 1973.

Soglian, Pier Maria. '*Otia* umanistici in Val Calepio.' *La Rivista di Bergamo* 18 (Summer 1999): 56–61.

Sornaga, Ettore. 'Quattro secoli e mezzo … le opere di S. Girolamo Miani a Bergamo.' *Atti del Ateneo di Scienze, Lettere, ed Arti di Bergamo* 43 (1982–3): 203–38.

Starn, Randolph. 'A Postmodern Renaissance.' *Renaissance Quarterly* 60, no. 1 (2007): 1–24.

Stone, Lawrence. 'The Educational Revolution in England, 1580–1640.' *Past and Present* 28 (1964): 41–80.

Strauss, Gerald. *Luther's House of Learning: Indoctrination of the Young in the German Reformation*. Baltimore: Johns Hopkins University Press, 1978.

Strauss, Gerald, and Richard Gawthrop. 'Protestantism and Literacy in Early Modern Germany.' *Past and Present* 104 (1984): 31–55.

Tagliabue, Mario. *Seminari Milanesi in terra bergamasca*. Milan: Tip. S. Lega Eucaristica, 1931.

Tagliaferri, Amelio, ed. *Atti del Convegno: Venezia e la terraferma attraverso le Relazioni dei Rettori (Trieste, 23–24 Ottobre 1980)*. Milan: Giuffrè, 1981.

Tallarigo, Carlo Maria. *Giovanni Pontano e I suoi tempi*. Naples: Domenico Morano, 1874.

Tamborini, Alessandro. *La compagnia e le scuole della Dottrina Cristiana*. Milan: Tipografia Arcivescovile Giovanni Daverio, 1939.

Taschini, Roberto. 'Popolazione e classi sociali a Bergamo tra XV e XVI secolo.' Tesi di laurea. Università di Padova, Facoltà di Economia e Commercio, relatore Gino Barbieri, 1970–1.

Tentorio, Marco. 'La "Methodus Studiorum" dei Somaschi nel 1741.' In *Il Cardinale Tolomeo Gallio e il suo Collegio, nel quarto centenario della sua fondazione, 1583–1983*. Como: Opera Pia Collegio Gallio, 1983.

- 'Saggio storico dello sviluppo dell'ordine Somasco dal 1569 al 1650.' Tesi di laurea. 2 vols. Università Cattolica del Sacro Cuore di Milano, Facoltà di Lettere e Filosofia, relatore Giovanni Soranzo, 1941.
- 'Somaschi.' In *Ordini e congregazioni religiose*, edited by M. Escobar, 609–30. Turin: n.p., 1951.
- 'Lo studio del greco nell'ordine somasco nel sec. XVIII.' *Rivista dell'ordine dei Padri Somaschi* 36 (1961): 24–31.
Terpstra, Nicholas. *Abandoned Children of the Italian Renaissance: Orphan Care in Florence and Bologna*. Baltimore and London: Johns Hopkins University Press, 2006.
- 'Apprenticeship in Social Welfare: From Confraternal Charity to Municipal Poor Relief in Early Modern Italy.' *Sixteenth Century Journal* 25 (Spring 1994): 101–20.
- *The Art of Executing Well: Rituals of Execution in Renaissance Italy*. Kirksville, MO: Truman State University Press, 2008.
- *Lay Confraternities and Civic Religion in Renaissance Bologna*. Cambridge: Cambridge University Press, 1994.
- *The Politics of Ritual Kinship: Confraternities and Social Order in Early Modern Italy*. Cambridge: Cambridge University Press, 1999.
Terpstra, Nicholas, and Konrad Eisenbichler, eds. *The Renaissance in the Streets, Schools, and Studies: Essays in Honour of Paul F. Grendler*. Toronto: University of Toronto Press, 2008.
Thorndike, Lynn. *History of Magic and Experimental Science*. 8 vols. New York: Columbia University Press, 1923–58.
Tiraboschi, Girolamo. *Storia della letteratura italiana*. 7 vols. Venice, 1796.
Tognon, Giuseppe. 'Intellettuali ed educazione del principe nel Quattrocento italiano: Il formarsi di una nuova pedagogia politica.' *Melanges de l'Ecole Francaise de Rome* 99 (1987): 405–33.
Torri, Tancredo. 'Artisti e studiosi bergamaschi all'Ateneo di Padova nei secoli.' *Giornale del Popolo* (Feb. 10 & 14, 1953), 3.
- *Dalle antiche Accademie all'Ateneo*. Bergamo: Stamperia di Gorle, 1975.
Toscani, Xenio. 'Le "Scuole della Dottrina Cristiana" come fattore di alfabetizzazione.' *Società e Storia* 7 (1984): 757–81.
- *Scuole e alfabetismo nello Stato di Milano da Carlo Borromeo alla Rivoluzione*. Milan: La Scuola, 1992.
- 'Catechisi e catechismi come fattore di alfabetizzazione in età moderna.' *Annali di storia dell'educazione* 1 (1994): 17–36.
Tramontin, Silvio. 'Gli inizi dei due seminari di Venezia.' *Studi veneziani* 7 (1965): 363–77.

- 'Ordini e Congregazioni Religiosi.' *Storia della cultura veneta,* vol. 4, pt. 1, 23–60. Vicenza: Neri Pozza, 1980.

Treccani degli Alfieri, Giovanni, ed. *Storia di Brescia.* 5 vols. Brescia: Fondazione Morcelli, 1961.

Trexler, Richard C. *Public Life in Renaissance Florence.* New York: Academic Press, 1980.

Turrini, Miriam. '"Riformare il mondo a vera vita christiana": Le scuole di catechismo nell'Italia del'500.' *Annali dell'Istituto Storico Italo-Germanico di Trento* 8 (1982): 407–89.

- 'La scuola di catechismo nell'Italia del Cinquecento: catechesi,"buoni costumi" ed alfabetizzazione.' Tesi di laurea. Università degli Studi di Bologna, Facoltà di Lettere e Filosofia, relatore Ottavia Niccoli, 1980–1.

- Il *'giovin signore' in collegio: I Gesuiti e l'educazione della nobilità nelle consuetudini del Collegio ducale di Parma.* Bologna: CLUEB, 2006.

Ugolini, U[golino?] *Di una pretesa cattedra pliniana a Brescia nei primi anni del secolo XVI.* Brescia, 1923.

Ulietti, Carlo. *Notizie storiche intorno al Seminario di Bergamo.* Bergamo: Tipografia Sonzogni, 1831.

Vaerini, Barnaba. *Scrittori di Bergamo Vescovi e Cardinali.* Bergamo, Tipografia Pagnoncelli, 1874.

Valota, Paola. 'Il Collegio Mariano di Bergamo nella seconda metà del Settecento.' *Bergomum* 89, no. 2 (1994): 99–221.

Vezzoli, Giovanni. 'Il collegio dei giuristi a Begamo nel XVI secolo.' Tesi di laurea. Università degli Studi di Milano, Facoltà di Giurisprudenza, relatore Antonio Padoa Schioppa, 1986–7.

Vistalli, Francesco. *Il Cardinale Cavagnis.* Bergamo: Istituto Italiano d'Arti Grafiche, 1913.

Vittori, Rodolfo. 'Le biblioteche di due maestri bergamaschi del Cinquecento.' *Bergomum* 96, no. 2 (2001): 23–56.

Vittori, Rodolfo and Pier Maria Soglian. 'Tra Bergamo e Basilea nel secondo '500: la Biblioteca di Rudolf von Salis e Claudia Grumelli.' *Annali di Storia moderna e contemporanea* 12 (2006): 9–55.

Volpi, Luigi. *Tre secoli di cultura bergamasca.* Bergamo: Edizione Orobiche, 1952.

Volpicelli, Luigi, ed. *Il Pensiero Pedagogico della Controriforma.* Florence: Sansoni, 1960.

Walker, David M., ed. *Oxford Companion to Law.* Oxford: Clarendon Press, 1988.

Weissman, Ronald F. 'Brothers and Strangers: Confraternal Charity in Renaissance Florence.' *Historical Reflections* 15 (Spring 1988): 27–45.

– *Ritual Brotherhood in Renaissance Florence*. New York: Academic Press, 1982.

Woodward, William H. *Studies in Education during the Age of the Renaissance*. Cambridge: University Press, 1906. Reprint New York: Russell & Russell, 1965.

– *Vittorino da Feltre and Other Humanist Educators*. New York: Teachers College, Columbia University Press, 1908. Reprint New York, 1963.

Woolfson, Jonathan. *Padua and the Tudors: English Students in Italy, 1485–1603*. Toronto: University of Toronto Press, 1998.

Zanardi, Mario, ed. *I Gesuiti e Venezia*. Padua: Editrice Gregoriana, 1994.

Zanchi, Goffredo. 'Dagli inizi del Cinquecento all'attuazione del Concilio di Trento.' In *Diocesi di Bergamo*, edited by A. Caprioli, A. Rimoldi, and L. Vaccaro, 161–79. Brescia: La Scuola, 1988.

– 'L'età post-Tridentina e il consolidarsi della tradizione bergamasca.' *Diocesi di Bergamo*, ed. A. Caprioli, A. Rimoldi, and L. Vaccaro, 181–200. Brescia: La Scuola, 1988.

Zanelli, Agostino. 'Del pubblico insegnamento in Brescia nei secoli XVI e XVII.' *Commentari dell'Ateneo di Brescia per l'anno 1896*: 24–53.

– 'Gabriele da Concoreggio e il Comune di Brescia.' *Archivio Storico Lombardo* 26 (1899): 60–86.

Zanocco, Rizieri. 'Le Origini del Seminario di Padova.' *Bollettino diocesano* 12 (1927): 349–55.

Zmora, Arie S. 'Schooling in Renaissance Pistoia: Community and Civic Humanism in Small-Town Tuscany.' *Sixteenth Century Journal* 34 (2003): 761–77.

Zoppetti, Maria Mencaroni. 'Echi e Modelli: un omaggio a Bartolomeo Colleoni negli affreschi di casa Passi in Bergamo.' In *Bartolomeo Colleoni e il territorio bergamasco*, edited by Lelio Pagani, 137–60. Bergamo: Edizioni dell'Ateneo, 2000.

Index